Fodor's 04

NEW YORK CITY

Where to Stay and Eat
for All Budgets

Must-See Sights
and Local Secrets

Ratings You Can Tru

D1341064

Fodor's Travel Publications New … Auckland
www.fodors.com

FODOR'S NEW YORK CITY 2004
Editors: William Travis, Amanda Theunissen

Editorial Contributors: Lynne Arany, Sarah Cupp, Michael B. de Zayas, John J. Donohue, Lesa Griffith, Elise Harris, Evelyn Kanter, Natasha Lesser, Andrea Meyer, Margaret Mittelbach, Jennifer Paull, Tom Steele
Maps: David Lindroth, *cartographer;* Rebecca Baer and Robert P. Blake, *map editors*
Design: Fabrizio La Rocca, *creative director;* Guido Caroti, *art director;* Melanie Marin, *senior photo editor*
Production/Manufacturing: Colleen Ziemba
Cover Photo (Wollman rink, Central Park): Walter Bibikow/Age Fotostock

COPYRIGHT

ISBN 1-4000-1251-1

ISSN 0736-9395

SPECIAL SALES

Fodor's Travel Publications are available at special discounts for bulk purchases for sales promotions or premiums. Special editions, including personalized covers, excerpts of existing guides, and corporate imprints, can be created in large quantities for special needs. For more information, contact your local bookseller or write to Special Markets, Fodor's Travel Publications, 1745 Broadway, New York, NY 10019. Inquiries from Canada should be directed to your local Canadian bookseller or sent to Random House of Canada, Ltd., Marketing Department, 2775 Matheson Boulevard East, Mississauga, Ontario L4W 4P7. Inquiries from the United Kingdom should be sent to Fodor's Travel Publications, 20 Vauxhall Bridge Road, London SW1V 2SA, England.

AN IMPORTANT TIP & AN INVITATION

Although all prices, opening times, and other details in this book are based on information supplied to us at press time, changes occur all the time in the travel world, and Fodor's cannot accept responsibility for facts that become outdated or for inadvertent errors or omissions. So **always confirm information when it matters,** especially if you're making a detour to visit a specific place. Your experiences—positive and negative—matter to us. If we have missed or misstated something, **please write to us.** We follow up on all suggestions. Contact the New York City editor at editors@fodors.com or c/o Fodor's at 1745 Broadway, New York, NY 10019.

PRINTED IN THE UNITED STATES OF AMERICA

10 9 8 7 6 5 4 3 2 1

DESTINATION NEW YORK CITY

It has been called the "greatest city in the world" so many times—usually by its own politicians, its own media figures, its own men and women in the street—that the claim may seem empty. But that slogan takes on new life when inverted: New York is civilization's greatest world within a city. It feels as though everything is here. It's not, of course, but that's a trifling observation. What truly matters is the overpowering impression that New York gives of being both a mirror and a magnet for all of humanity and all that humanity does. Come and see for yourself: New York is the world's beating heart.

Karen Cure

Karen Cure, Editorial Director

CONTENTS

ABOUT THIS BOOK

	There's no doubt that the best source for travel advice is a like-minded friend who's just been where you're headed. But with or without that friend, you'll have a better trip with a Fodor's guide in hand. Once you've learned to find your way around its pages, you'll be in great shape to find your way around your destination.
SELECTION	Our goal is to cover the best properties, sights, and activities in their category, as well as the most interesting communities to visit. We make a point of including local food-lovers' hot spots as well as neighborhood options, and we avoid all that's touristy unless it's really worth your time. You can go on the assumption that everything you read about in this book is recommended wholeheartedly by our writers and editors. Flip to **On the Road with Fodor's** to learn more about who they are. It goes without saying that no property mentioned in the book has paid to be included.
RATINGS	Orange stars ★ denote sights and properties that our editors and writers consider the very best in the area covered by the entire book. These, the best of the best, are listed in the **Fodor's Choice** section in the front of the book. Black stars ★ highlight the sights and properties we deem **Highly Recommended,** the don't-miss sights within any section. Fodor's Choice and Highly Recommended options are usually listed on the title page of the chapter covering that section. Use the index to find complete descriptions. In cities, sights pinpointed with numbered map bullets ❶ in the margins tend to be more important than those without bullets.
SPECIAL SPOTS	**Pleasures & Pastimes** focuses on types of experiences that reveal the spirit of the destination. Watch for **Off the Beaten Path** sights. Some are out of the way, some are quirky, and all are worth your while. If the munchies hit while you're exploring, look for **Need a Break?** suggestions.
TIME IT RIGHT	Wondering when to go? Check **On the Calendar** up front and chapters' **Timing** sections for weather and crowd overviews and best days and times to visit.
SEE IT ALL	Use Fodor's exclusive **Great Itineraries** as a model for your trip. (For a good overview of the entire destination, follow those that begin the book, or mix regional itineraries from several chapters.) **Good Walks** guide you to important sights in each neighborhood; ⚑ indicates the starting points of walks and itineraries in the text and on the map.
BUDGET WELL	Hotel and restaurant price categories from **¢ to $$$$** are defined in the opening pages of each chapter—expect to find a balanced selection for every budget. For attractions, we always give standard adult admission fees; reductions are usually available for children, students, and senior citizens. Look in **Discounts & Deals** in Smart Travel Tips for information on destination-wide ticket schemes.
BASIC INFO	**Smart Travel Tips** lists travel essentials for the entire area covered by the book; city- and region-specific basics end each chapter. To find the best way to get around, see the transportation section; see individual modes of travel ("By Car," "By Train") for details. We assume you'll check Web sites or call for particulars.

ON THE MAPS	**Maps** throughout the book show you what's where and help you find your way around. Black and orange numbered bullets ❶ ❶ in the text correlate to bullets on maps.
BACKGROUND	In general, we give background information within the chapters in the course of explaining sights as well as in **CloseUp** boxes and in **Understanding New York City** at the end of the book. To get in the mood, review the suggestions in **Books & Movies.**
DON'T FORGET	**Restaurants** are open for lunch and dinner daily unless we state otherwise; we mention dress only when there's a specific requirement and reservations only when they're essential or not accepted—it's always best to book ahead. **Hotels** have private baths, phone, TVs, and air-conditioning and operate on the European Plan (a.k.a. EP, meaning without meals). We always list facilities but not whether you'll be charged extra to use them, so when pricing accommodations, find out what's included.
SYMBOLS	

Many Listings

- ★ Fodor's Choice
- ★ Highly recommended
- ✉ Physical address
- ✥ Directions
- 📫 Mailing address
- ☎ Telephone
- 📠 Fax
- 🌐 On the Web
- ✉ E-mail
- 🎫 Admission fee
- ⏲ Open/closed times
- ▶ Start of walk/itinerary
- Ⓜ Metro stations
- 💳 Credit cards

Outdoors

- ⛳ Golf
- ⛺ Camping

Hotels & Restaurants

- 🏨 Hotel
- 🛏 Number of rooms
- 🛎 Facilities
- 🍽 Meal plans
- ✕ Restaurant
- ✍ Reservations
- 👔 Dress code
- 🚬 Smoking
- 🍷 BYOB
- ✕🏨 Hotel with restaurant that warrants a visit

Other

- 👶 Family-friendly
- ℹ Contact information
- ⇨ See also
- ✉ Branch address
- ☞ Take note

ON THE ROAD WITH FODOR'S

A trip takes you out of yourself. Concerns of life at home completely disappear, driven away by more immediate thoughts—about, say, what marvels will beguile the next day, or where you'll have dinner. That's where Fodor's comes in. We make sure that you know all your options, so that you don't miss something that's around the next bend just because you didn't know it was there. Because the best memories of your trip might have nothing to do with what you came to New York City to see, we guide you to sights large and small all over the five boroughs. You might set out to explore the Metropolitan Museum of Art, but back at home you find yourself unable to forget watching the sun sink below the skyline from the Brooklyn Bridge or strolling through Central Park. With Fodor's at your side, serendipitous discoveries are never far away.

Our success in showing you every corner of New York City is a credit to our extraordinary writers. Although there's no substitute for travel advice from a good friend who knows your style, our contributors are the next best thing—the kind of people you would poll for travel advice if you knew them.

New York native **Lynne Arany** is well-practiced in the art of uncovering the less-known gems in New York's cultural scene. Author of the *Little Museums* guidebook, contributor to the *New York Times,* and freelance travel writer and editor, she's covered areas from Scotland to the southwestern United States. But she most enjoys the serendipity of the search here at home.

Sarah Cupp is a staff writer for the *New York Times* index, covering sports. A freelance writer and editor for various publications and media outlets, she is also writing a nonfiction book about sports and religion. Sarah lives in Manhattan and roots for the New York Mets.

Michael de Zayas, updater of the Exploring Manhattan chapter, has worked at two of the city's more venerable institutions, the Metropolitan Museum of Art and the *New York Post.* Since earning a master of fine arts degree from Sarah Lawrence College, he has lived in the East Village, Midtown, and on the Upper West Side.

John J. Donohue has called the city home for more than 10 years and is the nightlife editor of "Goings on About Town" section of the *New Yorker.* His favorite hours to wander the streets are between 6 PM and 6 AM.

Manhattan-based dining writer **Lesa Griffith** has eaten her way around the world from Honolulu to Dakar and continues to do so in the five boroughs. She's a former editor of the *Time Out Eating & Drinking Guide.*

A native New Yorker and longtime Brooklyn resident, **Elise Harris,** our lodging updater, has never lived farther from the city than Princeton, NJ. She recently traded in her gig as an editor at *Out* magazine for a daily commute to the New York Public Library, where she does freelance journalism.

Outdoor activities and sports updater **Evelyn Kanter** has reported on all aspects of her hometown as a reporter for WCBS Radio and WABC-TV and contributing editor to *New York* magazine. A native New Yorker, she writes often about adventure travel; her articles have appeared in the *New York Times, Travel + Leisure,* and *Skiing,* among others. She lives on the Upper West Side.

Former Fodor's editor **Natasha Lesser** lives in Park Slope, Brooklyn, with her husband and daughter. She loves exploring the neighborhoods of New York's outer boroughs, which contain both old favorites and unexpected delights.

Andrea Meyer writes about film and entertainment for *Interview, Time Out New York, indieWIRE,* the *New York Post,* and reports on relationships and celebrities for *Glamour.* Born in Los Angeles, Andrea has lived in downtown New York for more than nine years and is proud to call the East Village her home.

Margaret Mittelbach has written about all aspects of the city, including upper Manhattan, which she covered for our Exploring Manhattan chapter.

Fodor's editor **Jennifer Paull** regularly scours the city for plum finds for the Shopping chapter, turning up everything from ostrich eggs to cult-favorite vinyl.

For more than five years, **Tom Steele** has covered the New York entertainment and restaurant scenes for *Fodor's New York City, Time Out New York,* and *Out* magazine. He lives in Manhattan.

WHAT'S WHERE

A New Yorker may casually mention that a bar is "downtown," which generally means below 14th Street, but when pressed for specifics, he or she can narrow that down to a neighborhood as quaint-sounding as "Alphabet City" or "NoLita." New York is full of neighborhoods, some defined by a landmark or ethnic heritage, some barely in the same form in which they began, others invented for commercial gain and successfully spreading their boundaries. A few in-between blocks toss their hat in with whichever nearby area is hottest at the moment. This guide checks into all the boroughs of the Big Apple, but naturally focuses on the core, Manhattan. Its long, thin stretch is covered here from south to north, from Wall Street and the East Village to Morningside Heights and Harlem.

Wall Street & the Battery

Nearly at the southern tip of Manhattan and clustered around the New York and American stock exchanges, Wall Street is both the name of the downtown financial nexus and a thoroughfare. The grand and hulking architecture wedged into these blocks truly does merit comparison to canyons. The Dutch began the colony of Nieuw Amsterdam on these narrow streets, and a century and a half later, George Washington was sworn in on Wall Street as the United State's first president. Luckily, the destruction that leveled the nearby World Trade Center did not physically damage the area. The absolute tip of the island is leafy Battery Park, full of war monuments and benches on which to rest and catch a harbor breeze.

The Seaport & the Courts

New York's days as a great 19th-century haven for clipper ships are preserved in lower Manhattan at South Street Seaport, centered on Fulton Street at the East River and crowned by the Brooklyn Bridge. On the cobblestone pedestrian streets and wooden docks, street performers compete with tall masted ships and retail stores for audiences' attention. Just blocks west of the seaport, you can take in the majestic court buildings of the City Hall area, some of which you might recognize from the TV show *Law and Order.*

Little Italy & Chinatown

No longer the large community it once was, Little Italy is now basically confined to Mulberry Street between Canal and Broome streets. A few remaining Italian-American families and touristy eateries keep traditions alive, such as September's San Gennaro festival and summer sidewalk dining. Chinatown has grown north of its original boundary of Canal Street, spilling into much of what was once Little Italy, and also farther east into the Lower East Side, a formerly Jewish neighborhood. As you head east from Broadway along Canal Street, Chinese discount stalls and jewelry stores increase in number, and to the south, a carnival-like atmosphere reigns on the small streets, which are packed with purveyors of untold varieties of pungent fish, unusual vegetables, and pastries. Between residents shopping for groceries and tourists looking for bargains and an exotic experience, it's slow moving on the sidewalks on weekends.

SoHo & TriBeCa

An eye-pleasing neighborhood of cast-iron buildings and a few Belgian brick streets, SoHo (*S*outh of *Ho*uston Street) is bounded on its other three sides by Lafayette Street, Canal Street, and 6th Avenue. Artists transformed SoHo's late 19th-century factories into loft studios in the 1960s, and many of the galleries that followed have since been replaced by cushy restaurants and high-fashion boutiques. Sidewalk vendors and young window-shoppers keep the scene from getting too rarified. To the south and west, TriBeCa (the *Tri*angle *Be*low *Ca*nal Street) extends roughly as far as Murray Street and east to West Broadway. The broader streets of TriBeCa have a neighborhood feel, with a sprinkling of pricey restaurants and precious specialty shops, and many converted factory buildings. The World Trade Center stood just to the south of this residential area.

Greenwich Village

The crazy-quilt pattern of narrow, tree-lined streets known to New Yorkers simply as "the Village" remains true to its 19th-century heritage as a haven for bohemians, students, artists, actors, carousers, and tourists. Extending from 14th Street south to Houston Street and from the piers of the Hudson River east to 5th Avenue, it's one of the best parts of the city to wander for hours. Jazz clubs and sing-along piano bars line Grove Street, where a destitute Thomas Paine spent his last days, and literary legends have left their mark at old speakeasies and taverns. The Village is still stomping grounds of one of the largest gay communities in the country (specifically on Sheridan Square and Christopher Street).

The East Village & the Lower East Side

Once an edgy neighborhood of immigrants, artists, and punks, the East Village was hit with a wave of gentrification in the 1990s that is now lapping Avenue C, the penultimate avenue of sub-neighborhood Alphabet City. NYU students and young executives have joined the harmonious mélange that frequents the Polish and Ukrainian coffee shops, black-box theaters, trendy pasta bars, and St. Mark's Place—a raggedy stretch of vintage stores, fetish shops, and sidewalk vendors. The area is bounded by 14th Street on the north, 4th Avenue or the Bowery on the west, Houston Street on the south, and the park-lined East River.

Saunter south of Houston Street and you'll enter the Lower East Side, once the cramped stepping-stone of many of New York's immigrant groups, and where the legacy of Jewish immigrants remains strongest in discount clothing, fabric, design stores, and even a century-old knish bakery on Houston Street. Young clothing designers and hip bars and restaurants are now filling the storefronts of residential buildings on streets such as Eldridge and Ludlow. Preserving the history of the area is the Lower East Side Tenement Museum.

Murray Hill, Flatiron District & Gramercy

In the nascent years of the skyscraper, two of New York's most distinctive structures wowed New Yorkers within the Flatiron District: the 21-story Fuller Building (now known as the Flatiron Building) wedged into the tight triangle created by 5th Avenue, Broadway, and 23rd Street, and the Metropolitan Life Insurance Company's 693-ft tower soaring above Madison Square Park. Within walking distance of this commercial area are the brownstone mansions and town houses of Gramercy, in the East 20s, and of Murray Hill, in the East 30s. Moneyed families such as the Roosevelts and Morgans made their homes here in the mid-19th century. The southern gateway to these neighborhoods is Union Square, surrounded by restaurants, stores, and a farmers' green market.

Chelsea

Like its London district namesake, New York's Chelsea maintains a villagelike personality, with quiet streets graced by lovingly renovated town houses. The neighborhood stretches from 6th Avenue west to the Hudson River, and from 14th Street to the upper 20s. Chelsea has always been congenial to writers and artists, and it has also embraced a multicultural population for decades; the neighborhood has largely supplanted the Village as the center of gay (mostly male) life in the city. Restaurants and shops on 8th Avenue are filled with well-toned "Chelsea Boys." The contemporary art scene thrives in spacious warehouse galleries west of 10th Avenue from West 20th to West 29th streets.

42nd Street

From west to east, this famous street is like a symphony of movements. It starts off slightly slow and seedy before a rapid crescendo to the tacky razzle-dazzle at Times Square, glaringly bright every day of the year. Thirty or so major Broadway theaters are nearby, in an area bounded roughly by West 41st and 53rd streets between 6th and 9th avenues. Before and after the show, critics, actors, directors, playwrights, and spectators come to dine on Restaurant Row (46th Street between 8th and 9th avenues) and along 9th Avenue in Hell's Kitchen. Midway across the island, the street's pulse gradually calms to the tree-lined stretch of Bryant Park and the New York Public Library. The pace picks up east of 5th Avenue, with high-rise offices, Grand Central Terminal, and the glorious Chrysler Building. Finally, the strident energy subsides near the genteel residences of Tudor City, the stately United Nations headquarters, and the balcony over the East River.

Rockefeller Center & Midtown Skyscrapers

Except perhaps for the sweeping panoramas to be seen from the Hudson River or the New York harbor, no other city scene so clearly says "New York" than the 19-building complex known as Rockefeller Center. These 22 acres of prime real estate (between 5th and 7th avenues and 47th and 52nd streets) are full of keepsake photo shots such as the ice-skating rink and towering Christmas tree fronting the GE building, the fan-staging area outside NBC's *Today Show,* and the pink-and-blue neon marquis of Radio City Music Hall. St. Patrick's Cathedral, Saks Fifth Avenue, and the rest of midtown's gleaming skyscrapers are just walk signs away.

5th Avenue & 57th Street

One of the world's great shopping districts, 5th Avenue north of Rockefeller Center, and 57th Street between Lexington Avenue and 7th Avenue are where you'll find some of the crème de la crème of designer boutiques and the biggest names in New York retailing. Follow Holly Golightly's lead in *Breakfast at Tiffany's* and come to look even if you know you won't buy. But there are also places on 5th Avenue where even a student can afford a knockoff look. Music aficionados of different bandwidths make their way to West 57th Street for either Carnegie Hall or the Hard Rock Cafe.

The Upper East Side

Between Park and 5th avenues is where Old Money resides, as well as the tony restaurants and social clubs that serve as extensions of luxurious town houses. Historic district designation has ensured that much of the Upper East Side between East 59th and 78th streets hasn't strayed from its turn-of-the-20th-century good taste, but whatever pushes the envelope of acceptability is sure to be on view at the Whitney Museum of American Art, a cantilevered modern fortress. Steel yourself for the clash of desire and resources when viewing the wares of Madison Avenue's haute couture boutiques. East of Park Avenue are the former tenements of the working class, now, alongside modern towers, mostly home to singles and young families.

Museum Mile

Once called Millionaire's Row, the stretch of 5th Avenue along Central Park between East 79th and 104th streets is still home to more millionaires—and billionaires—than any other street in the city. It earned its nickname Museum Mile for the world-class collections of art and artifacts scattered along its length (some housed in the former mansions of industrialists and philanthropists). The only building built by Frank Lloyd Wright in New York is the Solomon R. Guggenheim Museum, between East 88th and 89th streets. Whatever you do, don't leave without visiting at least a few galleries in the largest art museum in the western hemisphere, the Metropolitan Museum of Art, at East 82nd Street.

Central Park

This 843-acre patch of rolling countryside is where Manhattanites escape from the urban jungle and reconnect with nature. Nowhere does a rippled pond, peeping duckling, or crimson leaf seem more precious and remarkable than against a backdrop of high-rises. Named a National Historic Landmark in 1965, Central Park serves the city's most soothing vistas and opportunities for just about any outdoor activity. There are some very New York twists here though: white clothing is required for the croquet course, and at the open-air disco just off the northeast corner of the Sheep Meadow, rollerbladers move with figure-skaters' liquid grace. Buskers, massage practitioners, and remote-controlled miniature sailboats are some of the other pleasant distractions. The rectangular park is bordered by 59th and 110th streets, and 5th Avenue and Central Park West (which is what 8th Avenue becomes above West 59th Street).

The Upper West Side

Ornate prewar buildings line the residential boulevards of Riverside Drive, West End Avenue, and Central Park West and the commercial thoroughfare of Broadway, providing a stately backdrop for the lines of patrons awaiting a table during weekend brunch hours. Weaving between baby strollers, aspiring actors, and Juilliard students hustling off to their auditions and rehearsals, walk up busy Columbus Avenue at least as far as the American Museum of Natural History, whose pink-granite corner towers guard a four-block tract. Across the street is the New-York Historical Society, whose changing exhibits might highlight anything from paintings of New York social scenes to evidence gathered for the Julius and Ethel Rosenberg espionage trial. At night, Lincoln Center for the Performing Arts is what draws many to the area.

Morningside Heights

Rising up between the Upper West Side and Harlem, Morningside Heights is home to the ivied buildings of Columbia University, one of the nation's oldest, and to the magnificent French Gothic Cathedral of St. John the Divine, which in addition to religious services sponsors music performances of all genres. Two of the most visited buildings alongside Riverside Park are here: Grant's Tomb and Riverside Church.

Harlem

An important influence on American culture, Harlem has been a hotbed of African-American and Hispanic-American culture and life for nearly a century. Music is a big part of the cultural draw, be it gospel services at Baptist churches or amateur nights on the stage of the Apollo Theatre. The collection of the Schomburg Center for Research in Black Culture includes early jazz and blues recordings. Harlem extends north from 110th Street to about 145th Street (the border of Manhattanville); the most interesting sights on the tourist trail fall on the West Side roughly between 116th and 135th streets.

GREAT ITINERARIES

New York City in 5 Days

Enjoying everything New York City has to offer during a short trip is more than a challenge, it's an impossibility. Whether your bent is sightseeing or shopping, museums or music, New York does indeed have it all. In five days you can see only the best of the best.

DAY 1

Begin a day dedicated to New York icons with a bird's-eye view atop the Empire State Building. Stroll up 5th Avenue past the leonine guardians of the New York Public Library and step inside to behold the gleaming Main Reading Room. Forty-second Street takes you east to the beaux arts Grand Central Terminal, a hub of frenetic activity and architectural wonder. Move on to the Chrysler Building, an art deco stunner, and continue east to the United Nations. Make your way west across 49th Street to the triumvirate of Saks Fifth Avenue, Rockefeller Center, and St. Patrick's Cathedral. Shopping, ice-skating at the Rockefeller rink, or visiting a nearby museum could fill your day until dusk, a good time to walk south on 7th Avenue toward the bright lights of Times Square.

⏲ Rush hour is a contact sport in Grand Central Terminal and Wednesday's foot traffic through Times Square can grind nearly to a standstill as audiences pour in and out of Broadway matinees.

DAY 2

Set off in search of history via ferry to the Statue of Liberty and Ellis Island. An early start helps you beat the crowds and after a thorough visit complete with guided tours, you can expect to return six hours later. Back in Manhattan, walk through the Wall Street area, home of the colonial-era Fraunces Tavern and mid-19th-century Trinity Church. St. Paul's Chapel is Manhattan's oldest surviving church building and site of September 11 remembrances. Just north is the neo-Gothic Woolworth Building (don't miss the splendid gilded lobby) and City Hall. The perfect place to take in the sunset is the esplanade along Battery Park City, easily accessed via Chambers Street. For dinner, choose among TriBeCa's many restaurants.

⏲ There may be fewer crowds waiting for the ferry on weekdays.

DAY 3

Fine art and the finer things in life beckon, starting at the magnificent Metropolitan Museum of Art. You could easily spend a whole day here, but you'll exhaust yourself if you do. Luckily, just behind the museum lies beautiful Central Park, where you can collapse onto a bench, rowboat, or meadow and watch the world go by. For a romantic carriage ride through the park, hail a hansom cab at the park's south end, across from The Plaza hotel and the F.A.O. Schwarz toy store, both extravagances worth a peek. World-class shopping awaits on 5th Avenue and 57th Street.

⏲ The Metropolitan Museum of Art is closed Monday.

DAY 4

First thing this morning, head west to the American Museum of Natural History. Take a gander at the dinosaurs and stop by John Lennon's last home, the Dakota apartment building on Central Park West at 72nd Street. Walk into lush, green Central Park itself to see its Shakespeare Garden, Belvedere Castle, Bethesda Fountain, and Wildlife Center (more familiarly known as the Central Park Zoo). After your dose of fresh air, shop 'til you drop along 5th Avenue and 57th Street. Then treat yourself to dinner followed by a performance at Carnegie Hall or Lincoln Center for the Performing Arts.

⏲ Do this any day.

DAY 5

Do what many New Yorkers like to do on their days off—wander. Make your way to Chinatown for a dim sum breakfast or tapioca-filled soft drink. From here head north to SoHo and NoLita for galleries and chic boutiques and restaurants. Farther east, the Lower East Side is a former immigrant enclave where you'll find the Lower East Side Tenement Museum and bargain shopping on Orchard Street. If you haven't eaten by now, hit a café a few blocks north in the happening East Village, home to yet more shops and vintage stores. From Union Square, walk up Broadway to the fashionable Flatiron District with its inimitable Flatiron Building. Have dinner in one of the neighborhood's noted restaurants.

⏲ This is fine any day, though many Orchard Street shops are closed Saturday.

If You Have More Time

Brooklyn has as much personality as Manhattan and provides a great view of the New York skyline from the Brooklyn Bridge and the Promenade in historic Brooklyn Heights. If you're here for the sunset, check out the evening's world-class entertainment at the Brooklyn Academy of Music. Other daytime attractions in the borough are the Brooklyn Museum of Art and the Brooklyn Botanic Garden, both right next to a subway line. Art galleries are sprouting in hip Williamsburg, a short train ride from Manhattan's 14th Street, and the world's most famous modern art is now being exhibited at the Museum of Modern Art's temporary home in Queens. Back in Manhattan, another

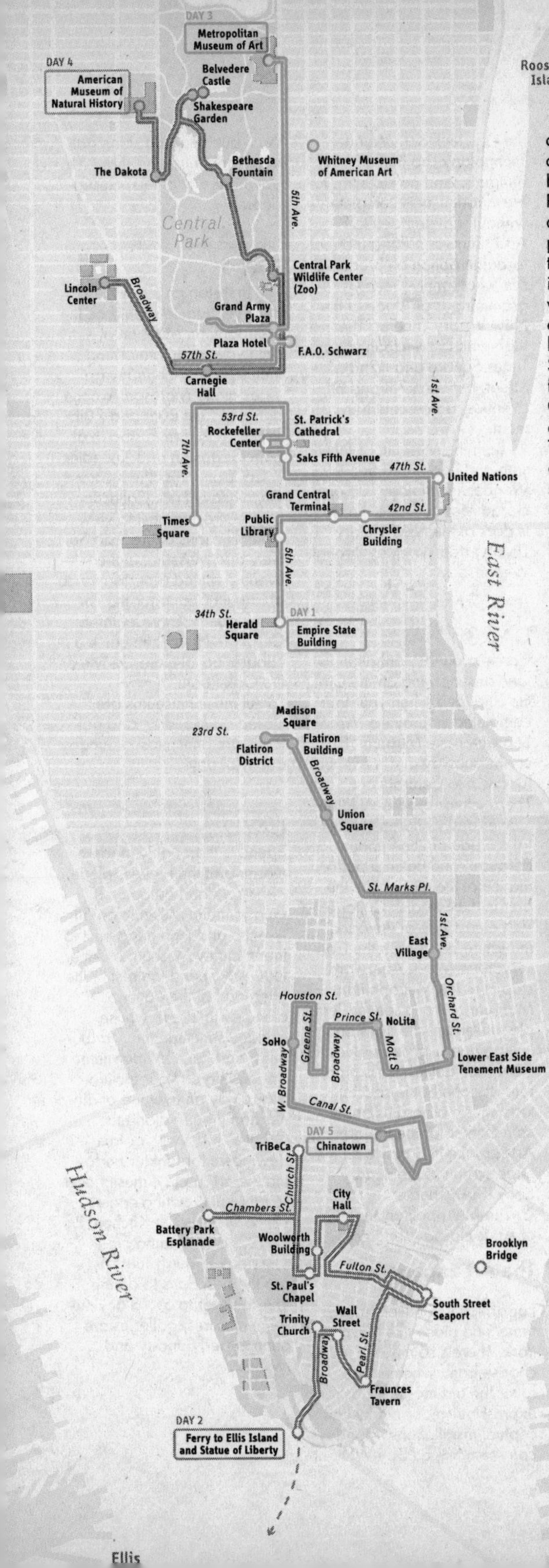

day sees another side of the city uptown. In Morningside Heights you'll find Riverside Park overlooking the Hudson and the Gothic work-in-progress Cathedral of St. John the Divine, as well as the ivory towers of Columbia University. Come back down to earth in Harlem, whose rich history is documented at the Schomburg Center near the famous Abyssinian Baptist Church. Other landmarks include the legendary Apollo Theatre, Striver's Row, the Studio Museum in Harlem, and soul-food restaurants such as Sylvia's.

If You Have 3 Days

For a small bite of the Big Apple, begin your first day at the Empire State Building, Metropolitan Museum of Art, and Central Park. Exit the park's south end at 5th Avenue and work your way through the stores until Rockefeller Center. Drop your loot at the hotel and then take a jaunt through neon-lit Times Square. On the second day take an early ferry trip to the Statue of Liberty and Ellis Island, and then walk the Wall Street area up until City Hall. Board an N or R train to 8th Street, where you can begin a tour of Washington Square Park and Greenwich Village. Follow the itinerary for Day 5 on your last day in town, which hits some great spots for clothing, art, and souvenirs.

A Kid's-Eye View of New York

New York bursts with fantastic activities and sights for tots and teenagers alike. Best of all, these stops appeal to adults as well. Two double-decker bus companies with hop-on, hop-off service and a water taxi service make getting around the city convenient and fun. Both have money-saving family packages that include MetroCards for public transportation, so consider your options when buying tickets.

DAY 1

Start off with a trip to that perennial favorite, the American Museum of Natural History, to see the genuinely awesome dinosaurs. Afterward take a subway ride down to 34th Street, in the front car for a cool view of the tracks. Teens might want to browse the affordable fashions at H & M, or you can head straight to the observatory deck of the nearby Empire State Building. Board a double-decker bus or take a subway down to SoHo, location of the New York City Fire Museum and the Children's Museum of the Arts. Adventurous eaters love dinner in Chinatown, where roast ducks hang in the windows and tapioca balls fill colorful shakes.

⏲ The Children's Museum of the Arts is closed Monday and Tuesday.

DAY 2

Begin the day on the first ferry out to the Statue of Liberty and Ellis Island. In warm weather, head next to South Street Seaport, which serves up fast food, tall ships, chain stores, and street performers. In winter, take the double-decker bus up to Rockefeller Center where ice-skating and the Christmas tree are special treats. There's more fun to be had at the nearby Museum of Television and Radio and at the high-tech SonyWonder Technology Lab in the Sony Building. And no kid's trip to New York City is complete without a pilgrimage to F.A.O. Schwarz. For a more affordable option on Broadway, see what family-friendly programming is on stage at the New Victory Theater. The high wattage of cleaned-up Times Square and 42nd Street, between 7th and 8th avenues, is free entertainment.

⏲ Both the Museum of Television and Radio and Sony-Wonder Technology Lab are closed Monday, and the stage is dark at the New Victory Theater from Monday through Wednesday.

DAY 3

Cruise around Manhattan island this morning on the Circle Line, and when your tour's completed stop by the *Intrepid* Sea-Air-Space Museum. Pick up the subway at 8th Avenue for a trip to Central Park. There, check out the Wildlife Center and Children's Zoo, take a ride on the famous carousel, and catch a performance at the marionette theater in the Swedish Cottage. At the east side of the park, miniature boats skim the Conservatory Water. Afterward stop in at the Metropolitan Museum of Art to see the Temple of Dendur, the arms and armor, and oversize statues in the Greek galleries. As night falls, try one of the special kids' music programs at Lincoln Center for the Performing Arts or take in a movie on the huge screen at the nearby Sony IMAX Theater.

⏲ The Metropolitan Museum of Art is closed Monday.

The Art Experience

For art lovers of every taste, there's no place like New York. There's so much to choose from, whether you favor the old masters, abstract expressionism, or quirky conceptual installations. Mondays can seem like a "Day Without Art," but there are some galleries and museums that take advantage of others' closed doors.

DAY 1

The first stop on every aesthete's schedule should be the Metropolitan Museum of Art. Limit yourself to a morning, then head for the many galleries along Madison Avenue between East 80th and 70th streets—be sure to stop in at both Gagosian and Knoedler & Co. Don't miss the masterpiece-heavy Frick Collection before strolling east to view the collections at the Asia Society and Museum. In the evening attend a performance at Lincoln Center for the Performing Arts, City Center, or Carnegie Hall. Then catch a cabaret act at Café Carlyle or the Oak Room.

⏲ All these museums are closed on Monday, and galleries are often closed Sunday and Monday.

DAY 2

Spend a thoroughly modern morning at the Neue Galerie New York and Solomon R. Guggenheim Museum on 5th Avenue and then head east to the Whitney Museum of American Art. Spend the rest of the afternoon at the galleries along 57th Street, whose standouts include the Marlborough and Pace Wildenstein. Depending on your inclination, enjoy an evening of dinner and theater along the Great White Way, or taxi downtown for funkier performance art, a play, music, or a reading at a cutting-edge venue such as The Kitchen, P. S. 122, or La Mama Etc.

⏲ Friday through Tuesday are the best days to do this tour in order to avoid any museum closures; galleries are often closed Sunday and Monday.

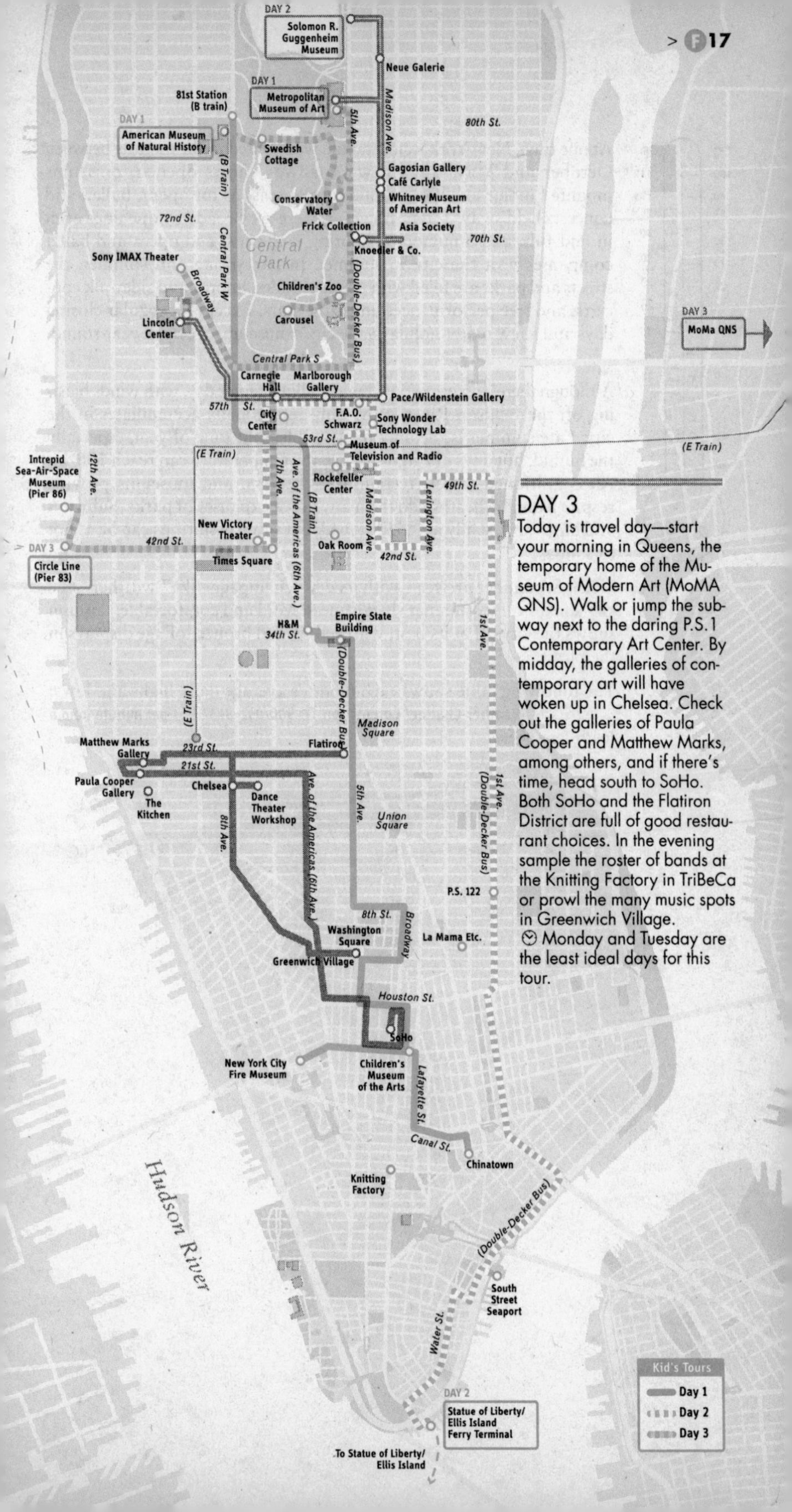

DAY 3

Today is travel day—start your morning in Queens, the temporary home of the Museum of Modern Art (MoMA QNS). Walk or jump the subway next to the daring P.S.1 Contemporary Art Center. By midday, the galleries of contemporary art will have woken up in Chelsea. Check out the galleries of Paula Cooper and Matthew Marks, among others, and if there's time, head south to SoHo. Both SoHo and the Flatiron District are full of good restaurant choices. In the evening sample the roster of bands at the Knitting Factory in TriBeCa or prowl the many music spots in Greenwich Village.

⏲ Monday and Tuesday are the least ideal days for this tour.

WHEN TO GO

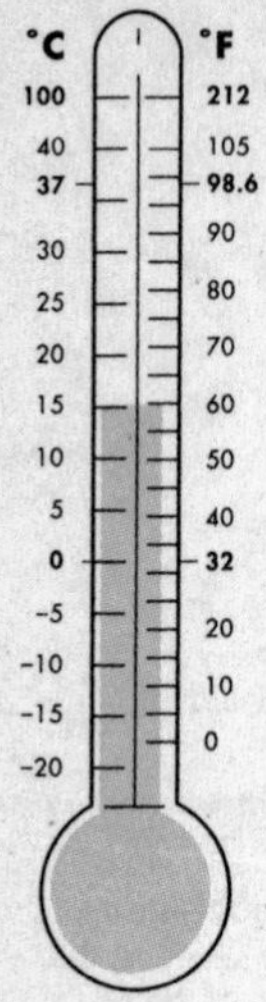

At one time, New York's cultural life was limited to the months between October and May, when new Broadway shows opened, museums mounted major exhibitions, and formal seasons for opera, ballet, and concerts held sway. Today, however, there are Broadway openings even in mid-July, and a number of touring orchestras and opera and ballet companies visit the city in summer. In late spring and summer, the streets and parks are filled with ethnic parades, impromptu sidewalk concerts, and free performances under the stars. Except for regular closing days and a few major holidays, the city's museums are open year-round.

Climate

Although there's an occasional bone-chilling winter day, with winds blasting off the Hudson River, snow only occasionally accumulates in the city. Late summer is the only really unpleasant time of year, especially the humid, hot days of August (when the temperature can reach 100°F). Air-conditioned stores, restaurants, theaters, and museums provide respite from the heat; so do the many green expanses of parks. Subways and buses are usually air-conditioned, but subway stations can be as hot as saunas.

When September arrives—with its dry "champagnelike" weather—the city shakes off its summer sluggishness. Mild and comfortable, autumn shows the city off at its best, with yellow and bronze foliage displays in the parks.

The following table shows each month's average daily highs and lows:

Forecasts **Weather Channel Connection** ☎ **900/932–8437, 95¢ per minute from a Touch-Tone phone.**

Jan.	38F	3C	May	72F	22C	Sept.	76F	24C
	25	–4		54	12		60	16
Feb.	40F	4C	June	80F	27C	Oct.	65F	18C
	27	–3		63	17		50	10
Mar.	50F	10C	July	85F	29C	Nov.	54F	12C
	35	2		68	20		41	5
Apr.	61F	16C	Aug.	84F	29C	Dec.	43F	6C
	44	7		67	19		31	–1

ON THE CALENDAR

NYC & Company–Convention and Visitors Bureau (✉ 810 7th Ave., between W. 52nd and W. 53rd Sts., 3rd floor, Midtown West ☎ 212/484–1222 or 212/397–8200 📠 212/245–5943 🌐 www.nycvisit.com) has exact dates and times for many of the events listed below, and the bureau's Web site has more information on free activities.

WINTER

Early Jan.	The nine-day New York National Boat Show (☎ 212/216–2000 🌐 www.javitscenter.com), at the Jacob Javits Convention Center shows off the latest in pleasure craft (power- and sailboats), yachts, and other nautical equipment.
Late Jan.	Leading dealers in the field of visionary art—also sometimes called naïve art or art of the self-taught—exhibit their wares at the Outsider Art Fair (☎ 212/777–5218) at the Puck Building in SoHo.
Late Jan.–early Feb.	The Chinese New Year, celebrated over two weeks, includes extravagant banquets and a colorful paper-dragon dance that snakes through Chinatown.
Early Feb.	In the invitational Annual Empire State Building Run-Up (☎ 212/860–4455) on February 4, runners scramble up the 1,576 stairs from the lobby of the Empire State Building to the 86th-floor observation deck.
	Nearly 3,000 well-bred canines and their human overseers take over Madison Square Garden for the Westminster Kennel Club Dog Show (☎ 212/465–6741 or 800/455–3647 🌐 www.westminsterkennelclub.org), the nation's second-longest-running animal event (after the Kentucky Derby).
Feb.	Hulking bikes of all varieties are on display at the New York International Motorcycle Show (☎ 212/216–2000 🌐 www.javitscenter.com) at the Jacob Javits Center.
Feb. 14	During the Valentine's Day Marriage Marathon (☎ 212/736–3100 Ext. 377), couples marry atop the Empire State Building.
Early Mar.	The gargantuan Artexpo (☎ 888/322–5226 🌐 www.artexpos.com), at the Jacob Javits Center, includes cultural performances from around the world.
Mar. 17	New York's first St. Patrick's Day Parade (☎ 212/484–1222) took place in 1762, making this boisterous tradition one of the city's oldest annual events. The parade heads up 5th Avenue, from 44th Street to 86th Street.

SPRING

Late Mar.	At the International Asian Art Fair (☎ 212/642–8572 🌐 www.haughton.com), 60 dealers from around the world exhibit furniture, sculptures, bronzes, ceramics, carpets, jewelry, and more from the Middle East, Southeast Asia, and the Far East.
	The Triple Pier Antique Show (☎ 212/255–0020) lures more than 600 antiques dealers to Piers 88, 90, and 92, offering everything from art glass to furniture. There's a reprise of the event in November, as well.

Late Mar.–early Apr.	The week before Easter, the Macy's Flower Show (☎ 212/494–5432) creates lush displays in its flagship emporium and sets its Broadway windows abloom. Exquisite flower arrangements are also on display in Rockefeller Center.
	The Jacob Javits Center is host to the annual New York International Auto Show (☎ 212/216–2000 🌐 www.javitscenter.com), where hundreds of the latest and hottest cars, along with auto oddities, get drivers' motors running.
	Easter Sunday As in the classic Fred Astaire movie, you can don an extravagant hat and strut up 5th Avenue in the Easter Promenade. The excitement centers around St. Patrick's Cathedral, at 51st Street.
Early Apr.	Every spring, the three-ring Ringling Bros. and Barnum & Bailey Circus (☎ 212/465–6741 🌐 www.ringling.com) comes to town. Just before opening night, the Animal Walk takes the show's four-legged stars from their train at Penn Station along 34th Street to Madison Square Garden; it happens around midnight but is well worth waiting up for.
Mid-Apr.	For more than 40 years book-lovers have been hitting their jackpot at the Antiquarian Book Fair (☎ 212/777–5218 🌐 www.sanfordsmith.com), held at the Seventh Regiment Armory on the Upper East Side. Nearly 200 book exhibitors display first editions, rare volumes, manuscripts, autographs, letters, atlases, drawings, and maps, with prices from $25 to more than $25,000.
Late Apr.	The Cherry Blossom Festival (☎ 718/623–7200 🌐 www.bbg.org) at the Brooklyn Botanic Garden takes place during the trees' peak flowering and includes Taiko drumming groups, traditional Japanese dance and arts, and bento box lunches for picnicking.
Early May	About 30,000 cyclists turn out for the annual Bike New York: The Great Five Boro Bike Tour (☎ 212/932–2453 🌐 www.bikenewyork.org). The low-key, 42-mi tour begins in Battery Park and ends with a ride across the Verrazano-Narrows Bridge. A ferry brings cyclists back to Manhattan.
	The International Fine Art Fair (☎ 212/642–8572 🌐 www.haughton.com) brings dealers from all over the country to the Seventh Regiment Armory, where they show off exceptional paintings, drawings, and sculptures from the Renaissance to the 20th century.
Mid-May	Congregation Shearith Israel (the Spanish and Portuguese Synagogue—the landmark home of America's oldest Orthodox Jewish congregation) sponsors a one-day Sephardic Fair (✉ Central Park W, at W. 70th St., Upper West Side ☎ 212/873–0300 🌐 www.shearith-israel.org), where you can watch artists making prayer shawls and crafting jewelry, potters throwing wine cups, and scribes penning marriage contracts.
Mid-May	On the second or third Saturday in May, booths of the Ninth Avenue Food Festival (☎ 212/484–1222) line 20 blocks of 9th Avenue (from West 37th Street to West 57th Street) and cook up every conceiv-

	able type of food. Most of 9th Avenue's many food stores and restaurants participate, selling samples of their wares as well as specially prepared delicacies.
Late May	Navy ships from the United States and abroad are joined by Coast Guard ships during Fleet Week (☎ 212/245–0072) for a parade up the Hudson River. After the ships dock, they are open to the public. It all happens at the *Intrepid* Sea-Air-Space Museum during the week before Memorial Day.
	For more than half a century, Memorial Day has marked the start of the Washington Square Outdoor Art Exhibit (☎ 212/982–6255), an open-air arts-and-crafts fair with some 600 exhibitors who set up in the park and on surrounding streets. The action continues for two weekends, from noon to sundown.
Early June	The Belmont Stakes (☎516/488–6000 🌐www.nyracing.com/belstakes), New York's thoroughbred of horse races, and a jewel in the Triple Crown, comes to Long Island's Belmont Park Racetrack.
Early–mid-June	The New York Jazz Festival (☎ 212/219–3006 🌐 www.jazfest.com), which began more than 10 years ago as an alternative to the JVC Jazz Festival, sponsors numerous performances of classic, acid, Latin, and avant-garde jazz at clubs and public spaces around town. The Knitting Factory (74 Leonard St.) in TriBeCa is a main venue.
Mid-June	During the National Puerto Rican Day Parade (☎ 718/401–0404), dozens of energetic bands send their rhythms reverberating down 5th Avenue, as huge crowds cheer them on.
SUMMER	
Late June	Lesbian and Gay Pride Week (☎ 212/807–7433 🌐 www.nycpride.org) includes the world's biggest annual gay pride parade down 5th Avenue, a film festival, and hundreds of other activities.
	JVC Jazz Festival New York (☎ 212/501–1390) brings giants of jazz and new faces alike to Carnegie Hall, Lincoln Center, the Beacon Theater, Bryant Park, and other theaters and clubs about town.
June–Aug.	Every Monday night filmgoers throng Bryant Park, the backyard of the New York Public Library's Humanities Center, for the Bryant Park Film Festival (☎ 212/512–5700 🌐 www.bryantpark.org). The lawn turns into a picnic ground as fans of classic films claim space hours before show time, which is at dusk.
	In Central Park, Summer Stage (☎ 212/360–2777 🌐 www.summerstage.org) presents free weekday evening and weekend afternoon blues, Latin, pop, African, and country music, dance, opera, and readings.
	Arrive early for a spot. Shakespeare in the Park (☎ 212/539–8500 or 212/539–8750 🌐 www.publictheater.org), sponsored by the Joseph Papp Public Theater at Central Park's Delacorte Theater, tackles the Bard and other classics, often with star performers.

	The New York Philharmonic (☎ 212/875–5656 🌐 www.newyorkphilharmonic.org) chips in with free concerts in various city parks.
	Celebrate Brooklyn (☎ 718/855–7882), New York's longest-running free performing arts festival, brings pop, jazz, rock, classical, klezmer, African, Latin, and Caribbean multicultural music, as well as spoken-word and theatrical performances, to the band shell in Brooklyn's Prospect Park.
July	The streets around Brooklyn's Our Lady of Mt. Carmel Church are full of Italian festivities for two weeks, beginning the first Thursday in July. A highlight of the Giglio e Paradiso festival (✉ Our Lady of Mt. Carmel 275 N. 8th St., Williamsburg ☎ 718/384–0223 for festival information) is when men of the community carry a 65-ft spire (on which a band is playing) down the street.
	Lincoln Center Festival (☎ 212/875–5928 🌐 www.lincolncenter.org) is an international summer performance event lasting several weeks; it includes classical music concerts, contemporary music and dance presentations, stage works, and non-Western arts.
	Midsummer Night Swing (☎ 212/875–5766 🌐 www.lincolncenter.org) transforms Lincoln Center's Fountain Plaza into an open-air dance hall. Top big bands provide jazz, Dixieland, R&B, calypso, and Latin rhythms for dancers of all ages; dance lessons are given each night.
	The Washington Square Music Festival (☎ 212/431–1088) is a series of Tuesday evening free outdoor classical, jazz, and big-band concerts.
July 4	Lower Manhattan celebrates Independence Day (☎ 212/484–1222) with the Great 4th of July Festival, which includes arts, crafts, ethnic food, and live entertainment.
	South Street Seaport also puts on a celebration. Macy's 4th of July Fireworks (☎ 212/494–4495) fill the night sky over the East River. The best viewing points are FDR Drive from East 14th to 41st streets (access via 23rd, 34th, and 48th streets) and the Brooklyn Heights Promenade. The FDR Drive is closed to traffic, but arrive early, as police sometimes restrict even pedestrian traffic.
Aug.	Lincoln Center Out-of-Doors (☎ 212/875–5108 🌐 www.lincolncenter.org) is a series of music, dance, and family-oriented events lasting almost the entire month.
	Harlem Week (☎ 212/862–7200), the world's largest black and Hispanic festival, runs throughout the month. Come for the food, concerts, gospel events, a film festival, children's festival, an auto show, and a bike tour.
	The music of Mozart and his peers wafts through Lincoln Center during the Mostly Mozart (☎ 212/875–5030 🌐 www.lincolncenter.org) festival. Afternoon and evening concerts are presented at reasonable prices.

Late Aug.–early Sept.	The U.S. Open Tennis Tournament (☎ 888/673–6849 🌐 www.usopen.org), in Flushing Meadows–Corona Park, Queens, is one of the city's premier annual sport events.
Labor Day weekend	A Caribbean revel modeled after the harvest carnival of Trinidad and Tobago, the West Indian-American Day Carnival (☎ 718/625–1515 🌐 www.nycarnival.org), on Labor Day in Brooklyn, is the centerpiece of a week's worth of festivities. Celebrations include salsa, reggae, and calypso music performances, as well as Monday's gigantic Mardi Gras–style parade of floats, elaborately costumed dancers, stilt walkers, and West Indian food and music.
Early Sept.	Broadway on Broadway (☎ 212/563–2929) brings some of the best current musical theater to the streets for a free two-hour outdoor concert held in Times Square.
Sept.	Garlands and lights bedeck Little Italy's Mulberry Street and environs for the Feast of San Gennaro (☎ 212/768–9320 🌐 www.littleitalynyc.com), the city's oldest, grandest, largest, and most crowded *festa,* held in honor of the patron saint of Naples.
	Every other September, Jim Henson Productions brings the International Festival of Puppet Theater (☎ 212/794–2400 🌐 www.henson.com) to Manhattan. The next festival will take place in 2004. This festival delights children and adults alike; it has impressed critics as well, winning both Obie and Drama Desk awards.
FALL	
Late Sept.	Some 200 publishers set up displays along 5th Avenue from 48th to 57th streets for New York Is Book Country (☎ 212/207–7242 🌐 www.nyisbookcountry.com), where you can buy new fall releases, meet authors, admire beautiful book jackets, and enjoy live entertainment and bookbinding demonstrations. Bring the children.
Late Sept.–mid-Oct.	Begun in 1963, the New York Film Festival (☎ 212/875–5600 🌐 www.filmlinc.com) is the city's most prestigious annual film event. Cinephiles pack various Lincoln Center venues, and advance tickets to afternoon and evening screenings are essential to guarantee a seat.
Oct.–Dec.	The Brooklyn Academy of Music (BAM) Next Wave Festival (☎ 718/636–4100 🌐 www.bam.org) attracts artsy crowds with its program of local and international cutting-edge dance, opera, theater, and music. You can see such "regulars" as Phillip Glass, John Cale, Lou Reed, and the German dance-theater troupe of Pina Bausch.
Oct.	The Columbus Day Parade (☎ 212/249–9923) is held each year around October 12, normally on 5th Avenue between 44th and 86th streets.
	Considered one of the world's top art fairs, the International Fine Art and Antique Dealers Show (☎ 212/642–8572 🌐 www.haughton.com) brings dealers from the United States and Europe, who show treasures dating from antiquity to the 20th century at the Seventh Regiment Armory.
	The Feast day of St. Francis of Assisi (October 4) is honored at the Cathedral Church of St. John the Divine with the blessing of animals, both household pets and the more exotic sort.

Oct. 31	Thousands of revelers, many in bizarre but brilliant costumes or manipulating huge puppets, march up 6th Avenue (from Spring to West 23rd streets) in the rowdy Greenwich Village Halloween Parade (☎ 845/758–5519 🌐 www.halloween-nyc.com).
Nov.–Jan.	The Radio City Christmas Spectacular (☎ 212/247–4777 🌐 www.radiocity.com) features the famed Rockettes at Radio City Music Hall.
Early Nov.	Since 1883, the National Horse Show (☎ 212/465–6741 🌐 www.nhs.org) has featured the best in equestrian competition.
	The New York City Marathon (☎ 212/860–4455 🌐 www.nyrrc.org), the world's largest, begins on the Staten Island side of the Verrazano-Narrows Bridge and snakes through all five boroughs before finishing in front of Tavern on the Green in Central Park. New Yorkers turn out in droves to cheer on the runners.
Nov. 11	On Veteran's Day (☎ 212/484–1222) a parade marches down 5th Avenue to Madison Square Park. Following the parade, there's a service held at the Eternal Light Memorial in the park.
Thanksgiving Day	The Macy's Thanksgiving Day Parade (☎ 212/494–4495) is a New York tradition, held the fourth Thursday in November. Watch huge balloons float down Central Park West from West 77th Street to Broadway and Herald Square.
Late Nov.	Several days after Thanksgiving, an enormous Christmas tree is mounted in Rockefeller Center, just above the golden Prometheus statue. Thousands of people gather to watch the ceremonial tree lighting (☎ 212/332–7654).
Late Nov.–early Jan.	Every year the Christmas window displays on view at Saks Fifth Avenue (✉ 611 5th Ave., between E. 49th and E. 50th Sts. Midtown East) and Lord & Taylor (✉ 424 5th Ave., between W. 38th and W. 39th Sts. Midtown West) are more inventive and festive than ever.
Late Dec.	A Giant Hanukkah Menorah (✉ 5th Ave. and 59th St. Midtown East ☎ 212/736–8400) is lighted at Grand Army Plaza.
New Year's Eve	The famous ball drop in Times Square (☎ 212/768–1560 🌐 www.timessquarebid.org) is televised all over the world.
	Arrive early, and dress warm! First Night (☎ 212/788–2000 🌐 www.nycvisit.com), a city-sponsored event that takes place in all five boroughs, includes dancing, live music, magicians, jugglers, arts and crafts, and other entertainment in a variety of alcohol-free venues.
	In Central Park, a rowdy Midnight Run (☎ 212/860–4455 🌐 www.nyrrc.org) sponsored by the New York Road Runners Club begins at Tavern on the Green. Some celebrants dress up in costume.

Architecture

Nothing evokes New York City more dramatically than its ever-evolving peaks of steel, glass, and concrete. Save yourself a cramped neck by beholding your favorite skyscraper from a distance, whether from the deck of a cruise boat or the Staten Island Ferry, or the boardwalk of another masterpiece of 19th-century architecture, the Brooklyn Bridge. Few buildings built prior to the mid-19th century have survived the perpetual swing of wrecking balls, but the Financial District has a few—St. Paul's Chapel, Trinity Church, and Federal Hall. Fans of art deco can wander in and out of the Empire State Building, the Chrysler Building, and Rockefeller Center. Modern buildings that play with curves include Philip Johnson's rose-color "Lipstick Building" at 3rd Avenue and East 53rd Street, Frank Lloyd Wright's Guggenheim Museum at 5th Avenue and East 89th Street, and the ski jump–like Grace Building by Skidmore, Owings & Merrill, at West 42nd Street, between 5th and 6th avenues.

Dining

From early in the morning to the moment dinner is served, star chefs fuss over seasonings, sauces, and broths with which to seduce your tongue. For the fairest of prices, stand-up counters and narrow holes-in-the-wall deliver the authentic taste of faraway lands. New York, like Paris, is a movable feast. To enjoy it within a fine establishment such as those of chef Daniel Boulud or restaurateur Danny Meyer, make reservations well in advance, or on shorter notice, you may be able to slip in for a cost-saving, but just as delectable lunch. Overspending your budget is not a prerequisite to eating well in this town. Sample kimchi at a Korean restaurant, snack on the crispest-ever french fries at a Belgian bistro, gobble up a pastrami sandwich or a bagel and schmear at a Jewish deli, or finally have a go at escargot or tripe at a 24-hour brasserie.

Museums

The settings of New York's museums can be as impressive as their collections—from the *Intrepid* Sea-Air-Space Museum aboard an aircraft carrier on the Hudson River to the chunks of European monasteries that make up the Cloisters, a collection of medieval art and objéts. To better imagine the laundry lines, pushcarts, barrels, and clamor of Little Italy and the Lower East Side during the late 1800s, take a boat trip to the immigrant processing center–turned–museum, Ellis Island, or squeeze through the narrow rooms of the Lower East Side Tenement Museum. On the opposite end of the spectrum, the rich collections of industrial barons and financiers such as Henry Clay Frick and J. P. Morgan are on view in their former mansions and private libraries. But if the city held no other museum than the colossal Metropolitan Museum of Art, you could still occupy yourself for days roaming its labyrinthine corridors. A plethora of art museums cover every borough of the city, so familiarize yourself with their permanent and upcoming exhibitions to best prioritize your viewing.

Performing Arts

New York has always been an epicenter of the arts. The city's nickname, "The Big Apple," is said to have been coined by jazz musicians, and you can hear them pour their soul into the great American music genre from the West Village's basements to Harlem's lounges. As the Times Square renaissance continues with no end in sight, Broadway's theaters are booked solid with shows that seem more rewarding every season. Just as vital and important as the blockbuster musicals is off-Broadway drama, where more than a few Tony Award–winning megahits originated. Tickets to productions that include actors as accomplished as Willem DaFoe, William H. Macy, and Frances McDormand are usually about half of those on the well-traveled Great White Way. Brooklyn hosts the world's most accomplished and avant-garde acting troupes, dance companies, and directors at the Brooklyn Academy of Music (BAM). Classical music is still centered on Manhattan's West Side, between Carnegie Hall, and the New York Philharmonic at Lincoln Center.

Shopping

Whether you're planning to run your credit cards up to the max or just window-shop, New York is a veritable shopping orgy. Everywhere, the ambience is part of the experience, and stores are stage sets—the elaborate Ralph Lauren mansion, the minimalist Calvin Klein boutique, super-charged NikeTown, endlessly eclectic ABC Carpet & Home. Bookstores are legion, including secondhand specialists like the Strand, with 8 mi of books. Even though you can get a lot of shopping done under one roof at Bloomingdales, Macy's, Saks Fifth Avenue, Henri Bendel, or Bergdorf Goodman, your feet will cover miles between their floors. SoHo and NoLita are where to go for pricy gifts and funky shoes and clothes, and the Meatpacking District now has hangers holding cuts of designer threads. Mayor Bloomberg may be cutting back on the city's recycling, but vintage and secondhand stores still freshen up castoffs from au-courant fashionistas of the *Sex and the City* vein.

FODOR'S CHOICE

Fodor's Choice ★

The sights, restaurants, hotels, and other travel experiences on these pages are our editors' top picks—our Fodor's Choices. They're the best of their type in the area covered by the book—not to be missed and always worth your time. In the destination chapters that follow, you will find all the details.

LODGING

$$$$ **The Carlyle.** Everything about this landmark suggests refinement, from the first-rate service to the artfully framed Audubons in the rooms. Bemelmans Bar and Café Carlyle are destinations unto themselves.

$$$$ **Four Seasons.** Towering over 57th Street, this I. M. Pei spire houses palatial, soundproof guest rooms with 10-ft ceilings, English sycamore walk-in closets, and blond-marble baths whose immense tubs fill in 60 seconds.

$$$$ **The Lowell.** Many of the suites have working fireplaces in this small gem on a tree-lined Upper East Side street. The Pembroke Room serves a stunning tea, and the Post House is renowned for steaks.

$$$–$$$$ **Mercer Hotel.** Imagine yourself in a minimalist SoHo loft apartment at this downtown hotel with dark African woods and high-tech light fixtures. The decadent two-person tubs, surrounded by mirrors, steal the show.

$$–$$$$ **Inn at Irving Place.** The tea salon of this grand pair of 1830s town houses near Gramercy Park evokes a gentler New York, as do the ornamental fireplaces, four-poster beds, and embroidered linens.

$$–$$$$ **W Times Square.** This super-sleek 57-floor monolith with in-room DVD players puts a premium on futuristic style and ultrahip bustle in its restaurant and bar.

$–$$$$ **The Paramount.** The bohemian, fashionable, yet cost-conscious clientele check out these theatre district digs. Inside at the Mezzanine Restaurant, you can enjoy cocktails or dinner while gazing down on the action below.

$–$$ **Roger Williams Hotel.** Its cavernous Rafael Viñoly–designed lobby—dubbed "a shrine to modernism" by *New York* magazine—highlights this stylish Murray Hill hotel.

¢–$$ **The Gershwin.** Young, foreign travelers flock to this budget hotel–cum–hostel, housed in a converted 13-story Greek revival building. Pop art on each floor augments the brightly colored rooms.

$ **Howard Johnson's Express Inn.** At the nexus of East Village and Lower East Side nightlife, the economical Express is perfect if you want to check out the downtown scene.

BUDGET LODGING

¢–$ **Larchmont Hotel.** Inside this beaux arts town house, rooms have a tasteful safari theme and share bathrooms. For the price and the old New York feel of West 11th Street, this Greenwich Village gem is all anyone needs.

RESTAURANTS

$$$$	**Craft.** Crafting your ideal meal here is like picking and choosing from a gourmand's well-stocked kitchen. The simple yet intriguing menu is exceptionally prepared.
$$$$	**Daniel.** Daniel Boulud's grand dining room presents French classics as well as the chef's own brilliant inventions, such as scallops in black tie (dressed with truffles).
$$$$	**Gramercy Tavern.** Tom Colicchio's seasonal menu offers a respite from the fusion food that's trendy around town. There's an emphasis on game and fish roasted on the bone. Save room for dessert.
$$$$	**Jean-Georges.** Dramatic picture windows give you a view of Central Park from this sleek, modernist dining room as Jean-Georges Vongerichten casts his culinary spell over some of the most astonishing dishes you'll ever taste.
$$$$	**Le Bernardin.** This trend-setting French seafood restaurant serves deceptively simple dishes, such as Spanish mackerel tartare with osetra caviar, in a plush, teak-paneled dining room.
$$$$	**Union Pacific.** Chef Rocco DiSpirito's dining room stands out as a favorite among serious food lovers. Every meal on the seasonal prix-fixe menu is an education in exotic ingredients and flavor combinations.
$$$–$$$$	**Gotham Bar&Grill.** Chef Alfred Portale practically invented "New York architectural cuisine," and he remains the genre's best practitioner—not a drop of flavor is ever lost in the process of arranging the strikingly beautiful presentations.
$$$	**Babbo.** This is Italian food as it was meant to be, updated, and after your first bite of the ethereal homemade pasta or tender suckling pig you'll know why critics rave.
$$$	**Peter Luger Steak House.** If you're after the best porterhouse steak in New York, then Peter Luger's is well worth the trip to Brooklyn. The beefsteak tomato and onion salad, and creamed spinach are perfect sides.
$$–$$$	**Nobu.** Nobu Matsuhisa's dramatic food makes this New York's most famous Japanese restaurant. Both the classic Japanese sushi and the more contemporary dishes are worth waiting for (you'll have to reserve a month in advance).

BUDGET RESTAURANTS

¢–$	**Moustache.** Salad filled pitas, rolled before your eyes, are popular draws to this appealing Middle Eastern restaurant, in both east and west village locations.
¢–$	**Sweet 'n' Tart Café & Restaurant.** Dim sum prepared to order, creative specialties, familiar standbys, and curative teas promise a flavorful experience.

AFTER HOURS

Bowery Ballroom. P. J. Harvey, Shelby Lynne, and Superchunk are among the performers who have appeared at this premier midsize concert venue.

Campbell Apartment. Enjoy a cocktail and executive high style from an overstuffed chair at this restored 1930 former elegant private office.

The Carlyle. At this discreetly sophisticated spot on the Upper East Side, Eartha Kitt and Bobby Short occasionally perform; Monday night belongs to Woody Allen and his clarinet.

Club Shelter. This warehouse-like space is the home to some of the best dancing in the city.

Royalton. A hidden entrance and ultra-modern decor make this a stylishly-hip spot for sipping vodka and champagne.

Village Vanguard. The quintessential jazz venue, where you can still feel the vibes of Monk, Coltrane, and Davis.

ARCHITECTURE

Chrysler Building. An art deco, William Van Alen–designed masterpiece built between 1928 and 1930, the Chrysler Building is one of New York's most iconic and beloved skyscrapers. It's at its best at dusk, when the stainless-steel spires glow, and at night, when its illuminated geometric design looks like the backdrop to a Hollywood musical.

Empire State Building. Atop the 86th-floor observatory (1,050 ft high) you can see up to 80 mi on a clear day. But at night the city's lights are dazzling. The French architect Le Corbusier said, "It is a Milky Way come down to earth." The definitive New York icon is equally stunning from afar.

Grand Central Terminal. The world's largest railway station and the nation's busiest is, as critic Tony Hiss has said, "as a crossroads, a noble building . . . and an ingenious piece of engineering." Inside its majestic space, a celestial map of the zodiac constellations covers the robin's egg–blue ceiling (the major stars actually glow with fiber-optic lights).

CHURCHES

Cathedral Church of St. John the Divine. The largest Gothic cathedral in the world carries the Portal of Paradise, which depicts St. John witnessing the Transfiguration of Jesus, and 32 biblical characters, all intricately carved in stone. The cathedral has changing museum and art-gallery displays and presents a full calendar of secular (classical, folk, solstice) concerts.

St. Patrick's Cathedral. The Gothic, double-spired, Roman Catholic cathedral of New York is one of the city's largest (seating approximately 2,400) and most striking churches.

FOR KIDS

Ice-skating, Rockefeller Center. The outdoor skating rink at Rockefeller Center is utterly romantic, especially when the enormous Christmas tree towers above.

MONUMENTS

Ellis Island Museum. If JFK airport seems daunting and chaotic, imagine disembarking into the international arrival hall at Ellis Island in the late 1800s. Interactive displays cover 400 years of immigration, the slave trade, and may provide links to your own ancestors. Enjoy a fabulous view and a stop at the Statue of Liberty while ferrying to the island.

Statue of Liberty. Presented to the United States in 1886 as a gift from France, she has become a near-universal symbol of freedom and democracy, standing a proud 152-ft high, on top of an 89-ft pedestal (executed by Richard Morris Hunt), on Liberty Island.

MUSEUMS

Metropolitan Museum of Art. Works of art from all over the world and every era of human creativity are part of this elegant and expansive treasure chest. When canvas and marble overwhelm you, turn to the temples, courtyard gardens, and silky dresses that also make up the collections.

MoMA QNS. With a fresh coat of bright blue paint, the former Swingline staple factory, temporary home of the Museum of Modern Art (MoMA), provides an unusual, industrial space for MoMA's peerless collection of 20th-century art.

Solomon R. Guggenheim Museum. Frank Lloyd Wright's landmark museum building displays an inspiring collection of Impressionist works including Matisse and van Gogh. Changing exhibitions focus on artists ranging from Norman Rockwell to Jeff Koons.

QUINTESSENTIAL NEW YORK

Bethesda Fountain. Few New York views are more romantic than the one from the top of the magnificent stone staircase that leads down to the ornate, three-tier fountain.

Cabaret. See a celebrity on stage or sitting next to you at one of the intimate cabaret rooms such as the Carlyle, Oak Room, or Joe's Pub.

Loeb Boathouse. Floating in a rowboat, on a quiet lake, surrounded by greenery . . . admiring the Manhattan skyline. It's an unforgettable experience.

SoHo. The elegant cast-iron buildings, occasional cobblestone street, art galleries, and clothing stores make this a wonderful area in which to shop, drink, and dream of a more glamorous life.

Walking over the Brooklyn Bridge. Begin admiring the Manhattan skyline from the Brooklyn Heights Promenade before setting out for a leisurely hour's stroll on the Brooklyn Bridge's boardwalk. Traffic is beneath you, and the views along the East River and harbor are wide open.

Washington Square Park. In a city without backyards, residents live their lives publicly, and if people-watching isn't entertainment enough in this Greenwich Village park, there are jugglers, magicians, and guitarists to circle round on the weekend.

A Yankees Game. Cheer on the winning Bronx Bombers alongside their devoted fans (or dare to root for the other team).

SHOPPING

Madison and 57th. Here's where the glossy flagships of international and American designers close ranks.

Nolita. One of the few neighborhoods that has withstood the chains, this is the place for unique boutiques.

ABC Carpet & Home. Each floor swarms with distinctive style, from the ornate accessories jumbled downstairs to the '60s mod squadrons above.

Barneys New York. Skate through for a cram session on the new darlings and the evergreen favorites of the design world.

B & H Photo Video and Pro Audio. Join the pros in perusing the equipment here.

Century 21. You can strike fashion gold among these packed racks of discounted goods.

Enchanted Forest. The toys here show—and inspire—real imagination.

Kate's Paperie. Wood pulp never looked so good as it does in these cards, wrapping papers, and albums.

Kiehl's Since 1851. The original source breeds cult-favorite lotions, conditioners, and cleansers.

Tiffany & Co. Talk about true blue—Tiffany's remains the consummate place for glittering gems and silver baubles.

THEME PARKS

Coney Island. Sideshows, old roller coasters, a boardwalk, a beach, and the original Nathan's Famous—what more could you ask for on a sunny afternoon in Brooklyn?

WHERE ART COMES FIRST

Brooklyn Academy of Music. America's oldest performing arts center is a premier performing arts mecca.

Carnegie Hall. A concert at this Italian Renaissance–style, 2,804-seat auditorium is a sublime experience.

Clementine. Works from up-and-coming artists are shown in this intimate Chelsea spot.

Film Forum. Come to watch anything from new releases to restored classics at this popular art-house-repertory theater.

Metropolitan Opera. From October to mid-April, this titan opera company performs with an intensity and quality that rival the world's finest symphonic orchestras. All performances, including operas sung in English.

WILDLIFE

The Bronx Zoo. One urban jungle deserves another. Only at the world's largest urban zoo is there room for gorillas to lumber around a 6½-acre simulated rain forest, or tigers and elephants to roam nearly 40 acres of open meadows.

SMART TRAVEL TIPS

Finding out about your destination before you leave home means you won't squander time organizing everyday minutiae once you've arrived. You'll be more streetwise when you hit the ground as well, better prepared to explore the aspects of New York City that drew you here in the first place. The organizations in this section can provide information to supplement this guide; contact them for up-to-the-minute details. Happy landings!

ADDRESSES

To locate the cross street that corresponds to a numerical avenue address, or to find the avenue closest to a numerical street address, check the phone book's "Address Locator." This handy chart provides relatively simple calculations for finding Manhattan addresses.

AIR TRAVEL TO & FROM NEW YORK

Schedules and fares for air service to New York vary from carrier to carrier and, sometimes, from airport to airport. For the best prices and for nonstop flights, consult several airlines. Generally, more international flights go in and out of Kennedy Airport, more domestic flights go in and out of LaGuardia Airport, and Newark Airport serves both domestic and international travelers.

BOOKING

When you book, **look for nonstop flights** and **remember that "direct" flights stop at least once.** Try to avoid connecting flights, which require a change of plane. Two airlines may operate a connecting flight jointly, so ask whether your airline operates every segment of the trip; you may find that the carrier you prefer flies you only part of the way. To find more booking tips and to check prices and make on-line flight reservations, log on to www.fodors.com.

CARRIERS

There's an abundance of large and small airlines with flights to and from New York City.

Major Airlines Domestic carriers: **America West** ☎ 800/235–9292 www.americawest.com. **American** ☎ 800/433–7300 www.americanairlines.com. **Continental** ☎ 800/525–0280 www.continental.com. **Delta** ☎ 800/221–1212 www.delta.com. **Northwest/KLM** ☎ 800/225–2525 www.nwa.com. **United** 800/241-6522 www.united.com. **US Airways** 800/428-4322 www.usairways.com.

International Carriers **British Airways** 800/247-9297; 0845/77-333-77 in the U.K. www.britishairways.com. **Canadian Airlines** 888/247-2262 www.aircanada.ca. **Qantas** 800/227-4500; 13-1313 in Australia www.qantas.com. **Virgin Atlantic Airways** 800/862-8621; 01293/450-150 in the U.K. www.virgin.com.

Smaller Airlines **Jet Blue** 800/538-2583 www.jetblue.com. **Midwest Express** 800/452-2022 www.midwestexpress.com.

CHECK-IN & BOARDING

Always **ask your carrier about its check-in policy.** Plan to arrive at the airport about two hours before your scheduled departure time for domestic flights and 2½ to 3 hours before international flights. You may need to arrive earlier if you're flying from one of the busier airports or during peak air-traffic times. To avoid delays at airport-security checkpoints, try not to wear any metal. Jewelry, belt and other buckles, steel-toe shoes, barrettes, and underwire bras are among the items that can set off detectors.

Assuming that not everyone with a ticket will show up, airlines routinely overbook planes. When everyone does, airlines ask for volunteers to give up their seats. In return, these volunteers usually get a several-hundred-dollar flight voucher, which can be used toward the purchase of another ticket, and are rebooked on the next flight out. If there are not enough volunteers, the airline must choose who will be denied boarding. The first to get bumped are passengers who checked in late and those flying on discounted tickets, so **get to the gate and check in as early as possible,** especially during peak periods.

Always **bring a government-issued photo ID to the airport;** even when it's not required, a passport is best.

CUTTING COSTS

The least expensive airfares to New York City are priced for round-trip travel and must usually be purchased in advance. Airlines generally allow you to change your return date for a fee; most low-fare tickets, however, are nonrefundable. It's smart to **call a number of airlines and check the Internet;** when you are quoted a good price, **book it on the spot**—the same fare may not be available the next day, or even the next hour. Always **check different routings** and look into using alternate airports. Also, price off-peak flights, which may be significantly less expensive than others. Travel agents, especially low-fare specialists (⇨ Discounts and Deals), are helpful.

Consolidators are another good source. They buy tickets for scheduled flights at reduced rates from the airlines, then sell them at prices that beat the best fare available directly from the airlines. Sometimes you can even get your money back if you need to return the ticket. Carefully read the fine print detailing penalties for changes and cancellations, purchase the ticket with a credit card, and **confirm your consolidator reservation with the airline.**

When you **fly as a courier,** you trade your checked-luggage space for a ticket deeply subsidized by a courier service. There are restrictions on when you can book and how long you can stay. Some courier companies list with membership organizations, such as the Air Courier Association and the International Association of Air Travel Couriers; these require you to become a member before you can book a flight.

Consolidators **AirlineConsolidator.com** 888/468-5385 www.airlineconsolidator.com; for international tickets. **Best Fares** 800/576-8255 or 800/576-1600 www.bestfares.com; $59.90 annual membership. **Cheap Tickets** 800/377-1000 or 888/922-8849 www.cheaptickets.com. **Expedia** 800/397-3342 or 404/728-8787 www.expedia.com. **Hotwire** 866/468-9473 or 920/330-9418 www.hotwire.com. **Now Voyager Travel** 45 W. 21st St., 5th Floor, New York, NY 10010 212/459-1616 212/243-2711 www.nowvoyagertravel.com. **Onetravel.com** www.onetravel.com. **Orbitz** 888/656-4546 www.orbitz.com. **Priceline.com** www.priceline.com. **Travelocity** 888/709-5983; 877/282-2925 in Canada; 0870/876-3876 in the U.K. www.travelocity.com.

Courier Resources **Air Courier Association/Cheaptrips.com** 800/282-1202 www.aircourier.org or www.cheaptrips.com. **International Association of Air Travel Couriers** 308/632-3273 www.courier.org. **Now Voyager Travel** 315 W. 49th St. Plaza Arcade, New York, NY 10019 212/459-1616 212/262-7407 www.nowvoyagertravel.com.

ENJOYING THE FLIGHT

State your seat preference when purchasing your ticket, and then repeat it when you confirm and when you check in. For more legroom, you can request one of the few emergency-aisle seats at check-in, if you are capable of lifting at least 50 pounds—a Federal Aviation Administration requirement of passengers in these seats. Seats behind a bulkhead also offer more legroom, but they don't have under-seat storage. Don't sit in the row in front of the emergency aisle or in front of a bulkhead, where seats may not recline.

Ask the airline whether a snack or meal is served on the flight. If you have dietary concerns, **request special meals when booking.** These can be vegetarian, low-cholesterol, or kosher, for example. It's a good idea to pack some healthful snacks and a small (plastic) bottle of water in your carry-on bag. On long flights, try to maintain a normal routine, to help fight jet lag. At night, **get some sleep.** By day, **eat light meals, drink water** (not alcohol), and **move around the cabin** to stretch your legs. For additional jet-lag tips consult *Fodor's FYI: Travel Fit & Healthy* (available at bookstores everywhere).

Smoking policies vary from carrier to carrier. Many airlines prohibit smoking on all of their flights; others allow smoking only on certain routes or certain departures. Ask your carrier about its policy.

FLYING TIMES

Some sample flying times are: from Chicago (3½ hours), London (7 hours), Los Angeles (6 hours), Sydney via Los Angeles (21 hours).

HOW TO COMPLAIN

If your baggage goes astray or your flight goes awry, complain right away. Most carriers require that you **file a claim immediately.** The Aviation Consumer Protection Division of the Department of Transportation publishes *Fly-Rights*, which discusses airlines and consumer issues and is available on-line.

Airline Complaints **Aviation Consumer Protection Division** ✉ U.S. Department of Transportation, C-75, Room 4107, 400 7th St. NW, Washington, DC 20590 ☎ 202/366-2220 🌐 www.dot.gov/airconsumer. **Federal Aviation Administration Consumer Hotline** ✉ for inquiries: FAA, 800 Independence Ave. SW, Room 810, Washington, DC 20591 ☎ 800/322-7873 🌐 www.faa.gov.

RECONFIRMING

Check the status of your flight before you leave for the airport. You can do this on your carrier's Web site, by linking to a flight-status checker (many Web booking services offer these), or by calling your carrier or travel agent.

SECURITY

Due to increased security measures in all of the area's airports, airlines are asking passengers to arrive three hours before an international flight, and two hours before a domestic flight. Be sure to bring a government-issued photo identification, such as a passport or driver's license. There are tight restrictions on what is allowed in carry-on luggage (⇨ Packing). Avoid wearing clothes with metal accessories and be prepared to remove your shoes for inspection.

AIRPORTS & TRANSFERS

The major gateways to New York City are LaGuardia Airport (LGA) and JFK International Airport (JFK) in the borough of Queens, and Newark International Airport (EWR) in New Jersey. Cab fares will generally be higher to and from Newark Airport, and LaGuardia is closer to Manhattan than JFK. The Air Train link between Penn Station in Manhattan and Newark Airport makes the smooth journey in less than 30 minutes.

Airport Information **JFK International Airport** ☎ 718/244-4444 🌐 www.jfkairport.com. **LaGuardia Airport** ☎ 718/533-3400 🌐 www.laguardiaairport.com. **Newark International Airport** ☎ 973/961-6000 or 888/397-4636 🌐 www.newarkairport.com.

AIRPORT TRANSFERS

Air-Ride Transportation Information Service provides detailed, up-to-the-minute recorded information on how to reach your destination from any of New York's airports. Note that if you arrive after midnight at any airport, you will likely wait a very long time for a taxi. Consider calling a car service as there is no shuttle service at that time.

Transfer Information **Air-Ride Transportation Information Service** ☎ 800/247-7433 🌐 www.panynj.gov/aviation.html.

TRANSFERS—CAR SERVICES

Car services (⇨ Taxis and Car Services) can be a great deal because the driver will often meet you on the concourse or in the baggage-claim area and help you with your luggage. The flat rates and tolls are often comparable to taxi fares, but some car services will charge for parking and waiting time at the airport. To eliminate these expenses, other car services require that you telephone their dispatcher when you land so they can send the next available car to pick you up. New York City Taxi and Limousine Commission rules require that all car services be licensed and pick up riders only by prior arrangement; if possible, **call 24 hours in advance for reservations,** or at least a half day before your flight's departure. Gypsy cab drivers often solicit fares outside the terminal; it's a risky choice, and even if you do have a safe ride you'll pay more than the going rate.

Car Reservations **Carmel Car Service** ☎ 212/666-6666 or 800/922-7635 🌐 www.carmelcarservice.com. **Executive Town Car & Limousines** ☎ 516/538-8551 or 800/716-2799. **Gotham Limousine** ☎ 212/868-4733 or 800/993-0050. **London Towncars** ☎ 212/988-9700 or 800/221-4009. **Manhattan International Limo** ☎ 718/729-4200 or 800/221-7500. **Mirage Limousine Service** ☎ 212/744-9700. **Skyline** ☎ 212/741-3711 or 800/567-5957. **Tel Aviv Car and Limousine Service** ☎ 212/777-7777 or 800/222-9888.

TRANSFERS—TAXIS & SHUTTLES

Outside the baggage-claim area at each of New York's major airports is a taxi stand where a uniformed dispatcher helps passengers find taxis (⇨ Taxis and Car Services). Cabs are not permitted to pick up fares anywhere else in the arrivals area, so if you want a taxi, take your place in line. Shuttle services generally pick up passengers from a designated spot along the curb.

New York Airport Service runs buses between JFK and LaGuardia airports, and buses from those airports to Grand Central Terminal, Port Authority Bus Terminal, Penn Station, and hotels between 33rd and 57th streets in Manhattan. The cost range is between $10 and $15. Buses operate from 6 AM to 11:10 PM from the airport; between 5 AM and 10 PM going to the airport. A $5 bus leaves either airport at the top of the hour for Long Island Railroad's Jamaica Station. The ride between both airports and the station is 30 minutes.

SuperShuttle vans travel to and from Manhattan to JFK, LaGuardia, and Newark. These blue vans will stop at your home, office, or hotel. Courtesy phones are at the airports. For travel to the airport, the company requests 24-hour advance notice, which you can arrange yourself or through a hotel concierge. Fares range from $13 to $22.

Shuttle Service **New York Airport Service** ☎ 718/875-8200 🌐 www.nyairportservice.com. **SuperShuttle** ☎ 212/258-3826 or 800/258-3826 🌐 www.supershuttle.com.

TRANSFERS FROM JFK INTERNATIONAL AIRPORT

Taxis charge a flat fee of $35 plus tolls (which may be as much as $4) to Manhattan only, and take 35–60 minutes. Prices are $16–$55 for trips to other locations in New York City. You should also tip the driver.

AirTrain JFK links to the A subway line at Howard Beach station, and by early summer of 2003, AirTrain JFK will also serve Jamaica Station (where the Long Island Railroad as well as three subway lines in the adjacent Sutphin Boulevard/Archer Avenue station connect to Manhattan). AirTrain JFK runs 24 hours, leaving Howard Beach station every 4 minutes during peak times and every 12 minutes during low traffic times, and will leave Jamaica Station every 10 minutes. From midtown Manhattan, the longest trip to JFK will be via the A train (under an hour); the quickest trip will be with the Long Island Railroad (about 30 minutes). When traveling to the Howard Beach station, be sure to take the A train marked FAR ROCKAWAY or ROCKAWAY PARK, **not** LEFFERTS BOULEVARD.

JFK Transfer Information **AirTrain JFK** ☎ 718/244-4444 🌐 www.airtrainjfk.com. **Long Island Railroad** Jamaica Station ✉ 146 Archer Ave., at Sutphin Ave. ☎ 718/217-5477.

TRANSFERS FROM LAGUARDIA AIRPORT

Taxis cost $15–$30 plus tip and tolls (which may be as high as $4) to most destinations in New York City, and take at least 20–40 minutes. Group taxi rides to Manhattan are available at taxi dispatch lines just outside the baggage claim areas during most travel hours (except on Saturday and holidays). Group fares run $9–$10 per person (plus a share of tip and tolls).

For $2 you can ride the M-60 public bus (there are no luggage facilities on this bus) to 116th Street and Broadway, across from Columbia University in Manhattan. From there, you can transfer to the No. 1 subway to midtown. Alternatively, you can take Bus Q-48 to the Main Street subway station in Flushing, where you can transfer to the No. 7 train. Allow at least 90 minutes for the entire trip to midtown.

Triboro Coach Corp. runs its Q-33 line from the airport to the Jackson Heights subway stop in Queens, where you can transfer to the E or F train; it also stops at the Roosevelt Avenue–Jackson Heights station, where you can pick up the No. 7 subway line. The cost is $2.

LaGuardia Transfer Information **Triboro Coach Corp.** 718/335-1000 www.triborocoach.com.

TRANSFERS FROM NEWARK AIRPORT

Taxis to Manhattan cost $35–$55 plus tolls ($8) and take 20 to 45 minutes. "Share and Save" group rates are available for up to four passengers between 8 AM and midnight—make arrangements with the airport's taxi dispatcher. From Manhattan, there's an extra $10 surcharge.

AirTrain Newark is an elevated light rail system that connects to New Jersey Transit and Amtrak trains at the Newark International Airport Station. Total travel time to Penn Station in Manhattan is approximately 20 minutes and costs $11.15. AirTrain runs from 5 AM to 2 AM daily, and there are no additional fees when you purchase a connecting ticket through New Jersey Transit or Amtrak.

New Jersey Transit Airlink buses leave Newark Airport every 20 to 30 minutes from 6:15 AM to 1:45 AM, for Penn Station in Newark, New Jersey. The ride takes about 20 minutes, and the fare is $4 (be sure to have exact change). From there, you can catch PATH trains, which run to Manhattan 24 hours a day. The trains run every 10 minutes on weekdays, every 15 to 30 minutes on weeknights, and every 20 to 30 minutes on weekends. Trains travel along 6th Avenue in Manhattan, making stops at Christopher Street, West 9th Street, West 14th Street, West 23rd Street, and West 33rd Street. The fare is $2.

Olympia Trails buses leave for Grand Central Terminal and Penn Station in Manhattan about every 20 minutes until midnight. The trip takes roughly 45 minutes, and the fare is $11. Between the Port Authority and Newark, buses run every 20 to 30 minutes. The fare is $11.

Newark Airport Information **AirTrain Newark** 888/397-4636 or 800/626-7433 www.airtrainnewark.com. **New Jersey Transit Airlink** 973/762-5100 www.njtransit.state.nj.us. **Olympia Trails** 212/964-6233 or 718/622-7700 www.olympiabus.com. **PATH Trains** 800/234-7284 www.pathrail.com.

BOAT & FERRY TRAVEL

The Staten Island Ferry runs across New York Harbor between Whitehall Street in lower Manhattan and St. George terminal in Staten Island. The 25-minute ride is free and from it you can get a wonderful view of the Financial District skyscrapers and the Statue of Liberty.

New York Water Taxi, in addition to serving commuters, shuttles tourists to the city's many waterfront attractions between the West Side, lower Manhattan, the South Street Seaport, and Brooklyn's waterfront parks. The hop-on, hop-off ticket (good for 24 hours) for adults is $15 and includes a one-day pass for public transportation.

NY Waterway is primarily a commuter service but also has sightseeing cruises. Its *Yankee Clipper* and *Mets Express* ferries take passengers from Manhattan and New Jersey to Yankee Stadium and Shea Stadium for $14 round-trip. Its service between the World Financial Center on the Hudson River to Pier 11 on Wall Street is free. NY Waterway also travels to Hoboken, New Jersey, from three Manhattan piers.

FARES & SCHEDULES

Boat & Ferry Information **Circle Line/Harbor Cruises** 212/269-5755 www.statueoflibertyferry.com. **New York Water Taxi (NYWT)** 212/742-1969 www.newyorkwatertaxi.com. **NY Waterway** 212/564-8846 or 800/533-3779 www.nywaterway.com. **Staten Island Ferry** 718/390-5253 or 718/815-2628.

BUS TRAVEL TO & FROM NEW YORK CITY

Most long-haul and commuter bus lines feed into the Port Authority Terminal, on 8th Avenue between West 40th and 42nd streets. You must purchase your ticket at a ticket counter, not from the bus driver, so give yourself enough time to wait in a line. Six bus lines, serving northern New Jersey and Rockland County, New York, make daily stops at the George Washington Bridge Bus Station from 5 AM to 1 AM. The station is connected to the 175th Street Station on the A line of the subway, which travels down the West Side of Manhattan.

Bus Information **Adirondack, Pine Hill, and New York Trailways** ☎ 800/225-6815 ⊕ www.trailways.com. **Bonanza Bus Lines** ☎ 800/556-3815 ⊕ www.bonanzabus.com. **Greyhound Lines Inc.** ☎ 800/231-2222 ⊕ www.greyhound.com. **Martz Trailways** ☎ 800/233-8604 ⊕ www.martztrailways.com. **New Jersey Transit** ☎ 973/762-5100 ⊕ www.njtransit.state.nj.us. **Peter Pan Trailways** ☎ 413/781-2900 or 800/343-9999 ⊕ www.peterpanbus.com. **Shortline** ☎ 800/631-8405 ⊕ www.shortlinebus.com. **Vermont Transit** ☎ 802/864-6811 or 800/451-3292 ⊕ www.vermonttransit.com.

BUS TRAVEL WITHIN NEW YORK CITY

Most city buses follow easy-to-understand routes along the Manhattan street grid. Routes go up or down the north–south avenues, or east and west on the major two-way crosstown streets: 96th, 86th, 79th, 72nd, 57th, 42nd, 34th, 23rd, and 14th. Most bus routes operate 24 hours, but service is infrequent late at night. Traffic jams can make rides maddeningly slow. Certain bus routes provide "Limited-Stop Service" during weekday rush hours, which saves travel time by stopping only at major cross streets and transfer points. A sign posted at the front of the bus indicates it has limited service; ask the driver whether the bus stops near where you want to go before boarding.

To find a bus stop, **look for a light-blue sign (green for a limited bus)** on a green pole; bus numbers and routes are listed, with the stop's name underneath.

FARES & SCHEDULES

Bus fare is the same as subway fare: $2. MetroCards (⇨ Public Transportation) allow you one free transfer between buses or from bus to subway; when using a token or cash, you can **ask the driver for a free transfer coupon,** good for one change to an intersecting route. Legal transfer points are listed on the back of the slip. Transfers generally have time limits of two hours. You cannot use the transfer to enter the subway system.

Route maps and schedules are posted at many bus stops in Manhattan and at major stops throughout the other boroughs. Each of the five boroughs of New York has a separate bus map; they are available from some station booths, but rarely on buses. The best places to obtain them are the MTA booth in the Times Square Visitors Center, or the information kiosks in Grand Central Terminal and Penn Station.

Bus Information **Metropolitan Transit Authority (MTA) Travel Information Center** ☎ 718/330-1234 ⊕ www.mta.nyc.ny.us. **MTA Status Information Hot Line** ☎ 718/243-7777, updated hourly.

PAYING

Pay your bus fare when you board, with exact change in coins (no pennies, and no change is given) or with a MetroCard.

BUSINESS HOURS

New York is very much a 24-hour city. Its subways and buses run around the clock, and plenty of services are available at all hours and on all days of the week.

BANKS & OFFICES

Banks are open weekdays 9 AM–3 PM or 9 AM–3:30 PM, and some have late hours one day a week or are open Saturday morning. *See* Mail and Shipping for post office hours.

MUSEUMS & SIGHTS

Museum hours vary greatly, but most of the major ones are open Tuesday–Sunday and keep later hours on Tuesday or Thursday evening.

PHARMACIES

Pharmacies are generally open early in the morning and remain open until at least 6 PM or 7 PM. Most chain drugstores, such as Duane Reade, CVS, and Rite-Aid, have a number of locations that keep late hours or are open 24 hours.

SHOPS

Stores are generally open Monday–Saturday from 10 AM to 6 PM or 7 PM, but neighborhood peculiarities do exist and many retailers remain open until 8 PM or even later. Sunday hours are common in most areas of the city. Many stores on the Lower East Side and in the Diamond District on West 47th Street close on Friday afternoon and all day Saturday for the Jewish Sabbath, but some are open Sunday.

CAMERAS & PHOTOGRAPHY

There are plenty of photography opportunities in New York, and you may have to shoot fast or several times if you want to avoid passersby filling the frame. Some people may be sensitive about having their pictures taken without their consent, so ask permission first. The *Kodak Guide to Shooting Great Travel Pictures* (available at bookstores everywhere) is loaded with tips.

Photo Help **Kodak Information Center** ☎ 800/242-2424 🌐 www.kodak.com.

EQUIPMENT PRECAUTIONS

Don't pack film and equipment in checked luggage, where it is much more susceptible to damage. X-ray machines used to view checked luggage are extremely powerful and therefore are likely to ruin your film. Try to **ask for hand inspection of film,** which becomes clouded after repeated exposure to airport X-ray machines, and **keep videotapes and computer disks away from metal detectors.** Always **keep film, tape, and computer disks out of the sun.** Carry an extra supply of batteries, and **be prepared to turn on your camera, camcorder, or laptop** to prove to airport security personnel that the device is real.

CAR RENTAL

Rates in New York City begin at around $70 a day and $350 a week for an economy car with air-conditioning, automatic transmission, and unlimited mileage. This does not include tax on car rentals, which is 13.25%. Rental costs are lower just outside New York City, specifically in places like Hoboken, New Jersey, and Yonkers, New York. The Yellow Pages are also filled with a profusion of local car-rental agencies, some renting secondhand vehicles. If you're traveling during a holiday period, make sure that a confirmed reservation guarantees you a car.

Major Agencies **Alamo** ☎ 800/327-9633 🌐 www.alamo.com. **Avis** ☎ 800/331-1212; 800/879-2847 or 800/272-5871 in Canada; 0870/606-0100 in the U.K.; 02/9353-9000 in Australia; 09/526-2847 in New Zealand 🌐 www.avis.com. **Budget** ☎ 800/527-0700; 0870/156-5656 in the U.K. 🌐 www.budget.com. **Dollar** ☎ 800/800-4000; 0124/622-0111 in the U.K., where it's affiliated with Sixt; 02/9223-1444 in Australia 🌐 www.dollar.com. **Hertz** ☎ 800/654-3131; 800/263-0600 in Canada; 0870/844-8844 in the U.K.; 02/9669-2444 in Australia; 09/256-8690 in New Zealand 🌐 www.hertz.com. **National Car Rental** ☎ 800/227-7368; 0870/600-6666 in the U.K. 🌐 www.nationalcar.com.

CUTTING COSTS

For a good deal, **book through a travel agent who will shop around.** Also, **price local car-rental companies**—whose prices may be lower still, although their service and maintenance may not be as good as those of major rental agencies—and **research rates on the Internet.** Remember to ask about required deposits, cancellation penalties, and drop-off charges if you're planning to pick up the car in one city and leave it in another. If you're traveling during a holiday period, also make sure that a confirmed reservation guarantees you a car.

Local Agencies **Autorent** ☎ 212/315-1555 🌐 www.autorentonline.com. **New York Rent-A-Car** ☎ 212/799-1100 or 800/697-2227 🌐 www.nyrac.com.

INSURANCE

When driving a rented car you are generally responsible for any damage to or loss of the vehicle. You also may be liable for any property damage or personal injury that you may cause while driving. Before you rent, see what coverage you already have under the terms of your personal auto-insurance policy and credit cards.

For about $10 to $25 a day, rental companies sell protection, known as a collision- or loss-damage waiver (CDW or LDW), that eliminates your liability for damage to the car; it's always optional and should never be automatically added to your bill. In New York State, which has outlawed the sale of the CDW and LDW altogether, you pay for only the first $100 of damage to the rental car.

REQUIREMENTS & RESTRICTIONS

In New York you must be 18 to rent a car. Some agencies in Manhattan require a minimum age of 25. When picking up a car, non-U.S. residents will need a reservation voucher for any prepaid reservations that were made in the traveler's home country, a passport, a driver's license, and a travel policy that covers each driver.

SURCHARGES

Before you pick up a car in one city and leave it in another, **ask about drop-off**

charges or one-way service fees, which can be substantial. Note, too, that some rental agencies charge extra if you return the car before the time specified in your contract. To avoid a hefty refueling fee, **fill the tank just before you turn in the car,** but be aware that gas stations near the rental outlet may overcharge. It's almost never a deal to buy the tank of gas that's in the car when you rent it; the understanding is that you'll return it empty, but some fuel usually remains. Surcharges may apply if you're under 25 or if you take the car outside the area approved by the rental agency. You'll pay extra for child seats (about $6 a day), which are compulsory for children under five, and usually for additional drivers (about $10 per day).

CAR TRAVEL

If you plan to drive into Manhattan, try to avoid the morning and evening rush hours (a problem at the crossings into Manhattan) and lunch hour. The deterioration of the bridges to Manhattan, especially those spanning the East River, mean repairs will be ongoing for the next few years. Listen to traffic reports on the radio (⇨ Media) before you set off, and don't be surprised if a bridge is partially or entirely closed.

Driving within Manhattan can be a nightmare of gridlocked streets, predatory motorists, and seemingly suicidal jaywalkers. Narrow and one-way streets are common, particularly downtown, and can make driving even more difficult. The most congested streets of the city lie between 14th and 59th streets and 3rd and 8th avenues.

GASOLINE

Fill up your tank when you have a chance—gas stations are few and far between. If you can, **fill up at stations outside of the city,** where prices are anywhere from 10¢ to 50¢ cheaper per gallon. The average price of a gallon of regular unleaded gas is $1.60, although prices can vary from station to station. In Manhattan, you can refuel at stations along the West Side Highway and 11th Avenue south of West 57th Street and along East Houston Street. Some gas stations in New York require you to pump your own gas; others provide attendants. In New Jersey, the law states an attendant must pump your gas.

PARKING

Free parking is difficult to find in midtown, and violators may be towed away literally within minutes. All over town, parking lots charge exorbitant rates—as much as $15 for two hours. If you do drive, **try not to use your car much for traveling within Manhattan.** Instead, park it in a guarded parking garage for at least several hours; the sting of hourly rates lessens somewhat if a car is left for a significant amount of time. If you find a spot on the street, be sure to **check parking signs carefully,** as rules differ from block to block.

ROAD CONDITIONS

New York City streets are in generally good condition, although there are enough potholes and bad patch jobs to make driving a little rough at times, such as on Canal Street. Road and bridge repair seems to go on constantly, so you may encounter the occasional detour or a bottleneck where a three-lane street narrows to one lane. Heavy rains can cause street flooding in some areas, most notoriously on the Franklin Delano Roosevelt Drive (known as the FDR and sometimes as the East River Drive), where the heavy traffic can grind to a halt when lakes suddenly appear on the road. Traffic can be very heavy anywhere in the city at any time, made worse by the bad habits—double-parking, sudden lane changes, etc.—of some drivers. Drivers don't slow down for yellow lights here—they speed up to make it through the intersection.

RULES OF THE ROAD

On city streets the speed limit is 30 mi per hour, unless otherwise posted. There's no right turn on red allowed within the city limits. Be alert for one-way streets and "no left turn" intersections. There's a ban on single-occupancy vehicles coming into Manhattan between 6 AM and 10 AM on weekdays (except holidays) via the Brooklyn Bridge, Manhattan Bridge, Williamsburg Bridge, Brooklyn Battery Tunnel, and Holland Tunnel.

The law requires that front-seat passengers wear seat belts at all times. Children under 16 must wear seat belts in both the front and back seats. Always **strap children under age five into approved child-safety seats.** It is illegal to use a handheld cell phone while driving in New York State. Police will immediately seize the car of any DWI (driving while intoxicated) offenders in New York City.

CHILDREN IN NEW YORK

Even though much of New York is focused on the adult pursuits of making money and spending it on the finer things in life, kids can run riot in this city, too. Cultural institutions include programs for introducing children to the arts, large stores put on fun promotional events, and many attractions, from skyscrapers to museums, engage the whole family. For listings of children's events, consult *New York* magazine, *Time Out New York,* and the free weekly *Village Voice* newspaper. The Friday *New York Times* "Weekend" section also includes children's activities. Other good sources on happenings for youngsters are the monthly magazines *New York Family* and *Big Apple Parent,* both available free at toy stores, children's museums, and other places around town where parents and children are found. If you have access to cable television, check the local all-news channel *NY1,* where you'll find a spot aired several times daily that covers current and noteworthy children's events. *Fodor's Around New York City with Kids* (available in bookstores everywhere) can help you plan your days together.

If you are renting a car, don't forget to **arrange for a car seat** when you reserve. For general advice about traveling with children, consult *Fodor's FYI: Travel with Your Baby* (available in bookstores everywhere).

Publications **Big Apple Parent** ☎ 212/889-6400 🌐 www.parentsknow.com. **Fodor's Travel Publications** ☎ 800/533-6478 🌐 www.fodors.com. **New York Family** ☎ 914/381-7474 🌐 www.parenthoodweb.com.

BABY-SITTING

Avalon Healthcare is prepared to take very young children off your hands—at least for the day. Rates are $16 an hour for one to two children of any age, and there is a flat fee of $17.50 an hour to care for three or more children. There's also a $3 transportation charge ($8 after 8 PM, $15 after midnight).

For children over age two, the Baby Sitters' Guild will schedule sightseeing tours for a flat fee of $100. Regular baby-sitting rates are $15 an hour for one child, $17 for two children, and $20 for three children, plus a $4.50 transportation charge ($7 after midnight). More than 16 languages are spoken by staff members. Minimum booking is for four hours.

Agencies **Avalon Healthcare** ☎ 212/245-0250 🌐 www.avalonhealthcare.com. **Baby Sitters' Guild** ☎ 212/682-0227 🌐 www.babysittersguild.com.

FLYING

Experts agree that it's a good idea to use safety seats aloft for children weighing less than 40 pounds. Airlines set their own policies: if you use a safety seat, U.S. carriers usually require that the child be ticketed, even if he or she is young enough to ride free, because the seats must be strapped into regular seats. And even if you pay the full adult fare for the seat, it may be worth it, especially on longer trips. Do **check your airline's policy about using safety seats during takeoff and landing.** Safety seats are not allowed everywhere in the plane, so get your seat assignments as early as possible.

When reserving, **request children's meals or a freestanding bassinet** (not available at all airlines) if you need them. But note that bulkhead seats, where you must sit to use the bassinet, may lack an overhead bin or storage space on the floor.

PUBLIC TRANSPORTATION

Children under six ride for free on MTA buses and subways. If you're pushing a stroller, don't struggle through a subway turnstile; **ask the station agent to buzz you through the gate** (make sure the attendant sees you swipe your MetroCard at the turnstile first). Keep a sharp eye on your young ones while on the subway. At some stations there is a gap between the train doors and the platform. During rush hour crowds often try to push into spaces that look empty—but are actually occupied by a stroller. Unfortunately New York riders are not known to give up their seats for children, or for someone carrying a child.

SIGHTS & ATTRACTIONS

Places that are especially appealing to children are indicated by a rubber-duckie icon (🐤) in the margin.

WHERE TO STAY

Rooms in New York are small by national standards, so ask just how large the room is into which you're adding a cot or foldout couch. Most hotels in New York allow children under a certain age to stay in their parents' room at no extra charge, but others charge for them as extra adults; be sure to **find out the cutoff age for children's discounts.**

COMPUTERS ON THE ROAD

Some hotels in New York provide access to data ports and Web TV. For specific information inquire before making reservations.

CONCIERGES

Concierges, found in many hotels, can help you with theater tickets and dinner reservations: a good one with connections may be able to get you seats for a hot show or prime-time dinner reservations at the restaurant of the moment. You can also turn to your hotel's concierge for help with travel arrangements, sightseeing plans, services ranging from aromatherapy to zipper repair, and emergencies. Always, **always tip** a concierge who has been of assistance (⇨ Tipping).

New York is *the* place to get whatever you need or want, whenever you may need or want it. The problem for visitors and residents alike has always been just how to perform this trick without burning too big a hole in your pocket. For a fee, New York Concierge can help. The cost begins with a $35 single-service charge and hourly rates of $50 for concierge assistance; whether your need is dire or whimsical, the sky's the limit.

New York Concierge ☎ 212/590-2530 🌐 www.nyconcierge.com.

CONSUMER PROTECTION

Whether you're shopping for gifts or purchasing travel services, **pay with a major credit card** whenever possible, so you can cancel payment or get reimbursed if there's a problem (and you can provide documentation). If you're doing business with a particular company for the first time, **contact your local Better Business Bureau and the attorney general's offices** in your state and (for U.S. businesses) the company's home state as well. Have any complaints been filed? Finally, if you're buying a package or tour, always **consider travel insurance** that includes default coverage (⇨ Insurance).

BBBs **Council of Better Business Bureaus** ✉ 4200 Wilson Blvd., Suite 800, Arlington, VA 22203 ☎ 703/276-0100 📠 703/525-8277 🌐 www.bbb.org.

CUSTOMS & DUTIES

IN AUSTRALIA

Australian residents who are 18 or older may bring home A$400 worth of souvenirs and gifts (including jewelry), 250 cigarettes or 250 grams of cigars or other tobacco products, and 1,125 ml of alcohol (including wine, beer, and spirits). Residents under 18 may bring back A$200 worth of goods. Members of the same family traveling together may pool their allowances. Prohibited items include meat products. Seeds, plants, and fruits need to be declared upon arrival.

Australian Customs Service Regional Director, Box 8, Sydney, NSW 2001 ☎ 02/9213-2000 or 1300/363263; 02/9364-7222 or 1800/803-006 quarantine-inquiry line 📠 02/9213-4043 🌐 www.customs.gov.au.

IN CANADA

Canadian residents who have been out of Canada for at least seven days may bring in C$750 worth of goods duty-free. If you've been away fewer than seven days but more than 48 hours, the duty-free allowance drops to C$200. If your trip lasts 24 to 48 hours, the allowance is C$50. You may not pool allowances with family members. Goods claimed under the C$750 exemption may follow you by mail; those claimed under the lesser exemptions must accompany you. Alcohol and tobacco products may be included in the seven-day and 48-hour exemptions but not in the 24-hour exemption. If you meet the age requirements of the province or territory through which you reenter Canada, you may bring in, duty-free, 1.5 liters of wine *or* 1.14 liters (40 imperial ounces) of liquor *or* 24 12-ounce cans or bottles of beer or ale. Also, if you meet the local age requirement for tobacco products, you may bring in, duty-free, 200 cigarettes and 50 cigars. Check ahead of time with the Canada Customs and Revenue Agency or the Department of Agriculture for policies regarding meat products, seeds, plants, and fruits.

You may send an unlimited number of gifts (only one gift per recipient, however) worth up to C$60 each duty-free to Canada. Label the package UNSOLICITED GIFT—VALUE UNDER $60. Alcohol and tobacco are excluded.

Canada Customs and Revenue Agency ✉ 2265 St. Laurent Blvd., Ottawa, Ontario K1G 4K3 ☎ 800/461-9999, 204/983-3500, 506/636-5064 🌐 www.ccra.gc.ca.

IN NEW ZEALAND

All homeward-bound residents may bring back NZ$700 worth of souvenirs and gifts; passengers may not pool their allowances, and children can claim only the concession on goods intended for their own use. For those 17 or older, the duty-free allowance also includes 4.5 liters of wine or beer; one 1,125-ml bottle of spirits; and either 200 cigarettes, 250 grams of tobacco, 50 cigars, *or* a combination of the three up to 250 grams. Meat products, seeds, plants, and fruits must be declared upon arrival to the Agricultural Services Department.

New Zealand Customs ✉ Head office: The Customhouse, 17-21 Whitmore St., Box 2218, Wellington ☎ 09/300-5399 or 0800/428-786 🌐 www.customs.govt.nz.

IN THE U.K.

From countries outside the European Union, including the United States, you may bring home, duty-free, 200 cigarettes or 50 cigars; 1 liter of spirits or 2 liters of fortified or sparkling wine or liqueurs; 2 liters of still table wine; 60 ml of perfume; 250 ml of toilet water; plus £145 worth of other goods, including gifts and souvenirs. Prohibited items include meat products, seeds, plants, and fruits.

HM Customs and Excise ✉ Portcullis House, 21 Cowbridge Rd. E, Cardiff CF11 9SS ☎ 0845/010-9000 or 0208/929-0152; 0208/929-6731 or 0208/910-3602 complaints 🌐 www.hmce.gov.uk.

DISABILITIES & ACCESSIBILITY

New York has come a long way in making life easier for people with disabilities. At most street corners, curbs dip to allow wheelchairs to roll along unimpeded. Many restaurants, shops, and movie theaters with step-up entrances have wheelchair ramps. And though some New Yorkers may rush past those in need of assistance, you'll find plenty of people who are more than happy to help you get around. Hospital Audiences, Inc. staffs the *HAI Hotline* weekdays 9 AM–5 PM, with information on transportation, hotels, restaurants, and cultural venues. Big Apple Greeters has tours of New York City tailored to visitors' personal preferences.

The Andrew Heiskell Library for the Blind and Physically Handicapped houses an impressive collection of braille, large-print, and recorded books in a layout designed for people with vision impairments.

Local Resources **Andrew Heiskell Library** ✉ 40 W. 20th St., between 5th and 6th Aves., Flatiron District ☎ 212/206-5400 🌐 www.nypl.org/branch. **Big Apple Greeters** ✉ 1 Centre St., Suite 2035, Lower Manhattan, New York, NY 10007 ☎ 212/669-2896 🌐 www.bigapplegreeter.org. **HAI Hotline** ☎ 212/284-4100 🌐 www.hospaud.org.

PUBLICATIONS

Access for All ($5), published by Hospital Audiences, Inc., lists theaters, museums, and other cultural institutions that have wheelchair access and services for people with hearing or vision impairments.

Hospital Audiences, Inc. ☎ 212/575-7676; 212/575-7673 TDD 🌐 www.hospaud.org.

RESERVATIONS

When discussing accessibility with an operator or reservations agent, **ask hard questions.** Are there any stairs, inside *or* out? Are there grab bars next to the toilet *and* in the shower/tub? How wide is the doorway to the room? To the bathroom? For the most extensive facilities meeting the latest legal specifications, **opt for newer accommodations.** If you reserve through a toll-free number, consider also calling the hotel's local number to confirm the information from the central reservations office. Get confirmation in writing when you can.

SIGHTS & ATTRACTIONS

Most public facilities in New York City, whether museums, parks, or theaters, are wheelchair-accessible. Some attractions have tours or programs for people with mobility, sight, or hearing impairments.

TRANSPORTATION

Other than at major subway exchanges, most stations are still all but impossible to navigate; people in wheelchairs should stick to public buses, most of which have wheelchair lifts at the rear door and "kneelers" at the front to facilitate getting on and off. Bus drivers will provide assistance.

Reduced fares are available to all disabled passengers displaying a Medicare card. Visitors to the city are also eligible for the same Access-a-Ride program benefits as New York City residents. Drivers with disabilities may use windshield cards from their own state or any Canadian province to park in designated handicapped spaces.

Complaints **Aviation Consumer Protection Division** (⇨ Air Travel) for airline-related problems. **Departmental Office of Civil Rights** ✉ for general inquiries, U.S. Department of Transportation, S-30, 400 7th St. SW, Room 10215, Washington, DC 20590 ☎ 202/366-4648 🖷 202/366-9371 🌐 www.dot.gov/ost/docr/index.htm. **Disability Rights Section** ✉ NYAV, U.S. Department of Justice, Civil Rights Division, 950 Pennsylvania Ave. NW, Washington, DC 20530 ☎ ADA information line 202/514-0301; 800/514-0301; 202/514-0383 TTY; 800/514-0383 TTY 🌐 www.ada.gov. **U.S. Department of Transportation Hotline** ☎ for disability-related air-travel problems, 800/778-4838 or 800/455-9880 TTY.

TRAVEL AGENCIES

In the United States, the Americans with Disabilities Act requires that travel firms serve the needs of all travelers. Some agencies specialize in working with people with disabilities.

Travelers with Mobility Problems **Access Adventures** ✉ 206 Chestnut Ridge Rd., Scottsville, NY 14624 ☎ 585/889-9096 ✉ dltravel@prodigy.net, run by a former physical-rehabilitation counselor. **Accessible Vans of America** ✉ 9 Spielman Rd., Fairfield, NJ 07004 ☎ 877/282-8267; 973/808-9709 reservations 🖷 973/808-9713 🌐 www.accessiblevans.com. **CareVacations** ✉ No. 5, 5110-50 Ave., Leduc, Alberta, Canada, T9E 6V4 ☎ 780/986-6404 or 877/478-7827 🖷 780/986-8332 🌐 www.carevacations.com, for group tours and cruise vacations. **Flying Wheels Travel** ✉ 143 W. Bridge St., Box 382, Owatonna, MN 55060 ☎ 507/451-5005 🖷 507/451-1685 🌐 www.flyingwheelstravel.com.

Travelers with Developmental Disabilities **Sprout** ✉ 893 Amsterdam Ave., New York, NY 10025 ☎ 212/222-9575 or 888/222-9575 🖷 212/222-9768 🌐 www.gosprout.org.

WHERE TO STAY

Despite the Americans with Disabilities Act, the definition of accessibility seems to differ from hotel to hotel. Some properties may be accessible by ADA standards for people with mobility problems but not for people with hearing or vision impairments, for example.

If you have mobility problems, ask for the lowest floor on which accessible services are offered. If you have a hearing impairment, check whether the hotel has devices to alert you visually to the ring of the telephone, a knock at the door, and a fire/emergency alarm. Some hotels provide these devices without charge. Discuss your needs with hotel personnel if this equipment isn't available, so that a staff member can personally alert you in the event of an emergency.

If you're bringing a guide dog, get authorization ahead of time and write down the name of the person with whom you spoke.

Most hotels in New York comply with the Americans with Disabilities Act. When you call to make reservations, specify your needs and make sure the hotel can accommodate them. Your best bet will be with newer and chain hotels.

DISCOUNTS & DEALS

In the numerous tourist-oriented publications that you can pick up at hotels and attractions, you'll find coupons good for discounts of all kinds, from dining and shopping to sightseeing and sporting activities. Cut-rate theater tickets are sold at TKTS (⇨ Performing Arts *in* Chapter 3) booths in Times Square and lower Manhattan. Some major museums have free-admission evenings once a week.

Be a smart shopper and **compare all your options** before making decisions. A plane ticket bought with a promotional coupon from travel clubs, coupon books, and direct-mail offers or purchased on the Internet may not be cheaper than the least expensive fare from a discount ticket agency. And always keep in mind that what you get is just as important as what you save.

DISCOUNT RESERVATIONS

To save money, **look into discount reservations services** with Web sites and toll-free numbers, which use their buying power to get a better price on hotels, airline tickets (⇨ Air Travel), even car rentals. When booking a room, always **call the hotel's local toll-free number** (if one is available) rather than the central reservations number—

you'll often get a better price. Always ask about special packages or corporate rates.

Airline Tickets **Air 4 Less** ☎ 800/AIR4LESS; low-fare specialist.

Hotel Rooms **Accommodations Express** ☎ 800/444-7666 or 800/277-1064 ⊕ www.accommodationsexpress.com. **Central Reservation Service** (CRS) ☎ 800/555-7555 or 800/548-3311 ⊕ www.roomconnection.net. **Quikbook** ☎ 800/789-9887 ⊕ www.quikbook.com. **RMC Travel** ☎ 800/245-5738 ⊕ www.rmcwebtravel.com. **Steigenberger Reservation Service** ☎ 800/223-5652 ⊕ www.srs-worldhotels.com. **Travel Interlink** ☎ 800/888-5898 ⊕ www.travelinterlink.com. **Turbotrip.com** ☎ 800/473-7829 ⊕ www.turbotrip.com.

PACKAGE DEALS

Don't confuse packages and guided tours. When you buy a package, you travel on your own, just as though you had planned the trip yourself. Fly/drive packages, which combine airfare and car rental, are often a good deal. In cities, ask the local visitor's bureau about hotel packages that include tickets to major museum exhibits or other special events.

SIGHTSEEING

If you have diverse interests, **consider purchasing a CityPass.** CityPass is a packet of tickets to top-notch attractions in New York—the Empire State Building, the Guggenheim Museum, the American Museum of Natural History, the Museum of Modern Art, the Whitney Museum of American Art, Circle Line Cruises, and the *Intrepid* Sea-Air-Space Museum—which will save you half the cost of each individual ticket. The packet is good for nine days from first use, and will allow you to beat long ticket lines at some attractions. You can buy a CityPass at any of the participants' ticket offices.

CityPass ☎ 888/330-5008 ⊕ www.citypass.com. **NYC & Company-Convention & Visitors Bureau** ✉ 810 7th Ave., between W. 52nd and W. 53rd Sts., 3rd floor, Midtown West ☎ 212/484-1222 or 212/397-8200 📠 212/245-5943 ⊕ www.nycvisit.com, weekdays 8:30 AM–6 PM, weekends 9 AM–5 PM.

EMERGENCIES

New Yorkers are sympathetic to out-of-towners in need of help. **Dial 911** for police, fire, or ambulance services in an emergency (TTY is available for persons with hearing impairments). Many New Yorkers carry cell phones, so consider asking someone to make the call for you if you are unable to do so yourself.

Hospitals **Bellevue** ✉ 462 1st Ave., at E. 30th St., Gramercy ☎ 212/562-4141. **Beth Israel Medical Center** ✉ 1st Ave. at E. 16th St., Gramercy ☎ 212/420-2000. **Cabrini Medical Center** ✉ 227 E. 19th St., between 2nd and 3rd Aves., Gramercy ☎ 212/995-6620. **Lenox Hill Hospital** ✉ 100 E. 77th St., between Lexington and Park Aves., Upper East Side ☎ 212/434-3030. **Mount Sinai Hospital** ✉ Madison Ave. at E. 100th St., Upper East Side ☎ 212/241-7171. **New York Hospital-Cornell Medical Center** ✉ 525 E. 68th St., at York Ave., Upper East Side ☎ 212/746-5454. **New York University Hospital Downtown (Formerly Beekman Downtown)** ✉ 170 William St., between Beekman and Spruce Sts., Lower Manhattan ☎ 212/312-5000. **New York University Medical Center** ✉ 550 1st Ave., at E. 32nd St., Murray Hill ☎ 212/263-5550. **St. Luke's-Roosevelt Hospital** ✉ 9th Ave. at 59th St., Midtown West ☎ 212/523-6800. **St. Vincent's Hospital** ✉ 7th Ave. and W. 12th St., Greenwich Village ☎ 212/604-7997.

Hot Lines **Mental Health** ☎ 212/219-5599 or 800/527-7474. **Sex Crimes Report Line** ☎ 212/267-7273. **Special Victims Liaison Unit** ☎ 212/267-7273. **Victims Services** ☎ 212/577-7777.

24-Hour Pharmacies **CVS** ✉ 342 E. 23rd St., between 1st and 2nd Aves., Gramercy ☎ 212/505-1555 ✉ 630 Lexington Ave., at E. 53rd St., Midtown East ☎ 917/369-8688 ⊕ www.cvs.com. **Duane Reade** ✉ 485 Lexington Ave., at E. 47th St., Midtown East ☎ 212/682-5338 ⊕ www.duanereade.com. **Genovese** ✉ 1299 2nd Ave., at E. 68th St., Upper East Side ☎ 212/772-0104 ⊕ www.genovese.com. **Rite-Aid** ✉ 303 W. 50th St., at 8th Ave., Midtown West ☎ 212/247-8736 ⊕ www.riteaid.com.

GAY & LESBIAN TRAVEL

Attitudes toward same-sex couples are very tolerant in Manhattan, perhaps less so in parts of the outer boroughs. Chelsea and Greenwich Village are the most prominently gay neighborhoods, but gay men and lesbians feel right at home almost everywhere. The world's biggest gay pride parade takes place on 5th Avenue each June.

For details about the gay and lesbian scene, consult *Fodor's Gay Guide to the USA* (available in bookstores everywhere).

PUBLICATIONS

For listings of gay events and places, check out *HX, MetroSource, Next, New York Blade,* and the *Village Voice,* all distributed free in many shops and clubs throughout Manhattan. Magazines *Paper* and *Time Out New York* have a gay-friendly take on what's happening in the city. For details about the gay and lesbian scene, consult *Fodor's Gay Guide to the USA* (available in bookstores everywhere).

Local Information **Gay and Lesbian National Hotline** ☎ 212/989-0999 🌐 www.glnh.org. **Lesbian and Gay Community Services Center** ✉ 208 W. 13th St., between 7th and 8th Aves., Greenwich Village ☎ 212/620-7310 🌐 www.gaycenter.org.

Gay- & Lesbian-Friendly Travel Agencies **Different Roads Travel** ✉ 8383 Wilshire Blvd., Suite 520, Beverly Hills, CA 90211 ☎ 323/651-5557 or 800/429-8747 (Ext. 14 for both) 📠 323/651-3678 ✉ lgernert@tzell.com. **Kennedy Travel** ✉ 130 W. 42nd St., Suite 401, New York, NY 10036 ☎ 212/840-8659, 800/237-7433 📠 212/730-2269 🌐 www.kennedytravel.com. **Now, Voyager** ✉ 4406 18th St., San Francisco, CA 94114 ☎ 415/626-1169 or 800/255-6951 📠 415/626-8626 🌐 www.nowvoyager.com. **Skylink Travel and Tour** ✉ 1455 N. Dutton Ave., Suite A, Santa Rosa, CA 95401 ☎ 707/546-9888 or 800/225-5759 📠 707/636-0951; serving lesbian travelers.

GUIDEBOOKS

Plan well and you won't be sorry. Guidebooks are excellent tools—and you can take them with you. You may want to check out color-photo-illustrated *Fodor's Exploring New York City* and *Compass American Guide: Manhattan,* thorough on culture and history, and pocket-size *Citypack New York City,* with a supersize city map. *Flashmaps New York City* is loaded with theme maps, and *Fodor's CITYGUIDE New York City,* for residents, with colorful listings. All are available at on-line retailers and bookstores everywhere.

HOLIDAYS

Major national holidays are New Year's Day (Jan. 1); Martin Luther King Jr. Day (3rd Mon. in Jan.); Presidents' Day (3rd Mon. in Feb.); Memorial Day (last Mon. in May); Independence Day (July 4); Labor Day (1st Mon. in Sept.); Columbus Day (2nd Mon. in Oct.); Thanksgiving Day (4th Thurs. in Nov.); Christmas Eve and Christmas Day (Dec. 24 and 25); and New Year's Eve (Dec. 31).

INSURANCE

The most useful travel-insurance plan is a comprehensive policy that includes coverage for trip cancellation and interruption, default, trip delay, and medical expenses (with a waiver for preexisting conditions).

Without insurance you'll lose all or most of your money if you cancel your trip, regardless of the reason. Default insurance covers you if your tour operator, airline, or cruise line goes out of business. Trip-delay covers expenses that arise because of bad weather or mechanical delays. Study the fine print when comparing policies.

U.K. residents can buy a travel-insurance policy valid for most vacations taken during the year in which it's purchased (but check preexisting-condition coverage).

Always **buy travel policies directly from the insurance company**; if you buy them from a cruise line, airline, or tour operator that goes out of business you probably won't be covered for the agency or operator's default, a major risk. Before making any purchase, **review your existing health and home-owner's policies** to find what they cover away from home.

Travel Insurers In the U.S.: **Access America** ✉ 6600 W. Broad St., Richmond, VA 23230 ☎ 800/284-8300 📠 804/673-1491 or 800/346-9265 🌐 www.accessamerica.com. **Travel Guard International** ✉ 1145 Clark St., Stevens Point, WI 54481 ☎ 715/345-0505 or 800/826-1300 📠 800/955-8785 🌐 www.travelguard.com.

FOR INTERNATIONAL TRAVELERS

For information on customs restrictions, *see* Customs and Duties.

CONSULATES

Australia **The Australian Consulate General** ✉ 150 E. 42nd St., 34th floor, between Lexington and 3rd., Midtown East, New York, NY 10017 ☎ 212/351-6500 📠 212/351-6501 🌐 www.australianyc.org.

Canada **Canadian Consulate General** ✉ 1251 Ave. of the Americas, between W. 49th and W. 50th Sts., Midtown West, New York, NY 10020 ☎ 212/596-1628 📠 212/596-1793 🌐 www.canada-ny.org.

New Zealand **New Zealand Consulate-General** ✉ 780 3rd Ave., Suite 1904, between E. 48th and E. 49th Sts., Midtown East, New York, NY 10017 ☎ 212/832-4038 📠 212/832-7602 🌐 www.un.int/newzealand.

United Kingdom **British Consulate-General** ✉ 845 3rd Ave., between E. 51st and E. 52nd Sts., Midtown East, New York, NY 10022 ☎ 212/745-0200 📠 212/745-3062 🌐 www.britainusa.com/ny.

CURRENCY

The dollar is the basic unit of U.S. currency. It has 100 cents. Coins include the copper penny (1¢); the silvery nickel (5¢), dime (10¢), quarter (25¢), and half-dollar (50¢); and the golden $1 coin, replacing a now-rare silver dollar. Bills are denominated $1, $5, $10, $20, $50, and $100, all green and identical in size; designs vary.

CURRENCY EXCHANGES

Currency-exchange booths are located throughout Manhattan, especially in touristy areas such as Grand Central Terminal (main concourse), South Street Seaport, and Times Square. Banks will also exchange money, but they have shorter hours (many banks close at 3 PM on weekdays and shut down entirely on weekends).

Exchange Offices **Chase Foreign Currency Department** ☎ 212/935-9935. **Chequepoint USA** ☎ 212/750-2400. **Thomas Cook Currency Services** ☎ 800/287-7362.

ELECTRICITY

The U.S. standard is AC, 110 volts/60 cycles. Plugs have two flat pins set parallel to each other.

EMERGENCIES

For police, fire, or ambulance, **dial 911** (0 in rural areas).

INSURANCE

Britons and Australians need extra medical coverage when traveling overseas.

Insurance Information In the U.K.: **Association of British Insurers** ✉ 51 Gresham St., London EC2V 7HQ ☎ 020/7600-3333 🖷 020/7696-8999 🌐 www.abi.org.uk. In Australia: **Insurance Council of Australia** ✉ Insurance Enquiries and Complaints, Level 3, 56 Pitt St., Sydney, NSW 2000 ☎ 1300/363683 or 02/9251-4456 🖷 02/9251-4453 🌐 www.iecltd.com.au. In Canada: **RBC Insurance** ✉ 6880 Financial Dr., Mississauga, Ontario L5N 7Y5 ☎ 800/565-3129 🖷 905/813-4704 🌐 www.rbcinsurance.com. In New Zealand: **Insurance Council of New Zealand** ✉ Level 7, 111-115 Customhouse Quay, Box 474, Wellington ☎ 04/472-5230 🖷 04/473-3011 🌐 www.icnz.org.nz.

MAIL & SHIPPING

You can buy stamps and aerograms and send letters and parcels in post offices. Stamp-dispensing machines can occasionally be found in airports, bus and train stations, office buildings, drugstores, and the like. You can also deposit mail in the stout, dark blue, steel bins at strategic locations everywhere and in the mail chutes of large buildings; pickup schedules are posted.

For mail sent within the United States, you need a 37¢ stamp for first-class letters weighing up to 1 ounce (23¢ for each additional ounce) and 23¢ for postcards. You pay 80¢ for 1-ounce airmail letters and 70¢ for airmail postcards to most other countries; to Canada and Mexico, you need a 60¢ stamp for a 1-ounce letter and 50¢ for a postcard. An aerogram—a single sheet of lightweight blue paper that folds into its own envelope, stamped for overseas airmail—costs 70¢.

To receive mail on the road, have it sent c/o General Delivery at your destination's main post office (use the correct five-digit ZIP code). You must pick up mail in person within 30 days and show a driver's license or passport.

PASSPORTS & VISAS

When traveling internationally, **carry your passport** even if you don't need one (it's always the best form of ID) and **make two photocopies of the data page** (one for someone at home and another for you, carried separately from your passport). If you lose your passport, promptly call the nearest embassy or consulate and the local police.

Visitor visas aren't necessary for Canadian or European Union citizens, or for citizens of Australia who are staying fewer than 90 days.

Australian Citizens **Passports Australia** ☎ 131-232 🌐 www.passports.gov.au. **United States Consulate General** ✉ MLC Centre, Level 59, 19-29 Martin Pl., Sydney, NSW 2000 ☎ 02/9373-9200; 1902/941-641 fee-based visa-inquiry line 🌐 usembassy-australia.state.gov/sydney.

Canadian Citizens **Passport Office** ✉ to mail in applications: 200 Promenade du Portage, Hull, Québec J8X 4B7 ☎ 819/994-3500 or 800/567-6868 🌐 www.ppt.gc.ca.

New Zealand Citizens **New Zealand Passports Office** ✉ For applications and information, Level 3, Boulcott House, 47 Boulcott St., Wellington ☎ 0800/22-5050 or 04/474-8100 🌐 www.passports.govt.nz. **Embassy of the United States** ✉ 29 Fitzherbert Terr., Thorndon, Wellington ☎ 04/462-6000 🌐 usembassy.org.nz. **U.S. Consulate General** ✉ Citibank Bldg., 3rd floor, 23 Customs St. E, Auckland ☎ 09/303-2724 🌐 usembassy.org.nz.

U.K. Citizens **U.K. Passport Service** ☎ 0870/521-0410 🌐 www.passport.gov.uk. **American Consulate General** ✉ Queen's House, 14 Queen St., Belfast, Northern Ireland BT1 6EQ ☎ 028/9032-8239 📠 028/9024-8482 🌐 www.usembassy.org.uk. **American Embassy** ✉ for visa and immigration information (enclose an SASE), Consular Information Unit, 24 Grosvenor Sq., London W1 1AE ✉ to submit an application via mail, Visa Branch, 5 Upper Grosvenor St., London W1A 2JB ☎ 09068/200-290 recorded visa information or 09055/444-546 operator service, both with per-minute charges; 0207/499-9000 main switchboard 🌐 www.usembassy.org.uk.

TELEPHONES

All U.S. telephone numbers consist of a three-digit area code and a seven-digit local number. Within many local calling areas, you dial only the seven-digit number. Within some area codes, you must dial "1" first for calls outside the local area. To call between area-code regions, dial "1" then all 10 digits; the same goes for calls to numbers prefixed by "800," "888," "866," and "877"—all toll free. For calls to numbers preceded by "900" you must pay—usually dearly.

For international calls, dial "011" followed by the country code and the local number. For help, dial "0" and ask for an overseas operator. The country code is 61 for Australia, 64 for New Zealand, 44 for the United Kingdom. Calling Canada is the same as calling within the United States. Most local phone books list country codes and U.S. area codes. The country code for the United States is 1.

For operator assistance, dial "0." To obtain someone's phone number, call directory assistance at 555-1212 or occasionally 411 (free at public phones). To have the person you're calling foot the bill, phone collect; dial "0" instead of "1" before the 10-digit number.

At pay phones, instructions often are posted. Usually you insert coins in a slot (usually 25¢–50¢ for local calls) and wait for a steady tone before dialing. When you call long-distance, the operator tells you how much to insert; prepaid phone cards, widely available in various denominations, are easier. Call the number on the back, punch in the card's personal identification number when prompted, then dial your number.

INTERNET SERVICES

You can check your e-mail or surf the Internet at cafés, copy centers, and libraries. By far the most well equipped and cheapest is easyInternetCafé in Times Square, which has a staggering 800 computer terminals; it's open 24 hours a day, seven days a week.

Internet Cafés **Cyber Cafe, SoHo** ✉ 273 Lafayette St., at Prince St., SoHo ☎ 212/334-5140 🌐 www.cybercafe.com. **Cyber Cafe, Times Square** ✉ 250 W. 49th St., between 8th Ave. and Broadway, Midtown West ☎ 212/333-4109 🌐 www.cyber-cafe.com. **easyInternetCafé** ✉ 234 W. 42nd St., between 7th and 8th Aves., Midtown West ☎ 212/398-0775 or 212/398-0724 🌐 www.easyeverything.com/usa. **Internet Cafe** ✉ 82 E. 3rd St., between 1st and 2nd Aves., East Village ☎ 212/614-0747 🌐 www.bigmagic.com.

Other Internet Locations **Cyberfelds at Village Copier** ✉ 20 E. 13th St., between 5th Ave. and University Pl., Greenwich Village ☎ 212/647-8830 🌐 www.cyberfelds.com. **Kinko's** ✉ 191 Madison Ave., at E. 34th St., Murray Hill ☎ 212/685-3831 🌐 www.kinkos.com. **The New York Public Library-Mid-Manhattan Library** ✉ 455 5th Ave., at E. 40th St., Midtown East ☎ 212/340-0833 🌐 www.nypl.org.

LIMOUSINES

You can rent a chauffeur-driven car from one of many limousine services. Companies usually charge by the hour or a flat fee for sightseeing excursions.

Limousine Services **All State Car and Limousine Service** ☎ 212/741-7440. **Bermuda Limousine International** ☎ 212/249-8400. **Carey Limousines** ☎ 212/599-1122. **Chris Limousines** ☎ 718/356-3232 or 800/542-1584. **Concord Limousines, Inc.** ☎ 212/230-1600 or 800/255-7255 🌐 www.concordlimo.com. **Gotham Limousine** ☎ 212/868-4733 or 800/385-1033. **London Towncars** ☎ 212/988-9700 or 800/221-4009 🌐 www.londontowncars.com. **Mirage Limousine** ☎ 212/744-9700.

MAIL & SHIPPING

Post offices are open weekdays 8 AM–5 PM or 8 AM–6 PM and Saturday until 1 PM. There are dozens of branches in New York, many of which provide abbreviated Saturday hours as well. You'll usually find the shortest lines at the smaller branches. The main post office on 8th Avenue is open daily 24 hours.

Post Offices **J.A. Farley General Post Office** ✉ 8th Ave. at W. 33rd St., Midtown West 10116 ☎ 212/967-8585.

MEDIA

NEWSPAPERS & MAGAZINES

The major newspapers in New York are the *Daily News, Newsday, New York Post, New York Sun, New York Times, Wall Street Journal,* and the *New York Observer,* as well as the *Village Voice*—a free publication. Local magazines include the *New Yorker, New York,* and *Time Out New York*. All of these are widely available at newsstands and shops around town.

RADIO & TELEVISION

Some of the major radio stations include *WBGO-FM* (88.3; jazz), *WBLS-FM* (107.5; R&B), *WKTU-FM* (103.5; urban), *WPLJ* (95.5; pop and rock), *WQXR-FM* (96.3; classical), and *WXRK-FM* (92.3; rock). Talk stations include *WNEW-FM* (102.7), *WNYC-AM* (820; National Public Radio), *WNYC-FM* (93.9; classical), *WNYE-FM* (91.5), and *WOR-AM* (710). News stations include *WABC-AM* (770), *WCBS-AM* (880), and *WINS-AM* (1010).

The city has its own 24-hour cable TV news station, *New York 1* (Channel 1), available through Time Warner Cable, with local and international news announcements around the clock. Weather forecasts are broadcast "on the ones" (1:01, 1:11, 1:21, etc.).

MONEY MATTERS

In New York, it's easy to get swept up in a debt-inducing cyclone of $60 per-person dinners, $80 theater tickets, $25 nightclub covers, $10 cab rides, and $300 hotel rooms. But one of the good things about the city is that there's such a wide variety of options, you can spend in some areas and save in others. Generally, prices in the outer boroughs are lower than those in Manhattan. Within Manhattan, a cup of coffee can cost from 50¢ to $4, a pint of beer from $3 to $7, and a sandwich from $3.50 to $10.

The most generously bequeathed treasure of the city is the arts. The admission fee at the Metropolitan Museum of Art is a suggestion; those who can't afford it can donate a lesser amount and not be snubbed. In summer a handful of free music, theater, and dance performances, as well as films (usually outdoors) fill the calendar each day.

Prices throughout this guide are given for adults. Substantially reduced fees are almost always available for children, students, and senior citizens.

ATMS

Cash machines are abundant throughout all the boroughs and are found not only in banks but in many grocery stores, Laundromats, delis, and hotels. But beware, many bank ATMs charge users a fee of up to $1.75, and the commercial ATMs in retail establishments can charge even more. Be careful to remain at the ATM until you complete your transaction, which may require an extra step after receiving your money.

CREDIT CARDS

Throughout this guide, the following abbreviations are used: **AE**, American Express; **D**, Discover; **DC**, Diners Club; **MC**, MasterCard; and **V**, Visa.

Reporting Lost Cards **American Express** ☎ 800/441-0519. **Diners Club** ☎ 800/234-6377. **Discover** ☎ 800/347-2683. **MasterCard** ☎ 800/622-7747. **Visa** ☎ 800/847-2911.

PACKING

In New York, jackets and ties are required for men in some restaurants; in general, New Yorkers tend to dress a bit more formally than their West Coast counterparts for special events. Jeans and sneakers are acceptable for casual dining and sightseeing just about anywhere in the city. Always **come with sneakers or other flat-heeled walking shoes** for pounding the New York pavement. In winter, you will need a warm coat, hat, scarf, and gloves. Bring shorts for summer, which is quite humid in New York. In spring and fall, pack at least one warm jacket and sweater, since moderate daytime temperatures can drop after nightfall.

Do **pack light,** because porters and luggage trolleys can be hard to find at New York airports. And **bring a fistful of quarters to rent a trolley.**

In your carry-on luggage, **pack an extra pair of eyeglasses or contact lenses and enough of any medication** you take to last a few days longer than the entire trip. You may also ask your doctor to write a spare prescription using the drug's generic name, as brand names may vary from country to country. In luggage to be checked, **never pack prescription drugs, valuables, or undeveloped film.** And don't forget to carry with you the addresses of offices that handle refunds of lost traveler's checks. Check *Fodor's How to Pack* (available at on-line retailers and bookstores everywhere) for more tips.

To avoid customs and security delays, carry medications in their original packaging. Packing requirements are far more stringent than they were before September 11, 2001. Don't pack any sharp objects in your carry-on luggage, including knives of any size or material, scissors, manicure tools, and corkscrews, or anything else that might arouse suspicion. Check *Fodor's How to Pack* (available in bookstores everywhere) for more tips.

To avoid having your checked luggage chosen for hand inspection, don't cram bags full. The U.S. Transportation Security Administration suggests packing shoes on top and placing personal items you don't want touched in clear plastic bags.

CHECKING LUGGAGE

You're allowed to carry aboard one bag and one personal article, such as a purse or a laptop computer. Make sure what you carry on fits under your seat or in the overhead bin. Get to the gate early, so you can board as soon as possible, before the overhead bins fill up.

Baggage allowances vary by carrier, destination, and ticket class. On international flights, you're usually allowed to check two bags weighing up to 70 pounds (32 kilograms) each, although a few airlines allow checked bags of up to 88 pounds (40 kilograms) in first class. Some international carriers don't allow more than 66 pounds (30 kilograms) per bag in business class and 44 pounds (20 kilograms) in economy. On domestic flights, the limit may be 50 pounds (23 kilograms) per bag. Most airlines won't accept bags that weigh more than 100 pounds (45 kilograms) on domestic or international flights. Check baggage restrictions with your carrier before you pack.

Airline liability for baggage is limited to $2,500 per person on flights within the United States. On international flights it amounts to $9.07 per pound or $20 per kilogram for checked baggage (roughly $640 per 70-pound bag) and $400 per passenger for unchecked baggage. You can buy additional coverage at check-in for about $10 per $1,000 of coverage, but it often excludes a rather extensive list of items, shown on your airline ticket.

Before departure, **itemize your bags' contents** and their worth, and label the bags with your name, address, and phone number. (If you use your home address, cover it so potential thieves can't see it readily.) Include a label inside each bag and **pack a copy of your itinerary.** At check-in, **make sure each bag is correctly tagged** with the destination airport's three-letter code. Because some checked bags will be opened for hand inspection, the U.S. Transportation Security Administration recommends that you leave luggage unlocked or use the plastic locks offered at check-in. TSA screeners place an inspection notice inside searched bags, which are re-sealed with a special lock.

If your bag has been searched and contents are missing or damaged, file a claim with the TSA Consumer Response Center as soon as possible. If your bags arrive damaged or fail to arrive at all, file a written report with the airline before leaving the airport.

Complaints U.S. Transportation Security Administration Consumer Response Center ☎ 866/289–9673 🌐 www.tsa.gov.

PUBLIC TRANSPORTATION

When it comes to getting around New York, you'll have your pick of transportation in almost every neighborhood. The subway and bus networks are thorough, although getting across town can take some extra maneuvering. If you're not pressed for time, take a public bus (⇨ Bus Travel Within New York City); they generally are slower than subways, but you can also see the city as you travel. Yellow cabs (⇨ Taxis and Car Services) are abundant, except at the rush hour of 4:30–5 PM, when many are off-duty (shift change time). Like a taxi ride, the subway (⇨ Subway Travel) is a true New York City experience and often the quickest way to get around. But New York is really a walking town, and depending on the time of day and your destination, hoofing it could be the easiest and most enjoyable option. During weekday rush hours (from 7:30 AM to 9:30 AM and 5 PM to 7 PM, **avoid the**

jammed midtown area, both in the subways and on the streets—travel time on buses and taxis can easily double.

Subway and bus fares are $2, although reduced fares are available for senior citizens and people with disabilities during non-rush hours.

If you plan to use the subway often, your best option is to use a MetroCard, a plastic card with a magnetic strip, which you can swipe through the reader at the turnstile and the cost of the fare is automatically deducted. You can **transfer free from bus to subway or subway to bus with the MetroCard.** You must start with the MetroCard and use it again within two hours to complete your trip. MetroCards are sold at all subway stations and at some stores—look for an "Authorized Sales Agent" sign. The MTA sells two kinds of MetroCards: unlimited-ride and pay-per-ride. Seven-day unlimited-ride MetroCards ($21) allow bus and subway travel for a week. If you will ride more than 12 times, this is the card to get. The one-day unlimited-ride Fun Pass ($7) is good from the day of purchase through 3 AM the following day and is only sold by neighborhood MetroCard merchants and MetroCard vending machines at stations (not through the station agent). When you purchase a pay-per-ride card worth $10, you get 6 rides for the price of 5). The advantage of pay-per-ride over unlimited ride is that the card can be shared between riders; unlimited-ride MetroCards can only be used once at the same station or bus route in an 18-minute period.

You can buy or add money to a MetroCard at a MetroCard vending machine. They are available at most subway station entrances (usually near the station booth). Major credit cards, ATM/debit cards, or cash may all be used.

Schedule & Route Information **Metropolitan Transit Authority (MTA) Travel Information Line** ☎ 718/330–1234 or 718/596–8585 🌐 www.mta.nyc.ny.us.

REST ROOMS

Public rest rooms in New York are few and far between, and they run the gamut when it comes to cleanliness. Facilities in Penn Station and Grand Central Terminal are not only safe but surprisingly clean and well maintained. Rest rooms in major subway stations remain largely sealed off, though there is one at Union Square. Two clean pay-toilets (25¢) are at the adjacent Herald and Greely squares on West 34th and West 32nd streets.

As a rule, **head for midtown department stores, museums, or the lobbies of large hotels to find the cleanest bathrooms.** Public atriums, such as the Citicorp Center and Trump Tower, also provide good public facilities, as do Bryant Park and the many Barnes & Noble bookstores and Starbucks coffee shops in the city. Restaurants usually reserve their rest rooms just for patrons, but if you're dressed well and look as if you belong, you can often just sail right in. Be aware that cinemas, Broadway theaters, and concert halls have limited amenities, and there are often long lines before performances and during intermissions.

SAFETY

New York City is one of the safest large cities in the country, outranking both Denver and San Francisco in 2002. However, do not let yourself be lulled into a false sense of security. As in any large city, travelers in New York remain particularly easy marks for pickpockets and hustlers.

In the wake of the World Trade Center disaster, security has been heightened throughout the city. As a result, never leave any bags unattended, and expect to have you and your possessions inspected thoroughly in places like airports, sports stadiums, museums, and tourist sites.

Do **ignore the panhandlers** on the streets (some aggressive, many homeless), people who offer to hail you a cab (they often appear at Penn Station, Port Authority, and Grand Central Terminal), and limousine and gypsy cab drivers who (illegally) offer you a ride.

Keep jewelry out of sight on the street; better yet, **leave valuables at home.** Don't wear gold chains or gaudy jewelry, even if it's fake. Men are advised to **carry wallets in front pants pockets** rather than in their back pockets. When in bars or restaurants, never hang your purse or bag on the back of a chair or put it underneath the table.

Be sure to **avoid deserted blocks in unfamiliar neighborhoods.** A brisk, purposeful pace helps deter trouble wherever you go.

The subway runs round-the-clock and is generally well trafficked until midnight (even later on Friday and Saturday nights), and overall it is much safer than it once was. If you do take the subway at night, ride in the center car, with the conductor, and wait on the center of the platform or right in front of the station agent. Watch out for unsavory characters lurking around the inside or outside of stations, particularly at night, and if a fellow passenger makes you nervous while on the train, trust your instincts and change cars. At any time of day, don't engage in verbal exchanges with aggressive riders who may accuse others of anything from pushing to taking up too much space. When you're waiting for a train, **stand far away from the edge of the subway platform,** especially when trains are entering or leaving the station. Once the train pulls into the station, **avoid empty cars.** When disembarking from a train, **stick with the crowd** until you reach the street.

The nationwide Traveler's Aid Service helps crime victims, stranded travelers, and wayward children, and works closely with the police. Its office at JFK airport is staffed daily 9 AM to 8 PM.

LOCAL SCAMS

Someone who appears to have had an accident at the exit door of a bus may flee with your wallet or purse if you attempt to give aid. The individual who approaches you with a complicated story is probably playing a confidence game and hopes to get something from you. Also **beware of strangers jostling you in crowds,** or someone tapping your shoulder from behind. Never play or place a bet on a sidewalk card game, shell game, or guessing game—they are all rigged to get your cash, and they're illegal.

SENIOR-CITIZEN TRAVEL

The Metropolitan Transit Authority (MTA) offers lower fares for passengers 65 and over. **Show your Medicare card to the bus driver or station agent,** and for the standard fare ($2) you will be issued a MetroCard and a return-trip ticket.

To qualify for age-related discounts, **mention your senior-citizen status up front** when booking hotel reservations (not when checking out) and before you're seated in restaurants (not when paying the bill). Be sure to have identification on hand. When renting a car, ask about promotional car-rental discounts, which can be cheaper than senior-citizen rates.

Educational Programs **Elderhostel** ✉ 11 Ave. de Lafayette, Boston, MA 02111-1746 ☎ 877/426-8056; 978/323-4141 international callers; 877/426-2167 TTY 🖷 877/426-2166 🌐 www.elderhostel.org.

MTA Reduced Fare hot line ☎ 718/243-4999 🌐 www.mta.nyc.ny.us.

SIGHTSEEING TOURS

A guided tour can be a good way to get a handle on this sometimes overwhelming city, to explore out-of-the-way areas to which you might not want to venture on your own, or get in-depth exposure to a particular facet of the city's history, inhabitants, or architecture.

BOAT TOURS

In good weather, a Circle Line Cruise is one of the best ways to get oriented. Once you've finished the three-hour, 35-mi circumnavigation of Manhattan, you'll have a good idea of where things are and what you want to see next. Narrations are as interesting and individualized as the guides who deliver them. The Circle Line operates daily, and the price is $25. Semi-Circle cruises, a limited tour, also run daily; the price is $20.

NY Waterway runs harbor cruises for $19. Dates and times vary, but the cruises run year-round; the Twilight Cruise operates from May through late December. The 54-seat vessels of the New York Water Taxi are available for custom charters with dining and dancing. A variety of themed cruises, from baseball to Broadway, are also available.

Several cruises leave from South Street Seaport's Pier 16. The cargo schooner *Pioneer* makes 1½- or 2-hour voyages Tuesday through Sunday, from May to September. Seaport Liberty Cruises run daily, hour-long sightseeing tours of New York Harbor and lower Manhattan; the cost is $13. There are also two-hour cruises with live jazz and blues on Wednesday and Thursday nights, from April through September. For serious water fans there are four- and six-hour Saturday trips aboard the wooden *W. O. Decker* tugboat, operated by the South Street Seaport Museum. Adult fare starts at $125.

The Spirit of New York sets out on lunch ($30–$45) and dinner ($50–$85) cruises. The meal is accompanied by live music and dancing. Private parties can also be arranged.

World Yacht Cruises serves Sunday brunch ($42) on two-hour cruises, and dinner ($67–$79) on three-hour cruises. The Continental cuisine is restaurant quality, prepared by some of New York's leading chefs, and there's music and dancing on board. The cruises run daily from April through December, and weekends only from January through March (weather permitting). Reservations are necessary.

Circle Line Cruise ✉ Pier 83 at W. 42nd St., Midtown West ☎ 212/563-3200 🌐 www.circleline.com. **New York Water Taxi** (NYWT) ☎ 212/742-1969 🌐 www.newyorkwatertaxi.com. **NY Waterway** ✉ Pier 78 at W. 38th St. and 12th Ave., Midtown West ☎ 800/533-3779 🌐 www.nywaterway.com. ***Pioneer*** ✉ Pier 16 at South Street Seaport, Lower Manhattan ☎ 212/748-8786 🌐 www.southstseaport.org. **Seaport Liberty Cruises** ✉ Pier 16 at South Street Seaport, Lower Manhattan ☎ 212/630-8888 or 212/563-3200 🌐 www.circleline.com. ***The Spirit of New York*** ✉ Pier 61 at W. 23rd St. and 12th Ave., Chelsea ☎ 212/742-7278 🌐 www.spiritcruises.com. ***W. O. Decker* Tugboat** ✉ Pier 16 at South Street Seaport, Lower Manhattan ☎ 212/748-8786 🌐 www.southstseaport.org. **World Yacht Cruises** ✉ Pier 81 at W. 41st St. and 12th Ave., Midtown West ☎ 212/630-8100 🌐 www.worldyacht.com.

BUS TOURS

Gray Line New York runs a number of "hop-on, hop-off" double-decker bus tours in various languages, including a downtown Manhattan loop, upper Manhattan loop, Harlem gospel tour, and evening tours of the city. Packages include entrance fees to attractions and one-day MetroCards. The company also books sightseeing cruises, as well as day trips to Atlantic City, West Point, and other locations in the New York area.

New York Double-Decker Tours runs authentic London double-deck buses year-round, 9 AM–6 PM in summer, 9 AM–3 PM in winter, making stops every 15–30 minutes. Tickets, which are valid for boarding and reboarding all day for five days, cost $26 for a downtown loop, $26 for an uptown loop, and $40 for a combination ticket. For all tours, you can hop on and off as often as you like.

Gray Line New York ✉ Port Authority Bus Terminal, 625 8th Ave., at 42nd St., Midtown West ☎ 800/669-0051 🌐 www.graylinenewyork.com. **New York Double-Decker Bus Tours** ✉ 72-25 Queens Blvd., Woodside, Queens ☎ 718/361-5788 🌐 www.nydecker.com.

HELICOPTER TOURS

Liberty Helicopter Tours has three pilot-narrated tours from $49 to $155 per person.

Liberty Helicopter Tours ✉ Heliport, W. 30th St. at 12th Ave., Midtown West ☎ 212/465-8905 🌐 www.libertyhelicopters.com.

PRIVATE GUIDES

Arthur Marks creates customized tours on which he sings show tunes about the city. Walk of the Town will tailor a tour to your interests; special themes include "Cops, Crooks, and the Courts" and "When Harlem was Jewish." Tours are available by appointment only.

Arthur Marks ☎ 212/673-0477. **Walk of the Town** ☎ 212/222-5343.

SPECIAL-INTEREST TOURS

Art Tours of Manhattan custom-designs walking tours of museum and gallery exhibits as well as artists' studios and lofts.

Bite of the Big Apple Central Park Bicycle Tour organizes two-hour bicycle trips through Central Park with stops along the way, including Strawberry Fields and the Belvedere Castle.

Ellen Sax Tours & Events arranges architectural sightseeing, visits to museums, galleries, the theater district, the financial district, and other neighborhoods in Manhattan for groups of six or more.

The Gracie Mansion Conservancy Tour will show you the 1799 house, official residence of New York City mayors since 1942. The mansion is open to the public on Wednesday; the tours run late March–mid-November, and reservations are mandatory. There's a suggested $4 donation.

Harlem Spirituals leads bus and walking tours and Sunday gospel trips to Harlem. Also in Harlem, you can trace the history of jazz backstage at the Apollo Theatre.

The Lower East Side Tenement Museum runs a tour of the Lower East Side, retracing its history as an immigrant community; it's available Saturday and Sunday, April through December.

Opera buffs tour scenery and costume shops and the stage area with The Metropolitan Opera House Backstage.

Quintessential New York has more than a dozen specialty tours for groups of six or more, each with a behind-the-scenes take. For example, during "The Artist Colony: SoHo" tour, guests visit an artist's studio and an antique dealer's workshop. Another plus is the chauffeured car.

The South Street Seaport Museum has tours of historic ships and the waterfront, as well as predawn forays through the fish market.
Apollo Theatre ☎ 212/531-5305 🌐 www.apollotheatre.org. **Art Tours of Manhattan** ☎ 609/924-0408. **Bite of the Big Apple** ☎ 212/541-8759. **Ellen Sax Tours** ☎ 212/832-0350 ✉ esax@erols.com. **Gracie Mansion Conservancy Tour** ☎ 212/570-4751. **Harlem Spirituals** ☎ 212/757-0425 🌐 www.harlemspirituals.com. **Lower East Side Tenement Museum** ☎ 212/431-0233 🌐 www.tenement.org. **Metropolitan Opera House Backstage** ☎ 212/769-7020 🌐 www.operaed.org. **Quintessential New York** ☎ 212/595-6510 🌐 www.qny.com. **South Street Seaport Museum** ☎ 212/748-8590 🌐 www.southstseaport.com.

WALKING TOURS: GUIDED

Adventure on a Shoestring is an organization dating from 1963 that explores New York neighborhoods. Weekend tours run rain or shine, and cost $5 per person. Reservations are a must. The wisecracking PhD candidates of Big Onion Walking Tours lead themed tours such as "Riot & Rebellion" and "The Multi-Ethnic Eating Tour: From Naples to Bialystock to Beijing" in addition to neighborhood walks. The Downtown Alliance conducts free, history-rich tours of the Wall Street area on Thursday and Saturday at noon. Meet on the steps of the National Museum of the American Indian at Bowling Green. Radical Walking Tours, based on a book by Bruce Kayton, visits sites of activism and revolution, such as prohibition-banned speakeasies, old meeting houses of the Black Panthers, and former communist gathering places.

The Municipal Art Society conducts a series of walking tours on weekdays and both bus and walking tours on weekends. It also sponsors "Discover New York" tours, which highlight the city's architecture and history. New York City Cultural Walking Tours focuses on the city's architecture and history. Tours are run every Sunday from March to December; private tours can be scheduled throughout the week. Urban Explorations runs tours with an emphasis on architecture and landscape design. Chinatown is a specialty.

River to River Walking Tours specializes in lower Manhattan on its 2½-hour walking excursions. The Urban Park Rangers conducts free weekend walks and workshops in city parks.

The knowledgeable Joyce Gold has been conducting tours for more than 25 years. Regular historical walks include "Greenwich Village Highlights" and "5th Avenue Gold Coast." The contributions of immigrants and artists to various neighborhoods are often highlighted in other tours.
Adventure on a Shoestring ☎ 212/265-2663. **Big Onion Walking Tours** ☎ 212/439-1090 🌐 www.bigonion.com. **Downtown Alliance** ☎ 212/606-4064 🌐 www.downtownny.com. **Joyce Gold** ☎ 212/242-5762 🌐 www.nyctours.com. **Municipal Art Society** ☎ 212/935-3960; 212/439-1049 for recorded information 🌐 www.mas.org. **New York City Cultural Walking Tours** ☎ 212/979-2388 🌐 www.nycwalk.com. **Radical Walking Tours** ☎ 718/492-0069. **River to River Walking Tours** ☎ 212/321-2823. **Urban Explorations** ☎ 718/721-5254. **Urban Park Rangers** ☎ 212/628-2345 🌐 www.nycparks.org.

WALKING TOURS: SELF-GUIDED

Pop one of the Talk-a-Walk cassettes ($9.95 per tape, plus $2.90 for shipping and handling for up to four tapes) into your Walkman and start strolling to an in-your-ear history of lower Manhattan or the Brooklyn Bridge. For a narrated tour of Central Park, pick up an audio guide from the bike rental shop Pedal Pusher.
Pedal Pusher ✉ 1306 2nd Ave., between E. 68th and E. 69th Sts., Upper East Side ☎ 212/288-5592. **Talk-a-Walk** ✉ Sound Publishers, 30 Waterside Plaza, Suite 10D, E. 23rd at 3rd Ave., Gramercy, New York, NY 10010 ☎ 212/686-0356.

STUDENTS IN NEW YORK

New York is home to such major schools as Columbia University, New York University, Fordham University, and the City College of New York. With other colleges scattered throughout the five boroughs, plus a huge population of public and private high-schoolers, it's no wonder the city is rife with discounts for students. Wherever you go, especially museums, sightseeing attractions, and performances, identify yourself as a student up front and ask if a discount is available. However, **be prepared to show your ID** as proof of age.

A great program for teens between the ages of 13 and 18 is High 5 For The Arts. Five-dollar tickets to all sorts of performances are sold on-line, and also at Ticketmaster outlets in the city, including at music stores such as HMV and Tower Records. Tickets are either for a single teen (Fridays and weekends) or for a teen and his or her guest of any age (Monday–Thursday). Write to receive a free catalog of events, check it out on-line, or pick one up at Barnes & Noble bookstores, Tower Records, The Wiz, or at the lobby of High 5's office. These $5 tickets cannot be bought over the phone or at the venue box offices. With the $5 museum pass, a teen can bring a guest of any age to participating museums any day of the week; these tickets are available only at the Ticketmaster outlets.

IDs & Services STA Travel ✉ 10 Downing St., New York, NY 10014 ☎ 212/627-3111 or 800/777-0112 🖷 212/627-3387 🌐 www.sta.com. Travel Cuts ✉ 187 College St., Toronto, Ontario M5T 1P7, Canada ☎ 416/979-2406, 800/592-2887, 866/246-9762 in Canada 🖷 416/979-8167 🌐 www.travelcuts.com.

SUBWAY TRAVEL

The 714-mi subway system operates 24 hours a day and serves most of the places you'll want to visit. It's cheaper than a cab, and during the workweek it is often faster than either taxis or buses. The trains are clean and well lighted, and air-conditioned cars predominate on every line. Still, the New York subway is not problem-free. Many trains are crowded, and the older ones are noisy. Homeless people sometimes take refuge from the elements by riding the trains, and panhandlers abound. Although trains usually run frequently, especially during rush hours, you never know when some incident somewhere on the line may stall traffic.

Most subway entrances are at street corners and are marked by lampposts with an illuminated Metropolitan Transit Authority (MTA) logo or globe-shape green or red lights—green means open and red means closed (though colors don't always correspond to reality). Subway lines are designated by numbers and letters, such as the 3 line or the A line. Some lines run "express" and skip stops, and others are "locals" and make all stops. Each station entrance has a sign indicating the lines that run through the station. Some entrances are also marked "uptown only" or "downtown only." Before entering subway stations, **read the signs carefully.** One of the most frequent mistakes visitors make is taking the train in the wrong direction. Maps of the full subway system are posted in every train car and usually on the subway platform (though these are sometimes out-of-date). You can usually pick up free maps at station booths.

The collapse of the World Trade Center damaged the subway lines 1, 9, 2, and 3, which have readjusted their routes. As a result of ongoing repairs to the Manhattan Bridge, train lines that used to travel over it have new routes and there are new lines replacing them as well. For the most up-to-date information, call the MTA's Travel Information Center or visit their Web site, www.mta.nyc.ny.us. Alternatively, ask a station agent.

FARES & TRANSFERS

Subway fare is the same as bus fare: $2. (At presstime, a court case to roll back the fare to $1.50 was pending.) You can transfer between subway lines an unlimited number of times at any of the numerous stations where lines intersect. If you use a MetroCard (⇨ Public Transportation) to pay your fare, you can also transfer to intersecting MTA bus routes for free. Transfers generally have time limits of two hours.

PAYING

Pay your subway fare at the turnstile, using a MetroCard that you can purchase at the station booth or from a vending machine.

SMOKING

Smoking is not allowed on New York City subways or in subway stations.

Subway Information Metropolitan Transit Authority (MTA) Travel Information Center ☎ 718/330-1234 🌐 www.mta.nyc.ny.us. MTA Lost Property Office ☎ 212/712-4500. MTA Status information hot line ☎ 718/243-7777, updated hourly.

TAXES

The city charges tax on hotel rooms (13.625%), rental cars (13.625%), and parking in commercial lots or garages (18.625%).

SALES TAX

New York City's 8.625% sales tax applies to almost everything you can buy retail, including restaurant meals. Prescription drugs and nonprepared food bought in grocery stores are tax exempt.

TAXIS & CAR SERVICES

There are several differences between taxis (cabs) and car services, or livery cabs: a taxi is yellow and a car-service sedan is not. In addition, taxis run on a meter, while car services charge a flat fee. And by law, car services are not allowed to pick up passengers unless you call for one first.

Taxis can be extremely difficult (if not impossible) to find in Brooklyn, Queens, Bronx, and Staten Island. As a result, you may have no choice but to call a car service. Always **determine the fee** beforehand when using a car service sedan; a 10%–15% tip is customary above that.

Yellow cabs are in abundance almost everywhere in Manhattan, cruising the streets looking for fares. They are usually easy to hail on the street or from a taxi rank in front of major hotels, though finding one at rush hour or in the rain can take some time. Even if you're stuck in a downpour or at the airport, **do not accept a ride from a gypsy cab.** If a cab is not yellow and does not have an aqua-color plastic medallion riveted to the hood, you could be putting yourself in danger by getting into the car.

You can see if a taxi is available by checking its rooftop light; if the center panel is lit and the side panels are dark, the driver is ready to take passengers. Taxi fares cost $2 for the first ⅕ mi, 30¢ for each ⅕ mi thereafter, and 20¢ for each minute not in motion. A 50¢ surcharge is added to rides begun between 8 PM and 6 AM. There is no charge for extra passengers, but you must pay any bridge or tunnel tolls incurred during your trip (sometimes a driver will personally pay a toll to keep moving quickly, but that amount will be added to the fare when the ride is over). Taxi drivers expect a 15% to 20% tip.

To avoid unhappy taxi experiences, **try to know where you want to go and how to get there before you hail a cab.** A few cab drivers are dishonest, and not all know the city as well as they should. Direct your cab driver by the cross streets of your destination (for instance, "5th Avenue and 42nd Street"), rather than the numerical address, which means little to many drivers. Also, speak simply and clearly to make sure the driver has heard you correctly—this will save you time, money, and aggravation. A quick pre-call to your destination will give you cross-street information, as will a quick glance at a map marked with address numbers. You can also find the cross street of many Manhattan addresses using the conversion chart found in the front section of the Yellow Pages.

Car Services **Carmel** ☎ 212/666–6666. **Highbridge Car Service** ☎ 212/927–4600. **Tel-Aviv** ☎ 212/777–7777.

TELEPHONES

Avoid making calls from your hotel room, because you may be charged a higher rate than usual for direct-dial calls or a surcharge on credit card calls. Public pay phones are easily found on the street and in hotels, bars, and restaurants.

Make sure that the pay phone is labeled as a Verizon telephone; the unmarked varieties are notorious change-eaters. There are also public credit card phones scattered around the city. If you want to consult a directory or make a more leisurely call, pay phones in the lobbies of office buildings or hotels (some of which take credit cards) are a better choice.

The area codes for Manhattan are 212, 646, and 917. For Brooklyn, Queens, the Bronx, and Staten Island, the area codes are 718 and 347. The area codes 917, 347, and 646 are also used for many cellular phones and pagers in all five boroughs.

TIME

New York operates on Eastern Standard Time. When it is noon in New York it is 9 AM in Los Angeles, 11 AM in Chicago, 5 PM in London, and 3 AM the following day in Sydney.

TIPPING

The customary tipping rate is 15%–20% for taxi drivers and waiters; bellhops are usually given $2 per bag in luxury hotels, $1 per bag elsewhere. Hotel maids should be tipped $2 per day of your stay. A doorman who hails or helps you into a cab can be tipped $1–$2. You should also tip your hotel concierge for services rendered; the size of the tip depends on the difficulty of your request, as well as the quality of the concierge's work. For an ordinary dinner reservation or tour arrangements, $3–$5 should do; if the concierge scores seats at a popular restaurant or show or performs unusual services (getting your laptop repaired, finding a good allergist, etc.), $10 or more is appropriate.

Waiters should be tipped 15%–20%, though at higher-end restaurants, a solid 20% is more the norm. Many restaurants add a gratuity to the bill for parties of six or more. Ask what the percentage is if the menu or bill doesn't state it. Tip $1 per drink you order at the bar, though if at an upscale establishment, those $15 martinis might warrant a $2 tip.

TOURS & PACKAGES

Because everything is prearranged on a prepackaged tour or independent vacation, you spend less time planning—and often get it all at a good price.

BOOKING WITH AN AGENT

Travel agents are excellent resources. But it's a good idea to collect brochures from several agencies, as some agents' suggestions may be influenced by relationships with tour and package firms that reward them for volume sales. If you have a special interest, **find an agent with expertise in that area**; the American Society of Travel Agents (ASTA; ⇨ Travel Agencies) has a database of specialists worldwide.

Make sure your travel agent knows the accommodations and other services of the place being recommended. Ask about the hotel's location, room size, beds, and whether it has a pool, room service, or programs for children, if you care about these. Has your agent been there in person or sent others whom you can contact?

Do some homework on your own, too: local tourism boards can provide information about lesser-known and small-niche operators, some of which may sell only direct.

BUYER BEWARE

Each year consumers are stranded or lose their money when tour operators—even large ones with excellent reputations—go out of business. So **check out the operator.** Ask several travel agents about its reputation, and try to **book with a company that has a consumer-protection program.** (Look for information in the company's brochure.) In the United States, members of the National Tour Association and the United States Tour Operators Association are required to set aside funds to cover payments and travel arrangements in the event that the company defaults. It's also a good idea to choose a company that participates in the American Society of Travel Agents' Tour Operator Program; ASTA will act as mediator in any disputes between you and your tour operator.

Remember that the more your package or tour includes, the better you can predict the ultimate cost of your vacation. Make sure you know exactly what is covered, and **beware of hidden costs.** Are taxes, tips, and transfers included? Entertainment and excursions? These can add up.

i Tour-Operator Recommendations **American Society of Travel Agents** (⇨ Travel Agencies). **National Tour Association** (NTA) ✉ 546 E. Main St., Lexington, KY 40508 ☎ 859/226-4444 or 800/682-8886 📠 859/226-4404 🌐 www.ntaonline.com. **United States Tour Operators Association** (USTOA) ✉ 275 Madison Ave., Suite 2014, New York, NY 10016 ☎ 212/599-6599 or 800/468-7862 📠 212/599-6744 🌐 www.ustoa.com.

TRAIN TRAVEL

For information about traveling by subway within New York City, *see* Subway Travel.

Metro-North Commuter Railroad trains take passengers from Grand Central Terminal to points north of New York City, both in New York State and Connecticut. Amtrak trains from across the United States arrive at Penn Station. For trains from New York City to Long Island and New Jersey, take the Long Island Railroad and New Jersey Transit, respectively; both operate from Penn Station. All of these trains generally run on schedule, although occasional delays occur. Smoking is not permitted on any train.

i Train Information **Amtrak** ☎ 800/872-7245 🌐 www.amtrak.com. **Long Island Railroad** ☎ 718/

217-5477 🌐 www.mta.nyc.ny.us/lirr. **Metro-North Commuter Railroad** ☎ 212/532-4900 🌐 www.mta.nyc.ny.us/mnr. **New Jersey Transit** ☎ 973/762-5100 🌐 www.njtransit.com. **PATH** ☎ 800/234-7284 🌐 www.panynj.gov.

Train Stations **Grand Central Terminal** ✉ E. 42nd St. at Park Ave., Midtown East ☎ 212/340-2210 🌐 www.grandcentralterminal.com. **Penn Station** ✉ W. 31st to W. 33rd Sts., between 7th and 8th Aves., Midtown West ☎ no phone.

TRAVEL AGENCIES

A good travel agent puts your needs first. Look for an agency that has been in business at least five years, emphasizes customer service, and has someone on staff who specializes in your destination. In addition, **make sure the agency belongs to a professional trade organization.** The American Society of Travel Agents (ASTA)—the largest and most influential in the field with more than 20,000 members in some 140 countries—maintains and enforces a strict code of ethics and will step in to help mediate any agent-client disputes involving ASTA members if necessary. ASTA (whose motto is "Without a travel agent, you're on your own") also maintains a Web site that includes a directory of agents. (If a travel agency is also acting as your tour operator, *see* Buyer Beware *in* Tours and Packages.)

Local Agent Referrals **American Society of Travel Agents** (ASTA) ✉ 1101 King St., Suite 200, Alexandria, VA 22314 ☎ 703/739-2782 or 800/965-2782 24-hr hot line 📠 703/739-3268 🌐 www.astanet.com. **Association of British Travel Agents** ✉ 68-71 Newman St., London W1T 3AH ☎ 020/7637-2444 📠 020/7637-0713 🌐 www.abtanet.com. **Association of Canadian Travel Agents** ✉ 130 Albert St., Suite 1705, Ottawa, Ontario K1P 5G4 ☎ 613/237-3657 📠 613/237-7052 🌐 www.acta.ca. **Australian Federation of Travel Agents** ✉ Level 3, 309 Pitt St., Sydney, NSW 2000 ☎ 02/9264-3299 📠 02/9264-1085 🌐 www.afta.com.au. **Travel Agents' Association of New Zealand** ✉ Level 5, Tourism and Travel House, 79 Boulcott St., Box 1888, Wellington 6001 ☎ 04/499-0104 📠 04/499-0786 🌐 www.taanz.org.nz.

VISITOR INFORMATION

The Grand Central Partnership (a sort of civic Good Samaritans' group) has installed a number of unstaffed information kiosks near Grand Central Terminal, loaded with maps and helpful brochures on attractions throughout the city. There are also seasonal outdoor carts sprinkled throughout the area (there is one near Vanderbilt Avenue and East 42nd Street), staffed by friendly, knowledgeable, multilingual New Yorkers. The 34th Street Partnership runs a kiosk on the concourse level at Penn Station (33rd Street and 7th Avenue); there's even a cart at the Empire State Building (5th Avenue at 34th Street.)

Contact the New York City visitor information offices for brochures, subway and bus maps, MetroCards, a calendar of events, listings of hotels and weekend hotel packages, and discount coupons for Broadway shows. The Downtown Alliance has information on the area encompassing City Hall south to Battery Park, and from the East River to West Street. For a free booklet listing New York City attractions and tour packages, contact the New York State Division of Tourism.

City Information **Brooklyn Information & Culture Inc.** ✉ 647 Fulton St., 2nd floor, Brooklyn 11217 ☎ 718/855-7882 🌐 www.brooklynX.org. **Downtown Alliance** ✉ 120 Broadway, Suite 3340, between Pine and Thames, Lower Manhattan 10271 ☎ 212/566-6700 📠 212/566-6707 🌐 www.downtownny.com. **NYC & Company-Convention & Visitors Bureau** ✉ 810 7th Ave., between W. 52nd and W. 53rd Sts., 3rd floor, Midtown West ☎ 212/484-1222 or 212/397-8200 📠 212/245-5943 🌐 www.nycvisit.com, weekdays 8:30 AM–6 PM, weekends 9 AM–5 PM. **Times Square Visitors Center** ✉ 1560 Broadway, between 46th and 47th Sts., Midtown West ☎ 212/768-1560 🌐 www.timessquarebid.org, daily 8 AM–8 PM.

Statewide Information **New York State Division of Tourism** 📪 Box 2603, Albany, NY 12220 ☎ 518/474-4116 or 800/225-5697 🌐 www.iloveny.state.ny.us.

Government Advisories **Consular Affairs Bureau of Canada** ☎ 800/267-6788 or 613/944-6788 🌐 www.voyage.gc.ca. **U.K. Foreign and Commonwealth Office** ✉ Travel Advice Unit, Consular Division, Old Admiralty Building, London SW1A 2PA ☎ 020/7008-0232 or 020/7008-0233 🌐 www.fco.gov.uk/travel. **Australian Department of Foreign Affairs and Trade** ☎ 02/6261-1299 Consular Travel Advice Faxback Service 🌐 www.dfat.gov.au. **New Zealand Ministry of Foreign Affairs and Trade** ☎ 04/439-8000 🌐 www.mft.govt.nz.

WALKING

The cheapest, sometimes the fastest, and usually the most interesting way to explore this city is by walking. Because New Yorkers by and large live in apartments rather than in houses, and travel by cab, bus, or subway rather than by private car, they end up walking quite a lot. As a result, street life is a vital part of the local culture. On crowded sidewalks, people gossip, snack, browse, cement business deals, make romantic rendezvous, encounter long-lost friends, and fly into irrational quarrels with strangers. It's a wonderfully democratic hubbub.

A typical New Yorker walks quickly and focuses intently on dodging cars, buses, bicycle messengers, construction sites, and other pedestrians. Although this might make natives seem hurried and rude, they will often come to the aid of a lost pedestrian, so **don't hesitate to ask a passerby for directions.**

WEB SITES

Do check out the World Wide Web when planning your trip. You'll find everything from weather forecasts to virtual tours of famous cities. Be sure to **visit Fodors.com,** a complete travel-planning site. You can research prices and book plane tickets, hotel rooms, rental cars, vacation packages, and more. In addition, you can post your pressing questions in the Travel Talk section. Other planning tools include a currency converter and weather reports, and there are loads of links to travel resources.

If you want to find out what's going on around town, New York Citysearch supplies comprehensive, searchable events listings. The Official New York City Web site has plenty of links to agencies, services, and cultural activities. To learn about the city in greater depth, go to the New York Public Library. To figure out subway directions to any New York address, consult the New York Subway Finder. The *New York Times* has reviews of current movies and theater, as well as music, dance, art listings, and show times. For more on traveling to New York City, the NYC & Company Convention & Visitors Bureau is a good source of basic sightseeing and lodging information, and a good place to find out about special offers.

Web Addresses **Fodor's.com** www.fodors.com. **New York Citysearch** www.nycitysearch.com. **New York Public Library** www.nypl.org. **New York Subway Finder** www.krusch.com/nysf.html. **NYC & Company** www.nycvisit.com. ***New York Times*** www.nytimes.com or www.nytoday.com. **Official New York City Web site** nyc.gov.

CONVERSIONS

DISTANCE

KILOMETERS/MILES

To change kilometers (km) to miles (mi), multiply km by .621. To change mi to km, multiply mi by 1.61.

km to mi	mi to km
1 = .62	1 = 1.6
2 = 1.2	2 = 3.2
3 = 1.9	3 = 4.8
4 = 2.5	4 = 6.4
5 = 3.1	5 = 8.1
6 = 3.7	6 = 9.7
7 = 4.3	7 =11.3
8 = 5.0	8 =12.9

METERS/FEET

To change meters (m) to feet (ft), multiply m by 3.28. To change ft to m, multiply ft by .305.

m to ft	ft to m
1 = 3.3	1 = .30
2 = 6.6	2 = .61
3 = 9.8	3 = .92
4 = 13.1	4 = 1.2
5 = 16.4	5 = 1.5
6 = 19.7	6 = 1.8
7 = 23.0	7 = 2.1
8 = 26.2	8 = 2.4

WEIGHT

KILOGRAMS/POUNDS

To change kilograms (kg) to pounds (lb), multiply kg by 2.20. To change lb to kg, multiply lb by .455.

kg to lb	lb to kg
1 = 2.2	1 = .45
2 = 4.4	2 = .91
3 = 6.6	3 = 1.4
4 = 8.8	4 = 1.8
5 = 11.0	5 = 2.3
6 = 13.2	6 = 2.7
7 = 15.4	7 = 3.2
8 = 17.6	8 = 3.6

GRAMS/OUNCES

To change grams (g) to ounces (oz), multiply g by .035. To change oz to g, multiply oz by 28.4.

g to oz	oz to g
1 = .04	1 = 28
2 = .07	2 = 57
3 = .11	3 = 85
4 = .14	4 = 114
5 = .18	5 = 142
6 = .21	6 = 170
7 = .25	7 = 199
8 = .28	8 = 227

CLOTHING SIZE

WOMEN'S CLOTHING

US	UK	EUR
4	6	34
6	8	36
8	10	38
10	12	40
12	14	42

WOMEN'S SHOES

US	UK	EUR
5	3	36
6	4	37
7	5	38
8	6	39
9	7	40

MEN'S SUITS

US	UK	EUR
34	34	44
36	36	46
38	38	48
40	40	50
42	42	52
44	44	54
46	46	56

MEN'S SHIRTS

US	UK	EUR
14½	14½	37
15	15	38
15½	15½	39
16	16	41
16½	16½	42
17	17	43
17½	17½	44

MEN'S SHOES

US	UK	EUR
7	6	39½
8	7	41
9	8	42
10	9	43
11	10	44½
12	11	46

TEMPERATURE

METRIC CONVERSIONS

To change centigrade or Celsius (C) to Fahrenheit (F), multiply C by 1.8 and add 32. To change F to C, subtract 32 from F and multiply by .555.

°F	°C
0	-17.8
10	-12.2
20	-6.7
30	-1.1
32	0
40	+4.4
50	10.0
60	15.5
70	21.1
80	26.6
90	32.2
98.6	37.0
100	37.7

LIQUID VOLUME

LITERS/U.S. GALLONS

To change liters (L) to U.S. gallons (gal), multiply L by .264. To change U.S. gal to L, multiply gal by 3.79.

L to gal	gal to L
1 = .26	1 = 3.8
2 = .53	2 = 7.6
3 = .79	3 = 11.4
4 = 1.1	4 = 15.2
5 = 1.3	5 = 19.0
6 = 1.6	6 = 22.7
7 = 1.8	7 = 26.5
8 = 2.1	8 = 30.3

EXPLORING MANHATTAN

1

FODOR'S CHOICE

Bethesda Fountain, *Central Park*
Cathedral Church of St. John the Divine, *Morningside Heights*
Chrysler Building, *Midtown East*
Ellis Island, *Lower Manhattan*
Empire State Building, *Murray Hill*
Grand Central Terminal, *Midtown East*
Metropolitan Museum of Art, *Upper East Side*
Solomon R. Guggenheim Museum, *Upper East Side*
St. Patrick's Cathedral, *Midtown East*
Statue of Liberty, *Lower Manhattan*

HIGHLY RECOMMENDED

American Folk Art Museum, *Midtown West*
American Museum of Natural History, *Upper West Side*
Brooklyn Bridge, *Lower Manhattan*
Carnegie Hall, *Midtown West*
The Dakota, *Upper West Side*
Frick Collection, *Upper East Side*
Lincoln Center, *Upper West Side*
The Mall, *Central Park*
Mott Street, *Little Italy*
Museum of the City of New York, *Upper East Side*
New York Public Library (NYPL) Humanities and Social Sciences Library, *Midtown West*
St. Bartholomew's Church, *Midtown East*
St. Luke's Place, *Greenwich Village*
Strivers' Row, *Harlem*
Stuyvesant Street, *Greenwich Village*
Times Square, *Midtown West*
Washington Square Park, *Greenwich Village*

Updated by Andrea Meyer, Margaret Mittelbach, and Michael de Zayas

MANHATTAN IS, ABOVE ALL, A WALKER'S CITY. Along its busy streets, an endless variety of sights unfolds everywhere you go. Attractions, many of them world-famous, crowd close together on this narrow island, and because the city can only grow up, not out, the new simply piles on top of the old. Manhattan's character changes every few blocks, so quaint town houses stand shoulder to shoulder with sleek glass towers, gleaming gourmet supermarkets sit around the corner from dusty thrift shops, and chic bistros inhabit the storefronts of soot-smudged warehouses. Many visitors, beguiled into walking a little farther, then a little farther still, often have stumbled upon their trip's most memorable moments.

Our walking tours cover a great deal of ground, yet they only scratch the surface of the city. If you plod dutifully from point to point, nose buried in this book, you'll miss half the fun. Look up at the tops of skyscrapers, and you'll see a riot of mosaics, carvings, and ornaments. Step into the lobby of an architectural landmark and study its features; take a look around to see the real people who work, live, or worship there today. Peep down side streets, even in crowded midtown, and you may find fountains, greenery, and sudden bursts of flowers. Find a bench or ledge on which to perch and take time just to watch the crowd passing by. New York has so many faces that every visitor can discover a different one.

When it comes to getting around New York, you'll have your pick of transportation in almost every neighborhood. The subway and bus networks are thorough, although getting across town can take some extra maneuvering. If you're not pressed for time, take a public bus; they generally are slower than subways, but you can also see the city as you travel. Yellow cabs are abundant, except at the rush hour of 4:30–5 PM, when many are off duty (shift change time). Like a taxi ride, the subway is a true New York City experience and often the quickest way to get around. But New York is really a walking town, and depending on the time of day and your destination, hoofing it could be the easiest and most enjoyable option.

Getting Your Bearings

The map of Manhattan has a Jekyll-and-Hyde aspect. The rational Dr. Jekyll part prevails above 14th Street, where the streets form a regular grid pattern, imposed in 1811. Numbered streets run east and west (crosstown), and broad avenues, most of them also numbered, run north (uptown) and south (downtown). The chief exceptions are Broadway and the thoroughfares that hug the shores of the Hudson and East rivers. Broadway runs the entire length of Manhattan. At its southernmost end it follows the city's north–south grid; at East 10th Street it turns and runs on a diagonal to West 86th Street, then at a lesser angle until West 107th Street, where it merges with West End Avenue.

Fifth Avenue is the east–west dividing line for street addresses: on either side, addresses begin at 1 where a street intersects 5th Avenue and climb higher in each direction, in regular increments. For example, 1 East 55th Street is just east of 5th Avenue, 99 East 55th Street is at Park (the equivalent of 4th) Avenue, 199 East 55th Street is at 3rd Avenue, and so on; likewise, 1 West 55th Street is just west of 5th Avenue, 99 West 55th Street is at 6th Avenue (also known as Avenue of the Americas), 199 West 55th Street is at 7th Avenue, and so forth. Above 59th Street, where Central Park interrupts the grid, West Side addresses start numbering at Central Park West, an extension of 8th Avenue. Avenue addresses are much less regular, for the numbers begin wherever each avenue begins and increase at different increments. An address at 552 3rd Avenue, for example, will not necessarily be anywhere near 552 2nd

Manhattan Neighborhoods
E.125th St.
HARLEM
Marcus Garvey Park
Columbia University
W.116th St.
Randalls Island
MORNINGSIDE HEIGHTS
Morningside Park
E.110th St.
E.106h St.
Wards Island
Henry Hudson Pkwy.
Riverside Dr.
Broadway
Amsterdam Ave.
W.96th St.
E.96th St.
UPPER WEST SIDE
UPPER EAST SIDE
Central Park West
W.86th St.
E.86th St.
Gracie Mansion
Riverside Park
Central Park
Metropolitan Museum of Art
Columbus Ave.
E.79th St.
American Museum of Natural History
Hudson River
West End Ave.
Park Ave.
E.72nd St.
W.72nd St.
Lexington Ave.
FDR Dr.
Roosevelt Island
E.65th St.
QUEEN
Lincoln Center
E.59th St.
Queensboro Bridge
W.57th St.
E.57th St.
Rockefeller Center
5th Ave.
E.50th St.
1st Ave.
11th Ave.
10th Ave.
9th Ave.
8th Ave.
Grand Central Terminal
United Nations
Times Square
W.42nd St.
Lincoln Tunnel
Port Authority Bus Terminal
E.42nd St.
Queens-Midtown Tunnel
MIDTOWN
Madison Ave.
3rd Ave.
2nd Ave.
Javits Convention Center
W.34th St.
Madison Square Garden
Empire State Building
East River
MURRAY HILL
W.23rd St.
7th Ave.
Ave. of the Americas
E.23rd St.
CHELSEA
Flatiron Building
GRAMERCY
W.14th St.
Union Sq.
E.14th St.
Hudson River
West Side Hwy.
GREENWICH VILLAGE
EAST VILLAGE
Washington Sq.
E. Houston St.
Williamsburg Bridge
W. Houston St.
NOLITA
LOWER EAST SIDE
SOHO
LITTLE ITALY
Canal St.
Holland Tunnel
TRI-BECA
CHINA-TOWN
Manhattan Bridge
NEW JERSEY
Chambers St.
West St.
W. Broadway
Brooklyn Bridge
World Trade Center Site
LOWER MANHATTAN
South Street Seaport
BROOKLY
Battery Park
Brooklyn-Battery Tunnel

Avenue. Even many New Yorkers cannot master the complexities of this system, so they give addresses in terms of intersections: 5th Avenue and 55th Street, for instance, or 55th Street between 9th and 10th avenues.

Below 14th Street—the area settled before the 1811 grid was decreed—Manhattan streets reflect the disordered personality of Mr. Hyde. They may be aligned with the shoreline, or they may twist along the route of an ancient cow path. Below 14th Street you'll find West 4th Street intersecting West 11th Street, Greenwich Street running roughly parallel to Greenwich Avenue, and Leroy Street turning into St. Luke's Place for one block and then becoming Leroy again. There's an East Broadway and a West Broadway, both of which run north–south and neither of which is an extension of plain old Broadway. Logic won't help you below 14th Street; only a good street map and good directions will.

You may also be confused by the way New Yorkers use *uptown, downtown,* and *midtown.* These terms refer both to locations and to directions. Uptown means north of wherever you are at the moment; downtown means to the south. But uptown, downtown, and midtown are also specific parts of the city. Unfortunately, no consensus exists about where these areas are: Downtown may mean anyplace from the tip of lower Manhattan through Chelsea. Midtown is generally known to be between 34th and 59th streets.

A similar situation exists with *East Side* and *West Side.* Someone may refer to a location as "on the East Side," meaning somewhere east of 5th Avenue. A hotel described as being "on the West Side" may be on West 42nd Street. But when New Yorkers speak of the East Side or the West Side, they usually mean the respective areas above 59th Street on either side of Central Park. Be prepared for misunderstandings.

WALL STREET & THE BATTERY

Island city that it is, much of Manhattan strangely turns its back on the rushing waters that surround it—not so the Battery. In Battery Park, you can stroll alongside the water and look out on the confluence of the Hudson and East River estuaries where bustling seaborne commerce once glutted the harbor that built the "good city of old Manhatto," Herman Melville's moniker from the second chapter of *Moby-Dick.* It was here that the Dutch established the colony of Nieuw Amsterdam in 1625; the first capitol building of the United States was built on Wall Street in 1789; and George Washington was sworn in on its steps as president. The city did not really expand beyond these precincts until the middle of the 19th century.

No matter how far the city and population have grown, much of what New York is known for—money and skyscrapers—remains at its old starting point. Wall Street, both an actual street and a shorthand name for the vast financial center that clusters around the New York and American stock exchanges, continues to dominate much of Lower Manhattan. It's fitting that this setting of feverish entrepreneurship and capitalism is within sight of enduring symbols of America: the Statue of Liberty and Ellis Island, port of entry for countless immigrants, looking for a new life in a new land.

The famous skyline of lower Manhattan was permanently altered after the terrorist attacks on the World Trade Center on September 11, 2001. Surrounding buildings were destroyed as well, and some businesses and residents moved elsewhere; but most stayed if they could, and many new faces have since moved to the area, helping to restore its busy storefronts and streets. Despite its changed profile and the difficulties businesses and residents have faced, lower Manhattan is slowly rebuilding itself and will continue to do so in the years to come.

Numbers in the text correspond to numbers in the margin and on the Lower Manhattan map.

a good walk

At the tip of the island, the **Staten Island Ferry** 1 affords a big-picture perspective on Wall Street and the Battery, and you can double the ride's scenic pleasures by taking it at sunset. Just north of the terminal, the white columns and curved brick front of the 1793 **Shrine of St. Elizabeth Ann Seton at Our Lady of the Rosary** 2 are dwarfed by the high-rise behind it. The house was once one of many mansions lining State Street. Across the street from the shrine, the verdant **Battery Park** 3 curves up the west side of the island. It's filled with sculptures and monuments, including the circular **Castle Clinton National Monument** 4. The venerable fort is the place to buy tickets for ferries to the **Statue of Liberty** 5 and **Ellis Island** 6. From Castle Clinton, walk away from the water, following the path running alongside the rose-filled Hope Garden to *The Sphere*, by Fritz Koenig. The damaged bronze sculpture once stood at the center of the World Trade Center plaza. The path ends near **Bowling Green** 7, an oval greensward at the foot of Broadway that in 1733 became New York's first public park. It provides an excellent view up Broadway of the formidable Canyon of Heroes, site of many a ticker-tape parade. While you're here, duck inside the Cunard Building at 25 Broadway to see the superb ceiling frescoes by Ezra Winter. Now a post office, this Renaissance-style building completed in 1921 once was the booking hall for the great ocean liners owned by Cunard. On the south side of Bowling Green is the beaux arts Alexander Hamilton U.S. Custom House, home of the **National Museum of the American Indian** 8.

Follow Whitehall Street (the continuation of Broadway) down the east side of the museum. A left turn onto Bridge Street will bring into focus a block of early New York buildings. As you approach Broad Street, the two-tone Georgian **Fraunces Tavern** 9 will appear on the right, on Pearl Street. Across Pearl Street, the plaza of 85 Broad Street pays homage to urban archaeology with a transparent panel in the sidewalk at the corner of Pearl and Coenties Slip, showing the excavated foundations of the 17th-century Stadt Huys, the Old Dutch City Hall. The course of old Dutch Stone Street is marked in the lobby with a line of brown paving stones.

Next head north on Pearl Street to **Hanover Square** 10, a quiet tree-lined plaza. Leading south is Stone Street, the oldest paved street in the city. A small alley off Stone Street is Mill Lane, where New York's first Sephardic Jewish community was forced to worship secretly in a mill during the mid-1600s. Turn right off Mill Lane onto South William and walk until you hit its triangular convergence with Beaver Street. On the right, 20 Exchange Place towers and adds street-level interest with weighty art deco doorways depicting the engines of commerce. On the corner to your left is the elegant entrance to the legendary Delmonico's restaurant. Two blocks farther north, William Street crosses **Wall Street** 11. For a jaw-dropping display of the money that built Manhattan, take a look at the massive arcade of 55 Wall Street, now home of the Regent Wall Street Hotel.

One block west on Wall Street, where Broad Street becomes Nassau Street, a statue of George Washington stands on the steps of the **Federal Hall National Memorial** 12. Across the street is an investment bank built by J. P. Morgan in 1913. By building only four stories, Morgan was in ef-

Lower Manhattan
Promenade
Franklin St.
Leonard St.
Worth St.
Thomas St.
Hudson St.
Staple St.
Old New York Life Insurance Company Headquarters
Hogan St.
Lafayette St.
Federal Plaza
Duane St.
Reade St.
Elk St.
Centre St.
Foley Square
Pearl St.
Hayes Pl.
Baxter St.
Mulberry St.
Mott St.
CHINATOWN
Henry St.
Catherine Slip
Madison St.
St. James Pl.
FDR Drive
Brooklyn Bridge
Stuyvesant High School
West St. Overpass
Chambers St.
A,C,
1,2,3,9
J,M,Z
4,5,6
Warren St.
Park Pl. W.
Murray St.
Greenwich St.
West Broadway
Church St.
Broadway
Brooklyn Bridge Walkway
Pace University
City Hall Park
Park Pl.
N,R,W
2,3
Barclay St.
Park Row
Spruce St.
Beekman St.
New York Mercantile Exchange
Vesey St.
North End Ave.
Hudson River Park
West St. (Closed)
World Trade Center Site
Ann St.
Fulton St.
A,C
4,5
Gold St.
Dover St.
Peck Slip
Pearl St.
Beekman St.
Fulton Fish Market
Titanic Memorial
SOUTH STREET SEAPORT
Pier 17
Pier 16
Hoboken Ferry Terminal
World Financial Center
North Cove Yacht Harbor
West Side Highway
Dey St.
John St.
Cortlandt St.
Maiden Lane
Nassau St.
Platt St.
Burling Slip
Liberty St.
Cedar St.
Louise Nevelson Plaza
Thames St.
Chase Manhattan Plaza
William St.
Albany St.
Carlisle St.
Trinity Pl.
Wall St.
55 Wall St.
Pine St.
Depyster St.
BATTERY
Rector St.
33
31
30
32
28
27
26
25
29
24
23
17
16
18
22
15
14
12
11
13

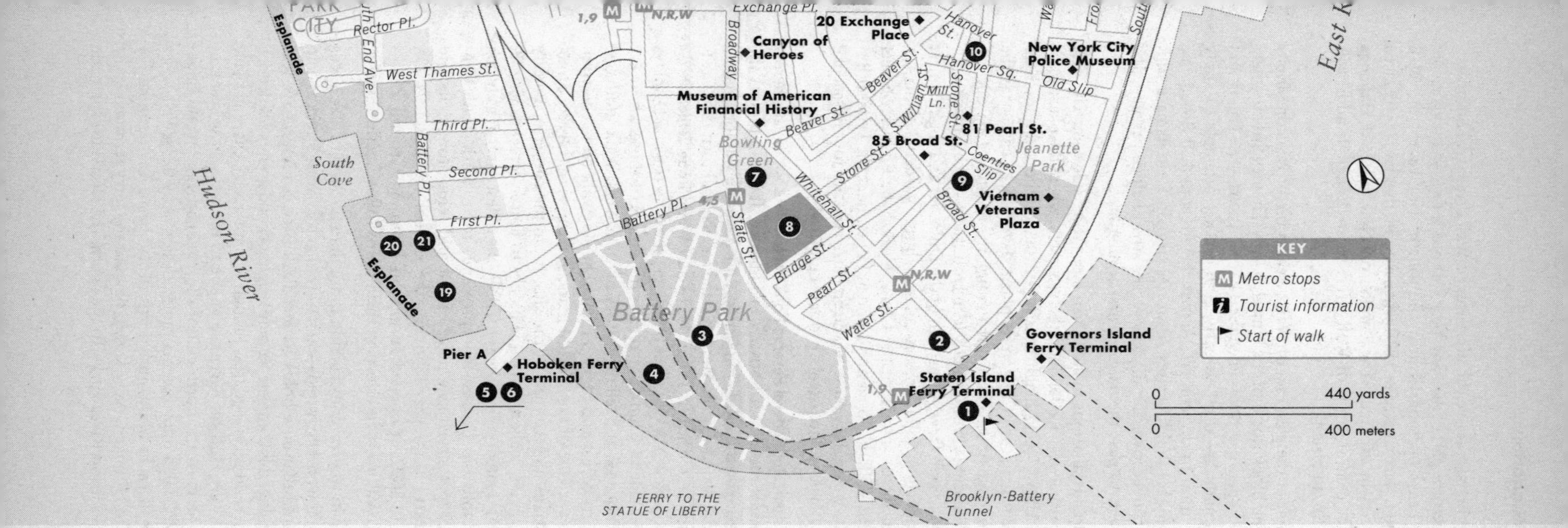

Wall Street & the Battery ▼

- Battery Park 3
- Bowling Green 7
- Castle Clinton National Monument 4
- Ellis Island 6
- Federal Hall National Memorial 12
- Federal Reserve Bank of New York 15
- Fraunces Tavern 9
- Hanover Square 10
- Museum of Jewish Heritage–A Living Memorial to the Holocaust 20
- National Museum of the American Indian 8
- New York Stock Exchange 13
- Robert F. Wagner Jr. Park 19
- St. Paul's Chapel 17
- Shrine of St. Elizabeth Ann Seton at Our Lady of the Rosary 2
- Skyscraper Museum ... 21
- Staten Island Ferry 1
- Statue of Liberty 5
- Trinity Church 14
- Wall Street 11
- World Financial Center 18
- World Trade Center Site 16

The Seaport & the Courts ▼

- African Burial Ground 32
- Brooklyn Bridge 29
- City Hall 25
- City Hall Park 24
- Criminal Courts Building 33
- Municipal Building 28
- New York County Courthouse 31
- South Street Seaport Historic District 22
- Surrogate's Court 27
- Tweed Courthouse 26
- U.S. Courthouse 30
- Woolworth Building 23

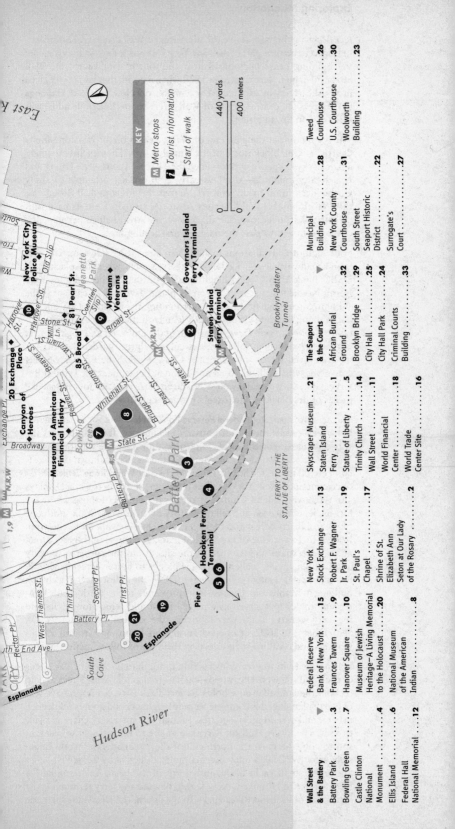

fect declaring himself above the pressures of Wall Street real estate values. Soon to become part of the New York City Stock Exchange expansion, the building bears pockmarks near the fourth window on the Wall Street side; these were created in 1920 when a bomb that had been placed in a pushcart nearby exploded. The temple-front **New York Stock Exchange (NYSE)** 13 is the central shrine of Wall Street (even though its address is officially on Broad Street).

The focal point at the west end of Wall Street is the brownstone **Trinity Church** 14. One block north of the church is tiny Thames Street, where a pair of skyscrapers playfully called the Thames Twins—the Trinity and U.S. Realty buildings—displays early-20th-century attempts to apply Gothic decoration to skyscrapers. Across the street at 120 Broadway, the 1915 Equitable Building rises 30 stories straight from its base with no setback; its overpowering shadow on the street helped persuade the city government to pass the nation's first zoning law.

Four sculpture installations make for an interesting side tour. The first is on Broadway between Cedar and Liberty streets, where the black-glass HSBC Bank USA (1971) heightens the drama of the red-and-silver Isamu Noguchi sculpture *Cube* in its plaza. Two blocks east, near the William Street edge of the plaza surrounding the 65-story Chase Manhattan Bank Building (1960), stands Jean Dubuffet's striking black-and-white *Group of Four Trees*. Just south of the Dubuffet and slightly inset is another Noguchi installation, a circular sculpture garden with his signature carved stones. North of the Chase plaza, where Liberty Street converges with William Street and Maiden Lane under the Federal Reserve Bank, the triangular Louise Nevelson Plaza contains four missilelike pieces of her black-welded-steel abstract sculpture.

The massive, rusticated **Federal Reserve Bank of New York** 15, directly across the street, recalls the Palazzo Strozzi in Florence, Italy, and looks the way a bank ought to: solid, imposing, and absolutely impregnable. Walk west past Broadway on Maiden Lane (which will turn into Cortlandt Street) to Church Street. There, the 16-acre **World Trade Center site** 16 once contained New York's tallest buildings, the twin towers. Displays along the west side of Church Street list the names of those who were lost on September 11, and tell the history of the towers. Walk south one block to Liberty Street and make a right. The sidewalk and pedestrian bridge (to Tower One of the World Financial Center) on Liberty Street allow pedestrians a close view of the site. From the corner of Liberty and Church streets, walk north three blocks to Fulton Street to visit **St. Paul's Chapel** 17 (enter on Broadway). This is the oldest surviving church building in Manhattan. Because of its proximity to the World Trade Center site, the chapel served as a place of rest and refuge for rescue and recovery workers in the year following the September 11 attacks. On September 11, 2002, it opened an exhibit honoring Ground Zero's workers and recalling their efforts in the months following the disaster.

During the twin towers' construction more than a million cubic yards of rock and soil were excavated—then moved across West Street to help reclaim the land that now holds Battery Park City. An impressive feat of urban planning, this complete 92-acre neighborhood houses residences, offices, and several green squares, though it's not a very exciting place to visit. The lovely Hudson River esplanade to the west is the best reason to come here. At the north end of the esplanade, the **World Financial Center (WFC)** 18, a four-tower complex designed by Cesar Pelli, rises above the small yacht basin. Just north of the basin is a terminal for ferry service to Hoboken, New Jersey. Beyond the ferry terminal is the south end of Hudson River Park. To the south, the riverside esplanade begins in the residential part of Battery Park City and connects with **Robert F. Wagner Jr. Park** 19, home to the **Museum of Jewish Heritage—A Living Memorial to the Holocaust** 20. Especially noteworthy among the artwork populating the esplanade are Ned Smyth's columned plaza with chessboards and the South Cove (a collaborative effort), a curved stage set of wooden piers and a steel-frame lookout quietly reminiscent of Lady Liberty's crown. Just across Battery Place from the Holocaust Museum is the **Skyscraper Museum** 21, where a history of Manhattan's verticality is waiting to be explored.

TIMING The Manhattan side of this tour takes most of a day—allow a lot more time to ferry out to the Statue of Liberty and Ellis Island. Visit on a weekday to capture the district's true vitality—but expect to be jostled on the crowded sidewalks if you stand still too long. If you visit on a weekend, on the other hand, in some areas you'll feel like a lone explorer in a canyon of buildings. The perimeter of the World Trade Center site is most crowded on the weekends. When visiting Liberty and Ellis islands, start early, preferably taking the first ferry to beat the crowds. The best place to end the day is on the Hudson River, watching the sun set.

What to See

3 **Battery Park.** Jutting out as if it were Manhattan's green toe, Battery Park (so named because a battery of 28 cannons was placed along its shore in colonial days to fend off the British) is built on landfill and has gradually grown over the centuries to its present 22 acres. The park's main structure is Castle Clinton National Monument, the takeoff point for ferries to the Statue of Liberty and Ellis Island. The interior of the park is loaded with various monuments and statues, some impressive, some downright obscure. Starting near the Staten Island Ferry Terminal, head north along the water's edge to the East Coast Memorial, a statue of a fierce eagle that presides over eight granite slabs inscribed with the names of U.S. servicemen who died in the western Atlantic during World War II. Climb the steps of the East Coast Memorial for a fine view of the main features of New York Harbor; from left to right: Governors Island, a former Coast Guard installation whose future is somewhat undecided; hilly Staten Island in the distance; the Statue of Liberty, on Liberty Island; Ellis Island, gateway to the New World for generations of immigrants; and the old railway terminal in Liberty State Park, on the mainland in Jersey City, New Jersey. On crystal-clear days you can see all the way to Port Elizabeth's cranes, which seem to mimic Lady Liberty's stance. Continue north past a romantic **statue of Giovanni da Verrazano,** the Florentine merchant who in 1524 piloted the ship that first sighted New York and its harbor. The Verrazano-Narrows Bridge, between Brooklyn and Staten Island, is visible from here, just beyond Governors Island. It's so long that the curvature of the earth had to be figured into its dimensions. At the park's northernmost edge, Marisol's bronze tribute to the American Merchant Marine in WWII is a dramatic depiction of three sailors trying to rescue a man in the water. Just beyond the sculpture is a white tented ferry terminal to Hoboken, New Jersey. Facing the terminal is Pier A, the last Victorian fireboat pier in the city. The building is undergoing restoration that will eventually transform it into a visitor and shopping center. Its clock tower, erected in 1919, was the nation's first World War I memorial. There are plenty of places to sit and rest in the leafy park, and two tiers of wood benches line the promenade. ⊠ *Broadway and Battery Pl., Lower Manhattan.*

7 **Bowling Green.** This oval greensward at the foot of Broadway became New York's first public park in 1733. On July 9, 1776, a few hours after citizens learned about the signing of the Declaration of Independence,

rioters toppled a statue of British king George III that had occupied the spot for 11 years; much of the statue's lead was melted down into bullets. In 1783, when the occupying British forces fled the city, they defiantly hoisted a Union Jack on a greased, uncleated flagpole so it couldn't be lowered; patriot John Van Arsdale drove his own cleats into the pole to replace the flag with the Stars and Stripes. The copper-top subway entrance here is the original one, built in 1904–05.

4 **Castle Clinton National Monument.** This circular red-stone fortress, built in 1811, first stood on an island 200 ft from shore as a defense for New York Harbor. In 1824 it became Castle Garden, an entertainment and concert facility that reached its zenith in 1850 when more than 6,000 people (the capacity of Radio City Music Hall) attended the U.S. debut of the Swedish Nightingale, Jenny Lind. After landfill connected it to the city, Castle Clinton became, in succession, an immigrant processing center, an aquarium, and now a restored fort, museum, and ticket office for ferries to the **Statue of Liberty** and **Ellis Island.** (The ferry ride is one loop; you can get off at Liberty Island, visit the statue, then board any ferry and continue on to Ellis Island, boarding another boat once you have finished exploring the historic immigration facility there.) Inside the old fort are dioramas of lower Manhattan in 1812, 1886, and 1941. Outside the landward entrance is a statue titled ***The Immigrants,*** at the beginning of a broad mall that leads back across the park. At the other end of the mall stands the **Netherlands Memorial Flagpole,** which depicts Dutch traders offering beads to Native Americans in 1626 for the land on which to establish Fort Amsterdam. Inscriptions describe the event in English and Dutch. If you're catching a ferry, be sure to leave adequate time for security checks, which include X-ray machines. Large packages and oversize bags and backpacks will not be permitted on board. ☎ *212/344–7220 for Castle Clinton; 212/269–5755 for ferry information* *Castle Clinton free; ferry $10 round-trip* *Daily 8:30–5, ferry departures daily every 45 mins 9:30–3:30; more departures and extended hrs in summer.*

6 Fodor'sChoice ★ **Ellis Island.** Between 1892 and 1924, approximately 12 million men, women, and children first set foot on U.S. soil at this 27½-acre island's federal immigration facility. By the time Ellis Island closed in 1954, it had processed the ancestors of more than 40% of Americans living today. The island's main building, now a national monument, reopened in 1990 as the **Ellis Island Immigration Museum.** More than 30 galleries of artifacts, photographs, and taped oral histories chronicle the immigrant experience, from what someone's native village was like to where a particular national group took root in America and what industries employed them. Check at the visitors desk for free film tickets, ranger tour times, or special programs. You can rent an audio guide or follow a ranger tour up to the white-tiled **Registry Room** (Great Hall), where immigrants awaited processing and inspectors screened out "undesirables"—unmarried women, the utterly destitute, and people suffering from contagious diseases. The ground-level **Railroad Ticket Office** has several interactive exhibits and three-dimensional representations on the *Peopling of America.* At a computer terminal in the **American Family Immigration Center,** you can search Ellis Island's records for your own ancestors (a $5 fee). Outdoors is the **American Immigrant Wall of Honor,** where the names of more than 500,000 immigrant Americans are inscribed along a promenade facing the Manhattan skyline. The names include Miles Standish, Priscilla Alden, George Washington's grandfather, Irving Berlin—it's possible to add a family member's name to the wall, too. ☎ *212/363–3200 for Ellis Island; 212/883–1986 for Wall of Honor information* *www.ellisisland.org* *Free* *Daily 9:30–5; extended hrs in summer.*

12 **Federal Hall National Memorial.** The site of this memorial is rich with both the country's and the city's history. The City Hall here hosted the 1765 Stamp Act Congress and, beginning in 1789, served as the Federal Hall of the new nation. On its balcony, George Washington took his oath as the country's first president. After the capital moved from New York to Philadelphia in 1790, the Federal Hall reverted to New York's City Hall, then was demolished in 1812 when the present City Hall was completed. The present Greek revival building, built as a U.S. Custom House in 1842, was modeled on the Parthenon. On the steps stands an 1883 statue of George Washington. His likeness was rendered by noted sculptor and relative of the president, John Quincy Adams Ward. Inside the hall is a museum with exhibits on New York and Wall Street. Guided tours are available, and you can also pick up brochures that lead you on themed self-guided walking tours of downtown. ✉ *26 Wall St., at Nassau St., Lower Manhattan* ☎ *212/825–6888* 🌐 *www.nps.gov/feha* 🎫 *Free* 🕑 *Weekdays 9–5.*

15 **Federal Reserve Bank of New York.** Built in 1924 and enlarged in 1935, this neo-Renaissance structure made of sandstone, limestone, and ironwork goes five levels underground. The gold ingots in the vaults here are worth roughly $140 billion—reputedly a third of the world's gold reserves. Tours of the bank include the gold vault, the trading desk, and "FedWorks," an interactive multimedia exhibit center where you can track trades that you "make." Computer terminals and displays provide almost as much information as an Economics 101 course—explaining such points as what the Federal Reserve Bank does (besides store gold), what the money supply is, and what causes inflation. ✉ *33 Liberty St., between William and Nassau Sts., Lower Manhattan* ☎ *212/720–6130* 🌐 *www.newyorkfed.org* 🎫 *Free* 🕑 *1-hr tour by advance (at least 1 wk) reservation, weekdays 9:30–2:30.*

9 **Fraunces Tavern.** Redbrick along one side, cream-color brick along another, the tavern's main building is a stately colonial house with a white-marble portico and coffered frieze, built in 1719 and converted to a tavern in 1762. It was the meeting place for the Sons of Liberty until the Revolutionary War, and in 1783 George Washington delivered a farewell address here to his officers celebrating the British evacuation of New York. Today a museum occupies the five-building complex. Fraunces Tavern contains two fully furnished period rooms and other displays of 18th- and 19th-century American history. The museum also offers family programs (such as crafts workshops and a scavenger hunt), lectures, and concerts. ✉ *54 Pearl St., at Broad St., Lower Manhattan* ☎ *212/425–1778* 🌐 *www.frauncestavernmuseum.org* 🎫 *$3* 🕑 *Tues., Wed., and Fri. 10–5; Thurs. 10–7; Sat. 11–5.*

10 **Hanover Square.** When the East River ran past present-day Pearl Street, this quiet tree-lined plaza stood on the waterfront and was the city's original printing-house square; on the site of 81 Pearl Street, William Bradford established the first printing press in the colonies. The pirate Captain Kidd lived in the neighborhood, and the Italianate sandstone-fronted **India House** (1851–54), a private club, and a restaurant and bar at No. 1, used to house the New York Cotton Exchange.

off the beaten path

Liberty Science Center. Across the Hudson River in Liberty State Park, New Jersey, this huge draw for children offers interactive educational experiences, including the Cardiac Classroom. Here kids immerse themselves in every aspect of cardiac surgery by communicating via video with specialists. Other highlights are an insect zoo, a 100-ft touch tunnel, an amazing 700-pound geodesic globe, the IMAX Dome Theater, and a 3-D laser show. ✉ *Liberty State Park, 251 Philip St., Jersey City, NJ* ☎ *201/200–1000* 🌐 *www.lsc.org* 🎫 *$10, IMAX Theater $9, 3-D laser show $3.50; combined admission to exhibits and theaters $16.50* ⏲ *Daily 9:30–5:30* ☞ *Call center for directions by car, PATH train, or ferry.*

Museum of American Financial History. On the site of Alexander Hamilton's law office (today the Standard Oil Building), this four-room museum displays artifacts of the financial market's history, including vintage ticker-tape machines and ticker tape from "Black Tuesday," October 29, 1929—the worst crash to date in the stock market's history. Temporary exhibits have focused on the career of J. P. Morgan and the artistry of African currency. ✉ *28 Broadway, north of Bowling Green, between Exchange Pl. and Beaver St., Lower Manhattan* ☎ *212/908–4110* 🌐 *www.financialhistory.org* 🎫 *$2* ⏲ *Tues.–Sat. 10–4.*

20 **Museum of Jewish Heritage—A Living Memorial to the Holocaust.** In a granite hexagon rising 85 ft above Robert F. Wagner Jr. Park, this museum pays tribute to the 6 million Jews who perished in the Holocaust. Kevin Roche and John Dinkeloo, architects, built the museum in the shape of the Star of David, with three floors of exhibits demonstrating the dynamism of 20th-century Jewish culture. Enter through a captivating multiscreen vestibule, perhaps best described as a storytelling gallery, that provides a context for the early-20th-century artifacts displayed on the first floor: elaborate screens hand-painted for the fall harvest festival of Sukkoth, wedding invitations, and tools used by Jewish tradesmen. Also intriguing is the use of original documentary film footage throughout the museum. The second floor details the rise of Nazism, anti-Semitism, and the ravages of the Holocaust. A gallery covers the doomed voyage of the *St. Louis,* a ship of German Jewish refugees that crossed the Atlantic twice in 1939 in search of a safe haven. Signs of hope are on display, as well, including a trumpet that Louis Bannet (the "Dutch Louis Armstrong") played for three years in the Auschwitz-Birkenau inmate orchestra. The third floor covers postwar Jewish life. The newly expanded east wing contains a theater, memorial garden, resource center, library, more galleries, classrooms, and a café. ✉ *18 1st Pl., Battery Park City, Lower Manhattan* ☎ *212/968–1800* 🌐 *www.mjhnyc.org* 🎫 *$7* ⏲ *Sun.–Wed. 10–5:45, Thurs. 10–8, Fri. and eve of Jewish holidays 10–3.*

8 **National Museum of the American Indian.** This museum, a branch of the Washington, D.C.–based Smithsonian Institution, is the first of its kind to be dedicated to Native American culture. The heritage of indigenous peoples of the western hemisphere is documented and explored through well-mounted exhibits, dance performances, lectures, readings, film, and crafts. Native Americans of all backgrounds participate in visiting programs and work at all levels of the staff. George Gustav Heye, a wealthy New Yorker, amassed most of the museum's collection—more than a million artifacts, including pottery, weaving, and basketry from the southwestern United States; painted hides from the Plains Indians of North America; carved jade from the Mexican Olmec and Maya cultures; and contemporary Native American paintings. The museum is in one of lower Manhattan's finest buildings: the beaux arts **Alexander Hamilton U.S. Custom House** (1907). From its base, massive granite columns rise to a pediment topped by a double row of statuary. Daniel Chester French, sculptor of Lincoln in the Lincoln Memorial in Washington, D.C., carved the lower statues, which symbolize continents (left to right: Asia,

the Americas, Europe, Africa). The upper row represents the major trading cities of the world. Inside, the display of white and color marble couldn't be more remarkable. The semicircular side staircases are equally breathtaking. Murals by Reginald Marsh completed in 1934 embellish the oval rotunda. ✉ *1 Bowling Green, between State and Whitehall Sts., Lower Manhattan* ☎ *212/514–3700* 🌐 *www.americanindian.si.edu* 🎫 *Free* ⏲ *Mon.–Wed. and Fri.–Sun. 10–5, Thurs. 10–8.*

off the beaten path

New York City Police Museum. Why are the police called cops? Why does a police badge have eight points? When was fingerprinting first used to solve a crime? Find the answers at this museum dedicated to New York's finest. The force's history from colonial times through the present is traversed with permanent and rotating exhibits, as well as interactive and sometimes chilling displays, including fingerprinting and forensic art stations, a drug-awareness display, and a tactics simulator. The Hall of Heroes honors police officers who have fallen in the line of duty, and a special memorial recognizes the 23 police officers, 13 Port Authority officers, and 343 firefighters who lost their lives on September 11, 2001. ✉ *100 Old Slip, near South St., Lower Manhattan* ☎ *212/480–3100* 🌐 *www.nycpolicemuseum.org* 🎫 *$5 suggested donation* ⏲ *Tues.–Sun. 10–5.*

1

⓲ **New York Stock Exchange (NYSE).** The largest securities exchange in the world, the NYSE nearly bursts from this relatively diminutive neoclassical 1903 building with an august Corinthian entrance—a fitting temple to the almighty dollar. Today's "Big Board" can handle a trillion shares of stock per day. In today's market-obsessed media, how those stocks perform each day is broadcast as news around the world. The third-floor interactive education center has been closed to the public since September 11, 2001. There are no immediate plans to reopen the center. Call for the most up-to-date information. ✉ *20 Broad St., between Wall St. and Exchange Pl., Lower Manhattan* ☎ *212/656–5165* 🌐 *www.nyse.com.*

⓳ **Robert F. Wagner Jr. Park.** This southern link in a chain of parks that stretches from Battery Park to Chambers Street features lawns, walks, garden beds, and benches with a panoramic view of the river and harbor. A stream of runners and rollerbladers flows by on the promenade. ✉ *Between Battery Pl. and Hudson River, Lower Manhattan.*

⓱ **St. Paul's Chapel.** The oldest (1766) public building in continuous use in Manhattan, this Episcopal house of worship, built of rough Manhattan brownstone, was modeled on London's St. Martin-in-the-Fields (a columned clock tower and steeple were added in 1794). A prayer service here followed George Washington's inauguration as president; Washington's pew is in the north aisle. The gilded crown adorned with plumes above the pulpit is thought to be the city's only vestige of British rule. St. Paul's and its 18th-century cemetery abut the World Trade Center site. For more than a year following the disaster, the chapel fence served as a shrine for visitors seeking solace. People from around the world left tokens of grief and support, or signed one of the large drop cloths that hung from the fence. After having served as a 24-hour refuge where rescue and recovery workers could eat, pray, rest, and receive counseling, the chapel reopened to the public in fall 2002 with an exhibit honoring Ground Zero's workers and recalling their efforts in the months following September 11. Call or check Trinity Church's Web site for current information on St. Paul's. ✉ *Broadway and Fulton St., Lower Manhattan* ☎ *212/602–0800* 🌐 *www.trinitywallstreet.org.*

2 **Shrine of St. Elizabeth Ann Seton at Our Lady of the Rosary.** The rectory of the shrine is a redbrick federal-style town house. With its distinctive portico, shaped to fit the curving street, it exemplifies the mansions that once lined the street. The house was built in 1793 as the home of the wealthy Watson family. Mother Seton and her family lived here from 1801 until the death of her husband in 1803. She joined the Catholic Church in 1805 and went on to found the Sisters of Charity, the first American order of nuns. In 1975 she became the first American-born saint. Masses are held here daily. ✉ *7 State St., near Whitehall St., Lower Manhattan* ☎ *212/269–6865* ⏲ *Weekdays 7–5, weekends 9–3.*

21 **Skyscraper Museum.** On the ground floor within the Ritz-Carlton Hotel, this museum celebrates Manhattan's varied architectural heritage and examines the historical forces and individuals that have shaped its successive skylines. Through exhibitions, lectures, and publications, tall buildings are explored as objects of design, products of technology, sites of construction, investments in real estate, and places of work and residence. "Manhattan Timeformations," a project available on the Web site, uses computer models and interactive animations to depict the dynamic relationship between skyscrapers and geology, landfill, settlement patterns, real estate cycles, and more. Walking tours are available by appointment only. ✉ *39 Battery Pl., Battery Park City, Lower Manhattan* ☎ *212/968–1961* 🌐 *www.skyscraper.org* ☞ *Call for admission fee and open hrs.*

1 **Staten Island Ferry.** The best transit deal in town is the Staten Island Ferry, a free 20- to 30-minute ride across New York Harbor, which provides great views of the Manhattan skyline, the Statue of Liberty, the Verrazano-Narrows Bridge, and the New Jersey coast. The classic blue-and-orange ferries embark on various schedules: every 15 minutes during rush hours, every 20–30 minutes most other times, and every hour on weekend nights and mornings. Since November 2001, cars have not been permitted on the ferry, though this may change. ✉ *State and South Sts., Lower Manhattan* ☎ *718/390–5253.*

Fodor's Choice ★

5 **Statue of Liberty.** Millions of American immigrants first glimpsed their new land when they laid eyes on the Statue of Liberty, a national monument that still awes all those who encounter it. *Liberty Enlightening the World,* as the statue is officially named, was sculpted by Frederic-Auguste Bartholdi and presented to the United States in 1886 as a gift from France. Since then she has become a near-universal symbol of freedom and democracy, standing a proud 152-ft high, on top of an 89-ft pedestal (executed by Richard Morris Hunt), on Liberty Island. Emma Lazarus's sonnet "The New Colossus" ("Give me your tired, your poor, your huddled masses . . .") is inscribed on a bronze plaque at the statue's base. Gustav Eiffel designed the statue's iron skeleton.

At press time, due to heightened security measures, the museum, pedestal, and stairwell to the crown were closed, but do visit for an inspiring ranger-led tour around the statue. Heightened security at the ferry departure point (Castle Clinton) will add time to your trip. If or when it reopens, the statue is accessible in two ways: an elevator ascends 10 stories to the viewing area atop the pedestal, and 354 double-helix steps (the equivalent of a 22-story building) climb to the crown. The park service occasionally closes off the line to the crown as early as 2, so it's vital to catch an early ferry (the earliest leaves at 8:45, but times vary seasonally). Exhibits inside the museum illustrate the statue's history, including videos of the view from the crown. In summer, come prepared to contend with the heat, both outside waiting in line and inside the statue. There are also life-size models of Lady Liberty's face and foot for peo-

ple who are blind to feel and a pleasant outdoo
Lower Manhattan ☎ *212/363–3200; 212/269–*
🌐 *www.nps.gov/stli* 🎫 *Free; ferry $10 round-t*
hrs in summer.

⓮ **Trinity Church.** The present Trinity Church, th
Anglican parish was established here in 169
Richard Upjohn. It ranked as the city's tallest building
second half of the 19th century. The three huge bronze doors were designed by Richard Morris Hunt to recall Lorenzo Ghiberti's doors for the Baptistery in Florence, Italy. The church's Gothic revival interior is light and elegant. On the church's north and south sides is a 2½-acre graveyard: Alexander Hamilton is buried beneath a white-stone pyramid, and a monument commemorates Robert Fulton, the inventor of the steamboat (he's buried in the Livingston family vault, with his wife). A museum outlines the church's history, and there's a bookstore and gift shop. A daily tour is offered at 2. ✉ *74 Trinity Pl. (Broadway at the head of Wall St.), Lower Manhattan* ☎ *212/602–0800* 🌐 *www.trinitywallstreet.org* ⏲ *Weekdays 8:30–6, weekends 8:30–4.*

off the beaten path

Vietnam Veterans Memorial. At this 14-ft-high, 70-ft-long rectangular memorial (1985), moving passages from news dispatches and the letters of military service people have been etched into a wall of greenish glass. The brick plaza around it is often desolate on weekends. ✉ *End of Coenties Slip between Water and South Sts., Lower Manhattan.*

⓫ **Wall Street.** Named after a wooden wall built across the island in 1653 to defend the Dutch colony against the Native Americans (mostly Algonquins), ⅓-mi-long Wall Street is arguably the most famous thoroughfare in the world—shorthand for the vast, powerful financial community that clusters around the New York and American stock exchanges. "The Street," as it's also widely known, began its financial career with stock traders conducting business along the sidewalks or at tables beneath a sheltering buttonwood tree. Today it's a dizzyingly narrow canyon—look to the east and you'll glimpse a sliver of East River waterfront; look to the west and you'll see the spire of Trinity Church, tightly framed by skyscrapers. For a clear lesson in the difference between Ionic and Corinthian columns, look at **55 Wall Street,** now the location of the Regent Wall Street hotel. The lower stories were part of an earlier U.S. Custom House, built in 1836–42; it was literally a bullish day on Wall Street when oxen hauled its 16 granite Ionic columns up to the site. When the National City Bank took over the building in 1899, it hired architects McKim, Mead & White to redesign the building and in 1909 added the second tier of columns but made them Corinthian.

⓲ **World Financial Center (WFC).** The four towers of this complex, 34–51 stories high and topped with different geometric shapes, were designed by Cesar Pelli and continue to serve as company headquarters for the likes of American Express and Dow Jones. The sides of the buildings facing the World Trade Center towers were damaged during the September 11 attacks, but have been fully restored. The elegant **Winter Garden** atrium, which once connected to the World Trade Center via a pedestrian bridge over West Street (the bridge was destroyed and the east side of the atrium was severely damaged on September 11), has been restored with a new wall of windows on its east side and is once again open to the public with an array of shops, cafés, and restaurants. At the south end of the WFC complex, a footbridge connects One WFC to the intersection of Liberty and Washington streets. The windows on the footbridge provide the closest view of the World Trade Center site.

At the northwest corner of the World Financial Center, the **New York Mercantile Exchange** (✉ 1 North End Ave., at Vesey St., Lower Manhattan ☎ 212/299–2000 Free ⏲ weekdays 9–5) houses the world's largest energy and precious-metals market. A ground-floor museum details the history of the exchange; a second-floor gallery with a 150-ft-long window overlooks the trading floors. At North Cove Harbor you can board a **New York Water Taxi** (☎ 201/985–8000), which will take you for a quick trip across the Hudson to New Jersey's Liberty State Park (a great place for a picnic), and just to the north of it is a New York Waterway terminal for ferry service to either Wall Street or Hoboken, New Jersey. It's a $3, 10-minute ride to Frank Sinatra's hometown. ✉ *West St. between Vesey and Liberty Sts., Lower Manhattan.*

16 **World Trade Center site.** On September 11, 2001, terrorist hijackers steered two commercial jets into the World Trade Center's 110-story towers, demolishing them and five outlying buildings, and killing nearly 3,000 people. Dubbed Ground Zero, the fenced-in 16-acre work site that emerged from the rubble has come to symbolize the personal and historical impact of the attack. In an attempt to grasp the reality of the destruction, to pray, or simply to witness history, visitors come to the site for a glimpse of what is left, clustering at the fence surrounding the site. Temporary panels listing the names of those who died in the attacks and recounting the history of the twin towers have been mounted along the fence on the west side of Church Street.

The World Trade Center (WTC) was a seven-building, 12-million-square-ft complex resembling a miniature city, with more than 430 companies from 28 countries engaged in a wide variety of commercial activities, including banking and finance, insurance, transportation, import and export, customs brokerage, trade associations, and representation of foreign governments. The daytime population of the WTC included 50,000 employees and 100,000 business and leisure visitors. Underground was a mall with nearly 100 stores and restaurants and a network of subway and other train stations. The twin towers were New York's two tallest buildings, the fourth tallest in the world after Kuala Lumpur's Petronas Towers, Shanghai's Jin Mao Building, and the Sears Tower in Chicago. The two 1,350-ft towers, designed by Minoru Yamasaki and built in 1972–73, were more engineering marvel than architectural masterpiece. To some they were an unmitigated design fiasco; to others their brutalist design and sheer magnitude gave them the beauty of modern sculpture, and at night when they were lighted from within, they were indeed beautiful strokes on the Manhattan skyline. Whether they were admired or reviled, the towers endured as a powerful symbol of American ingenuity, success, and dominance in the world marketplace.

THE SEAPORT & THE COURTS

New York's role as a great seaport is easiest to understand downtown, with both the Hudson River and East River waterfronts within walking distance. Although the deeper Hudson River came into its own in the steamship era, the more sheltered waters of the East River saw most of the action in the 19th century, during the age of clipper ships. This era is preserved in the South Street Seaport restoration, centered on Fulton Street between Water Street and the East River. Only a few blocks away you can visit another seat of New York history: the City Hall neigh-

A NEW BREEZE IS BLOWING, DOWN BY THE RIVERSIDE

NEW YORK IS A CITY OF ISLANDS, *surrounded by ocean, bay, river, and sound. The entire waterfront of the five boroughs measures 578 mi, making it the longest and most diverse of any municipality in the country. Down by the water, the air is salty and fresh, the views exhilarating, the mood peaceful and quiet. Yet downtown, pedestrian-friendly access to the Hudson River didn't come about until 1999, a year after the Hudson River Park Trust was created. The thin ribbon of park currently runs from Battery Park as far north as Gansevoort Street in the Meatpacking District, and is full of joggers, cyclists, and rollerbladers. Some of the piers were being used for the cleanup effort at the World Trade Center site, but they have all returned to their recreational role. Since the spring of 2003, three new piers off Greenwich Village (45 and 46 at Charles Street, and 51 at Jane Street) provide grassy lawns for napping, fields for playing, and a water-theme playground. Greenspace advocates have also spruced up the Empire-Fulton Ferry State Park in Brooklyn's industrial DUMBO neighborhood, which has incredible views of the East River between the Brooklyn and Manhattan bridges.*

Though New Yorkers are now spending leisure time by the water, New York grew up as a shipping and shipbuilding town. The Port of New York was first centered near the South Street Seaport on the East River, where the 18th-century streetscape and historic sailing vessels recall the clipper-ship era. Street names suggest the contours of Manhattan before settlers filled in the wetlands: Pearl Street, where mother-of-pearl shells were collected; Water Street; and Front Street. The port then moved to the wider, less turbulent Hudson River, where Robert Fulton launched the first steamboat in 1807. After the opening of the Erie Canal in 1825, which connected it to the Great Lakes and the West for trade, the city became the preeminent port in the country, the gateway to the continent for exports and imports, the "golden door" for immigrants. In the late 1800s, New York Harbor, crisscrossed with ferries, barges, tugs, canal boats, freighters, and passenger liners, was the busiest in the world. Until the Brooklyn Bridge was completed in 1883, even Manhattanites and Brooklynites couldn't visit each other except by ferries that landed at Fulton Street in lower Manhattan and Fulton Ferry Landing in DUMBO.

On the Hudson River, where older generations once boarded grand ocean liners to make a two-week journey across the Atlantic, New Yorkers are once again using boat travel—this time to commute within their own city. In response to subway routes that were crippled in the September 11 attacks, increased ferry service is providing commuters a transportation method that harkens back to the 1800s. In addition to the 200-plus-capacity boats of New York Waterways, the small, 54-seat New York Water Taxis are serving both rush-hour travelers and tourists. The taxi vessels are designed to create a minimal wake and provide easy access for both bicyclists and wheelchair users. New York Water Taxi service will connect such far-flung spots as the Intrepid *Sea-Air-Space Museum, Chelsea Piers Sports and Entertainment Complex, the South Street Seaport, and the Fulton Ferry Landing in Brooklyn.*

At the West Side Highway and Christopher Street, walk out on Greenwich Village's popular pier to take in the view back toward the fading vestiges of a Victorian-era waterfront: a panorama of warehouses (many converted to apartments and clubs) and smaller buildings that house cheap hotels and seedy bars. At 14th Street, remember Herman Melville, who worked as a customs inspector nearby. Just south of the Chelsea Piers complex, note the remains of the pier house where the Titanic *was scheduled to conclude its maiden voyage. In summer, check out the piers that spring to life with public events—movies, dances, and food festivals. Contact the* ***Hudson River Park Trust*** *(☎ 212/627–2020 🌐 www.hudsonriverpark.org) for information. For kayaking on the Hudson, see Chapter 7.*

borhood, which includes Manhattan's magisterial court and government buildings.

Numbers in the text correspond to numbers in the margin and on the Lower Manhattan map.

a good walk

Begin at the intersection of Water and Fulton streets. Water Street was once the shoreline; the latter thoroughfare was named after the ferry to Brooklyn, which once docked at its foot (the ferry itself was named after its inventor, Robert Fulton [1765–1815]). Extending to the river is the 11-block **South Street Seaport Historic District** 22, which is grounded on 19th-century landfill.

Return to Fulton Street and walk away from the river to Broadway, to St. Paul's Chapel. If you're facing north, forking off to the right is Park Row, which was known as Newspaper Row from the mid-19th to early-20th centuries, when most of the city's 20 or so daily newspapers had offices here. In tribute to that past, a statue of Benjamin Franklin (who was, after all, a printer) stands in front of Pace University, farther east on Park Row. Two blocks north of Fulton Street, on Broadway, is one of the finest skyscrapers in the city, the Gothic **Woolworth Building** 23, for which Frank Woolworth paid $13 million—in cash.

Wedged between Broadway and Park Row is triangular **City Hall Park** 24, originally the town common, which gives way to a slew of government offices. **City Hall** 25, built between 1803 and 1812, is unexpectedly modest. Lurking directly behind it is the **Tweed Courthouse** 26, named for the notorious politician William Marcy "Boss" Tweed.

On the north side of Chambers Street, east of the Tweed Courthouse, sits an eight-story beaux arts château, the 1911 **Surrogate's Court** 27, also called the Hall of Records. Across Centre Street from the château is the city government's first skyscraper, the imposing **Municipal Building** 28, built in 1914 by McKim, Mead & White. Just steps south of the Municipal Building, a ramp curves up into the pedestrian walkway over the **Brooklyn Bridge** 29. The river-and-four-borough views from the bridge are wondrous.

Foley Square, a name that has become synonymous with the New York court system, opens out north of the Municipal Building. On the right, the orderly progression of the Corinthian colonnades of the **U.S. Courthouse** 30 and the **New York County Courthouse** 31 is a fitting reflection of the epigraph carved in the latter's frieze: THE TRUE ADMINISTRATION OF JUSTICE IS THE FIRMEST PILLAR OF GOOD GOVERNMENT. Turn to look across Foley Square at Federal Plaza, which sprawls in front of the gridlike skyscraper of the Javits Federal Building. The black-glass box to the left houses the U.S. Court of International Trade. South of it, at the corner of Duane and Elk streets, is the site of the **African Burial Ground** 32.

Continue north up Centre Street past neoclassical civic office buildings to 100 Centre Street, the **Criminal Courts Building** 33, a rather forbidding construction with art moderne details. In contrast, the Civil and Municipal Courthouse (1960), across the way at 111 Centre Street, is an uninspired modern cube, although it, too, has held sensational trials. On the west side of this small square, at 60 Lafayette Street, is the slick black-granite Family Court, built in 1975, with its intriguing angular facade.

Walk west onto Leonard Street, south of the Family Court, and take a look at the ornate Victorian building that runs the length of the block on your left. This is the old New York Life Insurance Company headquarters, an 1870 building that was remodeled and enlarged in 1896 by

McKim, Mead & White. The ornate clock tower facing Broadway is occupied by the avant-garde Clocktower Gallery and is used as studio space by artists, who sometimes host exhibitions of their work. The stretch of Broadway south of here is the subject of what is believed to be the oldest photograph of New York. The picture focuses on a paving project—to eliminate the morass of muddy streets—that took place in 1850.

TIMING You can easily spend a half day at the Seaport, or longer if you browse in shops. Completing the rest of the walking tour takes about 1½ hours. The real Seaport, known as the Fulton Fish Market, which sells wholesale fish to the city's restaurants and grocery stores, opens well before the sun rises and clears out shortly after. Unless you're really interested in wholesale fish, you're best off visiting the Seaport when its other attractions are open. Try to do this during the week, so that the government offices will be open, too. Also, consider walking across the Brooklyn Bridge in the late afternoon for dramatic contrasts of light.

What to See

32 **African Burial Ground.** This grassy corner is part of the original area used to inter the city's earliest African-Americans—an estimated 20,000 were buried here until the cemetery was closed in 1794. The site was discovered during a 1991 construction project, and by an act of Congress it was made into a National Historic Landmark, dedicated to the people who were enslaved in the city between 1626 and Emancipation Day in New York, July 4, 1827. ✉ *Duane and Elk Sts., Lower Manhattan.*

★ 29 **Brooklyn Bridge.** "A drive-through cathedral" is how the critic James Wolcott describes one of New York's noblest and most recognized landmarks. Spanning the East River, the Brooklyn Bridge connects Manhattan island to the once-independent city of Brooklyn. Before its opening, Brooklynites had only the Fulton Street Ferry to shuttle them across the river. John Augustus Roebling—a visionary architect, legendary engineer, metaphysical philosopher, and fervid abolitionist—is said to have first conceived of the bridge on an icy winter's day in 1852, when the frozen river prevented him from getting to Brooklyn. Though by no means the first person so inconvenienced, Roebling the bridge builder was perfectly qualified to rectify the matter. Roebling spent the next 30 years designing, raising money for, and building what would be one of the first steel suspension bridges—and what was for several years one of the world's longest. Alas, its construction was fraught with peril. Work began in 1867; two years later Roebling died of gangrene after a wayward ferryboat rammed his foot while he was at work on a pier. His son, Washington, took over the project and was himself permanently crippled—like many others who worked on the bridge underwater, he suffered from the bends, or decompression sickness. With the help of his wife, Emily, Washington nonetheless saw the bridge's construction through to completion.

The long struggle to build the bridge so captured the imagination of the city that when it opened in 1883 it was promptly crowned the "Eighth Wonder of the World." Its twin Gothic-arch towers, with a span of 1,595½ ft, rise 272 ft from the river below; the bridge's overall length of 6,016 ft made it four times longer than the longest suspension bridge of its day. From roadway to water is about 133 ft, high enough to allow the tallest ships to pass. The roadway is supported by a web of steel cables, hung from the towers and attached to block-long anchorages on either shore.

A walk across the bridge's promenade—a boardwalk elevated above the roadway and shared by pedestrians, in-line skaters, and bicyclists—takes about 40 minutes, from Manhattan's civic center to the heart of Brooklyn Heights. It's well worth traversing for the astounding views. Midtown's jumble of spires and the Manhattan Bridge loom to the north. Mostly newer skyscrapers crowd lower Manhattan, while the tall ships docked at their feet, at South Street Seaport, appear to have sailed in straight from the 19th century. Governors Island sits forlornly in the middle of the harbor, which sweeps open dramatically toward Lady Liberty and, off in the distance, the Verrazano-Narrows Bridge (its towers are more than twice as tall as those of the Brooklyn Bridge). A word of caution to pedestrians: do obey the lane markings on the promenade—pedestrians on the north side, bicyclists on the south—as the latter are moving quickly and will not be pleased if you get in their way.

25 **City Hall.** Reflecting the classical refinement and civility of Enlightenment Europe, New York's surprisingly decorous City Hall is a diminutive palace with a facade punctuated by arches and columns and a cupola crowned by a statue of Lady Justice. Built between 1803 and 1812, it was originally clad in white marble only on its front and sides. The back was faced in more modest brownstone because city fathers assumed the city would never grow farther north than this. Limestone now covers all four sides. A sweeping marble double staircase leads from the domed rotunda to the second-floor public rooms. The small, Victorian-style **City Council Chamber** in the east wing has mahogany detailing and ornate gilding; the **Board of Estimate Chamber,** to the west, has colonial paintings and church-pew-style seating; and the **Governor's Room** at the head of the stairs, used for ceremonial events, is filled with historic portraits and furniture, including a writing table that George Washington used in 1789 when New York was the U.S. capital. The **Blue Room,** which was traditionally the mayor's office, is on the ground floor and is now used for mayoral press conferences.

Although the building looks genteel, the City Hall politicking that goes on there can be rough and tumble. News crews can often be seen jockeying on the front steps, as they attempt to interview city officials. City Hall is open to the public for tours. ✉ *City Hall Park, Lower Manhattan* ☎ *212/788–6865 for tour information* 💵 *Free* ⏲ *Tours by advance (1–2 wks) reservation, weekdays 10, 11, and 2.*

24 **City Hall Park.** Originally used as a sheep meadow, this green spot was known in colonial times as the Fields or the Common. It went on to become a graveyard for the impoverished, the site of an almshouse, and then the home of the notorious Bridewell jail before it became a park. Even as a park, the locale was far from peaceful: it hosted hangings, riots, and political demonstrations. A bronze statue of patriot Nathan Hale, who was hanged in 1776 as a spy by the British troops occupying New York City, stands facing City Hall. ✉ *Between Broadway, Park Row, and Chambers St., Lower Manhattan.*

33 **Criminal Courts Building.** Fans of crime fiction, whether on television, in the movies, or in novels, may recognize this rather grim art deco tower, which is connected by a skywalk (New York's Bridge of Sighs) to the detention center known as the Tombs. In *The Bonfire of the Vanities,* Tom Wolfe wrote a chilling description of this court's menacing atmosphere. ✉ *100 Centre St., at Hogan St., Lower Manhattan.*

28 **Municipal Building.** Who else but the venerable architecture firm McKim, Mead & White would the city government trust to build its first skyscraper in 1914? The roof section alone is 10 stories high, bristling with towers and peaks and topped by a 25-ft-high gilt statue of Civic Fame. New Yorkers come here to pay parking fines and get marriage

licenses (and to get married, in a civil chapel on the second floor). An immense arch straddles Chambers Street (traffic used to flow through here). ✉ *1 Centre St., at Chambers St., Lower Manhattan.*

31 **New York County Courthouse.** With its stately columns, pediments, and 100-ft-wide steps, this 1912 classical temple front is yet another spin-off on Rome's Pantheon. It deviates from its classical parent in its hexagonal rotunda, shaped to fit an irregular plot of land. The 1957 courtroom drama *Twelve Angry Men* was filmed here; the courthouse also hosts thousands of marriages a year. ✉ *60 Centre St., at Foley Sq., Lower Manhattan.*

22 **South Street Seaport Historic District.** Had it not been declared a historic district in 1967, this charming, cobblestone corner of New York with the city's largest concentration of early-19th-century commercial buildings would likely have been gobbled up by skyscrapers. In the early 1980s the Rouse Company, which had already created Boston's Quincy Market and Baltimore's Harborplace, was hired to restore and adapt the existing buildings, preserving the commercial feel of centuries past. The result is a hybrid of historical district and shopping mall. Many of its streets' 18th-, 19th-, and early-20th-century architectural details re-create the city's historic seafaring era.

At the intersection of Fulton and Water streets, the gateway to the Seaport, stands the ***Titanic* Memorial,** a small white lighthouse that commemorates the sinking of the RMS *Titanic* in 1912. Beyond it, Fulton Street, cobbled in blocks of Belgian granite, turns into a busy pedestrian mall. Just to the left of Fulton, at 211 Water Street, is **Bowne & Co. Stationers,** a reconstructed working 19th-century print shop. Continue down Fulton to Front Street, which has wonderfully preserved old brick buildings—some dating from the 1700s. On the south side of Fulton Street is the seaport's architectural centerpiece, **Schermerhorn Row,** a redbrick terrace of Georgian- and federal-style warehouses and countinghouses built in 1811–12. Some upper floors house gallery space, and the ground floors are occupied by upscale shops, bars, and restaurants. Also here is the visitor center and gift shop of the **South Street Seaport Museum** (☎ 212/748–8600 ⏲ Apr.–Sept., Fri.–Wed. 10–6, Thurs. 10–8; Oct.–Mar., Wed.–Mon. 10–5), which hosts walking tours, hands-on exhibits, and fantastic creative programs for children, all with a nautical theme. ✉ *Visitor center 211 Water St., South Street Seaport* ☎ *212/732–7678 for events and shopping information* 🌐 *www.southstseaport.org* 🎫 *$5 to ships, galleries, walking tours, Maritime Crafts Center, films, and other seaport events.*

Cross South Street, once known as the Street of Ships, under an elevated stretch of the FDR Drive to **Pier 16,** where historic ships are docked, including the *Pioneer,* a 102-ft schooner built in 1885; the *Peking,* the second-largest sailing bark in existence; the iron-hulled *Wavertree;* and the lightship *Ambrose.* The Pier 16 ticket booth provides information and sells tickets to the museum, ships, tours, and exhibits. Pier 16 also hosts frequent concerts and performances and is the departure point for various cruises, including the **Seaport Music Cruise** (☎ 212/630–8888 🎫 $20 and up), featuring jazz and blues; the Circle Line's **Seaport Liberty Cruise** (☎ 212/563–3200 🎫 $13), a one-hour sightseeing trip; and **"The Beast"** (☎ 212/563–3200 🎫 $16), a 30-minute speedboat ride out to the Statue of Liberty.

To the north is **Pier 17,** a multilevel dockside shopping mall featuring standard-issue national chain retailers such as Express and Victoria's Secret, among others. Its weathered-wood rear decks make a splendid spot from which to sit and contemplate the river.

As your nose will surmise, the blocks along South Street north of the museum complex still house a working fish market, which has been in operation since the early 1800s. Hundreds of species of fish—from swordfish to sea urchin roe—are sold by the fishmongers of the **Fulton Fish Market.** Get up early (or stay up late) if you want to see it: the action begins around 3 AM and ends by 8 AM. ☎ *212/748–8786* ✉ *$12* ⏲ *1st and 3rd Wed. of every month, depending on weather, at 6 AM; tours by reservation only.*

need a break?

The cuisine at the fast-food stalls on Pier 17's third-floor **Promenade Food Court** is eclectic: Pizza on the Pier, Daikichi Sushi, Simply Seafood, and Salad Mania. What's really spectacular is the view from the tables in a glass-walled atrium.

27 **Surrogate's Court–Hall of Records.** This 1911 building is the most ornate of the City Hall court trio. In true beaux arts fashion, sculpture and ornament seem to have been added wherever possible to the basic neoclassical structure, yet the overall effect is graceful rather than cluttered. Filmmakers sometimes use its elaborate lobby in opera scenes. A courtroom here was the venue for *Johnson v. Johnson,* where the heirs to the Johnson & Johnson fortune waged their bitter battle. ✉ *31 Chambers St., at Centre St., Lower Manhattan.*

26 **Tweed Courthouse.** Under the corrupt management of notorious politician William Marcy "Boss" Tweed (1823–78), this Anglo-Italianate gem, one of the finest designs in the City Hall area, took some $12 million and nine years to build (it was finally finished in 1872, but the ensuing public outrage drove Tweed from office). Although it is imposing, with its columned classical pediment outside and seven-story octagonal rotunda inside, almost none of the boatloads of marble that Tweed had shipped from Europe made their way into this building. Today it houses municipal offices; it has also served as a location for several films, most notably *The Verdict.* ✉ *52 Chambers St., between Broadway and Centre St., Lower Manhattan.*

30 **U.S. Courthouse.** Cass Gilbert built this courthouse in 1936, convinced that it complemented the much finer nearby Woolworth Building, which he had designed three decades earlier. Granite steps climb to a massive columned portico; above this rises a 32-story tower topped by a gilded pyramid, not unlike that with which Gilbert crowned the New York Life building uptown. Julius and Ethel Rosenberg were tried for espionage at this courthouse, and hotel queen Leona Helmsley went on trial here for tax evasion. ✉ *40 Centre St., at Foley Sq., Lower Manhattan.*

23 **Woolworth Building.** Called the Cathedral of Commerce, this ornate white terra-cotta edifice was, at 792 ft, the world's tallest building when it opened in 1913. The lobby's extravagant Gothic-style details include sculptures set into the portals to the left and right; one represents an elderly F. W. Woolworth pinching his pennies, while another depicts the architect, Cass Gilbert, cradling in his arms a model of his creation. Glittering mosaic tiles fill the dome and archways. ✉ *233 Broadway, between Park Pl. and Barclay St., Lower Manhattan.*

LITTLE ITALY & CHINATOWN

Mulberry Street is the heart of Little Italy; in fact, at this point it's virtually the entire body. In 1932 an estimated 98% of the inhabitants of this area were of Italian birth or heritage, but since then the growth and expansion of Chinatown to the south have encroached on the Italian neighborhood to such an extent that merchants and community leaders of the Little Italy Restoration Association (LIRA) negotiated with Chinatown to let at least Mulberry remain an all-Italian street. Since the late 1990s, trendy shops and restaurants have sprouted in what were Little Italy's northern reaches, and the area is now known as NoLita (*No*rth of *Li*ttle *Ita*ly).

In the second half of the 19th century, when Italian immigration peaked, the neighborhood stretched from Houston to Canal streets and the Bowery to Broadway. During this time Italians founded at least three Italian parishes, including the Church of the Transfiguration (now almost wholly Chinese); they also operated an Italian-language newspaper, *Il Progresso.*

In 1926 immigrants from southern Italy celebrated the first Feast of San Gennaro along Mulberry Street—a 10-day street fair that still takes place every September. Dedicated to the patron saint of Naples, the festival transforms Mulberry Street into a virtual alfresco restaurant, as wall-to-wall vendors sell traditional fried sausages and pastries. The community's other big festival celebrates St. Anthony of Padua in June; the church connected to that festival is at Houston and Sullivan streets, in what is now SoHo. These festivals are two of the few reminders of Little Italy's vibrant history as the neighborhood continues to change. If you want the flavor of a truly Italian neighborhood, visit Arthur Avenue in the Bronx—or rent a video of the Martin Scorsese movie *Mean Streets,* which was filmed in Little Italy in the early 1970s.

Visually exotic and full of inexpensive wares and gadgets, Chinatown is a popular tourist attraction, but it's also a real, vital community where roughly a quarter of the city's population of 400,000 Chinese still lives. Its main businesses are restaurants, retail stores, and garment factories; roughly half of its residents speak little or no English. Historically, Chinatown was divided from Little Italy by Canal Street, the bustling artery that links the Holland Tunnel (to New Jersey) and the Manhattan Bridge (to Brooklyn). However, since the late 20th century an influx of immigrants from the People's Republic of China, Taiwan, and especially Hong Kong has swelled Manhattan's Chinese population, and Hong Kong residents have poured capital into Chinatown real estate. Chinatown now spills over its traditional borders into Little Italy to the north and the formerly Jewish Lower East Side to the east. However, due to ever-rising rents in Chinatown proper, newly arrived immigrants are increasingly making their homes in the boroughs of Brooklyn and Queens.

The first Chinese immigrants were primarily railroad workers who came from the West in the 1870s to settle in a limited section of the Lower East Side. For nearly a century anti-immigration laws prohibited most men from having their wives and families join them; the neighborhood became known as a "bachelor society," and for years its population remained static. It was not until the end of World War II, when Chinese immigration quotas were increased, that the neighborhood began the expansion that is evident today.

Economically, Chinatown was probably the hardest hit neighborhood in Manhattan, outside Wall Street, following the attacks on the World Trade Center. Partly because of Chinatown's very insular and self-reliant nature, all of its major industries have suffered in the aftermath. To the casual visitor, however, the area still appears to be a lively marketplace crammed with souvenir shops and restaurants in funky pagoda-style buildings and crowded with pedestrians day and night. From fast-food noodles or dumplings to sumptuous Hunan, Szechuan, Cantonese, Mandarin, and Shanghai feasts, every imaginable type of Chinese cuisine is served here. Sidewalk markets burst with stacks of fresh seafood and strangely shaped fruits and vegetables. Food shops proudly display their wares: if America's motto is "A chicken in every pot," then Chinatown's must be "A roast duck in every window."

Numbers in the text correspond to numbers in the margin and on the Little Italy, Chinatown, SoHo & TriBeCa map.

a good walk

Start your tour at the corner of Mott and Prince streets, among the pricey, jewel-box-size boutiques and cafés that form chic NoLita. Mulberry, Mott, and Elizabeth streets between Houston and Kenmare streets are the core of this largely gentrified neighborhood that has weaved itself into the increasingly less visible mix of family-owned Italian, Latino, and Asian businesses. Windows artfully dressed with everything from wrist bags to baby clothes continue to debut, making the area a zestier sort of SoHo. Among these neighborhood debutantes sits the stately dowager, **St. Patrick's Old Cathedral** 1, the oldest Roman Catholic church in New York City. Tour the church and walk west on Prince Street to **Mulberry Street** 2; then walk south to Broome Street. East of Mulberry Street, the building at 375 Broome Street is known for its sheet-metal cornice that bears the face of a distinguished, albeit anonymous, bearded man.

To see the ornate Renaissance revival, former **New York City Police Headquarters** 3, walk west on Broome Street to Centre Street, and south to Grand Street. Next, head east to the corner of Grand and Mulberry streets and stop to get the lay of the land. Facing north (uptown), on your right you'll see a series of multistory houses from the early 19th century, built long before the great flood of immigration hit this neighborhood between 1890 and 1924. Turn and look south along the east side of Mulberry Street to see Little Italy's trademark railroad-apartment tenement buildings.

On the southeast corner of Grand Street, E. Rossi & Co., established in 1902, is an antiquated little shop that sells housewares, espresso makers, embroidered religious postcards, and jocular Italian T-shirts. Two doors east on Grand Street is Ferrara's, a pastry shop opened in 1892 that ships its creations—cannoli, peasant pie, Italian rum cake—all over the world. Continue south on Mulberry to see another survivor of the pre-tenement era, the two-story, dormered brick Van Rensselaer House, now Paolucci's Restaurant. Built in 1816, it's a prime example of the Italian federal style.

One block south of Grand Street, on the corner of Hester and Mulberry streets, you'll reach the site of what was once Umberto's Clam House (now Ristorante Da Gennaro), best known as the place where in 1973 mobster Joey Gallo was munching scungilli when he was fatally surprised by a task force of mob hit men. Turn left onto Hester Street to visit yet another Little Italy institution, Puglia, a restaurant where guests sit at long communal tables, sing along with house entertainers, and enjoy southern Italian specialties with quantities of homemade wine. One street west, on Baxter Street about three-quarters of a block toward Canal Street, stands the **San Gennaro Church** 4, which each September sponsors Little Italy's keynote event, the annual Feast of San Gennaro.

The restaurants and markets of Chinatown abound on Canal Street, and on weekends the crowds move at a snail's pace on the sidewalk, which is lined with street vendors. If Chinese food products intrigue you, stop to browse in Kam Man, at 200 Canal Street. A good place to get oriented is the **Museum of Chinese in the Americas (MoCA)** 5, in a century-old schoolhouse at the corner of Bayard and Mulberry streets. Catercorner from the museum is **Columbus Park** 6. This gathering spot occupies the area once known as the Five Points, the tough 19th-century slum ruled by Irish gangs that provided the backdrop for Martin Scorsese's film *Gangs of New York,* starring Daniel Day-Lewis. One block east of Mulberry Street, **Mott Street** 7 is another main drag of the neighborhood. On the corner of Mott and Mosco streets, you'll find the **Church of the Transfiguration** 8, established in 1801.

Just north of the church is a sign for Pell Street, a narrow lane of wall-to-wall restaurants whose neon signs stretch halfway across the thoroughfare. To the right off Pell is **Doyers Street** 9, the site of turn-of-the-20th-century gang wars. At the end of Doyers you'll find the **Bowery** 10. Cross the street to **Chatham Square** 11, then, from Kim Lau Square, continue past Park Row onto St. James Place to find two remnants of this neighborhood's pre-Chinatown past. On St. James Place is the **First Shearith Israel graveyard** 12, the first Jewish cemetery in the United States. Walk a half block farther, turn left on James Street, and you'll see St. James Church, a stately 1837 Greek revival edifice where Al Smith, who rose from this poor Irish neighborhood to become New York's governor and a 1928 Democratic presidential candidate, once served as altar boy.

Return to Chatham Square and walk north up the Bowery to **Confucius Plaza** 13, which is graced by a statue of the Chinese sage, beneath which are his words, "The World Is a Commonwealth." Then cross the Bowery back to the west side of the street; at the corner of Pell Street stands 18 Bowery, which is one of Manhattan's oldest homes—a federal and Georgian structure built in 1785 by meat wholesaler Edward Mooney. Farther north up the Bowery, a younger side of Chinatown is shown at the **Asian American Arts Centre** 14, which displays current work by Asian-American artists.

Continue north. At the intersection of the Bowery and Canal Street, a grand arch and colonnade designed by Carrère and Hastings in 1910 mark the entrance to the Manhattan Bridge, which leads to Brooklyn (the pedestrian and bike path over the bridge is accessed from the south). This corner was once the center of New York's diamond district. Today most jewelry dealers have moved uptown, but you can still find some pretty good deals at jewelers on the Bowery and the north side of Canal Street.

TIMING Since Little Italy consists of little more than one street, a tour of the area shouldn't take more than one hour. Most attractions are food-related, so plan on visiting around lunchtime. A fun time to visit is during the San Gennaro festival, which runs for two weeks each September, starting the first Thursday after Labor Day. Come on a weekend to see Chinatown at its liveliest; locals crowd the streets from dawn 'til dusk, along with a slew of tourists. For a more relaxed experience, opt for a weekday. Allowing for stops at the two local museums and a lunch break, a Chinatown tour will take about two additional hours.

What to See

14 **Asian American Arts Centre.** This space has impressive contemporary works by Asian-American artists, annual Chinese folk-art exhibitions during the Chinese New Year, Asian-American dance performances, and videotapes of Asian-American art and events. The center also sells unique art objects from Asia. The inconspicuous entrance is to the right of the McDonald's. A steep flight of stairs leads to the gallery. ✉ *26 Bowery, 3rd*

floor, between Bayard and Pell Sts., Chinatown ☎ *212/233–2154* 🎫 *Free* ⏲ *Mon.–Wed. and Fri. 12:30–6:30, Thurs. 12:30–7:30.*

10 **Bowery.** Now a commercial thoroughfare lined with stores selling light fixtures and secondhand restaurant equipment, this broad boulevard was a farming area north of the city in the 17th century. Its name derives from *bowerij,* the Dutch word for farm. As the city's growing population moved northward, the Bowery became a broad, elegant avenue lined with taverns and theaters. In the late 1800s the placement of an elevated subway line over the Bowery and the proliferation of saloons and brothels led to its demise; by the early 20th century it had become infamous as a skid row full of indigents and crime. After 1970 efforts at gentrification had some effect, and some of the neighborhood's indigent population dispersed. Today the Bowery is undergoing further gentrification.

11 **Chatham Square.** Ten streets converge at this labyrinthine intersection crisscrossed by pedestrian walkways and traffic lights. Standing on an island in the eye of the storm is the **Kim Lau Arch,** honoring Chinese casualties in American wars. A statue on the square's eastern edge pays tribute to a Quin Dynasty official named Lin Zexu. The 18-ft, 5-inch-tall granite statue reflects Chinatown's growing population of mainland immigrants and their particular national pride: the Fujianese minister is noted for his role in sparking the Opium War by banning the drug. The base of his statue reads: PIONEER IN THE WAR AGAINST DRUGS. On the far end of the square, at the corner of Catherine Street and East Broadway, stands a bank that was built to resemble a pagoda.

8 **Church of the Transfiguration.** Built in 1801 as the Zion Episcopal Church, this is an imposing Georgian structure with Gothic windows. It's now a Chinese Catholic church distinguished by its trilingualism: mass is said in Cantonese, Mandarin, and English. ✉ *29 Mott St., at Mosco St., Chinatown* ☎ *212/962–5157.*

need a break?

Across from the Church of the Transfiguration, at the corner of Mott and Mosco streets, a red shack holds **Hong Kong Egg Cake Company,** where Ms. Cecilia Tam makes mouthwatering small, round egg cakes for $1 a portion. Sample Chinese pastries, rice dumplings wrapped in banana leaves, yam cakes, and other sweet treats at local favorite **May May Chinese Gourmet Bakery** (✉ 35 Pell St., off Mott St., Chinatown, ☎ 212/267–0733). A colorful flag hangs outside the entrance of the **Chinatown Ice Cream Factory** (✉ 65 Bayard St., between Mott and Elizabeth Sts., Chinatown ☎ 212/608–4170), where the flavors range from red bean to litchi to green tea. Prepare to eat your scoop on the run, since there's no seating.

6 **Columbus Park.** Mornings bring groups of elderly Chinese practicing the graceful movements of tai chi to this shady, paved space; during afternoons the park's tables fill for heated games of mah-jongg. One hundred years ago the then-swampy area was known as the **Five Points**—after the intersection of Mulberry Street, Anthony (now Worth) Street, Cross (now Park) Street, Orange (now Baxter) Street, and Little Water Street (no longer in existence)—and was notoriously ruled by dangerous Irish gangs. In the 1880s a neighborhood-improvement campaign brought about the park's creation.

13 **Confucius Plaza.** North of Chatham Square, a bronze statue of Confucius presides before the redbrick high-rise apartment complex named for him. The statue was originally opposed by leftist Chinese immigrants,

who considered the sage a reactionary symbol of Old China. ✉ *Intersection of the Bowery and Division St., Chinatown.*

❾ **Doyers Street.** The "bloody angle"—a sharp turn halfway down this little alleyway—was the site of turn-of-the-20th-century battles between Chinatown's Hip Sing and On Leon tongs, gangs who fought for control over the local gambling and opium trades. Today the street is among Chinatown's most colorful, lined with tea parlors and barbershops.

⓬ **First Shearith Israel graveyard.** Consecrated in 1656 by the country's oldest Jewish congregation, this small burial ground bears the remains of Sephardic Jews (of Spanish-Portuguese extraction) who emigrated from Brazil in the mid-17th century. You can peek through the gates here and at the second and third Shearith Israel graveyards on West 11th Street in Greenwich Village and West 21st Street in Chelsea, respectively. ✉ *55 St. James Pl., Chinatown.*

★ ❼ **Mott Street.** The main commercial artery of Chinatown, Mott Street has appeared in innumerable movies and television programs as the street that exemplifies the neighborhood. Chinatown began in the late 1880s when Chinese immigrants (mostly men) settled in tenements in a small area that included the lower portion of Mott Street as well as nearby Pell and Doyers streets. Today the busy street overflows with fish and vegetable markets, restaurants, bakeries, and souvenir shops.

Opened in 1891, **32 Mott Street General Store,** historically known as Quong Yuen Shing & Co., is one of Chinatown's oldest curio shops, with porcelain bowls, teapots, and cups for sale.

❷ **Mulberry Street.** Crowded with restaurants, cafés, bakeries, imported-food shops, and souvenir stores, Mulberry Street, between Broome and Canal streets, is where Little Italy lives and breathes. The blocks between Houston and Spring streets fall within the neighborhood of NoLita.

need a break? You can savor cannoli and other sweet treats at **Caffe Roma** (✉ 385 Broome St., at Mulberry St., Little Italy ☎ 212/226–8413), a traditional neighborhood favorite with wrought-iron chairs and a pressed-tin ceiling.

❺ **Museum of Chinese in the Americas (MoCA).** In a century-old schoolhouse that once served Italian-American and Chinese-American children, MoCA is the first U.S. museum devoted to preserving the history of the Chinese people throughout the western hemisphere. The permanent exhibit—*Where is Home? Chinese in the Americas*—explores the Chinese-American experience through displays of artists' creations, personal and domestic artifacts, and historical documentation. Slippers for binding feet, Chinese musical instruments, a reversible silk gown (circa 1900) worn at a Cantonese opera performance, and antique business signs are some of the unique objects on display. Changing exhibits fill a second room. MoCA sponsors workshops, walking tours, lectures, and family events. Its archives (open by appointment only), dedicated to Chinese-American history and culture, include 2,000 volumes. ✉ *70 Mulberry St., at Bayard St., 2nd floor, Chinatown* ☎ *212/619–4785* 🌐 *www.moca-nyc.org* *$3 suggested admission* ⏲ *Tues.–Sun. noon–5.*

❸ **New York City Police Headquarters.** This magnificent Renaissance revival structure with baroque embellishments and a striking dome served as the New York City police headquarters from its construction in 1909 until 1973. In 1988 it was converted into a high-priced condominium complex. It's known to New Yorkers today as "240 Centre Street," and its big-name residents have included Cindy Crawford, Winona Ryder, and Steffi Graf, among others. ✉ *240 Centre St., between Broome and Grand Sts., Little Italy.*

⚑ ❶ **St. Patrick's Old Cathedral.** The first cornerstone of the original St. Pat's was laid in 1809, making it the oldest Roman Catholic church in the city. It was completed in 1815 and restored following a fire in 1866. The first American cardinal, John McCloskey, received his red hat in this building, and Pierre Toussaint, a former slave, who, as a freed man, donated most of his earnings to the poor, was buried in the graveyard. He was reburied at St. Patrick's Cathedral on 5th Avenue in 1983, prior to his veneration by Pope John Paul II. ✉ *233 Mott St., between Houston and Prince Sts., NoLita* ☎ *212/226–8075* ⏲ *Mon., Tues., Thurs. 8–1 and 3:30–6; Fri. 8–1 and 3:30–9; Sat. 8–1; Sun. 8–4.*

❹ **San Gennaro Church.** Every September San Gennaro Church—officially called the Most Precious Blood Church, National Shrine of San Gennaro—sponsors the Feast of San Gennaro, the biggest event in Little Italy. The century-old church's richly painted, jewel-box-like interior is worth a glance, especially the replica of the grotto at Lourdes. The church is open for services on weekends. For a visit during the week, see the rector at 109 Mulberry Street. ✉ *113 Baxter St., near Canal St., Little Italy* ☎ *212/768–9320 festival information; 212/226–6427 church.*

SOHO & TRIBECA

Today the names of these two downtown neighborhoods are synonymous with a certain style—an amalgam of black-clad artist types, young Wall Streeters, expansive loft apartments, chic boutiques, and packed-to-the-gills restaurants. It's all very urban, very cool, very now. Before the 1970s, though, these two areas were virtual wastelands. SoHo (so named because it is the district *So*uth of *Ho*uston Street, roughly bounded by Lafayette, Canal Street, and 6th Avenue) was regularly referred to as "Hell's Hundred Acres" because of the many fires that raged through the untended warehouses crowding the area. It was saved by two factors: first, preservationists here discovered the world's greatest concentration of cast-iron architecture and fought to prevent demolition; and second, artists discovered the large, cheap, well-lighted spaces that cast-iron buildings provide.

All the rage between 1860 and 1890, cast-iron buildings were popular because they did not require massive walls to bear the weight of the upper stories. Since there was no need for load-bearing walls, these buildings had more interior space and larger windows. They were also versatile, with various architectural elements produced from standardized molds to mimic any style—Italianate, Victorian Gothic, neo-Grecian, to name but a few visible in SoHo. At first it was technically illegal for artists to live in their loft studios, but so many did that eventually the zoning laws were changed to permit residence.

By 1980 SoHo's galleries, trendy shops, and cafés, together with its marvelous cast-iron buildings and vintage Belgian-block pavements (the 19th-century successor to traditional cobblestones), had made SoHo such a desirable area that only the most successful artists could afford it. Seeking similar space, artists moved downtown to another half-abandoned industrial district, for which a new, SoHo-like name was invented: TriBeCa (the *Tri*angle *Be*low *Ca*nal Street, although in effect it goes no farther south than Murray Street and no farther east than West Broadway). The same scenario has played itself out again, and TriBeCa's rising rents are already beyond the means of most artists, who have moved instead to west Chelsea and the Meatpacking District, Long Island City, areas of Brooklyn, or New Jersey. In SoHo, meanwhile, the arrival of large chain stores such as Pottery Barn and J. Crew has given some blocks the feeling of an outdoor shopping mall. On a single block of Broadway, the Museum of African Art has moved to Queens and the Guggenheim Museum SoHo has been replaced by a Prada store that cost more than $35 million to design.

Numbers in the text correspond to numbers in the margin and on the Little Italy, Chinatown, SoHo, TriBeCa map.

a good walk

Starting at Houston (pronounced *how*-ston) Street, walk south down Broadway, stopping to browse the stores and vendor stands between Houston and Prince streets. The sole remaining museum on the block is the **New Museum of Contemporary Art** 15, devoted exclusively to living artists. Within the **Prada** 16 store at 575 Broadway, Dutch architect Rem Koolhaas has created a high-tech setting for the Italian house of fashion. Several art galleries share these blocks as well, most notably at 568 Broadway, which houses 10 galleries, and the trendy Armani Exchange store on the ground level.

Just south of Prince Street, 560 Broadway on the east side of the block is another popular exhibit space, home to a dozen or so galleries. Across the street at No. 561, Ernest Flagg's 1904 Little Singer Building shows the final flower of the cast-iron style, with wrought-iron balconies, terra-cotta panels, and broad expanses of windows. One block south of the Little Singer Building, between Spring and Broome streets, a cluster of lofts that were originally part of the 1897 New Era Building share an art nouveau copper mansard at No. 495. At the northeast corner of Broadway and Broome Street is the **Haughwout Building** 17, a restored classic of the cast-iron genre. At the southeast corner of Broadway and Broome Street, the former Mechanics and Traders Bank (486 Broadway) is a Romanesque and Moorish revival building with half-round brick arches.

If you have youngsters in tow, head east on Grand Street two blocks to the **Children's Museum of the Arts** 18, where the interactive exhibits provide a welcome respite from SoHo's mostly grown-up pursuits. Otherwise, walk west on Grand Street three short blocks to discover several of SoHo's better exhibition spaces clustered on the south end of Greene and Wooster streets near Grand and Canal streets. These include Deitch Projects (76 Grand St.), the Drawing Center (35 Wooster St.), and Spencer Brownstone (39 Wooster St.).

From here you may continue north on Wooster Street for Prince Street shops or first head east one block to Greene Street, where cast-iron architecture is at its finest. The block between Canal and Grand streets represents the longest row of cast-iron buildings anywhere. Handsome as they are, these buildings were always commercial, containing stores and light manufacturing firms, principally in the textile trade. (Notice the iron loading docks and the sidewalk vault covers that lead into basement storage areas.) Two standout buildings on Greene Street are the so-called **Queen of Greene Street** 19 and the **King of Greene Street** 20. Even the lampposts on Greene Street are architectural gems: note their turn-of-the-20th-century bishop's-crook style, adorned with various cast-iron curlicues from their bases to their curved tops.

Greene Street between Prince and Spring streets is notable for the SoHo Building (Nos. 104–110); towering 13 stories, it was the neighborhood's tallest building until the SoHo Grand Hotel went up in 1996. At Prince Street, walk one block west to Wooster Street, which between Prince and Spring is a retail paradise. Like a few other SoHo streets,

Little Italy, Chinatown, SoHo & TriBeCa
W. Houston St.
GREENWICH VILLAGE
Downing St.
1,9
Houston St.
King St.
Hudson St.
Varick St.
Charlton St.
Vandam St.
Spring St.
NYC Fire Museum
Dominick St.
Broome St.
Holland Tunnel Entrance
Canal St.
Washington St.
Watts St.
Desbrosses St.
Holland Tunnel Exit
Greenwich St.
Vestry St.
Laight St.
Hubert St.
TRIBECA
Ericsson Pl.
N. Moore St.
Franklin St.
West St.
New York Mercantile Exchange
Jay St.
Staple St.
Harrison St.
West Side Hwy.
Stuyvesant High School
Chambers St.
Warren St.
Murray St.
1,2,3,9
A,C
C,E
A,C,E
MacDougal St.
Ave. of the Americas (Sixth Ave.)
Sullivan St.
Thompson St.
West Broadway
Wooster St.
Greene St.
Mercer St.
Broadway
Prince St.
N,R,W
Little Singer Building
SoHo Building
SOHO
Spring St.
OK Harris
New Era Building
Broome St.
Drawing Center
Grand St.
Howard St.
N,R,W,Q
Lispenard St.
Walker St.
White St.
Franklin St.
Leonard St.
Worth St.
Thomas St.
Church St.
F,V
21
15
16
20
17
22
19
24
23
25
26

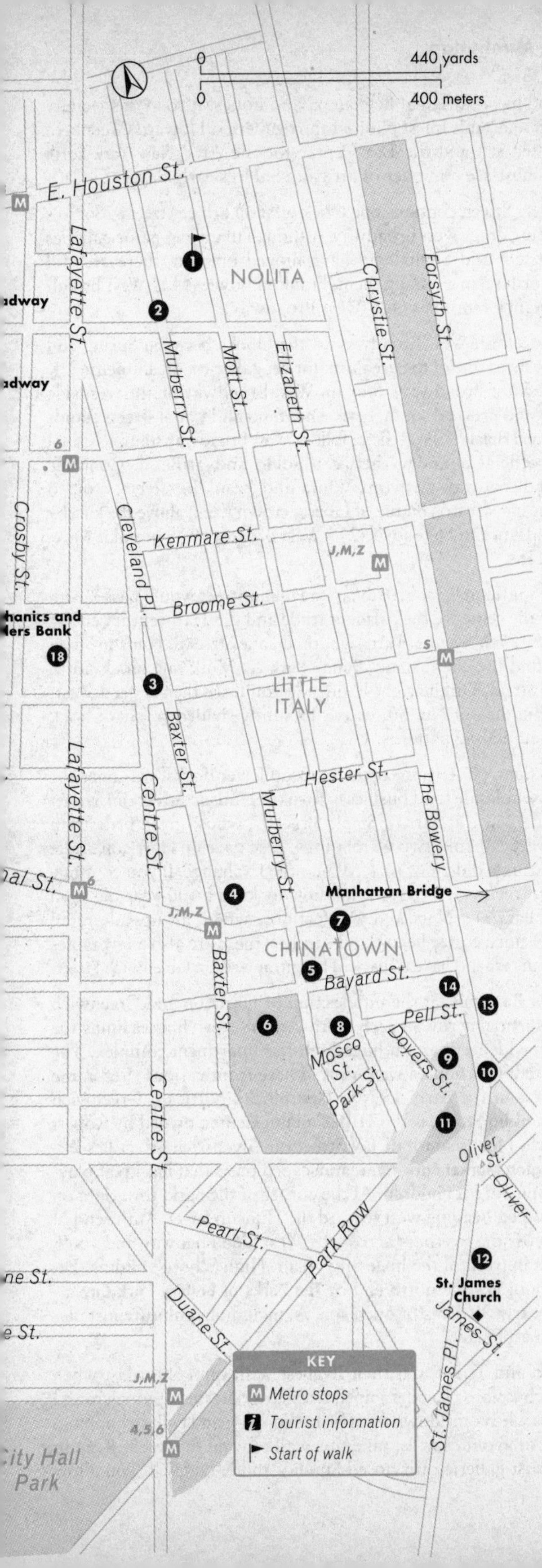

Little Italy & Chinatown

- Asian American Arts Centre 14
- The Bowery 10
- Chatham Square 11
- Church of the Transfiguration 8
- Columbus Park 6
- Confucius Plaza 13
- Doyers Street 9
- First Shearith Israel graveyard 12
- Mott Street 7
- Mulberry Street 2
- Museum of Chinese in the Americas (MoCA) 5
- New York City Police Headquarters 3
- St. Patrick's Old Cathedral 1
- San Gennaro Church 4

SoHo & TriBeCa

- Children's Museum of the Arts 18
- Duane Park 23
- Haughwout Building 17
- King of Greene Street 20
- New Museum of Contemporary Art 15
- New York Earth Room 21
- The Parks of Battery Park City 26
- Prada 16
- Queen of Greene Street 19
- SoHo Grand Hotel 22
- Staple Street 24
- Washington Market Park 25

Wooster still has its original Belgian paving stones. Also in this vicinity is one of Manhattan's finest photography galleries, Howard Greenberg (120 Wooster St.) and the Dia Center for the Arts' **New York Earth Room** 21, a must-see reminder of art from SoHo's early days.

From Wooster Street, continue one block west on Prince Street to SoHo's main shopping drag, West Broadway. Although many big-name galleries such as Castelli and Sonnabend have moved uptown, there are still holdouts worth seeing, among them, Franklin Bowles (431 West Broadway) and Nancy Hoffman (429 West Broadway).

Continue south on West Broadway to the blocks between Spring and Broome streets to one of the area's major art galleries, the immense OK Harris (383 West Broadway). Stay on West Broadway on the west side of the street and proceed south; between Grand and Canal streets stands the **SoHo Grand Hotel** 22. From here, follow West Broadway south to Canal Street, the official boundary between SoHo and TriBeCa. Continue down West Broadway. Between White and Franklin streets, stop to marvel at the life-size iron Statue of Liberty crown rising above the kitschy white-tile entrance to El Teddy's (219 West Broadway), a popular Mexican restaurant.

Continuing south on West Broadway to Duane Street, you'll pass Worth Street, once the center of the garment trade and the 19th-century equivalent of today's 7th Avenue. Turn right on Duane Street to Hudson Street and you'll find the calm, shady **Duane Park** 23. Walk one block north on Hudson Street. On the right-hand side you'll see the art deco Western Union Building at No. 60, where 19 subtly shaded colors of brick are laid in undulating patterns.

The area to the west (left), near the Hudson River docks, was once the heart of the wholesale food business. Turn off Hudson Street onto quiet Jay Street and pause at narrow **Staple Street** 24, whose green pedestrian walkway overhead links two warehouses. Also gaze up Harrison Street toward the ornate old New York Mercantile Exchange. If you continue west on Jay Street, you'll pass the loading docks of a 100-year-old food wholesaler, Bazzini's Nuts and Confections, where an upscale retail shop peddles nuts, coffee beans, and candies; there are also a few tables where you can rest and have a snack. The entrance is on Greenwich Street.

Just north of Bazzini's, at the intersection of Harrison and Greenwich streets, is a surprising row of early-19th-century town houses lining the side of Independence Plaza, a huge high-rise apartment complex. The three-story redbrick houses were moved here from various sites in the neighborhood in the early 1970s. Two blocks north on Greenwich Street, at Franklin Street, is the TriBeCa Film Center, owned by Robert De Niro. Two blocks south of Jay Street on Greenwich Street lies 2½-acre **Washington Market Park** 25, a landscaped oasis that has great playground equipment for children. At the corner of the park, turn right on Chambers Street, heading west toward the Hudson River. At the end of the block, cross the overpass across the West Side Highway and you'll find yourself in front of the huge Stuyvesant High School building. Behind the school lies the north end of **The Parks of Battery Park City** 26, which has nearly 30 acres of open spaces, including sculpture installations and an esplanade.

TIMING To see SoHo and TriBeCa at their liveliest, visit on a Saturday, when the fashion-conscious crowd is joined by smartly dressed uptowners and suburbanites who come down for a little shopping and gallery hopping. If you want to avoid crowds, take this walk during the week. Keep in mind that most galleries are closed Sunday and Monday. If you allow time for browsing in a few galleries and museums, as well as a stop for lunch, this tour can easily take up to an entire day.

What to See

off the beaten path

Charlton Street. The city's longest stretch of redbrick town houses preserved from the 1820s and 1830s runs along the north side of this street, which is west of 6th Avenue and south of West Houston Street and has high stoops, paneled front doors, leaded-glass windows, and narrow dormer windows all intact. While you're here, stroll along the parallel King and Vandam streets for more fine federal houses. This quiet enclave was once an estate called Richmond Hill, whose various residents included George Washington, John and Abigail Adams, and Aaron Burr.

1

18 **Children's Museum of the Arts.** In a bi-level space in SoHo, children ages 1–10 can amuse and educate themselves with various activities, including a ball pond with colored physio balls; play acting in costume; music making with real instruments; and art making, from computer art to old-fashioned painting, sculpting, and collage. ✉ *182 Lafayette St., between Grand and Broome Sts., SoHo* ☎ *212/274–0986* 🌐 *www.cmany.org* *$5, Thurs. 4–6 pay as you wish* ⏲ *Wed., Fri., and weekends noon–5, Thurs. noon–6.*

23 **Duane Park.** The city bought this calm, shady triangle from Trinity Church in 1797 for $5. Cheese, butter, and egg warehouses surrounded this oasis for more than 100 years. ✉ *Bordered by Hudson, Duane, and Staple Sts., TriBeCa.*

need a break?

For a real New York story, duck into the **Odeon** (✉ 145 West Broadway, TriBeCa ☎ 212/233–0507), an art deco restaurant-bar. With black-and-red banquettes, chrome mirrors, and neon-lighted clocks, this place has a distinctively slick atmosphere. Come for a drink at the bar or a snack anytime from noon to 2 AM.

17 **Haughwout Building.** Nicknamed the Parthenon of Cast Iron, this five-story, Venetian palazzo–style structure was built in 1857 to house Eder Haughwout's china and glassware business. Each window is framed by Corinthian columns and rounded arches. Inside, the building once contained the world's first commercial passenger elevator, a steam-powered device invented by Elisha Graves Otis. Otis went on to found an elevator empire and made high-rises practical possibilities. ✉ *488–492 Broadway, at Broome St., SoHo.*

20 **King of Greene Street.** This five-story Renaissance-style 1873 building has a magnificent projecting porch of Corinthian columns and pilasters. Today the King (now painted ivory) houses the DBA Gallery and Alice's Antiques. ✉ *72–76 Greene St., between Spring and Broome Sts., SoHo.*

15 **New Museum of Contemporary Art.** The avant-garde exhibitions here, all by living artists (many from outside the United States), are often innovative and socially conscious. The well-stocked bookstore and the free basement gallery devoted to interactive art (all of which can be touched) are more than enough to get you in the door. Readings, performance art, and film and video screenings often take place here. ✉ *583 Broadway, between W. Houston and Prince Sts., SoHo* ☎ *212/219–1222* 🌐 *www.newmuseum.org* *$6; half price Thurs. 6 PM–8 PM* ⏲ *Tues., Wed., and Fri.–Sun. noon–6; Thurs. noon–8.*

need a break?

Space Untitled Espresso Bar (✉ 133 Greene St., south of W. Houston St., SoHo ☎ 212/260–8962) serves caffeine, smoothies, sweets, and sandwiches, as well as wine and beer, in a large gallery space.

off the beaten path

New York City Fire Museum. Real firefighters give the tours here, and the collection of firefighting tools from the 18th, 19th, and 20th centuries includes hand-pulled and horse-drawn apparatus, engines, sliding poles, uniforms, and fireboat equipment. Since the attack on the World Trade Center, when New York's Bravest lost 343 members while rescuing civilians, the museum has been crowded, particularly on Saturday. A memorial exhibit featuring photos, paintings, children's artwork, and found objects all relating to the attacks on September 11, 2001, are also on view. Guided tours for 12 or more can be made by appointment. ✉ *278 Spring St., near Varick St., SoHo* ☎ *212/691–1303* 🌐 *www.nycfiremuseum.org* *$5 suggested donation* *Tues.–Sat. 10–5, Sun. 10–4.*

21 **New York Earth Room.** Walter de Maria's 1977 avant-garde work consists of 140 tons of gently sculpted soil (22 inches deep) filling 3,600 square ft of space of the Dia Center for the Arts' second-floor gallery. Fans of de Maria's work shouldn't miss his *Broken Kilometer,* a few blocks away at 393 West Broadway. ✉ *141 Wooster St., between W. Houston and Prince Sts., SoHo* ☎ *212/473–8072* *Free* *Jan.–mid-June and mid-Sept.–Dec., Wed.–Sun. noon–3 and 3:30–6.*

26 **The Parks of Battery Park City.** A landscaped oasis with grassy areas, playgrounds, promenades and walkways, and handball and basketball courts, this park on the river stretches from Battery Park to Chambers Street. Between May and October, there are nearly 800 activities to take part in, from kids' pick-up soccer games to drumming circles and dance performances. At the end of Vesey Street is a playground and the Irish Hunger Memorial, created in remembrance of the "Great Irish Famine and Migration" of 1845–52. One of many public art installations is ***The Real World*** by Tom Otterness, at the end of Chambers Street. Tiny cartoonish creatures in bronze go about their playful and naughty business in a story-book setting, which ultimately pokes fun at the area's capitalist ethos. Beyond Stuyvesant High School (1992) on Chambers Street is the start of **Hudson River Park's** esplanade, which will eventually extend north to 59th Street. This landscaped ribbon of asphalt fills with bikers, joggers, and rollerbladers, especially on weekends. Benches along the path are terrific spots from which to watch the sun set over New Jersey. At present the completed esplanade runs as far as Gansevoort Street in the Meatpacking District north of Greenwich Village. There's a temporary path stretching between West 14th and 34th streets, and pedestrian access is as far as West 59th Street, though not always along the water. Several piers along the river are being built or rehabilitated for public use. ✉ *Entrances at Chambers St. and Rector Street bridge* ☎ *212/267–9700* 🌐 *www.bpcparks.org.*

16 **Prada.** OMA, the Dutch architecture firm led by Rem Koolhaas, delves into the relations among theory, design, and sheer consumerism at Prada's SoHo store. You may find the technological gizmos and display innovations more fascinating than the latest clothing. A sweeping sine curve of zebrawood dips into a set of oversize steps, creating a continuum from the ground floor to the basement. Metal display cages hung from the ceiling can be rolled along tracks to reconfigure the space; a seamless glass elevator glides between floors. Souped-up dressing rooms

have doors that change from clear to opaque; inside, turn slowly in front of a plasma screen to see a video image of how the back of an outfit looks. Strips of video screens elsewhere on the selling floor show arty film clips, and pink resin stripes the shelving areas. And the exposed white spackling? Intentional. ✉ *575 Broadway, at Prince St., SoHo* ☎ *212/334–8888* 🌐 *www.prada.com* ⏲ *Mon.–Sat. 11–7, Sun. noon–6.*

need a break?

Diagonally across from the Prada Store, **Dean & DeLuca** (✉ 560 Broadway, at Prince St., SoHo ☎ 212/431–1691), the gourmet emporium, brews superb coffee and tea and sells yummy pastries at a premium, but it's standing room only.

1

19 **Queen of Greene Street.** The regal grace of this 1873 cast-iron beauty is exemplified by its dormers, columns, window arches, projecting central bays, and Second Empire–style roof. ✉ *28–30 Greene St., between Grand and Canal Sts., SoHo.*

22 **SoHo Grand Hotel.** The first major hotel to appear in the area since the 1800s, the 1996, 15-story SoHo Grand pays tribute to the neighborhood's architectural history, particularly the cast-iron historic district. Bill Sofield's industrial-chic yet warm decor complements the original 19th-century structure. A 17th-century French stone basin serves as a "dog bar" at the hotel's entrance, signaling that pets are welcome. A staircase—made of translucent bottle glass and iron and suspended from the ceiling by two cables—links the entryway with the second-floor lobby, which has 16-ft-high windows and massive stone columns supporting the paneled mercury mirror ceiling. ✉ *310 West Broadway, between Canal and Grand Sts., SoHo* ☎ *212/965–3000.*

need a break?

For a delicious light lunch, head to **Snack** (✉ 105 Thompson St., between Prince and Spring Sts., SoHo ☎ 212/925–1040) for tasty Greek sandwiches and salads. On sunny days, get it to go and park yourself on a bench at the Vesuvio Playground down the block.

24 **Staple Street.** Little more than an alley, Staple Street was named for the eggs, butter, cheese, and other staple products unloaded here by ships in transit that didn't want to pay duty on any extra cargo. Framed at the end of the alley is the redbrick **New York Mercantile Exchange** (✉ 6 Harrison St.), with a corner tower topped by a bulbous roof. On the ground floor is the acclaimed French restaurant Chanterelle.

TriBeCa Film Center. Robert De Niro created this complex of editing, screening, and production rooms, where Miramax Films, Steven Spielberg, Quincy Jones, and De Niro keep offices. Like many of the other stylish and renovated buildings in this area, it's a former factory, the old Coffee Building. On the ground floor is the TriBeCa Grill restaurant, also owned by De Niro. ✉ *375 Greenwich St., between Franklin and N. Moore Sts., TriBeCa.*

25 **Washington Market Park.** This much-needed recreation space was named after the great food market that once sprawled over the area. It's now a green, landscaped stretch with a playground and a gazebo across from a public elementary school. At the corner, a stout little red tower resembles a lighthouse, and iron ship figures are worked into the playground fence—reminders of the neighborhood's long-gone dockside past. ✉ *Greenwich St. between Chambers and Duane Sts., TriBeCa.*

GREENWICH VILLAGE

Greenwich Village, which New Yorkers invariably speak of simply as "the Village," enjoyed a raffish reputation for years. The area was originally a rural outpost of the city—a haven for New Yorkers during early-9th-century smallpox and yellow fever epidemics—and many of its blocks still look relatively pastoral, with brick town houses and low-rises, tiny green parks and hidden courtyards, and a crazy-quilt pattern of narrow, tree-lined streets (some of which follow long-ago cow paths). In the mid-19th century, however, as the city spread north of 14th Street, the Village became the province of immigrants, bohemians, and students (New York University [NYU], today the nation's largest private university, was planted next to Washington Square in 1831). Its politics were radical and its attitudes tolerant, which is one reason it became a home to such a large lesbian and gay community.

Several generations of writers and artists have lived and worked here: in the 19th century, Henry James, Edgar Allan Poe, Mark Twain, Walt Whitman, and Stephen Crane; at the turn of the 20th century, O. Henry, Edith Wharton, Theodore Dreiser, and Hart Crane; and during the 1920s and '30s, John Dos Passos, Norman Rockwell, Sinclair Lewis, John Reed, Eugene O'Neill, Edward Hopper, and Edna St. Vincent Millay. In the late 1940s and early 1950s, the abstract expressionist painters Franz Kline, Jackson Pollock, Mark Rothko, and Willem de Kooning congregated here, as did the Beat writers Jack Kerouac, Allen Ginsberg, and Lawrence Ferlinghetti. The 1960s brought folk musicians and poets, notably Bob Dylan and Peter, Paul, and Mary.

Today, block for block, the Village is still one of the most vibrant parts of the city. Well-heeled professionals occupy high-rent apartments and town houses side by side with bohemian, longtime residents—who pay cheap rents thanks to rent-control laws—as well as NYU students. Locals and visitors rub elbows at dozens of small restaurants, cafés spill out onto sidewalks, and an endless variety of small shops pleases everyone. Except for a few pockets of adult-entertainment shops and divey bars, the Village is as scrubbed as posher neighborhoods.

Numbers in the text correspond to numbers in the margin and on the Greenwich Village, the East Village, and the Lower East Side map.

a good walk

Begin your tour of Greenwich Village at the foot of 5th Avenue at Washington Memorial Arch in **Washington Square Park** 1. Most buildings bordering the leafy square belong to NYU. On Washington Square North, between University Place and MacDougal Street, stretches **The Row** 2, two blocks of lovingly preserved Greek revival and federal-style town houses.

At the corner of Washington Square South and Thompson Street you'll see the square-towered **Judson Memorial Church** 3. One block east, at La Guardia Place, NYU's rebuilt student center stands on the site of a boardinghouse that had been nicknamed the House of Genius for the talented writers who lived there over the years: Theodore Dreiser, O. Henry, and Eugene O'Neill, among others. Another block east is the hulking red sandstone Bobst Library, built in 1972, which represents an abortive attempt to create a unified campus look for NYU as envisioned by architects Philip Johnson and Richard Foster. At one time plans called for all the Washington Square buildings to be refaced in this red stone; the cost proved prohibitive. On the east side of the square, you can take in a contemporary art exhibit at **Grey Art Gallery** 4, housed in NYU's main building.

Greenwich Village ▼

The East Village & The Lower East Side ▼

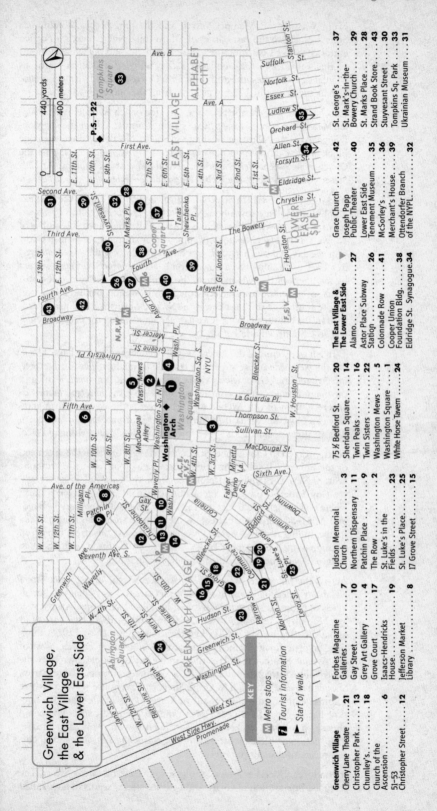

From Washington Memorial Arch and the park, cross Washington Square North to the east corner of 5th Avenue, where there's a portico entrance to 7–13 Washington Square North. Beyond the white columns of this entrance is the small, attractive Willy's Garden. A statue of Miguel de Cervantes, the author of *Don Quixote,* stands at the far end. The likeness, cast in 1724, was a gift from the mayor of Madrid.

Another half a block north, on the east side of 5th Avenue, is **Washington Mews** 5, a cobblestone private street. A similar Village mews, MacDougal Alley, lies between Washington Square North and 8th Street, one block west. Continue up the west side of 5th Avenue; you'll pass the **Church of the Ascension** 6, a Gothic revival brownstone building. At 12th Street you can stop in the **Forbes Magazine Galleries** 7.

Backtrack to West 11th Street and turn right to see one of the best examples of a Village town-house block. One exception to the 19th-century redbrick town houses here is the modern, angled front window of 18 West 11th Street, usually occupied by a stuffed bear whose outfit changes day to day. This house was built after the original was destroyed in a 1970 explosion of a basement bomb factory, which had been started by members of the Weathermen, the revolutionary faction of the Students for a Democratic Society. Toward 6th Avenue, behind a low wall on the south side of the street, is the Second Shearith Israel graveyard, used by the country's oldest Jewish congregation after the original cemetery in Chinatown and before the one in Chelsea.

Turn left on Avenue of the Americas (6th Avenue) and go south one block. On the west side of the street, the triangle formed by West 10th Street, 6th Avenue, and Greenwich Avenue originally held a market, a jail, and the magnificent towered courthouse that is now the **Jefferson Market Library** 8. West of 6th Avenue on 10th Street is the wrought-iron gateway to a tiny courtyard called **Patchin Place** 9; around the corner, on 6th Avenue just north of 10th Street, is a similar cul-de-sac, Milligan Place.

Next, proceed to Christopher Street, which veers off from the south end of the library triangle. Christopher Street has long been the symbolic heart of New York's gay and lesbian community. Within a few steps you'll see **Gay Street** 10 on your left. Continue on to cross Waverly Place, where on your left you'll pass the 1831 brick **Northern Dispensary** 11 building. At **51–53 Christopher Street** 12, the historic Stonewall riots marked the beginning of the gay rights movement. Across the street is a green triangle named **Christopher Park** 13, not to be confused with **Sheridan Square** 14, another landscaped triangle to the south.

Across the busy intersection of 7th Avenue South, Christopher Street has many cafés, bars, and stores; several cater to a gay clientele, but all kinds of people traverse the narrow sidewalks. Two shops worth a visit are McNulty's Tea and Coffee Co. (No. 109), with a large variety of tea and coffee blends, and Li-Lac Chocolate Shop (No. 120), a longtime favorite for its homemade chocolate and butter crunch. West of 7th Avenue South, the Village turns into a picture-book town of twisting tree-lined streets, quaint houses, and tiny restaurants. Starting from Sheridan Square West, follow Grove Street past the house at No. 59 where Thomas Paine died—now the site of Marie's Crisis Cafe—and the onetime home (No. 45) of poet Hart Crane. At the next corner you could choose to follow Bleecker Street northwest toward Abingdon Square. This section of Bleecker Street is full of crafts and antiques shops, coffeehouses, and small restaurants.

If you forego Bleecker Street, continue your walk on Grove Street. The secluded intersection of Grove and Bedford streets seems to have fallen through a time warp into the 19th century. One of the few remaining clapboard structures in Manhattan is **17 Grove Street** 15. Around the same corner is **Twin Peaks** 16, an early-19th-century house that resembles a Swiss chalet. Heading west, Grove Street curves in front of the iron gate of **Grove Court** 17, a group of mid-19th-century brick-front residences.

Return to Bedford Street, turn right, and walk until you get to No. 86. Behind the unmarked door is **Chumley's** 18, a former speakeasy. Continue a couple of blocks farther to the oldest house in the Village, the **Isaacs-Hendricks House** 19. The place next door, **75½ Bedford Street** 20, at 9½ ft wide, is New York's narrowest house. Bedford Street intersects Commerce Street, one of the Village's most romantic untrod lanes, and home to the historic **Cherry Lane Theatre** 21. Across the street, past the bend in the road, stand two nearly identical brick houses separated by a garden and popularly known as the **Twin Sisters** 22.

Turn left onto Barrow Street and then right onto Hudson Street, so named because this was originally the bank of the Hudson River. The block to the northwest is owned by **St. Luke's in the Fields** 23. Writer Bret Harte once lived at 487 Hudson Street, at the end of the row. If your feet are getting tired, you can head north on Hudson Street for four blocks and take a rest at the legendary **White Horse Tavern** 24, at 11th Street.

Two blocks south of Barrow Street, turn left at **St. Luke's Place** 25 (this is Leroy Street west of Hudson Street), a one-block row of classic 1860s town houses. Across 7th Avenue South, St. Luke's Place becomes Leroy Street again, which terminates in an old Italian neighborhood at Bleecker Street. Because of all the touristy shops and crowds, Bleecker Street between 6th and 7th avenues seems more vital these days than Little Italy does. For authentic Italian ambience, step into one of the fragrant Italian bakeries, such as A. Zito & Sons (No. 259) and Rocco's (No. 243), or look inside the old-style butcher shops, such as Ottomanelli & Sons (No. 285) and Faicco's (No. 260). In a town that's fierce about its pizza, some New Yorkers swear by John's Pizzeria (No. 278), the original in a chain of four branches citywide. Be forewarned, however: no slices; whole pies only.

Head east on Bleecker Street to Carmine Street and the Church of Our Lady of Pompeii, where Mother Cabrini, a naturalized Italian immigrant who became the first American saint, often prayed. When you reach Father Demo Square (at Bleecker Street and 6th Avenue), head up 6th Avenue to West 3rd Street and check out the basketball courts, where city-style basketball is played in all but the very coldest weather. Turn down West 3rd Street and check out the illustrious Blue Note, where jazz greats play. The next intersection brings you to MacDougal Street, once home to several illustrious names. The two houses at 127 and 129 MacDougal Street were built for Aaron Burr in 1829; notice the pineapple newel posts, a symbol of hospitality. Louisa May Alcott wrote *Little Women* while living at 130–132 MacDougal Street. The Provincetown Playhouse at No. 133 premiered many of Eugene O'Neill's plays.

Head south on MacDougal to reach Caffe Reggio (No. 119), one of the Village's first coffeehouses. Its interior hasn't changed much since it opened in 1927. At Minetta Tavern (No. 113), a venerable Village watering hole, turn right onto Minetta Lane, which leads to narrow Minetta Street, another former speakeasy alley. Both streets follow the course of Minetta Brook, which once flowed through this neighborhood and still bubbles deep beneath the pavement. The foot of Minetta Street returns you to the corner of 6th Avenue and Bleecker Street, the stomping grounds of 1960s-era folksingers (many performed at the now-defunct Folk City, one block north on West 3rd Street). Partly because of the proximity of NYU, this area still attracts a young crowd to its cafés, bars, jazz clubs, coffeehouses, theaters, and cabarets.

TIMING Greenwich Village lends itself to a leisurely pace, so allow yourself most of a day to explore its backstreets and stop at shops and cafés.

What to See

21 **Cherry Lane Theatre.** One of the original off-Broadway houses, this 1817 building was converted into a theater in 1923, thanks to Edna St. Vincent Millay and a group of theater artists. Over the years it has hosted American premieres of works by O'Neill, Beckett, Ionesco, Albee, Pinter, and Mamet. The playhouse still contains the original audience seats. ✉ *38 Commerce St., at Barrow St., Greenwich Village* ☎ *212/989–2020.*

13 **Christopher Park.** Those taking a break in this small triangular retreat share the space with the life-size sculptures of George Segal—that of a lesbian couple sitting on a bench and of gay male partners standing and conversing. The bronze statue is of Civil War general Philip Henry Sheridan. ✉ *Bordered by W. 4th, Grove, and Christopher Sts., Greenwich Village.*

18 **Chumley's.** A speakeasy during the Prohibition era, this still-secret tavern behind an unmarked door on Bedford Street retains its original ambience with oak booths, a fireplace once used by a blacksmith, and a sawdust-strewn floor. For years Chumley's attracted a literary clientele (John Steinbeck, Ernest Hemingway, Edna Ferber, Simone de Beauvoir, and Jack Kerouac), and the book covers of their publications were proudly displayed (and still appear) on the walls. There's another "secret" entrance in Pamela Court, accessed at 58 Barrow Street around the corner. ✉ *86 Bedford St., near Barrow St., Greenwich Village* ☎ *212/675–4449.*

6 **Church of the Ascension.** A mural depicting the Ascension of Jesus and stained-glass windows by John LaFarge, as well as a marble altar sculpture by Augustus Saint-Gaudens, are the highlights of this 1841 Gothic revival–style brownstone church designed by Richard Upjohn. In 1844 President John Tyler married Julia Gardiner here. ✉ *36–38 5th Ave., at 10th St., Greenwich Village* ☎ *212/254–8620* 🌐 *www.ascensionnyc.org* ⏲ *Weekdays noon–2 and 5:30–6:30.*

12 **51–53 Christopher Street.** On June 27, 1969, a gay bar at this address named the Stonewall Inn was the site of a clash between gay men and women (some in drag) and the New York City police. As the bar's patrons were being forced into police wagons, sympathetic gay onlookers protested and started fighting back, throwing beer bottles and garbage cans. Every June the Stonewall Riots are commemorated around the world with parades and celebrations that honor the gay rights movement. A clothing store now occupies No. 51; a bar named Stonewall is next door at No. 53. ✉ *51–53 Christopher St., between Waverly Pl. and 7th Ave. S, Greenwich Village.*

7 **Forbes Magazine Galleries.** The late publisher Malcolm Forbes's idiosyncratic personal collection fills the ground floor of the limestone Forbes Magazine Building, once the home of Macmillan Publishing. Exhibits change in the large painting gallery and one of two autograph galleries, while permanent highlights include U.S. presidential papers, more than 500 intricate toy boats, 10,000 toy soldiers, and some of the oldest Monopoly game sets ever made. Perhaps the most memorable permanent display contains exquisite items created by the House of Fabergé, including 12 jeweled eggs designed for the last of the Russian czars. ✉ 62

5th Ave., at 12th St., Greenwich Village ☎ *212/206–5548* *Free* ⏲ *Tues.–Sat. 10–4.*

need a break?

If you're yearning for a *pain au chocolat* or a madeleine, stop by **Marquet Pâtisserie** (✉ 15 E. 12th St., Greenwich Village ☎ 212/229–9313), a sleek, friendly café that serves irresistible French pastries, great coffee, and satisfying sandwiches, salads, and quiches.

10 **Gay Street.** A curved, one-block lane lined with small row houses from circa 1810, Gay Street is named after the *New York Tribune* editor who lived here with his wife and fellow abolitionist, Lucretia Mott. The black neighborhood was a stop on the Underground Railroad and would later become a strip of speakeasies. In the 1930s this darling thoroughfare and nearby Christopher Street became famous nationwide when Ruth McKenney published her somewhat zany autobiographical stories in the *New Yorker,* based on what happened when she and her sister moved to Greenwich Village from Ohio (they appeared in book form as *My Sister Eileen* in 1938). McKenney wrote in the basement of No. 14. Also on Gay Street, Howdy Doody was designed in the basement of No. 12. ✉ *Between Christopher St. and Waverly Pl., Greenwich Village.*

4 **Grey Art Gallery.** New York University's main building has a welcoming street-level space with changing exhibitions usually devoted to contemporary art. ✉ *100 Washington Sq. E, between Waverly Pl. and Washington Pl., Greenwich Village* ☎ *212/998–6780* *$2.50 suggested donation* ⏲ *Tues., Thurs., and Fri. 11–6; Wed. 11–8; Sat. 11–5.*

17 **Grove Court.** Built between 1853 and 1854, this enclave of brick-front town houses was originally intended as apartments for employees of neighborhood hotels. Grove Court used to be called Mixed Ale Alley because of the neighbors' propensity to pool beverages brought from work. It now houses more affluent residents. ✉ *10–12 Grove St., Greenwich Village.*

19 **Isaacs-Hendricks House.** Originally built as a federal-style wood-frame residence in 1799, this immaculate structure is the oldest remaining such house in Greenwich Village. Its first owner, Joshua Isaacs, a wholesale merchant, lost the farmhouse to creditors; the building then belonged to copper supplier Harmon Hendricks. The village landmark was remodeled twice; it received its brick face in 1836, and the third floor was added in 1928. ✉ *77 Bedford St., at Commerce St., Greenwich Village.*

8 **Jefferson Market Library.** After Frederick Clarke Withers and Calvert Vaux's magnificent, towered building was constructed in 1877, critics variously termed its hodgepodge of styles Venetian, Victorian, or Italian. Villagers, noting the alternating wide bands of red brick and narrow strips of granite, dubbed it the "lean bacon style." The structure, named after our third president, was built as a courthouse, and over the years it has harbored a number of government agencies (public works, civil defense, census bureau, police academy); it was on the verge of demolition when local activists saved it and turned it into a public library in 1967. Note the fountain at the corner of West 10th Street and 6th Avenue and the seal of The City of New York on the east front. Inside are handsome interior doorways and a graceful circular stairway. If the gate is open, visit the flower garden behind the library, a project run by local green thumbs on the former site of a women's prison. ✉ *425 6th Ave., at 10th St., Greenwich Village* ☎ *212/243–4334.*

3 **Judson Memorial Church.** Designed by celebrated architect Stanford White, this Italian Roman-Renaissance church has long attracted a con-

gregation interested in the arts and community activism. Funded by the Astor family and John D. Rockefeller and constructed in 1892, the yellow-brick and limestone building was the brainchild of Edward Judson, who hoped to reach out to the poor immigrants in adjacent Little Italy. The church has stained-glass windows designed by John LaFarge and a 10-story campanile. Inquire at the parish office for weekday access at 243 Thompson Street. ✉ *55 Washington Sq. S, at Thompson St., Greenwich Village* ☎ *212/477–0351* ⏲ *Weekdays 10–6.*

off the beaten path

Meatpacking District. Until the late 1990s, this area between the Hudson River and 9th Avenue, from Gansevoort Street north to West 14th Street, seemed immune to gentrification due to its rather industrial function and location far west. But rising rents elsewhere sent entrepreneurs and gallery owners hunting, and once the high-fashion shops, fine art galleries, and adorable bakeries moved in, swinging carcasses and their attendant odors no longer seemed to be much of a deterrent. Although the overnight beef and poultry movers for which the district is known are still here, as are the transvestite prostitutes who contribute to the area's fringe character, the seeds of chic continue to be sown by ambitious photographers, filmmakers, new-media wunderkinds, restaurateurs, and retailers in search of affordable space. Urbanites and celebrities with their fingers on the pulse followed suit and snatched up the large, unfinished warehouses of abandoned meat-processing plants and automotive stores for renovation as residences. The main drag for the rapidly multiplying eateries, galleries, shops, and nightclubs is West 14th Street (at the end of which, near the Hudson, Herman Melville was once a customs inspector). The entrenched meat market dominates the streets in the morning. The trade peaks on weekdays between 5 AM and 9 AM. ✉ *Between 9th Ave. and Hudson River, from Gansevoort St. north to 14th St., Greenwich Village.*

⓫ **Northern Dispensary.** Constructed in 1831, this triangular Georgian brick building originally served as a clinic for indigent Villagers. Edgar Allan Poe was a frequent patient. The structure has also housed a dental clinic and a nursing home for AIDS patients. Note that the Dispensary has *one* side on *two* streets (Grove and Christopher streets where they meet) and *two* sides facing *one* street—Waverly Place, which splits in two directions. ✉ *165 Waverly Pl., Greenwich Village.*

❾ **Patchin Place.** This little cul-de-sac off West 10th Street between Greenwich and 6th avenues has 10 diminutive 1848 row houses. Around the corner on 6th Avenue is a similar dead-end street, **Milligan Place,** consisting of four small homes completed in 1852. The houses in both quiet enclaves were originally built for the waiters (mostly Basques) who worked at 5th Avenue's high-society Brevoort Hotel, long since demolished. Patchin Place later attracted numerous writers, including Theodore Dreiser, e. e. cummings, Jane Bowles, and Djuna Barnes. John Reed and Louise Bryant also lived here. Milligan Place eventually became the address for several playwrights, including Eugene O'Neill.

❷ **The Row.** Built from 1829 through 1839, this series of beautifully preserved Greek revival town houses along Washington Square North, on the two blocks between University Place and MacDougal Street, once belonged to merchants and bankers, then writers and artists such as John Dos Passos and Edward Hopper. Now the buildings serve as NYU offices and faculty housing. Developers demolished 18 Washington Square North, once the home of Henry James's grandmother, and the setting for his novel *Washington Square*. (Henry himself was born just off the square, in a long-gone house on Washington Place.) The oldest building on the block, No. 20, was constructed in 1829 in the federal style, and with Flemish bond brickwork—alternate bricks inserted with the smaller surface (headers) facing out—which before 1830 was considered the best way to build stable walls. ✉ *1–13 and 19–26 Washington Sq. N, between University Pl. and MacDougal St., Greenwich Village.*

23 **St. Luke's in the Fields.** The first warden of the Episcopal parish of St. Luke's, which was constructed in 1822 as a country chapel for downtown's Trinity Church, was Clement Clarke Moore, author of "A Visit from St. Nicholas" (" 'Twas the night before Christmas . . ."). The chapel, an unadorned structure of soft-color brick, was nearly destroyed by fire in 1981, but a flood of donations, many quite small, from West Village residents financed restoration of the square central tower. Concerts by the St. Luke's Choir, a professional ensemble, and the Choristers, a choir made up of 25 boys and girls, are offered at Christmastime and in spring; both groups are featured regularly as part of the liturgy. The Barrow Street Garden on the chapel grounds is worth visiting in spring and summer. ✉ *487 Hudson St., between Barrow and Christopher Sts., Greenwich Village* ☎ *212/924–0562* ⏲ *Grounds open Tues.–Fri. 9–7, weekends 1–4.*

★ 25 **St. Luke's Place.** Shaded by graceful gingko trees, this street has 15 classic Italianate brownstone and brick town houses (1852–53). Novelist Theodore Dreiser wrote *An American Tragedy* at No. 16, and poet Marianne Moore resided at No. 14. Mayor Jimmy Walker (first elected in 1926) lived at No. 6; the lampposts in front are "mayor's lamps," which were sometimes placed in front of the residences of New York mayors. This block is often used as a film location, too: No. 12 was shown as the Huxtables' home on *The Cosby Show* (although the family lived in Brooklyn), and No. 4 was the setting of the Audrey Hepburn movie *Wait Until Dark*. Before 1890 the playground on the south side of the street was a graveyard where, according to legend, the dauphin of France—the lost son of Louis XVI and Marie Antoinette—is buried. ✉ *Between Hudson St. and 7th Ave. S, Greenwich Village.*

need a break?

The **Anglers and Writers Café** (✉ 420 Hudson St., at St. Luke's Pl., Greenwich Village ☎ 212/675–0810) lives up to its name with bookshelves, fishing tackle, and pictures of Door County, Wisconsin, hung on the walls. It's an ideal spot to linger over a pot of tea and a slice of cake.

15 **17 Grove Street.** William Hyde, a prosperous window-sash maker, built this clapboard residence in 1822; a third floor was added in 1870. Hyde added a workshop behind the house in 1833. The building has since served many functions; it housed a brothel during the Civil War. The structure is the Village's largest remaining wood-frame house. ✉ *17 Grove St., at Bedford St., Greenwich Village.*

20 **75½ Bedford Street.** Rising real estate rates inspired the construction of New York City's narrowest house—just 9½ ft wide—in 1873. Built on a lot that was originally a carriage entrance of the Isaacs-Hendricks House next door, this sliver of a building has been home to actor John Barrymore and poet Edna St. Vincent Millay, who wrote the Pulitzer prize-winning *Ballad of the Harp-Weaver* during her tenure here from 1923 to 1924. ✉ *75½ Bedford St., between Commerce and Morton Sts., Greenwich Village.*

⓮ **Sheridan Square.** Once an unused asphalt space, this green triangle was landscaped following an extensive dig by urban archaeologists, who unearthed artifacts dating to the Dutch and Native American eras. ✉ *Bordered by Washington Pl. and W. 4th, Barrow, and Grove Sts., Greenwich Village.*

⓰ **Twin Peaks.** In 1925 financier Otto Kahn gave money to a Village eccentric named Clifford Daily to remodel an 1835 house for artists' use. The building was whimsically altered with stucco, half-timbers, and the addition of a pair of steep roof peaks. The result was something that might be described as an imitation Swiss chalet. ✉ *102 Bedford St., between Grove and Christopher Sts., Greenwich Village.*

㉒ **Twin Sisters.** These attractive federal-style brick homes connected by a walled garden were said to have been erected by a sea captain for two daughters who loathed each other. Historical record insists that they were built in 1831 and 1832 by a milkman who needed the two houses and an open courtyard for his work. The striking mansard roofs were added in 1873. ✉ *39 and 41 Commerce St., Greenwich Village.*

❺ **Washington Mews.** This cobblestone private street is lined on one side with the former stables of the houses on The Row on Washington Square North. Writer Walter Lippmann and artist-patron Gertrude Vanderbilt Whitney (founder of the Whitney Museum) once had homes in the mews; today it's mostly owned by NYU. ✉ *Between 5th Ave. and University Pl., Greenwich Village.*

★ ❶ **Washington Square Park.** Earnest-looking NYU students, Frisbee players, street musicians, skateboarders, jugglers, chess players, and bench warmers—and those just watching the grand opera of it all—generate a maelstrom of playful activity in this physical and spiritual heart of the Village. This lively 9½-acre park started out as a cemetery, principally for yellow fever victims—an estimated 10,000–22,000 bodies lie below. In the early 1800s it was a parade ground and the site of public executions; bodies dangled from a conspicuous Hanging Elm that still stands at the northwest corner of the square. Made a public park in 1827, the square became the focus of a fashionable residential neighborhood and a center of outdoor activity. Two well-equipped and shady playgrounds attract gaggles of youngsters, dog owners congregate at the popular dog run, and tourists and locals alike are drawn toward the large central fountain where in spring and summer passersby and loungers can cool off in small sprays, or, when the fountain is dry, entertainers and musicians pass the hat. A huge outdoor art fair is held around the park's perimeter each spring and fall; a jazz series blooms in summer; and at the academic year's end the entire park absorbs New York University's graduating class, proud parents, and spent faculty.

Dominating the square's north end, the triumphal **Washington Memorial Arch** stands at the foot of glorious 5th Avenue. A wooden version of the Washington Arch designed by Stanford White was built in 1889 to commemorate the 100th anniversary of George Washington's presidential inauguration and was originally placed about half a block north of its present location. The arch was reproduced in Tuckahoe marble in 1892, and the statues—*Washington at War* on the left, *Washington at Peace* on the right—were added in 1916 and 1918, respectively. The civilian version of Washington is the work of Alexander Stirling Calder, father of the renowned artist Alexander Calder. Bodybuilder Charles Atlas modeled for *Peace.* ✉ *5th Ave. between Waverly Pl. and 4th St., Greenwich Village.*

24 **White Horse Tavern.** Built in 1880, this amiable bar occupies one of the city's few remaining wood-frame structures. Formerly a speakeasy and a seamen's tavern, the White Horse has been popular with artists and writers for decades; its best-known customer was Welsh poet Dylan Thomas, who had a room named for him here after his death in 1953. ✉ *567 Hudson St., at W. 11th St., Greenwich Village* ☎ *212/243–9260.*

THE EAST VILLAGE & THE LOWER EAST SIDE

The gritty dwellings of the East Village—an area bounded by East 14th Street on the north, 4th Avenue or the Bowery on the west, East Houston Street on the south, and the East River—have housed immigrant families since the mid-1800s, although the cultural composition of those families continues to change. The 1970s brought a counterculture of hippies, experimental artists, writers, and students who benefited from the inexpensive living spaces and the East Village's reputation as a progressive neighborhood. During the 1980s, artists fleeing skyrocketing real estate prices in SoHo brought in their wake new restaurants, shops, and somewhat cleaner streets. Longtime bastions of the arts, such as the Classic Stage Company, La MaMa E.T.C., and St. Mark's-in-the-Bowery Church were joined by newer institutions such as P.S. 122, and several "hot" art galleries opened in narrow East Village storefronts. But the gallery scene here lasted only a couple of years—just long enough to drive up rents substantially on some blocks but not long enough to drive out all the neighborhood's original residents. Today an interesting mix has survived: artistic types and longtime members of various immigrant enclaves, principally Polish, Ukrainian, Slovene, Puerto Rican, Dominican, Japanese, and Filipino groups, and the neighborhood's traditional gentrification frontier has pushed east from Avenue A to Avenue B. The once sketchy Alphabet City (named for its Avenues A, B, C, and D) now seems like a walk in the park, where good restaurants, stylish bars, and funky shops are as likely to be patronized by the marginally employed as by young financiers.

South of East Houston Street, the Lower East Side (bounded by the Bowery to the west and East Broadway to the south) was, from the mid-19th century to the early 1920s, home to millions of mostly European refugees and Jews seeking a haven from famine, wars, and political repression. It became, in 1870, one of the most densely populated districts in the world. Entire families worked in unregulated sweatshops, mostly in the needle trades, and lived in cold-water railroad tenements. The influx was stemmed following passage of restrictive immigration laws in the 1920s. Some streets, such as Orchard, Essex, Eldridge, Hester, and Norfolk, still retain reminders of this period, mostly in the form of family-owned shops that date to the 1900s. Since the mid-1990s, trendy boutiques, restaurants, and bars have proliferated the area, as artists and young professionals colonize streets that also house substantial Hispanic and Chinese communities. The storefronts of the Lower East Side are a colorful mix of dress shops, Puerto Rican bodegas, Chinese produce markets, and kosher restaurants, but at night the sidewalks belong to lounge lizards.

Numbers in the text correspond to numbers in the margin and on the Greenwich Village, the East Village & the Lower East Side map.

a good walk

Begin at the intersection of East 8th Street, 4th Avenue, and Astor Place, where you'll see two traffic islands. One of these contains an ornate cast-iron kiosk, a replica of a beaux arts subway entrance, which provides access to the uptown **Astor Place Subway Station** 26 . On the other traffic island stands the **Alamo** 27, a huge black cube.

Go straight east from the Alamo to **St. Marks Place** 28, the name given to 8th Street in the East Village. Second Avenue, which St. Marks crosses after one block, was called the Yiddish Rialto in the early part of the 20th century: at that time eight theaters between Houston and 14th streets presented Yiddish-language productions of musicals, revues, and heart-wrenching melodramas. Two survivors from that period are the Orpheum (126 2nd Ave., at 8th St.) and the neo-Moorish Yiddish Arts Theatre, now the multiscreen Village East Cinemas (189 2nd Ave., at 12th St.), which has preserved the original ornate ceiling. In front of the Second Avenue Deli (156 2nd Ave., at 10th St.), Hollywood-style squares have been embedded in the sidewalk to commemorate Yiddish stage luminaries.

Second Avenue is also home to a neighborhood landmark, **St. Mark's-in-the-Bowery Church** 29 on the corner of East 10th Street. From here you can take a short detour to admire the facades of handsome redbrick row houses on quiet **Stuyvesant Street** 30, which stretches southwest to East 9th Street. If you continue two blocks north up 2nd Avenue from the church, you'll reach the **Ukrainian Museum** 31.

Next, return south to 135 2nd Avenue, between East 9th Street and St. Marks Place, to see the **Ottendorfer Branch of the New York Public Library** 32. Continue east on either East 9th Street or St. Marks Place, toward Alphabet City. East 9th Street is full of small, friendly shops selling designer and vintage clothing, housewares, toys, music, and much more, while St. Marks Place between 1st Avenue and Avenue A is lined with inexpensive cafés catering to a late-night younger crowd.

At the northeast corner of 1st Avenue and East 9th Street stands P.S. 122, a former public school building transformed into a complex of spaces for avant-garde entertainment. At Avenue A is **Tompkins Square Park** 33, a fairly peaceful spot during the day.

If you walk south on Avenue A past East Houston Street, you'll run into the historical Lower East Side, now a gentrified enclave. Students and artists occupy tenements once belonging to entire families on such streets as Rivington and Clinton. Popular bars and clubs, especially along Ludlow Street, draw crowds well beyond these new locals on the weekends. On Orchard Street, a longtime shopping strip, bargains can still be haggled for on fabrics, leather goods, clothes, and more, but the face of the Orchard Street Garment District has been modernized by a younger generation of pricey fashion-furious boutiques such as Shop (105 Stanton St.) and Vlada (101 Stanton St.). Here and there you'll see reminders of the old days—the fading signs for defunct Jewish businesses, as well as for a few holdouts, such as Gertel's Bakery (53 Hester St.) and The Pickle Guys (49 Essex St.). Historic establishments such as Katz's Delicatessen (205 E. Houston St., at Ludlow St.), Ratner's Restaurant (138 Delancey St.), and the more upscale Russ & Daughters (179 E. Houston St., between Orchard and Allen Sts.) anchor the area firmly in its immigrant past. Two important synagogues, markers of time and tradition, are persevering renovations: the city's oldest synagogue, dating to 1850, the Shul of New York (172 Norfolk St., between Stanton and E. Houston Sts.), now the Angel Orensanz Center for the Arts, and, farther south, the **Eldridge Street Synagogue** 34, once the largest Jewish house of worship. On Orchard Street, the **Lower East Side Tenement Museum** 35 brings a bygone era to life.

Head back up into the East Village, to the corner of 1st Avenue and East 6th Street. The entire south side of East 6th Street between 1st and 2nd avenues belongs to a dozen or more Indian restaurants serving inexpensive subcontinental fare (New Yorkers joke that they all share a single kitchen). Continuing west on East 6th Street, past 2nd Avenue, turn right onto Taras Shevchenko Place (named for the Ukrainian Shakespeare) to East 7th Street and **McSorley's Old Ale House** 36. Just west of McSorley's is Surma, the Ukrainian Shop, and across the street is the copper-domed **St. George's Ukrainian Catholic Church** 37, whose interior is lightened by impressive stained-glass windows.

Across 3rd Avenue, the massive brownstone **Cooper Union Foundation Building** 38 houses a tuition-free school for artists, architects, and engineers and overlooks Cooper Square, an inhospitable space snubbed even by students. To the south are the offices of the *Village Voice* newspaper (36 Cooper Sq.), and around the corner on East 4th Street, the **Merchant's House Museum** 39.

One block west of Cooper Square is Lafayette Street. The long block between East 4th Street and Astor Place contains on its east side a grand Italian Renaissance–style structure housing the **Joseph Papp Public Theater** 40. Across the street note the imposing marble Corinthian columns fronting **Colonnade Row** 41, a stretch of four crumbling 19th-century Greek revival houses. Walk north to Astor Place and turn left to reach Broadway. Three blocks north lies **Grace Church** 42, which has a striking marble spire. If you continue along the same side of the street as the church, you'll pass a few of the many antiques stores in the area. You can end your walk at the popular **Strand Book Store** 43, the largest secondhand bookstore in the city and an absolutely necessary stop for anyone who loves to read. Clothing shops, shoe shops, and chain stores line Broadway south of Astor Place. Above street level the old warehouses here have mostly been converted into residential lofts.

TIMING Allow about three hours for the walk. If you plan to stop at museums, add one hour, and at least another hour to browse in shops along the way.

What to See

27 **Alamo.** Balanced on a post, the "Cube," as it is locally known, was one of the first abstract sculptures in New York City to be placed in a public space. Created by Bernard Rosenthal in 1967, the massive black cube made of steel was originally part of a temporary citywide exhibit, but it became a permanent installation thanks to a private donor. It's a constant hangout for skateboarders and pierced and studded youth. ✉ *On traffic island at Astor Pl. and Lafayette St., East Village.*

off the beaten path

Alphabet City. Beyond 1st Avenue, the north–south avenues all labeled with letters, not numbers, give this area its nickname. Alphabet City was once a burned-out territory of slums and drug haunts, but some blocks and buildings were gentrified during the height of the East Village art scene in the mid-1980s and again in the late '90s. The reasonably priced restaurants with their bohemian atmosphere on Avenues A, B, and C and the cross streets between them, attract all kinds. A close-knit Puerto Rican community lies east of Avenue A, but amid the Latin shops and groceries Avenue B is now a sort of far-out restaurant row. ✉ *Alphabet City extends approximately from Ave. A to the East River, between 14th and E. Houston Sts., East Village.*

need a break?

Casimir (✉ 103–105 Ave. B, between 6th and 7th Sts., East Village ☎ 212/358–9683) is an authentically cozy bistro where you can stop for a glass of wine and some pâté or heartier French favorites like roasted chicken and steak frites.

26 **Astor Place Subway Station.** At the beginning of the 20th century, almost every Interborough Rapid Transit (IRT) subway entrance resembled the ornate cast-iron replica of a beaux arts kiosk that covers the stairway leading to the uptown No. 6 train. In the station itself, authentically reproduced ceramic tiles of beavers, a reference to the fur trade that contributed to John Jacob Astor's fortune, line the walls. Milton Glaser, a Cooper Union graduate, designed the station's attractive abstract murals. ✉ *On traffic island at E. 8th St. and 4th Ave., East Village.*

41 **Colonnade Row.** Marble Corinthian columns front this grand sweep of four Greek revival mansions (originally nine) constructed in 1833, with stonework by Sing Sing penitentiary prisoners. In their time these once-elegant homes served as residences to millionaires John Jacob Astor and Cornelius Vanderbilt until they moved uptown. Writers Washington Irving, William Makepeace Thackeray, Charles Dickens, and Edmund White all stayed here at one time or another. Today three houses are occupied on street level by restaurants, while the northernmost building houses the Astor Place Theatre. ✉ *428–434 Lafayette St., between Astor Pl. and E. 4th St., East Village.*

38 **Cooper Union Foundation Building.** This impressive Italianate eight-story brownstone structure overlooks humble Cooper Square, where 3rd and 4th avenues merge into the Bowery. A statue of industrialist Peter Cooper, by Augustus Saint-Gaudens, presides here. Cooper founded this college in 1859 to provide a forum for public opinion and free technical education for the working class. Abraham Lincoln, Mark Twain, and Susan B. Anthony have all delivered speeches here. The foundation still offers tuition-free education in architecture, art, and engineering. Cooper Union was the first structure to be supported by steel railroad rails—rolled in Cooper's own plant. The Great Hall gallery is open to the public and presents changing exhibitions during the academic year. ✉ *7 E. 7th St., at 3rd Ave., East Village* ☎ *212/353–4200* *Free* ⏲ *Weekdays 11–7, Sat. noon–5.*

34 **Eldridge Street Synagogue.** This was the first Orthodox synagogue erected by the large number of Eastern European Jews who settled on the Lower East Side in the mid- to late 19th century. The lavish Moorish revival–style building has undergone a major restoration. Inside is an exceptional hand-carved ark of Italian walnut, a sculptured wooden balcony, and enormous brass chandeliers. Once the largest Jewish house of worship, it is now the Congregation K'hal Adath Jeshurun and Anshe Lubz. ✉ *12 Eldridge St., between Canal and Division Sts., Lower East Side* ☎ *212/219–0888* 🌐 *www.eldridgestreet.org* *$5* ⏲ *Tours Tues. and Thurs. 11:30 and 2:30, Sun. 11–4 on the hr.*

42 **Grace Church.** Topped by a finely ornamented octagonal marble spire, this Episcopal church, designed for free by James Renwick Jr., has excellent Pre-Raphaelite stained-glass windows. The building—a mid-19th-century example of an English Gothic revival church—fronts a small green yard facing Broadway. The church has been the site of many society weddings (including that of P. T. Barnum show member Tom Thumb). ✉ *802 Broadway, at E. 10th St., East Village* ☎ *212/254–2000* ⏲ *Weekdays noon–1; Sun. services at 9, 11, and 6.*

(40) **Joseph Papp Public Theater.** In 1854 John Jacob Astor opene… first free public library in this expansive redbrick and brownsto… ian Renaissance–style building. It was renovated in 1967 as the P… Theater to serve as the New York Shakespeare Festival's permanent hom… The theater opened its doors with the popular rock musical *Hair.* Under the leadership of the late Joseph Papp, the Public's five playhouses built a fine reputation for bold and innovative performances; the long-running hit *A Chorus Line* had its first performances here, as have many less commercial plays. Today, director and producer George C. Wolfe heads the Public, which continues to present controversial modern works and imaginative Shakespeare productions. The Public produces the free Shakespeare Festival every summer in Central Park's Delacorte Theater. ✉ *425 Lafayette St., between E. 4th St. and Astor Pl., East Village* ☎ *212/260–2400.*

(35) **Lower East Side Tenement Museum.** Step back in time and into the partially restored 1863 tenement building at 97 Orchard Street, where you can view the apartments of Natalie Gumpertz, a German-Jewish dressmaker (dating from 1878); the Confino family, Sephardic Jews from Kastoria, Turkey, which is now part of Greece (1916); the Rogarshevsky family from Eastern Europe (1918); and Adolph and Rosaria Baldizzi, Catholic immigrants from Sicily (1935). The tour through the Confino family apartment is designed for children, who are greeted by a costumed interpreter playing Victoria Confino. This is America's first urban living-history museum dedicated to the life of immigrants, and reservations are suggested for the guided tour. The museum also leads a walking tour around the Lower East Side. If you wish to forego the tours, you can watch a free historical slide show as well as a video with interviews of Lower East Side residents past and present. The gallery (free) has changing exhibits relating to the neighborhood's history. Tours are limited to 15 people. ✉ *90 Orchard St., at Broome St., Lower East Side* ☎ *212/431–0233,* *www.tenement.org* *Tenement and walking tours, each $9; Confino apartment tour $8* *Museum daily 11–5:30; tenement tours Tues.–Sun., call or visit Web site for schedule; Confino apartment tour weekends hourly noon–3; walking tour Apr.–Dec., weekends 1 and 2:30.*

(36) **McSorley's Old Ale House.** One of several pubs that claim to be New York's oldest, this often crowded saloon attracts many collegiate types enticed by McSorley's own brands of ale. McSorley's asserts that it opened in 1854; it didn't admit women until 1970. The mahogany bar, gas lamps, and potbelly stove all hark back to decades past. Joseph Mitchell immortalized the spot in the *New Yorker.* ✉ *15 E. 7th St., between 2nd and 3rd Aves., East Village* ☎ *212/473–9148.*

(39) **Merchant's House Museum.** Built in 1831–32, this redbrick house, combining federal and Greek revival styles, offers a rare glimpse of family life in the mid-19th century. Retired merchant Seabury Tredwell and his descendants lived here from 1835 right up until it became a museum in 1933. The original furnishings and architectural features remain intact; family memorabilia are also on display. The parlors have 13-ft ceilings with intricate plasterwork, freestanding Ionic columns, a mahogany pocket-door screen, and black-marble fireplaces. Self-guided tour brochures are always available, and guided tours are given on weekends. ✉ *29 E. 4th St., between the Bowery and Lafayette, East Village* ☎ *212/777–1089* *$5* *Thurs.–Mon. 1–5.*

(32) **Ottendorfer Branch of the New York Public Library.** Eager to improve the lives of fellow German immigrants then heavily populating the East Village, philanthropists Oswald and Anna Ottendorfer commissioned the construction of this library and adjacent German Dispensary (now

sant Polyclinic), which was designed by William Schickel in 1884. brary began as the German-language branch of the Free Circu- Library (hence the words FREIE BIBLIOTHEK UND LESEHALLE on its) and eventually became part of the city's public library system. ispensary is among the first buildings in New York to display or- tal terra-cotta, including busts of noted figures in medicine on the exterior. This landmark building, a designation that includes parts of its interior, was completely renovated in 2000. ✉ *135 2nd Ave., between St. Marks Pl. and E. 9th St., East Village* ☎ *212/674–0947.*

37 **St. George's Ukrainian Catholic Church.** Quite the standout on the block with its copper dome and three brightly colored religious murals on its facade, this ostentatious modern church serves as a central meeting place for the local Ukrainian community. Built in 1977, it took the place of the more modest Greek revival–style St. George's Ruthenian Church. An annual Ukrainian folk festival is held here in the spring. ✉ *30 E. 7th St., between 2nd and 3rd Aves., East Village* ☎ *212/674–1615* ⏲ *Daily 6–9.*

29 **St. Mark's-in-the-Bowery Church.** This charming 1799 fieldstone country church stands its ground against the monotonous city block system. The area was once Dutch governor Peter Stuyvesant's *bouwerie,* or farm, and the church occupies the former site of his family chapel. St. Mark's is the city's oldest continually used Christian church site, and both Stuyvesant and Commodore Perry are buried here. The Greek revival steeple and cast-iron front porch were later additions to the church; its interior had to be completely restored after a disastrous fire in 1978. Over the years St. Mark's has hosted progressive events, mostly in the arts. In the 1920s a pastor injected the Episcopal ritual with Native American chants, Greek folk dancing, and Eastern mantras. William Carlos Williams, Amy Lowell, and Carl Sandburg once read here, and Isadora Duncan, Harry Houdini, and Merce Cunningham also performed here. Today dancers, poets, and theater artists perform in the main sanctuary, where pews have been removed to accommodate them. ✉ *131 E. 10th St., at 2nd Ave., East Village* ☎ *212/674–6377.*

need a break?

Bright and bustling 24-hour **Veselka** (✉ 144 2nd Ave., at 9th St., East Village ☎ 212/228–9682), a longtime East Village hangout, serves muffins, Italian coffee, egg creams, and Ben & Jerry's ice cream alongside good, traditional Ukrainian fare such as borscht, pierogies, and veal goulash.

28 **St. Marks Place.** The longtime hub of the hip East Village, St. Marks Place is the name given to East 8th Street, between 3rd Avenue and Avenue A. During the 1950s beatniks such as Allen Ginsberg and Jack Kerouac lived and wrote in the area; the 1960s brought Bill Graham's Fillmore East concerts, the Electric Circus, and hallucinogenic drugs. The black-clad, pink-haired, or shaved-head punks followed, and the imaginatively pierced, heavily made-up goths have replaced them. Ethnic restaurants, jewelry stalls, and stores selling posters, incense, and curious clothing line up between 2nd and 3rd avenues. Despite NYU dorms in the vicinity, even the ubiquitous Gap chain couldn't take root on this raggedy and idiosyncratic street.

At 80 St. Marks Place, near 1st Avenue, is the Pearl Theatre Company, which performs classic plays from around the world. The handprints, footprints, and autographs of such past screen luminaries as Joan Crawford, Ruby Keeler, Joan Blondell, and Myrna Loy are embedded in the sidewalk. At 96–98 St. Marks Place (between 1st Avenue and Avenue

A) stands the building that was photographed for the cover of Led Zeppelin's *Physical Graffiti* album. The cafés between 2nd Avenue and Avenue A attract customers late into the night.

43 **Strand Book Store.** Serious book lovers the world over make pilgrimages to this secondhand book emporium with a stock of some 2 million volumes, including thousands of collector's items (the store's slogan is "8 Miles of Books"). Opened in 1929 by Ben Bass, the Strand was originally on 4th Avenue's Book Row until it moved in 1956 to its present location on Broadway (a second store is near South Street Seaport). Barely touched review copies of new books sell for 50% off. A separate rare-book room is on the third floor at 826 Broadway, to the immediate north of the main store. ✉ *828 Broadway, at E. 12th St., East Village* ☎ *212/473–1452* ⏲ *Main store Mon.–Sat. 9:30–10:30, Sun. 11–10:30; rare books Mon.–Sat. 9:30–6:20, Sun. 11–6.*

★ 30 **Stuyvesant Street.** This diagonal slicing through the block bounded by 2nd and 3rd avenues and East 9th and 10th streets is unique in Manhattan: it's the oldest street laid out precisely along an east–west axis. (This grid never caught on, and instead a street grid following the island's geographic orientation was adopted.) Among the handsome red-brick row houses are the federal-style **Stuyvesant-Fish House** (✉ 21 Stuyvesant St., East Village), which was built in 1804 as a wedding gift for a great-great-granddaughter of the Dutch governor Peter Stuyvesant, and **Renwick Triangle,** an attractive group of carefully restored one- and two-story brick and brownstone residences originally constructed in 1861.

Surma, the Ukrainian Shop. The exotic stock at this charming little store includes books, magazines, and greeting cards, as well as musical instruments, painted eggs, and an exhaustive collection of peasant blouses. ✉ *11 E. 7th St., between 2nd and 3rd Aves., East Village* ☎ *212/477–0729* ⏲ *Weekdays 11–6, Sat. 11–4; closed Mon. in summer.*

33 **Tompkins Square Park.** This leafy spot amid the East Village's crowded tenements is a release valve. The square takes its name from four-time governor Daniel Tompkins, an avid abolitionist and vice president under James Monroe, who once owned this land from 2nd Avenue to the East River. Its history is long and violent: the 1874 Tompkins Square Riot involved some 7,000 unhappy laborers and 1,600 police. In 1988 police followed mayor David Dinkins's orders to clear the park of the many homeless who had set up makeshift homes here, and homeless rights and antigentrification activists fought back with sticks and bottles. The park was renovated and reopened in 1992 with a midnight curfew, still in effect today. The park fills up with locals on mild days year-round, partaking in minipicnics; drum circles; the playground; and, for dog owners, a large dog run. East of the park at 151 Avenue B, near East 9th Street, stands an 1849 four-story white-painted brownstone, where renowned jazz musician Charlie Parker lived from 1950 to 1954. The Charlie Parker Jazz festival packs the park for one day in late August. ✉ *Bordered by Aves. A and B and E. 7th and E. 10th Sts., East Village.*

need a break?

At the northwest corner of the park is **Life Cafe** (✉ 343 E. 10th St., at Ave. B, East Village ☎ 212/477–8791), a hangout featured in the hit Broadway musical *Rent.* **De Robertis Pasticceria** (✉ 176 1st Ave., between E. 10th and E. 11th Sts., East Village ☎ 212/674–7137) serves exceptional cheesecake and cappuccinos in its original 1904 setting, complete with glistening mosaic tiles. Opened in 1894, **Veniero's Pasticceria** (✉ 342 E. 11th St., between 1st and 2nd Aves., East Village ☎ 212/674–7264) has rows and rows of fresh cannoli, fruit tarts, cookies, and other desserts in glass cases. **Tarallucci e Vino**

(✉ 163 1st Ave., at E. 10th St., East Village ☎ 212/388–1190) serves a perfect latte, deliciously addictive doughnuts, and great people-watching.

31 **Ukrainian Museum.** Ceramics, jewelry, hundreds of brilliantly colored Easter eggs, and an extensive collection of Ukrainian costumes and textiles are the highlights of this small collection, nurtured by Ukrainian Americans in exile throughout the years of Soviet domination. At press time, the museum was planning a move to new quarters at 222 East 6th Street in summer 2003, so call ahead. ✉ *203 2nd Ave., between E. 12th and E. 13th Sts., East Village* ☎ *212/228–0110* *$3* *Wed.–Sun. 1–5.*

MURRAY HILL, FLATIRON DISTRICT & GRAMERCY

As the city grew progressively north throughout the 19th century, one neighborhood after another had its fashionable heyday, only to fade from glory. But three neighborhoods, east of 6th Avenue roughly between 14th and 40th streets, have preserved much of their historic charm: Murray Hill's brownstone mansions and town houses; the Flatiron District's classic turn-of-the-20th-century skyscrapers around Madison Square; and Gramercy's London-like leafy square. The Flatiron District, which is bordered by Union Square to the south, is now anchored by retailers, and with Gramercy, shares many boutique hotels and perhaps some of the city's hottest restaurants. The Flatiron District is also an important center of the city's new-media technology companies and dot-coms—before the bubble burst on the dot-com frenzy, the area was often referred to in the press as "Silicon Alley." The only truly enduring must-see along this route is the Empire State Building, the symbol of an older but ever-impressive technology.

Numbers in the text correspond to numbers in the margin and on the Murray Hill, Flatiron District, and Gramercy map.

a good walk

Begin in Murray Hill at the corner of East 36th Street and Madison Avenue, where financier J. P. Morgan built his private **Morgan Library** 1 next to his residence. Today the collection is open to the public and includes old-master drawings, medieval manuscripts, illuminated books, and original music scores. Continuing down Madison Avenue, at East 35th Street you'll pass the **Church of the Incarnation** 2, a brownstone version of a Gothic chapel. Across the street and taking up the entire next block is the landmark **B. Altman Building/New York Public Library–Science, Industry, and Business Library (SIBL)** 3, home of the famous department store from 1906 to 1989 and now the site of the New York Public Library's most high-tech research center. The main entrance is on 5th Avenue.

Head for the corner of 5th Avenue and 34th Street where you can't miss the **Empire State Building** 4, one of the world's most recognizable silhouettes. Walk a block west on 34th Street to 6th Avenue: before you is Herald Square, and across the street is the venerable **Macy's** 5 department store. Amidst the hubbub the square tries to provide a bit of calm with trees, flowers, and movable, Paris-style tables and chairs. A spacious pedestrian thoroughfare has been built around it, along with an attractive period newsstand and—talk about a miracle on 34th Street—an automated public bathroom. The monument that features Minerva and a large bell—the two bronze men strike the bell on the hour—stood atop the *New York Herald* building, on the north end of the square, from 1895 to 1921. Walk south down Broadway, passing Herald

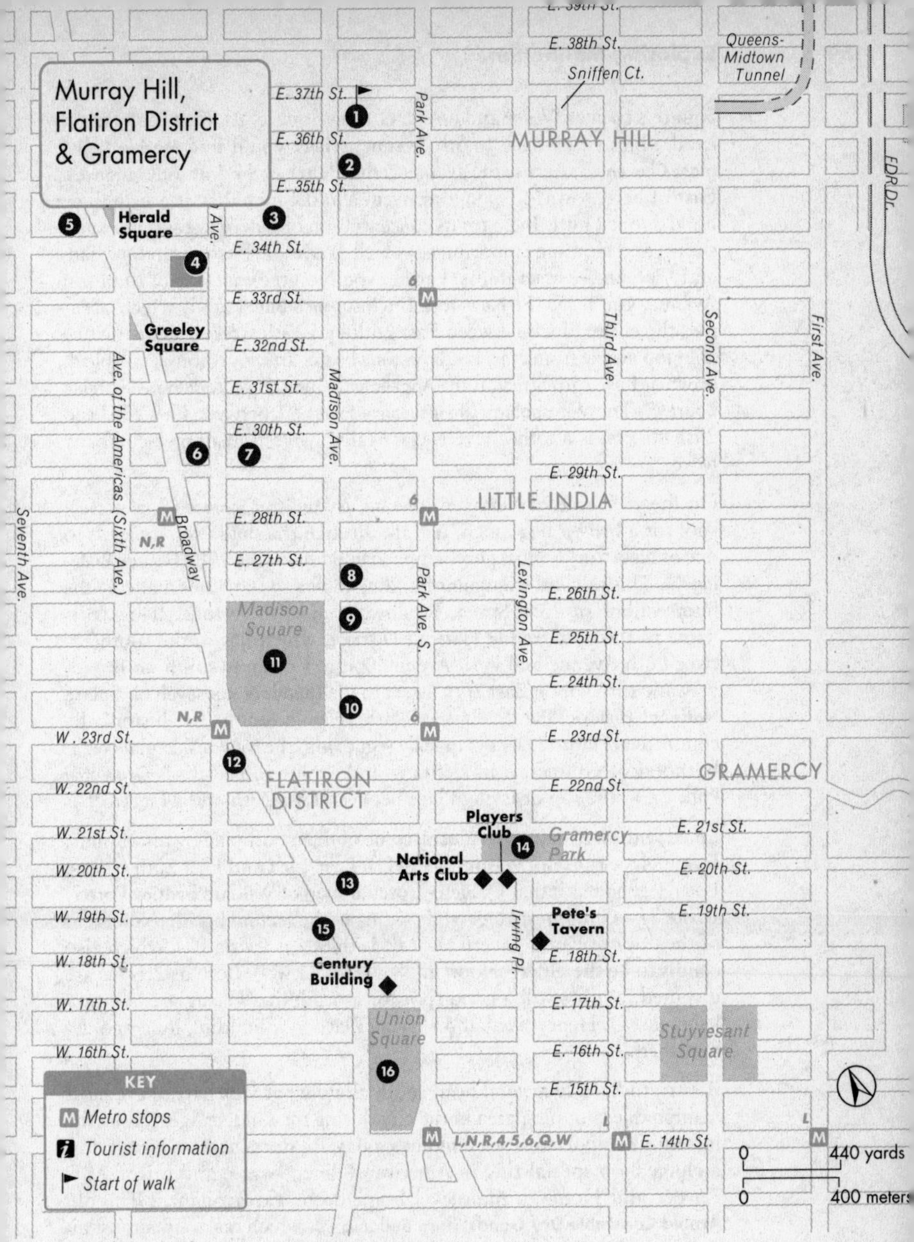

Appellate Division, New York State Supreme Court **9**

Arnold Constable Dry Goods Store Building **15**

B. Altman Building/ New York Public Library Science, Industry, and Business Library (SIBL) **3**

Church of the Incarnation **2**

Church of the Transfiguration. **7**

Empire State Building. **4**

Flatiron Building **12**

Gramercy Park **14**

Macy's **5**

Madison Square **11**

Marble Collegiate Church. **6**

Metropolitan Life Insurance Tower **10**

Morgan Library **1**

New York Life Insurance Building. **8**

Theodore Roosevelt Birthplace National Historic Site **13**

Union Square **16**

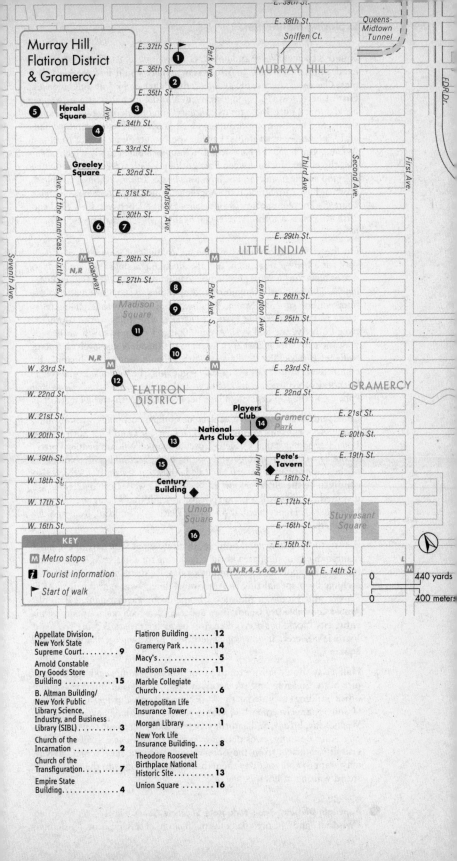

Square's twin at West 32nd Street, Greeley Square. At West 29th Street, head a block east back to 5th Avenue, where you'll find **Marble Collegiate Church** 6. Across the avenue is the **Church of the Transfiguration** 7. East of here, toward Lexington Avenue in the high 20s, is a neighborhood dubbed Little India for its concentration of Indian restaurants, spice shops, and clothing emporiums, as well as Middle Eastern, Indonesian, and Vietnamese restaurants. Farther south on the east side of Madison Avenue, you'll see the **New York Life Insurance Building** 8, which occupies the entire block between East 26th and 27th streets, its distinctive gold top visible from afar. The limestone beaux arts courthouse, one block down at East 25th Street, is the **Appellate Division, New York State Supreme Court** 9. The **Metropolitan Life Insurance Tower** 10, between East 23rd and 24th streets, is another lovely, classically inspired insurance-company tower.

On the west side of Madison Avenue, is **Madison Square** 11, a perfect spot for a brown-bag lunch. A walk through the shady square leads to one of New York's most photographed buildings—the 1902 **Flatiron Building** 12. This tall and triangular building tapers to the point made by the intersections of 23rd Street, Broadway, and 5th Avenue. It lends its name to the now trendy Flatiron District, which lies to the south between 6th Avenue and Park Avenue South. Continue south on Broadway and turn left on East 20th Street to the **Theodore Roosevelt Birthplace National Historic Site** 13. East of Park Avenue South, the historically commercial Flatiron District quickly segues into the tony residential neighborhood of Gramercy. Its defining and exclusive feature is **Gramercy Park** 14, at the top of Irving Place between East 20th and 21st streets.

Lined with charming row houses, some of them occupied by restaurants, Irving Place runs north–south between East 14th and East 20th streets. Local legend has it that O. Henry (pseudonym of William Sydney Porter) wrote *The Gift of the Magi* while sitting in the second booth to the right of the door at Pete's Tavern (129 E. 18th St., at Irving Pl.), which also claims to be the oldest saloon in New York (1864). Both assertions are disputed, but it's still a good spot for a drink in a Gaslight Era establishment. O. Henry lived at 55 Irving Place in a building long ago demolished.

Return to Broadway, and head south along what was part of *the* most fashionable shopping area in the city during the Gilded Age. Filling the incredible emporium-style buildings today are stores such as Fishs Eddy, a china shop specializing in American "diner"-ware, and pricey ABC Carpet and Home, a multilevel home-decor extravaganza. The old **Arnold Constable Dry Goods Store Building** 15, which takes up almost an entire city block, has been taken over by such retailers as Nine West and Victoria's Secret. If you continue down Broadway, it leads to **Union Square** 16.

TIMING Half a day should suffice for this tour. Allow 1½ hours each for the Empire State Building and the Morgan Library. Keep in mind that some office buildings included in the walk are open only during the week. The Union Square Greenmarket, a must-visit, is open all day every Monday, Wednesday, Friday, and Saturday. Before traipsing to the top of the Empire State Building, consider the weather and how it is likely to affect visibility. Sunsets from the observation deck are spectacular, so you may want to end your day there (but be sure to factor in the time you'll spend waiting in line).

What to See

9 **Appellate Division, New York State Supreme Court.** Figures representing "Wisdom" and "Justice" flank the main portal of this imposing Corinthian

courthouse, built in 1900, on the east side of Madison Square. Statues of great lawmakers of the past line the roof balustrade, including Moses, Justinian, and Confucius; a statue of Muhammad was removed in the 1950s at the request of local Islamic groups, as Islamic law forbids the representation of humans in sculpture or painting. Inside are exhibitions of New York historical ephemera, murals, and furniture by the Herter Brothers. ✉ *27 Madison Ave., entrance on E. 25th St., Flatiron District* ☎ *212/340–0400* ⏲ *Weekdays 9–5.*

15 **Arnold Constable Dry Goods Store Building.** Imagine yourself riding in a shining black carriage drawn by a set of four trotters, and you'll travel back in time to when this section of Broadway was the most fashionable strip of stores in New York. Arnold Constable was the Bloomingdale's of its era. Built in 1869–77 and designed by architect Griffith Thomas, this elegant five-story dry-goods building spans East 19th Street with entrances on both Broadway and 5th Avenue. A double-story mansard roof tops it, white marble covers the Broadway side, and a cast-iron facade hovers over 5th Avenue. Reoccupied by several clothing stores on the street level, this historic building again crackles with business. ✉ *881–887 Broadway, at E. 19th St., Flatiron District.*

3 **B. Altman Building/New York Public Library–Science, Industry, and Business Library (SIBL).** In 1906, department store magnate Benjamin Altman gambled that the fashionable shoppers who patronized his store at 6th Avenue and West 18th Street would follow him uptown to large new quarters on 5th Avenue and 34th Street, then a strictly residential street. They indeed came, and other stores followed, but then moved uptown again, to the 50s, leaving this trailblazer behind. In 1996, seven years after the bankruptcy and dismantling of the B. Altman chain, the New York Public Library transferred all scientific, technology, and business materials from its main 42nd Street building to a new state-of-the-art facility here, the **Science, Industry, and Business Library (SIBL).** This sleek and graceful high-tech library heeds Ruskin's words, "Industry without art is brutality," one of many quotations along the undulant upper wall inside the Madison Avenue lobby. Further demonstrating this philosophy is the artwork within Healy Hall, the 33-ft-high atrium that unites the two floors of SIBL. Downstairs a wall of TVs tuned to business-news stations and electronic ticker tapes beam information and instructions to patrons. Hundreds of computers wired to the Internet and research databases are the library's hottest tickets. Take a free half-hour tour Tuesday and Thursday at 2. Tours also take place each second and fourth Saturday of the month at 2. ✉ *188 Madison Ave., at E. 34th St., Murray Hill* ☎ *212/592–7000* 🌐 *www.nypl.org/research/sibl* ⏲ *Tues.–Thurs. 10–8, Fri.–Sat. 10–6.*

2 **Church of the Incarnation.** The 1864 Episcopal church where Delanos and Morgans once worshiped has a wealth of English- and American-designed stained glass. The north aisle's 23rd Psalm Window is by the Tiffany Glass works; the south aisle's two Angel windows, dedicated to infants, are by the William Morris Company of London. ✉ *209 Madison Ave., at E. 35th St., Murray Hill* ☎ *212/689–6350* 🌐 *www.churchoftheincarnation.org* ⏲ *Mass Wed. 12:15 and 6:30, Fri. 12:15; open Sun. after 11 AM mass.*

7 **Church of the Transfiguration.** Known as the Little Church Around the Corner, this Gothic revival church complex (1849–61) is set back in a shrub-filled New York version of an old English churchyard. It won its memorable nickname in 1870 when other area churches refused to bury actor George Holland, a colleague of well-known thespian Joseph Jefferson. Jefferson was directed to the "little church around the corner" to accomplish the burial, and the Episcopal institution has welcomed

literary and theater types ever since. The south transept's stained-glass window, by John LaFarge, depicts 19th-century superstar actor Edwin Booth as Hamlet, his most famous role. ✉ *1 E. 29th St., between 5th and Madison Aves., Murray Hill* ☎ *212/684–6770* 🌐 *www.littlechurch.org* ⏲ *Mon.–Sat. 8–6, Sun. after 11 AM mass.*

4 Fodor's Choice ★ **Empire State Building.** It may no longer be the world's tallest building (it currently ranks seventh), but it's certainly one of the best-known skyscrapers, its pencil-slim silhouette a symbol for New York City and, perhaps, the 20th century. The skyscraper craze of the 1920s generated a slew of buildings in Manhattan, each outstretching the next in the quest to claim the title of world's tallest building. Developer John Jacob Raskob was no different, asking architect William Lamb, "Bill, how high can you make it so it won't fall down?" The art deco behemoth opened on May 1, 1931, after a mere 13 months of construction; the framework rose at a rate of 4½ stories per week, making the Empire State Building the fastest-rising major skyscraper ever built. Many floors were left completely unfinished, however, so tenants could have them custom-designed. But the Great Depression delayed occupancy, and most of the building remained unfinished and empty, causing critics to deem it the "Empty State Building." The crowning spire was originally designed to dock dirigibles—another example of the period's soaring ambition—but after two failed attempts, the idea was set aside. In 1951 a TV transmittal tower was added to the top, raising the total height to 1,472 ft. Ever since the 1976 American bicentennial celebration, the top 30 stories have been spotlighted at night with colors honoring dozens of different holidays and events, including days that honor the various nationalities that make up the city's population. Some of the more recognizable lights include Martin Luther King Jr. Day (red, black, and green); Valentine's Day (all red); the Fourth of July and national holidays (red, white, and blue); Columbus Day (red, white, and green); Hanukkah (blue, white, and blue); and the Christmas season (red and green). For a year after September 11, 2001, the building stood lighted in red, white, and blue. The building has appeared in close to 200 movies, among them 1933's unforgettable *King Kong;* 1957's *An Affair to Remember,* in which Cary Grant waited impatiently at the top for his rendezvous with Deborah Kerr; and 1993's *Sleepless in Seattle,* in which Tom Hanks met Meg Ryan for the first time.

Today about 20,000 people work in the Empire State Building, and more than 3.3 million people visit its observation deck annually. Tickets are sold on the concourse level and on the building's Web site (a good way to avoid the considerable line); on your way up admire the illuminated panels depicting the Seven Wonders of the World—with the Empire State Building brazenly appended as number eight—in the three-story-high marble lobby. The 86th-floor observatory (1,050 ft high) is open to the air (expect heavy winds) and spans the building's circumference; on clear days you can see up to 80 mi. It's worth timing your visit for early or late in the day (morning is the least crowded time), when the sun is low on the horizon and the shadows are deep across the city. But at night the city's lights are dazzling. The French architect Le Corbusier said, "It is a Milky Way come down to earth." Really, both views are a must; one strategy is to go up just before dusk and witness both, as day dims to night. ✉ *350 5th Ave., at E. 34th St., Murray Hill* ☎ *212/736–3100 or 877/692–8439* 🌐 *www.esbnyc.com* 🎟 *$10* ⏲ *Daily 9 AM–midnight; last elevator up leaves at 11:15 PM.*

A major tourist attraction within the Empire State Building is the second-floor **New York Skyride.** A Comedy Central video presentation on the virtues of New York precedes a rough-and-tumble motion-simulator ride above and around some of the city's top attractions, which are projected on a two-story-tall screen. Since it's part helicopter video and part roller-coaster ride, children love it. The ride is not recommended for anyone who has trouble with motion sickness, and pregnant women are not admitted. ☎ *212/279–9777 or 888/759–7433* 🌐 *www.skyride.com* 💵 *$13.50; $19 for Skyride and Observatory* ⏲ *Daily 10–10.*

⓬ **Flatiron Building.** When completed in 1902, the Fuller Building, as it was originally known, caused a sensation. Architect Daniel Burnham made ingenious use of the triangular wedge of land and employed a revolutionary steel frame, which allowed for its 20-story, 286-ft height. Covered with a limestone and terra-cotta skin in the Italian Renaissance style, the ship's bow–like structure, appearing to sail intrepidly up the avenue, was the most popular subject of picture postcards at the turn of the 20th century. Winds invariably swooped down at its 23rd Street tip, billowing up the skirts of women pedestrians on 23rd Street, and local traffic cops had to shoo away male gawkers—coining the phrase "23 skiddoo." ✉ *175 5th Ave., bordered by E. 22nd and E. 23rd Sts., 5th Ave., and Broadway, Flatiron District.*

⓮ **Gramercy Park.** In 1831 Samuel B. Ruggles, an intelligent young real estate developer (he graduated from Yale at age 14), bought and drained a tract of what was largely swamp and created a charming park inspired by London's residential squares. Hoping that exclusivity would create demand, access to the park was limited only to those who would buy the surrounding lots. Sixty-six of the city's fashionable elite did just that, and no less than golden keys were provided for them to unlock the park's cast-iron gate. Although no longer golden, keys are still given only to residents; it is the city's only private park. Passersby can enjoy the carefully maintained landscaping through the 8-ft-high fence.

Lexington Avenue ends here, so vehicles rarely venture near and the block is quiet. Original 19th-century row houses in Greek revival, Italianate, Gothic revival, and Victorian Gothic styles surround the park's south and west sides. In the park stands a statue of actor Edwin Booth playing Hamlet; Booth lived at No. 16, which he purchased in 1888 to serve as the **Players Club** (✉ 16 Gramercy Park S, Gramercy), an association to elevate the then-low status of actors. Stanford White, the architect who renovated the club, was a member, as were many other nonactors. Other members over the years have included Mark Twain (who was once expelled, in error, for nonpayment of dues), John and Lionel Barrymore, Irving Berlin, Winston Churchill, Sir Laurence Olivier, Frank Sinatra, Walter Cronkite, Helen Hayes, and Richard Gere. The Players Club library holds one of the largest theater collections in America.

The **National Arts Club** (✉ 15 Gramercy Park S, Gramercy) was once the home of Samuel Tilden, a governor of New York and the 1876 Democratic presidential candidate. Calvert Vaux, codesigner of Central Park, remodeled this building in 1884, conjoining two houses and creating a 40-room mansion. Among its Victorian Gothic decorations are medallions outside portraying Goethe, Dante, Milton, and Benjamin Franklin. The club, founded in 1898 to bring together "art lovers and art workers," moved into the mansion in 1906. Early members included Woodrow Wilson and Theodore Roosevelt; Ethan Hawke and Martin Scorsese are more recent members. Although it is a private club (it has about 2,000 members), a number of rooms, which exhibit works from member artists, are open to the public—a great way to get a look around this exclusive property.

The austere gray-brown Friends Meeting House at 28 Gramercy Park South (1859) became the **Brotherhood Synagogue** in 1974, and a narrow plaza just east of the synagogue contains a Holocaust memorial. No. **19 Gramercy Park South** (1845) was the home in the 1880s of society doyenne Mrs. Stuyvesant Fish, a fearless iconoclast who shocked Mrs. Astor and Mrs. Vanderbilt when she reduced the time of formal dinner parties from several hours to 50 minutes, thus ushering in the modern social era. ✉ *Lexington Ave. between E. 20th and E. 21st Sts., Gramercy.*

❺ **Macy's.** On any given day about 30,000 people walk through the doors of the city's most famous (and the "World's Largest," according to its own boast) department store. Covering a full city block from 6th to 7th avenues between West 34th and 35th streets, with 11 floors and more than 2 million square ft of selling space, Macy's is a living retail legend. In 1902, half a century after whaling sailor Rowland Hussey Macy established a fancy dry-goods store at West 14th Street and 6th Avenue, the store moved to its current Herald Square site. Livestock was sold out of the main floor, but, equipped with the world's first modern escalators, Macy's introduced a new consumer phenomenon: vertical shopping. You can still ride these wooden steps today. Another promotional innovation was the Macy's Thanksgiving Day Parade, which stepped off in 1924. During its first decade, the large helium balloons for which the parade is known nationwide were released into the air and recovered by the public for prizes. Macy's continued to stay ahead of the curve in the 1940s and 1950s, when it sold prefabricated houses, airplanes, and automobiles out of the ninth floor, and when it popularized Scrabble after a Macy's buyer discovered the Brooklyn invention. The store was also the first retailer to promote such products as the Idaho baked potato and colored bath towels. ✉ *W. 34th St. between 6th and 7th Aves., Murray Hill* ☎ *212/695–4400* 🌐 *www.macys.com* ⏲ *Mon.–Sat. 10–8:30, Sun. 11–7; extended hrs Christmas season and sale days.*

⓫ **Madison Square.** With a picturesque view of some of the city's oldest and most charming skyscrapers (the Flatiron Building, Met Life Insurance Tower, and New York Life Insurance Building), this tree-filled 7-acre park mainly attracts dog owners and office workers, but it's a fine spot for people- or squirrel-watching, relaxing, and picnicking, too. Baseball was invented across the Hudson in Hoboken, New Jersey, but the city's first baseball games were played here circa 1845. On the north end an imposing 1881 statue by Augustus Saint-Gaudens memorializes Civil War naval hero Admiral Farragut. An 1876 statue of Secretary of State William Henry Seward (the Seward of the phrase "Seward's folly"—as Alaska was originally known) sits in the park's southwest corner, though it's rumored the sculptor placed a reproduction of the statesman's head on a likeness of Abraham Lincoln's body. ✉ *E. 23rd to E. 26th Sts. between 5th and Madison Aves., Flatiron District.*

❻ **Marble Collegiate Church.** Built in 1854 for the Reformed Protestant Dutch Congregation first organized in 1628 by Peter Minuit, the canny Dutchman who bought Manhattan from the Native Americans for the equivalent of $24, this impressive Romanesque revival church takes its name from the Tuckahoe marble that covers it. Dr. Norman Vincent Peale (*The Power of Positive Thinking*) was pastor here from 1932 to 1984. ✉ *1 W. 29th St., at 5th Ave., Murray Hill* ☎ *212/686–2770* 🌐 *www.marblechurch.org* ⏲ *Daily 10–noon and 2–4; Mass Sun. 11:15.*

❿ **Metropolitan Life Insurance Tower.** When it was added in 1909, the 700-ft tower, which re-creates the campanile of St. Mark's in Venice, made this 1893 building the world's tallest. Its clock's four dia stories high, and their minute hands weigh half a ton each; the quarter hour. A skywalk over East 24th Street links it to North Building. Its art deco loggias have attracted many film c the building has appeared in such films as *After Hours, Radio D* and *The Fisher King.* ✉ *1 Madison Ave., between E. 23rd and E. 24th Sts., Flatiron District.*

❶ **Morgan Library.** One of New York's most patrician museums, the Morgan is a world-class treasury of medieval and Renaissance illuminated manuscripts, old-master drawings and prints, rare books, and autographed literary and musical manuscripts. Many of the crowning achievements produced on paper, from the Middle Ages to the 20th century, are here: letters penned by John Keats and Thomas Jefferson; a summary of the theory of relativity in Einstein's own elegant handwriting; three Gutenberg Bibles; drawings by Dürer, da Vinci, Rubens, Blake, and Rembrandt; the only known manuscript fragment of Milton's *Paradise Lost;* Thoreau's journals; and original manuscripts and letters by Charlotte Brontë, Jane Austen, Thomas Pynchon, and many others. Originally built for the collections of Wall Street baron J. Pierpont (J. P.) Morgan (1837–1913), the museum has at its core a Renaissance-style palazzo, completed in 1906 by McKim, Mead & White, which houses the opulent period rooms of Morgan's original library. The **East Room** (the main library) has dizzying tiers of handsomely bound rare books, letters, and illuminated manuscripts. The **West Room,** Morgan's personal study, contains a remarkable selection of mostly Italian Renaissance furniture, paintings, and other marvels within its red-damask-lined walls.

Changing exhibitions, drawn from the permanent collection, are often highly distinguished. The library shop is within an 1852 Italianate brownstone, once the home of Morgan's son, J. P. "Jack" Morgan Jr., which is connected to the rest of the library by a graceful glass-roof garden court where lunch and afternoon tea are served. Outside on East 36th Street, the sphinx in the right-hand sculptured panel of the original library's facade was rumored to wear the face of architect Charles McKim. Exhibition tours are conducted free with admission Tuesday–Friday at noon. The library is closed for a redesign by architect Renzo Piano. It will reopen in 2006. ✉ *29 E. 36th St., at Madison Ave., Murray Hill* ☎ *212/685–0610* 🌐 *www.morganlibrary.org* 🎫 *$8 suggested donation* 🕒 *Tues.–Thurs. 10:30–5, Fri. 10:30–8, Sat. 10:30–6, Sun. noon–6.*

❽ **New York Life Insurance Building.** Cass Gilbert, better known for the Woolworth Building, capped this 1928 building with a gilded pyramid that is stunning when lighted at night. The soaring lobby's coffered ceilings and ornate bronze doors are equally grand. P. T. Barnum's Hippodrome (1890–1925) formerly occupied this site, and after that Madison Square Garden, designed by architect and playboy Stanford White. White was shot in the Garden's roof garden by Harry K. Thaw, a partner in White's firm and the jealous husband of actress Evelyn Nesbit, with whom White was purportedly having an affair—an episode more or less accurately depicted in E. L. Doctorow's book *Ragtime.* ✉ *51 Madison Ave., between E. 26th and E. 27th Sts., Flatiron District.*

off the beaten path

Sniffen Court. Just two blocks from the Morgan Library, the 10 Romanesque revival former brick carriage houses that line this easily overlooked cul-de-sac are equal parts Old London and New Orleans. Peer through the locked gate to admire them. ✉ *150–158 E. 36th St., between Lexington and 3rd Aves., Murray Hill.*

sevelt Birthplace National Historic Site. The 26th U.S. presi-
ly one from New York City—was born on this site in
iginal 1848 brownstone was demolished in 1916, but this
l replica, built in 1923, is a near-perfect reconstruction of
ere Teddy lived until he was 15 years old. Administered
nal Park Service, the house has a fascinating collection of
five Victorian period rooms. Saturday afternoon chamber
ts take place each fall, winter, and spring. ✉ *28 E. 20th St., between Broadway and Park Ave. S, Flatiron District* ☎ *212/260–1616* 🌐 *www.nps.gov/thrb* 🎫 *$3* ⏲ *Daily 9–5; guided tours 10–4.*

need a break?

A vegetarian restaurant in the style of a Japanese teahouse, **Zen Palate** (✉ 34 E. Union Sq., at E. 16th St., Flatiron District ☎ 212/614–9291) serves up an innovative culinary experience at moderate prices. Table service downstairs is fast paced; upstairs is a more formal dining room. The restaurant does not serve alcohol, but you can bring your own. On cool days warm up with marshmallowy hot chocolate at **The City Bakery** (✉ 3 W. 18 St., between 5th Ave. and Broadway, Flatiron District ☎ 212/366–1414).

16 **Union Square.** A park, meeting place, outdoor market, and home to some of the city's trendiest restaurants, this pocket of green space is the focus of a bustling residential and shopping neighborhood. The name "Union" originally signified that two main roads—Broadway and 4th Avenue—crossed here, but it took on a different meaning in the late 19th and early 20th centuries, when the square became a rallying spot for labor protests and mass demonstrations; many unions, as well as fringe political parties, moved their headquarters nearby. The park's community role was never more apparent than after the terrorist attacks on September 11, 2001, when the park became the city's primary gathering point for memorial services. Thousands of people nightly lighted candles, created posters and signs, and otherwise gathered for consolation. The statue of George Washington (1856, Henry Kirke Brown) at the north end of the park serenely overlooked the ceremonies. Other statues in the park include Abraham Lincoln (1866, Henry Kirke Brown) and the Marquis de Lafayette (1875, Frederic Auguste Bartholdi, who also sculpted the Statue of Liberty). A statue of Gandhi (1986, Kantilal B. Patel), usually wreathed with flowers, is now surrounded by its own garden in the southwest corner of the park.

Union Square is at its best on Monday, Wednesday, Friday, and Saturday (8–6), when the largest of the city's 28 **green markets** brings farmers and food purveyors from all over the Northeast. Crowds browse among the stands of fresh produce, flowers, plants, homemade bakery goods, cheeses, cider, New York State wines, and fish and meat. On the north end, the park's 1932 **Pavilion** is flanked by playgrounds and **Luna Park** (☎ 212/475–8464), an open-air restaurant open from mid-May through October.

New York University dormitories, movie theaters, and retail superstores occupy the handsome, restored 19th-century commercial buildings that surround the park. The run of diverse and imaginative architectural styles on the building at 33 Union Square West (the former name, the **Decker Building,** which is visible above the second floor's incised decoration) is, indeed, "fabulous"—it was the home of Andy Warhol's second Factory studio. The redbrick and white-stone **Century Building** (✉ 33 E. 17th St., Flatiron District), built in 1881, on the square's north side, is now a Barnes & Noble bookstore, which has preserved the building's original cast-iron columns and other architectural details. The building at 17th Street and Union Square East, now housing the New York Film Academy and the Union Square Theatre, was the final home of **Tammany Hall.** This organization, famous in its day as a fairly corrupt yet effective political machine, moved here just at the height of its power in 1929, but by 1943 it went bankrupt and had to sell the building. A block south on Union Square East is the former U.S. Savings Bank, now the Daryl Roth Theater. The southern block is dominated by an abstract timepiece on the exterior wall of the Virgin Records superstore. Stand under the colossal magic wand on the hour for a surprise. You have to be quite clever to read the digital clock made up of 15 changing numbers. A clue: at midnight, all the digits display "0." ✉ *E. 14th to E. 17th Sts. between Broadway and Park Ave. S, Flatiron District.*

CHELSEA

Like the London district of the same name, New York's Chelsea has preserved its villagelike personality. Both have their quiet nooks where the 19th century seems to live on; both have been havens for artists, writers, and bohemians—New York's notables include Louise Bourgeois and Susan Sontag. Until the 1830s one family's country estate occupied the area from West 19th to 28th streets and from 8th Avenue west. Clement Clarke Moore, the owner, realized the city was moving north and decided to divide his land into lots. With an instinctive gift for urban planning, he dictated a pattern of development that ensured street after street of graceful row houses. The New York neighborhood was named not after Chelsea itself but after London's Chelsea Royal Hospital, an old soldiers' home where Moore's grandfather once convalesced. A clergyman and classics professor, Moore is best known for his 1822 poem "A Visit from St. Nicholas"—"'Twas the night before Christmas . . ."

In the late 1990s and early 2000s Chelsea replaced SoHo as world art gallery headquarters. The former warehouse center west of 10th Avenue has drawn high-profile galleries for its cheaper rents and, above all, exaggerated spaciousness. The scene intensifies each month, expanding to the north and south of its epicenter at West 20th Street. New York's Chelsea is also catching up to London's upscale real estate, with townhouse renovations reclaiming side-street blocks. Restored historic cast-iron buildings on 6th Avenue house America's ubiquitous superstore tenants, who have helped revitalize the area. One-of-a-kind boutiques along 7th, 8th, and 9th avenues are sprinkled among unassuming grocery stores and other remnants of the neighborhood's immigrant past.

Today's Chelsea extends west of 5th Avenue from 14th to 29th streets. Eighth Avenue has surpassed Christopher Street in the West Village as New York's gay Main Street: shops, fitness clubs, and restaurants cater to a largely buff male clientele. Yet the thriving neighborhood has not pushed out the multicultural population that has lived here for decades.

Numbers in the text correspond to numbers in the margin and on the Chelsea map.

a good walk

Begin on the corner of 6th Avenue and West 18th Street. Sixth Avenue was once known as Ladies' Mile for its concentration of major department stores. After the stores moved uptown in the early 1900s, the neighborhood declined, and the grand old store buildings stood empty and dilapidated. The 1990s, however, brought a renaissance to the Flatiron District to the east, and 6th Avenue's grandest buildings once again purvey wares of all kinds. On the east side of the avenue, between West 18th and 19th streets, stands the former **Siegel-Cooper Dry Goods Store** ① ⚑.

B. Altman Dry Goods Store 2
Chelsea Hotel. . 13
Chelsea Piers Sports and Entertainment Complex. 11
Cushman Row . . 9
Dia Center for the Arts 10
404 West 20th Street 8
General Theological Seminary 6
Hugh O'Neill Dry Goods Store 3
James N. Wells House 7
Joyce Theater . . . 4
London Terrace Apartments . . . 12
St. Peter's Episcopal Church 5
Siegel-Cooper Dry Goods Store . 1

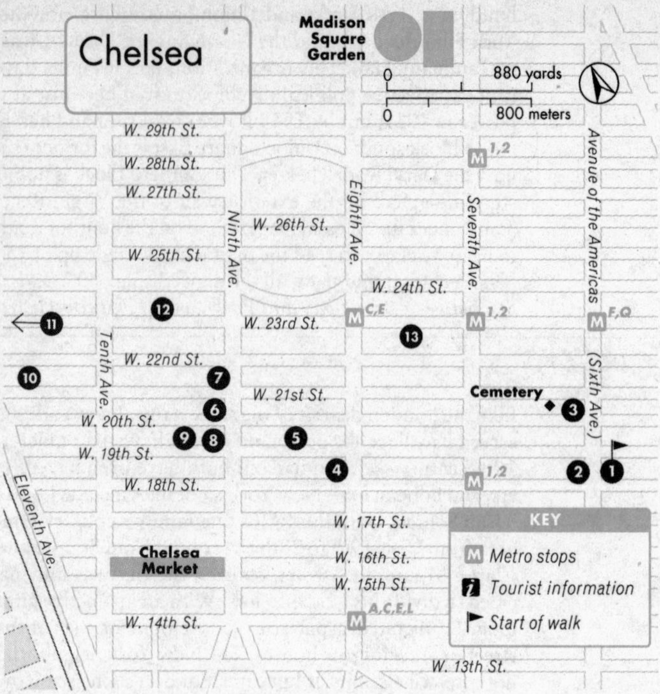

Between West 18th and 19th streets on the west side of the avenue is the 1877 cast-iron **B. Altman Dry Goods Store** 2, now occupied by Today's Man. Continue walking north to West 20th Street. The Gothic-style Church of the Holy Communion, an Episcopal house of worship dating from 1846, is on the northeast corner of the avenue. To the horror of some preservationists, it was converted into a nightclub, the Limelight, in the late 1980s. On the west side of the avenue between West 20th and 21st streets stands another former cast-iron retail palace, the **Hugh O'Neill Dry Goods Store** 3. If you turn left from 6th Avenue onto West 21st Street you'll come upon Third Cemetery of the Spanish & Portuguese Synagogue, Shearith Israel on the south side of the street. These days it's a rather neglected spot with upset marble gravestones, adjacent to a parking lot. In use from 1829 to 1851, it's one of three graveyards of this congregation in Manhattan.

Weekends, in parking lots catercorner on 6th Avenue between West 24th and 26th streets, you'll find the city's longest-running outdoor flea markets. Branching from 6th Avenue for almost a block in each direction along West 25th Street are smaller markets and an assortment of antiques shops. The Flower District roots itself along 6th Avenue from West 25th to West 29th streets, enlivening the sidewalks with impressive trees and plants.

Continue west to 8th Avenue, where the Chelsea Historic District officially begins. Its residential heart is between West 19th and West 23rd streets, from 8th to 10th avenues. To get a quick feel for 8th Avenue, head down to West 19th Street to the art deco **Joyce Theater** 4. Its presence, along with the burgeoning gay community here, helped attract many good moderately priced restaurants to the avenue.

On West 20th Street between 8th and 9th avenues, you'll find the brick parish house, fieldstone church, and rectory of 19th-century **St. Peter's**

Episcopal Church 5, home of the well-known Atlantic Theater Company. On the west side of 9th Avenue between 20th and 21st streets is the **General Theological Seminary** 6, the oldest Episcopal seminary in the United States. The man who first planned Chelsea in the mid-1800s lived in the **James N. Wells House** 7, on the northwest corner of West 21st Street.

Across the street from the seminary, **404 West 20th Street** 8 is the oldest house in the historic district. The residences next door, from 406 to 418 West 20th Street, are called **Cushman Row** 9 and are excellent examples of Greek revival town houses. Farther down West 20th Street, stop to look at the fine Italianate houses from Nos. 446 to 450. The arched windows and doorways are hallmarks of this style, which prized circular forms (no doubt because the expense required to build them showed off the owner's wealth). West 22nd Street has a string of handsome old row houses between 9th and 10th avenues.

Crossing 10th Avenue, you'll pass beneath old elevated train tracks; these form the eastern border to the vital Chelsea gallery scene. Between 10th and 11th avenues, from West 20th to 29th streets, although increasingly growing out in each direction from this core, you can spend an afternoon wandering in and out of ultrastylish art spaces. Admission to all galleries, save the Dia Center, is free. A good place to begin is on West 22nd Street at **Dia Center for the Arts** 10, the anchor of Chelsea's art community. East of Dia on West 22nd Street are quite a few galleries, including Matthew Marks Gallery and Pat Hearn Gallery, as well as the ultrahip Japanese fashion boutique Comme Des Garçons. One block down, on West 21st Street, is Paula Cooper Gallery. On the corner of West 24th Street and 11th Avenue is another transplant, Gagosian Gallery, one of the city's most influential and respected art dealers. Building No. 524 on West 26th Street is home to more than two dozen new galleries.

If you walk west on West 23rd Street, crossing the increasingly pedestrian-friendly West Side Highway (yes, this highway has stoplights), you'll come to the mammoth **Chelsea Piers Sports and Entertainment Complex** 11, the city's largest sports center. This prime piece of real estate on the Hudson River has views of New Jersey, and more important, the sunset over it. Many of those who can afford a membership here probably live in the **London Terrace Apartments** 12, a vast 1930 apartment complex on West 23rd Street between 10th and 9th avenues. Notice the lions on the arched entrances; from the side they look as if they're snarling, but from the front they have wide grins. During the 1880s and Gay '90s, West 23rd Street was the heart of the entertainment district, lined with theaters, music halls, and beer gardens. Today it's an undistinguished commercial thoroughfare. Among the relics of its heyday is the **Chelsea Hotel** 13, which is nevertheless better known for its seedy reputation.

TIMING You can tour Chelsea in two hours. Art appreciators should plan to spend the day, however, and take time to browse the galleries and stores and have a leisurely lunch. Typical gallery hours are Tuesday–Saturday 10–6, but it's best to call ahead about openings and closings. Most galleries are closed the entire month of August, and between Christmas and New Year's.

What to See

2 **B. Altman Dry Goods Store.** Built in 1877 with additions in 1887 and 1910, this ornate cast-iron giant originally housed B. Altman Dry Goods until the business moved in 1906 to its imposing quarters at 5th Avenue and 34th Street. ✉ *621 6th Ave., between W. 18th and W. 19th Sts., Chelsea.*

13 **Chelsea Hotel.** Constructed of red brick with lacy wrought-iron balconies and a mansard roof, this pleasingly out-of-place, 11-story neighborhood landmark opened in 1884 as a cooperative apartment house. It became a hotel in 1905, although it has always catered to long-term tenants, with a tradition of broad-mindedness that has attracted many creative types. Its literary roll call of former live-ins includes Mark Twain, Eugene O'Neill, O. Henry, Thomas Wolfe, Tennessee Williams, Vladimir Nabokov, Mary McCarthy, Brendan Behan, Arthur Miller, Dylan Thomas, William S. Burroughs, and Arthur C. Clarke (who wrote the script for *2001: A Space Odyssey* while living here). In 1966 Andy Warhol filmed a group of fellow artists, including Brigid Polk and Nico, in eight Chelsea Hotel rooms; the footage eventually became included in *The Chelsea Girls* (1967). The hotel was also seen on screen in *I Shot Andy Warhol* (1996) and *Sid and Nancy* (1986), a dramatization of the true-life Chelsea Hotel murder of Nancy Spungen, who was stabbed to death here, allegedly by her boyfriend, drugged punk rocker Sid Vicious. The shabby aura of the hotel is part of its allure. Read the commemorative plaques outside, then check out the eclectic collection of art in the lobby, some donated in lieu of rent by residents down on their luck. In the building's basement, accessible from the street, is the stylish bar Serena. ✉ *222 W. 23rd St., between 7th and 8th Aves., Chelsea* ☎ *212/243–3700* 🌐 *www.hotelchelsea.com.*

off the beaten path

Chelsea Market. In the former Nabisco plant, where the first Oreo cookies were made in 1912, nearly two dozen food wholesalers flank what is possibly the city's longest interior walkway in a single building—from 9th to 10th avenues. Admire the market's funky industrial design as you take in the delectable scents of the bread, wine, and meats sold here. ✉ *75 9th Ave., between W. 15th and W. 16th Sts., Chelsea* ☎ *no phone* ⏲ *Daily 8–8.*

11 **Chelsea Piers Sports and Entertainment Complex.** Beginning in 1910, the Chelsea Piers were the launching point for a new generation of big ocean liners, including the *Lusitania,* the British liner sunk by a German submarine in 1915. Even the *Titanic* planned to dock here at the end of its journey. Decades-long neglect ended with the transformation of the four old buildings along the Hudson River into a 1.7-million-square-ft, state-of-the-art sports and recreation facility, providing a huge variety of activities and several restaurants with river views, including the Chelsea Brewing Company, New York State's largest microbrewery. Private trips on the river via speedboat or yacht can be arranged by **Surfside 3 Marina** (☎ 212/336–7873). ✉ *Piers 59–62 on the Hudson River from 17th to 23rd Sts.; entrance at 23rd St., Chelsea* ☎ *212/336–6666* 🌐 *www.chelseapiers.com.*

9 **Cushman Row.** Built by dry-goods merchant and entrepreneur Don Alonzo Cushman, a friend of Clement Clarke Moore, who made a fortune developing Chelsea, this string of homes between 9th and 10th avenues represents some of the country's most perfect examples of Greek revival town houses. Original details include small wreath-encircled attic windows, deeply recessed doorways with brownstone frames, and striking iron balustrades and fences. Pineapples, a traditional symbol of welcome, perch atop the black iron newels in front of Nos. 416 and 418. ✉ *406–418 W. 20th St., between 9th and 10th Aves., Chelsea.*

10 **Dia Center for the Arts.** Dia is more like a contemporary art museum than the scores of Chelsea galleries it has helped draw to the neighborhood. Besides installations by diverse artists on its four floors of space, you might find an exhibit from Dia's permanent collection, which includes

creations by Joseph Beuys, Walter De Maria, Cy Twombly, Richard Serra, and Andy W the roof, which has a café and a two-way g Graham that invites contemplation of th brant bookstore designed by Cuban ar city's best art selections. There's also a mance space across the street. ✉ *548 11th Aves., Chelsea* ☎ *212/989–5566* 🌐 *w ⏲ Early Sept–mid June, Wed.–Sun. noon–6.*

need a break?

Wild Lily Tea Room (✉ 511A W. 22nd St., between 10th and 11th Aves., Chelsea ☎ 212/691–2258) is a tranquil Japanese art-cum-food shop, with an indoor koi pool. Teas with poetic names, such as Buddha's Finger and Pink Infusion, are served alongside salads, sandwiches, and desserts. For burgers and shakes, stop at **Empire Diner** (✉ 210 10th Ave., at W. 22nd St., Chelsea ☎ 212/243–2736), a gleaming stainless- steel hash house.

❽ **404 West 20th Street.** The oldest house in the historic district was built between 1829 and 1830 in the federal style. It still has one clapboard side wall; over the years it acquired a Greek revival doorway and Italianate windows on the parlor floor, and the roof was raised one story. ✉ *404 W. 20th St., at 9th Ave., Chelsea.*

❻ **General Theological Seminary.** The secretive grounds of this seminary are usually only discovered by stealth city explorers. The campus, which is hard to see behind the heavy exterior fencing, is accessible through the unremarkable 1960s-era building on 9th Avenue. Inside you'll find administrative offices, a bookstore, and the 240,000-volume **St. Mark's Library,** among the nation's greatest ecclesiastical libraries, with a world-class collection of Latin and English Bibles. When Chelsea developer Clement Clarke Moore divided his estate, he deeded a block-size section to the Episcopal seminary, where he taught Hebrew and Greek. Most of the school was completed in 1883–1902, when the school hired architect Charles Coolidge Haight, who pioneered the English Collegiate Gothic style, to design a campus to rival all other American colleges of the day. It worked. The hushed interior and the elm- and oak-graced lawns "sustain the pastoral illusion better than anything in New York besides Central Park," according to *New Yorker* architecture critic Paul Goldberger. ✉ *175 9th Ave., at W. 20th St., Chelsea* ☎ *212/243–5150* ⏲ *Grounds weekdays noon–3, Sat. 11–3; call for information on using the library.*

❸ **Hugh O'Neill Dry Goods Store.** Constructed in 1875, this cast-iron building, originally an emporium, features Corinthian columns and pilasters; its corner towers were once topped with huge bulbous domes. The name of the original tenant is proudly displayed on the pediment. ✉ *655–671 6th Ave., between W. 20th and W. 21st Sts., Chelsea.*

❼ **James N. Wells House.** This 1832 2½-story brick house was the home of Clement Clarke Moore's property manager, the man who planned Chelsea. Wells was responsible for the strict housing codes that created the elegant residential neighborhood by prohibiting stables and manure piles and requiring tree planting. ✉ *401 W. 21st St., between 9th and 10th Aves., Chelsea.*

need a break?

You can sit for hours without being disturbed at **Le Gamin** (✉ 183 9th Ave., at W. 21st St., Chelsea ☎ 212/243–8864), a rustic French café where soup-bowl-size café au lait, crepes, and salads are de rigueur.

Joyce Theater. When the former Elgin movie house dating to 1942 was gutted, what emerged in 1982 was this sleek modern theater with art deco touches. Today it's one of the city's leading modern-dance venues. ✉ *175 8th Ave., at W. 19th St., Chelsea* ☎ *212/242–0800.*

⓬ **London Terrace Apartments.** When this 20-story, block-long wall of red and black brick first opened in 1930, the doormen dressed as London bobbies. Today, the desirable 1,670 apartments are home to the fashion glitterati who work just up 7th Avenue in the Garment District. ✉ *W. 23rd to W. 24th Sts. between 9th and 10th Aves., Chelsea.*

❺ **St. Peter's Episcopal Church.** Built in 1836–38 on a rising tide of enthusiasm for Gothic revival architecture, the modest fieldstone St. Peter's is one of New York's first examples of early Gothic revival, though retaining elements of Greek revival style. To the left of the church, the brick **parish hall** is now the home of the Atlantic Theater Company, founded by playwright David Mamet. ✉ *344 W. 20th St., between 8th and 9th Aves., Chelsea* ☎ *212/929–2390.*

⚑ ❶ **Siegel-Cooper Dry Goods Store.** Built in 1896, much later than its neighbors, this impressive building adorned with glazed terra-cotta encompasses 15½ acres of space, and yet it was built in only five months. In its retail heyday, the store had an immense fountain on its main floor—a circular marble terrace with an enormous white-marble-and-brass replica of *The Republic,* the statue Daniel Chester French displayed at the 1883 Chicago World's Fair—which became a favorite rendezvous point for New Yorkers. During World War I the site was a military hospital. The building's splendid exterior ornamentation contrasts with its otherwise unremarkable brick facade. Today its principal tenants are Bed, Bath & Beyond, Filene's Basement, and T. J. Maxx. ✉ *620 6th Ave., between W. 18th and W. 19th Sts., Chelsea.*

need a break?

Petite Abeille (✉ 107 W. 18th St., near 6th Ave., Chelsea ☎ 212/604–9350) serves tasty café standards in addition to traditional Belgian waffles, chocolates, and cookies. Tintin, the Belgian comic book hero, brightens the walls.

42ND STREET

Few streets in America claim as many landmarks as midtown Manhattan's central axis, from Times Square, Bryant Park, and the main branch of the New York Public Library on its western half to Grand Central Terminal and the United Nations on its eastern flank. And few can claim as colorful a reputation. After World War II, 42nd Street took a nosedive, as once-grand theaters around Times Square switched from showing burlesque and legitimate theater to second-run and pornographic movies. With that decline came pickpockets, prostitutes, and the destitute, and the area became synonymous with tawdry blight.

But the street has been reincarnated, its metamorphosis starting slowly in the late 1980s and then proceeding more rapidly in the 1990s. First Bryant Park and then the block between 7th and 8th avenues were nurtured back to life. Forty-second Street is now poised to reclaim its fame as the mythical Broadway, with a steady stream of real estate deals and ground breakings; traffic-stopping celebrity appearances outside the Virgin Megastore and ABC and MTV studios; and new stores, hotels, and restaurants, many with entertainment themes, each visually louder than the last. The construction of the Condé Nast and Reuters buildings on Broadway and 7th Avenue, respectively, promises to maintain a significant intellectual presence amid the general gaiety. In Times Square itself, however, the neon lights shine brighter than ever—a local ordinance requires that massive billboard-style ads are included in all new construction. Some critics decry the "Disney-fication" of this part of town, but, really, what New York neighborhood is more appropriate for this over-the-top treatment?

Numbers in the text correspond to numbers in the margin and on the Midtown map.

a good walk

Begin at the corner of West 42nd Street and 8th Avenue, where the monolithic Port Authority Bus Terminal dispenses commuters, tourists, and those in search of some excitement onto the street or into the subway station beneath it. On the northwest corner of 8th Avenue and 43rd Street, a four-story bank building, empty for eight years, has been redesigned by Dutch architect Rem Koolhaas as the Second Stage Theater. On the southeast corner, a splashy 863-room Westin Hotel, designed by Miami's Arquitectonica, opened in late 2002. To the west, the block between 9th and 10th avenues presents a string of thriving off-Broadway playhouses, called Theatre Row. At 330 West 42nd Street stands the first McGraw-Hill Building, designed in 1931 by Raymond Hood, who later worked on Rockefeller Center, where there's a later McGraw-Hill building. The lobby is an art deco wonder of opaque glass and stainless steel. Literally the biggest attraction in Midtown West is the ***Intrepid* Sea-Air-Space Museum** 1, at West 46th Street and the Hudson River.

Of course, the big story is what's happening on 42nd Street between 8th and 7th avenues. Nine theaters once lined the street here, and for decades X-rated bookstores and peep shows were their only tenants. Some of these theaters have been immaculately restored or rehabilitated, their facades now beaming with high-wattage signs, while others await their turn. The E Walk complex stretches across the northwest portion of the street, comprising movie theaters, restaurants, arcades, and nightclubs.

East of E Walk on the same side of the street is a 10-story building of studios and theater space that bears the original facade of the Selwyn Theater (now the American Airlines Theatre), enhanced by a network of computer-controlled multicolor lights. The Times Square Theater is next door (No. 215), where for two decades after its 1920 opening, top hits such as *Gentlemen Prefer Blondes, The Front Page,* and *Strike Up the Band* were staged; Noël Coward's *Private Lives* opened here with Gertrude Lawrence, Laurence Olivier, and the author himself. Continuing east toward Times Square, you'll find the **Ford Center for the Performing Arts** 2 (which presents only a slim entrance on 42nd Street—the main facade is on 43rd Street and worth a detour) and the **New Victory Theater** 3, a reclaimed treasure that mounts theatrical productions for children. Across from the New Victory is the **New Amsterdam Theater** 4, resuscitated by the Walt Disney Company. Just to the west is **Madame Tussaud's New York** 5, where you can see life-size wax figures of major celebrities.

At the corner of 7th Avenue, the dazzling billboards of **Times Square** 6 will grab your attention to the north. Watch out for pedestrian traffic as you stop to gaze skyward. Head through Times Square to **Duffy Square** 7, a triangle between West 46th and 47th streets, the home of the TKTS discount Broadway ticket booth. On the east side of Broadway, the **Times Square Visitors Center** 8 in the historic Embassy Theater is a helpful all-in-one resource.

Next walk east on West 43rd Street toward 6th Avenue, where you'll pass **Town Hall** 9, one of the city's premier musical venues for much of the century. At 6th Avenue, visit the newly enlarged **International Center of Photography (ICP)** 10. Before returning to West 42nd Street, you may want to stroll by the hotels and clubs along West 44th Street. Walking east, you'll first see the comfortably understated **Algonquin Hotel** 11, an old celebrity haunt. Next door is the petite Iroquois Hotel (No. 49), where struggling actor James Dean lived in the early 1950s. Across the street from them is the Royalton Hotel (No. 44), a midtown hot spot that was stylishly redone by French designer Philippe Starck. Its neighbor, at 42 West 44th Street, the Association of the Bar of the City of New York, has one of the country's largest law libraries and an 1896 neoclassical facade resembling the courthouses. At 37 West 44th Street is the New York Yacht Club (1900), which until 1983 had displayed the America's Cup trophy for 150 years. The swelling beaux arts windows look just like the sterns of ships, complete with stone-carved water splashing over the sills. Farther east is the redbrick Harvard Club (No. 27); the Penn Club (No. 30), with its elegant blue awning, is on the other side of the street. And, yes, something on this block is open to the public: the General Society of Mechanics and Tradesmen Building (No. 20) has colonial-era objects on display. At the southwest corner of 5th Avenue and 44th Street, notice the 19-ft-tall 1907 sidewalk clock on a pedestal, a relic of an era when only the wealthy could afford watches.

At West 42nd Street between 5th and 6th avenues, steps rise into the shrubbery and trees of handsome **Bryant Park** 12, a perfect place to relax or picnic. The park stretches between West 42nd and West 40th streets and has been adopted as the backyard of all midtown workers. It's directly behind the magnificent beaux arts building that houses the **New York Public Library (NYPL) Humanities and Social Sciences Library** 13, the central research branch of the city's library system. A well-kept public bathroom is between the park and library, next to West 42nd Street. Across the street is the dramatically sloping facade of the Grace Building.

Continue east on 42nd Street to **Grand Central Terminal** 14. Park Avenue wraps around Grand Central on an elevated beltway and continues to the north. The once-problematic architectural space beneath the overpass, directly opposite Grand Central's main entrance, is now brightened by the Pershing Square Café. On the southwest corner of Park Avenue and East 42nd Street, the **Whitney Museum of American Art at Philip Morris** 15 takes up the large ground floor of the Philip Morris Building. Back across the overpass is the monumental space of the former Bowery Savings Bank (110 E. 42nd St.), built in 1923. With a five-story Romanesque arch and 70-ft-high marble columns, this indeed must have seemed, as critic Paul Goldberger has noted, "like the safest place in the world to place your dollars." At the corner of Lexington Avenue the 1929 Chanin Building (122 E. 42nd St.) flashes some inventive lobby detailing and floral art deco patterns on its facade.

Ask New Yorkers to name their favorite skyscraper, and most will choose the art deco **Chrysler Building** 16 at East 42nd Street and Lexington Avenue. Although the Chrysler Corporation itself moved out long ago, this graceful shaft culminating in a stainless-steel spire still captivates the eye and the imagination. On the south side of East 42nd Street and east one block, the ***Daily News* Building** 17, where the newspaper was produced until the spring of 1995, is another art deco tower with a lobby worth visiting. The modern **Ford Foundation Building** 18 on the next block encloses a 160-ft-high, ⅓-acre greenhouse that is open to the public.

Climb the steps along East 42nd Street between 1st and 2nd avenues to enter **Tudor City** 19, a self-contained complex of a dozen buildings with half-timbering and stained glass. From here you have a great view of the **United Nations Headquarters** 20. To end this walk on a quiet note, walk up 1st Avenue and turn left on East 47th Street, where you will find the **Japan Society** 21, a lovely oasis of fine and performing arts from Japan.

TIMING This long walk covers vastly different types of sights, from frenzied Times Square to bucolic Bryant Park, and from the ornate Grand Central Terminal to the sleek United Nations complex. If you start at the *Intrepid,* you could easily eat up half a day even before you reach 5th Avenue. The spectacle of Times Square is best appreciated at night.

What to See

11 **Algonquin Hotel.** Considering its history as a haunt of well-known writers and actors, this 1902 hotel is surprisingly unpretentious. Its most famous association is with the Algonquin Round Table, a witty group of literary Manhattanites who gathered in its lobby and dining rooms in the 1920s—a clique that included short-story writer and critic Dorothy Parker, humorist Robert Benchley, playwright George S. Kaufman, journalist and critic Alexander Woolcott, and actress Tallulah Bankhead. One reason they met here was the hotel's proximity to the former offices of the *New Yorker* magazine at 28 West 44th Street (the magazine now resides in the Condé Nast tower on Times Square). Come here for a cozy drink at the bar, dinner and cabaret performances in the intimate Oak Room, or just walk through the muraled lobby. ✉ *59 W. 44th St., between 5th and 6th Aves., Midtown West* ☎ *212/840–6800.*

off the beaten path

Beekman Place. This secluded and exclusive two-block-long East Side enclave has an aura of imperturbable calm. Residents of its elegant town houses have included the Rockefellers; Alfred Lunt and Lynn Fontanne; Ethel Barrymore; Irving Berlin; and, of course, Auntie Mame, a character in the well-known Patrick Dennis play (and later movie) of the same name. Steps at East 51st Street lead to an esplanade along the East River. ✉ *East of 1st Ave. between E. 49th and E. 51st Sts., Midtown East.*

12 **Bryant Park.** Midtown's only major green space has become one of the best-loved and most beautiful small parks in the city. Named for the poet and editor William Cullen Bryant (1794–1878), the 8-acre park was originally known as Reservoir Square (the adjacent main branch of the **New York Public Library** stands on the former site of the city reservoir). America's first World's Fair, the Crystal Palace Exhibition, was held here in 1853–54. Today London plane trees and formal flower beds line the perimeter of its central lawn. In temperate months the park draws thousands of lunching office workers; in summer it hosts live jazz and comedy concerts and sponsors free outdoor film screenings on Monday at dusk. At the east side of the park, near a squatting bronze cast of Gertrude Stein, is the open-air Bryant Park Café, which is open April 15–October 15, and the stylish Bryant Park Grill, which has a rooftop garden. The New York Chess Society sets up public tables near the west-end fountain in good weather (a sign set in the lawn reads SOCIABLE GAMES ARRANGED). In February and early September giant white tents spring up here for the New York fashion shows. ✉ *6th Ave. between E. 40th and E. 42nd Sts., Midtown West* ☎ *212/768–4242* 🌐 *www.bryantpark.org* ⊙ *Sept.–May, daily 7–7; June–Aug., daily 7* AM*–9* PM.

16 **Chrysler Building.** An art deco masterpiece designed by William Van Alen and built between 1928 and 1930, the Chrysler Building is one of New York's most iconic and beloved skyscrapers. It's at its best at dusk, when the stainless-steel spires glow, and at night, when its illuminated

Fodor's Choice ★

geometric design looks like the backdrop to a Hollywood musical. The Chrysler Corporation moved out in the mid-1950s, but the building retains its name and many automotive details: gargoyles shaped like car-hood ornaments sprout from the building's upper stories—wings from the 31st floor, eagle heads from the 61st. At 1,048 ft, the building only briefly held the world's-tallest title—for 40 days before the Empire State Building snatched it away. The Chrysler Building has no observation deck, but the dark lobby faced with African marble is worth a visit; the ceiling mural salutes transportation and human endeavor. The 32 Otis elevators are each lined with a different inlay of wood, each of which is from a different part of the world. ✉ *405 Lexington Ave., at E. 42nd St., Midtown East.*

17 ***Daily News* Building.** This Raymond Hood–designed art deco tower (1930) has brown-brick spandrels and windows that make it seem loftier than its 37 stories. The newspaper moved in 1995, but the famous, illuminated, 12-ft-wide globe set into a sunken space beneath a black dome in the lobby continues to impress adults and children alike. The floor is laid out like a gigantic compass, with bronze lines indicating mileage from New York to international destinations. ✉ *220 E. 42nd St., between 2nd and 3rd Aves., Midtown East.*

7 **Duffy Square.** This triangle at the north end of Times Square is named after World War I hero Father Francis P. Duffy (1871–1932), known as "the fighting chaplain," who later was pastor of Holy Cross Church on West 42nd Street. There's also a statue of George M. Cohan (1878–1942), who wrote "Yankee Doodle Dandy." The square is one of the best places for a panoramic view of Times Square's riotous assemblage of signs. At its north end the **TKTS discount ticket booth** sells discounted tickets to Broadway and off-Broadway shows. ✉ *In traffic island between W. 46th and 47th Sts., Midtown West.*

2 **Ford Center for the Performing Arts.** On the site of two classic 42nd Street theaters, the Ford Center incorporates a landmark 43rd Street exterior wall from the Lyric (built in 1903) and architectural elements from the Apollo (1910), including its stage, proscenium, and dome (the other parts of the theaters, which had fallen into disrepair, were demolished). A 1,006-seat orchestra, two 350-seat balconies, and a huge stage make it likely the Ford will continue to be a leading venue for large-scale productions. Such a future is in keeping with the Lyric's and Apollo's history: in the early part of the 20th century, the top talents on their stages included the Marx Brothers, Fred Astaire, Ethel Merman, and W. C. Fields. ✉ *213 W. 42nd St., between 7th and 8th Aves., Midtown West* ☎ *212/307–4100 for tickets.*

18 **Ford Foundation Building.** Home to one of the largest philanthropic organizations in the world, the Ford Foundation Building, built by Kevin Roche, John Dinkeloo & Associates in 1967, is best known for its glass-wall, 12-story-high atrium, which doubles as a ⅓-acre public greenhouse. Workers whose offices line the interior walls enjoy a placid view of its trees, terraced garden, and still-water pool. ✉ *320 E. 43rd St., between 1st and 2nd Aves., entrance on 42nd St., Midtown East* 🎫 *Free* ⏲ *Weekdays 9–5:30.*

off the beaten path

Garment District. This district, which runs along 7th Avenue between West 31st and 41st streets (where it's known as Fashion Avenue), teems with countless fabric, button, and notions shops, and warehouses, workshops, as well as showrooms that manufacture and finish mostly women's and children's clothing. On weekdays the streets are crowded with trucks and the sidewalks swarm with daredevil deliverymen wheeling garment racks between factories and subcontractors. Squeezing between this commerce are commuters on their way to **Pennsylvania Station** (✉ W. 31st to W. 34th Sts. between 7th and 8th Aves., Midtown West) to catch trains to New Jersey, Long Island, and via Amtrak, to anywhere. One prime example of the city that never sleeps is the **General Post Office** (✉ 8th Ave. and W. 33rd St., Midtown West ☎ 800/275–8777), open 24 hours a day, 365 days a year.

14 **Grand Central Terminal.** Grand Central is not only the world's largest railway station (76 acres) and the nation's busiest (500,000 commuters and subway riders use it daily), it's also one of the world's greatest public spaces, "justly famous," as critic Tony Hiss has said, "as a crossroads, a noble building . . . and an ingenious piece of engineering." A massive four-year renovation completed in October 1998 restored the 1913 landmark to its original splendor—and then some.

Fodor's Choice ★

The south side of East 42nd Street is the best vantage point from which to admire Grand Central's dramatic beaux arts facade, which is dominated by three 75-ft-high arched windows separated by pairs of fluted columns. At the top are a graceful clock and a crowning sculpture, *Transportation,* which depicts Mercury flanked by Hercules and Minerva. The facade is particularly beautiful at night, when bathed in golden light. Doors on Vanderbilt Avenue and on East 42nd Street lead past gleaming gold- and nickel-plated chandeliers to the cavernous **main concourse.** This majestic space is 200 ft long, 120 ft wide, and 120 ft—roughly 12 stories—high. Overhead, a celestial map of the zodiac constellations covers the robin's egg–blue ceiling (the major stars actually glow with fiber-optic lights). A marble staircase modeled after the Garnier stair at the Paris Opera is on the concourse's east end. Climb it to reach Metrazur restaurant. From this perch you can look across the concourse to the top of the opposite staircase, where diners treat themselves to either Cipriani or the mahogany-and-leather setting of Michael Jordan's The Steak House. Beyond those two restaurants to the left you'll find the Campbell Apartment, an extremely comfortable and stylish cocktail and cigar bar in what was once a rather secretive pied-à-terre.

The Grand Central Market on the east end of the main floor (a street entrance is on Lexington Avenue and East 43rd Street) is a great place to buy fresh fruit, fish, dairy goods, and breads. Dangling from its amazing inverted olive tree are 5,000 glass crystals. Dozens of restaurants (including an outpost of the popular Brooklyn deli, Junior's, and the mammoth Oyster Bar) and shops, many in spaces long closed to the public, make the downstairs **dining concourse** a destination in its own right.

Despite all its grandeur, Grand Central still functions primarily as a railroad station. Underground, more than 60 ingeniously integrated railroad tracks lead trains upstate and to Connecticut via Metro-North Commuter Rail. The subway connects here as well. The best (and worst) time to visit is at rush hour, when the concourse whirs with the frenzy of commuters dashing every which way. The most popular point for people to meet is at the central information kiosk, topped by a four-faced clock. The Municipal Arts Society (🌐 www.mas.org) leads architectural tours of the terminal from here. *Main entrance* ✉ *E. 42nd St. at Park Ave., Midtown East* ☎ *212/935–3960* 🌐 *www.grandcentralterminal.com* 🎫 *Tour free; donations to the Municipal Art Society accepted* ⏲ *Tours Wed. at 12:30; meet in front of information kiosk on main concourse.*

EVERYTHING YOU ALWAYS WANTED TO KNOW ABOUT THE SUBWAY

NEW YORK CITY HAS ALWAYS *had a reputation for innovation and speed, so it's not surprising that the world's first elevated railcar ran on tracks between Prince and 14th streets. The steam-powered train known as an "el" made its fledgling journey in 1832, marking the advent of New York City public transit. By the end of the 19th century, underground subways had arrived in cities around the world—but not in New York, the largest commercial and industrial metropolis in the world. "Public" transportation still consisted primarily of horse-drawn streetcars. The proposed subway system spent the last three decades of the 19th century on hold, a victim of bureaucratic corruption and incompetence.*

The stranglehold finally broke in 1894 when New Yorkers voted overwhelmingly for public ownership of the subway. This decision, one of the first major public issues decided by the city's people, gave the city ownership of the yet-to-be-built subway system's physical plant. At the groundbreaking ceremony on March 24, 1900, Mayor Robert A. Van Wyck used a silver spade from Tiffany's. Over the next four years, 12,000 mostly immigrant workers built the first tunnels. These laborers worked 10-hour days for 20¢ an hour. More than 50 men died and thousands were maimed while building what became the Interborough Rapid Transit (IRT) line. The 9.1 mi of track began at City Hall, continued north to Grand Central, crossed town, and then ran up Broadway to West 145th Street.

On October 27, 1904, the IRT finally opened. And while New York's subway was not the world's first, it was the first to use electric signals on all its tracks. A nickel bought a ticket, and in the IRT's first year, passengers took more than a billion rides. Turnstiles appeared in 1928, and it would be another 20 years before the fare rose to a dime. In 1953 tokens replaced tickets and the fare rose to 15¢. By the late 1990s the fare reached $1.50 and the new MetroCard allowed unlimited-ride options. In 2003, the fare was increased to $2 and tokens were discontinued.

Those original 9.1 mi of track have now grown to more than 700—more miles than any other subway system in the world. There are 5,800 subway cars, many of which have been replaced with new cars that feature digital displays and recorded messages that cheerfully advise, "Stand clear of the closings doors please." Riders still prefer the often amusing and grouchy exhortations of the live train operators. Yet to be crossed off New Yorkers' wish list are a 2nd Avenue subway line (to alleviate crowding on the 4, 5, and 6 lines) and an intelligible P.A. system on subway platforms.

The 24 subway lines operate 24 hours a day, 365 days a year. Changes in service due to repairs can last anywhere from a weekend to three years, and rerouted trains confound even locals. Carry a map with you as some platforms don't have one, or may contain an outdated one. Be aware that some lines change their routes at night or on the weekend; if you have any doubts while on the platform, stand in the middle in order to be near the train conductor's car when a train pulls into the station. You can pose a quick question through the conductor's open window. Though it's still not foolproof, the New York City subway services more than 1.5 billion rides a year, proving it is still one of this city's great bargains.

To learn more, visit ***The New York Transit Museum*** *(✉ Boerum Pl. at Schermerhorn St., Brooklyn Heights ☎ 718/243–3060 🌐 www.mta.nyc.ny.us/museum) in Brooklyn. The museum, housed in a decommissioned subway station, reopened in spring 2003 after extensive renovations. A new exhibition uses elements of a New York City intersection, and more than 200 trolley models are on display. Want some subway socks? Two of the museum's branches sell subway-related souvenirs. The* ***Grand Central Station gift store*** *(☎ 212/878–0106 ⏲ Weekdays 8–8, weekends 10–6), inside Grand Central, also has exhibitions. The* ***New York Transit Museum at Times Square*** *(✉ 1580 Broadway, between 46th and 47th Sts., Midtown West ☎ 212/730–4901 ⏲ Daily 8–8) sells souvenirs in the thick of Times Square.*

off the beaten path

Hell's Kitchen. As the name suggests, the first waves of immigrants in this area stretching from West 30th to 59th streets, and between the Hudson River and 8th Avenue, did not find the living easy. The gritty appellation came either from a gang that ruled the area in the late 1860s, or a nickname cops gave it in the 1870s. Though in the recent past, if you entered the city through the Port Authority Bus Terminal and Lincoln Tunnel, the rough-and-tumble neighborhood wasn't any more the inviting. Today Hell's Kitchen, or Clinton, has been on the up and up since the early 1990s. Along 9th Avenue, sidewalks are lined with perhaps the world's largest assortment of ethnic cafés, restaurants, and groceries. Argentina, Brazil, Indonesia, and Sri Lanka are just some of the countries represented. Each May, the 9th Avenue Food Festival brings tens of thousands of people to the closed street for exotic tasting treats. From West 34th to 39th streets between 11th Avenue and the West Side Highway, the massive **Jacob Javits Convention Center** (✉ 655 W. 34th St., at 11th Ave., Midtown West ☎ 212/216–2000) hosts business, trade, and entertainment events year-round.

1

need a break?

The pastry masters at **Poseidon Bakery** (✉ 629 9th Ave., near W. 44th St., Hell's Kitchen ☎ 212/757–6173) have been rolling out beautiful homemade phyllo dough and putting it to delectable use since 1923. The delicious and inexpensive breads and friendly service at **Amy's Bread** (✉ 672 9th Ave., at W. 46th St., Hell's Kitchen ☎ 212/977–2670) have quickly made it a New York institution.

⑩ **International Center of Photography (ICP).** This leading photography venue doubled its exhibition space in 2001 and moved its former uptown collection here. The expansion included a larger bookstore and the addition of a small café. Founded in 1974 by photojournalist Cornell Capa (photographer Robert Capa's brother), ICP's exhibits from its permanent collection of 45,000 works often focus on one genre (portraits, architecture, etc.) or the work of a single prominent photographer. ✉ *1133 6th Ave., at W. 43rd St., Midtown West* ☎ *212/857–0000* 🌐 *www.icp.org* *$9; Fri. 5–8 pay what you wish* ⏲ *Tues.–Thurs. 10–5, Fri. 10–8, weekends 10–6.*

⚑ ① ***Intrepid* Sea-Air-Space Museum.** Formerly the USS *Intrepid,* this 900-ft aircraft carrier is serving out its retirement as the centerpiece of Manhattan's only floating museum. An A-12 Blackbird spy plane, lunar landing modules, helicopters, seaplanes, and other aircraft are on deck. Docked alongside, and also part of the museum, are the *Growler,* a strategic-missile submarine; the *Edson,* a Vietnam-era destroyer; and several other battle-scarred naval veterans. Children will enjoy exploring the ships' skinny hallways and winding staircases, as well as manipulating countless knobs, buttons, and wheels. For an extra thrill (and an extra $5), they can try the Navy Flight Simulator and "land" an aircraft onboard. ✉ *Hudson River, Pier 86, 12th Ave. and W. 46th St., Midtown West* ☎ *212/245–0072* 🌐 *www.intrepidmuseum.org* *$13; free to active U.S. military personnel* ⏲ *May–Sept., weekdays 10–5, weekends 10–6; Oct.–Apr., Tues.–Sun. 10–5; last admission 1 hr before closing.*

㉑ **Japan Society.** The stylish and serene lobby of the Society has interior bamboo gardens linked by a second-floor waterfall. Works by well-known Japanese artists are exhibited in the second-floor gallery—past shows have included the first-ever retrospective of Yoko Ono's works. Cultural events, movies, lectures, language classes, concerts, and dramatic performances are also hosted. ✉ *333 E. 47th St., between 1st and 2nd Aves.,*

Midtown East ☎ *212/832–1155* 🌐 *www.japansociety.org* 🎟 *$5* ⏲ *Tues.–Fri. 11–6, weekends 11–5.*

❺ **Madame Tussaud's New York.** Go ahead, get close to Oprah, stare down Don King, and heckle Regis Philbin. You'll encounter all three celebs at this display of nearly 200 astoundingly lifelike historical, cultural, and popular characters in wax. The original Madame Tussaud's, which opened in London in 1835, is now England's top tourist draw; the opening of this branch on West 42nd Street confirms Times Square's status as New York's major entertainment destination. Inside, eerie Parisian tableaus, with a simulated guillotine and heads lying about cobblestone streets, make Halloween an excellent time to visit. But the realism of the American celebrities depicted in the "Opening Night Party" room is creepy all year: crowded with A-list celebs and a gawking swirl of tourists, the room induces a kind of vertigo, and you can't tell who's fake anymore—though Woody Allen, grinning alone in a corner, seems to get the last laugh. Via a film projected onto a domed 360-degree screening room, you can witness past events in New York. ✉ *234 W. 42nd St., between 7th and 8th Aves., Midtown West* ☎ *212/512–9600* 🌐 *www.madametussauds.com* 🎟 *$25* ⏲ *Daily 10–9; last ticket sold at 8.*

off the beaten path

Madison Square Garden. Sitting on top of the swarm of activity in Penn Station is this professional sports and entertainment behemoth, where athletes, rock stars, circus animals, and fans create a racket. If not to see an event, you can come here for a one-hour tour of the facilities—suites, locker rooms, and more. ✉ *W. 31st to W. 34th Sts. between 7th and 8th Aves., Midtown West* ☎ *212/465–5800* 🌐 *www.thegarden.com* 🎟 *$15* ⏲ *Tours daily 10–3.*

❹ **New Amsterdam Theater.** The street's most glorious theater, neglected for decades, triumphantly returned to life in 1997 following a breathtaking restoration. Built in 1903 by Herts & Tallant, the art nouveau theater had an innovative cantilevered balcony and was the original home of the Ziegfeld Follies. After years of decay—the flooded orchestra pit was home to an 8-ft tree complete with birds' nests—the theater's new tenant, the Walt Disney Company, had the 1,814-seat art nouveau interior painstakingly restored. Outside, the 1940s-vintage art deco facade dates to the theater's days as a movie house. The stage version of Disney's *The Lion King,* which opened in 1997 to critical accolades and commercial success, is likely to run here for years to come. If you can't get tickets, you can call ahead to join a group tour, which reveal the now-gorgeous theater contrasted with large mounted photographs documenting its pre-renovation disrepair. The theater's old, ruined state is also captured in the movie *Uncle Vanya on 42nd Street.* ✉ *214 W. 42nd St., between 7th and 8th Aves., Midtown West* ☎ *212/282–2900; 212/282–2907 for information on theater tours* ⏲ *Tour schedule varies; call for info* 🎟 *Tour admission $10.*

❸ **New Victory Theater.** The New Victory can make three unique claims: it was the first 42nd Street theater to be renovated as part of the revitalization of Times Square (1995), it's the oldest New York theater still in operation (since 1900), and it's the city's only theater devoted exclusively to productions for children and families. Special programs for teenagers, called VicTeens, include a night out with the cast. The theater was built by Oscar Hammerstein, who evidently passed down his interests to grandson Oscar Hammerstein II, who wrote the lyrics to such shows as *Oklahoma!* and *Carousel.* Acting legends Lionel Barrymore, Lillian Gish, Mary Pickford, and Tyrone Power strutted across the theater's stage, and in the 1930s it was Broadway's first burlesque house.

Today yellow-and-purple signs beckon from the elegant Venetian facade, and a gracious double staircase rises to a second-floor entry. Inside, garland-bearing cupids perch casually on the edge of the theater's dome above gilded deep-red walls. Unlike its neighboring theaters with long-running shows, the New Victory changes its productions every two weeks. ✉ *209 W. 42nd St., between 7th and 8th Aves., Midtown West* ☎ *646/223–3020 for tickets* 🌐 *www.newvictory.org.*

★ ⓭ **New York Public Library (NYPL) Humanities and Social Sciences Library.** This 1911 masterpiece of beaux arts design (Carrère and Hastings, architects) is one of the great research institutions in the world, with 6 million books, 12 million manuscripts, and 2.8 million pictures. But you don't have to crack a book to make it worth visiting: both inside and out, this stunning building, a National Historic Landmark, will take your breath away with its opulence.

Originally financed in large part by a bequest from New York governor Samuel J. Tilden, the library combined the resources of two 19th-century libraries: the Lenox Library and the Astor Library. The latter, founded by John Jacob Astor, was housed in a building downtown that has since been turned into the Joseph Papp Public Theater. Today the library anchors a network of close to 200 local branches throughout the city. You can see unusual behind-the-scenes collections, ranging from 19th- and early-20th-century menus to the personal library of magician Harry Houdini.

The grand entrance is at 5th Avenue just south of 42nd Street, where **two marble lions** guard a flagstone plaza. Mayor Fiorello La Guardia, who said he visited the facility to "read between the lions," dubbed them "Patience" and "Fortitude." Statues and inscriptions cover the white-marble neoclassical facade; in good weather the block-long grand marble staircase is a perfect spot to people-watch.

The library's bronze front doors open into the magnificent marble **Astor Hall,** flanked by a sweeping double staircase. Upstairs on the third floor, the magisterial **Rose Main Reading Room**—297 ft long (almost two full north–south city blocks), 78 ft wide, and just over 51 ft high—is one of the world's grandest library interiors. It has original chandeliers, oak tables, and bronze reading lamps that gleam as if they were new. Gaze up at the ceiling and you'll see murals of blue sky and puffy clouds, inspired by Tiepolo and Tintoretto. Exhibitions on photography, typography, literature, bookmaking, and maps are held regularly in the **Gottesman Exhibition Hall,** the **Edna B. Salomon Room,** the **Third Floor Galleries,** and the **Berg Exhibition Room.** Among the treasures you might see are Gilbert Stuart's portrait of George Washington, Charles Dickens's desk, and Charles Addams cartoons. Free one-hour tours leave Monday–Saturday at 11 and 2 from Astor Hall. ✉ *5th Ave. between E. 40th and E. 42nd Sts., Midtown West* ☎ *212/930–0800; 212/869–8089 for exhibit information* 🌐 *www.nypl.org* ⏲ *Thurs.–Sat. 10–6, Tues.–Wed. 11–7:30; exhibitions until 6.*

★ ❻ **Times Square.** Whirling in a chaos of competing lights and advertisements, Times Square is New York's white-hot energy center. Hordes of people, a mix of tourists and midtown workers, jostle for space on the sidewalks to walk and gawk. It would take hours of fixed concentration to really see what's going on here, in the confusion of lights, billboards, people, stores, and traffic. Like many New York City "squares," it's actually two triangles formed by the angle of Broadway slashing across 7th Avenue between West 42nd and 47th streets. Times Square (the name also applies to the general area, beyond the intersection of these streets) has been the city's main theater district since the turn of the 20th century: from West 44th to 51st streets, the cross streets west of Broadway are lined with some 30 major theaters; film houses joined the fray beginning in the 1920s.

Before the 1900s, this was New York's horse-trading center, known as Long Acre Square. Substantial change came with the arrival of the subway and the *New York Times,* then a less prestigious paper, which moved here in exchange for having its name grace the square. On December 31, 1904, the *Times* celebrated the opening of its new headquarters, at Times Tower, with a fireworks show at midnight, thereby starting a New Year's Eve tradition. Now resheathed in marble and called **One Times Square Plaza,** (✉ W. 42nd St. between Broadway and 7th Ave., Midtown West), the building is topped with the world's most famous rooftop pole, down which an illuminated 200-pound ball is lowered each December 31 to the wild enthusiasm of revelers below. (In the 1920s the *Times* moved to its present building, a green-copper-roof neo-Gothic behemoth, at 229 West 43rd Street.)

Times Square is hardly more sedate on the other 364 nights of the year. You'll be mesmerized by its usual high-wattage thunder: two-story-high cups of coffee that actually steam; a 42-ft-tall bottle of Coca-Cola; huge billboards of underwear models; mammoth, superfast digital displays of world news and stock quotes; on-location network studios; and countless other technologically sophisticated allurements. Zoning actually *requires* that buildings be decked out with ads, as they have been for nearly a century. The newest contributions to the electronic kinetics are visible in the sky-high Reuters headquarters (at the northwest corner of 7th Avenue and 42nd Street), and across 42nd Street from Reuters, at a new skyscraper known as 5 Times Square. No group magnifies all this energy better than the throngs of teens who gather each afternoon in front of MTV's studios in the heart of the square, hoping to be chosen to be part of the show "Total Request Live." TRL, as it's popularly known, is filmed live from the second-floor glass windows at West 44th Street and Broadway. Since such well-known acts as the Backstreet Boys, Eminem, and Britney Spears make regular rounds here, Times Square has become a mecca for youth. The traffic island in front of the Armed Forces Recruiting Office (in a shiny metal box with neon American flags) provides the best angles on the whole of Times Square's helter-skelter welter. ✉ *W. 42nd to W. 47th Sts. at Broadway and 7th Ave., Midtown West.*

❽ **Times Square Visitors Center.** When it opened in 1925, the Embassy Theater was an exclusive, high-society movie theater; a few years ago the lobby of this landmark theater was transformed into the city's first comprehensive visitor center. Beyond getting general Times Square information, you can buy sightseeing and theater tickets, MetroCards, and transit memorabilia; use ATMs; and log onto the Internet for free. There's also a video camera that shoots and e-mails instant photos. Free walking tours of Times Square are given Friday at noon. Perhaps most important, its rest rooms are the only facilities in the vicinity open to the nonpaying public. ✉ *1560 Broadway, between W. 46th and W. 47th Sts., Midtown West* ☎ *212/869–1890* 🌐 *www.timessquarebid.com* ⏲ *Daily 8–8.*

❾ **Town Hall.** Founded by suffragists in 1921 seeking a venue from which to educate women on political issues (Margaret Sanger was arrested here on November 12, 1921, while speaking about birth control), Town Hall instead quickly became one of the city's premier musical venues when its acoustics were accidentally discovered in its inaugural year. The landmark McKim, Mead & White federal revival building was designed with democracy in mind—there are no box seats and no obstructed views, giving rise to the phrase "not a bad seat in the house." A mix of musicians and entertainers performs here, from world music groups to Garrison Keillor. ✉ *123 W. 43rd St., between 6th and 7th Aves., Midtown West* ☎ *212/840–2824* ⏲ *Box office Mon.–Sat. noon–6 and until show time the night of the performance.*

19 **Tudor City.** Built between 1925 and 1928 to attract middle-income residents, this private "city" on a bluff above East 42nd Street occupies 12 buildings containing 3,000 apartments. Two of the buildings originally had no east-side windows, so the tenants wouldn't be forced to gaze at the slaughterhouses, breweries, and glue factories then crowding the shore of the East River. The terrace at the end of East 43rd Street now affords great views of the **United Nations Headquarters** and stands at the head of **Sharansky Steps** (named for Natan [Anatoly] Sharansky, the Soviet dissident). The steps run along **Isaiah Wall** (inscribed THEY SHALL BEAT THEIR SWORDS INTO PLOWSHARES); below are **Ralph J. Bunche Park,** named for the African-American former U.N. undersecretary, and **Raoul Wallenberg Walk,** named for the Swedish diplomat and World War II hero who saved many Hungarian Jews from the Nazis. ✉ *1st and 2nd Aves. from E. 40th to E. 43rd Sts., Midtown East.*

20 **United Nations Headquarters.** Officially an "international zone," not part of the United States, the U.N. Headquarters is a working symbol of global cooperation. The 18-acre riverside tract, now lushly landscaped, was bought and donated by oil magnate John D. Rockefeller Jr. in 1946. The headquarters were built in 1947–53 by an international team led by Wallace Harrison. The slim, 505-ft-tall green-glass **Secretariat Building;** the much smaller, domed **General Assembly Building;** and the **Dag Hammarskjöld Library** (1963) form the complex, before which fly the flags of member nations in alphabetical order, from Afghanistan to Zimbabwe, when the General Assembly is in session (mid-September to mid-December). Architecturally, the U.N. buildings are evocative of Le Corbusier (the influential French modernist was on the team of architects that designed the complex), and their windswept park and plaza remain visionary: there's a beautiful riverside promenade, a rose garden with 1,400 rosebushes, and sculptures donated by member nations.

An hour-long guided tour (given in 20 languages) is the main attraction; it includes the **General Assembly,** the **Security Council Chamber,** the **Trustee Council Chamber,** and the **Economic and Social Council Chamber,** though some rooms may be closed on any given day. Displays on war, nuclear energy, and refugees are also part of the tour; corridors overflow with imaginatively diverse artwork. Free tickets to assemblies are sometimes available on a first-come, first-served basis before sessions begin; pick them up in the General Assembly lobby. The **Delegates Dining Room** (☎ 212/963–7625) is open for a reasonably priced (up to $20) lunch weekdays (jackets required for men; reservations required at least one day in advance). The public concourse, one level down from the visitor entrance, has a coffee shop, gift shops, a bookstore, and a post office where you can mail letters with U.N. stamps. *Visitor entrance* ✉ *1st Ave. and E. 46th St., Midtown East* ☎ *212/963–7713* 🌐 *www.un.org* 🎫 *Tour $8.50* ☞ *Children under 5 not admitted* ⏲ *Tours daily 9:30–4:45; hr-long tours in English leave General Assembly lobby every 30 mins.*

15 **Whitney Museum of American Art at Philip Morris.** An enormous, 42-ft-high sculpture court with outstanding 20th-century sculptures, many of which are simply too big for the Whitney's uptown base, is the centerpiece of the museum's midtown branch. In the adjacent gallery five shows a year cover all aspects of American art. An espresso bar and seating areas make this an agreeable place to rest. ✉ *120 Park Ave., at E. 42nd St., Midtown East* ☎ *917/663–2453* 🎫 *Free* ⏲ *Sculpture court Mon.–Sat. 7:30* AM*–9:30* PM*, Sun. and holidays 11–7; gallery Mon.–Wed. and Fri. 11–6, Thurs. 11–7:30. Gallery talks Wed. and Fri. at 1.*

ROCKEFELLER CENTER & MIDTOWN SKYSCRAPERS

Athens has its Parthenon and Rome its Colosseum. New York's temples are its steel-and-glass skyscrapers. Many of them, including the Lever House and the Seagram Building, have been pivotal in the history of modern architecture, and the 19 limestone-and-aluminum buildings of Rockefeller Center constitute one of the world's most famous pieces of real estate.

Conceived by John D. Rockefeller during the Great Depression of the 1930s, the Rockefeller center complex—"the greatest urban complex of the 20th century," according to the *AIA Guide to New York City* architecture—occupies nearly 22 acres of prime real estate between 5th and 7th avenues and West 47th and 52nd streets. Its central cluster of buildings consists of smooth shafts of warm-hue limestone, streamlined with glistening aluminum. Plazas, concourses, and shops create a sense of community for the nearly quarter of a million people who use it daily. Restaurants, shoe-repair shops, doctors' offices, barbershops, banks, a post office, bookstores, clothing shops, variety stores—all are accommodated within the center, and all parts of the complex are linked by underground passageways.

Midtown now rivals the Wall Street area in its number of prestigious tenants. Rockefeller Center itself is a capital of the communications industry, containing the headquarters of a TV network (NBC), several major publishing companies (Time Warner, McGraw-Hill, Simon & Schuster), and the world's largest news-gathering organization, the Associated Press.

Numbers in the text correspond to numbers in the margin and on the Midtown map.

a good walk

This mile-long tour along six avenues and five streets is full of skyscrapers that can make the streets seem like canyon washes. An anchor of midtown Manhattan is Rockefeller Center (☎ 212/632–3975 for information, 🌐 www.rockefellercenter.com), one of the greatest achievements in 20th-century urban planning. Atlas stands sentry outside the classically inspired **International Building** (22) ⚑, on 5th Avenue between East 50th and 51st streets directly across from St. Patrick's Cathedral. Head one block south on 5th Avenue and turn west to walk along the **Channel Gardens** (23), a promenade of rock pools and seasonal flower beds. At the far end is the sunken **Lower Plaza** (24) and its famous gold-leaf statue of Prometheus. The backdrop to this scene is the 70-story **GE Building** (25), originally known as the RCA Building, whose entrance is guarded by another striking statue of Prometheus. Peer around the corner of West 50th Street to see the pink-and-blue neon sign of the titanic **Radio City Music Hall** (26) on 6th Avenue.

On the west side of 6th Avenue, from West 47th to 51st streets, stand four towers that form the **Rockefeller Center Extension** (27), part of a mid-1960s expansion. By West 52nd Street you've left the Rockefeller realm, but yet another monolith rises out of the landscape, the black **CBS Build-**

ing 28 (also known as Black Rock). From here it's a short stroll to a cluster of museums. Go east on West 52nd Street, passing the landmark **"21" Club** 29 before reaching the **Museum of Television and Radio** 30 next door. A shortcut through the outdoor public space close to the CBS Building or through a shopping arcade farther east, at 666 5th Avenue, takes you to West 53rd Street. Closer to 6th Avenue are the **Museum of Arts and Design** 31 and the **American Folk Art Museum** 32, which has made West 53rd Street its new digs. Despite the folk art museum's town house–like size, the artful building fills a void while its neighbor **Museum of Modern Art (MoMA)** 33 makes a foray into Queens while rebuilding. If you're in need of any tourist information, take a detour west to 7th Avenue, between 52nd and 53rd streets, to **NYC & Company Visitor Information Center** 34.

The true muse of midtown is not art, however, but business, as you'll see as you walk eastward. Immediately recognizable from afar by its Chippendale-style pediment is the elegant rose-granite tower known as the **Sony Building** 35, on Madison Avenue and East 55th Street. Farther east and a little south on Park Avenue stand two prime examples of the functionalist International Style: **Lever House** 36 and the **Seagram Building** 37, the only New York building designed by Ludwig Mies van der Rohe. Exhibiting a complementary restraint and classicism across the avenue from the Seagram Building is the monumental brick-and-limestone neo-Renaissance Racquet & Tennis Club (1916). One long block east on Lexington Avenue, between East 53rd and 54th streets, the luminous silvery shaft of the **Citicorp Center** 38 houses thousands more New Yorkers engaged in the daily ritual that built the city—commerce. To end your walk on a less material note, return to Park Avenue and turn southeast to 51st Street and **St. Bartholomew's Church** 39.

TIMING To see only the buildings, block out an hour and a half. Allow more time depending on your interest in the museums en route. At minimum you might spend 45 minutes in each of the museums—even then you'll only dip briefly into the collections. Start early in order to arrive at the Museum of Television and Radio when it opens, so you won't have to wait for a TV console on which to watch your shows. Keep in mind that some parts of Rockefeller Center are open only during the week.

What to See

★ 32 **American Folk Art Museum.** This museum has finally found a permanent home, and one within a work of art itself: an eight-story building designed in 2002 by heralded husband-and-wife team Tod Williams and Billie Tsein. The facade, consisting of 63 hand-cast panels of alloyed bronze, reveals individual textures, sizes, and plays of light. Inside, four gallery floors—dedicated to exhibitions and the collection of arts and decorative objects from the 18th century to the present day—are naturally lighted through a central skylight. Using multiple paths of circulation, an open atrium, and balconies of clear glass, you are treated to an architectural mix of intimacy and aspiration that echoes the folk art on display. Works include paintings, weather vanes, quilts, pottery, scrimshaw, and folk sculpture such as carousel animals and trade figures. ✉ *45 W. 53rd St., between 5th and 6th Aves., Midtown West* ☎ *212/265–1040* 🌐 *www.folkartmuseum.org* 🎫 *$9; free Fri. 6 PM–8 PM* ⏲ *Tues.–Thurs. and weekends 10–6, Fri. 10–8.*

28 **CBS Building.** The only high-rise designed by Eero Saarinen, Black Rock, as this 38-story building is known, was built in 1965. Its dark-gray granite facade actually helps to hold the building up, imparting a sense of towering solidity. ✉ *51 W. 52nd St., at 6th Ave., Midtown West.*

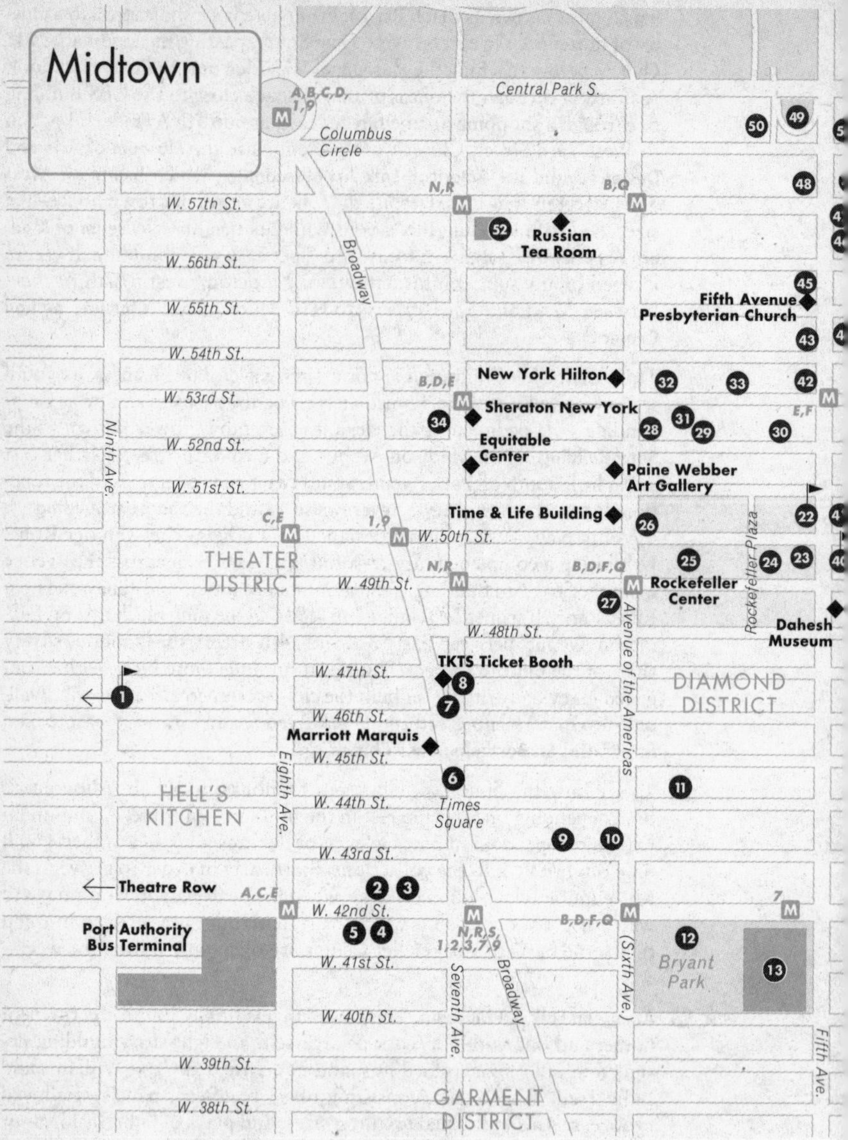

42nd Street

Algonquin Hotel **11**
Bryant Park **12**
Chrysler Building **16**
Daily News Building **17**
Duffy Square **7**
Ford Center for the Performing Arts **2**
Ford Foundation Building **18**
Grand Central Terminal **14**
International Center of Photography (ICP) **10**
Intrepid Sea-Air-Space Museum **1**
Japan Society **21**
Madame Tussaud's New York **5**
New Amsterdam Theater **4**
New Victory Theater **3**
New York Public Library Humanities and Social Sciences Library **13**
Times Square **6**
Times Square Visitors Center **8**
Town Hall **9**
Tudor City **19**
United Nations Headquarters **20**
Whitney Museum of American Art at Philip Morris **15**

Rockefeller Center & Midtown Skyscrapers

American Folk Art Museum **32**
CBS Building **28**
Channel Gardens **23**
Citicorp Center **38**
GE Building **25**
International Building **22**
Lever House **36**
Lower Plaza **24**
Museum of Arts and Design **31**

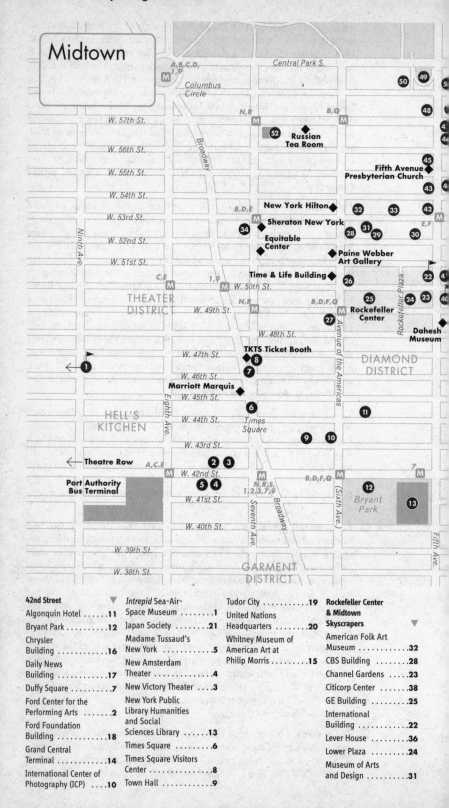

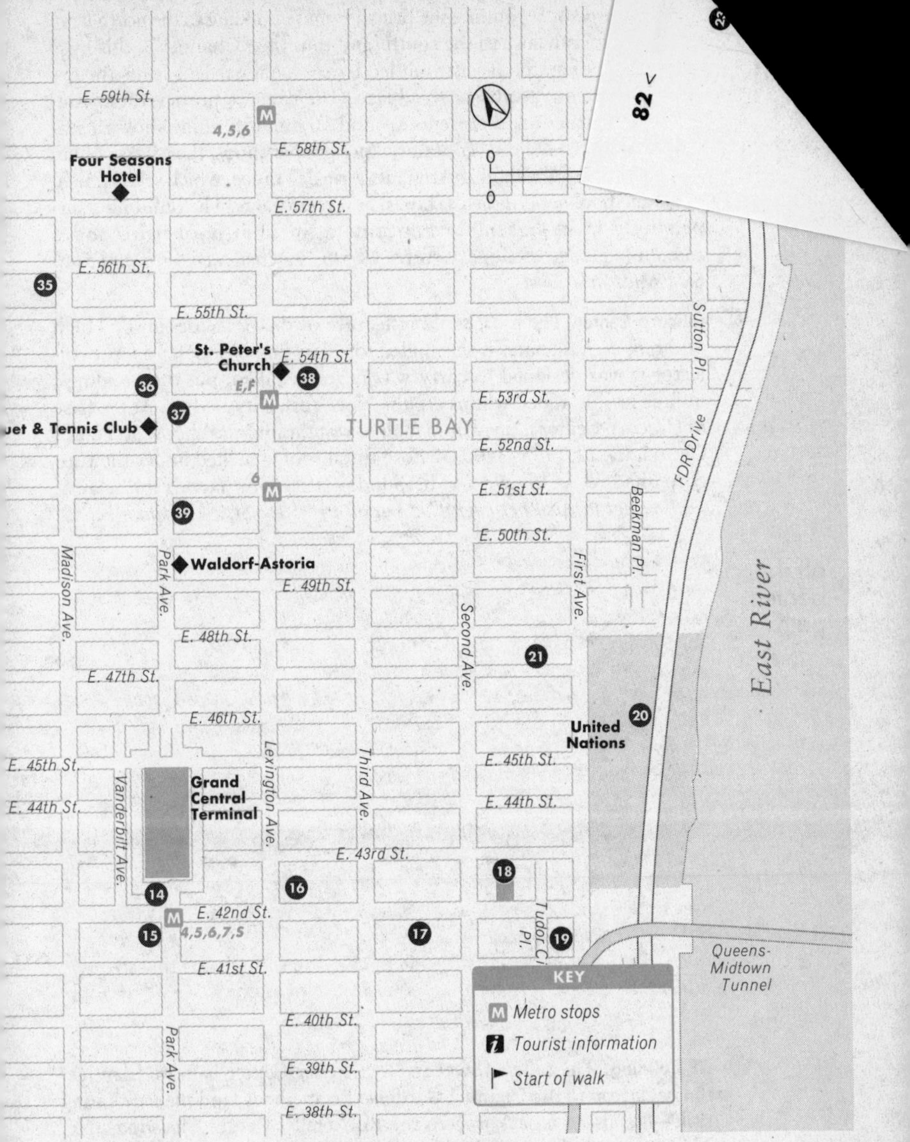

Museum of Modern Art (MoMA) 33
Museum of Television and Radio 30
NYC & Company Visitor Information Center 34
Radio City Music Hall 26
Rockefeller Center Extension 27
St. Bartholomew's Church 39
Seagram Building 37
Sony Building 35
"21" Club 29

5th Avenue & 57th Street
Bergdorf Goodman 48
Carnegie Hall 52
F.A.O. Schwarz 51
Grand Army Plaza 49
Henri Bendel 45
The Plaza 50
St. Patrick's Cathedral 41
St. Thomas Church 42
Saks Fifth Avenue 40
Takashimaya New York 44
Tiffany & Co. 47
Trump Tower 46
University Club 43

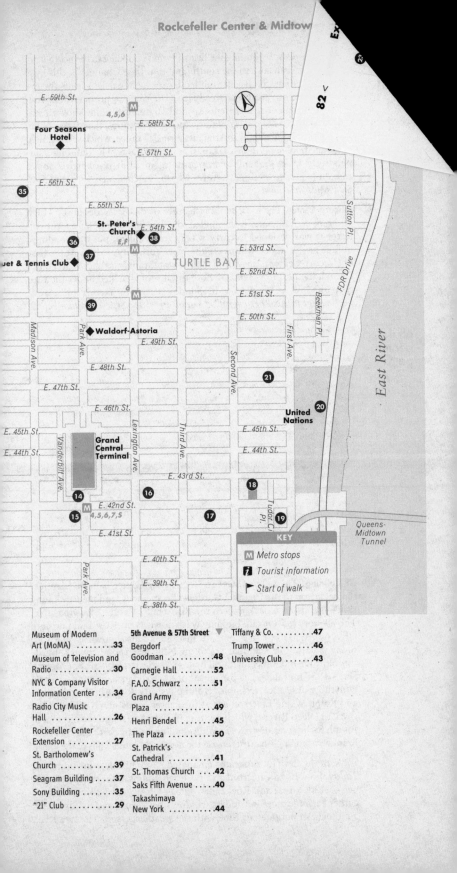

Channel Gardens. Separating the British Empire Building to the north from the Maison Française to the south (and thus the "Channel"), this busy promenade of six pools surrounded by seasonal gardens leads the eye from 5th Avenue to the Lower Plaza. The center's horticulturist conceived the gardens and presents around 10 often stunning shows a season. The French building contains, among other shops, the Metropolitan Museum of Art gift shop and the Librairie de France, which sells French-language books, periodicals, tapes, and recordings. The building's surprisingly large basement contains a Spanish bookstore and a foreign-language dictionary store. ✉ *5th Ave. between 49th and 50th Sts., Midtown West.*

38 **Citicorp Center.** The most striking feature of this 1977 design by Hugh Stubbins & Associates is the angled top. The immense solar-energy collector it was designed to carry was never installed, but the building's unique profile added whimsy to the New York City skyline. At the base of Citicorp Center is an atrium mall of restaurants and shops. **St. Peter's Church** (☎ 212/935–2200), whose tilted roof is tucked under the Citicorp shadow, is known for its Sunday afternoon jazz vespers, at 5. ✉ *Lexington Ave. between E. 53rd and E. 54th Sts., Midtown East.*

off the beaten path

Corporate-Sponsored Exhibits. Although it's not Museum Mile, midtown does benefit from companies that present free exhibits. The **Equitable Center** (✉ 787 7th Ave., at W. 51st St., Midtown West ☎ 212/554–4818) has an enormous Roy Lichtenstein work in its atrium and a gallery with excellent changing exhibits; it's open weekdays 11–6, Saturday noon–5. The **UBS Paine Webber Art Gallery** (✉ 1285 6th Ave., between W. 51st and W. 52nd Sts., Midtown West ☎ 212/713–2885), open weekdays 8–6, hosts four exhibits a year in the base of its building.

Diamond District. The relatively dowdy jewelry shops at street level on West 47th Street between 5th and 6th avenues are just the tip of the iceberg; upstairs, millions of dollars' worth of gems are traded, and skilled craftspeople cut precious stones. Wheeling and dealing goes on at fever pitch amongst the host of Hasidic Jews in severe black dress, beards, and curled side locks. So thronged is this street during the day that it becomes one of the slowest to navigate on foot in Manhattan.

25 **GE Building.** The tallest tower in Rockefeller Center is more than just the backdrop to the Channel Gardens, Prometheus, and the ice-skating rink—it's also the backdrop to the Rockefeller Center Christmas tree. The 70-story (850-ft-tall) building was known as the RCA Building until GE acquired its namesake company in 1986 (it's also known as 30 Rock): today it's also the headquarters of the NBC television network. Inside the lobby is a monumental mural by José María Sert, *American Progress.* Sert's 1937 mural depicts the muses of poetry, dance, and music along with those of science, technology, and physical effort. Abraham Lincoln and Ralph Waldo Emerson are at the center. Sert's mural replaced the work of Diego Rivera, which because it centered around the likeness of Joseph Stalin, was destroyed. Additional murals by Sert, and by Frank Brangwyn, an English artist, are on the north and south walls of the lobby.

Some of the first TV programs emanated from 30 Rock, including the *Today* show, broadcast from ground-floor studios at the southwest corner of 49th Street and Rockefeller Plaza. Crowds of perky onlookers gather each morning outside its windows between 7 and 9, hoping for a moment of national air time with the weatherperson. The two-level, monitor-spiked NBC Experience Store, directly across West 49th Street from the *Today* studio, is the departure point for 70-minute tours of the **NBC Studios** and of Rockefeller Center itself. Ticket information for other NBC shows is available here as well. To tour the area on your own, grab a free "Walking Tour of Rockefeller Center" pamphlet at the lobby's information desk. ✉ *30 Rockefeller Plaza, between 5th and 6th Aves. at 48th St., Midtown West* ☎ *212/664–7174* 💳 *Tour $17.50* ☞ *Children under 6 are not permitted* ⏲ *Tours depart from NBC store at street level of GE Bldg. every 15 mins Mon.–Sat. 8–7, Sun. 9–4:30. Thanksgiving–New Year's Day, Mon.–Sat. 8–10, Sun. 7–9.*

Poised above the GE Building's entrance doors on Rockefeller Plaza is a striking sculpture of Zeus by Lee Lawrie, the same artist who sculpted the big Atlas in front of the **International Building** on 5th Avenue. Inside, a dramatic mural entitled *Time,* by José María Sert, covers the ceiling of the foyer. Marble catacombs beneath Rockefeller Center house restaurants in all price ranges, from the formal Sea Grill to McDonald's; a post office and clean public rest rooms (scarce in midtown); and just about every kind of store. To find your way around the concourse, consult the strategically placed directories or obtain the free brochure "Walking Tour of Rockefeller Center" at the **GE Building information desk** (☎ 212/332–6868). When you've seen all there is to see, leave the GE Building from the 6th Avenue side to view the allegorical mosaics above that entrance. ✉ *Bounded by Rockefeller Plaza, 6th Ave., and 49th and 50th Sts., Midtown West.*

need a break?

Opposite the *Today* show studio, **Dean & DeLuca** (✉ 1 Rockefeller Plaza, at W. 49th St., Midtown West ☎ 212/664–1363) serves coffee, pastries, and sandwiches. Restaurateur Pino Luongo's **Tuscan Square** (✉ 16 W. 51st St., at Rockefeller Center, Midtown West ☎ 212/977–7777), a restaurant, wine cellar, espresso bar, and housewares and accessories market, delivers an old-world feel.

22 **International Building.** A huge statue of Atlas supporting the world stands sentry before this heavily visited Rockefeller Center structure, which houses many foreign consulates, international airlines, and a U.S. passport office. The lobby is fitted with Grecian marble. ✉ *5th Ave. between W. 50th and W. 51st Sts., Midtown West.*

36 **Lever House.** According to the *AIA Guide to New York City,* this 1952 skyscraper built for the Lever Brothers soap company is "where the glass curtain wall began." Gordon Bunshaft, of Skidmore, Owings & Merrill, designed a sheer, slim glass box that rests on the end of a one-story-thick shelf balanced on square chrome columns. The whole building seems to float above the street. Because the tower occupies only half the air space above the lower floors, its side wall reflects a shimmering image of its neighbors. ✉ *390 Park Ave., between E. 53rd and E. 54th Sts., Midtown East.*

24 **Lower Plaza.** Floating above this Rockefeller Center plaza, the great gold-leaf statue of the fire-stealing Greek hero **Prometheus** is one of the most famous sights in the complex. A quotation from Aeschylus—PROMETHEUS, TEACHER IN EVERY ART, BROUGHT THE FIRE THAT HATH PROVED TO MORTALS A MEANS TO MIGHTY ENDS—is carved into the red-granite wall behind. The sinkhole plaza was intended to serve as entrance to lower-level retail shops, but only succeeded with the public when the now-famous ice-skating rink was installed. Skaters line up October through April, and crowds gather above them on the Esplanade to watch their spins and spills. The rink gives way to an open-air café the

rest of the year. On the Esplanade's flagpoles, flags of the United Nations' members alternate with those of the American states. In December an enormous Christmas tree towers above. ✉ *Between 5th and 6th Aves. and W. 49th and W. 50th Sts., Midtown West* ☎ *212/332–7654 for the rink.*

31 **Museum of Arts and Design.** Formerly known as the American Craft Museum, this small museum showcases works of decorative arts, graphic and industrial design, and interdisciplinary genres that cross into sculpture, performance, and technology. You'll find works in clay, glass, fabric, wood, metal, paper, and even chocolate by contemporary American and international artisans. Recent exhibits have included works by Michael Graves and Frank Gehry. ✉ *40 W. 53rd St., between 5th and 6th Aves., Midtown West* ☎ *212/956–3535* 🌐 *www.americancraftmuseum.org* 🎫 *$8* 🕘 *Fri–Wed. 10–6, Thurs. 10–8.*

33 **Museum of Modern Art (MoMA).** If you've come by force of habit to 53rd Street looking for MoMA, you're in for quite a shock. The museum is now in Long Island City, Queens, while a major overhaul, led by Japanese architect Yoshio Taniguchi, is radically changing the look and feel of the 53rd Street site. Expected to be completed in spring 2004 (though the museum won't reopen until early 2005), renovations and additions will nearly double the museum's square footage. The museum moved to this block in 1939 and into a six-story building designed by Edward Durell Stone and Philip Goodwin. Their stylish former entrance, marked by the piano-shape canopy, will now serve as the entrance to the museum restaurant. The new main entrance will face West 54th Street with two new buildings: the eight-story Education and Research Center, and the Gallery Building, which will house the main galleries, including a second floor devoted to contemporary art. The Abby Aldrich Rockefeller Sculpture Garden, designed by Philip Johnson on the site of John D. Rockefeller's first New York home, will be used more boldly; the space around the garden will open dramatically into the museum. A final design touch incorporates Cesar Pelli's 1984 Museum Tower into the facade unit. ✉ *11 W. 53rd St., between 5th and 6th Aves., Midtown East* ☎ *212/708–9400* 🌐 *www.moma.org.*

need a break?

In the 1960s **Paley Park** (✉ 3 E. 53rd St., at 5th Ave., Midtown East) was the first of New York's vest-pocket parks—small open spaces squeezed between high-rise behemoths. A waterfall blocks out traffic noise, and feathery honey locust trees provide shade for relatively relaxing lunches. A snack bar opens when weather permits.

30 **Museum of Television and Radio.** Three galleries of photographs and artifacts document the history of broadcasting in this 1989 limestone building by Philip Johnson and John Burgee. A computerized catalog of more than 100,000 television and radio shows and commercials is the main draw; you can then view or listen to your picks in private screening rooms. ✉ *25 W. 52nd St., between 5th and 6th Aves., Midtown West* ☎ *212/621–6800 for general information and daily events; 212/621–6600 for other information* 🌐 *www.mtr.org* 🎫 *$10 suggested donation* 🕘 *Tues.–Wed. and Fri.–Sun. noon–6, Thurs. noon–8.*

34 **NYC & Company Visitor Information Center.** For tourist information, maps, tickets to attractions, souvenirs, and ATMs, stop by this bustling spot. ✉ *810 7th Ave., between W. 52nd and W. 53rd Sts., Midtown West* ☎ *212/484–1222* 🌐 *www.nycvisit.com* 🕘 *Weekdays 8:30–6, weekends 9–5.*

26 **Radio City Music Hall.** One of the jewels in the crown of Rockefeller Center, this 6,000-seat art deco masterpiece is America's largest indoor theater. Opened in 1932, it astonished the hall's Depression-era patrons with its 60-ft-high foyer, ceiling representing a sunset, and 2-ton chandeliers. The theater originally presented first-run movies in conjunction with live shows featuring the fabled Rockettes chorus line. In 1979 the theater was awarded landmark status. Its year-round schedule now includes major performers, awards presentations, and special events, along with its own Christmas and Easter extravaganzas. A $70 million renovation was completed in 1999 that gladdened critics and the public alike by, among other things, revealing the hall's originally intended gleaming colors. Very popular one-hour tours of the theater are conducted daily. ✉ *1260 6th Ave., at W. 50th St., Midtown West* ☎ *212/247–4777* 🌐 *www.radiocity.com* 🎫 *Tour $17* ⏲ *Tours Mon.–Sat. 10–5, Sun. 11–5, every 30 mins, performance schedule permitting.*

27 **Rockefeller Center Extension.** Twelve skyscrapers define 6th Avenue's west side, including these four nearly identical ones from West 47th to 51st streets built in the mid-1960s expansion of Rockefeller Center. Fountains and spacious street-level lobbies lessen the imposing solidity. The **1211 Building** at West 48th Street has a Fox News ticker tape larger than the NBC model on Rockefeller Plaza; Fox broadcasts many of its cable shows from the ground-floor glass studios. The sunken plaza of the **McGraw-Hill Building** between West 48th and 49th streets is notable for its 50-ft steel sun triangle that points to the seasonal positions of the sun at noon. The **Time & Life Building** stands between West 50th and 51st streets: CNN broadcasts many of its shows live from its first-floor glass studios here à la Fox. ✉ *6th Ave. between W. 47th and W. 51st Sts., Midtown West.*

★ 39 **St. Bartholomew's Church.** This handsome 1919 limestone-and-brick church, like the Racquet & Tennis Club two blocks north, represents a generation of midtown Park Avenue buildings long since replaced by such modernist landmarks as the Seagram and the Lever buildings. The incongruous juxtaposition plays up the church's finest features—a McKim, Mead & White Romanesque portal from an earlier (1904) church and the intricately tiled Byzantine dome. St. Bart's sponsors major music events throughout the year, including the summer's Festival of Sacred Music, with full-length masses and other choral works; an annual Christmas concert; and an organ recital series that showcases the church's 12,422-pipe organ, the city's largest. St. Bart's also runs a popular outdoor café. ✉ *109 E. 50th St., at Park Ave., Midtown East* ☎ *212/378–0200; 212/378–0248 for music-program information* 🌐 *www.stbarts.org* ⏲ *Church Mon.–Wed. 8:45–6, Thurs. 8:45–7:30, Sun. 8:45–8:30. Sunday services at 8, 9, 11, 5, and 7.*

need a break?

Café St. Bart's (✉ Park Ave. and E. 50th St., Midtown East ☎ 212/888–2664) is a charming and tranquil outdoor spot for a relatively inexpensive meal or a glass of wine or beer during the summer. The café serves breakfast and lunch weekdays year-round. Sunday brunches are also served year-round; Sunday dinner is served from April through December.

37 **Seagram Building.** Ludwig Mies van der Rohe (1886–1969), a leading interpreter of International Style architecture, built this simple, boxlike bronze-and-glass tower in 1958. The austere facade belies its wit: I-beams, used to hold buildings up, are here attached to the surface, representing the *idea* of support. The Seagram's innovative ground-level plaza, extending out to the sidewalk, has since become a common element in

urban skyscraper design. A 52nd Street entrance leads to one of New York's most venerated restaurants, the Four Seasons Grill and Pool Room. Even if you're not dining, peek in to see the Philip Johnson–designed dining room, a modernist masterpiece. Above the Grill Room's bar hangs a frighteningly sharp sculpture installation. ✉ *375 Park Ave., between E. 52nd and E. 53rd Sts., Midtown East* ☎ *212/572–7404* *Free* ⏲ *Tours Tues. at 3.*

35 **Sony Building.** Commissioned by AT&T, which has since decamped to New Jersey, the Sony Building was designed by Philip Johnson in 1984. Sony's rose-granite columns and its giant-size Chippendale-style pediment made the skyscraper an instant landmark. The first-floor arcade is home to Sony electronics stores; a restaurant; a café; and, to the delight of children, a talking robot. The **Sony Wonder Technology Lab** (☎ 212/833–8830 🌐 www.sonywondertechlab.com ⏲ Tues.–Wed. and Fri.–Sat. 10–6, Thurs. 10–8, Sun. noon–6; last entrance 30 mins before closing) on the fourth floor is a carnival of interactive exhibits, including a recording studio, and video-game and TV production studios. To save time and guarantee admission, call for a reservation. ✉ *550 Madison Ave., between E. 55th and E. 56th Sts., Midtown East* *Free* ⏲ *Sony Plaza daily 7 AM–11 PM.*

29 **"21" Club.** A trademark row of jockey statuettes parades along the wrought-iron balcony of this landmark restaurant, which has a burnished men's-club atmosphere and a great downstairs bar. After a period of decline in the 1980s, when its menu aged along with its wealthy clientele, "21" reinvented itself in the 1990s. Today the power brokers are back, along with the luster of the past. ✉ *21 W. 52nd St., between 5th and 6th Aves., Midtown West* ☎ *212/582–7200* 🌐 *www.21club.com.*

5TH AVENUE & 57TH STREET

Elegant shops and international fashion firms make this stretch of 5th Avenue just north of Rockefeller Center one of the world's great shopping districts. The rents and price tags rise even higher along East 57th Street, where there's a parade of exclusive boutiques and fine art galleries. Fifth Avenue's refined character has changed as brand-name stores with slick marketing schemes and loud decor have moved in. Theme restaurants dominate 57th Street west of 5th Avenue, though that fad is on the wane.

Numbers in the text correspond to numbers in the margin and on the Midtown map.

a good walk

Start right across the street from Rockefeller Center's Channel Gardens, at the renowned **Saks Fifth Avenue** 40, the flagship of the national chain. Across East 50th Street is the Gothic-style Roman Catholic **St. Patrick's Cathedral** 41. From outside, snap one of the city's most photographed views: the ornate white spires of St. Pat's against the black-glass curtain of Olympic Tower, a multiuse building of shops, offices, and luxury apartments at East 51st Street and 5th Avenue.

Cartier displays its wares in a jewel-box turn-of-the-20th-century mansion on the southeast corner of 52nd Street and 5th Avenue; similar houses used to line this street, and many of their residents were parishioners of **St. Thomas Church** 42, at the corner of West 53rd Street. Continuing north, you'll see the imposing bulk of the **University Club** 43 at the northwest corner of 54th Street. It shares the block with the Peninsula, one of the city's finer hotels. Across the street is **Takashimaya New York** 44, a branch of the elegant Japanese department store.

Fifth Avenue Presbyterian Church, a grand brownstone church (1875), sits on the northwest corner of 5th Avenue and 55th Street. On the same block is **Henri Bendel** 45, a bustling women's fashion store. Next door is Harry Winston (718 5th Ave.), with a spectacular selection of fine jewelry. Across the avenue is the Disney Store (No. 711), where you can buy everything Disney, from key chains to vacations.

Trump Tower 46, on the next block between East 56th and 57th streets, is an apartment and office building named for its self-promoting developer, Donald Trump. And finally, the jeweler that benefited so much from the cinematic image of Audrey Hepburn standing wistfully outside it, **Tiffany & Co.** 47. Around the corner on East 57th Street, NikeTown (No. 6) is a shrine to sports and sports marketing: TVs and scoreboards on the first floor let you keep track of how your team is doing. As you pass through the revolving doors of Tourneau TimeMachine (12 E. 57th St.), an audible ticking welcomes you to its four floors of timepieces. Between these two stores you can relax amid clusters of bamboo in the public atrium of 590 Madison Avenue, a five-side, 20-story sheath of dark gray-green granite and glass by Edward Larrabee Barnes. An Alexander Calder mobile hangs in the lobby.

Cross 57th Street and head back toward 5th Avenue on the north side of the street, with its stellar lineup of boutiques: the French classics Chanel, Hermès, and Christian Dior; the English Burberrys Ltd.; and the German Escada. The fragmented form of the white-glass Louis Vuitton Moët Hennesy headquarters (parent company and home of Dior) lends a lighthearted elegance to the street. Farther west are the watch store Swatch Timeship and the Original Levi's Store. The two **Bergdorf Goodman** 48 stores flank 5th Avenue: the extravagant women's boutiques are on the west side of the avenue between 57th and 58th streets, and the men's store is on the east side at 58th Street. Van Cleef & Arpels jewelers is within Bergdorf's West 57th Street corner.

Cross West 58th Street to **Grand Army Plaza** 49, the open space along 5th Avenue between 58th and 60th streets. Appropriately named **The Plaza** 50, the famous hotel stands at the western edge of this square. Across the street, on the southeast corner of 58th Street and 5th Avenue, is the legendary **F.A.O. Schwarz** 51 toy store, ensconced in the General Motors Building.

Now return to 57th Street and head west, where the glamour eases off a bit. The large red NO. 9 on the sidewalk, in front of 9 West 57th Street, was designed by Ivan Chermayeff. (If you approach it from the other direction, it resembles an "e," thereby orienting passersby—you're facing east.) Continuing west, you'll pass the Rizzoli Bookstore (No. 31), with a neoclassical-inspired ceiling as elegant as the art books it carries. Across 6th Avenue (New Yorkers *never* call it Avenue of the Americas, despite the street signs), you'll know you're in classical-music territory when you peer through the showroom windows at Steinway and Sons (109 W. 57th St.). Across the street stands what was the Russian Tea Room (150 W. 57th St.). Once the Czarina of ornamentation, the restaurant closed its doors in July 2002. Presiding over the southeast corner of 7th Avenue and West 57th Street, **Carnegie Hall** 52 has for decades reigned as a premier international concert hall.

TIMING This walk isn't long and can be completed in about 1½ hours. Add at least an hour for basic browsing and several more hours for serious shopping. Bear in mind that 5th Avenue is jam-packed with holiday shoppers from Halloween until New Year's.

What to See

48 **Bergdorf Goodman.** Good taste—at a price—defines this understated department store with dependable service. The seventh floor has room after exquisite room of wonderful linens, tabletop items, and gifts. *Main store ✉ 754 5th Ave., between W. 57th and W. 58th Sts., Midtown West ☎ 212/753–7300 ✉ men's store: 745 5th Ave., at E. 58th St., Midtown East.*

★ 52 **Carnegie Hall.** Musicians the world over have dreamed of playing Carnegie Hall ever since 1891, when none other than Tchaikovsky—direct from Russia—came to conduct his own work on opening night. Designed by William Barnet Tuthill, who was also an amateur cellist, this renowned concert hall was paid for almost entirely by Andrew Carnegie. Outside, the stout, square brown building has a few Moorish-style arches added, almost as an afterthought, to the facade. Inside, the simply decorated 2,804-seat white auditorium is one of the world's finest. The hall has attracted the world's leading orchestras and solo and group performers, from Arturo Toscanini and Leonard Bernstein (he made his triumphant debut here in 1943, standing in for New York Philharmonic conductor Bruno Walter) to Duke Ellington, Ella Fitzgerald, Judy Garland, Frank Sinatra, Bob Dylan, the Beatles (playing one of their first U.S. concerts)—and thousands of others.

Carnegie Hall was extensively restored in the 1980s; a subsequent mid-1990s renovation removed concrete from beneath the stage's wooden floor, vastly improving the acoustics. The work also increased the size of the lobby and added the small **Rose Museum** (✉ 154 W. 57th St., at 7th Ave., Midtown West ☎ 212/247–7800), which is free and open Thursday–Tuesday 11–4:30 and through intermission during concerts. Just east of the main auditorium, it displays mementos from the hall's illustrious history, such as a Benny Goodman clarinet and Arturo Toscanini's baton. A sensational concert series run by the hall's education department introduces children to classical music through informal sessions with performers, with a low $5 ticket price. You can take a guided one-hour tour of Carnegie Hall, or even rent it if you've always dreamed of singing from its stage. *✉ W. 57th St. at 7th Ave., Midtown West ☎ 212/247–7800 🌐 www.carnegiehall.org 🎫 $6 ⏲ Tours weekdays Oct.–June at 11:30, 2, and 3, performance schedule permitting.*

off the beaten path

Dahesh Museum. The Dahesh reopened in this new location in spring 2003 as an expanded museum of European academic art. Its collection is composed of 3,000 works donated by a Lebanese doctor named Dahesh (1909–84). The new museum (it was formerly tucked in a little-known second-floor exhibition space on 5th Avenue at 49th Street) houses an expanded shop, auditorium, Internet spaces, and an afternoon tearoom. Among the well-known painters represented are Bonheur, Bouguereau, Gérôme, and Troyon—all painters who have since been upstaged by their contemporaries, the impressionists, but who once claimed greater popularity. *✉ 580 Madison Ave., between W. 56th and W. 57th Sts., Midtown East ☎ 212/759–0606 🌐 www.daheshmuseum.org 🎫 Free ⏲ Tues.–Sat. 11–6.*

51 **F.A.O. Schwarz.** A wondrously fun selection of toys lies just beyond the fantastic mechanical clock standing inside the front doors of this famous toy-o-rama. Take a ride up a larger-than-life robot elevator for a view of the oversize decorations and role-playing employees. If the line to get in looks impossibly long, try walking around the block to the Madison Avenue entrance, where the wait may be shorter. Street dancers and drummers often perform on the plaza in front of the store. *✉ 767 5th Ave., at E. 58th St., Midtown East ☎ 212/644–9400 🌐 www.fao.com.*

49 **Grand Army Plaza.** The flower beds are attractive, but this square at the southeast corner of Central Park is most certainly the province of tourists and those catering to them. That's not to say a rest here isn't restorative, it's just not as prime a people-watching spot as other public spaces in New York. The **Pulitzer Fountain,** donated by publisher Joseph Pulitzer, dominates the southern portion of the square. Appropriately enough in this prosperous neighborhood, the fountain is crowned by a female figure representing Abundance. To the north prances Augustus Saint-Gaudens's gilded equestrian statue of Civil War general William Tecumseh Sherman. Real horses pull carriages through a southern loop of the park and are available at fixed prices ($34 for the first half hour, $10 each additional quarter hour). Across 60th Street is **Doris C. Freedman Plaza,** with outdoor sculpture courtesy of the Public Art Fund, at the grand Scholars' Gate. Follow the path from this gate direct to the entrance of the Central Park Zoo. The Plaza, the internationally famous hotel, stands at the square's western edge. ✉ *5th Ave. between W. 58th and W. 60th Sts., Midtown West.*

45 **Henri Bendel.** Chic Henri Bendel sells expensive women's clothing in a beautiful store, where inventive displays and sophisticated boutiques are hallmarks. You can have a meal in the second-floor café in front of the facade's René Lalique art-glass windows (1912) or view the windows from balconies ringing the four-story atrium. ✉ *712 5th Ave., between W. 55th and W. 56th Sts., Midtown West* ☎ *212/247–1100* ⏲ *Mon.–Wed. and Fri.–Sat. 10–7, Thurs. 10–8, Sun. noon–6.*

50 **The Plaza.** With Grand Army Plaza, 5th Avenue, *and* Central Park at its doorstep, this world-famous hotel claims one of Manhattan's prize real estate corners. A registered historical landmark built in 1907, The Plaza was designed by Henry Hardenbergh, who also built the Dakota apartment building on Central Park West. Here he concocted a birthday-cake effect of highly ornamented white-glazed brick topped with a copper-and-slate mansard roof. The hotel is home to Eloise, the fictional star of Kay Thompson's children's books, and has been featured in many movies, from Alfred Hitchcock's *North by Northwest* to *Plaza Suite.* ✉ *5th Ave. at W. 59th St., Midtown West* ☎ *212/759–3000.*

41 **St. Patrick's Cathedral.** The Gothic, double-spired, Roman Catholic cathedral of New York is one of the city's largest (seating approximately 2,400) and most striking churches. Dedicated to the patron saint of the Irish, the 1859 white marble-and-stone structure by architect James Renwick was consecrated in 1879. Additions over the years include the archbishop's house and rectory, the two 330-ft spires, and the intimate Lady Chapel. The original, predominantly Irish, members of the congregation made a statement when they chose the 5th Avenue location for their church: during the week, most of them came to the neighborhood only as employees of the wealthy. But on Sunday, at least, they could claim a prestigious spot for themselves. Among the statues in the alcoves around the nave is a modern depiction of the first American-born saint, Mother Elizabeth Ann Seton. The steps outside are a convenient, scenic rendezvous spot. Many of the funerals for fallen New York City police and firefighters were held here in the fall of 2001. ✉ *5th Ave. between E. 50th and E. 51st Sts., Midtown East* ☎ *212/753–2261 rectory* ⏲ *Daily 8 AM–8:45 PM.*

Fodor'sChoice ★

42 **St. Thomas Church.** This Episcopal institution with a grand, darkly brooding French Gothic interior was consecrated on its present site in 1916. The impressive huge stone reredos behind the altar holds the statues of more than 50 apostles, saints, martyrs, missionaries, and other church figures, all designed by Lee Lawrie. The church is also known for its men's and boys' choir; Christmas Eve services here are a seasonal high-

light. ✉ *5th Ave. at W. 53rd St., Midtown West* ☎ *212/757–7013* ⏲ *Daily 7–6.*

40 **Saks Fifth Avenue.** On a breezy day, the 14 American flags fluttering from the block-long facade of Saks's flagship store make for the most patriotic shopping scene in town (the flags have been proudly displayed for years). In 1926, the department store's move from its original Broadway location solidified midtown 5th Avenue's new status as a prestigious retail center. Saks remains a civilized favorite among New York shoppers. The eighth-floor Café SFA serves delicious light fare, with a view of Rockefeller Center, and the rooftop pools and gardens of the buildings flanking Channel Gardens. Saks's annual Christmas window displays, on view from late November through the first week of January, are among New York's most festive. ✉ *611 5th Ave., between E. 49th and E. 50th Sts., Midtown East* ☎ *212/753–4000* ⏲ *Mon.–Wed. and Fri.–Sat. 10–7, Thurs. 10–8, Sun. noon–6.*

44 **Takashimaya New York.** A tearoom, a florist within a garden atrium, and gifts and accessories that combine Eastern and Western styles make this six-floor branch of Japan's largest department store chain supremely elegant. ✉ *693 5th Ave., between E. 54th and E. 55th Sts., Midtown East* ☎ *212/350–0100* ⏲ *Mon.–Sat. 10–7, Sun. noon–5.*

47 **Tiffany & Co.** One of the most famous jewelers in the world and the quintessential New York store, Tiffany & Co. anchors the southeast corner of one of the city's great intersections. The fortresslike art deco entrance and dramatic miniature window displays have been a fixture here since 1940. Founded in 1837 at 237 Broadway, Tiffany slowly made its way uptown in six moves. The store's signature light-blue bags and boxes are perennially in style, especially on gift-giving occasions. A New York icon, Tiffany is immortalized in the 1961 Hollywood classic *Breakfast at Tiffany's,* in which a Givenchy-clad Audrey Hepburn emerges from a yellow cab at dawn to window-shop, coffee and Danish in hand. ✉ *727 5th Ave., at E. 57th St., Midtown East* ☎ *212/755–8000* 🌐 *www.tiffany.com.*

46 **Trump Tower.** As he has done with other projects, developer Donald Trump named this exclusive 68-story apartment and office building after himself. The grand 5th Avenue entrance leads into a glitzy six-story shopping atrium paneled in pinkish-orange marble and trimmed with lustrous brass. A fountain cascades against one wall, drowning out the clamor of the city, and trees and ivy climb the setbacks outside. ✉ *725 5th Ave., between E. 56th and E. 57th Sts., Midtown East.*

43 **University Club.** New York's leading turn-of-the-20th-century architects, McKim, Mead & White, designed this 1899 granite palace for an exclusive midtown club of degree-holding men. (The crests of various prestigious universities hang above its windows.) The club's popularity declined as individual universities built their own clubs and as gentlemen's clubs became less important on the New York social scene. Still, the seven-story Renaissance revival building (the facade looks as though it's three stories) is as grand as ever. Architectural critics rate this among Charles McKim's best surviving works. ✉ *1 W. 54th St., at 5th Ave., Midtown West.*

THE UPPER EAST SIDE

To many New Yorkers, the words "Upper East Side" connote old money, conservative values, and even snobbery. The neighborhood is certainly the epitome of the high-style, high-society way of life that exists for the privileged in any true cosmopolitan city. Alongside Central Park, between

5th and Lexington avenues, up to about East 96th Street or so, the trappings of wealth are everywhere apparent: well-kept buildings, children in private-school uniforms, nannies wheeling baby carriages, dog walkers, limousines, and doormen in braided livery.

But like all other New York neighborhoods, this one is diverse, too, and plenty of residents live modestly. The northeast section, which is known as Yorkville, is more affordable and ethnically mixed with a jumble of high and low buildings, old and young people. Until the 1830s, when the New York & Harlem Railroad and a stagecoach line began racing through, Yorkville was a quiet, remote hamlet with a large German population. Over the years it also welcomed waves of immigrants from Austria, Hungary, and Czechoslovakia, and a few local shops and restaurants keep up this European heritage, though their native-tongue customers have trickled down to a few surviving senior citizens. East of Lexington Avenue and between the 80s and 90s, young singles reign. On weekend nights, the scene in many bars resembles that of a fraternity and sorority reunion.

Numbers in the text correspond to numbers in the margin and on the Upper East Side & Museum Mile map.

a good walk

A fitting place to begin your exploration of the moneyed Upper East Side is that infamous shrine to conspicuous consumption, **Bloomingdale's** 1, at 59th Street between Lexington and 3rd avenues. Leaving Bloomingdale's, head west on East 60th Street toward 5th Avenue. As you cross Park Avenue, notice the wide, neatly planted median strip. Railroad tracks once ran aboveground here; they were not completely covered with a roadway until after World War I, and the grand, sweeping street that resulted became a distinguished residential address. Look south toward midtown, and you'll see the grand Helmsley Building, behind which rises the monolithic Met Life Building. Turn to look uptown, and you'll see a thoroughfare lined with massive buildings that are more like layers of mansions than apartment complexes. Colorful tulips and cherry blossoms in the spring and lighted pine trees in December make Park Avenue true to its name.

On the northwest corner of East 60th Street and Park Avenue is Christ Church United Methodist Church, built during the Depression but designed to look centuries old, with its random pattern of limestone blocks. Inside, the Byzantine-style sanctuary (open Sunday and holidays) glitters with golden mosaics. Continue west on 60th Street to pass a group of membership-only societies and clubs that have catered to the privileged since the 1800s. Although the clubs' memberships remain exclusive, their admirable architecture is there for all to see. The scholarly **Grolier Club** 2, with its fanciful grillwork curled over the doorway, is an exception in that it *is* open to the public. Continuing toward the park, you'll pass the **Harmonie Club** 3 on the south side of the street, and the even more lordly **Metropolitan Club** 4 on the north.

Take a right at 5th Avenue and walk alongside Central Park. At the corner of 61st Street you'll pass the Pierre, a hotel with a lovely mansard roof and tower that opened in 1930. Around the next corner at East 62nd Street is the **Knickerbocker Club** 5, another private social club. Across from it is the Fifth Avenue Synagogue, a limestone temple built in 1959. Its pointed oval windows are filled with stained glass in striking abstract designs. As you continue up 5th Avenue, at East 64th Street, you'll see the Central Park Zoo and the fortlike Arsenal, which houses the main offices of the New York City Department of Parks. At East 65th Street is another notable house of worship: **Temple Emanu-El** 6, one of the world's largest synagogues.

From 5th Avenue, turn right on East 66th Street, past the site of the house (3 E. 66th St.) where Ulysses S. Grant spent his final years. If presidential homes interest you, take a detour over to East 65th Street between Madison and Park avenues to Nos. 47 and 49, two connected town houses built in 1908 for Sara Delano Roosevelt and her son, Franklin, after his marriage to Eleanor. If you walk east another block on 65th Street, you'll reach the **China Institute** 7, where a small gallery exhibits Chinese art. From here, a short detour down Lexington Avenue will bring you to another singular gallery, the **Museum of American Illustration** 8, on East 63rd Street.

Back toward 5th Avenue, next door to Grant's house, at 5 East 66th Street, is the **Lotos Club** 9, a private arts and literature club. The large landmark apartment building (45 E. 66th St.) on the northeast corner of Madison Avenue and 66th Street was built from 1906 to 1908 with lovely Gothic-style detail. The red Victorian castle-fortress at East 66th Street and Park Avenue is the **Seventh Regiment Armory** 10. While often used as an exhibition space for art and antique shows, the armory is still owned by the military and was turned over to the National Guard for use as a command center following the September 2001 attack on the World Trade Center.

Although apartment buildings now prevail along Park Avenue, a few surviving mansions give you an idea of how the neighborhood once looked. The grand silvery-limestone palace on the southwest corner of East 68th Street and Park Avenue, built in 1919, now houses the prestigious Council on Foreign Relations. The **Americas Society** 11, which has a public art gallery, resides in a dark-redbrick town house on the northwest corner. The three buildings to the north—built between 1916 and 1926 and designed by three architects—maintain the same neo-Georgian design to create a unified block; the modern-day uses of these former homes add to the international flavor of the area. The Spanish Institute (No. 684) offers film series, lectures, and flamenco lessons. The Italian Cultural Institute (No. 686) sponsors readings, concerts, and performances. The Italian Consulate (No. 690) is home to the Italian diplomatic corps. Two blocks north, on the east side of Park Avenue, is the **Asia Society and Museum** 12, an educational center dedicated to the art of South, Southeast, and East Asia.

At this point, shoppers may want to get down to business on Madison Avenue between East 59th and 79th streets. The area is packed with haute couture designer boutiques, patrician art galleries, and unique stores specializing in fine wares from hair combs to truffles. Larger name stores such as Calvin Klein, DKNY, and Barneys, and the Giorgio Armani Boutique have also flocked to the prestigious neighborhood. Even if you're just window-shopping, it's fun to step inside the tony digs of Polo/Ralph Lauren in the landmark, French Renaissance–style Rhinelander mansion (built in 1898) at Madison Avenue and East 72nd Street. The aristocratic store has preserved the house's walnut fittings and outfitted it with Oriental rugs, chandeliers, period artwork, and antiques. Look for the distinctive **Whitney Museum of American Art** 13 looming on the right at East 75th Street—this striking building has a base smaller than its upper floors. Take at least two hours to view the collection. At Madison Avenue and 76th Street is the **Carlyle Hotel** 14, one of the city's most elite and discreet properties.

The final leg of this tour is several blocks away in Yorkville. Walk four blocks east on 78th Street, then north on 2nd Avenue, and east again on 86th Street. The quiet blocks of 78th Street between Park and 2nd avenues are home to rows of well-maintained Italianate town houses from the late 1800s. Many shops and restaurants line 2nd Avenue, some reflecting the area's Eastern European heritage. At East 81st Street the Yorkville Packing House (1560 2nd Ave.) is a Hungarian meat market that serves up fresh-made sausages. At East 86th Street, the German store Schaller & Weber (1654 2nd Ave.) entices with bratwurst, imported chocolates, and stollen. Secondhand stores in the area sell all sorts of odds and ends discarded by the well-to-do.

On East 86th Street and East End Avenue, the **Henderson Place Historic District** 15 includes 24 small-scale town houses built in the late 1880s. Across the street is **Carl Schurz Park** 16, overlooking the East River. **Gracie Mansion** 17, the mayor's house, sits at its north end.

TIMING This tour covers a lot of ground, although many sights merely warrant looking, not stopping. Allow about three leisurely hours for the walk. The art institutions—the Americas Society, the Asia Society and Museum, and the Whitney Museum—take more time.

What to See

11 **Americas Society.** This McKim, Mead & White–designed neo-federal town house was among the first on this stretch of Park Avenue (built 1909–11). It was commissioned by Percy Rivington Pyne, the grandson of financier Moses Taylor and a notable financier himself. From 1948 to 1963 the mansion housed the Soviet Mission to the United Nations. In 1965 it was saved from developers by the Marquesa de Cuevas (a Rockefeller descendant), who acquired the property and presented it to the Center for Inter-American Relations, now called the Americas Society, whose mission is to educate U.S. citizens about the rest of the western hemisphere. The society has frequent concerts and literary events; its art gallery hosts changing exhibits. ✉ *680 Park Ave., at 68th St., Upper East Side* ☎ *212/249–8950* 🌐 *www.americas-society.org* 🎟 *Free* ⏲ *Tues.–Sun. noon–6. Closed between exhibitions.*

12 **Asia Society and Museum.** The eight-story red-granite building that houses this museum and educational center complements Park Avenue's older, more traditional architecture. Founded in 1956, the society offers a regular program of lectures, films, and performances, in addition to permanent and changing exhibitions. The Asian art collection of Mr. and Mrs. John D. Rockefeller III forms the museum's major holdings. The collection includes South Asian stone and bronze sculptures; art from India, Nepal, Pakistan, and Afghanistan; bronze vessels, ceramics, sculpture, and paintings from China; Korean ceramics; and paintings, wooden sculptures, and ceramics from Japan. A glassed-in atrium, sculpture garden, café, and visitor center on the first floor make the Asia Society one of the Upper East Side's most inviting stops. ✉ *725 Park Ave., at 70th St., Upper East Side* ☎ *212/288–6400 for general information; 212/517–2742 for the box office* 🌐 *www.asiasociety.org* 🎟 *$7; free Fri. 6–9* ⏲ *Tues.–Thurs. and weekends 11–6, Fri. 11–9.*

1 **Bloomingdale's.** A New York institution, this noisy and crowded block-long behemoth sells everything from designer clothes to high-tech tea kettles in slick, sophisticated displays. Most selections are high quality, and sale prices on designer goods can be extremely satisfying. In addition to full his, hers, and home sections, Bloomingdale's has four restaurants, a chocolatier, and a coffee shop. ✉ *E. 59th St. and Lexington Ave., Upper East Side* ☎ *212/705–2000* 🌐 *www.bloomingdales.com* ⏲ *Weekdays 10–8:30, Sat. 10–7, Sun. 11–7; extended hrs Thanksgiving– Christmas.*

16 **Carl Schurz Park.** Once known as East End Park, this promontory was renamed in 1911 to honor Carl Schurz (1829–1906), a famous 19th-century German immigrant who eventually served the United States as

a minister to Spain, a major general in the Union Army, and a senator from Missouri. During the Hayes administration, Schurz was secretary of the interior; he later moved back to Yorkville and worked as editor of the *New York Evening Post* and *Harper's Weekly.*

From the park's southern entrance at East 86th Street, a curved stone staircase leads up to the wrought-iron railings at the edge of John Finley Walk, which overlooks the churning East River—actually just an estuary connecting Long Island Sound with Upper New York Bay. You can see the Triborough, Hell Gate, and Queensboro bridges; Wards, Randall's, and Roosevelt islands; and, on the other side of the river, Astoria, Queens. The view is so tranquil you'd never guess you're directly above the FDR Drive. Behind you along the walk are raised flower beds, recreation areas, and a playground. Although the park doesn't compare in size with the West Side's Riverside Park, Upper East Siders cherish it nonetheless. Stroll to the north end of the park to reach **Gracie Mansion,** where the city's mayor usually resides. The park tapers to an end at East 90th Street, where there's a dock from which ferryboats depart to lower Manhattan and up to Yankee Stadium. ✉ *E. 84th to E. 90th St. between East End Ave. and East River, Upper East Side.*

⓮ **Carlyle Hotel.** The mood here is English manor house. The elegant Café Carlyle regularly features top performers such as Bobby Short, Eartha Kitt, and Woody Allen (the latter on clarinet). The more relaxed Bemelmans Bar is known for its murals by Ludwig Bemelmans, the famed illustrator of the Madeline children's books. Stargazers, take note: this hotel's roster of the rich-and-famous has included George C. Scott, Steve Martin, and Princess Diana. In the early 1960s President John F. Kennedy frequently stayed here; rumor has it he entertained Marilyn Monroe in his rooms. ✉ *35 E. 76th St., at Madison Ave., Upper East Side* ☎ *212/744–1600* 🌐 *www.thecarlyle.com.*

❼ **China Institute.** A pair of fierce, fat stone lions guards the doorway of this pleasant redbrick town house, which houses a gallery and educational center. In addition to regular lectures, the institute hosts two annual exhibitions focusing on traditional Chinese art, including painting, calligraphy, folk art, architecture, and textiles. ✉ *125 E. 65th St., between Lexington and Park Aves., Upper East Side* ☎ *212/744–8181* 🌐 *www.chinainstitute.org* 🎫 *$3; free Tues. and Thurs. 6–8* ⏲ *Mon., Wed., Fri., and Sat. 10–5; Tues. and Thurs. 10–8; Sun. 1–5. Closed between exhibitions.*

⓱ **Gracie Mansion.** Surrounded by a small lawn and flower beds, this federal-style yellow-frame residence, the official home of the mayor of New York, still feels like a country manor house, which it was when built in 1799 by wealthy merchant Archibald Gracie. The Gracie family entertained many notables here, including Louis-Philippe (later king of France), President John Quincy Adams, the Marquis de Lafayette, Alexander Hamilton, James Fenimore Cooper, Washington Irving, and John Jacob Astor. The city purchased Gracie Mansion in 1887, and after a period of use as the Museum of the City of New York, Mayor Fiorello H. La Guardia made it the official mayor's residence in 1942. Don't expect to find New York City's current mayor Michael Bloomberg here, however; he chose to stay in his own residence rather than moving to Gracie Mansion when he took office in 2002. ✉ *Carl Schurz Park, East End Ave. opposite 88th St., Upper East Side* ☎ *212/570–4751* 🎫 *$7* ⏲ *Guided tours Wed. and Thurs. 10–3, starting every hr on the hr; all tours by advance reservation only.*

❷ **Grolier Club.** Founded in 1884, this private club is named after the 16th-century French bibliophile Jean Grolier. Its members are devoted to the bookmaking crafts; one of them, Bertram G. Goodhue, designed this neatly proportioned Georgian-style redbrick building in 1917. The club presents public exhibitions on subjects related to books and has a reference library of more than 100,000 volumes (open by appointment only). ✉ *47 E. 60th St., between Madison and Park Aves., Upper East Side* ☎ *212/838–6690* 🌐 *www.grolierclub.org* *Free* *Gallery Sept.–July, Mon.–Sat. 10–5. Closed between exhibitions.*

❸ **Harmonie Club.** Originally a private club for German Jews, the Harmonie has distinguished itself from the city's other men's clubs by allowing women at dinner since its inception in 1852. (Stephen Birmingham's *Our Crowd: The Great Jewish Families of New York* profiles the club's original generation.) The club's current building is a pseudo-Renaissance palace built in 1906 by McKim, Mead & White. ✉ *4 E. 60th St., between 5th and Madison Aves., Upper East Side.*

⓯ **Henderson Place Historic District.** This cozy block has preserved 24 of its original 32 Queen Anne–style town houses, which were built in the late 1880s for "people of moderate means." Richard Norman Shaw designed the stone-and-brick buildings to be comfortable yet romantic dwellings that combine elements of the Elizabethan manor house with classic Flemish details. Note the lovely bay windows, the turrets marking the corner of each block, and the symmetrical roof gables, pediments, parapets, chimneys, and dormer windows. ✉ *Henderson Pl. and East End Ave. between 86th and 87th Sts., Upper East Side.*

need a break?

DT-UT (✉ 1626 2nd Ave., at E. 84th St., Upper East Side ☎ 212/327–1327) is a coffee parlor with comfy chairs, sandwiches, s'mores, and pastries. The diner **Viand** (✉ 300 E. 86th St., at 2nd Ave., Upper East Side ☎ 212/879–9425) has superlative service and an extensive menu of treats.

❺ **Knickerbocker Club.** Built in 1915, this serene marble-trimmed redbrick and limestone mansion, the third home of the club—originally founded in 1874 by such wheeler-dealers as John Jacob Astor and August Belmont—was designed by Delano and Aldrich. ✉ *2 E. 62nd St., near 5th Ave., Upper East Side.*

❾ **Lotos Club.** This private club, which attracts devotees of the arts and literature, got its name in 1870 from the poem "The Lotos-Eaters" by Alfred Tennyson. Mark Twain and Andrew Carnegie were among the founding members. Its current home is a handsomely ornate beaux arts mansion originally built in 1900 by Richard Howland Hunt for a member of the Vanderbilt family. ✉ *5 E. 66th St., between 5th and Madison Aves., Upper East Side.*

❹ **Metropolitan Club.** With a lordly neoclassical edifice, this exclusive club was built in 1891–94 by the grandest producers of such structures—McKim, Mead & White. It was established by J. P. Morgan when a friend of his was refused membership in the Union League Club; its members today include leaders of foreign countries, presidents of major corporations, and former U.S. president Bill Clinton. ✉ *1 E. 60th St., near 5th Ave., Upper East Side.*

off the beaten path

Mount Vernon Hotel Museum and Garden. On property once owned by Colonel William Stephens Smith, the husband of Abigail Adams, daughter of former president John Adams, this 18th-century carriage house is now owned by the colonial Dames of America and largely restored to look as it did when it served as a bustling day hotel during the early 19th century (a time when the city's population was just beginning to boom). Eight rooms display furniture and artifacts of the federal and empire periods, and an adjoining garden is designed in 18th-century style. ✉ *421 E. 61st St., between York and 1st Aves., Upper East Side* ☎ *212/838–6878* 💵 *$5* ⏲ *Tues.–Sun. 11–4.*

8 **Museum of American Illustration.** This specialized museum was founded in 1901 to "promote and stimulate interest in the art of illustration, past, present, and future." The Society of Illustrators assembles eclectic exhibitions on everything from *New Yorker* cartoons and Norman Rockwell paintings to pictures from *Mad* magazine and children's books. ✉ *128 E. 63rd St., between Lexington and Park Aves., Upper East Side* ☎ *212/838–2560* 🌐 *www.societyillustrators.org* 💵 *Free* ⏲ *Tues. 9–8, Wed.–Fri. 9–5, Sat. noon–4.*

off the beaten path

Roosevelt Island. This 2-mi-long East River island, which lies parallel to Manhattan from East 48th to 85th streets, became a planned mixed-income residential project in the 1970s and now houses some 8,000 people. The island has a 19th-century lighthouse designed by James Renwick Jr. (architect of St. Patrick's Cathedral) and Blackwell House (1794), the fifth-oldest wooden house in Manhattan. Some fragments remain of the asylums, hospitals, and jails once clustered here, when it was known as Welfare Island and before that Blackwell's Island (Mae West and William "Boss" Tweed are among those who served time in Blackwell Penitentiary). Walkways follow the island's edge. The real treat, however, is the 4½-minute ride over on the aerial **Roosevelt Island Tramway** (☎ 212/832–4543 💵 $1.50); the entrance is at 2nd Avenue and 60th Street, a few blocks east of Bloomingdale's. For more about the island, visit www.roosevelt-island.ny.us.

10 **Seventh Regiment Armory.** The term "National Guard" derives from the Seventh Regiment, which has traditionally consisted of select New York men who volunteered for service. (The Seventh Regiment first used the term in 1824 in honor of the Garde National de Paris.) This huge structure, designed by Seventh Regiment veteran Charles W. Clinton in the late 1870s, is still used as an armory and was occupied by the National Guard after the attack on the World Trade Center in September 2001. Parts of the armory that aren't on duty serve various functions; a homeless shelter, the Seventh Regiment Mess and Bar, and numerous posh art and antique exhibitions also use its space. Both Louis Comfort Tiffany and Stanford White designed rooms in its surprisingly residential interior; go up the front stairs into the wood-paneled lobby and take a look around. Over the years, neglect and water damage have taken their toll on the building's interiors, earning the armory a place on the "100 Most Endangered Sites" list of the World Monuments Fund in 2000–01. A statewide commission is making plans for restoring this oft-overlooked architectural gem. ✉ *643 Park Ave., between 66th and 67th Sts., Upper East Side.*

6 **Temple Emanu-El.** The world's largest Reform Jewish synagogue seats 2,500 worshipers. Built in 1928–29 of limestone and designed in the Romanesque style with Byzantine influences, the building has Moorish and art deco ornamentation, and its sanctuary is covered with mosaics. A free museum displays artifacts detailing the congregation's history and Jewish life. ✉ *1 E. 65th St., at 5th Ave., Upper East Side* ☎ *212/744–1400* 🌐 *www.emanuelnyc.org* ⏲ *Sabbath services Fri. 5:15, Sat. 10:30; weekday services Sun.–Thurs. 5:30. Temple open daily 10–5. Museum open Sun.–Thurs. 10–4:30, Fri. 10–4, Sat. 1–4:30.*

13 **Whitney Museum of American Art.** This museum grew out of a gallery in the studio of the sculptor and collector Gertrude Vanderbilt Whitney, whose talent and taste were fortuitously accompanied by the wealth of two prominent families. She offered her collection of 20th-century American art to the Met, but they turned it down, so she established an independent museum in 1930. The current building, opened in 1966, is a minimalist gray-granite vault separated from Madison Avenue by a dry moat; it was designed by Marcel Breuer, a member of the Bauhaus school. The monolithic exterior is much more forbidding than the interior, where exhibitions offer an intelligent survey of 20th-century American works. The fifth floor's eight sleek galleries house "De Kooning to Mid-Century," featuring works by Reginald Marsh, George Bellows, Robert Henri, and Marsden Hartley. Notable pieces include Hopper's *Early Sunday Morning* (1930) and Bellows' *Dempsey and Firpo* (1924), several of Georgia O'Keeffe's dazzling flower paintings, and Alexander Calder's beloved sculpture *Circus* (1926–31). The second floor picks up chronologically where the fifth floor leaves off, with "Pollock to Today," more highlights from the permanent collection, including paintings and sculpture by such postwar and contemporary artists as Jackson Pollack, Jim Dine, Jasper Johns, Mark Rothko, Frank Stella, Chuck Close, Cindy Sherman, and Roy Lichtenstein. The famed Whitney Biennial, which showcases the most important developments in American art over the past two years, takes place in even-numbered years. The Whitney also has a branch across from Grand Central Terminal in midtown. ✉ *945 Madison Ave., at E. 75th St., Upper East Side* ☎ *212/570–3676* 🌐 *www.whitney.org* *$12; Fri. 6–9 pay what you wish* ⏲ *Tues.–Thurs. and weekends 11–6, Fri. 1–9.*

need a break?

The soft lighting, tasteful decor, and delicious, if somewhat pricey, pastries, chocolates, and drinks of **Payard Pâtisserie & Bistro** (✉ 1032 Lexington Ave., between E. 73rd and E. 74th Sts., Upper East Side ☎ 212/717–5252) are a perfect complement to a day on the Upper East Side. Take a seat at the small café tables up front.

MUSEUM MILE

Once known as Millionaires' Row, the stretch of 5th Avenue between East 79th and 104th streets has been fittingly renamed Museum Mile, for it now contains New York's most distinguished cluster of cultural institutions. The connection is more than coincidental: many museums are housed in what used to be the great mansions of merchant princes and wealthy industrialists. A large percentage of these buildings was constructed of limestone (it's cheaper than marble) and reflect the beaux arts style, which was very popular among the wealthy at the turn of the 20th century.

Numbers in the text correspond to numbers in the margin and on the Upper East Side, Museum Mile map.

a good walk

This walk up 5th Avenue, from East 70th to 105th Street, covers nearly 2 mi. If you walk on the west side of the avenue (crossing over to visit museums, of course), you'll be under the canopy of Central Park and have a good view of the mansions and apartments across the street. The **Frick Collection** 18 is housed at East 70th Street in an ornate, imposing beaux arts mansion. More former mansions follow, among them the New York University Institute of Fine Arts at 1 East 78th Street, a gleaming white-marble building modeled after a French hotel and built for tobacco magnate James B. Duke in 1912. One block farther north

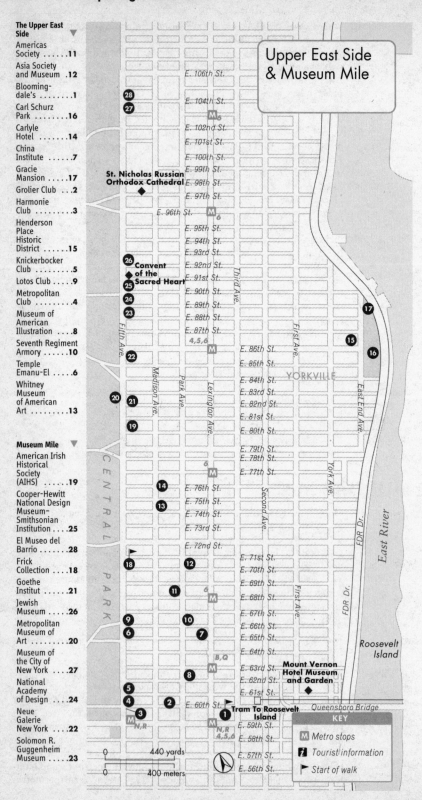

The Upper East Side

Museum Mile

is the French Renaissance–style facade of the Ukrainian Institute of America at 2 East 79th Street, which regularly hosts art exhibitions and concerts. At 80th Street is the **American Irish Historical Society (AIHS)** 19, another fine example of the French-influenced beaux arts style that was so popular at the turn of the 20th century.

From here you can't miss the **Metropolitan Museum of Art** 20, one of the world's largest art museums, making room for itself on Central Park's turf. Across from the Met, between East 82nd and 83rd streets, one beaux arts town house stands amid newer apartment blocks. It now belongs to the Federal Republic of Germany, represented by the **Goethe Institut** 21. At the corner of East 85th Street is 1040 5th Avenue, the former home of Jacqueline Kennedy Onassis, from which she could view Central Park and the reservoir that now bears her name. One block north, you'll encounter the **Neue Galerie New York** 22, a museum devoted to German and Austrian art in a 1914 Carrère and Hastings mansion.

At East 88th Street, Frank Lloyd Wright's striking **Solomon R. Guggenheim Museum** 23 is the architect's only major New York building. A block north stands the **National Academy of Design** 24, a prestigious museum and school of fine arts. At East 91st Street you'll find the former residence of industrialist Andrew Carnegie, now the **Cooper-Hewitt National Design Museum–Smithsonian Institution** 25. The huge Italianate limestone mansion across the street was constructed between 1914 and 1918 for financier Otto Kahn and his wife, Addie, noted patrons of the arts. Today it's home to the Convent of the Sacred Heart, a private girls school.

As you continue north, look for the **Jewish Museum** 26 at East 92nd Street; designed to look like a French Gothic–style château, it was originally built for financier Felix Warburg in 1908. The handsome, well-proportioned Georgian-style mansion on the corner of 5th Avenue and 94th Street was built in 1914 for another 5th Avenue magnate, Willard Straight, founder of *The New Republic* magazine. For some architectural variety, take a short walk east on 97th Street. The baroque-style St. Nicholas Russian Orthodox Cathedral (15 E. 97th St.), built in 1901–02, has onion-dome cupolas.

At East 103rd Street, the intimate **Museum of the City of New York** 27 has exhibits related to Big Apple history. One block north, **El Museo del Barrio** 28 highlights Latin American culture. After filling up on all this culture, you may want to head for nature: cross the street to Central Park's Conservatory Garden, a formal, enclosed tract in the rambling park, where you can sit on a bench and enjoy the scents of whatever's in bloom.

TIMING It would be impossible to do justice to all these collections in one outing; the Metropolitan Museum alone contains too much to see in a week, much less a day. Consider selecting one or two museums or exhibits in which to linger and simply walk past the others, appreciating their exteriors (this in itself constitutes a minicourse in architecture). Save the rest for another day—or for your next trip.

Be sure to pick the right day for this tour: most museums are closed at least one day of the week, usually Monday, and a few have free admission during extended hours on specific days. Others have drinks, snacks, or music during late weekend hours. During the annual "Museum Mile" celebration—held annually on the second or third Tuesday in June—5th Avenue closes to traffic, music fills the air, and museums open their doors, free to all, from 6 to 9 PM.

What to See

19 **American Irish Historical Society (AIHS).** U.S. Steel president William Ellis Corey, who scandalized his social class by marrying musical comedy star Mabelle Gilman, once owned this heavily ornamented, mansard-roof beaux arts town house; he died in 1934, and the building remained vacant until it was purchased and renovated by the AIHS (established 1897), which set up shop here in 1940. The society hosts frequent lectures, literary events, and concerts, and the library's holdings chronicle Irish and Irish-American history. Tours are usually available on request. ✉ *991 5th Ave., at E. 80th St., Upper East Side* ☎ *212/288–2263* 🌐 *www.aihs.org* 🎫 *Free* ⏲ *Library weekdays 10:30–5 (by appointment).*

25 **Cooper-Hewitt National Design Museum–Smithsonian Institution.** Industrialist Andrew Carnegie (1835–1919) sought comfort more than show when he built this 64-room house, designed by Babb, Cook & Williard, on what were the outskirts of town in 1901; this was the year he became the richest man in the world, and from the first-floor study Carnegie administered his extensive philanthropic projects. (Note the low doorways—Carnegie was only 5 ft 2 inches tall.) The core of the museum's collection was assembled in 1897—not by Carnegie—but by the two Hewitt sisters, granddaughters of inventor and industrialist Peter Cooper. Major holdings focus on aspects of contemporary and historical design, including drawings, prints, textiles, furniture, metalwork, ceramics, glass, woodwork, and wall coverings. The Smithsonian Institution took over the museum in 1967, and in 1976 the collection was moved into the Carnegie mansion. The changing exhibitions—which have covered such subjects as jewelry design and the construction of the Disney theme parks—are invariably enlightening and often amusing. In summer some exhibits make use of the museum's lovely garden. ✉ *2 E. 91st St., at 5th Ave., Upper East Side* ☎ *212/849–8400* 🌐 *www.si.edu/ndm* 🎫 *$8; free Tues. 5–9* ⏲ *Tues. 10–9, Wed.–Fri. 10–5, Sat. 10–6, Sun. noon–6.*

need a break? Supplying many of the city's best restaurants, **Ciao Bella Gelato Cafe** (✉ 27 E. 92nd St., between 5th and Madison Aves., Upper East Side ☎ 212/831–5555) has more than 20 flavors of superdense Italian-style ice cream. Fruit flavors like blueberry and blood orange vie for supremacy with traditional tastes like dark chocolate and pistachio.

28 **El Museo del Barrio.** *El barrio* is Spanish for "the neighborhood," and the museum, focusing on Latin American and Caribbean art, is fittingly located on the edge of East Harlem, where a largely Spanish-speaking, Puerto Rican community resides. Founded in 1969, the 8,000-object permanent collection includes numerous pre-Columbian artifacts, sculpture, film and video, and the museum's well-known *santos,* or saints—carved wooden folk-art figures from Puerto Rico. On permanent display is "Taíno: Ancient Voyagers of the Caribbean," which documents the vanished peoples of the islands through stone and ceramic artwork. ✉ *1230 5th Ave., between E. 104th and E. 105th Sts., Upper East Side* ☎ *212/831–7272* 🌐 *www.elmuseo.org* 🎫 *$5 suggested donation* ⏲ *Wed.–Sun. 11–5; extended hrs in summer.*

★ 18 **Frick Collection.** Coke-and-steel baron Henry Clay Frick (1849–1919) amassed this superb art collection far from the soot and smoke of Pittsburgh, where he made his fortune. The mansion was designed by Thomas Hastings and built in 1913–14. It opened as a museum in 1935 and expanded in 1977, but still resembles a gracious private home, albeit one with bona fide masterpieces in almost every room. The number of famous paintings is astounding, and many treasures bear special mention.

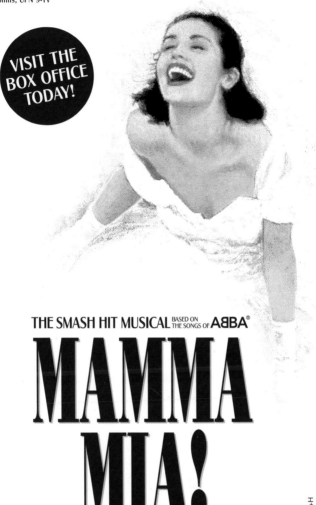

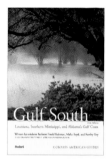

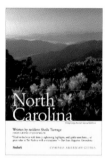

Édouard Manet's *The Bullfight* (1864) hangs in the Garden Court. Two of the Frick's three Vermeers—*Officer and Laughing Girl* (circa 1658) and *Girl Interrupted at Her Music* (1660–61)—hang by the front staircase. Fra Filippo Lippi's *The Annunciation* (circa 1440) hangs in the Octagon Room. Gainsborough and Reynolds portraits are in the dining room; canvases by Gainsborough, Constable, Turner, and Gilbert Stuart are in the library; and several Titians (including *Portrait of a Man in a Red Cap,* circa 1516), Holbeins, a Giovanni Bellini (*St. Francis in the Desert,* circa 1480), and an El Greco (*St. Jerome,* circa 1590–1600) are in the "living hall." Nearly 50 additional paintings, as well as much sculpture, decorative arts, and furniture, are in the West and East galleries. Three Rembrandts, including *The Polish Rider* (circa 1655) and *Self-Portrait* (1658), as well as a third Vermeer, *Mistress and Maid* (circa 1665–70), hang in the former; paintings by Whistler, Goya, Van Dyck, Lorrain, and David in the latter. A free video presentation introducing the collection runs every hour in the Music Room. The free "ArtPhone" audio tour guides you through the museum at your own pace and is available in several languages. When you're through, the tranquil indoor court with a fountain and glass ceiling is a lovely spot for a respite. ✉ *1 E. 70th St., at 5th Ave., Upper East Side* ☎ *212/288–0700* 🌐 *www.frick.org* 🎫 *$12* ☞ *Children under 10 not admitted* ⏲ *Tues.–Thurs. 10–6, Fri. 10–9, Sat. 10–6, Sun. 1–6.*

21 **Goethe Institut.** In a 1907 beaux arts town house, this German cultural center hosts art exhibitions as well as lectures, films, and workshops; its extensive library includes German newspapers and periodicals. ✉ *1014 5th Ave., between E. 82nd and E. 83rd Sts., Upper East Side* ☎ *212/439–8700* 🌐 *www.goethe.de/newyork* 🎫 *Exhibitions free* ⏲ *Library Tues. and Thurs. noon–7, Wed. and Fri.–Sat. noon–5. Gallery Mon., Wed., and Fri. 10–5; Tues. and Thurs. 10–7.*

26 **Jewish Museum.** One of the largest collections of Judaica in the world, the Jewish Museum explores the development and meaning of Jewish identity and culture over the course of 4,000 years. Housed in a graystone Gothic-style 1908 mansion, the exhibitions draw on the museum's collection of artwork and ceremonial objects, ranging from a 3rd-century Roman burial plaque to 20th-century sculpture by Elie Nadelman. The two-floor permanent exhibition, "Culture and Continuity: The Jewish Journey" displays nearly 1,000 objects. Special exhibitions focus on Jewish history and art. ✉ *1109 5th Ave., at E. 92nd St., Upper East Side* ☎ *212/423–3200* 🌐 *www.jewishmuseum.org* 🎫 *$8; Thurs. 5–8 pay what you wish* ⏲ *Sun. 10–5:45, Mon.–Wed. 11–5:45, Thurs. 11–8, Fri. 11–3.*

20 **Metropolitan Museum of Art.** The largest art museum in the western hemisphere (spanning four blocks, it encompasses 2 million square ft), the Met is one of the city's supreme cultural institutions. Its permanent collection of nearly 3 million works of art from all over the world includes objects from the Paleolithic era to modern times—an assemblage whose quality and range make this one of the world's greatest museums.

Fodor's Choice ★

The Met first opened its doors on March 30, 1880, but the original Victorian Gothic redbrick building by Calvert Vaux has since been encased in other architecture, which in turn has been encased. The majestic 5th Avenue facade, designed by Richard Morris Hunt, was built in 1902 of gray Indiana limestone; later additions eventually surrounded the original building on the sides and back. (You can glimpse part of the museum's original redbrick facade in a room to the left of the top of the main staircase and on a side wall of the ground-floor European Sculpture Court.)

The 5th Avenue entrance leads into the **Great Hall,** a soaring neoclassical chamber that has been designated a landmark. Past the admission booths, a wide marble staircase leads up to the **European paintings** galleries, whose 2,500 works include Botticelli's *The Last Communion of St. Jerome* (circa 1490), Pieter Brueghel's *The Harvesters* (1565), El Greco's *View of Toledo* (circa 1590), Johannes Vermeer's *Young Woman with a Water Jug* (circa 1660), Velázquez's *Juan de Pareja* (1648), and Rembrandt's *Aristotle with a Bust of Homer* (1653). The arcaded **European Sculpture Court** includes Auguste Rodin's massive bronze *The Burghers of Calais* (1884–95).

The **American Wing,** in the northwest corner, is best approached from the first floor, where you enter through a refreshingly light and airy garden court graced with Tiffany stained-glass windows, cast-iron staircases by Louis Sullivan, and a marble federal-style facade taken from the Wall Street branch of the United States Bank. Take the elevator to the third floor and begin working your way down through the rooms decorated in period furniture—everything from a Shaker retiring room to a federal-era ballroom to the living room of a Frank Lloyd Wright house—and American paintings.

In the realm of 20th-century art, the Met was a latecomer, allowing the Museum of Modern Art and the Whitney to build their collections with little competition until the Metropolitan's contemporary art department was finally established in 1967. The Met has made up for lost time, however, and in 1987 it opened the three-story **Lila Acheson Wallace Wing.** Pablo Picasso's portrait of Gertrude Stein (1906) is the centerpiece of this collection. The **Iris and B. Gerald Cantor Roof Garden,** above this wing, open from May to late October, showcases 20th-century sculptures and provides a refreshing break with its unique view of Central Park and the Manhattan skyline.

Those with a taste for classical art should proceed to the left of the Great Hall on the first floor to see the **Greek galleries.** Grecian urns and mythological marble statuary are displayed beneath a skylighted, barrel-vaulted stone ceiling that forms one of the grandest museum spaces in the city. Although renovations are still in progress, Roman galleries are slated to open behind the Greek galleries, with a court for Roman sculpture, and space for the museum's collection of rare Roman wall paintings excavated from the lava of Mt. Vesuvius. The Met's awesome **Egyptian collection,** spanning some 4,000 years, is on the first floor, directly to the right of the Great Hall. Here you'll find papyrus pages from the Egyptian Book of the Dead, stone coffins engraved in hieroglyphics, and mummies. The collection's centerpiece is the **Temple of Dendur,** an entire Roman-period temple (circa 15 BC) donated by the Egyptian government in thanks for U.S. help in saving ancient monuments. Placed in a specially built gallery with views of Central Park, the temple faces east, as it did in its original location, and a pool of water has been installed at the same distance from it as the Nile once stood. Another spot suitable for contemplation is directly above the Egyptian treasures, in the **Asian galleries:** the Astor Court Chinese garden reproduces a Ming dynasty (1368–1644) scholar's courtyard, complete with water splashing over artfully positioned rocks.

Also on the first floor are the **Medieval galleries.** The Gothic sculptures, Byzantine enamels, and full-size baroque choir screen built in 1763 are impressive and may whet your appetite for the thousands of medieval objects displayed at the Cloisters, the Met's annex in Washington Heights. From the Medieval galleries continue straight on until you enter the cool, skylighted white space of the **Lehman Wing,** where the exquisite, mind-bogglingly large personal collection of the late donor, investment banker Robert Lehman, is displayed in rooms resembling those of his West 54th Street town house. The collection's strengths include old-master drawings; Renaissance paintings by Rembrandt, El Greco, Petrus Christus, and Hans Memling; French 18th-century furniture; and 19th-century canvases by Goya, Ingres, and Renoir. Even at peak periods, crowds tend to be sparse here. To the north of the Medieval Galleries is the **Arms & Armor** exhibit, which is full of chain mail, swords, shields, and fancy firearms. On the ground floor, the **Costume Institute** has changing exhibits of clothing and fashion spanning seven centuries that focus on subjects ranging from undergarments to Gianni Versace.

Although it exhibits roughly only a quarter of its vast holdings at any one time, the Met offers more than you can reasonably see in one visit. Focus on two to four sections and know that, somewhere, there's an empty exhibit that just might be more rewarding than the one you can't see due to the crowds. Walking tours and lectures are free with your admission contribution. Tours covering various sections of the museum begin about every 15 minutes on weekdays, less frequently on weekends; they depart from the tour board in the Great Hall. Self-guided audio tours can be rented at a desk in the Great Hall and often at the entrance to major exhibitions. Lectures, often related to temporary exhibitions, are given frequently. ✉ *5th Ave. at 82nd St., Upper East Side* ☎ *212/535–7710* 🌐 *www.metmuseum.org* 🎫 *$12* 🕐 *Tues.–Thurs. and Sun. 9:30–5:30, Fri. and Sat. 9:30–9.*

need a break?

The very popular Belgian café chain, **Le Pain Quotidien** (✉ 1131 Madison Ave., between E. 84th and E. 85th Sts., Upper East Side ☎ 212/327–4900), has a large, wide-plank pine communal table for croissants, tarts, brioche, and café au lait or simple meals of soup, open-face sandwiches, or salads. The quintessential Upper East Side café, **E.A.T.** (✉ 1064 Madison Ave., between E. 80th and E. 81st Sts., Upper East Side ☎ 212/772–0022), serves everything from carrot soup and tabbouleh salad to roast lamb sandwiches and chopped liver. The light and airy room bustles with diners from 7 AM to 10 PM daily.

★ 27 **Museum of the City of New York.** Unique aspects of the city are drawn together in this massive Georgian mansion built in 1930. From the Dutch settlers of Nieuw Amsterdam to the present day, with period rooms, dioramas, films, prints, paintings, sculpture, and clever displays of memorabilia, this museum's got it all. Special exhibits take up most of the space—don't expect an overarching account of city history. An exhibit on Broadway illuminates the history of American theater with costumes, set designs, and period photographs; the noteworthy toy gallery has several meticulously detailed dollhouses. Maps, nautical artifacts, Currier & Ives lithographs, and furniture collections constitute the rest of the museum's permanent displays. Weekend programs are oriented especially for kids. ✉ *1220 5th Ave., at E. 103rd St., Upper East Side* ☎ *212/534–1672* 🌐 *www.mcny.org* 🎫 *$7 suggested donation* 🕐 *Wed.–Sat. 10–5, Sun. noon–5.*

24 **National Academy of Design.** Since its founding in 1825, the Academy has required each member elected to its Museum and School of Fine Arts (the oldest art school in New York) to donate a representative work of art. This criterion produced a strong collection of 19th- and 20th-century American art, as members have included Mary Cassatt, Samuel F. B. Morse, Winslow Homer, John Singer Sargent, Frank Lloyd Wright, Jacob Lawrence, I. M. Pei, Robert Rauschenberg, Jennifer Bartlett, Chuck Close, and Red Grooms. Art and architecture shows highlight

both the permanent collection and loan exhibits. The collection's home is a stately 19th-century mansion donated in 1940 by sculptor and academy member Anna Hyatt Huntington and her husband Archer. Huntington's bronze, *Diana of the Chase* (1922), reigns triumphantly in the academy's foyer. ✉ *1083 5th Ave., between E. 89th and E. 90th Sts., Upper East Side* ☎ *212/369–4880* 🌐 *www.nationalacademy.org* 🎫 *$8; free Fri. 5–6* ⏲ *Wed.–Thurs. noon–5, Fri.–Sun. 11–6.*

22 **Neue Galerie New York.** Organized by the late art dealer Serge Sabarsky and cosmetics heir Ronald S. Lauder, the Neue Galerie specializes in early-20th-century German and Austrian art and design as epitomized by Gustav Klimt, Vasily Kandinsky, Paul Klee, Egon Schiele, and Josef Hoffman and other designers from the Wiener Werkstatte. The two-floor gallery, along with a café serving Viennese pastries and a top-notch design shop, are in a 1914 mansion designed by Carrère and Hastings, which was home to Mrs. Cornelius Vanderbilt III, the top social hostess of the Gilded Age. ✉ *1048 5th Ave., at E. 86th St., Upper East Side* ☎ *212/628–6200* 🌐 *www.neuegalerie.org* 🎫 *$10* ☞ *Children under 12 not admitted; under 16 must be accompanied by an adult* ⏲ *Mon. 11–6, Fri. 11–9, weekends 11–6.*

need a break?

In an elegant, high-ceilinged space adjacent to the Neue Galerie, **Café Sabarsky** (✉ 1048 5th Ave., at E. 86th St., Upper East Side ☎ 212/288–0665) serves Viennese coffee, cakes, strudel, and Sacher torte (Monday and Wednesday–Sunday 11–6). If you seek something more than a sugar fix, the savory menu includes trout crepes and goulash.

23 **Solomon R. Guggenheim Museum.** Frank Lloyd Wright's landmark museum building is visited as much for its famous architecture as it is for its superlative art. Opened in 1959, shortly after Wright died, the Guggenheim is an icon of modernist architecture, designed specifically to showcase—and complement—modern art. Outside the curvaceous building, Wright's attention to detail is strikingly evident—in the portholelike windows on its south side, the circular pattern of the sidewalk, and the smoothness of the hand-plastered concrete. Inside, under a 92-ft-high glass dome, a ¼-mi-long ramp spirals down past changing exhibitions. The museum has especially strong holdings in Vasily Kandinsky, Paul Klee, Marc Chagall, Pablo Picasso, and Robert Mapplethorpe. In its Tower galleries, double-high ceilings accommodate extraordinarily large art pieces, and the Tower's fifth-floor sculpture terrace has a view overlooking Central Park. On permanent display, the museum's Thannhauser Collection is comprised primarily of works by French impressionists and neo-impressionists including Matisse, van Gogh, Toulouse-Lautrec, and Cézanne. Changing exhibitions focus on artists ranging from Norman Rockwell to Jeff Koons. Since its founding, the museum has opened branches around the world, including the renowned Frank O. Gehry–designed Guggenheim Bilbao (1997) in Spain. ✉ *1071 5th Ave., between E. 88th and E. 89th Sts., Upper East Side* ☎ *212/423–3500* 🌐 *www.guggenheim.org* 🎫 *$12; Fri. 6–8 pay what you wish* ⏲ *Mon.–Wed. and weekends 10–5:45, Fri. 10–8.*

Fodor's Choice ★

CENTRAL PARK

For many residents, Central Park is the greatest—and most indispensable—part of New York City. Without the park's 843 acres of meandering paths, tranquil lakes, ponds, and open meadows, New Yorkers might be a lot less sane. Every day thousands of joggers, cyclists, in-line skaters, and walkers make their daily jaunts around the park's loop, the reservoir, and various other parts of the park. Come summertime the park serves as Manhattan's Riviera, with sun worshipers crowding every available patch of grass. Throughout the year pleasure seekers of all ages come to enjoy horseback riding, softball, ice-skating or roller-skating, rock climbing, croquet, tennis, bird-watching, boating, chess, checkers, theater, concerts, skateboarding, folk dancing, and more—or simply to escape the rumble of traffic, walk through the trees, and feel, at least for a moment, far from the urban frenzy.

No matter how close to nature New Yorkers feel when reveling in it, Central Park was in fact the first artificially landscaped park in the United States. The design was conceived in 1857 by Frederick Law Olmsted and Calvert Vaux, the founders of the landscape architecture profession in the United States. Their design was one of 33 submitted in a contest arranged by the Central Park Commission. The Greensward Plan, as it was called, combined pastoral, picturesque, and formal elements: open rolling meadows complement fanciful landscapes and grand, formal walkways. "It's up to us to turn democratic ideals into trees and dirt," said Vaux. The southern portion of the park has many formal elements, while the north end is deliberately more wild. Four transverse roads—at 66th, 79th, 86th, and 96th streets—were designed to carry crosstown traffic beneath the park's hills and tunnels so that park goers would not be disturbed, and 40 bridges were conceived—each with its own unique design and name—to give strollers easy access to various areas.

The job of constructing the park was monumental. Hundreds of residents were displaced, swamps were drained, and great walls of Manhattan schist were blasted. Thousands of workers were employed to move some 5 million cubic yards of soil and plant thousands of trees and shrubs in a project that lasted 16 years. Today, thanks to the efforts of the Central Park Conservancy, a private, not-for-profit organization, Olmsted and Vaux's green oasis looks better than ever.

In the years following the park's opening in 1859, more than half its visitors arrived by carriage. Today, with a little imagination, you can still experience the park as they did, by hiring a horse-drawn carriage at Grand Army Plaza or any other major intersection of Central Park South at 59th Street between 5th Avenue and Columbus Circle. Rates, which are regulated, are $34 for the first half hour and $10 for each additional quarter hour for up to four people. The official Web site for the park is www.centralparknyc.org.

Numbers in the text correspond to numbers in the margin and on the Central Park map.

a good walk

To explore the park on foot, begin at the southeast corner, at Grand Army Plaza, at 59th Street. The first path off the main road (East Drive) leads to **The Pond** ① ⚑, where Gapstow Bridge provides a great vantage point for the oft-photographed midtown skyscrapers. Heading north on the path, you'll come to **Wollman Memorial Rink** ②, whose popularity is second only to that of the rink at Rockefeller Center. Turn your back to the rink, and you'll see **The Dairy** ③, which serves as the park's main visitor center. As you walk up the hill to the Dairy, you'll pass the Chess and Checkers House to your left, where gamesters gather on weekends (playing pieces are at the Dairy).

As you leave the Dairy, to your right (west) is the Playmates Arch, which leads to a large area of ball fields and playgrounds. Coming through the arch, you'll hear the jaunty music of the antique **Friedsam Memorial Carousel** ④, the second oldest on the East Coast.

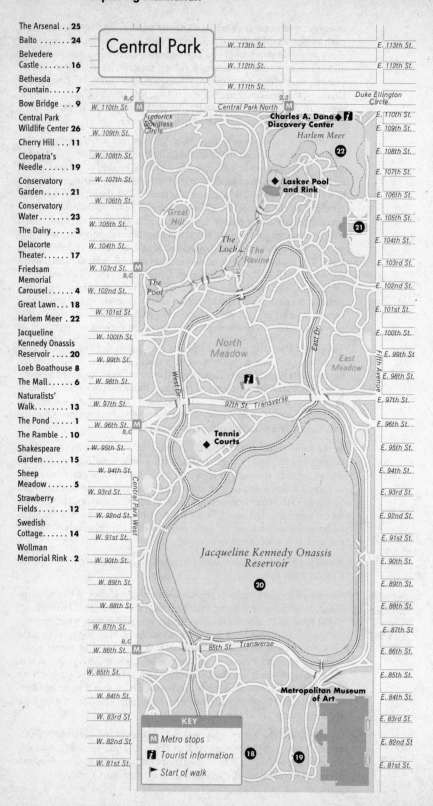

The Arsenal . . 25
Balto 24
Belvedere Castle 16
Bethesda Fountain 7
Bow Bridge . . . 9
Central Park Wildlife Center 26
Cherry Hill . . . 11
Cleopatra's Needle 19
Conservatory Garden 21
Conservatory Water 23
The Dairy 3
Delacorte Theater 17
Friedsam Memorial Carousel 4
Great Lawn . . . 18
Harlem Meer . 22
Jacqueline Kennedy Onassis Reservoir 20
Loeb Boathouse 8
The Mall 6
Naturalists' Walk 13
The Pond 1
The Ramble . . 10
Shakespeare Garden 15
Sheep Meadow 5
Strawberry Fields 12
Swedish Cottage 14
Wollman Memorial Rink . 2

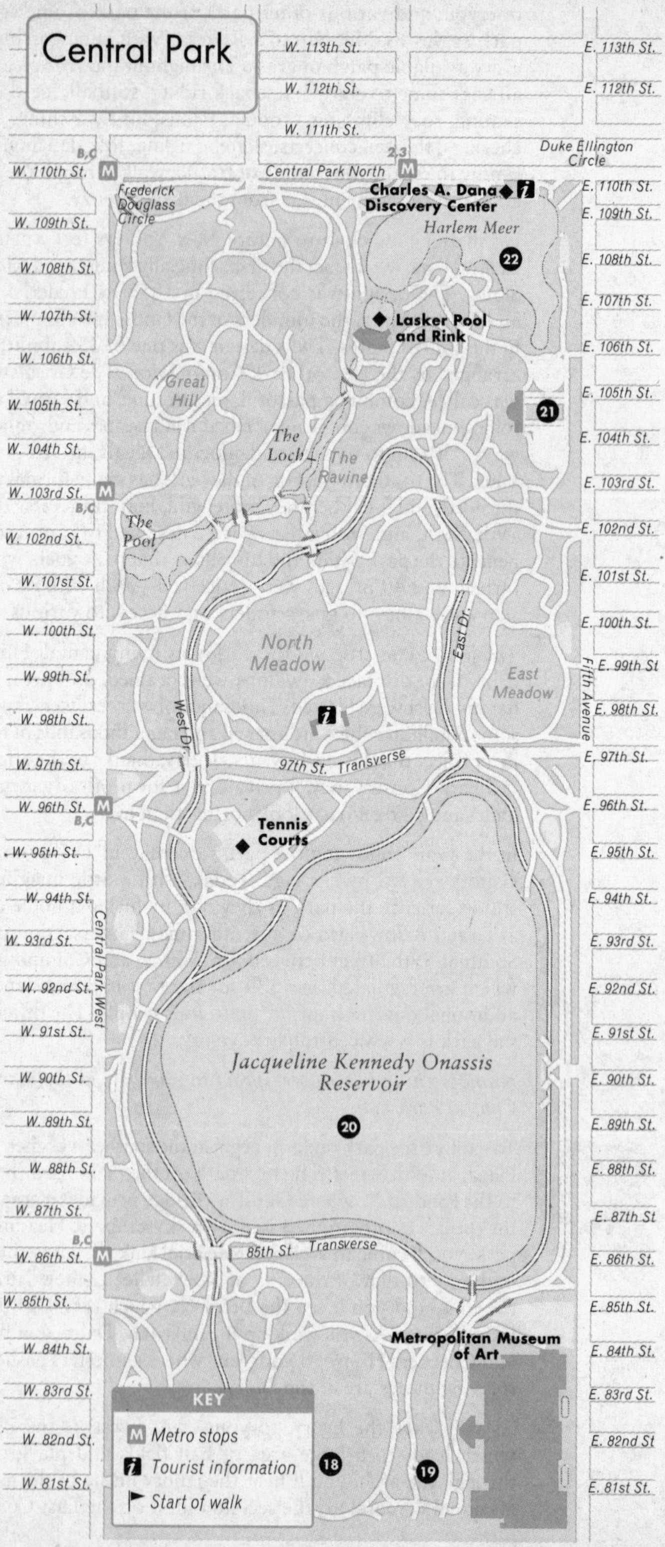

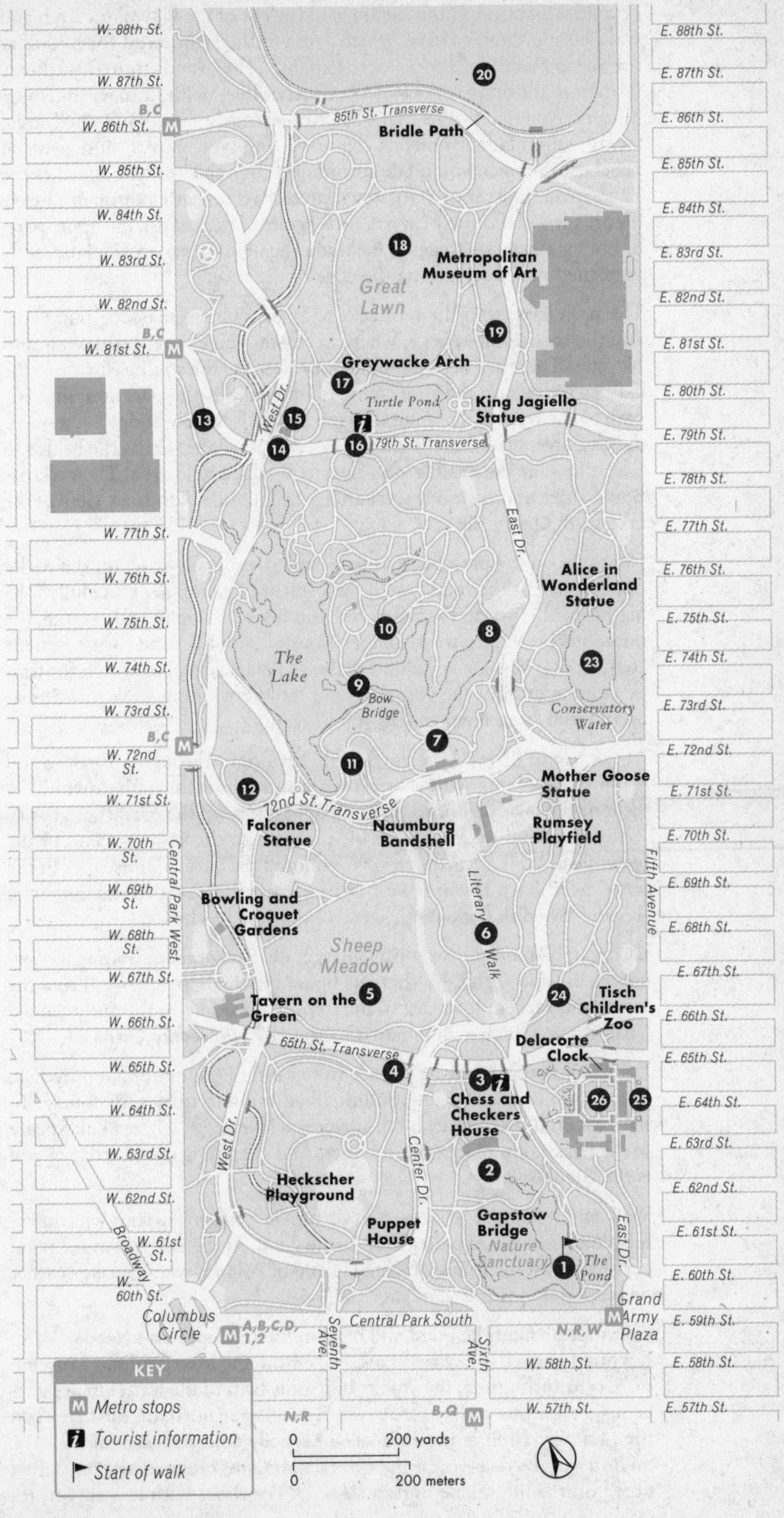
W. 88th St.
W. 87th St.
B,C
W. 86th St.
W. 85th St.
W. 84th St.
W. 83rd St.
W. 82nd St.
B,C
W. 81st St.
W. 77th St.
W. 76th St.
W. 75th St.
W. 74th St.
W. 73rd St.
B,C
W. 72nd St.
W. 71st St.
W. 70th St.
W. 69th St.
W. 68th St.
W. 67th St.
W. 66th St.
W. 65th St.
W. 64th St.
W. 63rd St.
W. 62nd St.
W. 61st St.
W. 60th St.
Broadway
Central Park West
Columbus Circle
A,B,C,D, 1,2
Seventh Ave.
Central Park South
Sixth Ave.
N,R,W
Grand Army Plaza
W. 58th St.
W. 57th St.
N,R
B,Q
E. 88th St.
E. 87th St.
E. 86th St.
E. 85th St.
E. 84th St.
E. 83rd St.
E. 82nd St.
E. 81st St.
E. 80th St.
E. 79th St.
E. 78th St.
E. 77th St.
E. 76th St.
E. 75th St.
E. 74th St.
E. 73rd St.
E. 72nd St.
E. 71st St.
E. 70th St.
E. 69th St.
E. 68th St.
E. 67th St.
E. 66th St.
E. 65th St.
E. 64th St.
E. 63rd St.
E. 62nd St.
E. 61st St.
E. 60th St.
E. 59th St.
E. 58th St.
E. 57th St.
Fifth Avenue
85th St. Transverse
Bridle Path
Metropolitan Museum of Art
Great Lawn
Greywacke Arch
Turtle Pond
King Jagiello Statue
79th St. Transverse
West Dr.
East Dr.
Alice in Wonderland Statue
The Lake
Bow Bridge
Conservatory Water
Mother Goose Statue
72nd St. Transverse
Falconer Statue
Naumburg Bandshell
Rumsey Playfield
Literary Walk
Bowling and Croquet Gardens
Sheep Meadow
Tavern on the Green
Tisch Children's Zoo
65th St. Transverse
Delacorte Clock
Chess and Checkers House
Center Dr.
Heckscher Playground
Puppet House
Gapstow Bridge
Nature Sanctuary
The Pond
KEY
Metro stops
Tourist information
Start of walk
0
200 yards
0
200 meters

From the carousel, climb the slope to the left of the Playmates Arch and walk beside Center Drive, which veers to the right. Stop for a look at the **Sheep Meadow** 5, a 15-acre expanse. The grand, formal walkway farther up the drive is **The Mall** 6, which is lined with statuary and magnificent American elms. The Mall opens up into a band-shell area, where rollerbladers practice figure-skating-type moves, and rows of benches often accommodate drumming circles. The road ahead is the 72nd Street transverse, a crosstown street. Pass beneath it through a lovely tile arcade—elaborately carved birds and fruit trees adorn the upper parts of both staircases—to get to **Bethesda Fountain** 7, set on an elaborately patterned paved terrace on the edge of the lake.

The path east from the terrace leads past Chinese massage purveyors and the **Loeb Boathouse** 8, where in season you can rent rowboats and bicycles. There are decent public rest rooms on the southeast side of the café as well as on the staircase leading to the Bethesda Fountain. The path to the west of the fountain's terrace leads to **Bow Bridge** 9, a splendid cast-iron bridge arching over a neck of the lake. Cross the bridge to take a look at **The Ramble** 10, a heavily wooded wild area. Then recross Bow Bridge and continue west along the lakeside path for a view of the lake from **Cherry Hill** 11.

Continue on the path back to the 72nd Street transverse; on the rocky outcrop across the road, you'll see a statue of a falconer gracefully lofting his bird. Turn to the right, and you'll see a more prosaic statue, the pompous bronze figure of Daniel Webster with his hand thrust into his coat. Cross West Drive behind Webster, being careful to watch for traffic coming around the corner. Tramp up the winding walk into **Strawberry Fields** 12, a memorial to John Lennon.

At the top of Strawberry Fields' hill, turn right through a rustic wood arbor thickly hung with wisteria vines and follow the path downhill. A view of the lake will open on your right. Start up the road that goes to 77th Street and take the path off the right to the southern end of the **Naturalists' Walk** 13. After you've explored the varied landscapes of the walk, head back toward West Drive. Cross the street to the authentic wooden **Swedish Cottage** 14, scene of marionette shows.

Rising up behind the Swedish Cottage, the **Shakespeare Garden** 15 covers the hillside with flora that has figured in the Bard's work. From the top of the garden, turn east to the steps that lead up to the aptly named Vista Rock, which is dominated by the 1872 **Belvedere Castle** 16.

Look out from the castle terrace over Turtle Pond, populated by fish, ducks, and in summer dragonflies, in addition to turtles, of course. To the left you'll see the back of the **Delacorte Theater** 17, where Shakespeare in the Park takes place each summer. And stretching out in front of you is the **Great Lawn** 18.

Walk out the south end of the terrace, turn left, and make your way downhill along the shaded path above Turtle Pond. At the east end of the pond curve left past the statue of King Jagiello of Poland, where groups gather on weekends for folk dancing.

Continue around the pond and head uphill to **Cleopatra's Needle** 19, an Egyptian obelisk just across East Drive from the Metropolitan Museum of Art (in springtime, the cherry blossoms behind the museum are gorgeous). Vigorous walkers may want to continue north on East Drive to the pathway circling the **Jacqueline Kennedy Onassis Reservoir** 20. A ½ mi north of the reservoir is the spectacular **Conservatory Garden** 21. Just north of it is the serene **Harlem Meer** 22. For those with less energy, return south from Cleopatra's Needle, following the path through Greywacke Arch under East Drive. Then angle right (south), around the back corner of the Metropolitan Museum, and take the first right.

After you pass the dog-walking stretch of Cedar Hill on the right, continue south to one of the park's most formal areas: the symmetrical stone basin of the **Conservatory Water** 23, which is often crowded with remote-control model sailboats. Climb the hill at the far end of the water, cross the 72nd Street transverse, and follow the path south. When you see a rustic wooden shelter atop an outcrop of rock, take the path on the right to see **Balto** 24, a bronze statue of the real-life sled dog. The path circles back to the Tisch Children's Zoo, after which you'll pass under the Denesmouth Arch to the elaborately designed Delacorte Clock. A path to the left will take you around to the front entrance of **The Arsenal** 25, which houses various exhibits and some great WPA-era murals. Just past the clock is the **Central Park Wildlife Center** 26, formerly known as the Zoo.

TIMING Allow three to four hours for this route so that you can enjoy its pastoral pleasures at a leisurely pace. The circular drive is closed to auto traffic weekdays 10–3 (except for the southeast portion of the road, up to 72nd Street) and 7–10, and weekends and holidays. Nonautomotive traffic is often heavy and sometimes fast moving, so always be careful when you're crossing the road, and stay toward the inside when you're walking. Weekends are the liveliest time in the park—free entertainment is everywhere, and the entire social microcosm is on parade.

Central Park has the lowest crime rate of any precinct in the city. Just use common sense and stay within sight of other park visitors. Take this walk only during the day, since the park is fairly empty after dark.

For a recorded schedule of park events, call 888/697–2757. For a schedule of walking tours in Central Park, call 212/360–2727. Or visit the park's Web site at www.centralparknyc.org. Directions, park maps, and event calendars can also be obtained from volunteers at two 5th Avenue information booths, at East 60th Street and East 72nd Street. Food for thought: although there are cafés connected with several attractions, as well as food stands near many park entrances, food choices are limited; a picnic lunch is usually a good idea.

What to See

25 **The Arsenal.** Built between 1847 and 1851 as a storage facility for munitions, the Arsenal predates the park and is the oldest extant structure within its grounds. Between 1869 and 1877 it was the early home of the American Museum of Natural History, and it now serves as headquarters of the Parks and Recreation Department. The downstairs lobby has WPA-era murals, an upstairs gallery has changing exhibits relating to park and natural-environmental design, and a small public library offers information about New York City parks and other attractions. Olmsted and Vaux's original plan for Central Park is in a display case on the third floor. ✉ *830 5th Ave., at E. 64th St., Central Park* ☎ *212/360–8111* 💲 *Free* ⏲ *Weekdays 9–5.*

24 **Balto.** This bronze statue commemorates Balto, a real-life sled dog who led a team of huskies that carried medicine for 60 mi across perilous ice to Nome, Alaska, during a 1925 diphtheria epidemic. The surface of the statue is shiny from being petted by thousands of children. ✉ *East of Center Dr. near Literary Walk and E. 67th St., Central Park.*

16 **Belvedere Castle.** Standing regally atop Vista Rock, Belvedere Castle was built in 1872 of the same gray Manhattan schist that thrusts out of the soil in dramatic outcrops throughout the park (you can examine

some of this schist, polished and striated by Ice Age glaciers, from the lip of the rock). From here you can also see the stage of Delacorte Theater and observe the picnickers and softball players on the Great Lawn. The castle, a typically 19th-century mishmash of styles—Gothic with Romanesque, Chinese, Moorish, and Egyptian motifs—was deliberately kept small so that when it was viewed from across the lake, the lake would seem bigger. (The Ramble's forest now obscures the lake's castle view.) Since 1919 it has been a U.S. Weather Bureau station; look for twirling meteorological instruments atop the tower. Inside, the Henry Luce Nature Observatory has nature exhibits, children's workshops, and educational programs. Free discovery kits containing binoculars, bird guides, maps, and sketching materials are available in exchange for two pieces of identification. ✉ *Midpark at 79th St. Transverse, Central Park* ☎ *212/772–0210* 🎫 *Free* ⏲ *Apr.–Oct., Tues.–Sun. 9–5; Nov.–Mar., Tues.–Sun. 10–4.*

❼ **Bethesda Fountain.** Few New York views are more romantic than the one from the top of the magnificent stone staircase that leads down to the ornate, three-tier Bethesda Fountain. You might recognize it from one of the many films that have been shot here. The fountain was dedicated in 1873 to commemorate the soldiers who died at sea during the Civil War. Named for the biblical pool in Jerusalem, which was supposedly given healing powers by an angel, it features the statue *The Angel of the Waters* rising from the center. The four figures around the fountain's base symbolize Temperance, Purity, Health, and Peace. Beyond the terrace stretches the lake, filled with swans and amateur rowboat captains. ✉ *Midpark at 72nd St. Tranverse, Central Park.*

Fodor's Choice ★

❾ **Bow Bridge.** This splendid cast-iron bridge arches over a neck of the lake between Bethesda Fountain and The Ramble. Stand here to admire the water's mirror image of vintage apartment buildings peeping above the treetops—a quintessential New York image. ✉ *Midpark north of 72nd St. Tranverse, Central Park.*

❻ ㉖ **Central Park Wildlife Center.** Even a leisurely visit to this small but delightful menagerie, home to more than 130 species, will only take about an hour. The biggest specimens here are the polar bears—go to the Bronx Zoo if you need tigers, giraffes, and elephants. Clustered around the central Sea Lion Pool are separate exhibits for each of the Earth's major environments. The Polar Circle features a huge penguin tank and polar-bear floe; the open-air Temperate Territory is highlighted by a pit of chattering monkeys; and the Rain Forest contains the flora and fauna of the tropics. The **Tisch Children's Zoo,** on the north side of the Denesmouth Arch, has interactive, hands-on exhibits where you can pet such domestic animals as pigs, sheep, goats, and cows. There's also an enchanted forest area, designed to thrill the six-and-under set. Above a redbrick arcade near the Zoo is the **Delacorte Clock,** a delightful glockenspiel that was dedicated to the city by philanthropist George T. Delacorte. Its fanciful bronze face is decorated with a menagerie of mechanical animals, including a dancing bear, a kangaroo, a penguin, and monkeys that rotate and hammer their bells when the clock chimes its tune every half hour. ✉ *Entrance at 5th Ave. and E. 64th St., Central Park* ☎ *212/439–6500* 🌐 *www.wcs.org/zoos/centralpark* 🎫 *$3.50* ☞ *No children under 16 admitted without adult* ⏲ *Apr.–Oct., weekdays 10–5, weekends 10:30–5:30; Nov.–Mar., daily 10–4:30.*

⓫ **Cherry Hill.** Originally a watering area for horses, this circular plaza with a small wrought-iron-and-gilt fountain is a great vantage point for the lake and the West Side skyline. ✉ *Midpark near 72nd St. Transverse, Central Park.*

19 **Cleopatra's Needle.** This hieroglyphic-covered obelisk that began life in Heliopolis, Egypt, around 1600 BC, has nothing to do with Cleopatra—it's just New York's nickname for the work. It was eventually carted off to Alexandria by the Romans in 12 BC, and landed here on February 22, 1881, when the khedive of Egypt made it a gift to the city. It stands behind the Metropolitan Museum, on the west side of East Park Drive. A century in New York has done more to ravage the Needle than millennia of globe-trotting, and the hieroglyphics have sadly worn away to a tabula rasa. The copper crabs supporting the huge stone at each corner almost seem squashed by its weight. ✉ *E. Park Dr. north of 79th St. Transverse, Central Park.*

21 **Conservatory Garden.** These magnificent formal gardens occupy 6 acres near Central Park's northeast corner, near the Harlem Meer. The conservatory's entrance is marked by elaborate wrought-iron gates that once graced the midtown 5th Avenue mansion of Cornelius Vanderbilt II. The **Central Garden,** in the classic Italian style, has a lawn bordered by yew hedges and cool crab-apple allées. Across the lawn is the large Conservatory Fountain, beyond which a semicircular wisteria-draped pergola rises into the hillside. The **North Garden,** in the French tradition, marshals large numbers of bedding plants into elaborate floral patterns. The three spirited girls dancing in the Untermeyer Fountain are at the heart of a great circular bed where 20,000 tulips bloom in spring and 2,000 chrysanthemums herald autumn. Perennials in the English-style **South Garden** surround a statue of characters from the classic children's book *The Secret Garden* by Frances Hodgson Burnett. ✉ *Near 5th Ave. and E. 105th St., Central Park* ☎ *212/360–2766* *Free* ⏲ *Daily 8–dusk.*

23 **Conservatory Water.** The sophisticated model boats that sail this Renaissance revival–style stone basin are raced each Saturday morning at 10, spring through fall. At the north end is one of the park's most beloved statues, José de Creeft's 1960 bronze sculpture of **Alice in Wonderland,** sitting on a giant mushroom with the Mad Hatter, March Hare, and leering Cheshire Cat in attendance; children clamber all over it. On the west side of the pond, a bronze statue of **Hans Christian Andersen,** the Ugly Duckling at his feet, is the site of storytelling hours on summer Saturdays at 11 AM. Model sailboats can be rented from a concession by the boat pond. ✉ *East side of park, from E. 73rd to E. 75th Sts., Central Park.*

3 **The Dairy.** When it was built in the 19th century, the Dairy sat amid grazing cows and sold milk by the glass. Today the Dairy's painted, pointed eaves, steeple, and high-pitched slate roof harbor the **Central Park Visitor Center,** which has exhibits on the park's history, maps, a park reference library, and information about park events. ✉ *Midpark south of 65th St. Transverse, Central Park* ☎ *212/794–6564* ⏲ *Apr.–Oct., Tues.–Sun. 10–5; Nov.–Mar., Tues.–Sun. 10–4.*

17 **Delacorte Theater.** Some of the best things in New York are, indeed, free—but have *long* lines—including summer performances by the Public Theater/New York Shakespeare Festival at this open-air stage. The casts seem to get more Hollywood-star-encrusted every year. Meryl Streep, Michelle Pfeiffer, Christopher Walken, Helen Hunt, Morgan Freeman, and Kevin Kline are just a few of the luminaries who have performed in the park. Tickets are free and are given out starting at 1 PM on the day of each show. Plan to line up by mid-morning or earlier if there have been good reviews; each person on line is allowed two tickets for that evening's performance. Same-day tickets are also given away at the Public Theater (425 Lafayette St., East Village) at 1 PM. ✉ *Midpark near*

W. 81st St., Central Park ☎ *212/539–8750 seasonal* ⏲ *Mid-June–Labor Day, Tues.–Sun. 8 PM.*

★ ❹ **Friedsam Memorial Carousel.** Remarkable for the size of its hand-carved steeds—all 57 are three-quarters the size of real horses—this carousel was built in 1908 and moved here from Coney Island in 1951. Today it's considered one of the finest examples of turn-of-the-20th-century folk art. The carousel's original Wurlitzer organ plays a variety of tunes, from old-time waltzes to polkas. ✉ *Midpark south of 65th St. Transverse, Central Park* ☎ *212/879–0244* *$1* ⏲ *Apr.–Nov., daily 10–6; Dec.–Mar., weekends 10–4:30, weather permitting.*

need a break?

At the **Ballfields Café** (✉ Midpark near W. 63rd St., Central Park), in the redbrick Ballplayers House south of the carousel, kids can order grilled cheese or peanut-butter-and-jelly sandwiches before or after a spin on the carousel. For the over-21 crowd, there's a wine and beer list.

⓲ **Great Lawn.** This 14-acre oval greensward has endured millions of footsteps, thousands of ball games, hundreds of downpours, dozens of concerts, and even the crush attending one papal mass. Yet, it's the stuff of a suburbanite's dream—perfectly tended turf (a mix of rye and Kentucky bluegrass), state-of-the-art drainage systems, automatic sprinklers, and careful horticultural monitoring. The area hums with action on weekends and most summer evenings, when its softball fields and picnicking grounds provide a much-needed outlet for city dwellers of all ages. ✉ *Midpark between 81st and 85th Sts., Central Park.*

㉒ **Harlem Meer.** Those who never venture beyond 96th Street miss out on two of the park's loveliest attractions: the Conservatory Garden and Harlem Meer, an 11-acre sheet of water where, in warmer months, as many as 100 people a day fish for stocked largemouth bass, catfish, golden shiners, and bluegills on a catch-and-release basis. At the meer's north end is the Victorian-style **Charles A. Dana Discovery Center,** where you can learn about geography, orienteering, ecology, and the history of the upper park. Within walking distance of the center are fortifications from the American Revolution and other historic sites, as well as woodlands, meadows, rocky bluffs, lakes, and streams. Fishing poles are available with identification from mid-April through October. ✉ *Between 5th and Lenox Aves. at Central Park N, Central Park* ☎ *212/860–1370* ⏲ *Discovery Center Apr.–Oct., Tues.–Sun. 10–5; Nov.–Mar., Tues.–Sun. 10–4.*

⑳ **Jacqueline Kennedy Onassis Reservoir.** Named for the former first lady, who frequently jogged in the area and lived nearby, this 106-acre body of water was built in 1862 to provide fresh water to Manhattan residents. Although it still contains 1 billion gallons, it's no longer used for drinking water—the city's main reservoirs are upstate. A 1.58-mi cinder path circling the lake is popular with runners year-round. If you come for some exercise, though, observe local traffic rules and run counterclockwise. Even if you're not training for the New York Marathon, it's worth visiting the reservoir for the stellar views of surrounding high-rises and the stirring sunsets; in spring and fall the hundreds of trees around it burst into color, and migrant waterfowl are plentiful. Just remember to look out for the athletes, as they have the right of way. ✉ *Midpark from 85th to 96th Sts., Central Park.*

❽ **Loeb Boathouse.** At the brick neo-Victorian boathouse on the park's 18-acre lake, you can rent a dinghy, take a ride in an authentic Venetian gondola, or pedal off on a rented bicycle. ✉ *Midpark at E. Park Dr.,*

Central Park ☎ 212/517–2233 Boat rental $10 per hr ($30 deposit); $30 per half hr for gondola rides; bicycle rental $6–$20 per hr, deposit required ⏲ Boats and bikes available Mar.–Oct., daily 10–5, weather permitting. Call for gondolier's schedule.

need a break?

The **Boathouse Cafe** (✉ Midpark at E. Park Dr., Central Park ☎ 212/517–2233) is an open-air restaurant and bar that serves lunch and dinner. An adjacent cafeteria dishes up a good cheap breakfast and lunch. In warm weather, the lake view from the Boathouse's terrace is nothing short of idyllic.

1

★ 6 **The Mall.** Around the turn of the 20th century, fashionable ladies and gentlemen used to gather to see and be seen on this broad, formal walkway. Today the Mall looks as grand as ever. The south end of its main path, the **Literary Walk,** is covered by the majestic canopy of the largest collection of American elms in North America and lined by statues of authors and artists such as Robert Burns, Shakespeare, and Sir Walter Scott. East of the Mall, behind the Naumburg Bandshell, is the site of **SummerStage,** a free summertime concert series. ✉ *Midpark between 66th and 72nd Sts., Central Park.*

13 **Naturalists' Walk.** Starting at the West 79th Street entrance to the park, this landscaped nature walk (through which you can wind your way toward the **Swedish Cottage,** the **Shakespeare Garden,** and **Belvedere Castle**) has spectacular rock outcrops; a stream that attracts bird life; a woodland area with various native trees; stepping-stone trails; and, thankfully, benches. ✉ *Off Central Park W between W. 77th and W. 81st Sts., Central Park.*

1 **The Pond.** Swans and ducks can sometimes be spotted on the calm waters of the Pond. For an unbeatable view of the city skyline, walk along the shore to **Gapstow Bridge.** From left to right you'll see the brown peak-roof Sherry-Netherland Hotel; the black-and-white CBS Building; the rose-color Chippendale-style top of the Sony Building; the black-glass shaft of Trump Tower; and, in front, the green gables of the Plaza hotel. ✉ *Central Park S and 5th Ave., Central Park.*

10 **The Ramble.** Designed to resemble upstate New York's Adirondack Mountain region, the Ramble is a heavily wooded, 37-acre area laced with twisting, climbing paths. This is prime bird-watching territory since it's a rest stop along a major migratory route, and shelters many of the more than 270 species of birds that have been sighted in the park. The Central Park Conservancy leads walking tours here. Because the Ramble is so dense and isolated, however, it's not a good place to wander alone or at night. ✉ *Midpark between E. 74th St. and 79th St. Transverse, Central Park* ☎ *212/360–2727 for tours.*

15 **Shakespeare Garden.** Inspired by the flora mentioned in the playwright's work, this somewhat hidden garden (between Belvedere Castle and the Swedish Cottage) is well worth a stop. Under the dedicated care of the gardener something is almost always blooming on the terraced hillside of lush beds. The fantastic spring bulb display beginning in March and June's peak bloom of antique roses are particularly stunning times to visit. The curving paths are furnished with handsome rustic benches, making this park-designated quiet zone a superb spot for a good read or contemplative thought. ✉ *W. Park Dr. and 79th St. Transverse, Central Park.*

5 **Sheep Meadow.** A sheep grazing area until 1934, this grassy 15-acre meadow is now a favorite of picnickers and sunbathers. It's a designated

quiet zone; the most vigorous sports allowed are kite flying and Frisbee tossing. Just west of the meadow, the famous **Tavern on the Green,** originally the sheepfold, was erected by Boss Tweed in 1870 and is now an overpriced restaurant frequented largely by tourists. ✉ *East of West Dr. and north of 65th St. Transverse, Central Park.*

need a break? The Moorish-style **Mineral Springs Pavilion** (✉ Midpark near W. 68th St., Central Park) at the north end of the Sheep Meadow was designed by Calvert Vaux and J. Wrey Mould, who also designed Bethesda Terrace. Built as one of the park's four refreshment stands in the late 1860s, the pavilion still has a snack bar. Behind it are the croquet grounds and lawn-bowling greens.

12 **Strawberry Fields.** This memorial to John Lennon, who penned the classic 1967 song "Strawberry Fields Forever," is sometimes called the "international garden of peace." Its curving paths, shrubs, trees, and flower beds donated by many countries create a deliberately informal landscape reminiscent of the English parks of Lennon's homeland. Every year on December 8, Beatles fans mark the anniversary of Lennon's death by gathering around the star-shape, black-and-white IMAGINE mosaic set into the pavement. Lennon's 1980 murder took place across the street at the Dakota apartment building, where he lived. ✉ *W. Park Dr. and W. 72nd St., Central Park.*

14 **Swedish Cottage.** This traditional Swedish schoolhouse was imported in 1876 for the Philadelphia Exhibition and brought to Central Park soon thereafter. Marionette theater is performed regularly to the delight of young park visitors. ✉ *W. Park Dr. north of 79th St. Transverse, Central Park* ☎ *212/988–9093* *$6* *Shows Tues.–Fri. 10:30 and noon; Sat. 1. No Sat. shows July–Aug.; call for reservations.*

2 **Wollman Memorial Rink.** Its music blaring out into the tranquillity of the park can be a bit of an intrusion, but you can't deny that the lower park makes a great setting for a spin on the ice. Even if you don't want to join in, you can stand on the terrace to watch ice-skaters throughout the winter. ✉ *E. Park Dr. south of 65th St. Transverse, Central Park* ☎ *212/439–6900* *$11 Fri.–Sun., $8.50 Mon.–Thurs.; skate rentals and lockers extra* *Nov.–Mar., Mon.–Tues. 10–2:30, Wed.–Thurs. 10–10, Fri.–Sat. 10 AM–11 PM, Sun. 10–9, weather permitting.*

THE UPPER WEST SIDE

The Upper West Side—never as exclusive as the tony East Side—has always had an earthy appeal. Although real estate prices have gone sky high (its restored brownstones and co-op apartments are among the city's most coveted residences), the Upper West Side is still a haven for families—albeit increasingly well-heeled ones—who give the area a pleasant, neighborhood feel. On weekends, stroller-pushing parents cram the sidewalks and shoppers jam the fantastic gourmet food stores and fashion emporiums that line Broadway. In the evenings, the action moves inside as singles from the city and suburbs mingle in bars and restaurants along Columbus and Amsterdam avenues. Altogether, the neighborhood's lively avenues, quiet tree-lined side streets, two flanking parks—Central on its east, Riverside on its west—and leading cultural complexes, such as the American Museum of Natural History and Lincoln Center, allow residents and visitors a great variety of things to do in a relatively compact area.

Numbers in the text correspond to numbers in the margin and on the Upper West Side & Morningside Heights map.

a good walk

The West Side story begins at **Columbus Circle** 1, the bustling intersection of Broadway, 8th Avenue, Central Park West, and Central Park South. Cars enter this enormous circle from any one of several directions (use caution and cross only at marked intersections). On the leafy southwest corner of Central Park, a line of horse-drawn carriages awaits passengers. If you're in the mood for an ecclesiastical outing, stop at the nearby **American Bible Society Gallery and Library** 2, home of the largest Bible collection in the United States.

With its parade of elegant, monumental apartment buildings on one side and Central Park on the other, Central Park West is one of the city's grandest avenues. In the 1930s the most coveted address along here was at the block-long Century (25 Central Park W), which went up in 1931, taking with it one of the last large lots below 96th Street—only two buildings have gone up on this stretch since then. The solid brick-and-limestone New York Society for Ethical Culture buildings (33 Central Park W and 2 W. 64th St.), built in 1902–10, host Sunday services as well as periodic lectures and concerts. From this corner, the view up the avenue is particularly handsome. Turn west on 64th Street; on your left, the West Side YMCA at No. 10 has a neo-Moorish portal with tiny carved figures representing the worlds of sports (golfers, tennis players) *and* religion (St. George slaying the dragon). As you approach Broadway, **Lincoln Center** 3, New York's premier performing arts venue, widens into view. On summer nights the brightly lighted fountain in the central plaza with the Metropolitan Opera House behind is a lovely sight.

On the east side of Columbus Avenue just below 66th Street stands the **American Folk Art Museum: Eva & Morris Feld Gallery** 4, a branch of the main museum. Around the corner at 77 West 66th Street is the headquarters of the ABC television network; ABC owns several buildings along Columbus Avenue as well, including some studios where news shows and soap operas are filmed, so keep an eye out for your favorite daytime doctors, tycoons, and temptresses. Up Columbus Avenue one block, turn right onto West 67th Street and head toward Central Park West, where just before the corner you'll encounter the Elizabethan front of the **Hotel des Artistes** 5. Across the street, just inside Central Park, is Tavern on the Green.

Walk north on the east (park) side of Central Park West for the best view of the stately apartment buildings that line the avenue. Mixed among them is the **Spanish & Portuguese Synagogue, Shearith Israel** 6 at West 70th Street, home of the country's oldest Jewish congregation. At 72nd Street cross back over Central Park West to get a close-up view of **The Dakota** 7, the châteaulike apartment building that presides over the block. Its neighbors to the north include several other famous apartment buildings. The Langham (135 Central Park W, at W. 73rd St.) is an Italian Renaissance–style high-rise that was designed by leading apartment architect Emery Roth in 1929–30. Roth also designed the twin-tower San Remo (145–146 Central Park W, at W. 74th St.), which was built in 1930; over the years, it has been home to Rita Hayworth, Dustin Hoffman, Raquel Welch, Paul Simon, Barry Manilow, Tony Randall, and Diane Keaton. The Kenilworth (151 Central Park W, at W. 75th St.), built in 1908, with its immense pair of ornate front columns, was once the address of Basil Rathbone (Hollywood's quintessential Sherlock Holmes) and Michael Douglas. The row of massive buildings along Central Park West breaks between West 77th and 81st streets to make room for the **American Museum of Natural History** 8. Across 77th Street is the **New-York Historical Society** 9. The final residential beauty on Central Park West by Emery Roth is the cubic Beresford (211 Central Park W, at W.

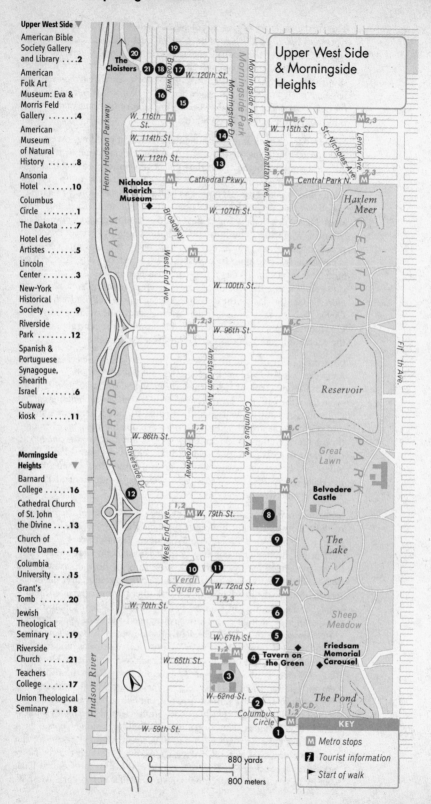

Upper West Side

American Bible Society Gallery and Library 2
American Folk Art Museum: Eva & Morris Feld Gallery 4
American Museum of Natural History 8
Ansonia Hotel 10
Columbus Circle 1
The Dakota 7
Hotel des Artistes 5
Lincoln Center 3
New-York Historical Society 9
Riverside Park 12
Spanish & Portuguese Synagogue, Shearith Israel 6
Subway kiosk 11

Morningside Heights

Barnard College 16
Cathedral Church of St. John the Divine 13
Church of Notre Dame . . 14
Columbia University 15
Grant's Tomb 20
Jewish Theological Seminary 19
Riverside Church 21
Teachers College 17
Union Theological Seminary 18

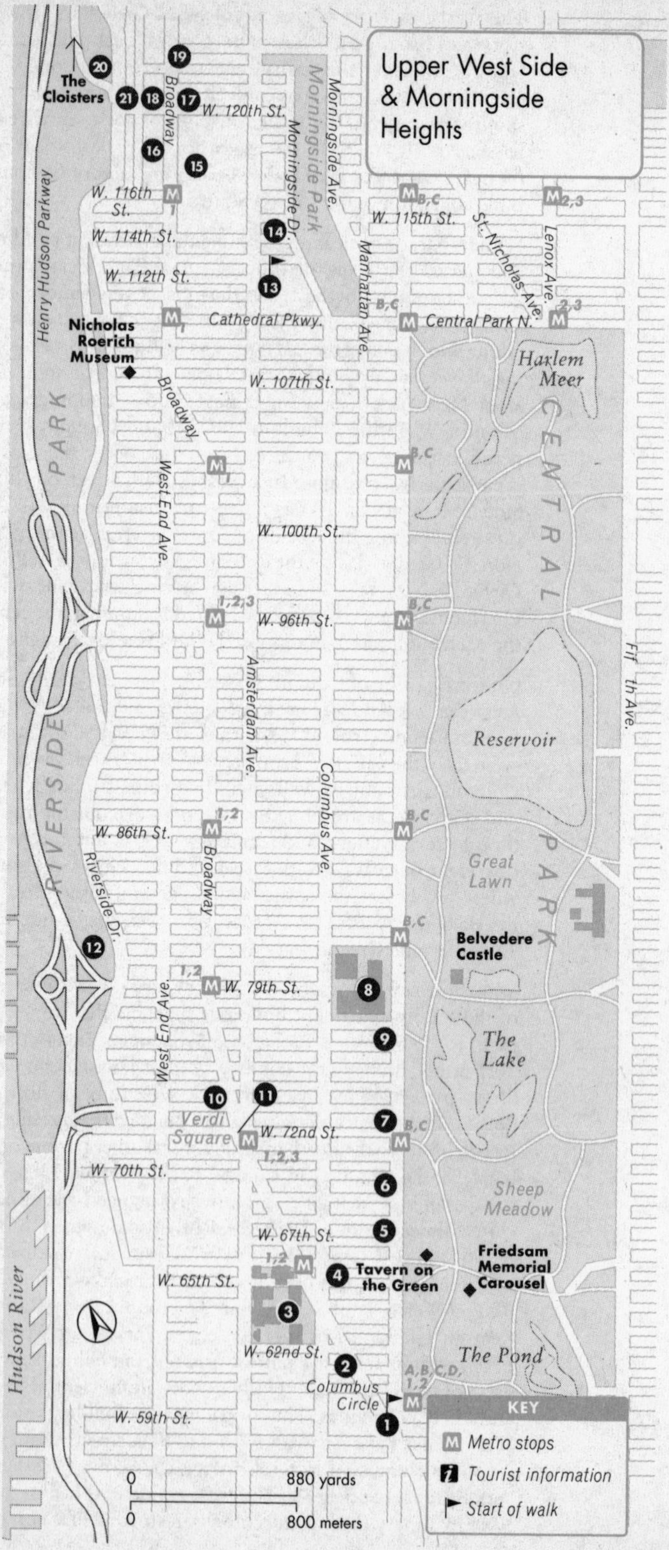

81st St.), built in 1929, whose lighted towers romantically haunt the night sky.

At this point you've covered the major institutions in the neighborhood. If you've had enough sightseeing, you could forsake the rest of this tour for a stroll through Central Park or for shopping along Columbus Avenue, which is directly behind the museum. Food lovers should head west to the numerous foodie shrines along the west side of Broadway, including Zabar's (2245 Broadway, between W. 80th and W. 81st Sts.), where shoppers battle it out for exquisite delicatessen items, prepared foods, gourmet groceries, coffee, and cheeses as well as cookware, dishes, and small appliances. One of the oldest seafood purveyors in New York, Citarella (2135 Broadway, at W. 75th St.) has expanded into a food-lover's fantasy with a vast selection of caviar, truffles, foie gras, and gourmet takeout. Next door at the bountiful but unpretentious Fairway Market (2127 Broadway, at W. 74th St.), snack food, cheeses, and produce practically overflow onto the street.

One block south of Fairway, at West 73rd Street and Broadway, are the white facade and fairy-castle turrets of the **Ansonia Hotel** ⑩, a turn-of-the-20th-century luxury building. At West 72nd Street, where Broadway cuts across Amsterdam Avenue, is triangular Verdi Square (named for Italian opera composer Giuseppe Verdi); here a marble statue of the composer is flanked by figures from Verdi's operas: *Aida, Otello,* and *Falstaff*. The triangle south of West 72nd Street is Sherman Square (named for Union Civil War general William Tecumseh Sherman); the **subway kiosk** ⑪ here is an official city landmark.

If you still feel like walking, blocks such as West 71st Street or West 74th Street between Broadway and Central Park West are perfect for casual strolling; or follow Riverside Drive up to West 116th Street and Columbia University in Morningside Heights. The latter leads past **Riverside Park** ⑫, which many neighborhood residents use as their backyard.

TIMING Charming tree- and brownstone-lined park blocks comprise this tour, which will easily take two or three hours at a relaxed clip. The exhibits at the American Folk Art Museum and the New-York Historical Society shouldn't take more than two hours to view, but the mammoth and often crowded American Museum of Natural History can eat up most of a day. In bad weather you might want to limit your itinerary to what's covered between Lincoln Center and the Museum of Natural History. If you're here on a Sunday, check out the upscale flea market at the southwest corner of West 77th Street and Columbus Avenue.

What to See

❷ **American Bible Society Gallery and Library.** With nearly 50,000 scriptural items in more than 2,000 languages, this is one of the largest Bible collections in the world outside the Vatican. The library, which can be toured by appointment, houses Helen Keller's massive 10-volume Braille Bible, leaves from a first-edition Gutenberg Bible, and a Torah from China. The public gallery puts on changing exhibitions of sacred art, ranging from stained glass to sculpture. ✉ *1865 Broadway, at W. 61st St., Upper West Side* ☎ *212/408–1200* 🌐 *www.americanbible.org* ⊙ *Bookstore and gallery Mon.–Wed. and Fri. 10–5, Thurs. 10–6, Sat. 10–5; gallery closed between exhibitions; library by appointment only.*

❹ **American Folk Art Museum: Eva & Morris Feld Gallery.** The changing exhibitions at this intimate museum (a branch of the American Folk Art Museum on West 53rd Street) include arts and decorative objects from the 18th century to the present day that are culled from all over the Americas. What's on show—folk paintings, textiles, outsider art, dolls, trade signs, weather vanes, and quilts—is frequently an extension of themes highlighted at the main museum. The gift shop has intriguing craft items, books, Christmas ornaments, and great cards. ✉ *2 Lincoln Sq., Columbus Ave. between W. 65th and W. 66th Sts., Upper West Side* ☎ *212/595–9533* 🌐 *www.folkartmuseum.org* 🎫 *$3 suggested admission* ⏲ *Mon. 11–6, Tues.–Sun. 11–7:30.*

★ ❽ **American Museum of Natural History.** With 42 exhibition halls and more than 32 million artifacts and specimens, this is the world's largest and most important museum of natural history. Dinosaur mania begins in the massive, barrel-vaulted **Theodore Roosevelt Rotunda,** where a 50-ft-tall skeleton of a barosaurus rears on its hind legs, protecting its fossilized baby from an enormous marauding allosaurus. Three spectacular dinosaur halls on the fourth floor—the **Hall of Saurischian Dinosaurs,** the **Hall of Ornithischian Dinosaurs,** and the **Hall of Vertebrate Origins**—use real fossils and interactive computer stations to present interpretations of how dinosaurs and pterodactyls might have behaved. In the **Hall of Fossil Mammals** interactive video monitors featuring museum curators explain what caused the woolly mammoth to vanish from the Earth and why mammals don't have to lay eggs to have babies. The **Hall of Biodiversity** focuses on Earth's wealth of plants and animals; its main attraction is the walk-through "Dzanga-Sangha Rainforest," a life-size diorama complete with the sounds of the African tropics—from bird calls to chain saws. The **Hall of Human Biology and Evolution**'s wondrously detailed dioramas trace human origins back to Lucy and feature a computerized archaeological dig and an electronic newspaper. The popular 94-ft blue whale model recently resurfaced when the revamped Hall of Ocean Life reopened as a "fully immersive marine environment," complete with shimmering blue lighting and whale song. For a taste of what the museum was like before computers and other high-tech wizardry was introduced, visit the softly lighted **Carl Akeley Hall of African Mammals,** where a small herd of elephants is frozen in time and surrounded by artful early-20th-century dioramas depicting beasts in their habitats.

The spectacular **Hayden Planetarium** is in a 90-ft aluminum-clad sphere that appears to float inside an enormous glass cube, which in turn is home to the **Rose Center for Earth and Space.** Models of planets, stars, and galaxies dangle overhead, and an elevator whisks you to the top of the sphere and the planetarium's **Sky Theater,** which—using "all-dome video"—transports you from galaxy to galaxy as if you were traveling through space. The sky show, "The Search for Life: Are We Alone?," narrated by Harrison Ford, is the most technologically advanced planetarium show in the world, incorporating up-to-the-minute scientific knowledge about the universe in computerized projections generated from a database of more than 2 billion stars. After the show, you descend a spiral walkway that tracks 13 billion years of the universe's evolution. The Rose Center also includes two major exhibits, the **Hall of the Universe,** in which black holes and colliding galaxies are explored through video and moving sculpture, and the **Hall of Planet Earth,** which explains the climate, geology, and evolution of our home planet with the help of more than 100 giant rocks from the ocean floor, glaciers, and active volcanoes. On Friday evening, 5:45–8:15, the Rose Center turns into a cocktail lounge, with tapas-style dining and live jazz under the "stars."

Films on the museum's 40-ft-high, 66-ft-wide **IMAX Theater** (☎ 212/769–5034 for show times) screen are usually about nature (climbing Mt. Everest, a safari in the Serengeti, or an underwater journey to the wreck of the *Titanic*) and cost $17, including museum admission. ✉ *Central Park W at W. 79th St., Upper West Side* ☎ *212/769–5200 for museum tickets and programs; 212/769–5100 for museum general information* 🌐 *www.amnh.org* 🎟 *Museum $12 suggested donation; museum and planetarium show combination ticket $21. Prices may vary for special exhibitions* ⏲ *Sat.–Thurs. 10–5:45; Fri. 10–8:45.*

need a break?

Big Nick's (✉ 2175 Broadway, at 77th St., Upper West Side ☎ 212/724–2010) pizza joint is a favorite with local youngsters. **H & H Bagels** (✉ 2239 Broadway, at W. 80th St., Upper West Side ☎ 212/595–8003) sells—and ships around the world—a dozen varieties of chewy bagels hot from the oven. They're at it 24 hours a day, 7 days a week.

10 **Ansonia Hotel.** This 1904 beaux arts masterpiece designed by Paul M. Duboy commands its corner of Broadway with as much architectural detail as good taste can stand. Inspiration for the former apartment hotel's turrets, mansard roof, and filigreed-iron balconies came from turn-of-the-20th-century Paris. Suites came without kitchens (and separate quarters for a staff that took care of the food). Designed to be fireproof, it has thick, soundproof walls that make it attractive to musicians; famous denizens of the past include Enrico Caruso, Igor Stravinsky, Arturo Toscanini, Florenz Ziegfeld, Theodore Dreiser, and Babe Ruth. Today, the Ansonia is a condominium apartment building. ✉ *2109 Broadway, between 73rd and 74th Sts., Upper West Side.*

off the beaten path

Children's Museum of Manhattan. In this five-story exploratorium, children ages 1–10 are invited to paint their own masterpieces, float boats down a "stream," and even film their own newscasts. To complement the exhibits, there are daily art workshops, science programs, and storytelling sessions. ✉ *212 W. 83rd St., between Broadway and Amsterdam Aves., Upper West Side* ☎ *212/721–1234* 🌐 *www.cmom.org* 🎟 *$6* ⏲ *Mid-June–Aug., Tues.–Sun. 10–5; mid-Sept.–mid-June, Wed.–Sun. 10–5.*

1 **Columbus Circle.** This busy intersection—where Broadway, 8th Avenue, Central Park West, and Central Park South all meet—gets its name from the 700-ton granite monument capped by a marble statue of Columbus in the middle of the tiny circular park at the center of the intersection. Lately, however, Columbus has taken a backseat—and been increasingly dwarfed—as the southwest quadrant of the circle has undergone a radical transformation with the construction of the AOL Time Warner Center. A 55-story, twin-towered supercomplex, the Center will house offices, studios for CNN, multimillion-dollar condos, a multistory marble-and-glass mall with high-end shops and restaurants, a Mandarin Oriental hotel, and a new concert hall for Jazz at Lincoln Center. The entire complex, designed by architect Rafael Viñoly, is slated for completion by the beginning of 2004. At a cost of $1.8 billion, the AOL Time Warner complex is the most expensive building project in U.S. history.

Northeast of the circle, standing guard over the entrance to Central Park, is the **Maine Monument,** whose gleaming equestrian figures perch atop a formidable limestone pedestal. At the monument's foot, horse-drawn cabs await fares through Central Park, and a small Victorian-style pavilion houses a 24-hour newsstand. The Trump International Hotel and Tower fills the wedge of land between Central Park West and Broadway; Donald Trump spent $250 million to gut this once marble-clad tower and rewrap it in a lamentable brown-glass curtain wall. Happily, it's also home to the self-named Jean-Georges restaurant, where the celebrity chef works his culinary magic. You can sometimes see his white-clad assistants furiously stirring and chopping in the window as you walk past on Broadway.

★ ❼ **The Dakota.** The most famous of all the apartment buildings lining Central Park West, the Dakota set a high standard for the many that followed it. Designed by Henry Hardenbergh, who also built the Plaza Hotel, the Dakota was so far uptown when it was completed in 1884 that it was jokingly described as being "out in the Dakotas." Indeed, this buff-color château, with picturesque gables and copper turrets, housed some of the West Side's first residents. The Dakota is often depicted in scenes of old New York, and it was by looking out of a window here that Si Morley was able to travel back in time in Jack Finney's *Time and Again*. Its slightly spooky appearance was played up in the movie *Rosemary's Baby.* The building's entrance is on West 72nd Street; the spacious, lovely courtyard is visible beyond the guard's station. At the Dakota's gate, in December 1980, a deranged fan shot John Lennon as he came home from a recording session. Other celebrity tenants have included Boris Karloff, Rudolf Nureyev, José Ferrer and Rosemary Clooney, Lauren Bacall, Rex Reed, Leonard Bernstein, Gilda Radner, and Connie Chung. ✉ *1 W. 72nd St., at Central Park W, Upper West Side.*

❺ **Hotel des Artistes.** Built in 1918 with an elaborate, mock-Elizabethan lobby, this "studio building," like several others on West 67th Street, was designed with high ceilings and immense windows, making it ideal for artists. Its tenants have included Isadora Duncan, Rudolph Valentino, Norman Rockwell, Noël Coward, Fannie Hurst, and contemporary actors Joel Grey and Richard Thomas; another tenant, Howard Chandler Christy, designed the lush, soft-tone murals in the ground-floor restaurant, Café des Artistes. ✉ *1 W. 67th St., at Central Park W, Upper West Side.*

★ ❸ **Lincoln Center.** A unified complex of pale travertine, Lincoln Center (built 1962–68) is the largest performing arts center in the world—so large it can seat nearly 18,000 spectators at one time in its various halls. Here maestro Lorin Maazel conducts Brahms and Beethoven, the American Ballet Theater performs *Swan Lake,* and Luciano Pavarotti sings arias and duets—and that's just an average day. The complex's three principal venues are grouped around the central Fountain Plaza: to the left, as you face west, is Philip Johnson's **New York State Theater,** home to the New York City Ballet and the New York City Opera. In the center, brilliantly colored Chagall murals are visible through the arched lobby windows of Wallace Harrison's **Metropolitan Opera House,** home to the Metropolitan Opera and the American Ballet Theater. And to the right is Max Abramovitz's **Avery Fisher Hall,** host to the New York Philharmonic Orchestra. A great time to visit the complex is on summer evenings, when hundreds of dancers trot and swing around the plaza during Midsummer Night Swing. One-hour guided tours, given daily, cover the center's history and wealth of artwork.

Lincoln Center encompasses much more than its three core theaters. Its major outdoor venue is **Damrosch Park,** on the south flank of the Met, where summer open-air festivals are often accompanied by free concerts at the **Guggenheim Bandshell.** In chillier months, the Big Apple Circus settles in. Accessible via the walk between the Metropolitan and Avery Fisher is the North Plaza—the best of Lincoln Center's spaces—with a massive Henry Moore sculpture reclining in a reflecting pool. The long lines and glass wall of Eero Saarinen's **Lincoln Center Theater** stand behind the pool. It is home to the **Vivian Beaumont Theater,** officially considered a Broadway house, despite its distance from the theater district.

Below it is the smaller **Mitzi E. Newhouse Theater,** where many award-winning plays originate. Next to the Lincoln Center Theater is the **New York Public Library for the Performing Arts** (☎ 212/870–1600), a research and circulating library with an extensive collection of books, records, videos, and scores on music, theater, and dance. An overpass leads from this plaza across West 65th Street to the world-renowned **Juilliard School** (☎ 212/769–7406) for music and theater; actors Kevin Kline, Robin Williams, and Patti LuPone studied here. An elevator leads down to street level and **Alice Tully Hall,** home of the Chamber Music Society of Lincoln Center and the New York Film Festival. Or turn left from the overpass and follow the walkway west to Lincoln Center's **Walter Reade Theater,** one of the finest places in the city to watch films. ✉ *W. 62nd to W. 66th St. between Broadway and Amsterdam Ave., Upper West Side* ☎ *212/546–2656 for general information; 212/875–5350 for tour schedule and reservations* 🌐 *www.lincolncenter.org* 🎫 *Tour $10.*

need a break?

Before or after a Lincoln Center performance, the pleasant **Cafe Mozart** (✉ 154 W. 70th St., between Broadway and Columbus Ave., Upper West Side ☎ 212/595–9797) has wine, pastries, Viennese schnitzel, and piano music. The simple setting and garden at **Café La Fortuna** (✉ 69 W. 71st St., between Columbus Ave. and Central Park W, Upper West Side ☎ 212/724–5846) is pepped up with opera music, memorabilia, tasty sandwiches, and espresso.

9 **New-York Historical Society.** Founded in 1804, the New-York Historical Society is the city's oldest museum and one of its finest research libraries, with a collection of 6 million pieces of art, literature, and memorabilia. Exhibitions shed light on New York's—and America's—history, everyday life, art, and architecture. Highlights of the collection include George Washington's inaugural chair, 500,000 photographs from the 1850s to the present, original watercolors for John James Audubon's *Birds of America,* the architectural files of McKim, Mead & White, and the largest U.S. collection of Louis Comfort Tiffany's lamps. The permanent exhibition in Dexter Hall, "Masterworks of the 19th Century" shows off one of the most in-depth collections of pre-20th-century American paintings in the world, including seminal landscapes by Hudson River School artists Thomas Cole, Asher Durant, and Frederic Church. There are usually also four or five changing exhibits on subjects ranging from colonial mapmaking to Victorian board games. If you still haven't gotten your fill, 40,000 of the society's most treasured pieces are on permanent display in the Henry Luce III Center for the Study of American Culture. ✉ *2 W. 77th St., at Central Park W, Upper West Side* ☎ *212/873–3400* 🌐 *www.nyhistory.org* 🎫 *Museum $6 suggested donation* ⏲ *Museum Tues.–Sun. 11–6; library Tues.–Sat. 10–5; library closed Sat. Memorial Day–Labor Day.*

12 **Riverside Park.** Long and narrow, tree-lined Riverside Park—laid out by Central Park's designers Olmsted and Vaux between 1873 and 1888—runs along the Hudson River from West 72nd to 159th streets. The park is best experienced on weekends, when Upper West Side residents and their children throng its walkways. From the corner of West 72nd Street and Riverside Drive—where a **statue of Eleanor Roosevelt** stands at the park's entrance—head down the ramp (through an underpass beneath the West Side Highway) to the **79th Street Boat Basin,** a rare spot in Manhattan where you can walk right along the river's edge and watch a flotilla of houseboats bobbing in the water. These boats must sail at least once a year to prove their seaworthiness. Behind the boat basin, the **Rotunda** is home in summer to the Boat Basin Cafe, an open-air spot

for a snack and river views. From the Rotunda, head up to the **Promenade,** a broad formal walkway extending a few blocks north from West 80th Street, with a stone parapet overlooking the river.

At the end of the Promenade, a community garden explodes with flowers. To the right, cresting a hill along Riverside Drive at West 89th Street, stands the Civil War **Soldiers' and Sailors' Monument** (1902, designed by Paul M. Duboy), an imposing 96-ft-high circle of white-marble columns. From its base is a view of Riverside Park, the Hudson River, and the New Jersey waterfront. ✉ *W. 72nd to W. 159th Sts. between Riverside Dr. and the Hudson River, Upper West Side.*

6 **Spanish & Portuguese Synagogue, Shearith Israel.** Built in 1897, this neoclassical edifice, with stained-glass windows by Louis Comfort Tiffany, is the fifth home of the oldest Jewish congregation in the United States, founded in 1654. A "Little Synagogue" inside is a replica of Shearith Israel's Georgian-style first synagogue (which was built on Mill Street in what is now the financial district) and is filled with original, 350-year-old furnishings. ✉ *2 W. 70th St., at Central Park W, Upper West Side* ☎ *212/873–0300* 🌐 *www.shearith-israel.org* ⏲ *Morning services weekdays 7:15, Sun. 8; call for times of evening services. Guided tours by appointment.*

11 **Subway kiosk.** This brick and terra-cotta building with rounded neo-Dutch molding is one of two remaining control houses from the original subway line (the other is at Bowling Green in lower Manhattan). Built in 1904–05, it was the first express station north of 42nd Street. Beneath it is one of the most heavily trafficked subway stations in Manhattan. ✉ *W. 72nd St. and Broadway, Upper West Side.*

need a break?

Gray's Papaya (✉ 2090 Broadway, at W. 72nd St., Upper West Side ☎ 212/799–0243) is a New York institution. Plastered with signs and slogans ("no gimmicks, no bull"), it serves up fruit smoothies and juicy, mustard-drenched hot dogs at dirt-cheap prices, 24 hours a day.

MORNINGSIDE HEIGHTS

On the high ridge north and west of Central Park, a cultural outpost grew up at the end of the 19th century, spearheaded by a triad of institutions: the relocated Columbia University, which developed the mind; St. Luke's Hospital, which cared for the body; and the Cathedral of St. John the Divine, which tended the soul. Idealistically conceived as an American Acropolis, the cluster of academic and religious institutions that developed here managed to keep these blocks stable during years when neighborhoods on all sides were collapsing. In the 1980s and 1990s, West Side gentrification reclaimed the area to the south, while the areas north and east of here began bouncing back as well. Within the gates of the Columbia or Barnard campuses or inside the hushed St. John the Divine or Riverside Church, New York City takes on a different character. This is an *uptown* student neighborhood—less hip than the Village, but friendly, fun, and intellectual.

Numbers in the text correspond to numbers in the margin and on the Upper West Side & Morningside Heights map.

a good walk

Broadway is the heartbeat of Morningside Heights, but many of the most remarkable sights will take you east and west of the main thoroughfare. Walk east from Broadway on West 112th Street and the massive **Cathedral Church of St. John the Divine** 13 ⚑ will gradually loom up before you.

From here swing east on West 113th Street to secluded Morningside Drive. You'll pass the beaux arts–baroque 1896 core of St. Luke's Hospital, which has sprouted an awkward jumble of newer buildings. On Morningside Drive at West 114th Street, the **Church of Notre Dame** (14) nestles into its corner with as much personality but far less bulk than the other churches on this tour. At West 116th Street, catercorner from Columbia University's President's House (60 Morningside Dr.), pause at the overlook on the right to gaze out at the skyline and down into Morningside Park which tumbles precipitously into a wooded gorge. Designed by Olmsted and Vaux of Central Park fame, the park went through many rough years due to neglect and crime in surrounding blocks, but efforts to improve it in the late 1990s have made the park a favorite destination for Columbia students.

Turn back toward Amsterdam Avenue on West 116th Street, and walk past the Law School's streamlined Greene Hall to the eastern gates of **Columbia University** (15). Across Broadway from Columbia proper is its sister institution, **Barnard College** (16). Institutes of higher learning abound as you follow Broadway on the east side of the street north to West 120th Street—on the right is **Teachers College** (17), a part of Columbia, and on the left is the interdenominational **Union Theological Seminary** (18). At the northeast corner of West 122nd Street and Broadway, behind a large blank-walled redbrick tower that fronts the intersection at an angle, is the **Jewish Theological Seminary** (19). Walk west on 122nd Street; between Claremont Avenue and Broadway the prestigious Manhattan School of Music (601 W. 122nd St.) is on your right, with musical instruments carved into the stone beneath its upper-story windows. Between Claremont and Riverside Drive is Sakura Park, a quiet formal garden, with cherry trees that achieve full, frothy bloom in spring.

Cross Riverside Drive at West 122nd Street into Riverside Park. The handsome white-marble **Grant's Tomb** (20) was once one of the city's most popular sights. The tomb's outdoor plaza is surrounded by colorful mosaic-tiled walls and benches (Pedro Silva and the City Arts Workshop, 1973) that depict taxi cabs, flowing fire hydrants, and city buildings. Back on the east side of Riverside Drive, the refined **Riverside Church** (21) seems the antithesis of the rougher hulk of the Cathedral of St. John the Divine. Keep strolling south and you'll be able to admire Riverside Park and the Hudson to your right, and a long row of magnificent stone apartment buildings to your left.

TIMING Allow yourself about two hours to leisurely walk the tour. To get the true flavor of the neighborhood, which is often student dominated, come during the week, when classes are in session. You'll be able to visit campus buildings and sample café life, and because the major churches on the tour are active weeklong, you won't miss seeing them in action.

What to See

(16) **Barnard College.** Established in 1889 and one of the former Seven Sisters women's colleges, Barnard has steadfastly remained single-sex and independent from Columbia, although its students can take classes there (and vice versa). Note the bear (the college's mascot) on the shield above the main gates at West 117th Street. Through the gates is **Barnard Hall,** which houses classrooms, offices, a pool, and dance studios. Its brick-and-limestone design echoes the design of Columbia University's buildings. To the right of Barnard Hall, a path leads through the narrow but neatly landscaped campus. ✉ *Entrance at Broadway and W. 117th St., Morningside Heights* ☎ *212/854–2014* 🌐 *www.barnard.edu* ⏲ *Student-led tours Mon.–Sat. at 10:30 and 2:30 when classes are in session.*

13 **Cathedral Church of St. John the Divine.** Everything about the cathedral is colossal, from its cavernous 601-ft-long nave, which can hold some 5,000 worshipers, to its 162-ft-tall dome crossing, which could comfortably contain the Statue of Liberty. Even though this divine behemoth is unfinished—the transepts and tower are the most noticeably uncompleted elements—it is already the largest Gothic cathedral in the world. To get the full effect of the building's size, approach it from Broadway on West 112th Street. On the wide steps climbing to the Amsterdam Avenue entrance, five portals arch over the entrance doors. The central Portal of Paradise depicts St. John witnessing the Transfiguration of Jesus, and 32 biblical characters, all intricately carved in stone. The 3-ton bronze doors below the portal open only twice a year—on Easter and in October for the Feast of St. Francis, when animals as large as elephants and camels are brought in, along with cats and dogs, to be blessed. The doors have relief castings of scenes from the Old Testament on the left and the New Testament on the right.

Fodor's Choice ★

The cathedral's first cornerstone was laid in 1892, and in 1911 a major change in architectural vision came at the hands of Ralph Adams Cram, a Gothic revival purist who insisted on a French Gothic style for the edifice (his work also shaped Princeton University and West Point). The granite of the original Romanesque-Byzantine design is visible inside at the crossing, where it has yet to be finished with the Gothic limestone facing. Note that the finished arches are pointed—Gothic—while the uncovered two are in the rounded Byzantine style. The **Great Rose Window** in the western facade, made from more than 10,000 pieces of colored glass, is the largest stained-glass window in the United States. Although work on the cathedral had continued for nearly 50 years, construction came to a halt when the United States entered World War II. Work did not resume again until 1979, by which time stonecutting had become something of a lost art in this country; in order to continue building, stonecutters came from Europe to train local craftspeople. As it stands, the cathedral is now about two-thirds complete—and it may stay that way for a while. In 2002, work was halted once again following a fire that damaged the north transept and burned down the cathedral's gift shop. Though the cathedral remains almost fully functional, the financial burden of the fire resulted in construction being abandoned for the time being.

Inside, along the cathedral's side aisles, some chapels are dedicated to contemporary issues such as sports, poetry, and AIDS. The **Saint Saviour Chapel** contains a three-panel bronze altar in white-gold leaf with religious scenes by artist Keith Haring (this was his last work before he died of AIDS in 1990). The more conventional **baptistry,** to the left of the altar, is an exquisite octagonal chapel with a 15-ft-high marble font and a polychrome sculpted frieze commemorating New York's Dutch heritage. The altar area expresses the cathedral's interfaith tradition and international mission—with menorahs, Shinto vases, and, in the **Chapels of the Seven Tongues** behind the altar, dedications to various ethnic groups. Seventeenth-century Barberini tapestries hang throughout the cathedral; two were damaged in the fire and are in the process of being conserved.

A precinct of châteaulike Gothic-style buildings, known as the **Cathedral Close,** is behind the cathedral on the south side. In a corner by the Cathedral School is the **Biblical Garden,** with perennials, herbs, and an arbor. Around the bend from here is a rose garden. Back at Amsterdam Avenue, the **Peace Fountain** depicts the struggle of good and evil. The forces of good, embodied in the figure of the archangel Michael, triumph by decapitating Satan, whose head hangs from one side. The fountain is encircled by small, whimsical animal figures cast in bronze from pieces sculpted by children.

Along with Sunday services (8, 9, 9:30, 11, and 6), the cathedral runs a score of community outreach programs, has changing museum and art-gallery displays, supports artists-in-residence and an early music consortium, and presents a full calendar of nonreligious (classical, folk, solstice) concerts. Christmastime programs and organ recitals are especially popular. ✉ *1047 Amsterdam Ave., at W. 112th St., Morningside Heights* ☎ *212/316–7540; 212/662–2133 box office; 212/932–7347 tours* 🌐 *www.stjohndivine.org* 💳 *Tours $3* ⏲ *Mon.–Sat. 8–6, Sun. 8–7; tours Tues.–Sat. at 11, Sun. at 1.*

need a break?

If St. John has filled your soul but your stomach is crying out for its share, head for the **Hungarian Pastry Shop** (✉ 1030 Amsterdam Ave., at W. 111th St., Morningside Heights ☎ 212/866–4230) for tasty desserts and coffee.

14 **Church of Notre Dame.** A French neoclassical landmark building (1911), this Roman Catholic church has a grand interior, including a replica of the French grotto of Lourdes behind its altar. It once served a predominantly French community of immigrants, but like the neighborhood, today's congregation is more ethnically diverse, with Irish, German, Italian, African-American, Hispanic, and Filipino members. The building is open 30 minutes before and after masses, which are held weekdays at 8 and 12:05; Saturday at 12:05 and 5:30; and Sunday at 8:30, 11:30, and 5:30. ✉ *405 W. 114th St., at Morningside Dr., Morningside Heights* ☎ *212/866–1500.*

off the beaten path

The Cloisters. Perched atop a wooded hill in Fort Tryon Park, near Manhattan's northernmost tip, the Cloisters houses the medieval collection of the Metropolitan Museum of Art in an appropriately medieval monastery-like setting. Colonnaded walks connect authentic French and Spanish monastic cloisters, a French Romanesque chapel, a 12th-century chapter house, and a Romanesque apse. An entire room is devoted to the richly woven and extraordinarily detailed 15th- and 16th-century Unicorn Tapestries—a must-see. Three enchanting gardens shelter more than 250 species of plants similar to those grown during the Middle Ages, including herbs and medicinals; the Unicorn Garden blooms with flowers and plants depicted in the tapestries. Concerts of medieval music are held here regularly, and an outdoor café decorated with 15th-century carvings serves biscotti and espresso (May–October). The Cloisters is easily accessible by public transportation: the M4 Cloisters–Fort Tryon Park bus provides a lengthy but scenic ride; catch it along Madison Avenue below West 110th Street, or on Broadway above West 110th Street, or take the A train to West 190th Street. ✉ *Fort Tryon Park, Inwood* ☎ *212/923–3700* 💳 *$12 suggested donation* ⏲ *Mar.–Oct., Tues.–Sun. 9:30–5:15; Nov.–Feb., Tues.–Sun. 9:30–4:45.*

15 **Columbia University.** This wealthy, private, coed Ivy League school was New York's first college when it was founded in 1754. Back then, before American independence, it was called King's College—note the gilded crowns on the black wrought-iron gates at the Amsterdam Avenue entrance. The herringbone-pattern brick paths of College Walk lead into the refreshingly open main quadrangle, dominated by the neoclassical **Butler Library** to the south and the rotunda-top **Low Memorial Library**

to the north. Butler, built in 1934, holds the bulk of the university's 7 million books. Low was built in 1895–97 by McKim, Mead & White, which laid out the general campus plan when the college moved here in 1897. Modeled on the Roman Pantheon, Low is now mostly offices, but on weekdays you can go inside to see its domed, templelike former Reading Room. Low Library also houses the visitor center, where you can pick up a campus guide or arrange a tour. The steps of Low Library, presided over by Daniel Chester French's statue *Alma Mater,* have been a focal point for campus life, not least during the student riots of 1968. The southwest corner of the quad is the site of Lerner Hall, Columbia's distinctly 21st-century **student center**, with a six-story glass atrium and ultramod glass catwalks. ✉ *Visitor center, north of W. 116th St. between Amsterdam Ave. and Broadway, in Low Memorial Library, Morningside Heights* ☎ *212/854–4900* 🌐 *www.columbia.edu* ⏲ *Weekdays 9–5. Tours begin 11 and 2 weekdays from Room 213, Low Library.*

Before Columbia moved here, this land was occupied by the Bloomingdale Insane Asylum; the sole survivor of those days is Buell Hall (1878), the gabled orange-red brick house, east of Low Library. North of Buell Hall is the interdenominational **St. Paul's Chapel** (☎ 212/854–1493 ⏲ Sept.–May, daily 10–10 when classes are in session, with services on Sun.; chapel closes at 5 during school breaks), an exquisite little Byzantine-style dome church with fine tile vaulting inside. It also has a 5,347-pipe organ, a marble terrazzo floor, and stained-glass windows depicting famous Columbia alumni.

need a break?

The exterior of **Tom's Restaurant** (✉ 2880 Broadway, at 112th St., Morningside Heights ☎ 212/864–6137) made frequent appearances on the TV show *Seinfeld.* Whether or not you are excited by its claim to fame, this diner is still a good place for a New York bite.

off the beaten path

Dyckman Farmhouse Museum. This gambrel-roofed Dutch colonial farmhouse (1784) is the last of its kind in Manhattan. Its six period rooms are furnished with 18th- and 19th-century Dutch and English antiques, and it's surrounded by a ½-acre park with flower and vegetable gardens. ✉ *4881 Broadway, at W. 204th St., Inwood* ☎ *212/304–9422* 🌐 *www.dyckman.org* 🎟 *$1* ⏲ *Tues.–Sun. 10–4.*

20 **Grant's Tomb.** This commanding position along the Hudson River, within Riverside Park, is the final resting place of Civil War general and two-term president Ulysses S. Grant and his wife Julia Dent Grant. Opened in 1897, almost 12 years after Grant's death, it was a more popular sight than the Statue of Liberty until the end of World War I. The towering granite tomb, the largest mausoleum in North America, is engraved with the words LET US HAVE PEACE, recalling Grant's speech to the Republican convention upon his presidential nomination. Under a small white dome, the Grants' twin black-marble sarcophagi are sunk into a deep circular chamber visible from above; minigalleries to the sides display photographs and Grant memorabilia. ✉ *Riverside Dr. and W. 122nd St., Morningside Heights* ☎ *212/666–1640* 🌐 *www.nps.gov/gegr* 🎟 *Free* ⏲ *Daily 9–5; 20-min tours run on the hr.*

19 **Jewish Theological Seminary.** The seminary was founded in 1886 as a training ground for rabbis, cantors, and scholars of Conservative Judaism, but this complex wasn't built until 1930. You can visit the seminary's excellent library and gallery, which have frequent exhibits of rare Hebrew manuscripts and historic documents. ✉ *3080 Broadway, at W. 122nd St., Morningside Heights* ☎ *212/678–8000* 🌐 *www.jtsa.edu* 🎟 *Free* ⏲ *Call for library and gallery hrs.*

need a break?

Just two blocks north of the Jewish Theological Seminary, **Toast** (✉ 3157 Broadway, between LaSalle St. and Tiemann Pl., Morningside Heights ☎ 212/662–1144) dishes up carefully crafted, quickie meals at very reasonable prices. The oversize grilled-vegetable, barbecue-pork, and steak sandwiches all come on freshly baked bread with home-style fries. Be sure to leave room for the cheesecake.

off the beaten path

Nicholas Roerich Museum. An 1898 Upper West Side town house is the site of this small, eccentric museum dedicated to the work of Russian artist Nicholas Roerich, who immigrated to New York in the 1920s and quickly developed an ardent following. Some 200 of his paintings hang here—notably some vast canvases of the Himalayas. He also designed sets for ballets, such as Stravinsky's *Rite of Spring,* photographs of which are also on view. Free chamber music concerts are usually held here on Sunday afternoon at 5. ✉ *319 W. 107th St., between Broadway and Riverside Dr., Morningside Heights* ☎ *212/864–7752* 🌐 *www.roerich.org* *Free; donations accepted* ⏲ *Tues.–Sun. 2–5.*

21 **Riverside Church.** In this modern (1930) Gothic-style edifice, the smooth, pale limestone walls are restrained, but the main entrance, on Riverside Drive, explodes with elaborate stone carvings modeled on the French cathedral of Chartres (as are many other details here). Inside, look at the handsomely ornamented main sanctuary and take the elevator to the top of the 22-story, 356-ft tower, with its 74-bell carillon, the largest in the world. Although affiliated with the American Baptist church and the United Church of Christ, Riverside is interdenominational, interracial, international, and very politically and socially conscious. Its calendar includes political and community events, dance and theater programs, and concerts, along with regular Sunday services. Call for hours and fees for the tower, which has been under renovation. ✉ *490 Riverside Dr., between W. 120th and W. 122 Sts., Morningside Heights* ☎ *212/870–6700 church; 212/870–6792 visitor center* 🌐 *www.theriversidechurchny.org* *Free* ⏲ *Visitor center Tues.–Sat. 10:30–5, Sun. 9:45–10:45 and 12:15–4; service Sun. 10:45.*

17 **Teachers College.** Redbrick Victorian buildings house Columbia University's Teachers College, founded in 1887 and still the world's largest graduate school in the field of education. Names of famous teachers throughout history line the frieze along the Broadway facade. ✉ *525 W. 120th St., Morningside Heights* ☎ *212/678–3710 visitor center* 🌐 *www.teacherscollege.edu* ⏲ *Tours Tues. and Fri. at 1, reservations recommended.*

18 **Union Theological Seminary.** Founded in 1836, this progressive, all-denominational seminary moved here, to its rough, gray, collegiate Gothic quadrangle, in 1910; it has one of the world's finest theological libraries. Step inside the main entrance, on Broadway at West 121st Street, and ask to look around the serene central quadrangle. ✉ *W. 120th to 122nd Sts. between Broadway and Claremont Ave., Morningside Heights* ☎ *212/662–7100* 🌐 *www.uts.columbia.edu.*

HARLEM

Harlem has been the capital of African-American culture and life for nearly a century. Originally called Nieuw Haarlem and settled by Dutch farmers, Harlem became a well-to-do suburb by the 19th century; many Jews moved here from the Lower East Side in the late 1800s, and black

New Yorkers began settling here in large numbers in about 1900, moving into a surplus of fine apartment buildings and town houses built by real estate developers for a middle-class white market that never materialized. By the 1920s Harlem had become the most famous black community in the United States.

In an astonishing confluence of talent known as the Harlem Renaissance, black novelists, playwrights, musicians, and artists—many of them seeking to escape discrimination and persecution in other parts of the country—gathered here. Black performers starred in chic Harlem jazz clubs—which, ironically, only whites could attend. Throughout the Roaring '20s, while whites flocked here for the infamous parties and nightlife, blacks settled in for the opportunity this self-sustaining community represented. But the Depression hit Harlem hard. By the late 1930s it was no longer a popular social spot for downtown New Yorkers, and many African-American families began moving out to houses in the suburbs of Queens and New Jersey.

By the 1960s Harlem's population had dropped dramatically, and many of those who remained were disillusioned enough with social injustices to join in civil rights riots. A vicious cycle of deteriorating housing, poverty, and crime turned the neighborhood into a simmering ghetto. Today, however, Harlem is restoring itself. Deserted buildings and yards of rubble still scar certain parts, but shining amid them are old jewels such as the refurbished Apollo Theatre, countless architecturally splendid churches, and cultural magnets such as the Studio Museum and Schomburg Center. Black (and, increasingly, white) professionals and young families are also restoring many of Harlem's classic brownstone and limestone buildings, bringing new life to the community. The economic turnaround has been billed as the second Harlem Renaissance. Commercial rental rates have doubled in recent years and brownstone and apartment rental rates have skyrocketed as the area becomes more racially diverse. Former president Bill Clinton chose West 125th Street as the site of his new office, and many residents have warmly greeted his arrival as evidence of a new era.

Note that the city's north–south avenues acquire different names in Harlem, commemorating heroes of black history: 6th Avenue becomes Lenox Avenue or Malcolm X Boulevard, 7th Avenue is Adam Clayton Powell Jr. Boulevard, and 8th Avenue is Frederick Douglass Boulevard; West 125th Street, the major east–west street, is Martin Luther King Jr. Boulevard. Many people still use the streets' former names, but the street signs use the new ones.

Numbers in the text correspond to numbers in the margin and on the Harlem map.

a good walk

Within a minute's walk of the West 116th Street No. 2/3 subway station are three houses of worship and a market. At the southwest corner of West 116th Street and Malcolm X Boulevard, you'll see a green aluminum onion dome at the top of the Malcolm Shabazz Masjid (102 W. 116th St.), a former casino that was converted in the mid-1960s to a black Muslim mosque, where El-Hajj Malik El-Shabazz (better known as Malcolm X) once preached. Past the mosque is the unassuming exterior of **Canaan Baptist Church of Christ** 1, where Martin Luther King Jr. delivered a sermon shortly before his death. Another neighborhood church known for its rousing Sunday gospel service is the **Memorial Baptist Church** 2, a block south on West 115th Street. Open every day of the week, the **Malcolm Shabazz Harlem Market** 3, on West 116th Street

Abyssinian Baptist Church .9
Apollo Theatre .7
Canaan Baptist Church of Christ 1
Malcolm Shabazz Harlem Market .3
Marcus Garvey Park 4
Memorial Baptist Church 2
Schomburg Center for Research in Black Culture ..8
Strivers' Row .10
Studio Museum in Harlem 6
Sylvia's Soul Food Restaurant 5

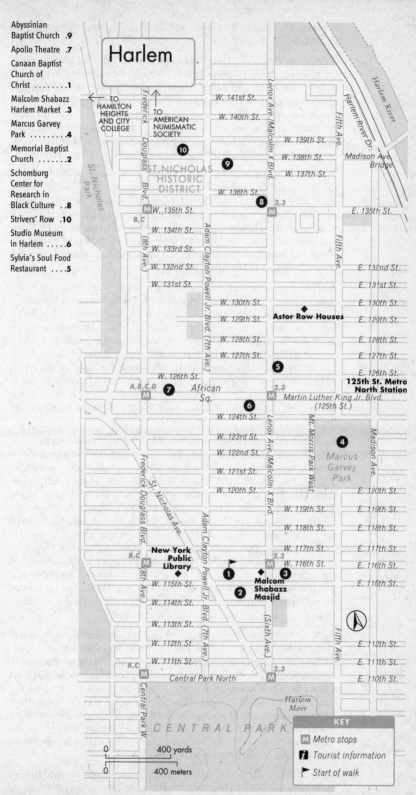

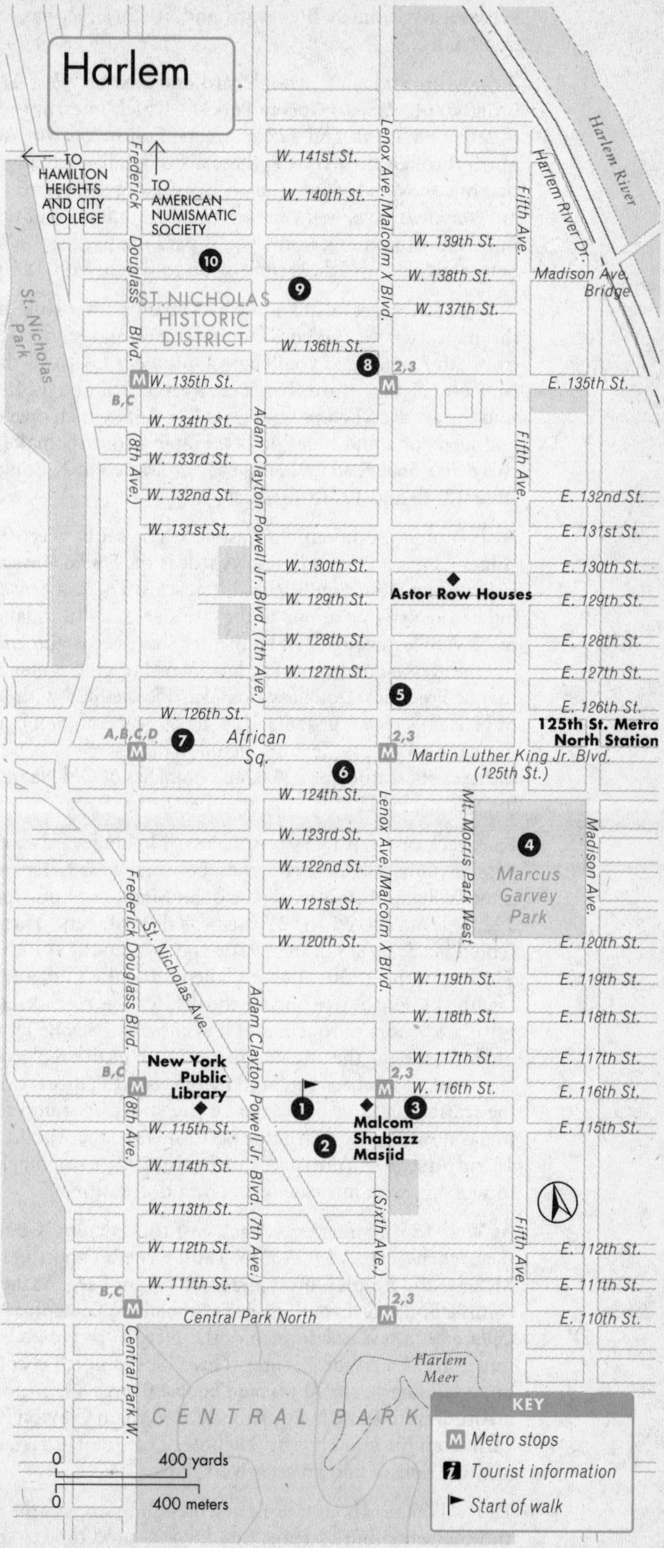

between Malcolm X Boulevard and 5th Avenue, has indoor and outdoor stalls.

A walk up Malcolm X Boulevard and east on West 120th Street will bring you to **Marcus Garvey Park** 4, which interrupts 5th Avenue between West 120th and 124th streets. Follow the 5th Avenue entrance north through the park to where a stone hill—actually the schist rock that once covered Manhattan—rises 70 ft up from street level to a lookout; on clear days you can see Yankee Stadium and the Empire State Building. Continuing north you'll pass the park's pool and bathhouse before picking up 5th Avenue again to reach West 125th Street.

West 125th Street (also known as Martin Luther King Jr. Boulevard) is the main artery of Harlem's cultural, retail, and economic life. Walk west from 5th Avenue and you'll pass a number of African-theme stores. On Malcolm X Boulevard, between West 125th and 124th streets, you'll find the art deco Lenox Lounge at No. 288, which opened in the 1930s and hosts jazz and blues nights. Hungry tourists make the pilgrimage to **Sylvia's Soul Food Restaurant** 5, on Malcolm X Boulevard, between West 126th and 127th streets.

A community standout on West 125th Street between Malcolm X and Adam Clayton Powell Jr. boulevards is the **Studio Museum in Harlem** 6. Continuing west, you'll pass the striking Theresa Towers office building before arriving at one of the city's great cultural landmarks, the famous **Apollo Theatre** 7. The theater has drawn audiences since 1913, but the glass-and-chrome Harlem USA shopping center a half block farther at Frederick Douglass Boulevard is credited with being a big part of Harlem's recent upswing. It's the largest complex built in Harlem in more than 30 years. Tenants include a nine-screen Magic Johnson movie theater with seating for 2,700, and branches of Old Navy, Modell's Sporting Goods, HMV Records, and the Disney Store.

Backtrack east to Adam Clayton Powell Jr. Boulevard and continue north, passing numerous large churches. Between West 131st and 132nd streets is the Williams Institutional (Christian Methodist Episcopal) Church (No. 2225). From 1912 to 1939 this was the Lafayette Theatre, which presented black revues in the 1920s and housed the WPA's Federal Negro Theater in the 1930s. Eubie Blake and Duke Ellington both got their big breaks here. A tree outside the theater was considered a lucky charm for black actors to touch, and it eventually became known as the Tree of Hope; though the original tree and then its live replacement were both cut down, it has been replaced by the colorful, abstract metal "tree" on the traffic island in the center of the street. A stump from the second tree is now a lucky charm for performers at the Apollo. To the west on 132nd Street is St. Aloysius Church (No. 209), a stunningly detailed house of worship with intricate terra-cotta decoration.

At West 135th Street cross back east to Malcolm X Boulevard. Notice the branch of the YMCA (No. 180); writers Langston Hughes, Claude McKay, and Ralph Ellison all rented rooms here. At the corner of Malcolm X Boulevard you'll find the **Schomburg Center for Research in Black Culture** 8, a research branch of the New York Public Library that also functions as a cultural center. Three blocks north is another neighborhood landmark, the **Abyssinian Baptist Church** 9, one of the first black institutions to settle in Harlem. Across Adam Clayton Powell Jr. Boulevard from the church is St. Nicholas Historic District, a handsome set of town houses known as **Strivers' Row** 10.

TIMING The walk takes about four hours, including stops at the Studio Museum and the Schomburg Center. Sunday is a good time to tour Harlem, especially if you'd like to attend one of the many church services celebrating with gospel music, and weekends in general are the liveliest time for walking around the neighborhood. If you do attend a church service, remember that most people are there to worship and don't think of themselves or their church as tourist attractions. Show up on time for services, and be respectful of ushers, who may ask you to sit in a special section; don't take pictures or videos; dress in your Sunday best (not shorts and flip-flops); make a contribution when the collection comes around; and be prepared to stay for the full service, which may last as long as two hours.

What to See

9 **Abyssinian Baptist Church.** A famous family of ministers—Adam Clayton Powell Sr. and his son, Adam Clayton Powell Jr., the first black U. S. congressman—has presided over this Gothic-style church, which moved here in the 1920s. Stop in on Sunday to hear the gospel choir and the fiery sermon of its present activist minister, Reverend Calvin Butts. The Coptic cross on the pulpit was a gift from Haile Selassie, then the king of Ethiopia. ✉ *132 Odell Clark Pl. (W. 138th St.), between Adam Clayton Powell Jr. and Malcolm X Blvds., Harlem* ☎ *212/862–7474* 🌐 *www.abyssinian.org* ⏲ *Sun. services 9 and 11* ☞ *Groups of 10 or more call ahead, as seating is limited.*

off the beaten path

American Numismatic Society. The society, founded in 1858, displays its vast collection of coins and medals, including many that date from ancient civilizations, in two public galleries at the Audubon Terrace Museum complex. ✉ *Audubon Terrace, Broadway at W. 155th St., Harlem* ☎ *212/234–3130* 🌐 *www.amnumsoc.org* 🎟 *Free; donations accepted* ⏲ *Tues.–Fri. 9–4:30.*

Hispanic Society of America. The Hispanic Society has the best collection of Spanish art outside the Prado in Madrid, with paintings, sculptures, manuscripts, and decorative artworks from Spain, Portugal, Latin America, and the Philippines—including pieces by Goya, El Greco, and Velázquez. ✉ *Audubon Terrace, Broadway between W. 155th and W. 156th Sts., Harlem* ☎ *212/926–2234* 🌐 *www.hispanicsociety.org* 🎟 *Free; donations accepted* ⏲ *Library Sept.–July, Tues.–Sat. 10–4:30; museum Sun. 1–4.*

7 **Apollo Theatre.** When it opened in 1913, it was a burlesque hall for white audiences only, but after 1934 music greats such as Billie Holiday, Ella Fitzgerald, Duke Ellington, Count Basie, Nat "King" Cole, Lionel Hampton, and Aretha Franklin performed at the Apollo. The theater fell on hard times and closed for a while in the early 1970s, but it has been renovated and in use again since 1983. The Apollo's current roster of stars isn't as consistent as it was in the past, but its regular Wednesday night amateur performances at 7:30 are as wild and raucous as they were in the theater's heyday. Former winners of Amateur Night include Sarah Vaughn, James Brown, and The Jackson Five. The Wall of Fame, in the lobby, is a giant collage of Apollo entertainers. Included in an hour-long guided tour is a spirited, audience-participation-encouraged oral history of the theater, with many inside stories about past performers, as well as a chance to perform in a no-boos-allowed "Amateur Night" show. Tour goers also get to touch what's left of the Tree of Hope (a stump) as they walk across the stage. A gift shop sells Apollo clothing, gift items, jewelry, and recordings. ✉ *253 W. 125th St., between Adam Clayton Powell Jr. and Frederick Douglass Blvds., Harlem* ☎ *212/749–5838 for performance schedules; 212/531–5337 for tours* 🎟 *Tours $8 weekdays, $10 weekends.*

need a break?

New York's favorite doughnut-shop chain, **Krispy Kreme** (✉ 280 W. 125th St., at Frederick Douglass Blvd., Harlem ☎ 212/531–0111), bakes the sweetest of sweets.

❶ **Canaan Baptist Church of Christ.** Gospel fans and visitors are welcome at the 10:45 Sunday service led by Reverend Wyatt Tee Walker, who is known internationally as a crusader for civil rights. Martin Luther King Jr. delivered his famous "A Knock at Midnight" sermon (penned in 1963) here one month before his assassination in 1968. ✉ *132 W. 116th St., between Malcolm X and Adam Clayton Powell Jr. Blvds., Harlem* ☎ *212/866–0301.*

off the beaten path

Hamilton Heights and City College. The beautiful neo-Gothic stone towers of City College decorate the ridge of Hamilton Heights, where wide sidewalks, quiet streets, green plantings, and well-maintained houses make the neighborhood a real charmer. City College's center is on West 138th Street and Convent Avenue. Its arched schist gates, green lawns, and white terra-cotta trim could easily be part of an Ivy League campus, but the college has always been a public institution (tuition was free until the mid-1970s). The pretty row houses and churches that comprise Hamilton Heights were built around the turn of the 20th century on land once owned by Alexander Hamilton. His federal-style house, known as **Hamilton Grange**, is at 287 Convent Avenue (near West 141st Street, about 100 yards south of its original location). To reach this neighborhood from Strivers' Row (West 138th and 139th streets), take a short walk uphill on 141st Street past St. Nicholas Park. ✉ *St. Nicholas Ave. to Hudson River, approx. W. 135th to W. 155th Sts., Harlem.*

❸ **Malcolm Shabazz Harlem Market.** This colorful indoor-outdoor bazaar, with more than 100 permanent stalls, specializes in imported African products, including Mali mud-cloth coats, skirts, and scarves, as well as West African masks and figurines, herbal soaps, leather bags, and contemporary paintings. In summer, a food kiosk serves up tasty Caribbean and Southern-style dishes. ✉ *52 W. 116th St., between Malcolm X Blvd. and 5th Ave., Harlem* ☎ *212/987–8131* 🌐 *www.harlemmarket.com* ⏲ *Daily 10–7.*

❹ **Marcus Garvey Park.** Originally Mount Morris Square, this rocky plot of land was renamed in 1973 after Marcus Garvey (1887–1940), who preached from nearby street corners and led the back-to-Africa movement. From the street, you can see its three-tier, cast-iron **watchtower** (Julius Kroel, 1856), the only remaining part of a now defunct citywide network used to spot and report fires in the days before the telephone. The handsome neoclassical row houses of the **Mount Morris Park Historic District** front the west side of the park and line side streets. ✉ *Interrupts 5th Ave. between W. 120th and W. 124th Sts., Madison Ave. to Mt. Morris Park W, Harlem* 🌐 *www.east-harlem.com/parks_mg.htm.*

❷ **Memorial Baptist Church.** The gospel choir fills the sanctuary with soulful, moving, often joyous gospel music during a two-hour service, which begins promptly at 10:45 on Sunday. You can learn to sing gospel, as well as study its rhythms and history by enrolling in a Saturday workshop run by the church. The free sessions are especially popular with the busloads of Japanese tourists making the weekend rounds in Harlem. ✉ *141 W. 115th St., between Malcom X and Adam Clayton Powell Jr. Blvds., Harlem* ☎ *212/663–8830.*

off the beaten path

Morris–Jumel Mansion. The oldest surviving private dwelling in Manhattan, this elegant 1765 Palladian-style mansion has nine period rooms with Georgian, federal, and French Empire furnishings. Originally the summer villa of British officer Roger Morris, it later briefly served as George Washington's headquarters during the American Revolution. In 1810, it was purchased by the French merchant Stephen Jumel, whose widow Eliza Bowen married Aaron Burr in the mansion's octagonal parlor. ✉ *65 Jumel Terr., at 160th St., east of St. Nicholas Ave., Washington Heights* ☎ *212/923–8008* 🌐 *www.preserve.org/hbt/morris/jumel.htm* *$3* ⏲ *Wed.–Sun. 10–4.*

New York Public Library 115th Street Branch. This striated, three-story Italian palazzo–style row house was designed by New York's fabled architectural firm, McKim, Mead & White, in 1908. The money for the construction of this and more than 60 other branch libraries was donated by Andrew Carnegie in 1901, and almost all of these were narrow, mid-block structures—because of Manhattan's expensive real estate. Look for the African-American heritage collection in the wooden display cases on the first floor. ✉ *203 W. 115th St., between Adam Clayton Powell Jr. and Frederick Douglass Blvds., Harlem* ☎ *212/666–9393* 🌐 *www.nypl.org/branch/man/hu.html* ⏲ *Tues. 11–7, Wed. 10–6, Thurs.–Fri. noon–6, Sat. 1–5.*

8 **Schomburg Center for Research in Black Culture.** The New York Public Library's Division of Negro Literature, History, and Prints first gained acclaim in 1926 when it acquired the vast collection of Arturo Alfonso Schomburg, a black scholar of Puerto Rican descent. Schomburg was curator in 1932–38, and, in 1940, when Schomburg died, the collection of more than 10,000 books, documents, paintings, and photographs recording black history was renamed in his honor. Later designated a research library, the ever-growing collection moved in 1980 into this modern redbrick building from the handsome Victorian next door (designed bMcKim, Mead & White), which is now a Schomburg exhibit hall. The collection has more than 5 million items, including rare manuscripts, art and artifacts, motion pictures, records, and videotapes. The Moving Image and Recorded Sound Division's music collection has early recordings of blues and jazz singers, as well as classic radio broadcasts, which can be heard in semiprivate listening booths. The Schomburg complex also includes the **American Negro Theatre,** gallery space for changing exhibitions on African-American history, and the **Langston Hughes Auditorium.** ✉ *515 Malcolm X Blvd., at W. 135th St., Harlem* ☎ *212/491–2200* 🌐 *www.schomburgcenter.org* *Free* ⏲ *Tues.–Wed. noon–8, Thurs.–Fri. noon–6, Sat. 10–6.*

need a break?

A good place for coffee and maybe a bite to eat, whether it's grits, a delicious dessert, or fried chicken, is **Pan Pan Restaurant** (✉ 500 Malcolm X Blvd., at W. 135th St., Harlem ☎ 212/926–4900).

★ 10 **Strivers' Row.** Since 1919, African-American doctors, lawyers, and other professionals have owned these elegant homes designed by such notable architects as Stanford White (his neo-Renaissance creations stand on the north side of West 139th Street). Behind each row are service alleys, a rare luxury in Manhattan. Musicians W. C. Handy ("The St. Louis Blues") and Eubie Blake ("I'm Just Wild About Harry") were among the residents here. The area, now officially known as the **St. Nicholas Historic District,** got its nickname because less affluent Harlemites felt that its residents were "striving" to become well-to-do. These quiet, tree-lined streets rank among the loveliest in Manhattan. ✉ *W. 138th and*

W. 139th Sts. between Adam Clayton Powell Jr. and Frederick Douglass Blvds., Harlem.

need a break?

If you're on Strivers' Row and you like fried chicken and sweet-potato pie, stop by the **Sugar Shack** (✉ 2611 Frederick Douglass Blvd., at W. 139th St., Harlem ☎ 212/491–4422). The Sunday brunch menu (waffles, biscuits, and gravy) is mouthwatering.

6 **Studio Museum in Harlem.** Focusing on African-American, Caribbean, and African art, this small museum houses a collection of paintings, sculpture (in a light-filled sculpture garden), and photographs (including historic photographs of Harlem by James Van Der Zee, popular in the 1930s, and works by Jacob Lawrence and Romare Bearden). The museum has changing exhibitions and special lectures and programs, and its gift shop is full of black American, Caribbean, and African-inspired books, posters, and jewelry. ✉ *144 W. 125th St., between Malcolm X and Adam Clayton Powell Jr. Blvds., Harlem* ☎ *212/864–4500* 🌐 *www.studiomuseuminharlem.org* 🎫 *$5 suggested admission* 🕓 *Wed.–Fri. and Sun. noon–6, Sat. 10–6.*

5 **Sylvia's Soul Food Restaurant.** Although there have been rumors about her retiring, personable Sylvia Woods still stays late most nights chatting with her customers. Southern specialties and cordiality are the rule here. When the restaurant opened in 1962, it seated 35. Now it's taken over an entire city block and can seat 450. Sylvia's own line of foods—including BBQ sauce and corn-bread mix—is now available at the restaurant and in neighborhood supermarkets. ✉ *328 Malcolm X Blvd., between W. 126th and W. 127th Sts., Harlem* ☎ *212/996–0660.*

EXPLORING THE OUTER BOROUGHS

2

FODOR'S CHOICE

Bronx Zoo, *The Bronx*
Coney Island, *Brooklyn*
MoMA QNS, *Queens*

HIGHLY RECOMMENDED

American Museum of the Moving Image, *Queens*
Brooklyn Borough Hall, *Brooklyn*
Brooklyn Botanic Garden, *Brooklyn*
Brooklyn Heights Promenade, *Brooklyn*
Brooklyn Museum of Art (BMA), *Brooklyn*
New York Botanical Garden, *The Bronx*
P.S.1 Contemporary Art Center, *Queens*
Prospect Park Audubon Center at the Boathouse, *Brooklyn*
Snug Harbor Cultural Center, *Staten Island*
Yankee Stadium, Highbridge, *The Bronx*

Updated by Natasha Lesser

WHEN MOST PEOPLE THINK OF NEW YORK, they think of Manhattan as "The City," and Brooklyn, Queens, the Bronx, and Staten Island as one big peripheral blob—the sticky, brown caramel surrounding the real Big Apple. Although Manhattan Island admittedly contains most of the sights that the city is known for, it's only one of the five boroughs (counties) that comprise New York City. Almost 80% of New York City's population doesn't live in Manhattan, and if you want to rub shoulders with native New Yorkers, you've got a much better chance in the boroughs. Within their expanses, there has always been room for immigrants. Nothing better illustrates the city's ethnic diversity (and divisions) than a subway ride: take the N or R from Queens, through Manhattan, and to Brooklyn, and you'll witness the ebb and tide of nations.

You'll also find that the outer boroughs are full of friendly neighborhoods, superb restaurants, and unique cultural attractions—museums, parks, and historical sights—all within a 45-minute subway ride from Manhattan. With such destinations as P.S.1 Contemporary Art Center and the Isamu Noguchi Garden Museum, Queens has become an art-lover's destination—even more so since the Museum of Modern Art made its temporary move here from midtown. The heavy hitters of the Bronx include the New York Botanical Garden, Bronx Zoo, and Yankee Stadium. In Brooklyn, the Brooklyn Museum of Art, Brooklyn Botanic Garden, and Coney Island are some of the main attractions. And for a view of the skyline and the Statue of Liberty, nothing beats the 20-minute, free ferry trip to Staten Island. Like the many Manhattanites who are making the exodus, you'll find that the outer boroughs are very desirable places to be.

THE BRONX

New York City's northernmost and only mainland borough (the others are all on islands) was the retreat of wealthy New Yorkers in the 19th century, when the area consisted of a picturesque patchwork of farms, market villages, and country estates. In the 1920s, the Bronx experienced a short-lived golden age: the new elevated subway line attracted an upwardly mobile population, and the Grand Concourse was fashioned as New York City's Champs-Elysées. Although the Bronx has a reputation as a gritty, down-and-out place, the borough is full of vital areas like the Italian neighborhood of Belmont. It has its cultural gems, too—a botanical garden, a world-renowned zoo, and, of course, Yankee Stadium, home of the celebrated Bronx Bombers.

The New York Botanical Garden, the Bronx Zoo & Belmont

Within the 5-mi vicinity covered in this tour, you can stroll among gardens of roses (250 kinds); watch red pandas swing from tree to tree; and sample biscotti at a third-generation bakery where patrons greet each other by name.

Numbers in the text correspond to numbers in the margin and on the New York Botanical Garden & Bronx Zoo map.

a good walk

The most direct route to the **New York Botanical Garden** 1 ⚑ is via Metro-North to the Botanical Garden stop, which is right across from the garden's pedestrian entrance (cross Kazimiroff Boulevard to the garden's Mosholu Gate). A cheaper alternative is to take the D train or the No. 4 to Bedford Park Boulevard. From the subway station continue east on Bedford Park Boulevard (a 10-minute walk) to the Kazimiroff Boulevard entrance of the garden. You may be tempted to spend most of the day here; when you do decide to leave the grounds, exit via the main gate near the Great Garden Clock. Turn left and walk along Southern Boulevard (10 minutes); turn left onto Fordham Road and continue (five minutes) to the Rainey Gate entrance of the **Bronx Zoo** 2—another must-see sight that could easily take up a day.

Exit the zoo via Southern Boulevard, turn right, and walk two blocks to East 187th Street; this will lead you straight into the heart of **Belmont** 3, an Italian neighborhood. You'll know you're in the right place when you see the imposing brick structure of **Our Lady of Mt. Carmel Roman Catholic Church** 4 (at Belmont Avenue and East 187th Street), the spiritual heart of the neighborhood—but for the true Belmont experience, take a walk through the **Arthur Avenue Retail Market** 5.

Fordham University 6 occupies a large plot of land north of Belmont. To get here, backtrack on Arthur Avenue to East Fordham Road (head toward the tall Gothic tower in the distance) and turn left. Although the college prefers that you take the official tour, you can sneak a peek at the handsome inner campus on your own, too; turn right on Bathgate Avenue, which leads to a college gate manned by a security guard. To return to Manhattan, continue west on East Fordham Road three blocks to chaotic Fordham Plaza, the "Times Square of the Bronx." From here, take Metro-North at East Fordham Road and Webster Avenue, or continue on East Fordham Road about four blocks more up to the Fordham Road subway station (at Grand Concourse) for the D train.

TIMING The Bronx Zoo and the New York Botanical Garden are each vast and interesting enough to merit half a day or more. If you want to visit both, start early and plan on a late lunch or early dinner in Belmont. Saturday is the best day to see the Italian neighborhood at its liveliest; on Sunday most stores are closed. The zoo and the garden are less crowded on weekdays—except Wednesday, when admission to both is free.

What to See

5 **Arthur Avenue Retail Market.** The market, in a building sheltering more than a dozen stalls, is one of the last bastions of old-time New York with a strong Italian-American presence. Here, amid piles of fresh produce, vendors still sell fresh beef hearts, rabbit, tripe, all kinds of olives, gnocchi *freschi* (fresh), *bufula* (buffalo) mozzarella, and low-price ceramic ware imported from Italy. Stop for a quick lunch—or at least a pizza square with toppings fresh from the market—at the Café al Mercato. *✉ 2344 Arthur Ave., at E. 187th St., Belmont ☎ 718/364–7681 ⏲ Mon.–Sat. 7–6 Ⓜ B, D, No. 4 to Fordham Rd., then Bx12 east; No. 2 or 5 to Pelham Pkwy., then Bx12 west; Metro-North to Fordham Rd., then shuttle bus to Belmont and Bronx Zoo.*

need a break?

At **Dominick's** (✉ 2335 Arthur Ave., at E. 187th St., Belmont ☎ 718/733–2807), there are no menus and no wine list. Instead, the question "What do you have?" is most often answered with "What do you want?" What you'll want is a heaping dish of spaghetti with meatballs along with crusty bread and wine poured from a jug. The same family has been cooking at Dominick's since the 1940s, serving loyal fans at congested communal tables.

3 **Belmont.** Often called the Little Italy of the Bronx, Belmont is much more of a real, thriving Italian neighborhood than its Manhattan counterpart. On Saturday afternoon, locals set off to buy freshly baked bread, homemade sausage, and fresh pasta. Don't be surprised to hear people speaking Italian—or Albanian: the neighborhood has become an enclave for this group as well. On Arthur Avenue, some of the gastronomic temp-

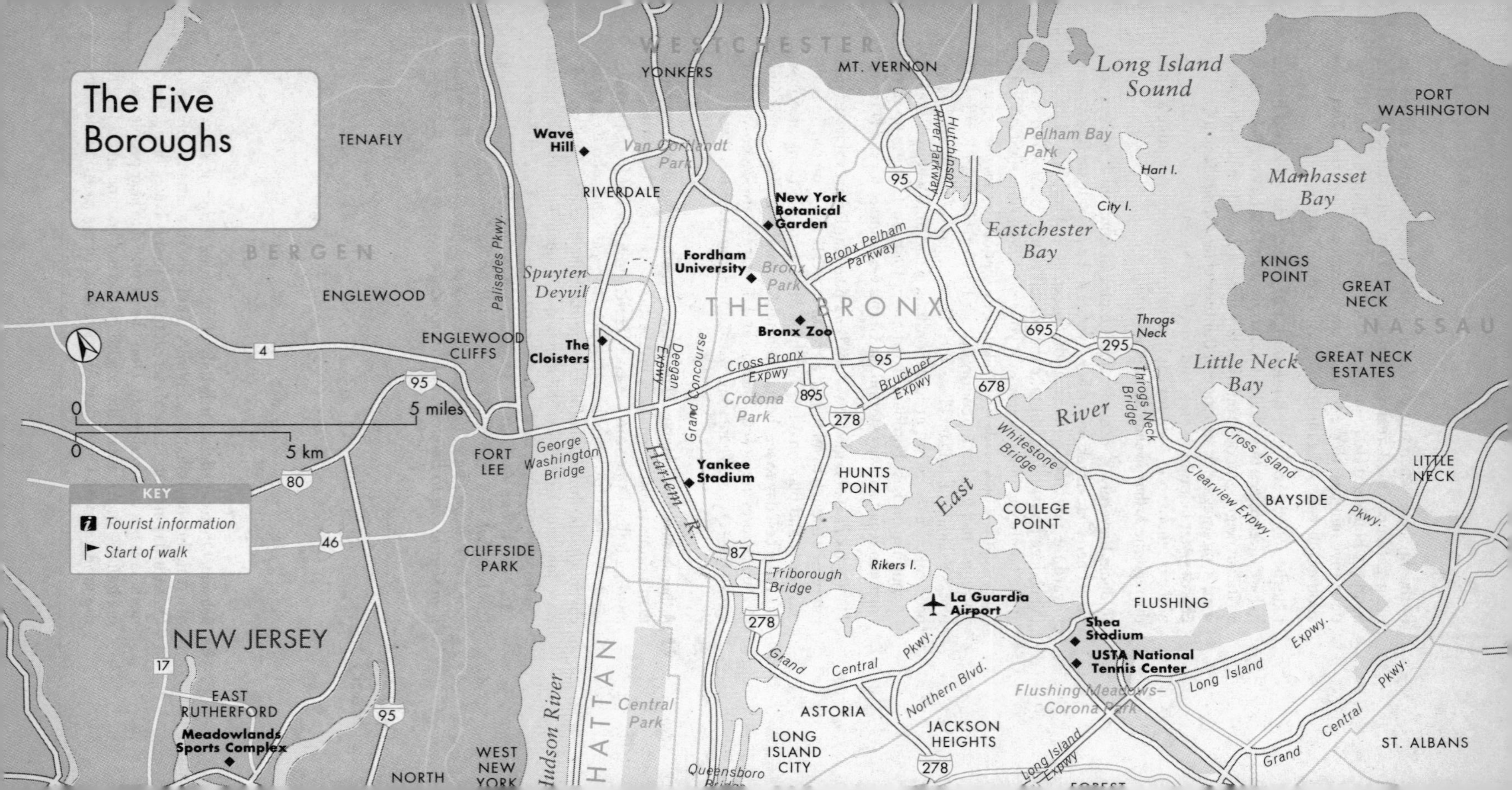
The Five Boroughs
KEY
Tourist information
Start of walk
0
5 miles
0
5 km
WESTCHESTER
YONKERS
MT. VERNON
Long Island Sound
PORT WASHINGTON
Manhasset Bay
KINGS POINT
GREAT NECK
NASSAU
GREAT NECK ESTATES
Little Neck Bay
LITTLE NECK
BAYSIDE
Cross Island Pkwy.
Clearview Expwy.
FLUSHING
Long Island Expwy.
Grand Central Pkwy.
ST. ALBANS
Shea Stadium
USTA National Tennis Center
Flushing Meadows–Corona Park
Throgs Neck
Throgs Neck Bridge
295
695
678
Whitestone Bridge
East River
COLLEGE POINT
La Guardia Airport
Rikers I.
JACKSON HEIGHTS
Northern Blvd.
278
ASTORIA
LONG ISLAND CITY
Queensboro Bridge
Triborough Bridge
87
HUNTS POINT
Bruckner Expwy
95
THE BRONX
Bronx Zoo
Bronx Park
Bronx Pelham Parkway
Hutchinson River Parkway
Pelham Bay Park
Hart I.
City I.
Eastchester Bay
New York Botanical Garden
Fordham University
Cross Bronx Expwy
895
Crotona Park
Yankee Stadium
Grand Concourse
Deegan Expwy
Harlem R.
Central Park
MANHATTAN
Hudson River
George Washington Bridge
The Cloisters
Spuyten Deyvil
RIVERDALE
Van Cortlandt Park
Wave Hill
Palisades Pkwy.
FORT LEE
CLIFFSIDE PARK
WEST NEW YORK
NORTH
ENGLEWOOD CLIFFS
ENGLEWOOD
TENAFLY
PARAMUS
BERGEN
4
80
46
NEW JERSEY
17
EAST RUTHERFORD
Meadowlands Sports Complex

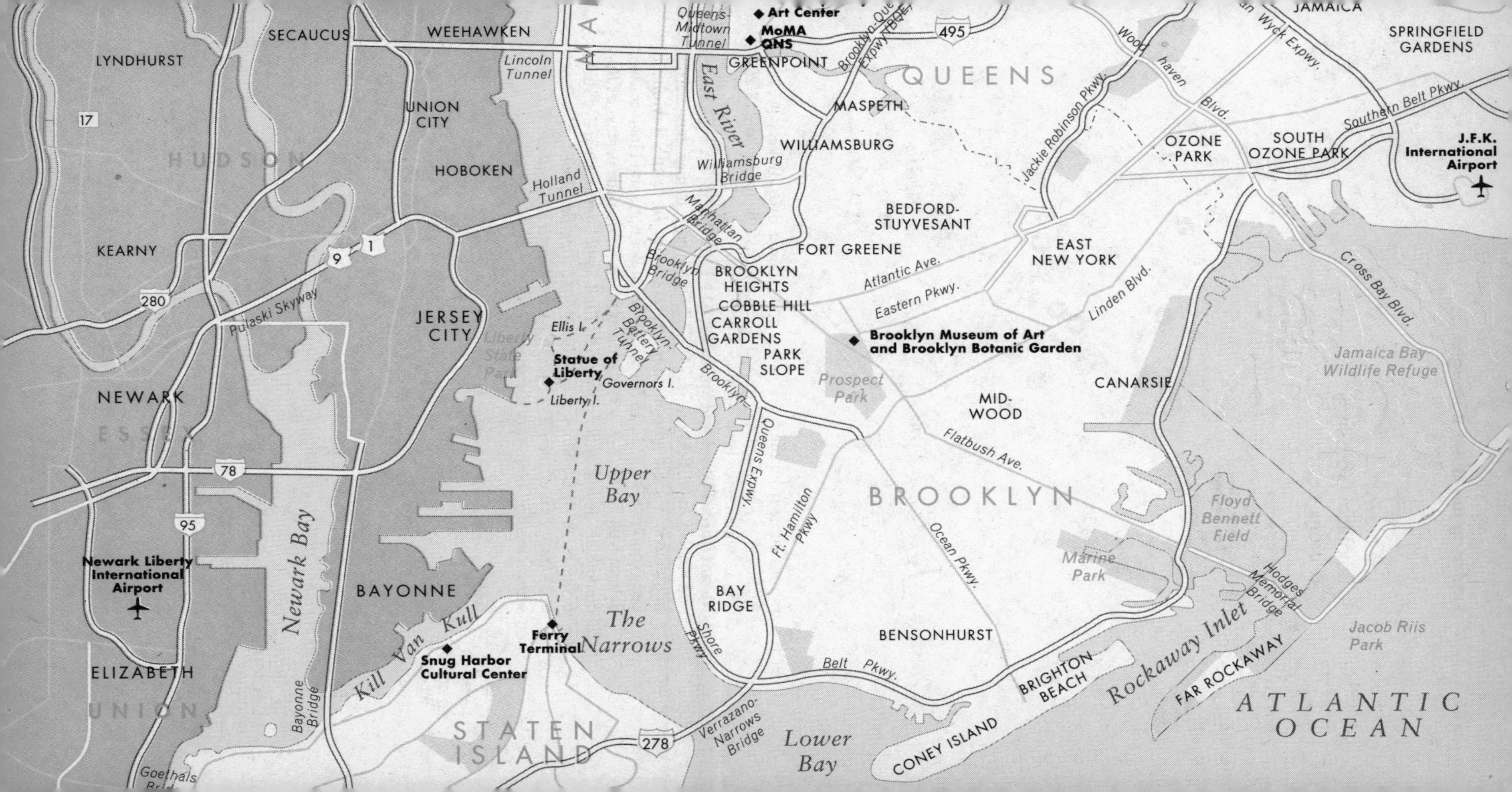
LYNDHURST
SECAUCUS
WEEHAWKEN
Lincoln Tunnel
Queens-Midtown Tunnel
Art Center
MoMA QNS
GREENPOINT
495
QUEENS
JAMAICA
SPRINGFIELD GARDENS
Van Wyck Expwy.
Woodhaven Blvd.
Southern Belt Pkwy.
J.F.K. International Airport
17
HUDSON
UNION CITY
HOBOKEN
Holland Tunnel
East River
Williamsburg Bridge
Brooklyn-Queens Expwy (BQE)
MASPETH
WILLIAMSBURG
Jackie Robinson Pkwy.
OZONE PARK
SOUTH OZONE PARK
KEARNY
9
1
280
Pulaski Skyway
Manhattan Bridge
Brooklyn Bridge
BEDFORD-STUYVESANT
FORT GREENE
BROOKLYN HEIGHTS
COBBLE HILL
CARROLL GARDENS
PARK SLOPE
Atlantic Ave.
Eastern Pkwy.
EAST NEW YORK
Linden Blvd.
Cross Bay Blvd.
JERSEY CITY
Liberty State Park
Ellis I.
Statue of Liberty
Liberty I.
Governors I.
Brooklyn-Battery Tunnel
Brooklyn-Queens Expwy.
Brooklyn Museum of Art and Brooklyn Botanic Garden
Prospect Park
CANARSIE
Jamaica Bay Wildlife Refuge
NEWARK
ESSEX
78
Upper Bay
MID-WOOD
Flatbush Ave.
BROOKLYN
Ft. Hamilton Pkwy
95
Newark Bay
Newark Liberty International Airport
BAYONNE
Floyd Bennett Field
Marine Park
Ocean Pkwy.
BAY RIDGE
Shore Pkwy
Kill Van Kull
Ferry Terminal
The Narrows
Snug Harbor Cultural Center
BENSONHURST
Hodges Memorial Bridge
Jacob Riis Park
ELIZABETH
UNION
Bayonne Bridge
Belt Pkwy.
BRIGHTON BEACH
Rockaway Inlet
FAR ROCKAWAY
ATLANTIC OCEAN
STATEN ISLAND
278
Verrazano-Narrows Bridge
Lower Bay
CONEY ISLAND
Goethals Bridge

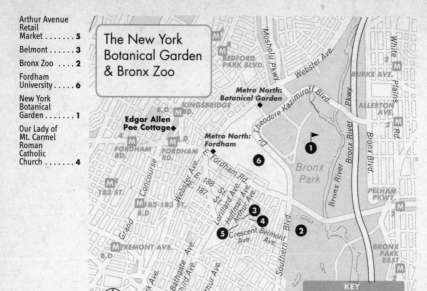

Arthur Avenue Retail Market 5
Belmont 3
Bronx Zoo 2
Fordham University 6
New York Botanical Garden 1
Our Lady of Mt. Carmel Roman Catholic Church 4

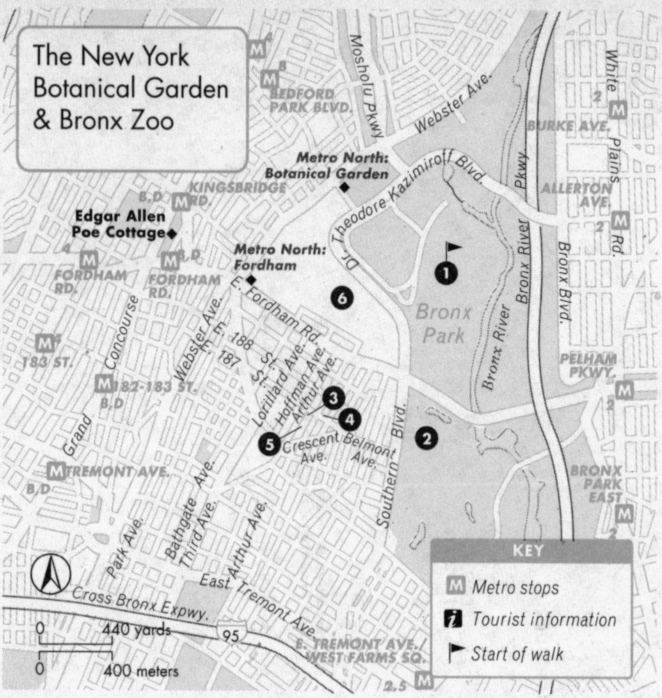

tations come from the brick ovens at **Madonia Bros. Bakery** (✉ 2348 Arthur Ave., between 187th and Crescent Sts., Belmont ☎ 718/295–5573), which have been turning out golden-brown loaves since 1918. **Mount Carmel Wines and Spirits** (✉ 612 E. 187th St., between Arthur and Hughes Aves., Belmont ☎ 718/367–7833) has a tremendous selection of Italian wines and grappas in beautiful bottles. **Borgatti's Ravioli and Egg Noodles** (✉ 632 E. 187th St., between Belmont and Hughes Aves., Belmont ☎ 718/367–3799) is known for its homemade pastas. ✉ *Bordered by E. Fordham Rd., Southern Blvd., and Crescent and 3rd Aves., Belmont* Ⓜ *B, D, No. 4 to Fordham Rd., then Bx12 east; No. 2 or 5 to Pelham Pkwy., then Bx12 west; Metro-North to Fordham Rd., then shuttle bus to Belmont and Bronx Zoo.*

need a break?

DeLillo Pastry Shop (✉ 606 E. 187th St., between Arthur and Hughes Aves., Belmont ☎ 718/367–8198) serves espresso and Italian pastries as well as superb Italian ices in summer (try the cappuccino–chocolate chip). At **Egidio's Pastry Shop** (✉ 622 E. 187th St., between Arthur and Hughes Aves., Belmont ☎ 718/295–6077) sample handmade Italian pastries, washed down with a strong shot of espresso. The homemade gelati next door are top-notch.

off the beaten path

Bronx Museum of the Arts. A walk along the Grand Concourse—a boulevard lined with art moderne apartment buildings—brings you to this collection of 20th-century works of art by African, African-American, Latin, Latin American, South Asian, and Asian-American artists. Keep an eye out for rotating exhibits and installations by contemporary local and international artists. Every third Friday night of the month, the party "Bounce" offers performances, new media installations, and dancing. The museum is a 15-minute walk from Yankee Stadium. ✉ *1040 Grand Concourse, at 165th St.* ☎ *718/681–6000* 🌐 *www.bxma.org* *$5 suggested donation; Wed. free*

Wed. noon–9, Thurs.–Sun. noon–6 Ⓜ No. 4 to 161st St.; B, D to 167th St.

2 Fodor's Choice ★ **Bronx Zoo.** Opened in 1899, this 265-acre spread is the world's largest urban zoo. The zoo's more than 4,500 animals, representing more than 600 species, mostly live in outdoor, parklike settings, often separated from onlookers by no more than a moat. One of the best exhibits is the **Congo Gorilla Forest,** a 6½-acre re-creation of an African rain forest with treetop lookouts, wooded pathways, lush greenery, and 400 animals—including two lowland gorilla troops, okapi, and red-river hogs. **Jungle World** is an indoor Asian tropical rain forest filled with white-cheeked gibbons, tree kangaroos, Malayan tapirs, and other exotic critters. In **Wild Asia,** open from April to October, tigers and elephants roam free on nearly 40 acres of open meadows and dark forests. Siberian tigers inhabit **Tiger World,** a setting that re-creates the Amur Valley, which borders China and Russia.

The **World of Darkness** is a windowless building that offers a rare glimpse into the nightlife of such nocturnal creatures as fruit-eating bats and naked mole rats. From late May to early October, a thousand butterflies and moths of 35 species dazzle visitors in the **Butterfly Zone.** Three different rides, including a monorail, an aerial tram, and the Zoo Shuttle, offer various perspectives of the grounds in summer. In winter, outdoor exhibitions are slightly modified, with fewer animals on view. The **Children's Zoo** ($2), open from April to October, has many hands-on learning activities, as well as a large petting zoo. Youngsters can see the world from an animal's perspective by crawling through a prairie dog tunnel and trying on a turtle's shell for size. If you're visiting the city with children during the holidays, don't miss the zoo's spectacular **Holiday Lights** ($7 mid-Nov.–mid-Dec., Fri.–Sun; mid-Dec.–early Jan., daily), when the zoo is ablaze with thousands of twinkling lights decorating 144 giant-size animal sculptures—from frogs to meerkats.

The easiest way to get to the zoo is to take the **Liberty Line** (☎ 718/652–8400) BxM11 express bus from mid-Manhattan, which runs up Madison Avenue; the one-way fare is $3 and exact change is required. You can also take the No. 2 subway to Pelham Parkway and walk three blocks west to the zoo's Bronx Parkway entrance, or take the No. 5 to East 180 Street and then transfer to the No. 2. ✉ *Bronx River Pkwy. and Fordham Rd., Fordham* ☎ *718/367–1010* 🌐 *www.wcs.org* *Apr.–Oct., Thurs.–Tues. $9; Nov.–Dec., Thurs.–Tues. $7; Jan.–Mar., Thurs.–Tues. $5; free Wed. year-round; Extra charge for some exhibits. Parking $7* *Apr.–Oct., weekdays 10–5, weekends 10–5:30; Nov.–Mar., daily 10–4:30; last ticket sold 1 hr before closing* Ⓜ *No. 2 to Pelham Pkwy. or No. 5 to 180 St. and transfer to No. 2; BxM11 express bus to zoo entrance.*

off the beaten path

City Island. At the extreme northeast end of the Bronx is a bona fide island of 230 acres. (To reach City Island, take the No. 6 subway to Pelham Bay Parkway and then catch the Bx29 bus.) In 1761, a group of local residents planned a port to rival New York's, but when that scheme hit the shoals, they returned to perennial maritime pursuits such as fishing and boatbuilding. City Island–produced yachts have included a number of America's Cup contenders. Connected to Pelham Bay Park by bridge, City Island has a maritime atmosphere, fishing-boat rentals, and hopping seafood restaurants. The 1½-mi-long City Island Avenue is the island's main strip. Near the bridge, off the avenue, is one group of restaurants; on the other end is another bunch, including **Johnny's Famous Reef Restaurant** (✉ 2 City

Island Ave. ☎ 718/885–2086), where fried fish, eaten inside or out, is the order of choice. Walk the length of the avenue or hop on the Bx29 bus.

Edgar Allan Poe Cottage. The Bronx County Historical Society maintains Poe's country retreat in Poe Park. It was here that Poe and his sickly wife, Virginia, sought refuge from Manhattan and from the vicissitudes of the writerly life between 1846 and 1849. The family was so impoverished that Poe's mother sometimes picked dandelions by the roadside for dinner. Poe wandered the countryside on foot and listened to the sound of the church bells at nearby St. John's College Church (now Fordham University); word has it that these bells inspired one of his most famous poems, "The Bells." ✉ *E. Kingsbridge Rd. and Grand Concourse, Norwood* ☎ *718/881–8900* 🌐 *www.bronxhistoricalsociety.org* *$3* *Sat. 10–4, Sun. 1–5* Ⓜ *No. 4 or D to Kingsbridge Rd.*

❻ **Fordham University.** A small enclave of distinguished Collegiate Gothic architecture in the midst of urban sprawl, this university opened in 1841 as a Jesuit college and was one of the country's preeminent schools. Fordham now has nearly 15,000 students in its undergraduate and graduate schools, including its campuses near Lincoln Center and in Tarrytown, New York. With ID, you can enter the grounds via Fordham Road at Third Avenue, adjacent to the Metro-North station, to see the **University Church,** whose stained glass was donated by King Louis Philippe of France (1773–1850); **Edward's Parade,** the quadrangle in the center of campus; and **Keating Hall,** sitting like a Gothic fortress in the center of it all. Maps are posted around the campus and are available in the security office in the Thebauld Hall Annex. Campus tours can be arranged through the office of undergraduate admission. ✉ *441 E. Fordham Rd., at 3rd Ave., Belmont* ☎ *800/367–3426, 718/817–1000, or 718/817–5946* 🌐 *www.fordham.edu* Ⓜ *B, D, No. 4 to Fordham Rd.; Metro-North to Fordham Rd.*

★ ⚑ ❼ **New York Botanical Garden.** Considered one of the leading botany centers of the world, this 250-acre garden built around the dramatic gorge of the Bronx River is one of the best reasons to make a trip to the Bronx. The garden was founded by Dr. Nathaniel Lord Britton and his wife, Elizabeth. After visiting England's Kew Gardens in 1889, they returned full of fervor to create a similar haven in New York.

The grounds encompass the historic **Lorillard Snuff Mill,** built by two French Huguenot manufacturers in 1840 to power the grinding of tobacco for snuff. Nearby, the Lorillards grew roses to supply fragrance for their blend. A path along the Bronx River from the mill leads to the garden's 50-acre **Forest,** the only surviving remnant of the forest that once covered New York City. Outdoor plant collections include the **Peggy Rockefeller Rose Garden,** with 2,700 bushes of more than 250 varieties; the spectacular **Rock Garden,** which displays alpine flowers; and the **Everett Children's Adventure Garden,** 8 acres of plant and science exhibits for children, including a boulder maze, giant animal topiaries, and a plant discovery center. Inside the historic **Enid A. Haupt Conservatory**—a Victorian-era glass house with 17,000 individual panes—are year-round recreations of misty tropical rain forests and arid African and North American deserts as well as changing exhibitions. In a semipermanent tent outside the conservatory is the **Gift Shop.** The **International Plant Science Center** incorporates both the **Herbarium** (open to researchers only), with its collection of more than 6.5 million plant specimens, and the **Metz Library,** which houses a collection of texts, illustrations, photographs, and other artifacts related to plant research and horticulture as well as an exhibition space.

To get to the Botanical Garden, take the Harlem-local-line train of **Metro-North** (☎ 212/532–4900) from Grand Central Terminal to the Botanical Garden stop; or take the B or D to the Bedford Park Boulevard–Lehman College stop or the No. 4 to Bedford Park Boulevard and walk about eight blocks east to the entrance on Kazimiroff Boulevard. By car, take the Bronx River Parkway, Exit 7W. A good way to see the garden is with the "Garden Passport" (🎫 $10), which gives you access to the Conservatory, Rock Garden, Native Plant Garden, Tram Tour, and Everett Children's Adventure Garden. ✉ *200th St. and Kazimiroff Blvd., Bedford Park* ☎ *718/817–8700* 🌐 *www.nybg.org* 🎫 *$3; free Sat. 10–noon and Wed.; Enid A. Haupt Conservatory $5; parking $5* ⏲ *Apr.–Oct., Tues.–Sun. 10–6; Nov.–Mar., Tues.–Sun. 10–4* Ⓜ *B, D, or No. 4 to Bedford Park Blvd.; Metro-North to Botanical Garden.*

2

❹ **Our Lady of Mt. Carmel Roman Catholic Church.** Rising like a beacon of faith above the neighborhood, this is the spiritual center of Belmont. In 1907, an Irish priest successfully petitioned the archdiocese for an Italian church to serve the new Italian immigrant community. Many residents of the neighborhood volunteered to help build the church in order to keep the costs down. ✉ *627 E. 187th St., between Hughes and Belmont Aves., Belmont* ☎ *718/295–3770* ⏲ *Weekdays 7–1 and 4–8, Sat. 7 AM–8 PM, Sun. 7–2 and 6–8:30* Ⓜ *B, D, No. 4 to Fordham Rd., then Bx12 east; No. 2 or 5 to Pelham Pkwy., then Bx12 west; Metro-North to Fordham Rd., then shuttle bus to Belmont and Bronx Zoo.*

off the beaten path

Wave Hill. In the mid- to late 19th century, Manhattan millionaires built summer homes in the Bronx suburb of Riverdale. Perched on a ridge above the Hudson River, the neighborhood commands stirring views of the New Jersey Palisades. Wave Hill, a former estate dating back to 1843, is now a 28-acre public garden and cultural center. At various times Theodore Roosevelt, Mark Twain, and Arturo Toscanini all rented the property, which was donated to the city in 1960. Today the greenhouse and conservatory, plus 18 acres of exquisite herb, wildflower, and aquatic gardens, attract green thumbs from all over the world. Grand beech and oak trees adorn wide lawns, and elegant pergolas are hidden along curving pathways. Additional draws are gardening and crafts workshops, a summertime dance series, changing art exhibitions, Sunday concerts in Armor Hall from fall to spring, and a popular café overlooking the river and Palisades. From Manhattan you can drive up the Henry Hudson Parkway to Exit 21 and follow the signs to Wave Hill. Or you can take the Metro-North Harlem-line train to the Riverdale stop and walk up West 254th Street to Independence Avenue, turn right, and proceed to the main gate. If you take the No. 1 or No. 9 train to 231st Street, transfer next to the Bx10 bus to 252nd Street and Riverdale Avenue. Cross the overpass and follow the signs to Wave Hill. ✉ *W. 249th St. and Independence Ave., Riverdale* ☎ *718/549–3200* 🌐 *www.wavehill.org* 🎫 *Mar.–Nov. $4, Sat. AM and Tues. free; Dec.–Feb. free* ⏲ *Mid-Apr.–May and Aug.–mid-Oct., Tues.–Sun. 9–5:30; June–July, Tues. 9–5:30, Wed. 9–dusk, Thurs.–Sun. 9–5:30; mid-Oct.–mid-Apr., Tues.–Sun. 9–4:30; free garden tours Sun. 2:15. Call for program schedule* Ⓜ *No. 1 or 9 train to 231st St., then Bx10 bus to 252nd St. and Riverdale Ave.; Metro-North Harlem line to Riverdale.*

off the beaten path

Yankee Stadium. Since Babe Ruth hit a home run in the park's inaugural game in 1923, Yankee Stadium has been one of baseball's most revered cathedrals. Many renovations later, the stadium still feels like the place where Lou Gehrig and Micky Mantle performed their heroic deeds. Take a tour of the stadium (arrive by 11:30 for the noon tour) or come for a game: the Yankees play ball between April and September. ✉ *161st St. and River Ave., Highbridge* ☎ *718/579–4531 tours; 718/293–6000 box office* 🌐 *www.yankees.com* *Tour $12* Ⓜ *B, D, No. 4 to 161st St.–Yankee Stadium.*

BROOKLYN

A sibling rivalry has existed between Brooklyn and Manhattan ever since the 1898 unification of Brooklyn with the rest of the city. Hardly Manhattan's wimpy sidekick, Brooklyn is a metropolis in its own right, full of world-class museums, spacious parks, landmark buildings, five-star restaurants, and lively neighborhoods. In fact, it's the most populous of all the boroughs, with nearly 2.5 million residents; even if it were sheared from the rest of New York, it would still be among the 20 largest cities in the United States.

Some of Brooklyn's neighborhoods are as trendy as downtown Manhattan. Williamsburg is a catwalk of stylish young people, who have built a lively nightlife scene. DUMBO, with its galleries and residential lofts, is Brooklyn's answer to SoHo. Over in working-class Italian Carroll Gardens, chefs trained at elite Manhattan restaurants have opened successful bistros. Fort Greene, with the Brooklyn Academy of Music as its anchor, is on the brink of becoming a performing arts enclave in full bloom. Brooklyn Heights, Cobble Hill, and Park Slope are favored more than ever by young families and professionals, who are drawn by the dignified brownstone- and tree-lined streets, handsome parks, cultural institutions, and the less frenetic pace of life.

Williamsburg

Starting around the turn of the 20th century, immigrants—largely Hasidic Jews, Poles, and Puerto Ricans—settled in this industrial section of Brooklyn along the East River, forming autonomous communities side by side. The artists and twenty- to thirtysomethings who are the neighborhood's newest residents have transformed it into Brooklyn's answer to the East Village. Most of the action—bars, restaurants, cafés, stores, and art galleries—can be found between Metropolitan Avenue and North 9th Street along **Bedford Avenue**, the main drag of bohemian Williamsburg. From Manhattan it takes just one stop into Brooklyn on the L train to be in the center of the scene. One of the first art galleries to open in the neighborhood, **Pierogi** (✉ 177 N. 9th St., between Bedford and Driggs Aves., Williamsburg ☎ 718/599–2144) displays changing exhibitions of works by local artists. **Galapagos** (✉ 70 N. 6th St., between Wythe and Kent Aves., Williamsburg ☎ 718/782–5188) is an all-in-one bar, art gallery, performance space, and movie house.

Brooklyn Heights, Cobble Hill & Carroll Gardens

"All the advantages of the country, with most of the conveniences of the city," ran the ads for a real estate development that sprang up in the 1820s just across the East River from downtown Manhattan. Brooklyn Heights—named for its enviable hilltop position—was New York's first suburb, linked to the city originally by ferry and later by the Brooklyn Bridge. Feverish construction led by wealthy industrialists and shipping magnates quickly transformed the airy heights into a fashionable upper-middle-class community. It was characterized by radical politics, as in abolitionist Henry Ward Beecher, and a leisurely, aristocratic ambience. In the 1940s and '50s, the area became a bohemian haven, home to writers including Carson McCullers, W. H. Auden, Arthur Miller, Truman Capote, Richard Wright, Alfred Kazin, Norman Mailer, and Hart Crane. Thanks to the vigorous efforts of preservationists in the 1960s, much of the Heights was designated New York's first historic district. Some 600 buildings more than 100 years old, representing a wide range of American building styles, are in excellent condition today.

A short hop across Atlantic Avenue from Brooklyn Heights, Cobble Hill is another quiet residential area of leafy streets lined with notable town houses built by 19th-century New York's upper middle class. A bit farther south, around President Street, Cobble Hill turns into the historically Italian, working-class section of Carroll Gardens, a neighborhood distinguished by deep blocks that allow for tiny front yards, and Smith Street's trendy boutiques and restaurants.

Numbers in the text correspond to numbers in the margin and on the Brooklyn Heights, Cobble Hill & Carroll Gardens map.

a good walk

From Manhattan, it takes about 40 minutes to walk across the Brooklyn Bridge and into Brooklyn Heights. At the bridge's Tillary Street terminus, turn right, walk two blocks to Cadman Plaza West, and swing right to Clark Street, where you'll see a subway entrance. To conserve energy, you can take the No. 2 or 3 subway from Manhattan to Clark Street, or the No. 4 or 5 to Borough Hall and walk up Court Street past the government buildings to Clark Street. From Clark Street take Henry Street one block to Pineapple Street. From here you'll be able to see the blue towers of the Manhattan Bridge, which links Brooklyn to Manhattan, and a view of the Brooklyn Bridge will soon come into view as you walk one block farther to Orange Street.

Turn left and on the north side of the block (the right-hand side) between Henry and Hicks streets is a formidable institution, the **Plymouth Church of the Pilgrims** 1, the center of abolitionist sentiment in the years before the Civil War. Turn right on Hicks Street and follow it to Middagh Street (pronounced *mid*-awe). At its intersection with Willow Street is **24 Middagh Street** 2, the oldest home in the neighborhood. Venture a few steps west on Middagh Street to see the Manhattan Bridge reaching over the East River in the shadow of the dominating Watchtower building. The neighborhood below the bridge is named for its location, **DUMBO** 3—*D*own *U*nder the *M*anhattan *B*ridge *O*verpass. Many of the buildings in this former industrial area have been turned into residential lofts, galleries, and artists' studios.

Backtrack on **Willow Street** 4 and observe the masterful local architecture between Clark and Pierrepont streets. As you turn right on Pierrepont Street heading toward the river, glance down **Columbia Heights** 5 to your right, where the brownstones are particularly elegant and well maintained.

Pierrepont Street ends at the **Brooklyn Heights Promenade** 6, one of the most famous vista points in all of New York City. After you've soaked in the views from the Promenade, turn up Montague Street. Look left to see Nos. 2 and 3 Pierrepont Place, two brick-and-brownstone palaces built in the 1850s. On your right lies Montague Terrace, where Thomas Wolfe lived when he was finishing *You Can't Go Home Again.* W. H. Auden lived on the top floor of the brownstone at 1 Montague Terrace.

Brooklyn Borough Hall 7
Brooklyn Heights Promenade 6
Brooklyn Historical Society 8
Christ Church .13
Cobble Hill Park 11
Columbia Heights 5
Court Street ..14
Dumbo 3
New York City Transit Museum 10
Our Lady of Lebanon Cathedral 9
Plymouth Church of the Pilgrims .1
Smith Street ..15
24 Middagh Street 2
Warren Place Workingmen's Cottages and Home and Tower "Model Tenements" ..12
Willow Street ..4

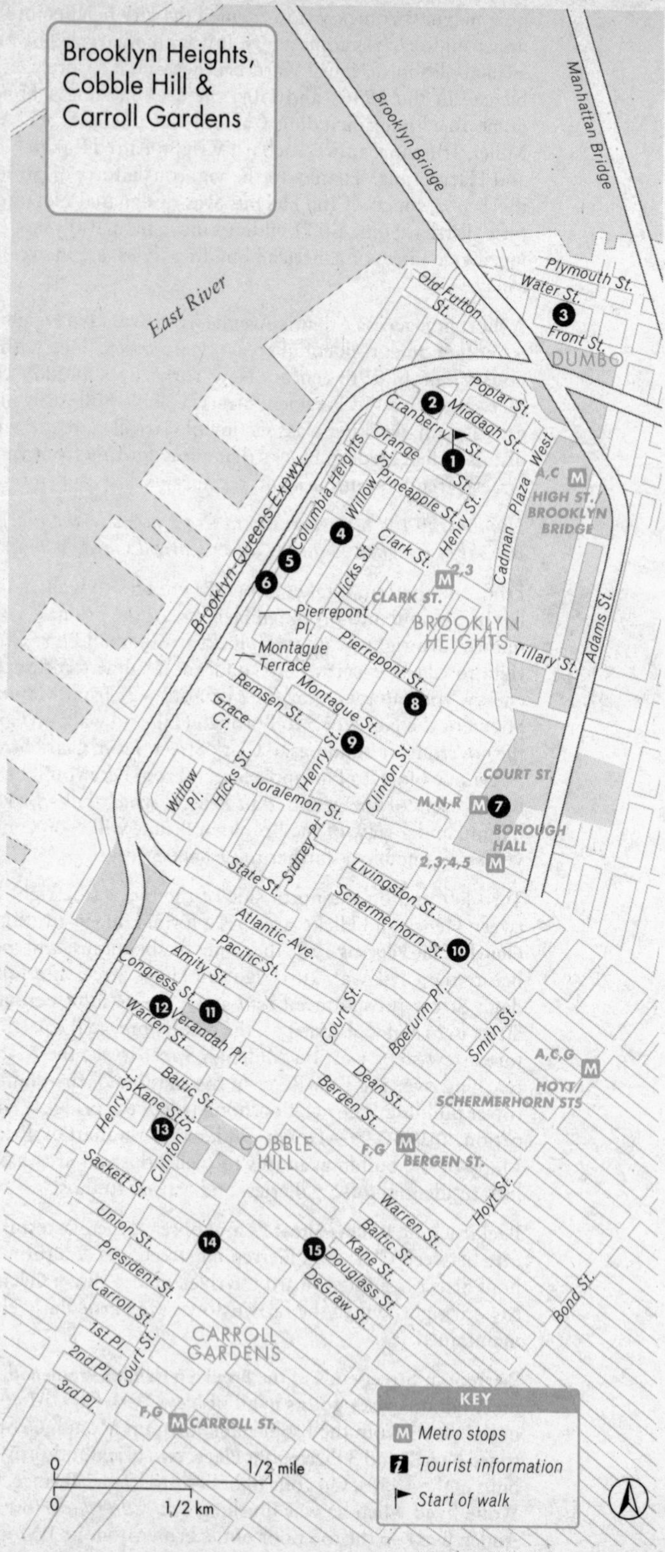

Continue east along this commercial spine of the Heights, past a variety of restaurants, coffee shops, and retail clothing and gift stores. At the northwest corner of Montague and Clinton streets is St. Ann's and the Holy Trinity Church, known for its early American stained-glass windows. Only the Congregation Hall is open for services; the rest of the church is closed indefinitely while money is raised for urgently needed repairs.

Beyond Clinton on the north side of Montague Street, note an interesting and eclectic row of banks: Chase, a copy of the Palazzo della Gran Guardia in Verona, Italy; and Citibank, looking like a latter-day Roman temple. Also remarkable is the art deco Municipal Credit Union. Farther down the street you'll find the historic **Brooklyn Borough Hall** 7, or you can detour a block north up Clinton Street to the elegant Romanesque redbrick **Brooklyn Historical Society** 8.

Return south along Clinton Street, and then turn right onto Remsen Street. At the corner of Remsen and Henry streets, stop to take in the Romanesque revival **Our Lady of Lebanon Cathedral** 9. Continue west on Remsen Street and then turn left onto Hicks Street to visit the 1847 Gothic revival Grace Church (254 Hicks St.). Across Hicks Street is Grace Court Alley, a traditional mews with a score of beautifully restored redbrick carriage houses, which were once stables for the mansions on Remsen and Joralemon streets.

Just a few more steps down Hicks Street, turn right and stroll down cobblestone Joralemon Street, noting Nos. 29–75, a line of modest brick row houses that delicately sidestep their way down the hill toward the river. Follow Willow Place between Joralemon and State streets, where the quietly elegant former Willow Place Chapel, built in 1876, stands. Nos. 43–49, four redbrick houses, are linked by a majestic two-story colonnade that looks transplanted from an antebellum Southern mansion.

Turn left on State Street and follow it back to Clinton Street. Make a left here and then the next right on Schermerhorn Street to visit the **New York City Transit Museum** 10. Otherwise turn right down Clinton to Atlantic Avenue, a busy thoroughfare with Middle Eastern food shops and restaurants. Farther east on Atlantic, between Hoyt and Bond streets, you can find more than a dozen antique-furniture stores and purveyors of modern housewares, including Breukelen and Bark.

Atlantic Avenue is the dividing line between the neighborhoods of Brooklyn Heights and Cobble Hill. For a taste of the latter, go two blocks south down Clinton Street to **Cobble Hill Park** 11, bordered by Congress Street and Verandah Place, a graceful row of converted stable buildings. On the way to the park you'll pass Amity Street, where Jennie Jerome, mother of Winston Churchill, was born in 1854 at No. 197. Three blocks south of Cobble Hill Park, Clinton Street is lined with Romanesque revival, neoclassical, and Italianate brownstones. Take a right at Warren Street and walk past Henry Street. On the right you'll see the charming **Warren Place Workingmen's Cottages and Home and Tower "Model Tenements"** 12. The Workingmen's Cottages, 24 beautiful Romanesque revival residences, stand on a side street marked by a small, hanging wooden sign. Circle the gardens and exit back onto Warren Street. Starting at 136 Warren, you'll see the Home and Tower "Model Tenements," two of the 19th century's most important architectural structures. Go back to Clinton Street and turn right. Two blocks down, at 320 Clinton Street, stands the Episcopal **Christ Church** 13, designed by Richard Upjohn.

Another four blocks down Clinton Street, near President Street, Cobble Hill gives way to the largely Italian neighborhood of Carroll Gardens. If you stroll down President or Carroll street, or 1st and 2nd places, you'll see the lovingly tended gardens where the abundance of religious statuary attests to the neighborhood's Catholic background. Or turn left (east) on DeGraw Street to **Court Street** 14, the neighborhood's main thoroughfare. One block east, **Smith Street** 15, with its stretch of funky shops and excellent restaurants, is also worth exploring.

To continue on to Park Slope, take the F train from the Carroll Street subway station (at the intersection of Carroll and Smith streets) three more stops toward Coney Island, to the 7th Avenue stop.

TIMING Allow three to four hours for a leisurely tour of these three neighborhoods; more if you stop for lunch, dinner, or both. Try to come on a sunny day, when the view from the Promenade is most spectacular.

What to See

★ 7 **Brooklyn Borough Hall.** Built in 1848, this Greek revival landmark is arguably Brooklyn's handsomest building. The hammered-brass top of the cast-iron cupola (a successor to the original wooden one, which burned in 1895) was restored by the same French craftsmen who restored the Statue of Liberty. The stately building is adorned with Tuckahoe marble both inside and out; other highlights are the square rotunda and the two-story beaux arts–style courtroom with plaster columns painted to look like wood. Today the hall serves as the office of Brooklyn's borough president. On Tuesday and Saturday a green market sets up on the flagstone plaza in front. ✉ *209 Joralemon St., at Court St., Brooklyn Heights* ☎ *718/802–3700* 🌐 *www.brooklyn-usa.org* 🎫 *Free* ⏲ *Call for tour information* Ⓜ *No. 2, 3, 4, or 5 to Borough Hall; N or R to Court St.*

★ 6 **Brooklyn Heights Promenade.** Stretching from Orange Street on the north to Remsen Street on the south, this ⅓-mi-long esplanade offers enthralling views of Manhattan. Find a bench and take in the view of the skyline, the Statue of Liberty, Ellis Island, and the Brooklyn Bridge, the transcendently impressive steel suspension bridge designed by John Augustus Roebling and completed in 1883. The small island to your left is Governors Island, a former Coast Guard base whose future fate has not yet been determined. Below you is the Brooklyn–Queens Expressway and Brooklyn's industrial waterfront. Ⓜ *No. 2 or 3 to Clark St.; A or C to High St.*

need a break? Serving lunch and dinner, the **Heights Café** (✉ 84 Montague St., at Hicks St., Brooklyn Heights ☎ 718/625–5555) is the spot for American fare in the Heights.

8 **Brooklyn Historical Society.** Completed in 1881, this elegant redbrick museum and library was the first major structure in New York to feature terra-cotta ornamentation, such as capitals, friezes, and lifelike busts. The building's exhibitions on Brooklyn history and culture and its impressive library are open to the public. Ongoing programs include weekend neighborhood walking tours; call for details. ✉ *128 Pierrepont St., at Clinton St., Brooklyn Heights* ☎ *718/222–4111* 🌐 *www.brooklynhistory.org* Ⓜ *No. 2. 3, 4, or 5 to Borough Hall; N or R to Court St.*

13 **Christ Church.** This sandstone Episcopal church, with its lean, tower-dominated facade, was designed by the prolific architect Richard Upjohn, who lived nearby at 296 Clinton Street. (He also designed Grace Church,

at 254 Hicks Street, and Our Lady of Lebanon Cathedral, at 113 Remsen Street) Inside, the pulpit, lectern, and altar are the work of Louis Comfort Tiffany. You can see the interior during services or by appointment. ✉ *320 Clinton St., at Kane St., Cobble Hill* ☎ *718/624–0083* ⏲ *Services weekdays noon, Wed. 6 PM, Sun. 10:30 and 11* Ⓜ *F or G to Bergen St.*

11 **Cobble Hill Park.** One of the city's first vest-pocket parks, this green space has marble columns at its entrances, antique benches and tables, and a playground. Bordering the park's south side is **Verandah Place,** a charming row of converted stable buildings; Thomas Wolfe once resided in the basement of No. 40 (one of his many residences in the borough). ✉ *Congress St. between Clinton and Henry Sts., Cobble Hill* Ⓜ *F or G to Bergen St.*

need a break?

Between Court and Clinton streets on Atlantic Avenue are a half dozen Middle Eastern markets and eateries. **Sahadi Importing** (✉ 187–189 Atlantic Ave., between Clinton and Court Sts., Brooklyn Heights ☎ 718/624–4550) has cheap and delicious dried fruits, nuts, candies, and olives to buy by the pound, among other snacks like spinach pies.

5 **Columbia Heights.** Among the majestic residences on this street, the brownstone grouping of **Nos. 210–220** is often cited as the most graceful in New York. Norman Mailer lives on this street, and from a rear window in **No. 111,** Washington Roebling, who in 1869 succeeded his father as chief engineer for the Brooklyn Bridge, directed the completion of the bridge from his sickbed. ✉ *Between Pierrepont and Cranberry Sts., Brooklyn Heights* Ⓜ *No. 2 or 3 to Clark St.; A or C to High St.*

14 **Court Street.** Court Street's activity whirls around its cafés, restaurants, bookstores, and old-fashioned bakeries. Fresh pasta, mozzarella, sausages, olives, and prepared dishes are available at a number of shops, including **Pastosa Ravioli** (✉ 347 Court St., at Union St., Carroll Gardens ☎ 718/625–7952), where the gnocchi is particularly recommended. **Caputo's Dairy** (✉ 460 Court St., between 3rd and 4th Pl., Carroll Gardens ☎ 718/855–8852) has a wide selection of homemade pastas and sauces. Italian sausages, *soppressata* (pork sausage), and homemade mozzarella are sold at **G. Esposito's & Sons** (✉ 357 Court St., between President and Union Sts., Carroll Gardens ☎ 718/875–6863), the neighborhood's best meat store. Ⓜ *F or G to Bergen St.; No. 2, 3, 4, or 5 to Borough Hall.*

need a break?

Marquet (✉ 221 Court St., at Warren St., Cobble Hill ☎ 718/852–9267) makes irresistible tarts and other French pastries. **Sweet Melissa Patisserie** (✉ 276 Court St., at Douglass St., Cobble Hill ☎ 718/855–3410) has sticky buns, madeleines, and finger sandwiches.

3 **DUMBO.** This neighborhood, in a former industrial area along the river, is named for its location—*D*own *U*nder the *M*anhattan *B*ridge *O*verpass. Residential lofts, artists' studios, and galleries now fill what were once warehouses. The waterfront park provides an unbeatable view of Manhattan framed by the Brooklyn and Manhattan bridges. The neighborhood has a few stores, cafés, bars, and restaurants, including the romantic River Café and Grimaldi's Pizzeria, as well its own gourmet ice cream parlor, the Brooklyn Ice Cream Factory. But mostly it retains its sparse, industrial feel. Ⓜ *F to York St.; A or C to High St.*

10 New York City Transit Museum. The museum, inside a converted 1930s subway station, has restored classic subway cars, an operating signal tower, more than 200 trolley models, and exhibits on the history of surface transportation and the subway's construction. Look for changing shows on all topics transportation-related. The museum shop, like the one in Grand Central Terminal, is a mother lode of subway-inspired memorabilia. ✉ *Boerum Pl. at Schermerhorn St., Brooklyn Heights* ☎ *718/694–5100* 🌐 *www.mta.info/museum* 💳 *$3* ⏲ *Tues.–Fri. 10–4, weekends noon–5* Ⓜ *No. 2, 3, 4, or 5 to Borough Hall; N or R to Court St.; A or C to Hoyt/Schermerhorn Sts.*

9 Our Lady of Lebanon Cathedral. One of the oldest Romanesque revival buildings in the country, this Congregational church was designed by Richard Upjohn in 1844. Its doors, which depict Norman churches, were salvaged from the 1943 wreck of the ocean liner *Normandie*. ✉ *113 Remsen St., at Henry St., Brooklyn Heights* ☎ *718/624–7228* ⏲ *Services weekdays noon; Sun. 9 AM and 11 AM; tours by appointment* Ⓜ *No 2 or 3 to Clark St.; No. 2, 3, 4, or 5 to Borough Hall; N or R to Court St.*

1 Plymouth Church of the Pilgrims. Thanks to the stirring oratory of Brooklyn's most eminent theologian, Henry Ward Beecher (brother of Harriet Beecher Stowe, author of *Uncle Tom's Cabin*), this house of worship was the vortex of antislavery sentiment in the years before the Civil War. Because it provided refuge to slaves, the church, which was built in 1849, was known as the Grand Central Terminal of the Underground Railroad in its latter years. Its windows, like those of many other neighborhood churches, were designed by Louis Comfort Tiffany. In the gated courtyard beside the church, a statue of Beecher depicts refugee slaves crouched in hiding behind the base. ✉ *Orange St. between Henry and Hicks Sts., Brooklyn Heights* ☎ *718/624–4743* ⏲ *Service Sun. 11 AM; tours by appointment* Ⓜ *No. 2 or 3 to Clark St.; A or C to High St.*

15 Smith Street. From humble beginnings, this otherwise low-key, semi-commercial street has become the center of this hip neighborhood full of fashionable boutiques and eclectic restaurants. Young designers and restaurateurs, some of whom trained with the best chefs in Manhattan, have set up shop here, drawn by the more affordable rents. The restaurants, from French bistros to refined New American, are some of Brooklyn's best. Ⓜ *F or G to Bergen or Carroll Sts.*

need a break?

Locals like the casual and inviting **Boerum Hill Food Company** (✉ 134 Smith St., between Bergen and Dean Sts., Boerum Hill ☎ 718/222–0140) for coffee and updated American fare at breakfast, lunch, or dinner. At **Café LULUc** (✉ 214 Smith St., between Butler and Baltic Sts., Boerum Hill ☎ 718/625–3815) enjoy a cappuccino, croissant, and other authentic French café cuisine. At **Halcyon** (✉ 227 Smith St., between Douglass and Butler Sts., Carroll Gardens ☎ 718/260–9299) order a coffee or a glass of wine and find a seat on one of the vintage couches and chairs. Records are sold in the back, and a DJ spins his or her picks. **Panino'teca** (✉ 275 Smith St., between Sackett and DeGraw Sts., Carroll Gardens ☎ 718/237–2728) specializes in panini sandwiches.

2 24 Middagh Street. This 1824 federal-style clapboard residence with a mansard roof is the oldest home in the neighborhood. Peer through a door in the wall on the Willow Street side for a glimpse of the cottage garden and carriage house in the rear. Ⓜ *No. 2 or 3 to Clark St.; A or C to High St.*

⑫ **Warren Place Workingmen's Cottages and Home and Tower "Model Tenements."** An early (1877) experiment in low-income, multifamily housing, these beautiful apartments by Brooklyn philanthropist Alfred Tredway White (1846–1921) prefigure the early-20th-century garden apartments built in Forest Hills, Sunnyside, and Jackson Heights, Queens. White's structures stand in marked contrast to the enormous, blocklike housing projects designed by later urban planners for low-income tenants. Now the Home and Tower apartments are the exclusive Cobble Hill Towers. The Workingmen's Cottages, which White built for higher-income workers, are one of the most secret and charming enclaves in New York City. Each building is less than 12 ft wide. Attesting to White's good works at his funeral, William Howard Taft remarked, "I don't know any other one in all that six million of New York City who would leave such a void as he does." ✉ *The Tower: 136–142 Warren St., Cobble Hill* ✉ *417–435 Hicks St., Cobble Hill* ✉ *The Home: 439–445 Hicks St., Cobble Hill* ✉ *129–135 Baltic St. Cobble Hill* Ⓜ *F or G to Bergen St.*

④ **Willow Street.** One of the prettiest and most architecturally varied blocks in Brooklyn Heights is Willow Street between Clark and Pierrepont streets. At **No. 22** stands Henry Ward Beecher's house—a prim Greek revival brownstone. **Nos. 155–159** are three brick federal row houses that were allegedly stops on the Underground Railroad. Ⓜ *No. 2 or 3 to Clark St.; A or C to High St.*

Park Slope & Prospect Park

Park Slope grew up in the late 1800s and is one of Brooklyn's most comfortable places to live today. Row after row of immaculate brownstones date from its turn-of-the-20th-century heyday, when Park Slope had the nation's highest per-capita income. Seventh Avenue, between Lincoln and 15th streets, is the neighborhood's main drag, with long-established restaurants, groceries, bookstores, shops, cafés, bakeries, churches, and real estate agents. Generating the better buzz are the restaurants, bars, and gift shops along still-gentrifying 5th Avenue. To get to the north end of the Slope, take the Q to 7th Avenue (at Flatbush Ave.) or the No. 2 or 3 to Grand Army Plaza; to get to the south Slope (roughly between 5th and 15th streets), take the F to 7th Avenue (at 9th Street).

The "Park" in Park Slope refers to 526-acre Prospect Park, designed by Frederick Law Olmsted and Calvert Vaux and completed in the late 1880s. It's rumored that the two liked this more naturalistic setting better than their previous creation, Manhattan's Central Park. The park is not as heavily used as Central Park and has very few vendors within it selling snacks and beverages. Nearby are the Grand Army Plaza, with its Soldiers' and Sailors' Memorial Arch; the stately Brooklyn Museum and Brooklyn Public Library; and the scenic Brooklyn Botanic Garden, a worthwhile destination any time of year.

Numbers in the text correspond to numbers in the margin and on the Park Slope & Prospect Park map.

a good walk

Begin at the north end of Park Slope, at Flatbush and 8th avenues. The Nos. 2 and 3 trains stop here (Grand Army Plaza). Walk down 8th Avenue to Lincoln Place, where the sumptuous Venetian-palace style of the **Montauk Club** ① proclaims its standing as one of Brooklyn's most prestigious clubs. Continue along 8th Avenue, stopping to look at the brownstones on side streets along the way (President and Carroll streets are especially handsome), until you reach **Montgomery Place** ②, with its remarkable row of Romanesque revival brownstones.

Brooklyn Botanic Garden **14**
Brooklyn Museum of Art (BMA) **15**
Brooklyn Public Library **12**
Eastern Parkway **13**
Grand Army Plaza **3**
Lefferts Historic House **10**
Litchfield Villa . . . **4**
Montauk Club **1**
Montgomery Place **2**
Prospect Park Audobon Society at the Boathouse **8**
Prospect Park Band Shell **6**
Prospect Park Carousel **9**
Prospect Park Zoo **11**
7th Avenue **16**
Tennis House **5**
Wollman Memorial Rink **7**

From the top of Montgomery Place, take a left and walk north along Prospect Park West back to **Grand Army Plaza** 3, whose center is dominated by the Soldiers' and Sailors' Memorial Arch, patterned on the Arc de Triomphe in Paris. Across from the plaza is the main entrance to Prospect Park, where winding paths and drives, undulating meadows, unexpected vistas, and woodlands serve up unanticipated pleasures at every turn. A good way to experience the park is to walk the entirety of its 3.3.-mi circular drive and make detours off it as you wish (just be careful on weekdays in winter when the drive is open to traffic). Joggers, skaters, and bicyclists have the drive to themselves daily 9–5 and 7–10 PM April–October and weekends year-round.

Immediately upon entering the park, veer right on the circular drive. Take a moment to peer down the 90-acre Long Meadow, one of New York's greatest open spaces and a haven for picnickers, kite fliers, and dogs (on leashes). Remarkably, more than 130 years after the park's construction, the view down the Long Meadow from here still takes in no buildings—only grass, trees, and sky. A short distance down the drive, just beyond a playground on your right, a small access road leads you to **Litchfield Villa** 4, an elaborate Italianate mansion and home of the park's administrative offices. Continuing on the drive, you'll come to two structures on your left—the Picnic House, frequently booked for weddings and sometimes for free performances, and the **Tennis House** 5, home to the Brooklyn Center for Urban Education.

To the left, beyond the groomed meadow, lies the Ravine, the wooded core of the park. Its wilderness demonstrates Olmsted's genius at juxtaposing vastly different landscapes. The majority of the Ravine is fenced off to protect the plantings, though one section by the waterfall is now open. Guided tours, given on weekends from April to November, are a good way to see the otherwise inaccessible parts of the park (contact the Prospect Park hot line for details, 718/965–8999, 🌐 www.

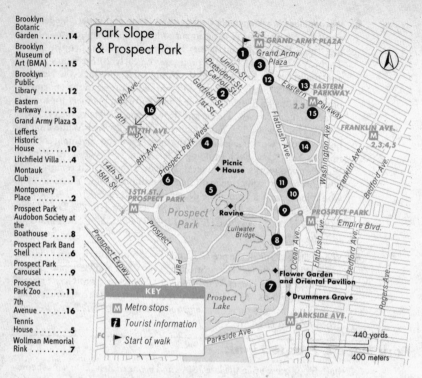

prospectpark.org). On the right side of the drive, near the 9th Street entrance, is the **Prospect Park Band Shell** 6, site of the park's enormously popular summer performing arts series.

The drive curves to the left around a half dozen baseball diamonds used by local leagues between Memorial Day and Labor Day; the diamonds mark the far southern end of Long Meadow. After a long downhill, the drive's view opens to the left onto the glorious 60-acre Prospect Lake, a refuge for waterfowl, including a few resident swans. Round the lake past the Ocean Parkway/Coney Island Avenue park entrance, and after a bit of the straightaway you'll come upon Drummers Grove on the right. This area has long been a weekend gathering spot for local African, Caribbean, and African-American musicians. Sunday afternoons when it's warm out, dozens of drummers and dancers jam, joined by an audience of sidetracked bicyclists, joggers, and skaters.

Just past the grove, on the left, is **Wollman Memorial Rink** 7. It's adjacent to the Flower Garden and Oriental Pavilion, the most formally laid-out part of the park. Once a graceful setting where people strolled to the strains of an orchestra, the area is now rather desolate. Moving on, you'll reach the **Prospect Park Audubon Center at the Boathouse** 8. The Boathouse sits opposite the Lullwater Bridge, creating an idyllic scene, particularly on evenings when the light is just right and the lake reflects an exact image of the building. Just steps from the Boathouse (on the left as you face the Cleft Ridge Span) is the lovely Camperdown Elm, immortalized by the poet Marianne Moore, who in the 1960s was an early park preservationist.

Not far beyond the Boathouse, on the eastern edge of the park (to your right), is the **Prospect Park Carousel** 9, and beyond that the **Lefferts Historic House** 10 and the **Prospect Park Zoo** 11. From here, you're just a short uphill walk away from Grand Army Plaza, at which point you'll have come full circle around the park.

East (to your right) of the park's Grand Army Plaza entrance stands the main branch of the **Brooklyn Public Library** 12. A couple of hundred yards farther down the grand **Eastern Parkway** 13 lie the entrances to two of Brooklyn's most important cultural offerings: the beautifully tended **Brooklyn Botanic Garden** 14, which occupies 52 acres, and the world-class **Brooklyn Museum of Art (BMA)** 15. To return to Manhattan, you can take the No. 2 or 3 subway lines from the Eastern Parkway–Museum station in front of the museum. If at any time you want to check out the shops and restaurants of Park Slope, head to **7th Avenue** 16, Park Slope's commercial center. From Grand Army Plaza, Union Street leads to the avenue.

TIMING You could easily spend a half day at the Brooklyn Museum or the Brooklyn Botanic Garden—and another three hours exploring Prospect Park. If you must squeeze everything into one trip, break up your wanderings with a visit to 7th Avenue, where restaurants and cafés abound. Weekends are the best time to observe local life and to enjoy the park, when it's closed to vehicles. On weekends and holidays throughout the year, from noon to 5 PM, the red "Heart of Brooklyn" trolley circles Prospect Park, leaving Wollman Rink on the hour and hitting the zoo, the Botanic Garden, the Band Shell, and most other sights. Best of all it's free and it connects with the Brooklyn Children's Museum's trolley. Prospect Park has heaps of information for the Brooklyn visitor on the Web at www.prospectpark.org, or call the park hot line at 718/965–8999.

What to See

★ ⓮ **Brooklyn Botanic Garden.** A major attraction at this 52-acre botanic garden, one of the finest in the country, is the beguiling **Japanese Garden**—complete with a blazing red *torii* gate and a pond laid out in the shape of the Chinese character for "heart." The Japanese cherry arbor here turns into a breathtaking cloud of pink every spring, and the Cherry Blossom Festival is perhaps the park's most popular weekend event. You can also wander through the **Cranford Rose Garden** (5,000 bushes, 1,200 varieties); the **Fragrance Garden,** designed especially for the blind; the **Shakespeare Garden,** featuring more than 80 plants immortalized by the Bard (including many kinds of roses); and **Celebrity Path,** Brooklyn's answer to Hollywood's Walk of Fame, with the names of New York stars—including Mel Brooks, Woody Allen, Mary Tyler Moore, Barbra Streisand, Mae West, and Maurice Sendak—inscribed on stepping-stones. The **Steinhardt Conservatory,** a complex of handsome greenhouses, holds thriving desert, tropical, temperate, and aquatic vegetation, as well as a display charting the evolution of plants over the past 140 million years. The extraordinary C. V. Starr Bonsai Museum in the Conservatory exhibits about 80 miniature Japanese specimens. Free tours are given weekends at 1 PM, except for holiday weekends (☎ 718/623–7220 for details). Entrances to the garden are on Eastern Parkway, just outside the subway station; on Washington Avenue, behind the Brooklyn Museum of Art (where there is also a fee parking lot); and on Flatbush Avenue at Empire Boulevard. ✉ *900 Washington Ave., between Flatbush Ave. and Empire Blvd., Prospect Heights* ☎ *718/623–7200* 🌐 *www.bbg.org* 🎫 *$3; free Tues. and Sat. before noon* ⏲ *Apr.–Sept., Tues.–Fri. 8–6, weekends 10–6; Oct.–Mar., Tues.–Fri. 8–4:30, weekends 10–4:30* Ⓜ *No. 2 or 3 to Eastern Pkwy.; Q to Prospect Park.*

off the beaten path

Brooklyn Children's Museum. This fully interactive museum for children has tunnels to walk through and animals to pet. Exhibitions cover topics ranging from city life to plant life and making patterns to making music. Free trolley service to the museum leaves Grand Army Plaza (corner of Union Street and Prospect Park West) at 15 minutes past the hour, and the Brooklyn Museum of Art at 25 minutes past the hour, from 10 to 5 on weekends. The trolley connects with the park's "Heart of Brooklyn" line. ✉ *145 Brooklyn Ave., at St. Marks Ave., Crown Heights* ☎ *718/735–4400* 🌐 *www.brooklynkids.org* 🎫 *$4 suggested donation* ⏲ *June–Aug., Mon. and Wed.–Sun. noon–5; Sept.–May, Wed.–Fri. 2–5, weekends 10–5* Ⓜ *No. 3 to Kingston Ave.; A to Nostrand Ave; C to Kingston-Throop Ave.*

★ ⓯ **Brooklyn Museum of Art (BMA).** A world-class museum, the BMA was founded in 1823 as the Brooklyn Apprentices' Library Association (Walt Whitman was one of its first librarians) and was a pioneer in the collection of non-Western art. With approximately 1.5 million pieces in its permanent collection, from Rodin sculptures to Andean textiles and Assyrian wall reliefs, it ranks as the second-largest art museum in New York—only the Met is larger. As you approach the massive, regal building designed by McKim, Mead & White (1893), look for the allegorical figures of Brooklyn and Manhattan, originally carved by Daniel Chester French for the Manhattan Bridge. The spectacular glass-fronted entranceway and the lobby were designed by Polshek Architects, the same firm that did the Rose Center for Earth and Space at the American Museum of Natural History.

Beyond the changing exhibitions, highlights include **Egyptian Art** (third floor), considered one of the best collections of its kind, and **African and**

Pre-Columbian Art (first floor). In the gallery of **American Painting and Sculpture** (fifth floor), *Brooklyn Bridge* by Georgia O'Keeffe hangs alongside nearly 200 first-rate works by Winslow Homer, John Singer Sargent, Thomas Eakins, George Bellows, and Milton Avery. The **Period Rooms** (fourth floor) include the complete interior of the Jan Martense Schenck House, built in the Brooklyn Flatlands section in 1675, as well as a Moorish-style room from the since-demolished 54th Street mansion of John D. Rockefeller. **Asian Art** (second floor) includes galleries devoted to Chinese, Korean, Indian, and Islamic works. On the third floor is the **Beaux-Arts Court,** a gracious, skylighted space where changing exhibits and events are held. Outdoors, the **Frieda Schiff Warburg Memorial Sculpture Garden** showcases architectural fragments from demolished New York buildings, including Penn Station. On the first Saturday of each month, "First Saturdays" offers a free evening of special programs, including live music, dancing, film screenings, and readings. ✉ *200 Eastern Pkwy., Prospect Heights* ☎ *718/638–5000* 🌐 *www.brooklynart.org* 💳 *$6 suggested donation* ⏲ *Wed.–Fri. 10–5, weekends 11–6; first Sat. of every month, except Sept., 6 PM–11 PM; call for program schedule* Ⓜ *No. 2 or 3 to Eastern Pkwy.*

need a break?

Before or after a visit to the Brooklyn Museum of Art or the Botanic Garden, dip into Prospect Heights for great diner fare and uncommonly friendly service at **Tom's Restaurant** (✉ 782 Washington Ave., at Sterling Pl., Prospect Heights ☎ 718/636–9738). The family business (since 1937) is closed Sunday and by 4 PM the rest of the week.

⓬ **Brooklyn Public Library.** Looking like a sleek, modern temple of learning with gold-leaf figures celebrating art and science, the facade of this grand edifice (1941) curves to embrace the roundabout between Eastern Parkway and Flatbush Avenue. Bright limestone walls, perfect proportions, and ornate decorative details make this a rare 20th-century New York building. The 15 bronze figures over the entrance, representing characters in American literature, were sculpted by Thomas Hudson Jones, who also designed the Tomb of the Unknown Soldier in Arlington National Cemetery. The small café inside is the nearest snack and coffee source to Prospect Park. ✉ *Grand Army Plaza at intersection of Flatbush Ave. and Eastern Pkwy., Prospect Heights* ☎ *718/230–2100* 🌐 *www.brooklynpubliclibrary.org* ⏲ *Mon.–Thurs. 9–8, Fri.–Sat. 9–6, Sun. 1–5* Ⓜ *No. 2 or 3 to Grand Army Plaza; Q to 7th Ave.*

⓭ **Eastern Parkway.** The world's first six-lane parkway originates at Grand Army Plaza. When Olmsted and Vaux conceived the avenue's design in 1866, in tandem with their plans for Prospect Park, they wanted it to mimic the grand sweep of the boulevards of Paris and Vienna. Today it continues to play an important role in Brooklyn culture: every Labor Day weekend Eastern Parkway hosts the West Indian American Day Parade, the biggest and liveliest carnival outside the Caribbean. Ⓜ *No. 2 or 3 to Grand Army Plaza.*

off the beaten path

Fort Greene. Young professionals, families, hipsters, and old-timers live side by side in this neighborhood full of brownstones. Anchored by the Brooklyn Academy of Music (BAM) and, down the street, the Mark Morris Dance Center, the area is fast becoming a performing arts destination. Funky bars and an eclectic range of restaurants, from French bistros to South African and Cambodian spots, are sprinkled throughout the neighborhood and off Lafayette Avenue, the area's spine. Fort Greene Park is another Olmsted and Vaux creation;

in summer, free concerts and dance parties are held there. Ⓜ *C to Lafayette Ave.; No. 2, 3, 4, or 5 or Q to Atlantic Ave.*

❸ **Grand Army Plaza.** Prospect Park West, Eastern Parkway, and Flatbush and Vanderbilt avenues radiate out from this geographic star. Crossing the broad streets around here can be dangerous; be careful. At the center of the plaza stands the **Soldiers' and Sailors' Memorial Arch** (☎ 718/965–8999 for information), honoring Civil War veterans and patterned after the Arc de Triomphe in Paris. Three heroic sculptural groupings adorn the arch: atop, a four-horse chariot by Frederick MacMonnies, so dynamic it seems about to catapult off the arch; to either side, the victorious Union Army and Navy of the Civil War. Inside are bas-reliefs of presidents Abraham Lincoln and Ulysses S. Grant, sculpted by Thomas Eakins and William O'Donovan, respectively. On some spring and fall weekends the top of the arch is accessible. To the northwest of the arch, Neptune and a passel of debauched Tritons leer over the edges of the **Bailey Fountain,** a popular spot for wedding-party photographs. On Saturday year-round, a green market sets up in the plaza; produce, flowers and plants, baked goods, cheese, and other foodstuffs attract throngs of locals. Ⓜ *No. 2 or 3 to Grand Army Plaza; Q to 7th Ave.*

❿ **Lefferts Historic House.** Built in 1783 and moved to Prospect Park in 1918, this gambrel-roof Dutch colonial farmhouse contains a historic house-museum. Rooms are furnished with antiques and period reproductions from the 1820s, the period when the house was last redecorated. The museum hosts all kinds of activities for kids; call for information. ✉ *Flatbush Ave. north of junction with Park Loop, Prospect Park* ☎ *718/789–2822* *Free* ⏲ *Apr.–Nov., Thurs.–Fri. 1–4, weekends 1–5* Ⓜ *Q to Prospect Park.*

❹ **Litchfield Villa.** The most important sight on the western border of Prospect Park, this Italianate mansion, built in 1857 for a prominent railroad magnate, was designed by Alexander Jackson Davis, considered the foremost architect of his day. It has housed the park's headquarters since 1883, but visitors are welcome to step inside and view the domed octagonal rotunda. ✉ *Prospect Park W and 5th St., Prospect Park* ☎ *718/965–8951* Ⓜ *F to 7th Ave.*

❶ **Montauk Club.** The home of a venerable club (and condominium apartments on its upper floors), this 1891 mansion designed by Francis H. Kimball is modeled on Venice's Ca' d'Oro and other Gothic Venetian palaces. It is Park Slope's most impressive building and easily rivals the showcase mansions on Manhattan's Upper East Side. You can view the building on three sides from the street; notice the friezes of Native American Montauks and the 19th-century private side entrance for members' wives. ✉ *25 8th Ave., at Lincoln Pl., Park Slope* Ⓜ *No. 2 or 3 to Grand Army Plaza; Q to 7th Ave.*

need a break?

On the north end of the Slope **Ozzie's Coffee & Tea** (✉ 57 7th Ave., at Lincoln Pl., Park Slope ☎ 718/398–6695) is a good local coffee joint. In warm weather, locals enjoying sipping their coffee outside on the benches at **Connecticut Muffin** (✉ 171 7th Ave., at 1st St., Park Slope ☎ 718/768–2022).

❷ **Montgomery Place.** This block-long street between 8th Avenue and Prospect Park West is considered to be one of Park Slope's finest; it's lined with stately town houses designed by the Romanesque revival genius C. P. H. Gilbert. Ⓜ *No. 2 or 3 to Grand Army Plaza; Q to 7th Ave.*

★ 8 **Prospect Park Audubon Center at the Boathouse.** Styled after Sansovino's 16th-century Library at St. Mark's in Venice, this impressive structure, built in 1905, looks out on the body of water known as the Lullwater. It now houses the Prospect Park Audubon Center, where you can learn about nature in the park through interactive exhibits, park tours, and educational programs especially for kids. On a nice day, take a ride on the electric boat or rent a pedal boat and head out onto the Lullwater and Prospect Lake. The café is always good for a break. ✉ *Entrance: Lincoln Rd. or Flatbush Ave. at Empire Blvd., Prospect Park* ☎ *718/287–3400 for Audubon Center; 718/282–7789 for pedal boats* 🌐 *www.prospectparkaudubon.org* *Audubon Center free; electric-boat tours $3* ⏲ *Audubon Center: Wed.–Thurs. 1–5, Fri.–Sun. 10–5; call for info about program and tour times. Café: Fri.–Sun. 10–5. Electric-boat tours: Apr.–Oct., Fri.–Sun. 10–4:30, every 30 mins. Pedal boats: mid-May–mid-Sept., weekends 11–5* Ⓜ *No. 2 or 3 to Grand Army Plaza; Q to Prospect Park.*

6 **Prospect Park Band Shell.** The Band Shell is the home of the annual **Celebrate Brooklyn Festival**, which from mid-June through the last weekend in August sponsors free films and concerts, from African-Caribbean jazz to Kurt Weill, from the Brooklyn Philharmonic to bluegrass and zydeco groups. A concessionaire sells hot meals and beverages, and the crowd either fills the seats or spreads out blankets on the small hill. ✉ *Prospect Park W and 9th St., Prospect Park* ☎ *718/965–8999 park hot line; 718/855–7882 Ext. 52 for Celebrate Brooklyn Festival* 🌐 *www.brooklynx.org/celebrate* *$3 suggested donation* ⏲ *Late June–Aug.; call for details* Ⓜ *F to 7th Ave.*

need a break?

A stone's throw from the park is **Dizzy's** (✉ 511 9th St., at 8th Ave., Park Slope ☎ 718/499–1966), serving classic diner fare and an abundant brunch, for which there's always a wait. Pick up unbeatable gourmet wraps (try the seared tuna) and other prepared foods at **Second Helpings** (✉ 448 9th St., near 7th Ave., Park Slope ☎ 718/965–1925). **Naidre's** (✉ 384 7th Ave., at 12th St., Park Slope ☎ 718/965–7585) makes stellar sandwiches, baked goods, and coffee.

9 **Prospect Park Carousel.** Horses, dragon-pulled chariots, and other colorful animals enliven the restored 1912 carousel, handcrafted by master carver Charles Carmel. ✉ *Flatbush Ave. at Empire Blvd., Prospect Park* ☎ *718/282–7789* *50¢ per ride* ⏲ *Apr.–May and Sept.–Oct., weekends 12–5; June–Aug., Thurs.–Fri 11–3, weekends 12–6* Ⓜ *No. 2 or 3 to Grand Army Plaza; Q to Prospect Park.*

11 **Prospect Park Zoo.** Small, friendly, and educational, this children's zoo off the main road of Prospect Park has a number of unusual and endangered species among its 390 inhabitants. The sea-lion pool is a hit with children, as are the indoor exhibits—"Animal Lifestyles," which explains habitats and adaptations, and "Animals in Our Lives," showcasing domesticated and farm animals. An outdoor discovery trail has a simulated prairie-dog burrow, a duck pond, and wallabies in habitat. ✉ *Flatbush Ave. at Empire Blvd., Prospect Park* ☎ *718/399–7339* 🌐 *www.prospectparkzoo.com* *$2.50* ⏲ *Apr.–Oct., weekdays 10–5, weekends 10–5:30; Nov.–Mar., daily 10–4:30 (last ticket 1/2 hr prior to closing)* Ⓜ *Q to Prospect Park.*

16 **7th Avenue.** Restaurants, groceries, bookstores, shops, cafés, bakeries, churches, real estate agents (one of the favorite neighborhood pastimes is window shopping for homes), and more line Park Slope's commercial spine from Flatbush Avenue roughly to 16th Street. At the north

end of the Slope, **Leaf & Bean** (✉ 83 7th Ave., between Union and Berkeley Sts., Park Slope ☎ 718/638–5791) carries tea, coffee, and lots of kitchen gadgets. **The Clay Pot** (✉ 162 7th Ave., between Garfield and 1st Sts., Park Slope ☎ 718/788–6564) is known for original wares and ornaments for the home and for one-of-a-kind wedding bands made by local artisans. Ⓜ *Q to 7th Ave.; F to 7th Ave.*

❺ **Tennis House.** The most prominent of several neoclassical structures in the park, this 1910 limestone and yellow-brick building postdates by 40 years the more rustic structures favored by Olmsted and Vaux, few of which survive. The Tennis House's most elegant features are the triple-bay Palladian arches on both its north and south facade, and its airy terra-cotta barrel-vaulted arcade on the south side. The building's large tiled central court has amazing acoustics—shout "hello" and listen to your voice bounce back at you. On the lower level, the **Brooklyn Center for the Urban Environment** has rotating exhibitions on urban issues and organizes Brooklyn walking tours. ✉ *Enter park at 9th St. and Prospect Park W, Prospect Park* ☎ *718/788–8549* *Free* ⏲ *Tennis House only, weekdays 9–5 and weekends noon–5; Tennis House and BCUE gallery, when an exhibition is up* Ⓜ *F to 7th Ave.*

❼ **Wollman Memorial Rink.** A smaller cousin to Wollman Rink in Central Park, this is one of Prospect Park's most popular destinations. Besides skating in winter, pedal-boat rentals are available here weekends and holidays from April through mid-October. ✉ *Enter park at Ocean Ave. and Parkside Ave., Park Slope* ☎ *718/287–6431 or 718/282–7789* *$4; $4 skate rental* ⏲ *Mid-Nov.–early Mar., Mon. 8:30–2; Tues. 8:30–5; Wed. 8:30–3; Thurs. 8:30–8; Fri. 8:30–9; Sat. 10–1, 2–6, and 7–10; Sun. 10–1 and 2–6* Ⓜ *Q to Parkside Ave.*

Coney Island

Fodor'sChoice ★

Named Konijn Eiland (Rabbit Island) by the Dutch for its wild rabbit population, Coney Island has a boardwalk, a 2½-mi-long beach, a legendary amusement park, a baseball stadium, and the city's only aquarium. Coney Island may have declined from its glory days in the early 1900s, when visitors lunched at a 34-room ocean-side hotel built in the shape of an elephant, glided across the nation's biggest dance floor at Dreamland, and toured a replica of old Baghdad called Luna Park. But it's still a great place to experience the sounds, smells, and sights of summer: hot dogs, suntan lotion, crowds, fried clams, and old men fishing the sea, not to mention the freak shows, the heart-stopping plunge of the king of roller coasters—the Cyclone—and the thwack of bats swung by Brooklyn's own minor league team, the Cyclones. A mile walk down the boardwalk takes you to Brighton Beach, an enclave of some 90,000 Russian, Ukrainian, and Georgian emigrés. On the streets here Russian is the language you'll hear most often.

a good walk

Coney Island is the last stop on the F, Q, and W trains in Brooklyn. The Coney Island boardwalk remains the hub of the action; amble along it to take in the local color. You'll find standard summer snacks here in the form of ice cream and saltwater taffy, but it is the chewy, deep-fried clams, hot dogs with spicy mustard, and ice-cold lemonade from **Nathan's Famous** ❶ that are truly synonymous with the Coney Island experience. Walk a bit farther west from Nathan's Surf Avenue location to reach **Keyspan Park** ❷, where the Brooklyn Cyclones, the borough's very own minor league team, play serious ball.

Head back along Surf Avenue past Nathan's to find a repository of times gone by: fire-eaters and sword swallowers carry on the traditions of what

Astroland 4
Brighton Beach Avenue. 7
Deno's Wonderwheel Park 5
Keyspan Park . . . 2
Nathan's Famous 1
New York Aquarium. 6
Sideshows by the Seashore and the Coney Island Museum. 3

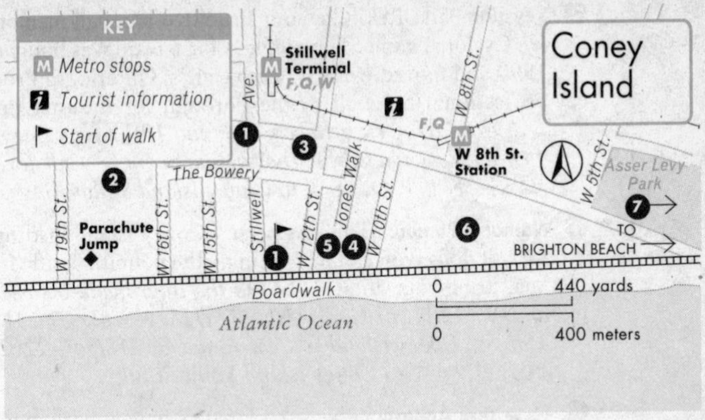

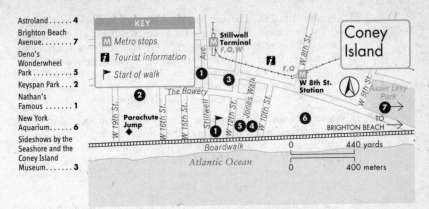

was once billed as the "World's Largest Playground" at **Sideshows by the Seashore and the Coney Island Museum** 3. The rickety septuagenarian Cyclone roller coaster at **Astroland** 4 and, farther down the boardwalk, the abandoned Space Needle–like structure, once the Parachute Jump, are testimony to this waning beachside culture. Be sure to take a ride on the Cyclone, which still packs a punch, or the ponderous Wonderwheel at **Deno's Wonderwheel Park** 5.

From the boardwalk, walk down West 10th Street back to Surf Avenue. Here beluga whales and some 10,000 plus other creatures of the sea make their home at the **New York Aquarium** 6. From the aquarium, walk about a mile east along the boardwalk to Brighton 1st Place, then head up to **Brighton Beach Avenue** 7, the heart of "Little Odessa." You can get back to Manhattan by taking the Q train from the Brighton Beach stop.

TIMING Coney Island is at its liveliest on weekends, especially in summer. Brighton Beach is a vibrant neighborhood year-round, though Saturday is its busiest shopping day. Allow most of a day for this trip, since the subway ride from Manhattan (one-way) takes at least an hour.

What to See

4 **Astroland.** The world-famous, wood-and-steel Cyclone is one of the oldest roller coasters still operating (it first rode in 1927); it was moved in 1975 to Astroland, which had recently opened as a "space-age" theme park. Today a visit is more like stepping into the past than the future, but the rides are still a thrill, as is the Skee-Ball. For certain hours you can buy a $14.99 "Pay One Price" ticket to the rides. *1000 Surf Ave., at W. 10th St., Coney Island 718/372–0275 www.astroland.com Call for seasonal hrs Free; $2–$5 per ride* M *F, Q, or W to Coney Island Stillwell Ave.*

7 **Brighton Beach Avenue.** The shops, bakeries, markets, and restaurants along Brighton Beach's main artery all cater to the neighborhood's substantial Russian community. This is the place to find knishes with every filling imaginable, borscht, *blinis* (small crepes or pancakes), and cups of dark-roast coffee, plus caviar at prices that can put Manhattan purveyors to shame. M *Q to Brighton Beach.*

5 **Deno's Wonderwheel Park.** You'll get a new perspective on the island from the Wonder Wheel, which was built in 1920. Though it appears tame, it will still quicken your heart rate. Other rides include the Spook-a-rama, the Thunderbolt, bumper cars, and a number of children's rides. *1025 Boardwalk, at W. 12th St., Coney Island 718/449–8836 www.wonderwheel.com Call for seasonal hrs Free; $4 per ride, 5 rides for $15* M *F, Q, or W to Coney Island Stillwell Ave.*

❷ Keyspan Park. Rekindle your Brooklyn baseball memories at a Brooklyn Cyclones game. This single A farm team was bought by the Mets in 1999 and moved from St. Catharine's, Ontario, to Brooklyn, bringing professional baseball to the borough for the first time since 1957. *1904 Surf Ave., between 16th and 19th Sts., Coney Island 718/449–8497 www.brooklyncyclones.com Call for game schedule $5–$8 F, Q, or W to Coney Island Stillwell Ave.*

❶ Nathan's Famous. This has been a Coney Island institution since 1916 for hot dogs (you can buy them by the pound), waffle fries, and lemonade. Bring your antacid. *On the Boardwalk between Stillwell Ave. and W. 12th St., Coney Island May–Sept. 1310 Surf Ave., at 15th St., Coney Island Year-round 718/946–2202 both locations F, Q, or W to Coney Island Stillwell Ave.*

❻ New York Aquarium. New York City's only aquarium is worth a trip in itself. Tropical fish, sea horses, and jellyfish luxuriate in large tanks; otters, walruses, penguins, and seals lounge on a replicated Pacific coast; a 180,000-gallon seawater complex hosts beluga whales; and dolphins and sea lions perform in the Aquatheater (May–October). There's a restaurant. *W. 8th St. and Surf Ave., Coney Island 718/265–3474 www.nyaquarium.com $11 Apr.–Memorial Day and Labor Day–Oct., weekdays 10–5, weekends 10–5:30; Memorial Day–Labor Day, weekdays 10–6, weekends 10–7; Nov.–Mar., daily 10–4:30; last ticket sold 45 mins prior to closing F, Q to W. 8 St.*

❸ Sideshows by the Seashore and the Coney Island Museum. Step right up for a lively circus sideshow, complete with a fire-eater, sword swallower, snake charmer, and contortionist. On the first Saturday after summer solstice, the cast of the sideshow, an amazing array of local legends, and a slew of outrageous New Yorkers take part in the **Mermaid Parade.** In a sometimes beautiful, sometimes absurd spectacle, imaginative floats and participants in wild costumes throng the Boardwalk and Surf Avenue to pay homage to the myth of the mermaid and the legend of the sea. Upstairs from Sideshows, the Museum has historic Coney Island memorabilia and a wealth of tourist information. *1208 Surf Ave., at W. 12th St., Coney Island 718/372–5159 for both www.coneyisland.com Sideshow $5; museum 99¢ Sideshows Memorial Day–Labor Day, Wed.–Fri. 2–8, weekends 1–11; Apr.–May and Sept., weekends 1–8. Museum weekends noon–5. Hrs vary, so call ahead F, Q, or W to Coney Island Stillwell Ave.*

QUEENS

Home of the La Guardia and John F. Kennedy international airports and many of Manhattan's bedroom communities, Queens is only seen by most visitors from the window of an airplane and cab. Named for Queen Catherine of Braganza, wife of Charles II, Queens was largely pro-British through the Revolutionary War. Today it's the largest of the city's five boroughs, accounting for a full third of the city's entire area. Its population of nearly 2,230,000 is the city's most diverse, and its countless ethnic neighborhoods continue to attract immigrants from all over the world. Its inhabitants represent almost all nationalities and speak scores of languages, from Hindi to Hebrew. Queens communities such as Astoria (Greek and Italian), Jackson Heights (Colombian, Mexican, and Indian), Sunnyside (Turkish and Romanian), and Flushing (Korean and Chinese) are fascinating to explore, particularly if you're interested in experiencing some of the city's tastiest—and least expensive—cuisine.

Note: Queens streets, drives, and avenues—altogether different thoroughfares—sometimes have the same numerical name; for instance, 30th Drive is not the same as 30th Avenue.

Astoria & Long Island City

Long Island City and Astoria, both just a few minutes from Manhattan, have emerged as the borough's destinations of choice for great museums and superb ethnic dining. Astoria is like an archaeological site—each layer contains a trace of the area's successive denizens, from moviemakers to Greek immigrants to young artists and professionals. In the 1920s, Hollywood was still a dusty small town when such stars as Gloria Swanson, Rudolph Valentino, and the Marx Brothers came to this part of Queens to work at "the Big House," Paramount's moviemaking center in the east. At that time the Kaufman-Astoria Studios were the largest and most important filmmaking studios in the country; today they remain the largest in the East, and they're still used for major films and television shows.

Originally German, then Italian, Astoria earned the nickname Little Athens in the late 1960s. Today there are also substantial numbers of Asians, Eastern Europeans, Irish, and Latino immigrants in Astoria, not to mention an ever-growing contingent of former Manhattan residents in search of cheaper rents. Here you can buy Cypriot cured olives and feta cheese from store owners who will tell you where to go for the best spinach pie, or you can sit outside at one of the many pastry shops, drink tall, frothy frappes, and watch the subway's elevated trains roll by. Astoria's a perfect pit stop for food either before or after seeing the museums of industrial Long Island City.

Numbers in the text correspond to numbers in the margin and on the Astoria, Long Island City map.

a good tour

By subway, take the E or V (weekdays only) from Manhattan to the 23rd Street–Ely Avenue stop in Long Island City or No. 7 to 45th Road–Courthouse Square for the **P.S.1 Contemporary Art Center** 1 ⚑. Or take the No. 7 train to the 33rd Street stop for **MoMA QNS** 2, the temporary space of the Museum of Modern Art. Jump back on the No. 7 to get between the two or ask at either institution for walking directions. A good option on weekends is to take the free Queens Artlink Bus (☎ 212/708–9750, 🌐 www.queensartlink.org), which runs between Manhattan and MoMA QNS and between many of the Long Island City museums; call for exact times.

In a large space not far from P.S.1 is the **Sculpture Center** 3: walk up Jackson Avenue to reach it. Or, if you're already at MoMA QNS, take 33rd Street one block to 43rd Avenue and turn right on 36th Street. The **Isamu Noguchi Garden Museum** 4 and **Museum for African Art** 5 have made temporary homes in the same building there. Backtrack to the 33rd Street subway station and take the No. 7 train to Queensboro Plaza. There, transfer to the N or W train to reach the Broadway stop in Astoria. You can eat lunch at one of the many restaurants and cafés up and down Broadway. Then walk (it's eight long blocks, about 20 minutes, from the Broadway subway station), hail a cab, or hop the Q104 bus toward the East River. At Vernon Boulevard and Broadway, the **Socrates Sculpture Park** 6 at first almost appears to be an urban hallucination, with its large, abstract artworks framed by Manhattan. Three blocks south on Vernon Boulevard, with its entrance on 33rd Road, the permanent site of the Isamu Noguchi Garden Museum is under reconstruction, possibly until Spring 2004.

American Museum of the Moving Image 7
Isamu Noguchi Garden Museum (temporary) 4
MoMA QNS 2
Museum for African Art 5
P.S.1 Contemporary Art Center 1
Sculpture Center .3
Socrates Sculpture Park 6

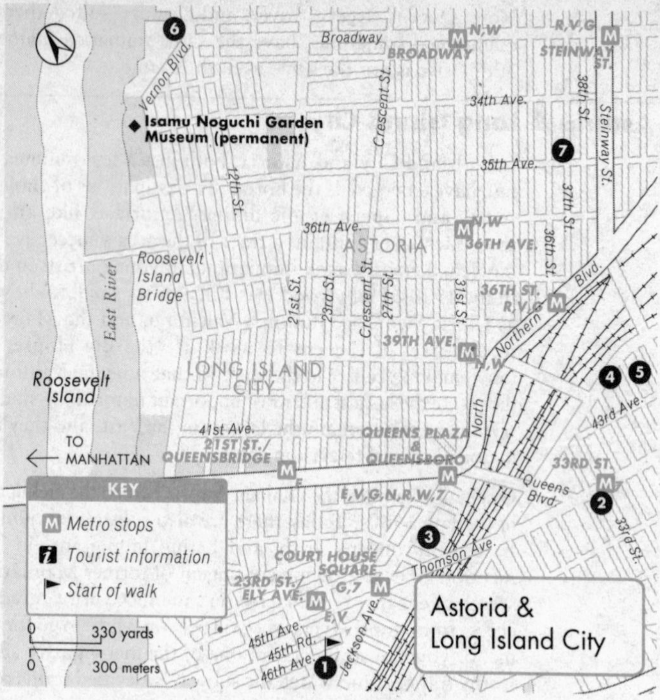

Return to Broadway and catch the Q104 bus to 36th Street; when you get off turn right and walk two blocks to 35th Avenue. Here you'll find the **American Museum of the Moving Image** 7, where it's easy to spend hours absorbed by the film-production exhibits and the regularly scheduled film series and directors' talks. Next door, the imposing 13-acre Kaufman-Astoria Studios has been used for the filming of such movies as *The Cotton Club* and television series such as *100 Centre Street,* the *Cosby Show,* and *Sesame Street.*

Head back to Broadway into the heart of the Greek community, between 31st and Steinway streets, where Greek pastry shops and coffee shops abound, and the elevated subway brings a constant stream of activity. Farther up, 30th Avenue is another busy thoroughfare with almost every kind of food store imaginable. The largest Greek Orthodox congregation outside Greece worships at St. Demetrios Cathedral, just off 30th Avenue. You could end your day with a fine dinner at one of Astoria's Greek restaurants (on or near Broadway) or venture to the Middle Eastern restaurants farther out on Steinway Street.

TIMING Greek Astoria is at its finest on Saturday, when sidewalk culture comes to life. To see all the art in Long Island City and Astoria, get an early start. Allow at least two hours each for leisurely visits to P.S.1 and MoMA QNS, and two for the American Museum of the Moving Image and a tour of Greek Astoria. It's something of a schlepp to the Socrates Sculpture Park (you may want to catch a cab). Be aware that a visit to two of these sights could fill up the better part of your day.

What to See

★ 7 **American Museum of the Moving Image.** Crossing the East River to Astoria for the nation's only museum devoted to the art, technology, and history of film, TV, and digital media is a worthwhile pilgrimage. Via artifacts, texts, live demonstrations, and video screenings, the core exhibition, "Behind the Screen," takes you step by step through the process of making movies. Interactive computers allow you to create animation, edit sound effects, dub dialogue, and add sound tracks. The museum's collection of movie memorabilia consists of more than 100,000 items, including the chariot used in *Ben Hur* and the Mohawk bald cap that Robert De Niro wore in *Taxi Driver.* Movie serials from the 1930s and '40s, such as Buck Rogers and Captain America, are shown daily in the 30-seat Tut's Fever Movie Palace. The museum also presents changing exhibits, lectures, and film programs, including retrospectives, Hollywood classics, and contemporary independent films. ✉ *35th Ave., between 36th and 37th Sts., Astoria* ☎ *718/784–0077* 🌐 *www.ammi.org* 🎟 *$8.50* ⏲ *Tues.–Fri. 10–5, weekends 11–6* Ⓜ *R, V (weekdays only), or G (weekends only) to Steinway St.; N or W to 36th St.*

need a break?

The hip, colorful **Café Bar** (✉ 32-90 36th St., at 34th Ave., Astoria ☎ 718/204–5273) is perfect for a snack, coffee, or an evening cocktail. **S'Agapo** (✉ 43-21 34th Ave., at 35th St., Astoria ☎ 718/626–0303) serves some of the best Greek food in Queens. At **Omonia Café** (✉ 32-20 Broadway, at 33rd St., Astoria ☎ 718/274–6650) you can watch the constant activity on Broadway while nursing coffee and honey-sweet pastries. Rotisserie-roasted lamb and other Greek classics can be had for a song at 24-hour diner **Uncle George's** (✉ 33-19 Broadway, at 34th St., Astoria ☎ 718/626–0593).

off the beaten path

Flushing Meadows–Corona Park. The site of both the 1939 and 1964 World's Fairs, this park is well worth the trek from Manhattan. A ride on the No. 7 subway from Times Square or Grand Central Station to the Willets Point–Shea Stadium stop puts you within walking distance of some of Queens' most exciting cultural and recreational institutions.

The **Queens Museum of Art** features contemporary art by local and international artists. But it's best known for its knock-your-socks-off New York City panorama, a 9,335-square-ft model of the five boroughs, made for the 1964 World's Fair. It faithfully replicates all the city's boroughs building by building, on a scale of 1 inch per 100 ft. The model's tiny brownstones and skyscrapers are updated periodically to look exactly like the real things. The museum has a "First Thursdays" program with live music, film screenings, and access to current exhibitions. In front of the museum is the awe-inspiring **Unisphere.** Made entirely of stainless steel for the 1964 World's Fair, this massive sculpture of the Earth is 140 ft high and weighs 380 tons. ✉ *Flushing Meadows–Corona Park, Flushing* ☎ *718/592–9700* 🌐 *www.queensmuseum.org* 🎟 *$5 suggested donation; $7 "First Thursdays"* ⏲ *Tues.–Fri. 10–5, weekends noon–5; first Thurs. of every month 10–8.*

The **New York Hall of Science** is a great place to take the kids. A top science museum, it has more than 160 hands-on experiments on subjects ranging from lasers to microbes. Outside, stations on the Science Playground coax youngsters into learning while they're horsing around—a seesaw, for example, becomes a lesson in balance and leverage. ✉ *111th St., at 46th Ave., Flushing* ☎ *718/699–0005* 🌐 *www.nyscience.org* 🎟 *$7.50; free Thurs. 2–5, Sept.–June* ⏲ *Sept.–June, Tues.–Wed. 9:30–2, Thurs.–Sun. 9:30–5; July–Aug., Tues.–Sun. 9:30–5.*

Children love the **Queens Wildlife Center,** where American animals roam in settings loosely approximating their natural habitats. The residents include spectacled bears, mountain lions, sea lions, bobcats, coyotes, bison, and elk. ✉ *53-51 111th St., at 53rd Ave., Flushing* ☎ *718/271–7761* 🌐 *www.wcs.org* 🎫 *$2.50* ⏲ *Daily 10–4:30; last ticket sold at 4.*

During baseball season, top the day off with a Mets game at **Shea Stadium** (☎ 718/507–8499 for a game schedule), just north of the park. If you're into tennis, catch such champs as Andre Agassi, Martina Hingis, and the Williams sisters at the U.S. Open Tournament on and around Labor Day at the **USTA National Tennis Center** opposite the Unisphere. Or play a match yourself at one of the 29 courts open to the public (☎ 718/760–6200 for court reservations and fees).

❹ **Isamu Noguchi Garden Museum.** This museum is dedicated to the work of Japanese-American sculptor Isamu Noguchi (1904–88). Until Spring 2004, the museum is in a temporary home near MoMA QNS while the main space undergoes renovation. The small, temporary space has changing exhibitions of Noguchi's pieces in stone, bronze, wood, clay, and steel; videos document his long career. The permanent building is a former photo engraving plant purchased by Noguchi in 1975 as a place to display his work. The large, open-air garden and two floors of gallery space provide ample room to show more than 250 pieces. ✉ *Temporary location: 36-01 43rd Ave., at 36th St., Long Island City (until Spring 2004)* ✉ *Permanent location: 32-37 Vernon Blvd., at 33rd Rd., Long Island City (Spring 2004)* ☎ *718/204–7088 or 718/721–1932* 🌐 *www.noguchi.org* 🎫 *$4 suggested donation* ⏲ *Mon., Thurs., Fri. 10–5, weekends 11–6* Ⓜ *Temporary location: No. 7 to 33rd St.; permanent location: N to Broadway, then 15-min walk west to Vernon Blvd.*

Fodor's Choice ★

❷ **MoMA QNS.** While the Museum of Modern Art (MoMA) undergoes a $650 million reconstruction of its famous West 53rd Street building (to be completed in 2005), its peerless collection of 20th-century art resides in the former Swingline staple factory, now painted a bright blue. The space has a contemporary, industrial feel, with its large, open galleries, sparse white walls, and polished concrete floors. Videos projected onto the walls in the lobby and along the ramp snaking up to the café add to the cutting-edge aesthetic. On display are highlights from the permanent collection as well as changing exhibitions. Once the museum heads back to midtown, the building will become the permanent home for conservation, research, and storage. ✉ *45-20 33rd St., at Queens Blvd., Long Island City* ☎ *718/389–4729* 🌐 *www.moma.org* 🎫 *$12; Fri. after 4 pay what you wish* ⏲ *Sat.–Mon. and Thurs. 10–5, Fri. 10–7:45* Ⓜ *No. 7 to 33rd St.*

❺ **Museum for African Art.** Dedicated to contemporary and traditional African art, the exhibits at this small but expertly conceived museum may include contemporary sculpture, ceremonial masks, architectural details, costumes, and textiles. ✉ *36-01 43rd Ave., at 36th St., Long Island City* ☎ *718/784–7700* 🌐 *www.africanart.org* 🎫 *$5* ⏲ *Mon. and Thurs.–Fri. 10–5, weekends 11–6* Ⓜ *No. 7 to 33rd St.*

★ ⚑ ❶ **P.S.1 Contemporary Art Center.** A pioneer in the alternative-space movement, P.S.1 rose from the ruins of an abandoned school in 1971 as a sort of community arts center for the future. Now a partner of the Museum of Modern Art, P.S.1 still focuses on community involvement, with studio spaces for resident artists and educational programs. In summer, its Sunday afternoon outdoor dance parties with vogue DJs attract a hip crowd. P.S.1's exhibition space is enormous, and every available corner is used—four-oddfloors, rooftop spaces, staircases and landings, bathrooms, the boiler room and basement, and outdoor galleries. Exhibitions reflect the center's mission to present experimental and formally innovative contemporary art, from the progressive and interactive to the incomprehensible. It's never dull. You can exit the museum via a 45-ft corkscrew slide. ✉ *22-25 Jackson Ave., at 46th Ave., Long Island City* ☎ *718/784–2084* 🌐 *www.ps1.org* 🎟 *$5* 🕑 *Thurs.–Mon. noon–6* Ⓜ *No. 7 to 45 Rd.–Courthouse Sq.; E, V (weekdays only), to 23rd St.–Ely Ave.; G to Court Sq.*

❸ **Sculpture Center.** The setting for this museum devoted to contemporary sculpture is a former trolley repair shop renovated by Maya Lin and David Hotson. The center is a resource for cutting-edge work, with its large indoor and outdoor exhibition spaces, sculpture library, and studios for visiting artists. ✉ *44-19 Purves St., at Jackson Ave., Long Island City* ☎ *718/361–1700* 🌐 *www.sculpture-center.org* 🎟 *$5 suggested donation* 🕑 *Thurs.–Mon. 11–6* Ⓜ *No. 7 to 45 Rd.–Courthouse Sq.; E, V (weekdays only), to 23rd St.–Ely Ave.; G to Court Sq.; R to Queens Plaza.*

❻ **Socrates Sculpture Park.** In 1985, local artist Mark DiSuvero and other residents rallied to transform what had been an abandoned landfill and illegal dump site into this 4½-acre park devoted to public art. The park was named in honor of the philosopher as well as the local Greek community. Today a superb view of the river and Manhattan frames huge works of art made of scrap metal, old tires, and other recycled products. You can climb on or walk through a number of the sculptures. ✉ *Vernon Blvd. at Broadway, Long Island City* ☎ *718/956–1819* 🌐 *www.socratessculpturepark.org* 🎟 *Free* 🕑 *Daily 10–sunset* Ⓜ *N to Broadway.*

STATEN ISLAND

Although Staten Island is a borough of New York City, it is, for many New Yorkers, a distant suburb. Staten Islanders number about 450,000, yet share a space that's 2½ times the size of Manhattan. Locals, many of whom are second- or third-generation residents, feel a strong allegiance to their borough. Despite its low profile, Staten Island has some real attractions, such as a phenomenal view of lower Manhattan and the Statue of Liberty afforded by a 20-minute ferry ride across New York Harbor—the only direct route to Manhattan from the island. Its small museums hold unexpected offerings, and its historic villages at Richmondtown and Snug Harbor give a sense of New York's past.

On weekdays and weekend afternoons you can catch the free Staten Island Ferry, 718/815–2628, at least every half hour. On weekend mornings until 11:30 AM, the ferries leave the southern tip of Manhattan at Whitehall Terminal every hour on the half hour; from 11:30 AM until 7:30 PM, they run every half hour. To get to Whitehall Terminal, take a No. 4 or 5 train to Bowling Green, or an N or R train to Whitehall.

Snug Harbor & Beyond

Just 2 mi from the ferry terminal, the restored sailor's community of Snug Harbor is by far the most popular of Staten Island's attractions. The colony of retired seamen was founded in 1831 at the bequest of wealthy shipowner Robert Richard Randall, and for the next 140 years it served as the nation's first maritime hospital and rest home. For a highly enjoyable outing, take the scenic ferry ride from Manhattan and visit Snug Harbor and two small but engaging nearby museums.

Numbers in the text correspond to numbers in the margin and on the Staten Island map.

Snug Harbor and Beyond
- Alice Austen House Museum 3
- Garibaldi-Meucci Museum 4
- Snug Harbor Cultural Center 1
- Staten Island Zoo 2

Richmondtown
- Historic Richmond-town 5
- Jacques Marchais Museum of Tibetan Art 6

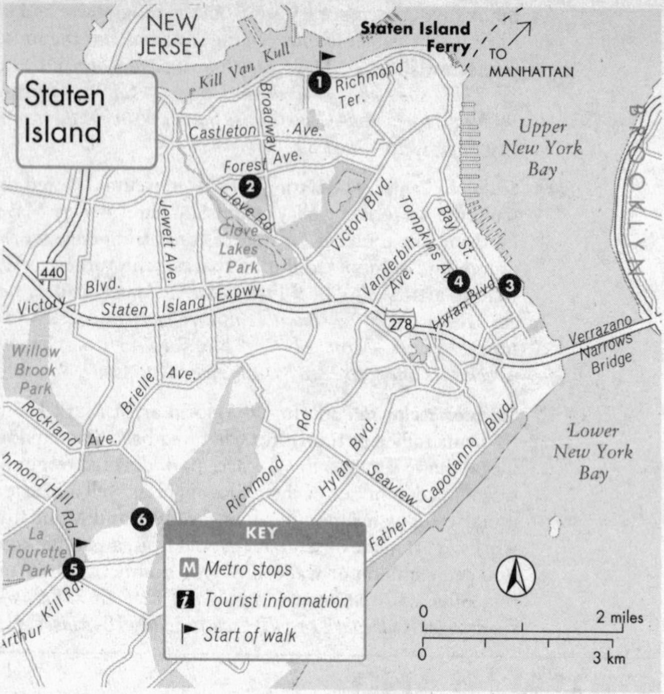

a good tour

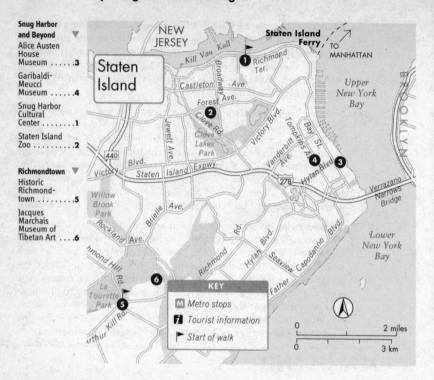

From the Staten Island Ferry terminal, a seven-minute (2-mi) ride on the S40 bus will take you to the **Snug Harbor Cultural Center** ❶, an 83-acre complex with an art gallery, a botanical garden, a children's museum, and a colorful history. Signal the driver as soon as you glimpse the black iron fence along the edge of the property. You can also grab a car service at the ferry terminal (the ride should cost you about $5). From Snug Harbor, you can catch the S40 bus to Richmond Terrace, and then change to the S53 (about a 20-minute trip) to see farm animals and a faux African savannah at the **Staten Island Zoo** ❷. Or take the S48 bus or taxi ($5) from the ferry terminal.

If you still have time after touring Snug Harbor and the zoo, return to the ferry terminal and catch the S51–Bay Street bus for the 15-minute ride to Hylan Boulevard to see turn-of-the-20th-century photographs in the ivy-covered **Alice Austen House Museum** ❸. For some Italian-American history, head to the **Garibaldi-Meucci Museum** ❹, where General Giuseppe Garibaldi lived in exile with his friend Antonio Meucci—the true inventor of the telephone. From the Alice Austen House, it's about a mile to the Garibaldi-Meucci Museum: take Bay Street to Chestnut Avenue and turn left. To get here from the ferry, take the S52 or S78 bus to Tompkins Avenue and Chestnut.

TIMING The Snug Harbor Cultural Center alone will take at least half a day, including the ferry commute; add to that the Alice Austen House and the Garibaldi-Meucci Museum, or the zoo, and you're in for a whole-day adventure. If you're interested in visiting both museums, plan your visit toward the end of the week, when they're both open.

What to See

❸ **Alice Austen House Museum.** Photographer Alice Austen (1866–1952) defied tradition when, as a girl of 10, she received her first camera as a gift from an uncle. Austen went on to make photography her lifetime avocation, documenting a vivid social history of Staten Island in the early part of the 20th century. She lived most of her life in this cozy, Dutch-style cottage known as Clear Comfort, and many of her photographs are on display. The museum also hosts changing contemporary and historical photography exhibits. The waterfront spot affords a great view of the Verrazano Bridge. ✉ *2 Hylan Blvd., at Edgewater St., Rosebank* ☎ *718/816–4506* 🌐 *www.aliceausten.org* *$2* ⏲ *Thurs.–Sun. noon–5* Ⓜ *S51 bus to Hylan Blvd.; walk 1 block east to water.*

4 **Garibaldi-Meucci Museum.** The house Antonio Meucci once called home is now a small museum full of letters and photographs of fiery Italian patriot Giuseppe Garibaldi. It also documents Meucci's invention of the telephone before Alexander Graham Bell and has changing exhibits related to Italian and Italian-American history. Appropriately, the museum is in the heart of the Italian neighborhood of Rosebank; the colorful **Our Lady of Mount Saint Carmel Society Shrine** is nearby, at 36 Amity Street. ✉ *420 Tompkins Ave., entrance on Chestnut Ave., Rosebank* ☎ *718/442–1608* *$3* ⏲ *Tues.–Sun. 1–5; call first* Ⓜ *From ferry, S52 or S78 bus to Tompkins Ave. and Chestnut.*

★ 1 **Snug Harbor Cultural Center.** Once part of a sprawling farm, then a home for "aged, decrepit, and worn-out sailors," this 83-acre property is based around a row of five columned Greek Revival temples, built between 1831 and 1880, and consists of 28 mostly restored historic buildings. The Main Hall—the oldest building on the property, dating from 1833—is home to the **Newhouse Center for Contemporary Art** (☎ 718/448–2500 Ext. 260 $3 ⏲ Wed.–Sun. 11–5), exhibiting contemporary work, normally within a historical context. Thus, older works often sit beside multidisciplinary pieces—in costume, video, mixed-media, and performance, among others—in the expansive space. Next door is the **John A. Noble Collection** (☎ 718/447–6490 $3 ⏲ Thurs.–Sun. 1–5), where an old seaman's dormitory has been transformed into classrooms; a library and archive; a printmaking studio; and galleries displaying maritime-inspired photography, lithographs, and artwork.

The cultural center grounds are graced by the **Staten Island Botanical Gardens,** which include a perennial garden, a greenhouse, a vineyard, 10 acres of natural marsh habitat, a rose garden, and a sensory garden with fragrant, touchable flowers and tinkling waterfalls intended for people with vision and hearing impairments. An authentic Chinese Scholars' Garden—hand-created by artisans from China and one of only two in the United States—has reflecting ponds, waterfalls, pavilions, and a teahouse. The Carl Grillo Glass House keeps tropical, desert, and temperate plant environments, and the Connie Gretz Secret Garden is wonderfully child-friendly in design, with castles and moats among the flowers. Call for special programs, held throughout the year. ☎ *718/273–8200* 🌐 *www.sibg.org* *Free; $5 for Chinese Garden and Secret Garden* ⏲ *Dawn–dusk; Chinese Garden, Glass House, and Secret Garden Tues.–Sun. 10–5.*

The **Staten Island Children's Museum,** also on the grounds, has five galleries with hands-on exhibitions introducing such topics as nature's food chains, storytelling, and insects. Portia's Playhouse, an interactive children's theater, invites youngsters to step up to the stage and try on costumes. ☎ *718/273–2060* *$5* ⏲ *Tues.–Sun. noon–5.*

The second-oldest hall in the city (after Carnegie, built in 1892) is Snug Harbor's **Music Hall** (☎ 718/815–7684), which has frequent performances, including an annual music festival. The former chapel houses the 210-seat **Veterans Memorial Hall** (☎ 718/815–7684), site of many indoor concerts and gatherings. The complex has a gift shop and a cafeteria. ✉ *1000 Richmond Terr., between Snug Harbor Rd. and Tyson Ave., Livingston* ☎ *718/448–2500* 🌐 *www.snug-harbor.org* *Cultural Center grounds free* ⏲ *Dawn–dusk; tours weekends at 2, meet at the gift shop* Ⓜ *S40 bus to Snug Harbor.*

need a break?

Adobe Blues (✉ 63 Lafayette St., off Richmond Terr., Snug Harbor ☎ 718/720–2583) is a bar and restaurant that serves up more than 200 beers, 40 types of tequila, and Southwestern fare.

❷ **Staten Island Zoo.** At this small but high-quality zoo you'll find a "South American" tropical forest, a serpentarium (reptile house), an aquarium, an "African Savannah at Twilight," and a children's center. ✉ *Barrett Park, 614 Broadway, West Brighton* ☎ *718/442–3100* 🌐 *www.statenislandzoo.org* *$5; pay as you wish Wed. 2–4:45* ⏲ *Daily 10–4:45; last admission 1 hr before closing* Ⓜ *S48 bus to Broadway and Forest, turn left on Broadway and walk 2 blocks.*

Richmondtown

Hilly and green, the scenic southern part of the island is far from the ferry terminal but worth the trip. Sprawling Historic Richmondtown takes you on a vivid journey into Staten Island's past, and the hilltop Jacques Marchais Museum of Tibetan Art transports you to the mountains of Asia.

a good tour

Take the S74–Richmond Road bus or a car service (which costs about $12) from the ferry terminal to **Historic Richmondtown** ❺ (a 30- to 40-minute trip), whose historic buildings date from the 17th, 18th, and 19th centuries. Afterward, grab lunch at the Parsonage restaurant or head to the **Jacques Marchais Museum of Tibetan Art** ❻, which has the largest collection of its kind outside Tibet. To get there, take the S74 bus or walk about a half mile east on Richmond Road to Lighthouse Avenue, where it's about a 15-minute walk uphill.

TIMING Set aside the better part of a day for Historic Richmondtown, and add on a couple of hours for the Tibetan Museum. If you take the bus, ask the driver about the return schedule. Both Historic Richmondtown and the Tibetan Museum are closed Monday and Tuesday and open afternoons only on weekends. Historic Richmondtown hosts a variety of seasonal events, including "Old Home Day" in October and a Christmas celebration.

What to See

❺ **Historic Richmondtown.** These 28 buildings, some constructed as early as 1685, others as late as the 19th century, are part of a 100-acre village that was the site of Staten Island's original county seat. Some of the buildings here have been relocated from different spots on the island—all brought together to provide a sense of Staten Island's rich history. The Staten Island Historical Society runs the site, and 12 buildings that have been restored are open to the public. Many, such as the Greek revival courthouse, which serves as the **visitor center** in summer, date from the 19th century; other architectural styles on-site range from Dutch colonial to Victorian Gothic revival. The **Staten Island Historical Society Museum,** built in 1848 as the second county clerk's and surrogate's office, now houses furniture, tools, photographs, and other Staten Island artifacts plus changing exhibitions about the island; it serves as the visitor center in winter. **Stephen's General Store,** built in 1837, looks much as it did in the mid-19th century. Adjacent is the late-19th-century **Stephen's House,** which is also filled with artifacts from the period. The

Voorlezer's House, built in 1695, is one of the oldest buildings on the site; it served as a residence as well as a place of worship and an elementary school.

During special events staff members demonstrate Early American crafts and trades such as printing, tinsmithing, basket making, and fireplace cooking. In summer you might want to make reservations for the traditional dinner (call for details), cooked outdoors and served with utensils of the specific period. Old Home Day in October shows off craftspeople at work; and December brings a monthlong Christmas celebration. A tavern on the historic village grounds hosts a Saturday night concert series showcasing ethnic and folk music; call for details. ✉ *441 Clarke Ave., Richmondtown* ☎ *718/351–1611* 🌐 *historicrichmondtown.org* 🎫 *$5* 🕐 *June–Aug., Mon. and Wed.–Sat. 10–5, Sun. 1–5; Sept.–May, Wed.–Sun. 1–5; call for tour times and for a schedule of events* Ⓜ *S74 bus to St. Patrick's Pl.*

6 **Jacques Marchais Museum of Tibetan Art.** One of the largest private, nonprofit collections of Tibetan and Himalayan sculpture, scrolls, and paintings outside of Tibet is displayed in this museum resembling a Tibetan monastery. Try to visit on a day when the monks bless the monastery—and you; call for times. ✉ *338 Lighthouse Ave., Richmondtown* ☎ *718/987–3500* 🌐 *www.tibetanmuseum.com* 🎫 *$5* 🕐 *Wed.–Sun. 1–5* Ⓜ *S74 bus to Lighthouse Ave. and walk uphill 15 min.*

THE ARTS

3

FODOR'S CHOICE

Brooklyn Academy of Music, *Brooklyn*
Carnegie Hall, *Midtown West*
Clementine, *Chelsea*
Film Forum, *Greenwich Village*
Metropolitan Opera, *Upper West Side*

HIGHLY RECOMMENDED

Bowery Poetry Club, *Lower East Side*
Dance Theater Workshop (DTW), *Chelsea*
Edwynn Houk, *Midtown East*
Gallery Onetwentyeight, *Lower East Side*
Joyce Theater, *Chelsea*
Leo Castelli, *Upper East Side*
Lincoln Center, *Upper West Side*
New York City Ballet (NYCB), *Upper West Side*
92nd St. Y, *Upper East Side*
P.S.122, *East Village*
SonyWonder Technology Lab, *Midtown East*
Walter Reade Theater, *Upper West Side*
The Ziegfeld, *Midtown West*

Updated by
Lynne Arany

NEW YORK CITY HAS A MAGNETIC PULL on artists and their audiences. From every corner of the Earth, artists gather here to commune with their peers, study the masters, check out the competition, and—with luck and hard work—present their talents to the city's eager audiences. Whether performing the classics or more experimental fare, artists of all disciplines and styles can find a niche here. And discerning patrons strive to keep up with the latest—from flocking to a concert hall to hear a world-class soprano deliver a flawless performance to crowding in a cramped basement bookstore to support young writers nervously stumbling over their own prose.

New York has somewhere between 200 and 250 legitimate theaters, and many more ad hoc venues—parks, churches, universities, museums, lofts, galleries, streets, rooftops, and even parking lots. The city also keeps up a revolving door of festivals and special events: summer jazz, one-act-play marathons, international film series, and musical celebrations from the classical to the avant-garde, to name just a few. It is this unrivaled wealth of culture and art that many New Yorkers cite as the reason why they're here.

FILM & TELEVISION

Film

On any given week New York City theaters screen all the major new releases, classics renowned and obscure, unusual foreign offerings, small independent flicks, hard-to-find documentaries, and cutting-edge video and experimental works.

Getting Tickets

Alas, New York may be the global capital of cineasts, so sold-out shows are common. It's a good idea to purchase tickets in advance, if possible. If you do arrive around show time, you may have to endure a line that winds around the block. Note that some queues are for people who have already bought their tickets; be sure to ask if the line is for ticket holders or ticket buyers.

For show times around the city, try **AOLMovieFone** (☎ 212/777–3456 🌐 www.moviefone.com), where you can check times and order tickets in advance with a credit card. Not all movie theaters participate, however, and there's a per ticket surcharge: on-line it's $1, by phone it's $1.50. **Newyork.citysearch.com** (🌐 newyork.citysearch.com) has current theater and movie listings.

First-Run & Mainstream Movies

Wherever you are in the city, you usually don't have to walk far before coming across a movie theater showing new releases. Tickets to most of these theaters are $9.50 or $10. Although there are no matinee discounts in Manhattan, discounts for seniors and children are usually available.

Two theaters preserve the flavor of grand old movie houses of times past. ★ **The Ziegfeld** (✉ 141 W. 54th St., between 6th and 7th Aves., Midtown West ☎ 212/765–7600) has a huge screen, brilliant red decor, an awesome sound system, and shows the latest blockbusters and is often host to their grand-opening galas as well. **Radio City Music Hall** (✉ 1260 6th Ave., at W. 50th St., Midtown West ☎ 212/247–4777), with its art deco setting, 34-ft-high screen, and 4,500-watt projector, is now only rarely used for movie screenings, though it does conduct tours.

In Times Square, the first-run house **Astor Plaza** (✉ W. 44th St., between Broadway and 8th Ave., Midtown ☎ 212/869–8340), though a bit frayed at the edges, may have the biggest screen in the city; the bonus is, all seats are discounted here. In the East Village, the **Village East Cinemas** (✉ 181–189 2nd Ave., at E. 12th St., East Village ☎ 212/529–6799) multiplex is housed in a restored Yiddish theater. Catch a film that's screening in the original stage area and check out the chandelier and Moorish-style ceiling trim and wall details there and in the lobby.

Independent, Foreign & Revival Films

New Yorkers have such a ravenous appetite for celluloid that even obscure, short-run indie films can expect a full house, and several cinemas reserve their screens soley for foreign and independent American releases. These genres are also frequently screened at performing arts centers, cultural societies, and museums, such as the Asia Society, Scandinavia House, the Japan Society, Alliance Francaise, and the Whitney Museum of American Art. But you'll most likely catch the alternative films downtown (screen sizes can vary at these theaters; most often they're small). Hometown directors who buck the Hollywood trends include Wes Anderson, Spike Lee, Jim Jarmusch, and Steve Buscemi.

The **American Museum of the Moving Image (AMMI)** (✉ 35th Ave. at 36th St., Astoria, Queens ☎ 718/784–0077 🌐 www.ammi.org) presents classic repertory and special series programming, such as films that were made in both silent and sound versions. A first stop for indie- and foreign-film fans is the **Angelika Film Center** (✉ 18 W. Houston St., at Mercer St., Greenwich Village ☎ 212/995–2000 🌐 www.angelikafilmcenter.com). **Anthology Film Archives** (✉ 32 2nd Ave., at E. 2nd St., East Village ☎ 212/505–5181 🌐 www.anthologyfilmarchives.org) consists of two theaters housed in a renovated courthouse. This "museum" is dedicated to preserving and exhibiting independent and avant-garde film, and features many foreign directors. The four-screen complex at **Brooklyn Academy of Music: BAM Rose Cinemas** (✉ 30 Lafayette Ave., at Ashland Pl. off Flatbush and Atlantic Aves., Fort Greene ☎ 718/623–2770) shows mostly first-run foreign-language and independent films and repertory programming.

Cinema Village (✉ 22 E. 12th St., between University Pl. and 5th Ave., Greenwich Village ☎ 212/924–3363) has three screens that show mostly independent films. The larger upstairs theater hosts somewhat more mainstream movies. In addition to premiering new releases, **Film Forum** (✉ 209 W. Houston St., between 6th Ave. and Varick St., Greenwich Village ☎ 212/727–8110 🌐 www.filmforum.com) hosts ongoing series of obscure films by directors such as William Castle or Samuel Fuller, never-before-seen cuts, and newly restored prints of classic works such as Orson Welles's *Touch of Evil* or the documentary on the Rolling Stones' 1969 tour *Gimme Shelter.* Within a space that was once a vaudeville theater, **Landmark's Sunshine Cinema** (✉ 143 E. Houston St., between 1st and 2nd Aves., Lower East Side ☎ 212/358–7709 🌐 www.LandmarkTheatres.com) has seven decent-size screens showing independent films. The venerable Thalia Theater was completely refurbished and reopened in 2002 as the **Leonard Nimoy Thalia at Symphony Space** (✉ 250 W. 95th St., at Broadway, Upper West Side ☎ 212/864–5400 🌐 www.symphonyspace.org). Count on them for series-style programming such as a selection of movies from directors with a singular point of view or a Brazilian film festival. While the Manhattan branch of the museum undergoes renovation, the Museum of Modern Art (MoMA) will continue its excellent program of classic films at **MoMA Film at the Gramercy Theatre** (✉ 127 E. 23rd St., at Lexington Ave., Gramercy ☎ 212/777–4900 🌐 www.moma.org).

Fodor'sChoice ★

FINDING OUT WHAT'S GOING ON

WITH SO MUCH TO CHOOSE from, you might want to consult the critics—and in New York, there's one on every corner. From the journalists serving up their picks and pans at the newsstands to the opinionated cabbie who whisks you off to your next destination, there's plenty to go by. To find out who or what's playing where, check out newyork.citysearch.com and the listings in the weekly publications. ***Time Out New York*** *provides the most comprehensive information, while the "Cue" section in the back of* ***New York*** *magazine is more selective.* ***The New Yorker*** *has long been known for its "Goings On About Town" section that contains limited, yet ruthlessly succinct reviews of theater, dance, art, music, film, and nightlife.* ***The Village Voice, The Onion,*** *and* ***New York Press*** *are free papers and have extensive listings as well.*

The New York Times *comes in pretty handy, especially on Friday, with its two "Weekend" sections (Fine Arts and Leisure; Movies and Performing Arts). The Sunday "Arts and Leisure" section has longer articles on everything from opera to sitcoms, plus theater and movie ads and a full, detailed survey of cultural events for the coming week.*

Paper *magazine dishes the trendiest of the trendy scenes, and many of the above-mentioned publications plus the* ***New York Blade*** *illuminate the ever-changing gay and lesbian arts scene.*

Just off Central Park and next to the Plaza Hotel, **The Paris** (✉ 4 W. 58th St., between 5th and 6th Aves., Midtown West ☎ 212/688–3800) is an exquisite showcase for much-talked-about new American and foreign releases.

The **Quad Cinema** (✉ 34 W. 13th St., between 5th and 6th Aves., Greenwich Village ☎ 212/255–8800 🌐 www.quadcinema.com) plays first-run art and foreign films on four relatively small screens. **The Screening Room** (✉ 54 Varick St., at Canal St., TriBeCa ☎ 212/334–2100 🌐 www.thescreeningroom.com) has two cozy theaters, both with a 1940s feel. Programming is generally small independents and the occasional nostalgia piece like *Breakfast at Tiffany's*. **Two Boots Pioneer Theater** (✉ 155 E. 3rd St., at Ave. A, East Village ☎ 212/254–3300 🌐 www.twoboots.com) consists of one comfy screening room (and a home-theater-size screen) that screens rare oldies, short films, and the odd independent. ★ The comfortable, modern auditorium of the **Walter Reade Theater** (✉ Lincoln Center, 165 W. 65th St., between Broadway and Amsterdam Ave., plaza level, Upper West Side ☎ 212/875–5600 🌐 www.filmlinc.com) has wonderful sight lines. It presents series devoted to "the best in world cinema" that run the gamut from silents and documentaries to retrospectives and recent releases, often on the same theme or from the same country. Live events—dance, readings, and more—are often held in conjunction with screenings. Purchase tickets at the box office or online up to four weeks in advance, and one week ahead if ordering by phone. Inquire about the once-monthly showing of open-captioned features for people who are deaf.

New York's leading annual film event is the **New York Film Festival** (☎ 212/875–5050 🌐 www.filmlinc.com), sponsored by the Film Society of Lincoln Center every September and October. Its program includes exceptional movies, most never before seen in the United States; the festival's hits usually make their way into local movie houses over the next couple of months. Each March, the Film Society of Lincoln Center joins forces with the Museum of Modern Art to produce **New Directors–New Films** (☎ 212/875–5050 🌐 www.filmlinc.com), giving up-and-coming directors their moment to flicker. Call ahead for the latest venue information.

On Monday nights in summer—usually August—you can bring a picnic and blankets to **HBO's Bryant Park Film Festival** (☎ 212/512–5700 🌐 www.bryantpark.org) just after sunset, when classics such as *On the Waterfront, Singing in the Rain,* and *King Kong* are screened for free. The lawn is always packed, so arrive early to secure a patch of green. Sponsored by the **Hudson River Park Conservancy** (☎ 212/533–7275 🌐 www.HudsonRiverPark.org), free classic and noir films such as *From Here to Eternity* are shown in the evenings at dusk on Wednesday at **Pier 54** (✉ off the West Side Hwy. at 13th St., Greenwich Village) and on Fridays at **Pier 25** (✉ off the West Side Hwy. at N. Moore St., TriBeCa) in July and August. First-come, first-served folding chairs are available, and at Pier 25 there's a barbecue stand and tables from which to enjoy the sunset, too.

Film for Children

Several museums sponsor special film programs aimed at families and children, including the Museum of Modern Art, the Museum of Television and Radio, and the American Museum of the Moving Image. Children marvel at the amazing nature and science films shown on the huge screen in the **IMAX Theater** (✉ Central Park W and W. 79th St., Upper West Side ☎ 212/769–5034 🌐 www.amnh.org) at the American Museum of Natural History. At the **Loews Lincoln Square Theater** (✉ 1998 Broadway, at W. 68th St., Upper West Side ☎ 212/336–5020) audience members strap on high-tech headgear that makes specially created feature films appear in 3-D.

★ **SonyWonder Technology Lab** (✉ 550 Madison Ave., between E. 55th and E. 56th Sts., Midtown East ☎ 212/833–7858 weekdays 🌐 www.sonywondertechlab.com), an interactive experience that uses multimedia presentations to demystify technology, shows free films for kids. Selections range from PG-13 thrillers to G-rated holiday classics (children under 17 must be accompanied by an adult). Call ahead for reserved tickets; remaining tickets are distributed at 5:45 PM on the day of showing.

Lincoln Center's **Walter Reade Theater** shows feature films for children on weekend afternoons and sponsors children's film festivals. The innovative series **Reel to Real** (☎ 212/875–5570 🌐 www.filmlinc.com) takes place on weekends from October to June. A typical program pairs a double billing of classic films—a collection of Betty Boop cartoons, for example—with a live dance or music performance.

Television

Tickets to tapings of television shows are free, but can be difficult to come by on short notice. Some shows, like Letterman, require that you send a postcard with your name, address, and phone number for each pair of tickets requested, at least a month and up to 10 months in advance. Even then, that card may be thrown into a lottery hopper. Others—as it is now with all NBC shows taped in New York—accept requests by e-mail or phone only. But in most cases, same-day standby tickets are available to people willing to wait in line for several hours, sometimes starting at 5 or 6 AM, depending on the level of celebrity involved at a particular taping.

The Caroline Rhea Show. Sweet Caroline took over from Rosie O'Donnell as of the fall 2002 season, and continues the celebrity-studded couch-chat format, along with some light and easy patter and comedic savvy. Tickets are available by a lottery system at 7:30 AM Monday through Thursday at the West 49th Street NBC Studios entrance to 30 Rockefeller Plaza. Or you can reserve tickets by phone or e-mail (☎ 212/664–3056). Children under five cannot attend; guests under 16 must be accompanied by an adult. ✉ *NBC Studios, Caroline Rhea Show, 30 Rockefeller Plaza, between 5th and 6th Aves., Midtown West 10112* ☎ *212/664–4444.*

The Daily Show with Jon Stewart. With a knowing smirk, the amiable Jon Stewart pokes fun at news headlines on this half-hour cable show. The program tapes from Monday through Thursday, and free tickets can be obtained by calling the Daily Show studios. Children under 18 cannot attend. ✉ *The Daily Show studios, 513 W. 54th St., between 10th and 11th Sts., Midtown West* ☎ *212/586–2477.*

It's Showtime at the Apollo. One of Harlem's most beloved landmarks hosts this raucous talent search where competitors must display both talent and nerves of steel. Tickets to tapings are free, but you must send a self-addressed stamped envelope in advance. Check out the Web site (🌐 www.showtimeinharlem.com) for additional information. ✉ *Tickets, 3 Park Ave., 40th floor, between E. 33rd and 34th Sts., 10016* ☎ *212/889–3532.*

Late Night with Conan O'Brien. This popular variety show hosted by O'Brien targets hip, savvy viewers and attracts consistently interesting guests. Standby tickets are available from Tuesday through Friday after 9 AM at the 49th Street side of 30 Rockefeller Plaza. Call the ticket information line (☎ 212/664–3056) for advance reservations. No one under 16 can attend a taping. ✉ *NBC Studios, Late Night with Conan O'Brien, 30 Rockefeller Plaza, between W. 49th and W. 50th Sts., Midtown West, 10112* ☎ *212/664–4444.*

The Late Show with David Letterman. David Letterman, known in some circles as the thinking man's Jay Leno, has a famously quirky, idiomatic manner that makes his show capable of real surprises. Call 212/247–6497 at 11 AM on tape days for standby tickets. You can sign-up for cancellation tickets on www.cbs.com or write for reservations: the request must be on a postcard, and the wait may be as much as a year. No one under 18 can attend. ✉ *Late Show Tickets, c/o Ed Sullivan Theater, 1697 Broadway, between 53rd and 54th Sts., Midtown West, 10019* ☎ *212/975–1003.*

Live! with Regis and Kelly. Talk-show veteran Regis Philbin and his co-host Kelly Rippa keep the sparks flying on this morning program, which books an eclectic roster of guests. Standby tickets become available weekdays at 7 AM at the **ABC studio** (✉ 71 Lincoln Sq., between W. 67th St. and Columbus Ave., Upper West Side). Otherwise, write for tickets a full year in advance. Children under 10 cannot attend. *Live! Tickets, Ansonia Station, Box 230777, 10023* ☎ *212/456–3537.*

MTV Studios. If you're between the ages of 18 and 24 you can be an audience member of **Total Request Live** (**TRL**) with host Carson Daly. This hugely popular show is taped weekdays at 4 PM on the second floor of the high-energy MTV studios in Times Square. For advance reservations, e-mail or call the TRL hot line. ✉ *1515 Broadway, at 43rd St., Midtown West* ☎ *212/398–8549.*

Saturday Night Live. Probably the most influential comedy variety show in the history of television—who else could coax Yankee shortstop Derek Jeter into full drag?—*SNL* continues to captivate audiences. This show tapes 20 times per season. Standby tickets are distributed on a first-come, first-served basis at 7 AM on the day of the show at the West 50th Street entrance to 30 Rockefeller Plaza. You may receive either standby for a dress rehearsal (7 PM arrival time) or the live show (10 PM arrival time). Written requests for tickets must be submitted in August; your card is then entered in ticket lotteries. You will be notified one to two weeks in advance if you're selected. No one under 16 may attend. ✉ *NBC Studios, Saturday Night Live, 30 Rockefeller Plaza, between 5th and 6th Aves., Midtown West, 10112* ☎ *212/664–4444.*

Today. The king of morning talk shows airs weekdays from 7 AM to 10 AM in the glass-enclosed, ground-level NBC studio at the corner of West 49th Street and Rockefeller Plaza. You can watch the action through the giant windows, and you may well be spotted on TV by friends back home, standing behind anchors Katie Couric and Matt Lauer. In summer, live performances by artists ranging from Elvis Costello to Tony Bennett are presented outdoors in the adjoining courtyard. ✉ *Rockefeller Plaza between W. 48th and W. 49th Sts., Midtown West.*

The View. Barbara Walter's experiment in televised water-cooler chitchat and celebrity gossip has been an unqualified hit. Join Star Jones (lawyer), Meredith Vieira (wife–mother), Joy Behar (irreverent comic), and, occasionally, Barbara Walters herself for an oftentimes outrageous hour of live television. Ticket requests (postcards only) need to be sent four to six months in advance; you may also request tickets on-line at www.abc.com. No one under 18 will be admitted. ✉ *Tickets, The View, 320 W. 66th St., at West End Ave., Upper West Side, 10023.*

PERFORMING ARTS

New York is indisputably the performing arts capital of America. In the course of a year, celebrated artists from around the world perform in the city's legendary concert halls and theaters. But the city's own artistic resources are what make the exciting performing arts scene here so terrific. Thousands of great actors, singers, musicians, and other artists populate the city, infusing New York's cultural scene with unparalleled levels of creative energy.

Getting Tickets

Scoring tickets to shows and concerts is fairly easy—unless, of course, you're dead set on attending the season's hottest events, which are often sold out months in advance. Generally, the box office is the best place to buy tickets, since in-house ticket sellers make it their business to know about their theaters and can point out (on a chart) where you'll be seated. It's always a good idea to purchase tickets in advance to avoid disappointment. You'll generally find that tickets are more readily available for evening performances from Tuesday through Thursday and matinees on Wednesday. Tickets for weekend matinees are tougher to secure. Most Broadway productions take Sunday and Monday nights off.

Major concerts and recitals, especially prime seats at venues such as the Metropolitan Opera, can cost twice as much as a Broadway play. For the most part, the top ticket price for musicals can cost as much as $100, and the best seats for nonmusicals can cost as much as $75. Promoters of some of Broadway's hottest productions—such as *The Producers*—are experimenting with pricing their choicest seats higher to discourage scalping. Ticket scalpers have reportedly sold tickets for as much as $200 to shows that were available at the box office for much less. Lately there has been an upswing in the selling of counterfeit tickets and tickets for seats that don't exist. Ticket scalping is against the law in New York.

Check the arts listings in the *New York Times* to see which ticket vendor is handling the production you want to see (newspaper ads generally specify which service you should use for a given event). To purchase tickets in advance from the box office, send a certified check or money order, several alternate dates, and a self-addressed, stamped envelope. You can also use a credit card to reserve tickets for Broadway and off-Broadway shows. Expect a surcharge of $8–$10 per ticket and an additional charge per order of $2.50–$3.50 if you use Ticketmaster or Telecharge. Both services have links to individual theater seating charts so you can see where your seats are before you buy a ticket. You can arrange to have your tickets mailed to you or held at the theater's box office.

The League of American Theatres and Producers is the organization behind the **Broadway Line** (☎ 888/276–2392 toll-free; 212/302–4111 in the tristate area 🌐 www.livebroadway.com), which gives information about show times, theater addresses, and ticket prices. For the phone service, once you've heard the information you seek, the line can connect you directly to Telecharge or Ticketmaster to buy tickets. **Center Charge** (☎ 212/721–6500) handles ticket orders for Lincoln Center's Avery Fisher and Alice Tully halls, for Jazz at Lincoln Center, as well as for Lincoln Center's summer festivals and the Big Apple Circus in the winter. **OffBroadwayonline** (🌐 www.offbroadwayonline.com) is a comprehensive site for information on off-Broadway and off-off-Broadway shows, including lots of special offers. **Telecharge** (☎ 212/239–6200 🌐 www.telecharge.com) handles a great many Broadway shows. **Ticketmaster** (☎ 212/307–4100 🌐 www.ticketmaster.com) handles New York State Theater, Town Hall, and Brooklyn Academy of Music tickets. Off- and off-off-Broadway theaters have their own joint box office called **Ticket Central** (✉ 416 W. 42nd St., between 9th and 10th Aves., Midtown West ☎ 212/279–4200 🌐 www.ticketcentral.org). It's open daily between 12 and 8. Although there are no discounts here, tickets to performances in these theaters are usually less expensive than Broadway tickets, and they cover events including theater, performance art, and dance. **Walt Disney Theatrical Productions** (☎ 800/755–4000 or 212/307–4747 🌐 www.disneyonbroadway.com) is the place to get tickets for the ever-growing number of popular Disney Broadway productions.

If you're in town without tickets, try visiting the **Broadway Ticket Center** (✉ 1560 Broadway, between W. 46th and W. 47th Sts., Midtown West ☎ no phone), at the Times Square Visitors Center, open daily 8–8 (ticket-window hours are Monday–Saturday 9–7 and Sunday 10–6). There are descriptions and videotaped excerpts from shows, theater-location maps, and a box office that handles same-day and advance tickets for most Broadway shows (*The Lion King* is not included) and several off-Broadway shows. Tickets are full price, with a $4.50 handling charge per ticket.

For those willing to pay top dollar to see that show or concert everyone's talking about but no one can get tickets for, try a ticket broker. You might have to pay $250 for tickets that would have cost $80 at the box office, but you can get last-minute seats for hot shows. **Continental Guest Services** (☎ 212/944–8910 or 800/299–8587 🌐 www.intercharge.com) is one of the best-known brokers in Manhattan. Also check the lobbies of major hotels for them and others.

DISCOUNT TICKETS Some theaters and performance spaces offer reduced rates for unsold tickets on the day of the performance, usually a half hour before curtain time. Other shows have front-row orchestra—or very rear balcony—seats available at a reduced price (about $20) the day of the performance. These discounts vary widely and are sometimes noted in the newspaper theater listings or ads. Occasionally, box offices offer same-day standing-room tickets ($10–$20) for sold-out shows (the Metropolitan Opera House sells standing-room tickets in advance); check with the particular theater for more information.

Some Broadway and off-Broadway shows sell reduced-price tickets for preview performances prior to the official opening night. Look at newspaper ads for discounted previews or consult the box office. Tickets for matinees may cost less, particularly on Wednesday. Reduced-price vouchers or tickets for dance, music, opera, and other performing arts may also be found at venues that offer discounted theater tickets.

Discounts on well-known long-running shows (such as *Beauty and the Beast* and *Phantom of the Opera*) are often available if you can lay your hands on a couple of "twofers"—discount-ticket coupons found at the Broadway Ticket Center. You can purchase half-price ticket vouchers at **NYC & Company Visitor Information Center** (✉ 810 7th Ave., between W. 52nd and W. 53rd Sts., Midtown West ☎ 212/484–1222) weekdays 8:30–6 and weekends 9–5. **City Hall Park Visitor Information Center** (✉ Broadway at the south end of City Hall Park, Lower Manhattan) sells half-price ticket vouchers weekdays 9–8 and weekends 10–8; it's closed in winter.

TKTS (✉ Duffy Sq., W. 47th St. and Broadway, Midtown West ✉ South Street Seaport, at the corner of Front and John Sts., in the rear of the Resnick/Prudential Building at 199 Water St., Lower Manhattan 🌐 www.tdf.org) is New York's best-known discount-ticket source. Operated by the Theatre Development Fund, the two TKTS booths sell day-of-performance tickets for Broadway and off-Broadway plays at 25%–50% off the usual price (plus a $2.50 service fee). The names of shows for which tickets are available are posted on electronic boards. You can pay with cash or traveler's checks; credit cards are not accepted.

For evening performances Monday–Saturday, the Duffy Square booth is open from 3 to 8; for Wednesday and Saturday matinee performances, from 10 to 2; for Sunday matinee and evening performances, from 11 to 7:30. Lines at Duffy Square can be long, especially on weekends, but the wait is generally pleasant (if the weather cooperates), as the bright lights and babble of Times Square surround you.

The South Street Seaport booth is open Monday–Saturday 11–6 and Sunday 11– 3:30. For matinees (on Wednesday, Saturday, and Sunday), you have to purchase tickets the day before the performance (which means matinee tickets are available to downtown customers before customers in midtown).

Playbill magazine's Web site **Playbill On-Line** (🌐 www.playbill.com) post regular discounts for Broadway and off-Broadway shows (along with restaurants and other deals). Options include saving a handling charge by bringing a printout of the offer to the box office or ordering by phone or directly through the site. The site has seating charts for all theaters.

Performing Arts Centers

New York's most renowned centers for the arts are tourist attractions in themselves.

Fodor'sChoice ★ America's oldest performing arts center, **Brooklyn Academy of Music** (⊠ 30 Lafayette Ave., at Ashland Pl. off Flatbush and Atlantic Aves., Fort Greene ☎ 718/636–4100 ⊕ www.bam.org), opened in 1859 and has a solid reputation for daring and innovative dance, music, opera, and theater productions. BAM's main performance spaces are the 2,100-seat Howard Gilman Opera House, a white-brick Renaissance Revival palace built in 1908, and the 874-seat Harvey Theater, a spartanly restored 1904 theater a block away at 651 Fulton Street. Acclaimed international companies are often on the bill. You can grab a bite at the BAMcafé, which is a venue for singers and musicians Thursday through Saturday nights. The **BAMbus** provides round-trip transportation between Manhattan and BAM for most events. Reservations are required (718/636–4100). The bus picks up passengers from the Whitney at Philip Morris (120 Park Ave., at East 42nd St., Midtown East) one hour prior to a performance.

Carnegie Hall (⊠ 881 7th Ave., at W. 57th St., Midtown West ☎ 212/247–7800 ⊕ www.carnegiehall.org) is one of the world's most famous concert halls. Performances are given in the beautifully restored 2,804-seat Isaac Stern Auditorium and the far more intimate Weill Recital Hall, where many young talents make their New York debuts, as well as the new Judy and Arthur Zankel Hall on the lower level. Although the emphasis is on classical music, Carnegie Hall also hosts jazz, pop, cabaret, and folk music concerts.

City Center (⊠ 131 W. 55th St., between 6th and 7th Aves., Midtown West ☎ 212/581–1212 ⊕ www.citycenter.org) has a neo-Moorish look (it was built in 1923 by the Ancient and Accepted Order of the Mystic Shrine and saved from demolition in 1943 by Mayor Fiorello La Guardia) and presents major dance troupes such as Alvin Ailey and Paul Taylor, as well as concert versions of classic American musicals. The Manhattan Theatre Club, with its highly regarded and popular program of innovative contemporary drama, also resides here.

The Kitchen (⊠ 512 W. 19th St., between 10th and 11th Aves., Chelsea ☎ 212/255–5793 ⊕ www.thekitchen.org) is *the* place for performance art, although multimedia, dance, and music have their moments, too.

★ **Lincoln Center** (⊠ W. 62nd to W. 66th Sts., Broadway to Amsterdam Ave., Upper West Side ☎ 212/546–2656 ⊕ www.lincolncenter.org) is a 16-acre complex that houses the Metropolitan Opera, New York Philharmonic, New York City Ballet, New York City Opera, Juilliard School, Lincoln Center Theater, New York Public Library for the Performing Arts, Film Society of Lincoln Center, Chamber Music Society of Lincoln Center, Jazz at Lincoln Center, School of American Ballet, the Vivian Beaumont Theater, Mitzi E. Newhouse Theater, and Walter Reade Theater. A variety of **Tours of Lincoln Center** (☎ 212/875–5350) are available starting at $10 per adult. The **Lincoln Center Festival** (☎ 212/875–5928) is a three-week summertime event. The programs include classical and contemporary music concerts, dance, film, and theater works. **Midsummer Night Swing** (☎ 212/875–5766) is a monthlong dance party that runs outdoors three or four nights per week from late June through July on the central Josie Robertson Plaza. To the beat of a live band, dancers swing, hustle, polka, merengue, salsa, tango, and more. Lincoln Center's longest running classical series is the **Mostly Mozart Festival** (☎ 212/875–5399) in August, featuring the music of Mozart and other classical favorites. Also in August, **Lincoln Center Out-of-Doors** (☎ 212/875–5108) is an almost nightly festival of free performances of music, dance, and special family programs taking place throughout the plaza and adjacent Damrosch Park. **Jazz at Lincoln Center** (☎ 212/258–9800) includes Jazz for Young People, an annual concert series hosted by Wynton Marsalis for children.

★ **P.S.122** (✉ 150 1st Ave., at E. 9th St., East Village ☎ 212/477–5288 🌐 www.ps122.org), housed in a former public school, has served as an incubator for talent like Eric Bogosian, Spalding Gray, Meredith Monk, and Blue Man Group. This scruffy, vibrant East Village venue presents exhibitions and productions that come and go quickly, and they're never boring. Look for its annual benefit performance marathon in February.

Classical Music

"Gentlemen," conductor Serge Koussevitzky once told the assembled Boston Symphony Orchestra, "maybe it's good enough for Cleveland or Cincinnati, but it's not good enough for New York." In a nutshell he described New York's central position in the musical world.

New York possesses not only the country's oldest symphony orchestra (the New York Philharmonic) but also three renowned conservatories—the Juilliard School, the Manhattan School of Music, and Mannes College of Music. Since the turn of the 20th century, the world's great orchestras and soloists have made Manhattan a principal stopping point.

New York's early music scene has increased dramatically over the last few years. A half dozen performing groups and presenting organizations stage early music concerts throughout the year in many venues, including various churches. In an average week, between 50 and 150 events appear in newspaper and magazine listings, and weekly concert calendars are published in all the major newspapers. Record and music shops serve as information centers.

Most venues also host children's programs. The **Little Orchestra Society** (☎ 212/971–9500 🌐 www.littleorchestra.org) organizes concerts that introduce classical music to children ages three–five at **Florence Gould Hall** (✉ 55 E. 59th St., between Park and Madison Aves., Midtown East ☎ 212/971–9500) and ages 5–12 at **Avery Fisher Hall at Lincoln Center.**

Concert Halls

The **Brooklyn Academy of Music (BAM)** (⇨ Performing Arts Centers) is the home of the Brooklyn Philharmonic, which under music director Robert Spano has the city's most adventurous symphonic programming. Both the Howard Gilman Opera House and the Harvey Theater have extraordinary acoustics. They are homes for the annual Next Wave Festival, which since its founding in 1982 has featured some of the most important concerts, dance events, and theatrical and opera productions, including new works by Philip Glass, Laurie Anderson, and Robert Wilson.

Fodor's Choice ★ **Carnegie Hall** (⇨ Performing Arts Centers) has operated for more than a century. Virtually every important musician of the 20th century performed in this Italian Renaissance–style building, often at the peak of his or her creative powers. Tchaikovsky conducted the opening night concert on May 5, 1891; Leonard Bernstein had his famous debut here; Vladimir Horowitz made his historic return to the concert stage; and world-class orchestras sound their very best here in the lush, perhaps incomparable, acoustics of the 2,804-seat auditorium. The Opera Orchestra of New York, under the direction of Eve Queler, puts on concert versions of rarely performed operas here several times a year, usually with superstar soloists.

Lincoln Center (⇨ Performing Arts Centers) is the city's musical nerve center, especially when it comes to the classics. In 2002 American conductor Lorin Maazel took the podium as the 22nd music director of the **New York Philharmonic** (☎ 212/875–5656). Maazel, who replaced maestro Kurt Masur, conducted the orchestra more than 100 times—including once as a child prodigy in the 1940s—before being named full-time music director. The NYP performs at Avery Fisher Hall from late September to early June. In addition to its concerts showcasing exceptional guest artists and the works of specific composers, the Philharmonic also schedules weeknight Rush Hour Concerts at 7:30 or 8 and Saturday Matinee Concerts at 2; these special events, offered throughout the season, last an hour and are priced lower than the regular subscription concerts. Rush Hour Concerts are followed by receptions with the conductor on the Grand Promenade, and Saturday Matinee Concerts feature discussions after the performances. A note for New York Philharmonic devotees: in season and when conductors and soloists are amenable, weekday orchestra rehearsals at 9:45 AM are open to the public on selected mornings for $14 (212/875–5656).

Intimate **Alice Tully Hall** (☎ 212/875–5050), Lincoln Center's "little white box," is considered to be as acoustically perfect as a concert hall can get. You can hear the Chamber Music Society of Lincoln Center, promising Juilliard students, Jazz at Lincoln Center, chamber music ensembles, music on period instruments, choral music, famous soloists, and concert groups.

Avery Fisher Hall (☎ 212/875–5030) follows the classic European rectangular pattern. To its stage come the world's great musicians; to its boxes, the black-tie-and-diamond-tiara set. Within the Library of the Performing Arts, **Bruno Walter Auditorium** (☎ 212/642–0142) often stages free concerts.

Other Venues

Aaron Davis Hall at City College (✉ W. 133rd St. at Convent Ave., Harlem ☎ 212/650–6900 🌐 www.aarondavishall.org) is an uptown venue for world music events and a variety of classical music and dance programs. In Brooklyn, **Bargemusic** (✉ Fulton Ferry Landing at Old Fulton and Furman Sts., Brooklyn Heights ☎ 718/624–2083 🌐 www.bargemusic.org) keeps chamber music groups busy year-round on an old barge with a fabulous view of the Manhattan skyline. New York's Ensemble for Early Music performs about 20 medieval and Renaissance music concerts in the **Cathedral of St. John the Divine** (✉ 1047 Amsterdam Ave., at W. 112th St., Morningside Heights ☎ 212/662–2133 🌐 www.stjohndivine.org).

At the **Church of the Ascension** (✉ 5th Ave. at W. 10th St., Greenwich Village ☎ 212/254–8553), Voices of Ascension, well known for its recordings, performs concerts of all periods. Choral and organ concerts take place at the **Church of St. Ignatius Loyola** (✉ 980 Park Ave., at E. 84th St., Upper East Side ☎ 212/288–2520) about twice a month from September to April with a special series at Christmastime. Single performances and seasonal series of sacred and secular music from the Middle Ages take place in the 12th-century chapel of the **Cloisters** (✉ Fort Tryon Park, Morningside Heights ☎ 212/650–2290).

Well known recitalists and chamber music groups perform at **Kaufmann Concert Hall** (✉ 92nd St. Y, 1395 Lexington Ave., at E. 92nd St., Upper East Side ☎ 212/996–1100 🌐 www.92ndsty.org).

The Kaye Playhouse (✉ Hunter College, E. 68th St. between Park and Lexington Aves., Upper East Side ☎ 212/772–4448) stages a varied program, including distinguished soloists, in a small concert hall.

Merkin Concert Hall (✉ Kaufman Center at Goodman House, 129 W. 67th St., between Broadway and Amsterdam Ave., Upper West Side ☎ 212/501–3330 🌐 www.ekcc.org) presents mostly chamber music ensembles.

The **Metropolitan Museum of Art** (✉ 1000 5th Ave., at E. 82nd St., Upper East Side ☎ 212/570–3949 🌐 www.metmuseum.org) holds three stages—the Temple of Dendur; the Grace Rainey Rogers Auditorium; and, at Christmas, the Medieval Sculpture Hall—with concerts by leading vocal, chamber, and jazz musicians. Other than Friday and Saturday evenings when the museum is open late, access is through the street-level entrance at East 83rd Street and 5th Avenue.

Miller Theatre (✉ Columbia University, Broadway at W. 116th St., Morningside Heights ☎ 212/854–1633 🌐 www.millertheatre.com) presents a varied program of jazz and classical performers, such as the New York Virtuosi Chamber Symphony.

Outdoor Music

All kinds of music waft through the air of the city's great outdoors. In the summertime both the Metropolitan Opera and the New York Philharmonic play free concerts in municipal parks, filling verdant spaces with the haunting strains of *La Bohème* or the thunder of the *1812 Overture*. For information call the **City Parks Special Events Hotline** (☎ 212/360–3456 or 888/697–2757).

From the middle of June through Labor Day, Prospect Park comes alive with the sounds of its annual **Celebrate Brooklyn Performing Arts Festival** (✉ 9th St. Band Shell, enter from 9th St. and Prospect Park W, Park Slope ☎ 718/855–7882 🌐 www.brooklynx.org). The enormously popular **Central Park SummerStage** (✉ Rumsey Playfield, 5th Ave. and E. 72nd St., Central Park ☎ 212/360–2777 🌐 www.summerstage.org) presents free programs, ranging from alternative rock to spoken word, from June through August. Arrive early to secure a seat or even a blanket spot. A **Jazzmobile** (☎ 212/866–4900) transports jazz and Latin music to parks throughout the five boroughs in July and August; Wednesday evening concerts are held at Grant's Tomb. The **Museum of Modern Art** (☎ 212/708–9480 🌐 www.moma.org) sponsors free Friday and Saturday evening concerts of 20th-century music mid-June through August at **Bryant Park** (✉ 42nd St. between 5th and 6th Aves.). Pier 16 at **South Street Seaport** (☎ 212/732–7678 🌐 www.southstseaport.org) is the setting for a cornucopia of concerts from Thursday through Saturday evenings from Memorial Day to Labor Day; it also sponsors holiday music programs from late November through January 1 on weekday evenings and weekend afternoons.

Dance

In a city that seems never to stop moving, dance is a thriving art form. On any given night, a wide variety of performances unfolds, be it of ballet, Japanese *butoh*, improvisation, or a dance-based Broadway show. Hard-core dance fans are often devoted to the virtuosity of ballet or the heady, experimental "downtown scene." Several New York–based companies blur the line, such as Merce Cunningham, the Mark Morris Dance Group, or Bill T. Jones–Arnie Zane Dance Company.

Ballet

Two powerhouse companies—the New York City Ballet and the American Ballet Theatre—continue to please and astonish huge audiences season after season. The intimate Joyce Theater (⇨ **Modern Dance**) hosts ballet companies focusing on contemporary works, including Eliot Feld's Ballet Tech, Ballet Hispanico, and Dance Theatre of Harlem.

The **American Ballet Theatre (ABT)** is renowned for its brilliant renditions of the great 19th-century classics (*Swan Lake, Giselle, The Sleeping Beauty,* and *La Bayardère*) as well as its eclectic contemporary repertoire, including works by all the 20th-century masters such as Balanchine, Tudor, Robbins, and de Mille. Since its inception in 1940, the company has included some of the great dancers, such as Mikhail Baryshnikov, Natalia Makarova, Rudolf Nureyev, Gelsey Kirkland, and Cynthia Gregory. The ballet has two New York seasons—eight weeks beginning in early May at its home in the Metropolitan Opera House and two weeks beginning in late October at City Center. The two theaters handle ticket orders for the ballet.

★ **New York City Ballet (NYCB),** founded in 1948, has two seasons. The winter season, which runs from mid-November through February, includes the beloved annual holiday production of George Balanchine's *The Nutcracker.* Its spring season lasts from late April through June. The company continues to stress the works themselves rather than individual performers, although that hasn't stopped a number of principal dancers (such as Kyra Nichols, Darci Kistler, Damian Woetzel, and Jock Soto) from standing out. The company has more than 90 dancers and performs and maintains an active repertoire of 20th-century works unmatched in the world, including works by Balanchine, Jerome Robbins, Ballet Master-in-Chief Peter Martins, and others. NYCB performs in Lincoln Center's **New York State Theater** (⊠ W. 62nd St. at Columbus Ave., Upper West Side ☎ 212/870–5570), where you can call for tickets and schedule information.

Modern Dance

The most innovative dance companies in the world perform in New York throughout the year, especially in fall and spring, showcasing the thrilling work of such legendary choreographers as Martha Graham, Merce Cunningham, Alvin Ailey, Mark Morris, Twyla Tharp, and Paul Taylor.

The **Brooklyn Academy of Music (BAM)** (⇨ Performing Arts Centers) hosts contemporary dance troupes as part of its Next Wave Festival every fall; this is where to catch the highly musical Mark Morris Dance Group or German choreographer Pina Bausch's sexy dance-theater company. At **City Center** (⇨ Performing Arts Centers) the modern masters such as Ailey ★ and Taylor hold sway. The newly renovated **Dance Theater Workshop (DTW)** (⊠ 219 W. 19th St., between 7th and 8th Aves., Chelsea ☎ 212/924–0077 🌐 www.dtw.org) serves as one of New York's most successful laboratories for new dance. **Danspace Project** (⊠ St. Mark's Church-in-the-Bowery, 131 E. 10th St., at 2nd Ave., East Village ☎ 212/674–8194 🌐 www.danspaceproject.org) sponsors a series of avant-garde choreography that runs from September through June.

★ In a former art deco movie house in Chelsea, the 500-seat **Joyce Theater** (⊠ 175 8th Ave., at W. 19th St., Chelsea ☎ 212/242–0800 🌐 www.joyce.org) presents soley dance. Its eclectic program includes tap, ballet, jazz, ballroom, and ethnic dance. Talented choreographers without mainstream appeal are spotlighted early in the year at the Altogether Different series. The Joyce SoHo (⊠ 155 Mercer St., between Houston and Prince Sts., SoHo ☎ 212/431–9233) hosts performances by up-and-coming local dancers. At the 92nd St. Y, the **Harkness Dance Project** (⇨ Readings and Lectures) presents emerging dance troupes with discussions following performances. Dance at **P.S.122** (⇨ Performing Arts Centers) often borders on performance art.

Opera

The greatest singers in the world all clamor to test their mettle at the Metropolitan Opera, where they can work alongside internationally admired directors and designers. The Met's lavish opera productions are sometime priced significantly lower than what you'd pay in Europe, but tickets are far from cheap (unless you buy standing room). Another opera right next door—the New York City Opera—isn't as fancy, but often strays from the classics to perform less common works.

Major Companies

These are good times for opera lovers in New York, as the city's two major companies, the Metropolitan Opera and New York City Opera, are winning raves. The titan of American opera companies, **Metropolitan Opera** brings the world's leading singers to its massive stage at Lincoln Center's **Metropolitan Opera House** (✉ W. 64th St. at Columbus Ave., Upper West Side ☎ 212/362–6000 🌐 www.metopera.org) from October to mid-April. Under the direction of James Levine, the Met's artistic director and principal conductor, and principal guest conductor Valery Gergiev, the opera orchestra performs with an intensity and quality that rival the world's finest symphonic orchestras. All performances, including operas sung in English, are unobtrusively subtitled on small screens (which can be turned off) on the back of the seat in front of you. For children, the Met presents its **Growing Up with Opera** program (☎ 212/769–7008).

Fodor's Choice ★

Tickets, such as the sought-after center box seats, can cost more than $200. There are many price tiers below that: for example, mid-range seats in the Family Circle might run about $80, and about 700 seats sell for closer to $30. Standing-room tickets for the week's performances go on sale on Saturday at 10 AM for even less. Weekday prices are slightly lower than weekend prices. Saturday matinee performances from December through the end of the season are broadcast live around the world on the Texaco-Metropolitan Opera International Radio Network.

Although not as widely known as the Met, the **New York City Opera** is just as vital to the city's operagoers as its more famous next-door neighbor. Under the leadership of artistic director Paul Kellogg, City Opera stages a diverse repertoire, including rarely seen baroque operas such as *Acis and Galatea* and *Rinaldo,* adventurous new works such as *Dead Man Walking,* and beloved classic operas such as *La Bohème, Carmen,* and the like. Placido Domingo and Beverly Sills began their careers at City Opera, and if recent performances from the likes of mezzo-soprano Joyce DiDonato are any indication, the next generation of great voices is following in their footsteps. City Opera performs from September through November and in March and April at Lincoln Center's **New York State Theater** (✉ W. 62nd St. at Columbus Ave., Upper West Side ☎ 212/870–5570 🌐 www.nycopera.com). All performances of foreign-language operas have supertitles—line-by-line English translations displayed above the stage.

Smaller Companies

The **Amato Opera Theatre** (✉ 319 Bowery, at E. 2nd St., East Village ☎ 212/228–8200) is an intimate, well-established showcase for rising singers. The theater seats only 107, and the performances of Verdi, Mozart, and other composers of the standard opera repertory are often sold out. **Brooklyn Academy of Music** is an outstanding venue for opera, particularly less famous baroque masterpieces by such composers as Rameau, Gluck, and Handel. **New York Gilbert and Sullivan Players** (✉ Symphony Space, 2537

Broadway, at W. 95th St., Upper West Side ☎ 212/769–1000; 212/864–5400 for box office) presents lively productions of Gilbert and Sullivan classics such as *Pirates of Penzance* and *The Mikado* performed with full orchestra. The **New York Grand Opera** (✉ 154 W. 57th St., near 7th Ave., Suite 125, Midtown West ☎ 212/245–8837) mounts free summer performances of operas by Verdi and other composers—with a full orchestra and professional singers—at Central Park SummerStage.

Opera aficionados should also keep track of the Carnegie Hall schedule for debuting singers and performances by the **Opera Orchestra of New York** (☎ 212/799–1982), which specializes in presenting concert versions of rarely performed operas, often with star soloists. A libretto of the opera is provided, and lights are kept up for those following along.

Theater

Broadway—not the Statue of Liberty or even the Empire State Building—is the city's number one tourist attraction. The renovation and restoration of some of the city's oldest and grandest theaters on and near 42nd Street has drawn New Yorkers' attention to the rebirth of Times Square. As in decades long past, everyone wants to be here, in the heart of the theater world.

The monthly **Broadway Theatre Guide,** published by the League of American Theatres and Producers is available at the Times Square Visitor Center (✉ 1560 Broadway, between W. 46th and W. 47th Sts., Midtown West); it may also be found at hotels around town. The **Broadway Line** (☎ 888/276–2392 toll-free; 212/302–4111 in CT, NJ, and NY) provides show times, plot summaries, theater addresses, and ticket prices. **NYC-ON STAGE** (☎ 212/768–1818), the Theatre Development Fund's 24-hour information service, covers performing arts events in all five boroughs. ***Time Out New York,*** a weekly newsstand "obsessive guide to impulsive entertainment," prints up-to-the minute Broadway, off-Broadway, and off-off-Broadway listings with reviews.

Playbill On-Line (🌐 www.playbill.com) is a good resource for both daily news and feature articles on Broadway and off-Broadway theater. It also links to the other theater-oriented sites, seating charts for all Broadway theaters, and access to discounts as well as Telecharge services. The magazine is available in hotels and theaters around town.

Broadway

To most people, New York theater means Broadway, that region roughly bounded by West 41st and West 52nd streets, between 7th and 9th avenues, where bright lights shine on newly restored theaters, gleaming entertainment complexes, theme stores, and restaurants. The names of the many theaters read like a roll call of American theater history: Edwin Booth, the Barrymores (Ethel, John, and Lionel), Eugene O'Neill, George Gershwin, Alfred Lunt and Lynn Fontanne, Helen Hayes, Richard Rodgers, and Neil Simon, among others.

Among the 40-odd theaters are some old playhouses as interesting for their history as for their current offerings. The handsomely renovated Selwyn is now known as the **American Airlines Theatre** (✉ 227 W. 42nd St., between 7th and 8th Aves., Midtown West ☎ 212/719–1300). After various reincarnations as a Venetian-style theater, burlesque hall, and pornographic movie house, it's now the home of the Roundabout Theatre Company, which is acclaimed for its revivals of classic plays and musicals.

The **Ford Center for the Performing Arts** (✉ 213–215 W. 43rd St., between 7th and 8th Aves., Midtown West ☎ 212/207–4100), a lavish 1,839-seat theater constructed on the site of two classic houses, the Lyric and the Apollo, incorporates original architectural elements from both theaters, along with state-of-the-art facilities to accommodate grand-scale musicals. The Walt Disney Company has refurbished the art nouveau **New Amsterdam** (✉ 214 W. 42nd St., between 7th and 8th Aves., Midtown West ☎ 212/282–2907), where Eddie Cantor, Will Rogers, Fanny Brice, and the Ziegfeld Follies once drew crowds. Today it's the den of *The Lion King*.

The **St. James** (✉ 246 W. 44th St., between Broadway and 8th Ave., Midtown West ☎ 212/269–6300), current home of Mel Brooks's juggernaut *The Producers,* is where Lauren Bacall was an usherette in the '40s and where a little show called *Oklahoma!* ushered in the era of the musical play.

Beyond Broadway

The best of New York theater is often found far away from 42nd Street. Off- and off-off-Broadway is where Eric Bogosian, Ann Magnuson, John Leguizamo, Danny Hoch, and Laurie Anderson often make their home. It's where you'll find crowd-pleasers such as the high-flying acrobatics of *De la Guarda* and the percussive dancing of *Stomp*. The longest-running play in American theater history, the romantic musical *The Fantasticks,* had its last curtain call at the Sullivan Street Playhouse in 2002, after 42 years.

In terms of quality and popularity, productions at many of the best-known off-Broadway theaters rival those seen in the larger houses on Broadway. In fact, some of Broadway's biggest hits had their start off-Broadway. Also off-Broadway you'll find venues staging performance art—a curious mélange of artistic disciplines blending music and sound, dance, video and lights, words, and whatever else comes to the performance artist's mind. The product is sometimes fascinating, sometimes stupefying. Performance art is almost exclusively a downtown, small-scale endeavor, although it's also showcased in the outer boroughs, especially Brooklyn.

The magazines and newspapers with a downtown orientation, such as *New York Press, New York Blade, Paper, Time Out New York,* the *Onion,* and the *Village Voice,* are an especially good source of information on what's going on off-off-Broadway and in performance art. Some off-Broadway venues sell tickets through the major agencies, but to obtain tickets to most off-off-Broadway and performance art events, contact the theater directly or try Ticket Central (212/279–4200).

The **Brooklyn Academy of Music** has built its considerable reputation on its annual **Next Wave Festival,** which takes place every November and December and stages avant-garde works of the highest professional standards. In the East Village the **Classic Stage Company** (✉ 136 E. 13th St., between 3rd and 4th Aves., East Village ☎ 212/239–6200) revives older works that still have relevance today. **De la Guarda** (✉ Daryl Roth Theatre, 20 Union Sq. E, at E. 15th St., Gramercy ☎ 212/239–6200), a wet and wild spectacle that mixes theater and circus, performs above and amidst an audience that stands and moves about during the entire show (children under eight are not permitted); purchase tickets through Telecharge.

The **Ensemble Studio Theatre** (✉ 549 W. 52nd St., between 10th and 11th Aves., Midtown West ☎ 212/247–3405), with its tried-and-true roster of players, develops new American plays. Each spring it presents a marathon of one-acts by prominent playwrights. **Here** (✉ 145 6th Ave., between Spring and Broome Sts., SoHo ☎ 212/647–0202 🌐 www.here.org) started in 1993 as a collaboration between two small theater companies and has grown into an arts center with café, art gallery, and three theaters. The company runs a free performance series sponsored by NBC that takes place from Monday through Thursday and is devoted to nurturing up-and-coming local performers.

With the help of its resident acting troupe, **Jean Cocteau Repertory** (✉ Bowery Lane Theatre, 330 Bowery, at Bond St., East Village ☎ 212/677–0060) revives classics by playwrights such as Beckett and Brecht. The **Joseph Papp Public Theater** (✉ 425 Lafayette St., south of Astor Pl., East Village ☎ 212/260–2400 🌐 www.publictheater.org) continues to present new, innovative theater. This is the theater whose productions of *Bring In 'Da Noise, Bring In 'Da Funk, The Wild Party,* and *On the Town* all went on to successful Broadway runs. In summer the Public heads to Central Park's **Delacorte Theater** (☎ 212/539–8750 [seasonal]) to mount free outdoor productions of plays by Shakespeare and others. Tickets for evening performances are distributed at around 1 PM on the day of the performance (to those who have been waiting several hours in line) downtown at the Public and uptown at the Delacorte. Ellen Stewart, also known—simply and elegantly—as La Mama, started the theater complex **La Mama E.T.C.** (✉ 74A E. 4th St., between Bowery and 2nd Ave., East Village ☎ 212/475–7710) in 1961. Over the past several decades, her East Village organization has branched out to import international innovators and has grown to include two theaters and a club. Productions include everything from African fables to new-wave opera to reinterpretations of the Greek classics. Past triumphs have included the original productions of *Godspell* and *Torch Song Trilogy.*

Manhattan Theatre Club (✉ City Center, 131 W. 55th St., between 6th and 7th Aves., Midtown West ☎ 212/581–1212 🌐 www.mtc-nyc.org), with two stages in the basement of City Center, presents some of the most talked-about new plays and musicals in town. Always interesting and often controversial works by Terrence McNally, Athol Fugard, August Wilson, and A. R. Gurney were all produced here. Call ahead, as most of the tickets go to subscribers. In the fall of 2003, MTC plans to also mount shows at the Biltmore Theatre. Lincoln Center's intimate 299-seat **Mitzi E. Newhouse** (✉ Lincoln Center, 150 W. 65th St., at Broadway, Upper West Side ☎ 212/239–6200 🌐 www.lct.org) stages slightly edgier works than the Broadway-size Vivian Beaumont upstairs, but it's not unusual for popular shows such as Tony-winning *Contact* to move from the Newhouse to the Beaumont.

The **New York Theater Workshop** (✉ 79 E. 4th St., between 2nd and 3rd Aves., East Village ☎ 212/460–5475 🌐 www.nytw.org) produces new work by playwrights such as Paul Rudnick, Tony Kushner, and Claudia Shear, whose play about Mae West, *Dirty Blonde,* premiered here before heading to Broadway. Jonathan Larson's musical, *Rent,* debuted here in 1996 before moving within three months to Broadway's Nederlander Theater. Hailed by the *New York Times* as "a first-class magician of the avant-garde," Richard Foreman oversees the **Ontological-Hysteric Theater** (✉ St. Mark's Church-in-the-Bowery, 131 E. 10th St., at 2nd Ave., East Village ☎ 212/533–4650), whose unconventional productions illuminate the human condition, often exploring the realm of dreams and nightmares. In summer the theater sponsors the Blueprint Series, which allows novice directors to test their skills in front of an audience.

Playwrights Horizons (✉ 416 W. 42nd St., between 9th and 10th Aves., Midtown West ☎ 212/564–1235 🌐 www.playwrightshorizons.org) produces promising new works, and it has the Pulitzers to prove it—for the plays *Driving Miss Daisy* and *The Heidi Chronicles* and the musical *Sunday in the Park with George*. The **Signature Theatre Company** (✉ 555 W. 42nd St., between 10th and 11th Aves., Midtown West ☎ 212/244–7529 🌐 www.signaturetheatre.org) devotes each season to works by a single playwright; past luminaries have included Lanford Wilson, Sam Shepard, and Maria Irene Fornes.

A four-theater cultural complex is home to the **Theater for the New City** (✉ 155 1st Ave., between E. 9th and E. 10th Sts., East Village ☎ 212/254–1109), which devotes its experimental productions to new playwrights. The complex also sponsors a free street-theater program, arts festivals, and a Christmas spectacular. The **Vineyard Theater** (✉ 108 E. 15th St., between Park Ave. S and Irving Pl., Gramercy ☎ 212/353–3366 🌐 www.vineyardtheatre.org), one of the best-regarded off-Broadway companies, knows how to pick a winner. Its productions of Paula Vogel's *How I Learned to Drive* and Edward Albee's *Three Tall Women* both won Pulitzers.

Theater for Children

Miss Majesty's Lollipop Playhouse (✉ Grove Street Playhouse, 39 Grove St., between W. 4th St. and 7th Ave. S, Greenwich Village ☎ 212/741–6436) brings fairy tales and nursery rhymes to life on weekend afternoons. **New Victory Theater** (✉ 209 W. 42nd St., between 7th and 8th Aves., Midtown West ☎ 646/223–3020 🌐 www.newvictory.org) programs plays, musical performances, and even mini-circuses. The **Paper Bag Players** (✉ The Kaye Playhouse, E. 68th St. between Park and Lexington Aves., Upper East Side ☎ 212/772–4448), the longest-running children's theater group in the nation, stages plays for children under 10. **Tada!** (✉ 120 W. 28th St., between 6th and 7th Aves., Chelsea ☎ 212/627–1732) is a popular children's group with a multiethnic perspective. **Theaterworks–USA** (✉ Promenade Theater, Broadway at W. 76th St., Upper West Side ☎ 212/647–1100) mounts original productions based on well-known children's books.

THE CIRCUS In addition to the big traveling shows that visit the city throughout the year, New York has three circuses of its very own. The **Big Apple Circus** (✉ Lincoln Center Plaza, Upper West Side ☎ 212/721–6500 or 800/922–3772 🌐 www.bigapplecircus.org) entertains kids and their families both in New York and in shows around the country. Sometimes the world-renowned **Cirque du Soleil** (🌐 www.cirquedusoleil.com) visits New York, and **Ringling Bros. and Barnum & Bailey Circus** (🌐 www.ringling.com) pitches its tents in Madison Square Garden in March. Look in the newspaper for dates, times, and ticket information.

PUPPET SHOWS **Marionette Theater** (✉ Swedish Cottage, W. Park Dr. north of 79th St. Transverse, Central Park ☎ 212/988–9093) entertains children Tuesday–Friday at 10:30 and noon, and Saturday at 1 (no Saturday show July–August); call for reservations. **Puppet Playhouse** (✉ Asphalt Green, 555 E. 90th St., between York and East End Aves., Upper West Side ☎ 212/369–8890) presents weekend shows of puppets and marionettes. The wooden marionettes at **Puppetworks** (✉ 338 6th Ave., at 4th St., Park Slope, Brooklyn ☎ 718/965–3391) perform classic children's stories in a 75-seat theater. Reservations are required for the weekend shows at 12:30 and 2:30.

READINGS & LECTURES

New York is still the center of American publishing, and as a result many writers find reason to settle here. Literary figures great and small personally share their work at the dozens of New York readings held each week. Readings sponsored by distinguished groups such as the Academy of American Poets, Dia Center for the Arts, the Poetry Project, the Poetry Society of America, and Poets House bring out some of the top names in contemporary literature, including John Updike, Don DeLillo, Toni Morrison, Frank McCourt, Philip Roth, and Kazuo Ishiguro. Readings in bookstores, libraries, bars, and theaters often are a chance to catch debuting talents. Authors read their recently published books at stores such as Barnes & Noble, Borders, Shakespeare & Co., Three Lives & Co., Urban Books, and Housing Works Used Book Café.

Informal poetry readings, sometimes with an open-mike policy that allows audience members to read their own work, crop up with frequency in coffeehouses and bars. These events are fairly popular, particularly with a younger crowd. There may be a low cover charge ($2–$5), and food and drink are usually available. For information on poetry readings around town, check the listings in *New York* magazine, *New York Press,* the *New Yorker, Time Out New York,* and the *Village Voice.*

★ "Poetry Czar" Bob Holman's **Bowery Poetry Club** (✉ 308 Bowery, at Bleecker St., Lower East Side ☎ 212/614–0505 🌐 www.bowerypoetry.com) serves up coffee and knishes along with its ingenious poetry events. Expect every permutation of the spoken word—and art and music, too.

The **Cornelia Street Café** (✉ 29 Cornelia St., between W. 4th and Bleecker Sts., Greenwich Village ☎ 212/989–9319) is a good bet for original poetry and fiction readings.

Dixon Place (✉ 258 Bowery, between Houston and Prince Sts., Lower East Side ☎ 212/219–0736 🌐 www.dixonplace.org), back down in its old location, sponsors readings regularly, some of which border on performance art.

One of the most influential and avant-garde reading series around town is **Nightlight**, held one Wednesday a month at the **Drawing Center** (✉ 35 Wooster St., between Grand and Broome Sts., SoHo ☎ 212/219–2166), an art space in SoHo. The **Ear Inn** (✉ 326 Spring St., between Greenwich and Washington Sts., SoHo ☎ 212/226–9060) holds poetry readings on Saturday afternoons.

For readings by gay and lesbian authors, contact the **Gay and Lesbian Community Services Center** (✉ 208 W. 13th St., between 6th and 7th Aves., West Village ☎ 212/620–7310), which sponsors readings by some of New York's—and the world's—most prominent gay writers.

The Kitchen (✉ 512 W. 19th St., between 10th and 11th Aves., Chelsea ☎ 212/255–5793 🌐 www.thekitchen.org) presents readings from the edges of the literary world. The **Knitting Factory** (✉ 74 Leonard St., between Broadway and Church Sts., TriBeCa ☎ 212/219–3055 🌐 www.knittingfactory.com) is a three-story arts complex that hosts a variety of spoken word and musical performances.

Makor (✉ 35 W. 67th St., between Central Park W and Columbus Ave., Upper West Side ☎ 212/601–1000 🌐 www.makor.org) is a sleek Jewish cultural arts center with excellent literary events geared toward a crowd in their twenties and thirties.

In its City Center home, **Manhattan Theatre Club** (✉ 131 W. 55th St., between 6th and 7th Aves., Midtown West ☎ 212/581–1212 🌐 www.mtc-nyc.org) sponsors **Writers in Performance**, a provocative program of dramatic readings and roundtable discussions that showcase novelists, poets, and playwrights from the United States and abroad.

Several branches of the New York Public Library present lectures and reading events. A monthly calendar of free library readings is available at each branch. A major reading and talk series is held at the **New York Public Library for the Performing Arts** (✉ 150 W. 65th St., between Columbus and Amsterdam Aves., Upper West Side ☎ 212/870–1630), at Lincoln Center, specializing in presentations by musicians, directors, singers, and actors. **The New Yorker Festival** (☎ 877/847–8693 🌐 festival.newyorker.com), held every fall since 2000, has become a must-attend event. Venues for readings, performances, discussions, and interviews are sprinkled throughout the city. Call for tickets early—they go fast. The **Nuyorican Poets Café** (✉ 236 E. 3rd St., between Aves. B and C, East Village ☎ 212/505–8183 🌐 www.nuyorican.org) schedules daily readings and hosts a Poetry Slam competition each Friday (you'll also find Latin jazz, comedy, and play readings here).

★ Authors, lyricists, playwrights, and poets take the stage at the **92nd St. Y** (✉ 1395 Lexington Ave., at E. 92nd St., Upper East Side ☎ 212/415–5500 🌐 www.92ndsty.org). A number of readings are held at **Symphony Space** (✉ 2537 Broadway, at W. 95th St., Upper West Side ☎ 212/864–5400 🌐 www.symphonyspace.org), including the Selected Shorts series of stories read by prominent actors and broadcast on National Public Radio.

ART GALLERIES

As America's art capital, New York has hundreds of galleries and thousands of artists. Exhibitions showcase artists ranging from established names, whose works can also be seen in major museum collections, to art-school graduates making their debut in group shows. Both midtown (5th Avenue and 57th Street) and the Upper East Side (the East 60s and 70s) have clusters of galleries showing anything from old masters to contemporary art. The most cutting-edge galleries, once concentrated in SoHo, have now migrated to the converted industrial spaces in Chelsea (in the West through the 20s, between 10th and 11th avenues) and have trickled south into the Meatpacking District in the West Village. Chic restaurants, bars, and haute-couture stores have followed in the galleries' footsteps here as well as in the East Village and the Lower East Side, where a hotbed of small start-up galleries is reestablishing a beachhead. Displaying work from emerging artists, the East Side galleries have a focus similar to the solid art scene that's been established in Brooklyn's Williamsburg, Greenpoint, and DUMBO sections.

Most Manhattan galleries are open Tuesday through Saturday. Brooklyn galleries are mostly open Friday through Sunday. To find out what's on view, consult the listings in *Time Out New York* or the *Village Voice*. Another helpful resource is the *Art Now Gallery Guide* (🌐 www.galleryguide.org), available at newsstands and in many galleries.

SoHo & TriBeCa

Ace. Just west of SoHo proper, Ace is a cavernous space where contemporary artists present large-scale works. Recent shows have included work by Sylvie Fleury, John Armleder, and fashion designer Issey Miyake. ✉ *275 Hudson St., between Spring and Canal Sts., SoHo* ☎ *212/255–5599.*

Art in General. This nonprofit organization often presents group exhibitions organized by guest curators. ✉ *79 Walker St., between Broadway and Lafayette St., TriBeCa* ☎ *212/219–0473* 🌐 *www.artingeneral.org.*

Deitch Projects. This energetic enterprise composed of two gallery spaces usually shows an emerging must-see plucked from the global art scene. Artists on view have included Cecily Brown, Teresita Fernandez, and Shazia Sikhander. ✉ *76 Grand St., between Greene and Wooster Sts., SoHo* ☎ *212/343–7300* ✉ *18 Wooster St., at Grand St., SoHo* ☎ *212/343–7300.*

Dia Center for the Arts: New York Earth Room. Conceptual artist Walter De Maria's installation, on view since 1977, consists of 250 cubic yards of dirt piled 22 inches deep. It's sublime. ✉ *141 Wooster St., between Houston and Prince Sts., SoHo* ☎ *212/473–8072* 🌐 *www.diacenter.org.*

Drawing Center. This nonprofit organization focuses on contemporary and historical sketches. Surprising works often push the envelope on what's considered drawing. ✉ *35 Wooster St., between Broome and Grand Sts., SoHo* ☎ *212/219–2166* 🌐 *www.drawingcenter.org.*

Howard Greenberg Gallery. This spot concentrates on vintage photographic art of all genres, from modernism, to photojournalism and street photography, to images created for advertising and industry. The adjacent Gallery 292, a more intimate space, houses portfolios, limited editions, and rare photography books. ✉ *120 Wooster St., between Prince and Spring Sts., SoHo* ☎ *212/334–0010* 🌐 *www.howardgreenberg.com.*

Nancy Hoffman. Contemporary painting, sculpture, drawing, prints, and photographic works by an impressive array of international artists are on display here. Gallery artists range from Robert Deese, known for his conceptual shaped canvases, to Yuko Shiraishi, whose abstract oil paintings explore different tones of a single color. ✉ *429 W. Broadway, between Prince and Spring Sts., SoHo* ☎ *212/966–6676* 🌐 *www.nancyhoffmangallery.com.*

OK Harris. This SoHo stalwart hosts a wide range of visual arts, from paintings to digitally enhanced photographs to trompe l'oeil reliefs, as well as antiques and collectibles. ✉ *383 W. Broadway, between Spring and Broome Sts., SoHo* ☎ *212/431–3600* 🌐 *www.okharris.com.*

Tony Shafrazi. Shafrazi is the exclusive representative of the estate of the painter Francis Bacon. Among the other artists shown here are Keith Haring, Dennis Hopper, Michael Ray Charles, and David LaChapelle. ✉ *119 Wooster St., between Prince and Spring Sts., SoHo* ☎ *212/274–9300.*

Lower East Side

ABC No Rio. Founded in 1980, this granddaddy of Lower East Side galleries exhibits art that is political in content and powerful in its imagery. ✉ *156 Rivington St., between Clinton and Suffolk Sts., Lower East Side* ☎ *212/254–3697* 🌐 *www.abcnorio.org.*

ATM Gallery. Smartly curated shows (by artist William Brady) include new and established artists, from paintings by Nancy Spero and the luminous photos of Benjamin Collier to sculptor-printmaker Peter Gourfain's razor-sharp engravings and Vince Roark's geometric drawings. ✉ *170 Ave. B, between 10th and 11th Sts., East Village* ☎ *212/375–0349* 🌐 *www.ATMGallery.com.*

★ **Gallery Onetwentyeight.** Inside the jewel-box space, artist Kazuko Miyamoto directs crisp and provocative group shows, such as the 2001 "Fetishistic," and solo forums, such as 2002's Steve Kwon show with its clean, yet compelling pencil drawings. ✉ *128 Rivington St., between Essex and Norfolk Sts., Lower East Side* ☎ *212/674–0244.*

Rivington Arms. A tiny space with a quirky and casual mind-set, this gallery shows pieces such as the photographic-sound works of collective Lansing-Dreiden and portrait paintings (on felt) by Jonah Koppel. ✉ *102 Rivington St., between Essex and Ludlow Sts., Lower East Side* ☎ *646/654–3213.*

The Scene Gallery. Opened in 2000, this fresh face on the western fringe of the Lower East Side art scene staged avant-garde collagist Charles Henri Ford's show in the lively spirit of his work; other shows are selected from an international group of artists working in a mix of media, from film and photography to sculpture and drawing, and include Godfried Donkor, Kaori Ukaji, and Julie Dogra-Brazell. ✉ *42 Rivington St., between Eldridge and Forsyth Sts., Lower East Side* ☎ *212/674–0508.*

Chelsea

Andrea Rosen. The gallery showcases young artists on the cutting edge, such as sculptor Andrea Zittel, painter John Currin, and photographer Wolfgang Tillmans. Most every form of artistic expression—from painting to film to performance—is explored here. ✉ *525 W. 24th St., between 10th and 11th Aves., Chelsea* ☎ *212/627–6000* 🌐 *www.andrearosengallery.com.*

Barbara Gladstone. Gladstone, the quintessential SoHo style maker, shows a range of interesting contemporary work, with paintings by Lari Pittman, photographs by Sharon Lockhart, and video by Gary Hill. ✉ *515 W. 24th St., between 10th and 11th Aves., Chelsea* ☎ *212/206–9300* 🌐 *www.gladstonegallery.com.*

Casey Kaplan. Kaplan has a keen eye for conceptual artists from around the globe. Among them is Anna Gaskell, who has made photos of young girls dressed in costume and engaged in some menacing but inexplicable activity. ✉ *416 W. 14th St., between 9th and 10th Aves., Chelsea* ☎ *212/645–7335* 🌐 *www.caseykaplangallery.com.*

Cheim & Read. This prestigious gallery represents modern painters and photographers such as Louise Bourgeois, and shows work by the late Jean-Michel Basquiat, Andy Warhol, and Diane Arbus. ✉ *547 W. 25th St., between 10th and 11th Aves., Chelsea* ☎ *212/242–7727.*

Fodor's Choice ★ **Clementine.** Works from artists to keep your eye on—especially painters and photographers—are shown in this intimate Chelsea spot, a favorite of cutting-edge connoisseurs. ✉ *526 W. 26th St., between 10th and 11th Aves., Chelsea* ☎ *212/243–5937* 🌐 *www.clementine-gallery.com.*

David Zwirner. Proving his finger is on the pulse of contemporary art, Zwirner shows works in all media by such emerging artists as Luc Tuymans, Stan Douglas, Thomas Ruff, Diana Thater, and Yutaka Sone, as well as such contemporary masters as Cy Twombly and Georg Baselitz. ✉ *525 W. 19th St., between 10th and 11th Aves., Chelsea* ☎ *212/727–2070* 🌐 *www.davidzwirner.com.*

Gagosian. This enterprising modern gallery has two branches in New York City, one in Beverly Hills, and one in London, all presenting works by heavy hitters, such as sculptor Richard Serra and the late pop art icon Roy Lichtenstein. ✉ *555 W. 24th St., at 11th Ave., Chelsea* ☎ *212/741–1111* ✉ *980 Madison Ave., between E. 76th and E. 77th Sts., Upper East Side* ☎ *212/744–2313* 🌐 *www.gagosian.com.*

Galerie Lelong. This Paris-based gallery, which in 2001 moved from its West 57th Street location to its new Chelsea digs, presents challenging installations such as Alfred Jaar's 2002 "Lament of the Images" and works by Andy Goldsworthy, Cildo Meireles, and Petah Coyne, among others. ✉ *528 W. 26th St., between 10th and 11th Aves., Chelsea* ☎ *212/315–0470.*

Chelsea

Andrea Rosen 12
Barbara Gladstone 6
Casey Kaplan 23
Cheim & Read 11
Clementine 4
David Zwirner 19
Gagosian 7
Galerie Lelong 4
Gavin Brown's Enterprise 22
Holly Solomon 20
Jack Shaiman 18
JG/Contemporary 2
Luhring Augustine 8
Marlborough 21
Mary Boone 9
Matthew Marks ...10, 15
Metro Pictures 6
Pace Wildenstein 5
Paula Cooper 16
Robert Miller 3
Sean Kelley 1
Sonnabend 13
Tanya Bonakdar 17
303 14

SoHo

Ace 24
Art in General 31
Deitch Projects 30
Drawing Center 29
Howard Greenberg 27
Nancy Hoffman 26
OK Harris 28
Tony Shafrazi 25

Gavin Brown's Enterprise. Smart and lively, this space has hosted the avant-garde performances of the duo of German artist-musicians, Fischerspooner, and a flea market for upstart artists selling both their clutter and their art. You can ruminate about the art at Passersby, a bar that Brown opened next door. ✉ *436 W. 15th St., between 9th and 10th Aves., Chelsea* ☎ *212/627–5258.*

Holly Solomon. Solomon's foresight is legendary—she was an early champion of photographer Robert Mapplethorpe—and now she shows works by artists such as William Wegman and Nick Waplington. ✉ *Room 425, Chelsea Hotel, 222 W. 23rd St., between 7th and 8th Aves., Chelsea* ☎ *212/941–5777.*

Jack Shainman. Both emerging and established artists are shown here. You might find works by Phil Frost, whose imagery is derived from graffiti. The duo of Aziz + Cucher make digital photos of figures with erased features, suggesting body imaging gone awry. ✉ *513 W. 20th St., between 10th and 11th Aves., Chelsea* ☎ *212/645–1701.*

JG/Contemporary. In the northernmost reaches of Chelsea, this gallery always surprises with contemporary artists ranging from the internationally established Dutch painter Karel Appel to Patrick Strzelec, who uses colored cast rubber tubes to define spatial relationships. ✉ *505 W. 28th St., between 10th and 11th Aves., Chelsea* ☎ *212/564–7662* 🌐 *www.jaygrimm.com.*

Luhring Augustine. Since 1985 owners Lawrence Luhring and Roland Augustine have worked with established and less well-known artists from Europe, Japan, and America. ✉ *531 W. 24th St., between 10th and 11th Aves., Chelsea* ☎ *212/206–9100* 🌐 *www.luhringaugustine.com.*

Mary Boone. A hot SoHo gallery during the 1980s, this venue now resides both uptown and in the newer flash point of Chelsea. Boone continues to show established artists such as Barbara Kruger and Eric Fischl, as well as newcomers Tom Sachs and Micha Klein. ✉ *541 W. 24th St., between 10th and 11th Aves., Chelsea* ☎ *212/752–2929* ✉ *745 5th Ave., 4th floor, between E. 57th and 58th Sts., Midtown East* ☎ *212/752–2929* 🌐 *www.maryboonegallery.com.*

Matthew Marks. At two Chelsea spaces Marks, one of the most influential art dealers in New York, shows prominent modern artists such as the painters Ellsworth Kelly and Willem de Kooning, as well as up-to-the-minute luminaries such as photographers Andreas Gursky, Inez van Lamsweerde, and Sam Taylor-Wood. ✉ *522 W. 22nd St., between 10th and 11th Aves., Chelsea* ☎ *212/243–0200* ✉ *523 W. 24th St., between 10th and 11th Aves., Chelsea* ☎ *212/243–0200* 🌐 *www.matthewmarks.com.*

Metro Pictures. The hottest talents in contemporary art shown here include Cindy Sherman, whose provocative and often disturbing photographs have brought her international prominence. ✉ *519 W. 24th St., between 10th and 11th Aves., Chelsea* ☎ *212/206–7100.*

Paula Cooper. SoHo pioneer Paula Cooper moved to Chelsea in 1996 and enlisted architect Richard Gluckman to transform a warehouse into a dramatic space with tall ceilings and handsome skylights. Now she has two galleries on the same block that showcase the minimalist sculptures of Carl André, the dot paintings of Yayoi Kusama, and the provocative photos of Andres Serrano, among other works. ✉ *534 W. 21st St., between 10th and 11th Aves., Chelsea* ☎ *212/255–1105* ✉ *521 W. 21st St., between 10th and 11th Aves., Chelsea* ☎ *212/255–5247.*

Robert Miller. Miller, a titan of the New York art world, represents the estates of some of the biggest names in modern painting and photography, such as Joan Mitchell, Robert Mapplethorpe, and Diane Arbus. ✉ *524 W. 26th St., between 10th and 11th Aves., Chelsea* ☎ *212/366–4774* 🌐 *www.robertmillergallery.com.*

Sean Kelly. Drop in here for works by top contemporary American and European artists including Marina Abramovic, Ann Hamilton, Cathy de Monchaux, and James Casebere. ✉ *528 W. 29th St., between 10th and 11th Aves., Chelsea* ☎ *212/239–1181* 🌐 *www.skny.com.*

Sonnabend. This pioneer of the SoHo art scene continues to show important contemporary artists in its Chelsea space, including Jeff Koons, Ashley Bickerton, and Californian conceptualist John Baldessari. ✉ *536 W. 22nd St., between 10th and 11th Aves., Chelsea* ☎ *212/627–1018.*

Tanya Bonakdar. This gallery presents such contemporary artists as Uta Barth, whose blurry photos challenge ideas about perception, and Ernesto Neto, a Brazilian artist who has made stunning room-size installations of large nylon sacks filled with spices. ✉ *521 W. 21st St., between 10th and 11th Aves., Chelsea* ☎ *212/414–4144* 🌐 *www.tanyabonakdargallery.com.*

303. International cutting-edge artists including photographers Doug Aitken, painter Sue Williams, and installation artist Karen Kilimnik are displayed here. ✉ *525 W. 22nd St., between 10th and 11th Aves., Chelsea* ☎ *212/255–1121* 🌐 *www.303gallery.com.*

Midtown–57th Street

David Findlay Jr. Fine Art. This gallery concentrates on American 19th- and 20th-century painters from John Singer Sargent to Arthur Dove to Andrew Wyeth. ✉ *41 E. 57th St., 11th floor, between 5th and Madison Aves., Midtown East* ☎ *212/486–7660.*

★ **Edwynn Houk.** The impressive stable of 20th-century photographers here includes Sally Mann, Lynn Davis, and Brassaï. The gallery also has prints by masters Edward Weston and Alfred Steiglitz. ✉ *745 5th Ave., between E. 57th and E. 58th Sts., Midtown East* ☎ *212/750–7070* 🌐 *www.houkgallery.com.*

Joseph Helman. Contemporary masters such as Claes Oldenburg, Robert Moskowitz, Joe Andoe, and Tom Wesselman are shown here. ✉ *20 W. 57th St., between 5th and 6th Aves., Midtown West* ☎ *212/245–2888.*

Lawrence Rubin Greenberg Van Doren Fine Art. This photography gallery continues to intrigue by featuring the works of young photographers or glamorous party pictures from Studio 54 to Cannes. ✉ *730 5th Ave., at E. 57th St., Midtown East* ☎ *212/445–0444.*

Marian Goodman. The excellent contemporary art here includes Jeff Wall's staged photographs presented on light boxes, South African artist William Kentridge's video animations, and Rebecca Horn's mechanized sculptures. A second gallery opened in Paris in 2000. ✉ *24 W. 57th St., between 5th and 6th Aves., Midtown West* ☎ *212/977–7160* 🌐 *www.mariangoodman.com.*

Marlborough. With galleries in London, Monte Carlo, Madrid, Santiago, and Boca Raton, the Marlborough empire also operates one of the largest and most influential galleries in New York City. The gallery represents modern artists such as Alex Katz, Magdalena Abakanowicz, and Paula Rego, and publishes prints by important 20th-century artists including Matisse, Picasso, Hockney, Johns, and Rauschenberg. ✉ *40 W. 57th St., between 5th and 6th Aves., Midtown West* ☎ *212/541–4900* ✉ *211 W. 19th St., between 7th and 8th Aves., Chelsea* ☎ *212/463–8634* 🌐 *www.marlboroughgallery.com.*

Pace Wildenstein. The giant gallery focuses on such modern and contemporary painters as Piet Mondrian, Julian Schnabel, and New York School painter Ad Reinhardt. Upstairs is **Pace Prints** (☎ 212/421–3237), where you can rifle through open racks of prints by artists such as Richard Diebenkorn, David Hockney, and Kiki Smith. Pace closed its SoHo location and moved much of its contents to its Chelsea space, which concentrates on up-to the minute contemporary artists, sculptors, and photographers. ✉ *32 E. 57th St., between Park and Madison Aves., Midtown East* ☎ *212/421–3292* ✉ *534 W. 25th St., between 10th and 11th Aves., Chelsea,* ☎ *212/929–7000.*

Peter Findlay. Covering 19th- and 20th-century works by European artists, this gallery shows pieces by Mary Cassatt, Paul Klee, and Alberto Giacometti. ✉ *41 E. 57th St., at Madison Ave., Midtown East* ☎ *212/644–4433* 🌐 *www.findlay.com.*

Spanierman. This venerable gallery deals in 19th- and early-20th-century American painting and sculpture. ✉ *45 E. 58th St., between Park and Madison Aves., Midtown East* ☎ *212/832–0208* 🌐 *www.Spanierman.com.*

Tibor de Nagy. Founded in 1950, this reputable gallery shows work by 20th-century artists such as Arthur Dove, Georgia O'Keeffe, Allen Ginsberg, and Trevor Winkfield. ✉ *724 5th Ave., between W. 56th and W. 57th Sts., Midtown West* ☎ *212/262–5050* 🌐 *www.tibordenagy.com.*

Upper East Side

David Findlay. Descend into a warren of rooms to view contemporary, color-soaked paintings. Represented artists include Pierre Lesieur, Roger Mühl, and (for a striking slice of New York streets) Tom Christopher. ✉ *984 Madison Ave., between E. 76th and E. 77th Sts., Upper East Side* ☎ *212/249–2909* 🌐 *www.davidfindlaygalleries.com.*

Hirschl & Adler. Although this gallery has a selection of European works, it is best known for its American paintings, prints, and decorative arts. Among the celebrated 19th- and 20th-century artists whose works are featured are: Thomas Cole, Frederick Church, Childe Hassam, John Storrs, and William Merritt Chase. ✉ *21 E. 70th St., between 5th and Madison Aves., Upper East Side* ☎ *212/535–8810* 🌐 *www.HirschlandAdler.com.*

Jane Kahan. Besides ceramics by Picasso (this gallery's specialty), you'll see works by 19th- and 20th-century artists such as Fernand Léger, Joan Miró, and Marc Chagall. ✉ *922 Madison Ave., between E. 73rd and E. 74th Sts., Upper East Side* ☎ *212/744–1490* 🌐 *www.janekahan.com.*

Knoedler & Company. Knoedler helped many great American collectors, including industrialist Henry Clay Frick, start their collections. Now its represented artists include 20th-century painters Helen Frankenthaler, Sean Scully, Donald Sultan, and John Walker. ✉ *19 E. 70th St., between 5th and Madison Aves., Upper East Side* ☎ *212/794–0550.*

★ **Leo Castelli.** Castelli, who passed away in 1999, was one of the most influential dealers of the 20th century. An early supporter of pop, minimalist, and conceptual art, he helped foster the careers of many important artists, including one of his first discoveries, Jasper Johns. The gallery moved here from SoHo and continues to show works by Roy Lichtenstein, Ed Ruscha, Jackson Pollock, and others. ✉ *59 E. 79th St., between Madison and Park Aves., Upper East Side* ☎ *212/249–4470* 🌐 *www.castelligallery.com.*

Margo Feiden. Illustrations by the late theatrical caricaturist Al Hirschfeld, who delighted readers of the *New York Times* for more than 60 years, are the draw here. ✉ *699 Madison Ave., between E. 62nd and E. 63rd Sts., Upper East Side* ☎ *212/677–5330* 🌐 *www.alhirschfeld.com.*

Michael Werner. This German art dealer mounts smart shows of such early-20th-century masters as Marcel Duchamp, Francis Picabia, and Henri Michaux in his refined, East Side town house. ✉ *4 E. 77th St., between 5th and Madison Aves., Upper East Side* ☎ *212/988–1623.*

Mitchell-Innes & Nash. This sleek spot specializing in contemporary, impressionist, and modern art presents the estates of Willem de Kooning,

Upper East Side
David Findlay . . 4
Gagosian 5
Hirschl & Adler 8
Jane Kahan 6
Knoedler & Company 7
Leo Castelli 1
Margo Feiden . 10
Michael Werner 3
Mitchell-Innes & Nash 2
Wildenstein & Co. 9

57th Street
David Findlay Jr. Fine Art 13
Edwynn Houk . 12
Joseph Helman 18
Lawrence Rubin Greenberg Van Doren Fine Art 15
Marian Goodman 17
Marlborough . 16
Mary Boone . . 12
Pace Wildenstein . . 14
Peter Findlay . 13
Spanierman . . 11
Tibor de Nagy 19

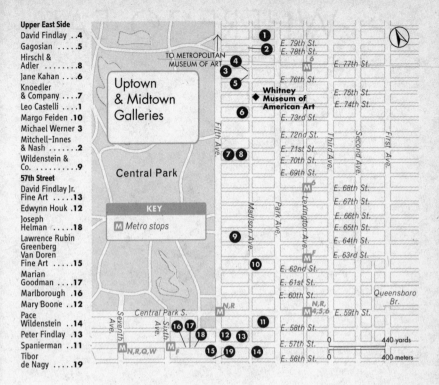

Tony Smith, and Jack Tworkov. ✉ *1018 Madison Ave., between 78th and 79th Sts., Upper East Side* ☎ *212/744–7400* 🌐 *www.miandn.com.*

Wildenstein & Co. This branch of the Wildenstein art empire was the first to take root in New York; its reputation for brilliant holdings was cemented by the acquisition of significant private museum-quality collections. Look for impressionist exhibitions. ✉ *19 E. 64th St., between 5th and Madison Aves., Upper East Side* ☎ *212/879–0500* 🌐 *www.wildenstein.com.*

Brooklyn

Bellwether. This nonprofit gallery started by a group of disenfranchised Yale graduates hosts shows by emerging and established local artists. ✉ *355 Grand St., between Havermeyer St. and Marcy Ave., Williamsburg* ☎ *718/387–3701* 🌐 *www.bellwethergallery.com.*

GAle GAtes et al. This warehouse space presents changing exhibitions that range from film, to theatrical projects, to sculpture, to performance art, to you name it. ✉ *37 Main St., between Front and Water Sts., DUMBO* ☎ *718/522–4596.*

Momenta Art. This artist-run, not-for-profit space presents changing exhibitions with a focus on emerging artists. ✉ *72 Berry St., between N. 9th and N. 10th Sts., Williamsburg* ☎ *718/218–8058* 🌐 *www.momentaart.org.*

Pierogi 2000. Here you'll find mostly solo shows of Williamsburg artists. Check out the Pierogi flatfiles, an installation that has been around the world—and back. ✉ *177 N. 9th St., between Bedford and Driggs Aves., Williamsburg* ☎ *718/599–2144* 🌐 *www.pierogi2000.com.*

WHERE TO EAT

4

FODOR'S CHOICE

Babbo, *Greenwich Village*
Craft, *Flatiron District*
Daniel, *Upper East Side*
Gotham Bar & Grill, *Greenwich Village*
Gramercy Tavern, *Flatiron District*
Jean-Georges, *Upper West Side*
Le Bernardin, *Midtown West*
Nobu, *TriBeCa*
Peter Luger Steak House, *Brooklyn*
Union Pacific, *Flatiron District*

HIGHLY RECOMMENDED

Aquavit, *Midtown West*
Blue Ribbon, *SoHo, Brooklyn*
Café Boulud, *Upper East Side*
Churrascaria Plataforma, *Midtown West*
Eleven Madison Park, *Flatiron District*
Ghenet, *NoLita*
JUdson Grill, *Midtown West*
Kuruma Zushi, *Midtown East*
Lombardi's, *Little Italy*
Magnolia Bakery, *Greenwich Village*
Maya, *Upper East Side*
Moustache, *Greenwich Village, East Village*
Pearl Oyster Bar, *Greenwich Village*
Picholine, *Upper West Side*
rm, *Upper East Side*
71 Clinton Fresh Food, *Lower East Side*
Sweet 'n' Tart Café & Restaurant, *Chinatown*
Takahachi, *East Village*
Veritas, *Flatiron District*

Updated By
Lesa Griffith
and Tom Steele

THE CITY'S LINGERING ECONOMIC doldrums have put a pinch on New Yorkers' purses, but not their voracious appetite for eating out. Because besides satisfying a taste for the finer things in life, restaurants serve Gothamites in other crucial ways. They are a key to exploring the city (the hunt through Queens streets for a bite after visiting MoMA QNS), a communication tool ("Let me tell you about this great little Thai place"), a source of cocktail-party one-upmanship ("You haven't been to Craft yet?!"), and act as extensions of minute kitchens and nonexistent dining rooms.

In a (dollar) sign of the times, a slew of mid-range restaurants serving well-executed soul-satisfying food have opened, such as Pfiff and Voyage. In addition, a wave of makeovers has made some haute eateries more accessible and affordable; for example, Alva morphed into the wildly popular Kitchen 22, featuring a wallet-friendly $25 prix-fixe menu.

Still, New York is about extremes, and although unemployment is at a high, the metropolis remains a mecca of the monied (after all, it's led by a billionaire mayor). So pricey menus haven't stopped new celebrity-chef restaurants such as Washington Park, L'Impero, and rm from opening and becoming hits.

Whether you decide to go for a steaming bowl of noodles in Chinatown or a chichi brasserie uptown, note that some of the dishes recommended in the following reviews may not be on the menu you receive when you sit down to eat. Chefs often change their menus with the season and with the availability of ingredients in the market. Use our recommendations as guidelines and you won't be disappointed.

MANHATTAN RESTAURANTS

Lower Manhattan

While the Financial District's post–September 11 physical recovery was remarkably speedy, psychologically the turnaround took a while—New Yorkers were understandably slow to return to the neighborhood to make merry. Now back up to speed, the restaurants in this most historic of the city's enclaves are largely busy lunch spots, expense-account dining rooms, and after-work watering holes, with the streets quiet by 9.

American

$$–$$$ ✕ **Delmonico's.** As the oldest restaurant in New York City, opened in 1827, Delmonico's is steeped in cultural, political, and culinary history. Eggs Benedict, lobster Newburg, and baked Alaska were invented here —and are still served. Inside the stately mahogany-paneled dining room, tuck into a 20-ounce boneless rib-eye steak smothered with frizzled onions, dry-aged and spoon tender, and don't forget to order creamed spinach on the side. ✉ *56 Beaver St., at William St., Lower Manhattan* ☎ *212/509–1144* *Reservations essential* ▭ *AE, DC, MC, V* ⊙ *Closed weekends.*

Contemporary

$$$–$$$$ ✕ **Bayard's.** Chef Eberhard Müller's austere, classic cooking fits well in this historic, nautical-theme setting. Some of the produce comes direct from his Long Island farm, and is incorporated into seasonal dishes such as celery root soup with walnut pesto, and roasted monkfish in a savory bacon broth. The restaurant, housed in a stately 1851 Italianate mansion, remains a private club at lunch. At dinner the energy of the room ranges from sedate to somnambulant. If you can't get a reservation for a fine meal anywhere on a Saturday night, remember you can probably get in here. And you'll be glad you could. ✉ *1 Hanover Sq., between Pearl and Stone Sts., Lower Manhattan* ☎ *212/514–9454* ✍ *Reservations essential* ▭ *AE, D, MC, V* ⊙ *Closed Sun. No lunch.*

French

¢–$$ ✕ **Les Halles.** Chef Anthony Bourdain has become famous not for his cooking, but for his best-selling books *Kitchen Confidential* and *A Cook's Tour* (the latter has spawned a Food Network show starring the reed-thin Bourdain). But the Financial District outpost of his original restaurant remains strikingly unpretentious, like a French bistro–cum–butcher shop. Butcher paper on the tables, French posters, and a tin ceiling contribute to the atmosphere. A good bet is the *côte de boeuf* with béarnaise sauce, a massive rib steak for two served on a wooden board. Other prime choices include crispy duck-leg confit and frisée salad, warm sausages with lentils, and heaping plates of garlicky cold cuts. ✉ *15 John St., between Broadway and Nassau St., Lower Manhattan* ☎ *212/285–8585* ▭ *AE, DC, MC, V* ⊙ *Closed Sun.*

Pan-Asian

$$–$$$ ✕ **Roy's New York.** Roy's New York is the only place in town where you're guaranteed to be able to order primo Pacific Ocean fish. The restaurant, part of Hawaii-born pioneering chef Roy Yamaguchi's growing empire of Pacific-Rim eateries, ships in Sandwich Island delicacies like opakapaka (snapper) and mahimahi a few times a week. The menu features such appetizers as skewered coconut shrimp, individual pizzas along the lines of a Chinese-style barbecued chicken pie, and rich entrées such as tender slow-braised char-broiled honey-mustard beef short ribs. Roy's is a culinary contrast to its largely meat-and-potatoes Wall Street neighbors. ✉ *130 Washington St., between Albany and Carlisle Sts., Lower Manhattan* ☎ *212/266–6262* ▭ *AE, D, DC, MC, V.*

Little Italy & Chinatown

As Chinatown encroaches from the south, Little Italy keeps getting littler, and from a culinary standpoint nobody's grieving the loss of tourist-trap Italian restaurants. Chinatown is known for cheap, authentic food in bare-bones surroundings. But a growing number of restaurants are paying attention to design and offering menus that show some creativity. Shanghai has replaced Cantonese and Szechuan as the cuisine of choice, and "bubble teas" (hot or cold drinks made from fruit or tea with chewy tapioca pearls) are all the rage.

Cafés

¢–$$ ✕ **Dragon Land Bakery.** Modern industrial design meets traditional Chinese pastry in this steel-lined bakery. Live fish and turtles inhabit the bolted, curio-cabinet tables; pastel-color bubble tea drinks fill the refrigerated case; and delicious, heated buns line a wall. ✉ *125 Walker St., at Baxter St., Chinatown* ☎ *212/219–2012* ✍ *Reservations not accepted* ▭ *No credit cards.*

¢ ✕ **Caffé Roma.** Arguably Manhattan's most authentic Italian coffeehouse, this favorite hangout has worn walls, marble tables, and strong cappuccino with plenty of foam. ✉ *385 Broome St., at Mulberry St., Little Italy* ☎ *212/226–8413* ▭ *No credit cards.*

¢ ✕ **Fay Da Bakery.** Although Chinatown is full of bakeries selling buns and other traditional pastries, this one stands out for its modern setting, excellent baked goods, and steaming hot cups of strong coffee, all for about $1. The savory BBQ pork buns and the sweet coconut-filled buns are the best. ✉ *83 Mott St., at Canal St., Chinatown* ☎ *212/791–3884* ▭ *No credit cards.*

In New York, deciding what to eat is as important as deciding what to see and do. The restaurants we list are the cream of the crop in each price category. If you're staying in midtown, note that most restaurants cater to the business crowd and the most practical breakfast and lunch options are the cafeteria-style delis that have both hot and cold sandwiches and salad bars with hot and cold dishes sold by the pound. The densest cluster of cheap eats is in the East Village. On the street, a hot pretzel from a vendor can come to the rescue between museum visits. To experience the town like a native, make dining a priority, and keep the following things in mind.

Children

Though it is unusual to see children in the dining rooms of Manhattan's most elite restaurants, dining with your youngsters in New York does not have to mean culinary exile. Many of the restaurants reviewed in this chapter are excellent choices for families. Upscale restaurants that offer some simple menu items and accommodating service, such as Osteria del Circo, Odeon, or "21" Club, can satisfy the pickiest adults and children alike. More casual options include Café Habana, Kitchenette, Serendipity 3, or Shopsin's General Store. For an interactive experience, consider Korean barbecue (such as Kang Suh), where you grill your own meal, or Brazilian *churrascaria* (such as Churrascaria Plataforma or Green Field Churrascaria), where waiters circulate with skewers of roasted meat. Most Chinese restaurants, such as Jing Fong, Great New York Noodletown, and Dim Sum Go Go, are child-friendly. And all of the New York steak houses—Gallagher's, The Palm, Peter Luger, and Sparks, for example—offer good, old-fashioned satisfaction in the form of onion rings, crispy potatoes, and creamed spinach. Some restaurants are so much fun they feel like they're simply made for children; *see* the "Treats for the Kids" box for a list of these.

Dress

While casual attire is acceptable most of the time, your concept of the term may change while in New York. In fact, the term most often used when you call and ask about the dress code is "casual chic." For example, Stella McCartney jeans are usually acceptable, while Levis are not. A few of the most formal places still require jackets and/or ties. As a rule, dress at restaurants in midtown and around Wall Street is more conservative than in other, more residential neighborhoods, especially at lunch. Shorts are appropriate only in the most casual spots. Don't be embarrassed to call and ask.

Hours

The city that never sleeps eats whenever it wants. Many restaurants stay open between lunch and dinner, some offer late-night seating, and still others serve around-the-clock. European and Latin American tourists are relieved that at least one American city allows them to dine as late as they do at home. Restaurants that serve breakfast often do so until noon.

Mealtimes

New Yorkers seem ready to eat at any hour. Many restaurants stay open between lunch and dinner, some offer late-night seating, and still others serve around-the-clock. European and Latin American tourists are relieved that at least one American city allows them to dine as late as they do at home. Restaurants in SoHo, TriBeCa, and the Village are likely to remain open late, while midtown spots and those in the theater and financial districts generally close earlier. A number of midtown restaurants are closed

Sunday. Unless otherwise noted, the restaurants listed in this guide are open daily for lunch and dinner.

Reservations

At the hottest restaurants reservations need to be made weeks in advance, no matter how well-connected the concierge at your hotel is. Tables are especially hard to come by if you want to dine between 7 and 9, or on Friday or Saturday night. Though it is by no means a guarantee, sometimes just showing up at a restaurant that has turned you away on the phone will get you a seat, if you are willing to wait for it. Last-minute cancellations and no-shows unexpectedly free up tables, and if you happen to be in the right place at the right time, one of those tables might be yours.

If you change your mind or your plans, cancel your reservation—it's only courteous, plus some of the busiest places have started to charge up to $25 a head for a no-show (they take a credit card number when you reserve). Many restaurants will ask you to call the day before or the morning of your scheduled meal to reconfirm: remember to do so or you could lose out. If your original time isn't ideal, ask when you confirm if a better one has become available. When you call, double-check that the information listed in these reviews hasn't changed. Credit card acceptance, hours of operation, chefs, and prices are subject to (and often do) change.

Smoking

As of March 30, 2003, smoking is prohibited in all enclosed public spaces in New York City, including restaurants and bars. There are also restaurants—often small establishments with a European staff and clientele—that ignore the law altogether and are known as havens for smokers.

Tipping

New Yorkers tip big, maybe because they can appreciate what it must be like to serve people as demanding and impatient as they are all day long. The rules are simple. Never tip the maître d' unless you're out to impress your guests or if you expect to pay another visit soon. In most restaurants, tip the waiter at least 15%–20%. (To figure the amount quickly, just double the tax noted on the check—it's 8.625% of your bill—and, if you like, add a little more.) Bills for parties of six or more sometimes include the tip already. Tip at least $1 per drink at the bar, and $1 for each coat checked.

What It Costs

Like the stock market, entrée prices in general have fallen: a rack of lamb that had inched over the $30 mark is now down to the high $20s. And the $60-plus prix-fixe menu has given way to the standard à la carte. Of course, the top-tier restaurants remain impervious to market changes—Daniel's prix-fixe menus start at $85. Many restaurants still charge $5–$10 for side dishes. Beware of the $10 bottle of water poured eagerly for unsuspecting diners.

If you are watching your budget, be sure to ask the price of daily specials recited by the waiter or captain. The charge for specials at some restaurants is noticeably out of line with the other prices on the menu. And of course, always review your bill. Even on computerized checks, mistakes do occur. No matter whose favor the mistake is in, it is a courtesy to bring it to your server's attention.

If you eat early or late you may be able to take advantage of a prix-fixe deal not offered at peak hours, and get more attentive service in the bargain. Most upscale restaurants offer fantastic lunch deals with special menus at cut-rate prices designed to give a true taste of the place. One dining bargain has become a New York institution. In 1992, the city's restaurants devised the idea of charging $19.92 for a prix-fixe lunch during the Democratic Convention in June. It was a huge success, and you can still find lunches (and some dinners) with prices tied to the year at restaurants throughout the city, not only during "Restaurant Week" in June and January, but all year-round.

Credit cards are widely accepted, but many restaurants (particularly smaller ones downtown) accept only cash. Our restaurant reviews indicate what credit cards are accepted (or not) at each establishment, but if you plan to use a credit card it is a good idea to double-check its acceptability when making reservations or before sitting down to eat.

WHAT IT COSTS

	$$$$	$$$	$$	$	¢
AT DINNER	over $35	$28–$35	$19–$27	$11–$18	under $10

Restaurant prices are for a main course at dinner, excluding sales tax of 8.625%.

Some restaurants are marked with a price range ($$–$$$, for example). This indicates one of two things: either the average cost straddles two categories, or if you order strategically, you can get out for less than most diners spend.

Wine

Gone for the most part are the hefty tomes filled with lists of historic vintages of French Bordeaux that used to be the norm at the city's top restaurants. Sommeliers all over the city are focusing on small-production, lesser-known wineries. Some are even keeping their wine lists purposefully small, so that they can change them frequently to match the season and the menu. Markups vary so much from bottle to bottle, restaurant to restaurant, that you should scan the entire list before making a selection. Half bottles are becoming more prevalent, and good wines by the glass are everywhere. If you are unfamiliar with the selection, don't hesitate to ask for recommendations. A well-trained waitstaff will know something about the wines they're serving, and many restaurants with no sommelier on staff designate special people to lend a hand.

¢ ✕ **Saint's Alp Teahouse.** Join the hip Asian youth crowding the small tables at Saint's Alp Teahouse, part of a Hong Kong–based international chain. They're here for bubble tea—frothy, pastel-color, flavored black or green tea speckled with beads of tapioca or sago (they look like tadpoles). Passion-fruit green tea with chewy tapioca is refreshing. You can also order snacks such as spring rolls, dumplings, or sweets. ✉ *51 Mott St., between Canal and Bayard Sts., Chinatown* ☎ *212/766–9889* ▭ *No credit cards.*

Chinese

¢–$$ ✕ **Funky Broome.** One of the new generation of Chinese restaurants, Funky Broome looks more like a high-tech Shiseido cosmetics shop than the Hong Kong–style eatery that it is. At night, the place bustles with young, hip neighborhood locals eating Cantonese comfort food like *congee* (rice gruel) topped with assorted meats and vegetables, and Sterno-heated mini-

Bayard's 3
Delmonico's . . .2
Les Halles 4
Roy's New York 1

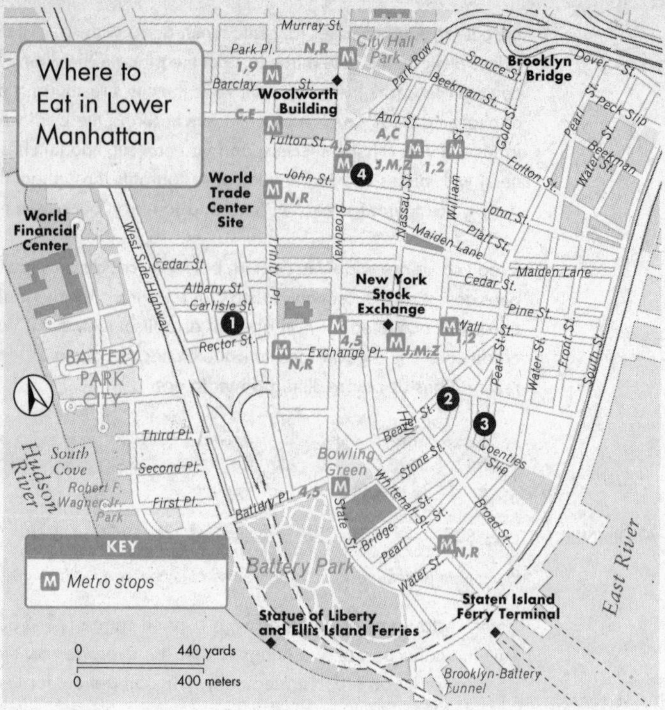

woks filled with sizzling stewlike dishes. Funky Broome, a marriage of NoLita cool and Chinatown taste, is an intriguing pit stop while touring the neighborhood. ✉ *176 Mott St., at Broome St., Little Italy* ☎ *212/941–8628* ▭ *AE, MC, V.*

¢–$$ ✕ **Great New York Noodletown.** Although the soups and noodles are unbeatable at this clean, no-frills restaurant, what you should order are the window decorations—the hanging lacquered ducks, roasted pork, and crunchy baby pig. All three are superb, especially if you ask for the pungent garlic-and-ginger sauce on the side. Seasonal specialties such as duck with flowering chives and salt-baked soft-shell crabs are excellent. So is the congee, available with any number of garnishes. Solo diners may end up at a communal table, but everyone ends up happy. ✉ *28 Bowery, at Bayard St., Chinatown* ☎ *212/349–0923* ✍ *Reservations essential* ▭ *No credit cards.*

¢–$$ ✕ **Joe's Shanghai.** Joe opened his first Shanghai restaurant in Queens, but buoyed by the accolades accorded his steamed soup dumplings—magically filled with a rich, fragrant broth and a pork or pork-and-crabmeat mixture—he saw fit to open in Manhattan's Chinatown, and then midtown. There's always a wait, but the line moves fast. Menu highlights include turnip shortcakes and dried bean curd salad to start, and succulent braised pork shoulder, ropey homemade Shanghai noodles, and traditional lion's head—rich pork meatballs braised in brown sauce—to follow. Other more familiar Chinese dishes are also excellent. ✉ *9 Pell St., between the Bowery and Mott St., Chinatown* ☎ *212/233–8888* ▭ *No credit cards.*

¢–$$ ✕ **Ping's Seafood.** It was only a matter of time before the personable chef-owner Chuen Ping Hui branched out from his Elmhurst restaurant to open not one, but two Manhattan outposts. Although the original location in Queens still has the most elaborate menu with the most extensive selection of live seafood, the Manhattan locales are more accessible both geographically and gastronomically. Helpful menus have pictures of most of the specialties. Among them are Dungeness crab in black bean sauce, crisp fried tofu, silken braised *e-fu* noodles, and Peking duck. Pricier than some other Chinatown haunts, these restaurants are also a notch above in setting and service. ✉ *22 Mott St., at Chatham Sq., Chinatown* ☎ *212/602–9988* *Reservations essential* ▭ *MC, V.*

¢–$ ✕ **Dim Sum Go Go.** Dim sum gets a creative spin at this sleek red-and-white spot. Dumplings go beyond steamed shrimp and pork with combos such as duck skin and crab in a spinach wrapper. The stars that mark certain menu items denote the restaurant's specialties, not "hot and spicy." There are also entrées such as panfried halibut with garlic sauce, and quail on baby bok choy. ✉ *5 East Broadway, at Chatham Sq., Chinatown* ☎ *212/732–0797* ▭ *AE, MC, V.*

¢–$ ✕ **Jing Fong.** Come to this authentic dim sum palace and pretend you're in Hong Kong. On weekend mornings hundreds of people crowd onto the escalator to Jing Fong's second-floor dining room. Chinese women call out in Cantonese (most don't speak English) while they push carts of dumplings, noodles, tofu, and a few things you might not want to order. The selection always includes *hargow* (steamed shrimp dumplings), *shu mai* (steamed pork dumplings), *chow fun* (wide rice noodles with dried shrimp or beef), sesame balls, and custard tarts. For the adventurous there are chicken feet, tripe, and snails. Arrive early to be sure you get the largest and freshest selection. ✉ *20 Elizabeth St., between Bayard and Canal Sts., Chinatown* ☎ *212/964–5256* ▭ *AE, MC, V.*

★ ¢–$ ✕ **Sweet 'n' Tart Café & Restaurant.** You'll be handed four different menus at this multilevel restaurant. One lists an extensive selection of dim sum prepared to order; another offers special dishes organized according to principles of Chinese medicine; a third lists more familiar sounding dishes, such as hot-and-sour soup; and the final one lists curative "teas" (more like soups or fruit shakes, really). Don't miss the yam noodle soup with assorted dumplings, or the fried rice with taro and Chinese sausage served in a bamboo container. The original café, with a more limited menu, is up the street, and some think it has better food. ✉ *20 Mott St., between Chatham Sq. and Pell St., Chinatown* ☎ *212/964–0380* ✉ *original café: 76 Mott St., at Canal St., Chinatown* ☎ *212/334–8088* ▭ *AE accepted at 20 Mott St. location; no credit cards at other locations.*

Italian

¢–$ ✕ **Bread.** At this stylish little paninoteca, owner Luigi Comandatore, a Mercer Kitchen alum, takes advantage of his location, buying top-notch ingredients from neighborhood purveyors such as Di Palo's Fine Foods and Balthazar Bakery to make perfect panini. Italian expats, windows open to the street in summer, and lots of red vino give Bread star lingering quality. ✉ *20 Spring St., between Elizabeth and Mott Sts., Little Italy* ☎ *212/334–1015* ▭ *AE, D, MC, V.*

Malaysian

¢–$ ✕ **New Indonesia & Malaysia Restaurant.** Malaysian restaurants are popping up like bamboo shoots in Chinatown and this dingy subterranean spot is the best. Locals crowd the dining room from morning (it opens at 8 AM) to night for the fragrantly spiced food. Indonesian-style chicken, crunchy in a sweet soy sauce; long-simmered beef *rendang*; and whole crabs swimming in a big bowl of spicy curry sauce and vermicelli are menu staples that get hearty nods of approval from anyone who's been to Jakarta or Kuala Lumpur. ✉ *18 Doyers St., at Pell St., Chinatown* ☎ *212/267–0088* ▭ *No credit cards.*

Pizza

★ $–$$ ✕ **Lombardi's.** Brick walls, red-and-white check tablecloths, and the aroma of thin-crust pies emerging from the coal oven set the mood for

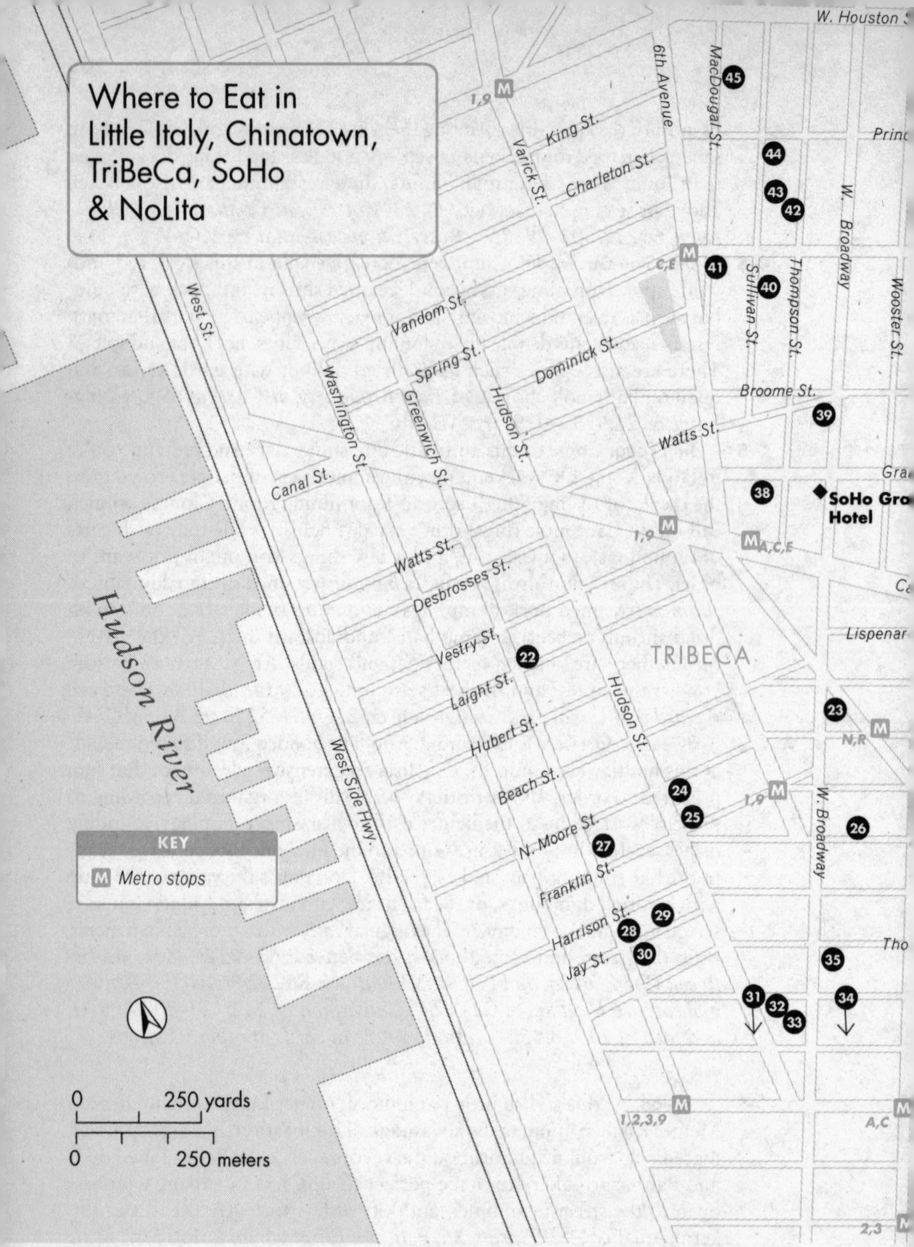

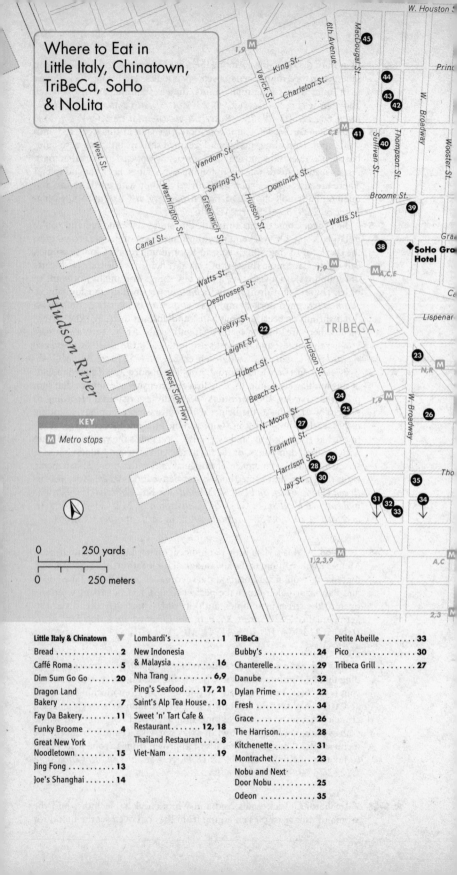

Little Italy & Chinatown ▼

- Bread 2
- Caffé Roma 5
- Dim Sum Go Go 20
- Dragon Land Bakery 7
- Fay Da Bakery. 11
- Funky Broome 4
- Great New York Noodletown 15
- Jing Fong 13
- Joe's Shanghai 14
- Lombardi's 1
- New Indonesia & Malaysia 16
- Nha Trang 6,9
- Ping's Seafood. . . . 17, 21
- Saint's Alp Tea House . . 10
- Sweet 'n' Tart Cafe & Restaurant. 12, 18
- Thailand Restaurant 8
- Viet-Nam 19

TriBeCa ▼

- Bubby's 24
- Chanterelle. 29
- Danube 32
- Dylan Prime 22
- Fresh 34
- Grace 26
- The Harrison. 28
- Kitchenette 31
- Montrachet. 23
- Nobu and Next Door Nobu 25
- Odeon 35
- Petite Abeille 33
- Pico 30
- Tribeca Grill 27

SoHo & NoLita

Aquagrill 41
Balthazar. 57
Blue Ribbon 43
Blue Ribbon Sushi 44
Café Habana 53
Café Lebowitz 3
Ceci Cela 56
Cendrillon 37
Fanelli 47
Le Gamin 45
Ghenet 51
Honmura An 50
Le Pain Quotidien 36
The Mercer Kitchen . . . 48
Newsbar 39
Peasant 54
Pepe Rosso To Go 40
Pfiff 38
Rialto 52
Rice 55
Savoy 46
Snack 42
Woo Lae Oak 49

some of the best pizza in Manhattan. Lombardi's has served pizza since 1905 (though not in the same location), and business has not died down a bit. The mozzarella is always fresh, resulting in an almost greaseless slice, and the toppings, such as homemade meatballs, pancetta, or imported anchovies, are also top quality. ✉ *32 Spring St., between Mott and Mulberry Sts., Little Italy* ☎ *212/941–7994* ▭ *No credit cards.*

Thai

¢–$$ ✕ **Thailand Restaurant.** It's hard to find a Thai restaurant in New York where everything is top-notch, but this large, popular Chinatown destination has a few terrific dishes. Among them are Penang duck in a fiery red curry sauce enriched with coconut milk and perfumed with opal basil, and shrimp simmered in your choice of red, green, or yellow curries. An order of steamed jasmine rice or sticky rice will help cool things off a little. ✉ *106 Bayard St., between Baxter and Mulberry Sts., Chinatown* ☎ *212/349–3132* ▭ *AE.*

Vietnamese

¢ ✕ **Nha Trang.** You can get a good meal at this inexpensive Vietnamese restaurant if you know how to order, so stick to the dishes you see others eating. Start with a steaming bowl of spicy sweet-and-sour seafood soup (the small order is enough for three or four people) and shrimp grilled on sugarcane. Follow that up with paper-thin pork chops grilled until crisp, and crunchy deep-fried squid served on a bed of shredded lettuce with a tangy dipping sauce. If the line is long, which it usually is, even with a second location around the corner, you may be asked to sit at a table with strangers. ✉ *87 Baxter St., between Bayard and Canal Sts., Chinatown* ☎ *212/233–5948* ✉ *148 Centre St., between Walker and White Sts., Chinatown* ☎ *212/941–9292* ▭ *No credit cards.*

¢ ✕ **Viet-Nam.** It may be difficult to find the little elbow of a street where this basement dive is located—tell cab drivers to turn right onto Pell Street from the Bowery and then left on Doyers—but after one bite of the tasty, cheap, and seductive Vietnamese food you'll remember how to get back. The sweet-and-sour dressing of the green papaya and beef jerky salad is positively addictive, as are the beef cubes with watercress, or anything served in the pungent black bean sauce. Genuinely proud of their food, the staff is extremely helpful, offering advice on what to order and help in how to eat some of the unusual dishes. ✉ *11–13 Doyers St., between the Bowery and Pell St., Chinatown* ☎ *212/693–0725* ▭ *AE.*

TriBeCa

This once industrial neighborhood attracts affluent residents seeking spacious lofts. The ground floors of these glamorized former warehouses and factories provide dramatic settings for some of the best restaurants in the city. Residents like Robert De Niro and Harvey Keitel can pop down to their favorite haunts. TriBeCa retains a ghostly, deserted feel at night—part of its charm—but the quiet will be shattered when you walk into one of the many fashionable dining rooms.

American

$$–$$$ ✕ **The Harrison.** Partners Danny Abrams and Jimmy Bradley's formula for the perfect neighborhood eatery, which they perfected at the Red Cat in Chelsea, works like a charm in TriBeCa. Even though the Harrison opened barely a month after September 11, its easy-to-digest American menu and warm, woody room made it a winner from the get-go. Expect well-executed dishes such as ricotta cavatelli, braised veal cheeks, and quail cassoulet, along with a selection of creative sides. ✉ *355 Greenwich St., at Harrison and Greenwich Sts., TriBeCa* ☎ *212/274–9310* ✍ *Reservations essential* ▭ *AE, D, MC, V* ⊙ *No lunch.*

American Casual

$ ✕ **Bubby's.** Crowds clamoring for coffee and freshly squeezed juice line up for brunch at this TriBeCa mainstay. The dining room is homey and comfortable with attractive furnishings and plate-glass windows; in summer, neighbors sit at tables outside with their dogs. For breakfast you can order grits, homemade granola, or such entrées as sour cream pancakes, and smoked trout with scrambled eggs. Eclectic comfort food—macaroni and cheese, southern fried chicken, meat loaf—make up the lunch and dinner menus. Be sure to get a piece of homemade pie for dessert. ✉ *120 Hudson St., at N. Moore St., TriBeCa* ☎ *212/219–0666* ▭ *AE, DC, MC, V.*

¢–$ ✕ **Kitchenette.** This small, comfy restaurant lives up to its name with tables so close together you're likely to make new friends. The dining room feels like a neighbor's breakfast nook, and the food tastes like your mom made it—provided she's a great cook. There are no frills, just good, solid cooking, friendly service, and a long line at peak times. For brunch don't miss the pancakes, cranberry-cinnamon swirl French toast, and thick-cut bacon. ✉ *80 West Broadway, at Warren St., TriBeCa* ☎ *212/267–6740* ▭ *AE* ⏲ *No dinner.*

Austrian

$$–$$$ ✕ **Danube.** Known for his virtuoso seasonal French cooking, David Bouley experiments in nouveau Austrian cuisine in a jewel box of a restaurant that evokes turn-of-the-20th-century Vienna. The elegant bar is alight with shimmering mosaic swirls, and the diminutive dining room is lined with sparkling Klimt reproductions. While signatures such as ravioli of Corinthian "Schlutzkrapfen" cheese with smoked hen-of-the-woods mushrooms still grace the menu, these days executive chef, and actual Austrian, Mario Lohninger is making his own headlines with dishes such as an intensely flavored oxtail consommé with bone marrow dumpling, and tuna-and-hamachi accented with onion pickled in key lime juice. The wine list is notable for hard-to-find Austrian and German labels. ✉ *30 Hudson St., at Duane St., TriBeCa* ☎ *212/791–3771* ✍ *Reservations essential* 👔 *Jacket and tie* ▭ *AE, D, MC, V* ⏲ *Closed Sun.*

Belgian

$–$$ ✕ **Petite Abeille.** This is the latest addition to this expanding chain of Belgian bistros. The menu tempts with salads, frites, sandwiches, omelets, poached salmon, and other light fare for early in the day. Come evening, sausages, *stoemp* (mashed sweet potatoes and veggies), steak, stew, and mussels satisfy. Two styles of waffles are always available: *de Bruxelles* (made fresh to order and topped with ice cream, whipped cream, and fresh fruit) and the true Belgian waffle, *de Liège* (imported from Belgium and reheated until the subtle caramelized sugar coating crunches and melts in your mouth). ✉ *134 West Broadway, between Duane and Thomas Sts., TriBeCa* ☎ *212/791–1360* ▭ *AE, MC, V.*

Contemporary

$$–$$$ ✕ **Tribeca Grill.** Anchored by the bar from the old Maxwell's Plum, this cavernous brick-wall restaurant displays art by Robert De Niro Sr., whose movie-actor son is one of restaurateur Drew Nieporent's partners. Chef Don Pintabona oversees the kitchen, but his contemporary American food doesn't seem as important to the nightly crowd of diners as does the prospect of sighting somebody famous. Still, you can eat well if you stick to the simplest dishes, such as braised short ribs or crisp baby chicken. Save room for the warm caramelized banana tart with chocolate malt ice cream; it's still the best. ✉ *375 Greenwich St., at Franklin St., TriBeCa* ☎ *212/941–3900* ✍ *Reservations essential* ▭ *AE, DC, MC, V* ⏲ *No lunch Sat.*

¢–$ ✕ **Grace.** The 40-ft-long mahogany bar will clue you in to Grace's cocktail prowess, but the kitchen's unusual and tasty array of small and large plates will keep you coming back for more. The menu hops from burgers to pork pot stickers to stuffed grape leaves with Lebne (tart Lebanese soft cheese) and marinated feta. If you're looking for a late-night snack, this is the place—the kitchen stays open until 4 AM. ✉ *114 Franklin St., between Church St. and West Broadway, TriBeCa* ☎ *212/343–4200* ▭ *AE, MC, V.*

French

$$$$ ✕ **Chanterelle.** Soft peach walls, luxuriously spaced tables, towering floral arrangements, and stylish servers set the stage for what is certainly the most understated of New York's fancy French restaurants. Unassuming service complements chef David Waltuck's simple creations. The delicious signature grilled seafood sausage will always be available, but the bulk of the prix-fixe menu is dictated by the season. (Hope for the roast sturgeon with bacon, pearl onions, and veal jus when you go.) Roger Dagorn, the restaurant's exceptional sommelier, can help find value in the discriminating, beautifully chosen wine list. ✉ *2 Harrison St., at Hudson St., TriBeCa* ☎ *212/966–6960* ✍ *Reservations essential* ▭ *AE, DC, MC, V* ⊗ *Closed Sun. No lunch Mon.*

$$–$$$ ✕ **Montrachet.** Every chef Drew Nieporent selects for this, his first (and one suspects dearest) restaurant, excels. Currently Harold Moore offers seasonal three- and five-course menus. If you're lucky, you'll be able to choose the marinated fluke with gingered vegetables and caviar to start, and follow it up with a horseradish-crusted salmon or a modern surf-n-turf of lobster and oxtails. Pastel walls, plush mauve banquettes, engaging works of art, and the occasional line cook traversing the dining room to the inconvenient walk-in refrigerator, set an unpretentious (some say dated) tone. The distinguished wine list emphasizes diminutive regional vineyards. ✉ *239 West Broadway, between Walker and White Sts., TriBeCa* ☎ *212/219–2777* ✍ *Reservations essential* ▭ *AE* ⊗ *Closed Sun. No lunch Mon.–Thurs. and Sat.*

$–$$$ ✕ **Odeon.** New York trendsetters change hangouts faster than they can press speed-dial on their cell phones, but this spot has managed to maintain its quality and flair for 20 years and counting. Even with the buzz at Keith McNally's other hot spots, Balthazar and Pastis, the neo–art deco room is still packed nightly with revelers. One change reflects a change in the diners: children are welcome these days. And the pleasant service, relatively low prices, and well-chosen wine list are always in style. The bistro-menu highlights include meaty crab cakes, grilled hanger steak, and wild-mushroom risotto. ✉ *145 West Broadway, between Duane and Thomas Sts., TriBeCa* ☎ *212/233–0507* ✍ *Reservations essential* ▭ *AE, D, MC, V.*

Japanese

$$–$$$ Fodor'sChoice ★ ✕ **Nobu.** Unless you're Robert De Niro (he's a partner and eats here regularly), you need to make reservations a month in advance at New York's most famous Japanese restaurant. A curved wall of river-worn black pebbles, a hand-painted beech floor, bare wood tables, and sculptural birch trees set the stage for Nobu Matsuhisa's dramatic food. (With a global empire to run, Nobu Matsuhisa has a stand-in: executive chef Edwin Ferrari.) The vast menu can take you down two paths. One road is the way to classic Japanese sushi and sashimi, among the best in town. Another leads you to contemporary dishes, such as the paper-thin hamachi spiced up with jalapeño or sea bass topped with black truffle slivers in a citrusy sauce of soy, butter, and *yuzu*. It's easiest to put yourself in the hands of the chef by ordering the *omakase omikase*—specify how much you want to spend (the minimum is $80 per person) and the kitchen

does the rest. Can't get reservations? Try your luck at Next Door Nobu, where diners can enjoy a slightly less-expensive menu on a first-come, first-served basis. ✉ *105 Hudson St., at Franklin St., TriBeCa* ☎ *212/219–0500; 212/219–8095 for same-day reservations* ✉ *Next Door Nobu, 105 Hudson St., at Franklin St., TriBeCa* ☎ *212/334–4445* *Reservations essential* ▭ *AE, DC, MC, V* ⊙ *No lunch weekends.*

Portuguese

$$–$$$ ✕ **Pico.** Calling this contemporary restaurant Portuguese is a bit of a stretch, but that's how the owners and chef characterize it, so who are we to argue? (Elements of the decor, such as colorful tiles, patterns, and tassels hope to reinforce the notion.) John Villa has created a modern menu that draws on the flavors of Portugal and its former colonies, Macao and Goa, but his refined sensibility and precise plating are firmly rooted in New York City. For authenticity's sake there is plenty of flaky salt cod, an impressively succulent suckling pig, and a rich and fragrant seafood and chorizo-sausage stew. But the rest is deliciously TriBeCa. ✉ *349 Greenwich St., between Harrison and Jay Sts., TriBeCa* ☎ *212/343–0700* ▭ *AE, DC, MC, V* ⊙ *Closed Sun. No lunch Sat.*

Seafood

$$–$$$ ✕ **Fresh.** Fish doesn't get any meatier than it does at Fresh, where you can get "prime rib" of swordfish, "baby back" halibut ribs, and "Kobe" bluefin tuna (sublimely fatty seared belly flesh). Chef Martin Burge, a former Gotham Bar & Grill chef de cuisine, has reinvented the seafood menu, preparing marine creatures—exotic and common—in surprising ways. Halibut cheeks are as tender as the foie gras with which they're paired; rillettes are made of mashed cod, smoked haddock, and potatoes; and Burge's take on fish-and-chips may be the best in the city. Of course, Fresh's offerings really are the catches of the day—one of the restaurant's co-owners is also the proprietor of Early Morning Seafood, which counts Alain Ducasse as a customer. ✉ *105 Reade St., at West Broadway, TriBeCa* ☎ *212/406–1900* ▭ *AE, MC, V* ⊙ *No lunch.*

Steak

$$–$$$$ ✕ **Dylan Prime.** This TriBeCa restaurant offers a softer, more sophisticated environment in which to enjoy steak than any of the legendary midtown steak houses. Dry-aged filet mignon is offered in 7- or 11-ounce portions, and rib eye comes in a 14-ounce slab. Sides, such as braised cranberry beans with roasted tomatoes and fricassee of wild mushrooms, are called "Accessories," and toppings for meat, such as Maytag blue cheese, are referred to as "Chapeaux." The chef, Bobby Duncan, dresses pork loin with an apple crust and dabbles in other creative compositions. Adjacent to the restaurant is a bar-lounge that serves shareable appetizers and finger foods. ✉ *62 Laight St., at Greenwich St., TriBeCa* ☎ *212/334–2274* ▭ *AE, DC, MC, V* ⊙ *No lunch weekends.*

SoHo & NoLita

Old-timers bemoan the fact that SoHo has evolved from red-hot art district to the world's chicest mall—Chanel and Prada have replaced Mary Boone and Gagosian (two seminal galleries that fled to Chelsea). But any way you shop it, the neighborhood still means good eating, whether you feel like charred burgers in an old artists' hangout (Fanelli's) or some Jean-Georges Vongerichten cuisine. Just be sure to wear your most up-to-the-minute ensemble. NoLita (*No*rth of *Li*ttle *Ita*ly), the trendy next-door neighborhood of small shops and restaurants, is reminiscent of a bygone SoHo, with fresh new eateries popping up every month. Expect beautiful crowds dressed in black and service that is refreshingly unpretentious given the clientele.

American

¢–$$ ✕ **Rialto.** The shabby-chic dining room with pressed-tin walls, plain wooden chairs, and burgundy banquettes provides a backdrop for the attractive crowd that makes this place hum. The food is interesting without being fussy, well suited to the noisy space where people-watching can often distract you from your plate. But those who like to eat will have no trouble focusing on such dishes as wild mushroom sausage or rosemary roasted chicken. The hamburger's pretty good, too. The lovely back garden is a great spot for alfresco summer dining; in winter it's canopied and heated. ✉ *265 Elizabeth St., between E. Houston and Prince Sts., NoLita* ☎ *212/334–7900* ⛵ *Reservations essential* ▭ *AE, MC, V.*

American Casual

¢–$ ✕ **Fanelli's.** A holdover from the days when SoHo was the stamping grounds of struggling artists rather than the owners of multimillion-dollar designer lofts, Fanelli's is a refreshingly weathered old pub. Housed in a building erected in 1857, when the area was known for brothels rather than boutiques, it is one of the most popular bar-restaurants in the city. Burgers, sandwiches, omelets, and pastas never tasted so subversive. The gorgeously timeworn original bar serves good draft beer to customers who can do without bizarre cocktails. ✉ *94 Prince St., at Mercer St., SoHo* ☎ *212/226–9412* ⛵ *Reservations not accepted* ▭ *AE, MC, V.*

Cafés

¢–$ ✕ **Le Gamin.** It's easy to confuse New York for Paris at this hip little haven, where the menu includes all the French-café standards: croque monsieur, quiche Lorraine, salade niçoise, crepes (both sweet and savory), and big bowls of café au lait. Service can be desultory, but the upside is that you're free to lounge for hours. ✉ *50 MacDougal St., between W. Houston and Prince Sts., SoHo* ☎ *212/254–4678* ▭ *AE, MC, V.*

¢–$ ✕ **Le Pain Quotidien.** This international Belgian chain brings its homeland ingredients with it, treating New Yorkers to crusty breads and delicious jams. Best of all is the Belgian chocolate sweetening the café mochas and hot chocolate. For a more substantial meal, take a seat at the long wooden communal table and sample hearty sandwiches like roast beef with caper mayonnaise or roasted turkey with herb dressing. ✉ *100 Grand St., at Mercer St., SoHo* ☎ *212/625–9009* ▭ *No credit cards.*

¢–$ ✕ **Snack.** Misleadingly named Snack serves big Greek flavors in SoHo. Local residents and shop owners come to the sliver of a storefront for vegetarian souvlaki and *papoutsakia* (half an eggplant stuffed with spicy ground beef and cheese). Don't expect a greasy gyro shack—Snack is a pretty space. You'll wish there were more than just a handful of chairs. ✉ *105 Thompson St., between Prince and Spring Sts., SoHo* ☎ *212/925–1040* ▭ *AE, MC, V.*

¢ ✕ **Ceci-Cela.** In New York, the search for good pain au chocolat ends here. The breakfast buns are flaky and have just the right touch of greasiness. The counter is constantly jammed with fans. In the woody back room you can sit down to hearty sandwiches, quiche, coffee, and pastries. Ceci-Cela normally closes at 7 PM, but stays open until 10 PM on Friday and Saturday—perfect for a postcinema discussion over dessert. ✉ *55 Spring St., between Lafayette and Mulberry Sts., NoLita* ☎ *212/274–9179* ▭ *No credit cards.*

¢ ✕ **Newsbar.** This ultracasual resting place has good coffee and tea, a generous selection of magazines, and CNN on the tube. ✉ *366 West Broadway, at Grand St., SoHo* ☎ *212/343–0053* ▭ *No credit cards.*

Contemporary

$$–$$$ ✕ **The Mercer Kitchen.** One of New York's premier chefs, Jean-Georges Vongerichten, runs this downtown outpost in the basement of the achingly hip Mercer Hotel. The sleek, modern, industrial space sizzles with the energy of the downtown elite (though these days the restaurant draws its share of average joes checking out the beautiful people). The dishes on the menu, which are more casual than at Vongerichten's other eateries, are grouped according to which section of the kitchen prepares them. Dinner might include black sea bass carpaccio (from the raw bar); Alsatian tarte flambé with *fromage blanc*, onions, and bacon (from the pizza oven); or roasted lobster with autumn vegetables (from the rotisserie). ✉ *Mercer Hotel, 99 Prince St., at Mercer St., SoHo* ☎ *212/966–5454* ✍ *Reservations essential* ▭ *AE, DC, MC, V.*

$$–$$$ ✕ **Savoy.** Chef-owner Peter Hoffman serves an eclectic mix of dishes inspired by the Mediterranean in this cozy restaurant on a quiet cobblestone corner. A bronze wire-mesh ceiling, arched wood accents, and blazing fireplace lend the downstairs space a country feel, the perfect setting for such down-to-earth dishes as grilled trout with herbed couscous or salt-crust-baked duck. Upstairs, the original tin ceiling, artwork, and open hearth are the backdrop for an expensive nightly prix-fixe menu, which includes a special grilled dish (cooked in the dining-room hearth). The wine list emphasizes small producers. ✉ *70 Prince St., at Crosby St., SoHo* ☎ *212/219–8570* ✍ *Reservations essential* ▭ *AE, MC, V* ⏲ *No lunch Sun.*

$–$$ ✕ **Pfiff.** Compact Pfiff, with its red vinyl banquettes, custom light fixtures (made by one of the partners who is a sculptor), and funky tunes, is one of those rare restaurants in which one could eat every night. The affordable menu reads familiar, but chef Matteo Riccardella gives everything an unexpected, delicious twist. Crème fraîche spiked with cinnamon and nutmeg adds kick to butternut squash soup. Nicely textured peanut-crusted ahi steak comes with an Asian accent of spicy Napa cabbage. And tender pork schnitzel is a crunch fest in a crisp breading, with cucumber salad and onion-filled truffled potato salad. Pfiff means "whistle" in German, and this is one place you won't blow off. ✉ *35 Grand St., at Thompson St., SoHo* ☎ *212/334–6841* ▭ *AE, D, DC, MC, V.*

Eclectic

★ $–$$$ ✕ **Blue Ribbon.** After more than a decade, Blue Ribbon remains *the* late-night food hangout. After the big boys—like Rocco, Bobby, and Mario—have closed their own kitchens, they still join the genial hubbub on occasion for some midnight specialness, namely the bone marrow with oxtail marmalade and the renowned raw bar platters. Flush trust funders, literary types, sassy singletons, austerely dressed designers—a good-looking gang fills this dark box of a room until 4 AM. The menu *appears* standard but it's not. Instead of the usual fried calamari, exceptionally tender squid is lightly sautéed in olive oil and garlic and served like a savory pudding in a Japanese rice bowl. Sweetbreads cleverly mix with shiitakes. As Eric and Bruce Bromberg's empire slowly grows (Blue Ribbon Sushi, Blue Ribbon Bakery, Blue Ribbon Brooklyn), so does its quality. ✉ *97 Sullivan St., between Prince and Spring Sts., SoHo* ☎ *212/274–0404* ✍ *Reservations not accepted* ▭ *AE, MC, V* ⏲ *No lunch.*

¢–$$ ✕ **Café Lebowitz.** Named after humorist Fran Lebowitz, owned by Brian McNally, and boasting customers like Robert De Niro, the très casual Café Lebowitz is prime dining real estate at dinner and brunch. On a weekday afternoon, though, it's a tranquil place for an espresso and apple strudel or a croque monsieur, and gazing at the NoLita chic passing by. At dinner, this quasi Viennese café is more of a steak-frites bistro with schnitzel and goulash thrown into the mix. ✉ *14 Spring St., at Elizabeth St., NoLita* ☎ *212/219–2399* ▭ *AE, D, MC, V.*

¢–$ ✕ **Rice.** All meals are built on a bowl of rice at this dark and narrow storefront where you can sit on chairs or bar stools while you dine at small tables. Choose from an array of rice varieties, such as basmati, brown, Thai black, or Bhutanese red, and create a meal by adding a savory topping such as Jamaican jerk chicken wings, warm lentil stew, or Indian chicken curry. The fresh, well-seasoned, budget-price menu affords a satisfying mix of multicultural cuisine and comfort food. ✉ *227 Mott St., between Prince and Spring Sts., SoHo* ☎ *212/226–5775* ✍ *Reservations not accepted* ▭ *No credit cards.*

Ethiopian

★ ¢–$$ ✕ **Ghenet.** New York has a steadily growing coterie of Ethiopian restaurants, and Ghenet is the most sophisticated of the lot. A rotating exhibit of local, African-inspired art hangs on the walls of this welcoming spot where the food is authentic and delicious. Order one of the combination platters to sample a variety of dishes, mounded on a platter lined with spongy *injera* flat bread, which is your edible utensil. In addition to the tasty poultry and meat options, there's a good selection of vegetarian dishes such as rich collard greens with Ethiopian spices, fiery potatoes and cabbage, and carrots in an onion sauce. ✉ *284 Mulberry St., between E. Houston and Prince Sts., NoLita* ☎ *212/343–1888* ▭ *AE, MC, V* ⊗ *Closed Mon. No dinner Sun.*

French

$–$$$ ✕ **Balthazar.** You're no longer guaranteed to sit next to a celebrity at Keith McNally's grand brasserie (younger sister Pastis has more star power), but it's still difficult to get an 8 PM reservation. The raw bar may be the best in town, with an outstanding selection of impossibly fresh crustaceans and bivalves. Nightly specials are French dishes that are as classic as the painstakingly accurate reproduction of a Parisian eatery. Steak tartare, steak frites, duck shepherd's pie—it's all good. Breakfast is a civilized affair, with croissants and pains au chocolat coming from the restaurant's own bakery (they're also on sale at the tiny adjacent shop). ✉ *80 Spring St., between Broadway and Crosby St., SoHo* ☎ *212/965–1414* ✍ *Reservations essential* ▭ *AE, MC, V.*

Italian

$$ ✕ **Peasant.** Though the name suggests otherwise, the crowd at this rustic-yet-hip restaurant is stylishly urban. Most of Frank DeCarlo's menu is prepared in a bank of wood-burning ovens, from which the heady aroma of garlic and smoke perfumes the room. The ovens also serve as the focal point of the dining room. Don't fill up on the crusty bread and fresh ricotta. Sizzling sardines (crisp on the outside, moist inside) arrive at the table in the terra-cotta pots in which they were baked. Rotisserie lamb is redolent with the scent of fresh herbs. ✉ *194 Elizabeth St., between Spring and Prince Sts., NoLita* ☎ *212/965–9511* ✍ *Reservations essential* ▭ *AE, MC, V* ⊗ *Closed Mon. No lunch.*

¢–$ ✕ **Pepe Rosso to Go.** A long list of specials changes daily here, but the menu always includes generously portioned pastas (prepared fresh in the open kitchen), antipasti, salads, entrées, and sandwiches. The gnocchi are as light as little clouds, the pesto sauce is fragrant with basil and garlic, and the veal is tender. Inexpensive wine is available in carafes or by the bottle. Dinner can cost less than $17 at any one of the four "Pepe" restaurants—quite possibly the best Italian value in the city. ✉ *149 Sullivan St., at W. Houston St., SoHo* ☎ *212/677–4555* ▭ *AE, MC, V.*

Japanese

$–$$$$ ✕ **Blue Ribbon Sushi.** If you're into fancy rolls crammed with everything stocked in the sushi bar and drizzled with various sauces, you'll like Blue Ribbon Sushi. While sushi purists may be disappointed, Blue Ribbon's dark, intimate nooks, stylized design, and servers with downtown attitude attract an equally stylish crowd who wait up to 45 minutes for a seat. Owned by the same people who own Blue Ribbon and its sisters, Blue Ribbon Sushi is also open late. A decent sake selection is served in traditional wooden boxes. ✉ *119 Sullivan St., between Prince and Spring Sts., SoHo* ☎ *212/343–0404* ✍ *Reservations not accepted* ▭ *AE, DC, MC, V.*

¢–$$ ✕ **Honmura An.** At Honmura An, the making of buckwheat *soba* noodles is an art, which you can watch being practiced in a glass-enclosed cube at the back of the teak-lined dining room. Like the best restaurants in Tokyo, where the original Honmura An still operates, this one focuses on doing one thing well. The true test of quality is the cold soba, served on square trays with a dipping sauce and a ladle full of cooking water you are expected to slurp as you eat. But everything on the menu is exquisite, including small tasting plates like sliced smoked duck, and signature soba sushi (noodles replace rice) made with mashed prawns and shiitakes. ✉ *170 Mercer St., between W. Houston and Prince Sts., SoHo* ☎ *212/334–5253* ✍ *Reservations essential* ▭ *AE, DC, MC, V* ⊙ *Closed Mon. No lunch Tues. and Sun.*

Korean

$–$$ ✕ **Woo Lae Oak.** If you thought Korean food was a cheap bowl of bibimbop, think again: Woo Lae Oak uses traditional flavors to create an elevated cuisine. The food is spicy and flavorful: kimchi burns the lips and prepares the palate for such dishes as *kesalmari* (Dungeness crab wrapped in spinach crepes), and *o ree mari* (duck slices wrapped in miso blini sweetened with a date sauce). But fans of tabletop grilling can still get their *bul go gi.* Since this is SoHo, the tables are dark marble slabs, the lighting is low, and attractive servers are dressed head to toe in black. ✉ *148 Mercer St., between Prince and W. Houston Sts., SoHo* ☎ *212/925–8200* ✍ *Reservations essential* ▭ *AE, DC, MC, V.*

Latin

¢–$ ✕ **Café Habana.** The simple Cuban-Latin menu at this small neighborhood hangout reflects the friendly, casual atmosphere: Cubano sandwiches, rice and beans, and *camarones al ajillo* (shrimp in garlic sauce), all at budget prices. Just try and get a seat, though: on any given night the sidewalk outside the cheery space with blue booths and pale green Formica tables is littered with belly-baring people waiting to get in. Some fans actually prefer **Café Habana to Go** around the corner, where the *tortas* and grilled corn are cheap and tasty. ✉ *17 Prince St., at Elizabeth St., NoLita* ☎ *212/625–2001* ▭ *AE, DC, MC, V* ✉ *229 Elizabeth St., between Houston and Prince Sts., NoLita* ☎ *212/625–2002* ▭ *AE, DC, MC, V.*

Philippine

$–$$ ✕ **Cendrillon Asian Grill and Marienda Bar.** Cendrillon means Cinderella in French, so the slipper-shape bar here is "fitting." Delicate inlay designs ornament the redbrick dining room's wood tables. Don't miss the spring rolls *(lumpia),* Asian barbecue (duck, spareribs, and chicken), black rice paella, or vinegary chicken adobo—the national dish of the Philippines. ✉ *45 Mercer St., between Broome and Grand Sts., SoHo* ☎ *212/343–9012* ▭ *AE, D, MC, V* ⊙ *Closed Mon.*

Seafood

$$–$$$ ✕ **Aquagrill.** For an island at the edge of the Atlantic Ocean, Manhattan has surprisingly few good seafood restaurants, especially downtown. But Aquagrill's friendly staff and extensive all-things-marine menu place it among the best. Chef-owner Jeremy Marshall mans the stove, while his wife, Jennifer, works the host stand. Specialties include roasted Dun-

geness crab cake napoleon and falafel-crusted salmon served on hummus with tomato and cucumber. Then there are the grilled fresh fish and a rotating selection of East and West Coast oysters. The chocolate tasting plate is a seductive end, but you may just want to have a few more *kumamotos:* they're sweet enough for a dessert. ✉ *210 Spring St., at 6th Ave., SoHo* ☎ *212/274–0505* ✍ *Reservations essential* ▭ *AE, DC, MC* ⊙ *Closed Mon.*

Greenwich Village

One of the most difficult Manhattan neighborhoods to navigate, Greenwich Village has enchanted many a tourist (and frustrated many a cab driver). Cornelia Street is a mini Restaurant Row, and tiny alcoves around the neighborhood have been transformed into serious eateries. To the far west, the Meatpacking District—where you can still see people carting around sides of beef—has blossomed into one of the most chic restaurant destinations in town.

American

$$ ✕ **Merge.** The city's most humorous chef, Sam DeMarco, who also runs First and District, does his most personal work at Merge. While you'll find his signature fun foods such as "lollipop" buffalo wings (a strategic snip makes all the meat bunch into a ball on the end of the bone) and mini burgers, the chef himself cooks American market-driven dishes in the new DeMarco's Room at the rear of the restaurant. And Sunday 4–11 PM, his Sopranos Dinner feeds the famished—course after course of hearty favorites such as *arancini* (rice balls) and *bresaola* (dried, salted beef fillet)—family style on large platters. It's one of the best bargains in the city at $28. When you've had enough, dash back to your hotel for a night of HBO. ✉ *142 W. 10th St., between Greenwich Ave. and Waverly Pl., Greenwich Village* ☎ *212/691–7757* ▭ *AE, MC, V* ⊙ *No lunch weekdays.*

$–$$ ✕ **Grange Hall.** Updated all-American cuisine, affordable prices, a friendly bar, and a room that alludes to the WPA style of architecture attract a lively local bar crowd to this former speakeasy on one of Greenwich Village's most charming, tucked-away streets. Order one of the small plates, such as potato pancakes with chive-spiked sour cream, for starters, or make an entire meal by ordering several of the sides. Entrées—including the center-cut pork chops and maple-glazed salmon—may be ordered by themselves or with a choice of soup or salad for a couple of dollars more. ✉ *50 Commerce St., at Barrow St., Greenwich Village* ☎ *212/924–5246* ✍ *Reservations essential* ▭ *AE, MC, V.*

$–$$ ✕ **Home.** Owners David Page and Barbara Shinn have re-created that mythic heartland home in this sliver of a storefront restaurant, where the walls are clapboard and the floorboards wide. Page's Midwestern background sets the menu's tone: perennial favorites include cornmeal-fried oysters, moist roast chicken, and juicy pork chops with butternut squash. And what's a home-cooked meal without some creamy chocolate pudding? Breakfast is served during the week, and brunch on weekends. ✉ *20 Cornelia St., between Bleecker and W. 4th Sts., Greenwich Village* ☎ *212/243–9579* ✍ *Reservations essential* ▭ *AE.*

Austrian

$$–$$$ ✕ **Wallsé.** For some, Kurt Gutenbrunner's modern Austrian menu at this neighborhood restaurant with a quasi–Wiener Werkstatt look is everything David Bouley's at Danube is not: soulful, and satisfying, with a strong emphasis on Austrian tradition and an urban New York attitude. It's hard to argue with such dishes as roesti with lobster; braised rabbit and spaetzle; perch with young leeks and horseradish; and Weiner

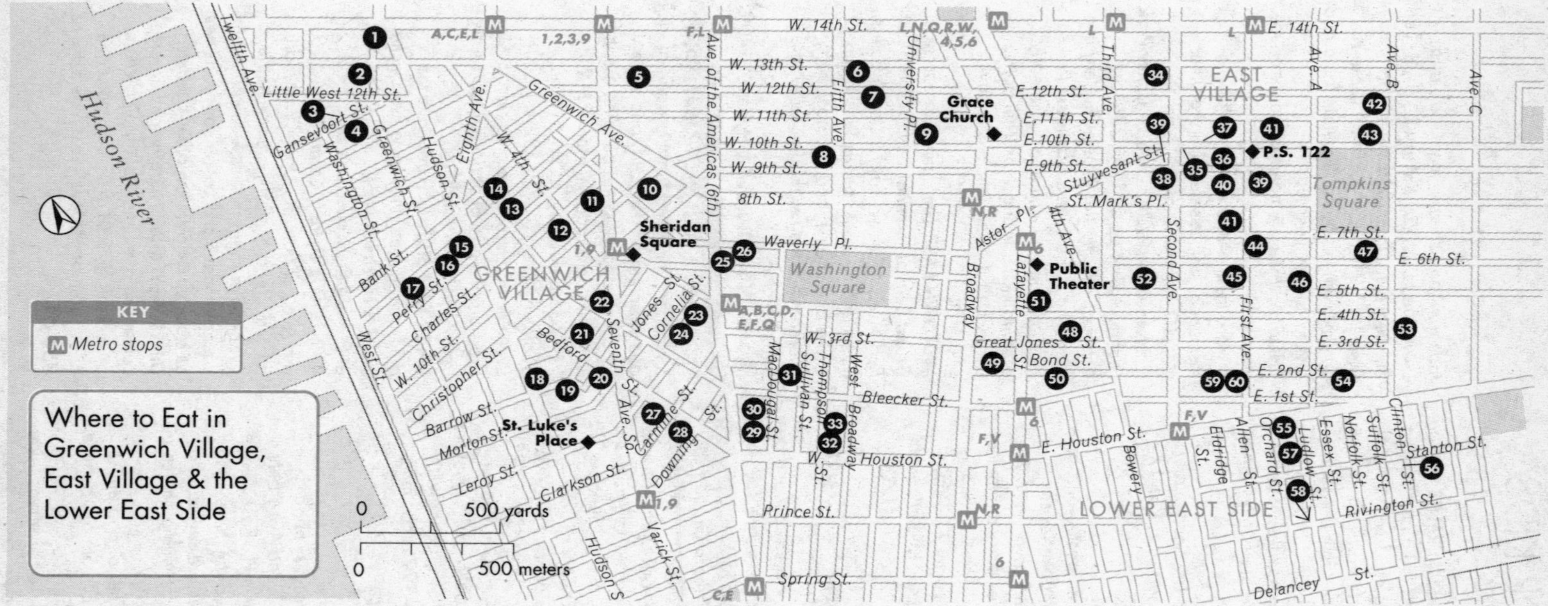

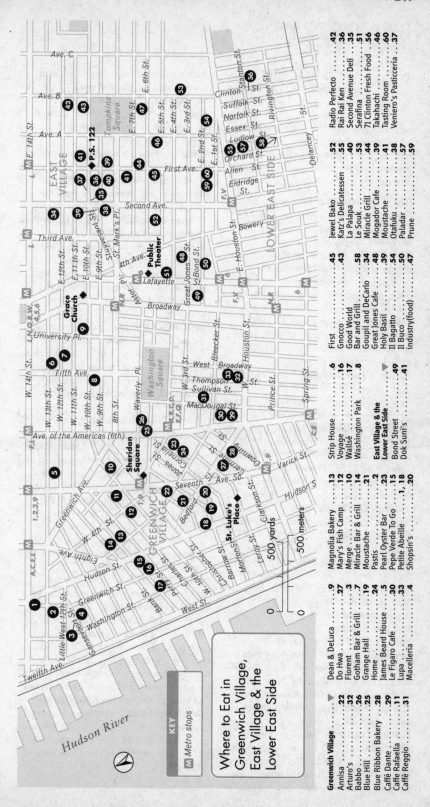

Where to Eat in Greenwich Village, East Village & the Lower East Side

Greenwich Village

- Annisa .22
- Arturo's .32
- Babbo .26
- Blue Hill .25
- Blue Ribbon Bakery .28
- Caffé Dante .29
- Caffe Rafaella .11
- Caffé Reggio .31
- Dean & DeLuca .9
- Do Hwa .27
- Florent .3
- Gotham Bar & Grill .7
- Grange Hall .19
- Home .24
- James Beard House .5
- Le Figaro Cafe .30
- Lupa .33
- Macelleria .4
- Magnolia Bakery .13
- Mary's Fish Camp .12
- Merge .10
- Miracle Bar & Grill .14
- Moustache .21
- Pastis .2
- Pearl Oyster Bar .23
- Pepe Verde To Go .15
- Petite Abeille .1, 18
- Shopsin's .20
- Strip House .6
- Voyage .16
- Wallsé .17
- Washington Park .8

East Village & the Lower East Side

- Bond Street .49
- Dok Suni's .41
- First .45
- Gnocco .43
- Good World Bar and Grill .58
- Goupil and DeCarlo .34
- Great Jones Cafe .48
- Holy Basil .39
- Il Bagatto .54
- Il Buco .50
- industry(food) .47
- Jewel Bako .52
- Katz's Delicatessen .55
- La Palapa .40
- Le Souk .53
- Miracle Grill .44
- Mogador Cafe .39
- Moustache .41
- Otafuku .38
- Paladar .57
- Prune .59
- Radio Perfecto .42
- Rai Rai Ken .36
- Second Avenue Deli .35
- Serafina .51
- 71 Clinton Fresh Food .56
- Takahachi .46
- Tasting Room .60
- Veniero's Pasticceria .37

TREATS FOR KIDS

NEW YORK RESTAURANTS *can be ill-equipped to handle families with young children. Waiters aren't used to braking for wayward tots, and little room between tables makes staying seated and low-volume conversation a courtesy to other diners. However, there are family-friendly options.*

LOWER MANHATTAN: *The South Street Seaport has a food court in its* ***Pier 17*** *(✉ 89 South St., South Street Seaport ☎ 212/732–7678).*

CHINATOWN: *Any of the restaurants here are good for children. Bakeries sell pastries both sweet and savory at 60¢ each, and several cafés carry the tactile treat of tapioca drinks. The flavors at the* ***Chinatown Ice Cream Factory*** *(✉ 65 Bayard St., between Mott and Elizabeth Sts., Chinatown ☎ 212/608–4170) include lychee and ginger.*

SOHO: Le Pain Quotidien *(✉ 100 Grand St., at Mercer St., SoHo ☎ 212/625–9009) is open for breakfast and has sandwiches, sweet treats, and hot chocolate. It closes by 7:30* PM.

TRIBECA: *The trendy* ***Tribeca Grand*** *(✉ 2 6th Ave., between Walker and White Sts., TriBeCa ☎ 212/519–6600) hotel has a room where children can watch movies while their parents brunch on Sunday.*

GREENWICH VILLAGE: Cones *(✉ 272 Bleecker St., between 6th and 7th Aves., Greenwich Village ☎ 212/414–1795) scoops European-style gelato.* ***Peanut Butter & Co.*** *(✉ 240 Sullivan St., between Bleecker and W. 3rd Sts., Greenwich Village ☎ 212/677–3995) has more than 10 varieties of peanut butter sandwiches, all served with carrot sticks and potato chips.*

EAST VILLAGE: *For a snack, head to* ***Pommes Frites*** *(✉ 123 2nd Ave., between E. 7th St. and St. Marks Pl., East Village ☎ 212/674–1234), a tiny hole-in-the-wall; the fabulous fries are served in a take-out cone and come with a choice of wild toppings.*

FLATIRON DISTRICT: *The roadhouselike* ***Chat 'n Chew*** *(✉ 10 E. 16th St., between 5th Ave. and Union Sq. W, Flatiron District ☎ 212/243–1616) serves huge portions of such American comfort food as macaroni and cheese, meat loaf, and overstuffed BLTs.* ***City Bakery*** *(✉ 3 W. 18th St., between 5th and 6th Aves., Flatiron District ☎ 212/366–1414 ⏲ Closed Sun. No dinner) has a lilliputian table and toys to occupy your kids.*

CHELSEA: *If you've managed to introduce your kids to Chelsea's art galleries, reward them with a burger at the old-fashioned, stainless-steel* ***Empire Diner*** *(✉ 210 10th Ave., at W. 22nd St., Chelsea ☎ 212/243–2736).* ***Trailer Park Lounge & Grill*** *(✉ 271 W. 23rd St., between 7th and 8th Aves., Chelsea) is a grown-up's Pee Wee's Playhouse that suits kids just fine. At lunch and in the early evening kids can snack on chili dogs, burgers, and other delicious trashy selections.*

MIDTOWN EAST: *The dining concourse at* ***Grand Central Terminal*** *(✉ E. 42nd St. at Park Ave., Midtown East) includes both sit-down and take-out options (and plenty of tables and chairs), and is a good alternative to the neighborhood's more formal dining.*

MIDTOWN WEST: Jekyll & Hyde *(✉ 1409 6th Ave., between W. 57th and W. 58th Sts., Midtown West ☎ 212/541–9505), a macabre multilevel fantasy world of trick doors, animated skeletons, and so-so food, will appeal to the budding Stephen Kings in your brood. At* ***Mars 2112*** *(✉ 1633 Broadway, at W. 51st St., Midtown West ☎ 212/582–2112), a five-minute bumpy spaceship ride to Mars precedes the arrival of decent food served up by Trekkie waitstaff.*

UPPER EAST SIDE: *Children love the dinosaur nuggets (they taste like chicken) at* ***E.J.'s Luncheonette*** *(✉ 1271 3rd Ave., at E. 73rd St., Upper East Side ☎ 212/472–0600).* ***Dylan's Candy Bar*** *(✉ 1011 3rd Ave., at 60th St., Upper East Side) is a child's (and dentist's) dream. At this Wonka-like sugar palace kids can eat ice-cream sundaes and cotton candy, as well as stock up on a billion other candies.*

UPPER WEST SIDE: *Huge, juicy burgers come with a multitude of topping choices at* ***Jackson Hole*** *(✉ 517 Columbus Ave., at W. 85th St., Upper West Side ☎ 212/362–5177).*

schnitzel, each prepared with a light hand and beautifully presented. Order at least one portion of the quark dumplings (steaming hot puffs of an ethereal dough served with buttered bread crumbs and fruit compote). ✉ *344 W. 11th St., at Washington St., Greenwich Village* ☎ *212/352–2300* ✍ *Reservations essential* ▭ *AE, MC, V* ⊙ *No lunch.*

Belgian

$–$$ ✕ **Petite Abeille.** There are only eight small tables in the original closet-size Hudson Street storefront, which remains the most inviting outpost of this expanding chain of Belgian bistros. The menu tempts with salads, frites, sandwiches, omelets, poached salmon, and other light fare for early in the day. Come evening, sausages, stoemp (mashed sweet potatoes and veggies), steak, stew, and mussels satisfy. Two styles of waffles are always available; de Bruxelles (made fresh to order and topped with ice cream, whipped cream, and fresh fruit) and the true Belgian waffle, de Liège (imported from Belgium and reheated until the subtle caramelized sugar coating crunches and melts in your mouth). ✉ *466 Hudson St., at Barrow St., Greenwich Village* ☎ *212/741–6479* ✉ *400 W. 14th St., at 9th Ave., Greenwich Village* ☎ *212/727–1505* ▭ *AE, MC, V.*

Cafés

¢–$ ✕ **Caffe Rafaella.** Parchment-paper lamp shades adorned with fluttering red fringe, variously hued marble-top tables, and an antiques-store assortment of chairs make this one of the homiest cafés in the city. ✉ *134 7th Ave. S, between 10th and Charles Sts., Greenwich Village* ☎ *212/929–7247* ▭ *No credit cards.*

¢–$ ✕ **Le Figaro Cafe.** A major beat hangout long ago, Le Figaro attracts herds of tourists and students now. On the weekend there's live jazz, but during the week (Wednesday and Thursday) you have to suffer karaoke. Middle Eastern music and belly dancers entertain in the back room on Sunday night. ✉ *184 Bleecker St., at MacDougal St., Greenwich Village* ☎ *212/677–1100* ▭ *MC, V.*

¢ ✕ **Caffè Dante.** A longtime Village haunt, this convivial spot has superlative espresso and knockout tiramisu. The regulars here have been coming for years. ✉ *79–81 MacDougal St., between W. Houston and Bleecker Sts., Greenwich Village* ☎ *212/982–5275* ▭ *AE, MC, V.*

¢ ✕ **Caffè Reggio.** In the neighborhood's oldest Italian coffeehouse (established 1927), a huge, antique espresso machine (from 1902) gleams among the tiny, packed tables. One of the paintings is an original from the school of Caravaggio. ✉ *119 MacDougal St., between W. 3rd and Bleecker Sts., Greenwich Village* ☎ *212/475–9557* ✍ *Reservations not accepted* ▭ *No credit cards.*

¢ ✕ **Dean & DeLuca.** Known for gourmet goodies, this small local chain is a spin-off of the SoHo gourmet market. Think fast as the line snakes past the gingerbread, cakes, cookies, sandwiches, and salads. ✉ *75 University Pl., at W. 11th St., Greenwich Village* ☎ *212/473–1908* ▭ *AE, MC, V.*

★ ¢ ✕ **Magnolia Bakery.** Sky-high home-style cakes, fabulous cupcakes, puddings, and pies keep this adorable bakery packed into the wee hours. They will even serve you a glass of milk to wash it all down. ✉ *401 Bleecker St., at W. 11th St., Greenwich Village* ☎ *212/462–2572* ▭ *AE, DC, MC, V.*

Contemporary

$$$–$$$$ ✕ **Gotham Bar & Grill.** A culinary landmark, Gotham Bar & Grill still thrills after 19 years. Celebrated chef Alfred Portale, who made the blueprint for architectural food, builds on a foundation of simple, clean flavors. On weekends, a steady stream of limos deposits people who come to gorge on transcendent dishes: no rack of lamb is more tender, no scal-

Fodor's Choice ★

lop sweeter. Portale (he's actually in the kitchen most weeknights) wrings maximum taste from the best the earth has to offer. A stellar 20,000-bottle cellar provides the perfect accompaniments—at a price. If you plan on splurging on the food of an American master, do it here. ✉ *12 E. 12th St., between 5th Ave. and University Pl., Greenwich Village* ☎ *212/620–4020* ✍ *Reservations essential* ▭ *AE, DC, MC, V* ⊙ *No lunch weekends.*

$$–$$$$ ✕ **Washington Park.** Hailed as a comeback kid, Jonathan Waxman, who in the 1980s brought California cuisine to New York via his hit restaurant Jams, is back on top with Washington Park. In Waxman's kitchen, the marriage of extreme seasonality and a classic foundation begets food of amazing lightness. Even a rich dish of foie gras gets a spa treatment of diced roasted apples and pears, rather than a cloying sauce. A skin-on sliver of pompano looks like a strip of bark, the firm white flesh's flavor brought out by capers, pepper, white wine, and lemon; it sounds familiar and simple yet tastes deep and complex. Although the menu is anything but budget, the staff doesn't put on airs. Knowledgeable sommelier Sean Toussaint (one of four) offers earnest guidance whether you can drop $40 or $400 on a bottle. ✉ *24 5th Ave., at 9th St., Greenwich Village* ☎ *212/529–4400* ✍ *Reservations essential* ▭ *AE, MC, V* ⊙ *No lunch.*

$$–$$$ ✕ **Annisa.** Dining at Annisa is an experience in sweetness and light: chef Anita Lo's ethereal, creative cooking is served in a spare bone-color room. Modern French technique mixes with Asian influences to create seared foie gras with soup dumplings, beef tenderloin awakened by a *sansho* peppercorn reduction, and pan-roasted chicken stuffed with pig's feet and truffles. The wine list, created by Roger Dagorn of Chanterelle, features the work of women wine makers and winery owners. From the innovative hors d'oeuvres to the delicate petit fours, Annisa raises the bar (and the price tag) on neighborhood dining. ✉ *13 Barrow St., between 7th Ave. and W. 4th St., Greenwich Village* ☎ *212/741–6699* ✍ *Reservations essential* ▭ *AE, MC, V* ⊙ *No lunch.*

$$ ✕ **Blue Hill.** Since it opened in 2000, this sophisticated chocolate-brown den of a restaurant hasn't stopped wowing critics and pedestrian eaters. Almost invisible from the quaint street, Blue Hill grabs your attention with chef Dan Barber's precisely cooked and elegantly constructed food—crabmeat lasagna, poached duck, and braised cod. Foams, purees, vinegars, hot and cold temperatures, hard and soft textures—these are the contrasting elements that elevate chef Barber's dishes to delectable heights. ✉ *75 Washington Pl., between Washington Sq. W and 6th Ave., Greenwich Village* ☎ *212/539–1776* ✍ *Reservations essential* ▭ *AE, DC, MC, V* ⊙ *No lunch.*

$–$$ ✕ **Voyage.** Scott Barton proves to be a chef to watch at Voyage, his new little West Village restaurant that gets everything just right. From the front lounge with the digital fireplace to the swank rear dining room (the padded walls make for great tête-à-têtes), Voyage makes you feel like one of the Beautiful People without all the fuss. Barton turns the familiar on its head, adding Caribbean, Indian, and French touches, to create something new. Sweet soft scallops are paired with crunchy sea beans in a grapefruit reduction and orange-scented olive oil. Voyage is a first-class trip at coach prices. ✉ *117 Perry St., at Greenwich St., West Village* ☎ *212/294–1000* ▭ *AE, MC, V* ⊙ *No lunch.*

Eclectic

$$$$ ✕ **James Beard House.** This landmark town house presents an extravagant dinner to the public almost every night. The James Beard Foundation, a nonprofit culinary organization, invites high-profile chefs from around the world to cook in what was once the home of the famous American cookbook author and television personality. Reservations must be made well in advance for the prepaid, prix-fixe dinners. All dinners begin at 7 PM with a cocktail reception, during which you can stand in the kitchen and watch the chefs in action. To find out what's on, visit www.jamesbeard.org. ✉ *167 W. 12th St., between 6th and 7th Aves., Greenwich Village* ☎ *212/675–4984* ✍ *Reservations essential* 🧥 *Jacket and tie* 💳 *AE, DC, MC, V* ☞ *Call ahead for schedule.*

¢–$ ✕ **Shopsin's General Store.** Welcome to the wacky world of Kenny Shopsin. In his tiny, dingy storefront restaurant you can sample more than 200 soups (up for Senegalese cherry?) or get thrown out if he doesn't like your attitude. There are also hundreds of entrées (each prepared à la minute). One of the best meals is breakfast. Offerings include homemade pumpkin pancakes, corn and cornmeal waffles, and a filling openface chorizo omelet. The coffee is good, but you have to help yourself, as you do to the jars of old-fashioned penny candy crowding a counter. Shopsin's is a true New York original. ✉ *63 Bedford St., at Morton St., Greenwich Village* ☎ *212/924–5160* 💳 *DC, MC, V* ⏲ *Closed weekdays 7 PM and weekends.*

French

$–$$$ ✕ **Blue Ribbon Bakery.** When the owners of Blue Ribbon and Blue Ribbon Sushi renovated this space they uncovered a 100-year-old coal-burning oven made from Italian tile and let it dictate the destiny of their restaurant. The bakery-restaurant has an eclectic menu featuring substantial sandwiches on homemade bread (from the oven, of course) and entrées that include trout and Cornish game hen. A whole section of the menu presents small plates of charcuterie, pâté, aged cheeses, and tapas-style dishes. The basement dining room (which has more atmosphere) is dark and intimate; upstairs is a Parisian-style café. ✉ *33 Downing St., at Bedford St., Greenwich Village* ☎ *212/337–0404* 💳 *AE, DC, MC, V.*

$–$$ ✕ **Pastis.** A spin-off of Balthazar in SoHo, Pastis looks like it was shipped in tile by tile from Paris. At night throngs of whippet-thin cell-phone-slinging boys 'n' girls gather at the bar up front sipping Pernods and martinis. The menu includes passable French dishes such as steak frites, *frisée aux lardons,* leeks vinaigrette, salmon in an herbal sauce, and excellent crusty bread (imported from Balthazar). Try to get a seat in the rear dining area, away from the milling bodies. The restaurant also serves a full breakfast menu—in summer, there's no better place for a hangover recovery than at an outdoor table. ✉ *9 9th Ave., at Little W. 12th St., Greenwich Village* ☎ *212/929–4844* ✍ *Reservations not accepted* 💳 *AE, DC, MC, V.*

¢–$$ ✕ **Florent.** When it's 4 AM and a slice of pizza on Bleecker Street just won't cut it, head to Florent, the true pioneer of dining in the Meatpacking District. Open each night until 5 AM (Thursday through Sunday it stays open 24 hours), this brushed-steel and Formica diner is always a blast—expect loud music, drag queens, and members of every walk of city life. The simple French menu features decent versions of everything you crave—onion soup, mussels steamed in white wine, blood sausage, pâté—and in the early morning hours you can also order from a full breakfast menu. ✉ *69 Gansevoort St., between Greenwich and Washington Sts., Greenwich Village* ☎ *212/989–5779* 💳 *No credit cards.*

Italian

$$–$$$ ✕ **Babbo.** Fodor'sChoice ★ After your first bite of the kitchen's ethereal homemade pasta or the tender suckling pig, you won't wonder why it's so hard to get reservations at Mario Batali's flagship restaurant (you'll need to make them before you arrive in New York). A five-course pasta tasting menu is the best way to get your fill of fresh noodles, such as the luscious lamb

and fresh mint "love letters," or the rich beef-cheek ravioli. Adventuresome eaters will rejoice in the delicious lamb's tongue salad or the custardy brain ravioli, but more timid diners gravitate toward such simple dishes as succulent whole fish baked in salt. And believe it or not, service is friendly. ✉ *110 Waverly Pl., between MacDougal St. and 6th Ave., Greenwich Village* ☎ *212/777–0303* ✍ *Reservations essential* ▭ *AE, MC, V* ⊙ *No lunch.*

$–$$$ ✕ **Macelleria.** Italian for "butcher shop," the name of this restaurant in the red-hot Meatpacking District presages the menu, which features Italian-style preparations of meat. The double-cut porterhouse for two is a deliciously aged piece of beef that comes with fresh-cut fries. Salads, pastas, side dishes, and other simple fare are skillfully prepared. The minimalist decor manages to feel simultaneously homey and chic with a stylish combination of brick, cement, and pine. As at many of the restaurants in this trendy destination neighborhood, the service can be sporadic. ✉ *48 Gansevoort St., between Greenwich and Washington Sts., Greenwich Village* ☎ *212/741–2555* ✍ *Reservations essential* ▭ *AE, MC, V.*

$ ✕ **Lupa.** Even the most hard-to-please Italian-food connoisseurs have a soft spot for Lupa, Mario Batali and Joseph Bastianich's "downscale" Roman trattoria (they also run high-end hits Babbo and Esca). Roughhewn wood, great Italian wines, and simple preparations of top-quality ingredients are what Lupa is about. People come repeatedly for dishes such as bucatini with sweet-sausage ragù, house-made salamis and hams, and fried baby artichokes. The front room of the restaurant is seated on a first-come, first-served basis, while reservations are taken for the back. ✉ *170 Thompson St., between Bleecker and W. Houston Sts., Greenwich Village* ☎ *212/982–5089* ▭ *AE, DC, MC, V* ⊙ *Closed Sun.*

¢–$ ✕ **Pepe Verde to Go.** A long list of specials changes daily here, but the menu always includes generously portioned pastas (prepared fresh in the open kitchen), antipasti, salads, entrées, and sandwiches. The gnocchi are as light as little clouds, the pesto sauce is fragrant with basil and garlic, and the veal is tender. Inexpensive wine is available in carafes or by the bottle. Dinner can cost less than $17 at any one of the four "Pepe" restaurants—quite possibly the best Italian value in the city. ✉ *559 Hudson St., between Perry and W. 11th Sts., Greenwich Village* ☎ *212/255–2221* ▭ *AE, MC, V.*

Korean

¢–$ ✕ **Do Hwa.** If anyone in New York is responsible for making Korean food cool, it is the mother-daughter team behind this perennially popular restaurant and its East Village sister, Dok Suni's. Jenny Kwak and her mother Myung Ja serve home cookin' in the form of *kalbi jim* (braised short ribs), *bibimbop* (a spicy, mix-it-yourself vegetable and rice dish), and other favorites that may not be as pungent as they are in Little Korea, but are satisfying nevertheless. ✉ *55 Carmine St., between Bedford and Bleecker Sts., Greenwich Village* ☎ *212/414–1224* ▭ *No credit cards* ⊙ *No lunch.*

Middle Eastern

★ ¢–$ ✕ **Moustache.** There's always a crowd waiting outside for one of the copper-top tables at this appealing Middle Eastern restaurant. The focal point is the pita, steam-filled pillows of dough rolled before your eyes and baked in a searingly hot oven. They are the perfect vehicle for the tasty salads—lemony chickpea and spinach, and hearty lentil and bulghur among them. For entrées, try the leg of lamb or merguez sausage sandwiches or, if you are feeling particularly hungry, tackle the *ouzi,* a large phyllo package stuffed with chicken and fragrant rice. Although the service can be slow, it's always friendly. ✉ *90 Bedford St., between Barrow and Grove Sts., Greenwich Village* ☎ *212/229–2220* ✍ *Reservations not accepted* ▭ *No credit cards.*

Pizza

$–$$$ ✕ **Arturo's.** Few guidebooks list this brick-walled Village landmark, but the jam-packed room and the smell of well-done pies augur a good meal to come. The pizza is terrific, cooked in a coal-fired oven. Basic pastas as well as seafood, veal, and chicken concoctions with mozzarella and lots of tomato sauce come at giveaway prices. Let everyone else stand in line at John's Pizzeria on Bleecker Street. ✉ *106 W. Houston St., near Thompson St., Greenwich Village* ☎ *212/677–3820* ▭ *AE, MC, V.*

¢–$ ✕ **Patsy's Pizzeria.** The original Patsy's opened back in 1933 in East Harlem, when the neighborhood was largely Italian. The pizzeria still serves some of the best slices in New York. The secret is in the thin, crisp, coal-oven-baked crust, topped with thick sauce and fresh toppings. ✉ *67 University Pl., between E. 10th and E. 11th Sts., Greenwich Village* ☎ *212/533–3500* ▭ *No credit cards.*

Seafood

$$ ✕ **Mary's Fish Camp.** The neighborhood's second New England fish house (the result of a split between Pearl Oyster Bar's partners) proves you can't have too much of a good thing. Casual Mary's Fish Camp usually has a wait for fried oysters, chowder, moist grilled catches of the day, and, of course, the sweet lobster roll with impeccable frites. A neighborhood favorite is the lobster potpie, which runs out early. ✉ *64 Charles St., at W. 4th St., Greenwich Village* ☎ *646/486–2185* ✍ *Reservations not accepted* ▭ *AE, MC, V* ⊙ *Closed Sun.*

★ $–$$ ✕ **Pearl Oyster Bar.** At long last, Pearl Oyster Bar, once no bigger than a bivalve, is expanding. Owner Rebecca Charles bought out the next door antiques shop to add 30 seats to her wildly popular restaurant. But chances are you'll still have a bit of a wait for the fresh seafood: chilled oysters to start, naturally, followed by bouillabaisse, a whole fish, or perhaps the famous lobster roll. Locals know to come by for a lazy lunch at the bar, when you can down some bluepoints and beer in peace. ✉ *18 Cornelia St., between Bleecker and W. 4th Sts., Greenwich Village* ☎ *212/691–8211* ▭ *MC, V* ⊙ *Closed Sun.*

Southwestern

$–$$ ✕ **Miracle Grill.** The margaritas are fabulous here, and the food reasonably priced and tasty—after all, this is where Bobby Flay got his start. Appetizers such as cornmeal-crusted catfish soft tacos are crowd pleasers. Entrée portions are huge, and vegetarians will appreciate the grilled or roasted vegetable dishes. ✉ *415 Bleecker St., between Bank and W. 11th Sts., Greenwich Village* ☎ *212/924–1900* ✍ *Reservations not accepted* ▭ *AE, MC, V* ⊙ *No lunch weekdays.*

Steak

$$–$$$$ ✕ **Strip House.** Judging by the pinup girl logo, the bordello-red walls, and the signature New York strip steak, the Strip House doesn't take itself too seriously. Still, it shows off the more sophisticated side of steak cookery. In addition to cuts of meat, chef David Walzog (who also oversees the meat at Michael Jordan's—The Steak House NYC, located in Grand Central Station) serves foie gras torchon and carpaccio appetizers. Nonbeef entrées—such as Dover sole and roast duck breast—and sides, such as melted heirloom tomatoes, and potatoes cooked in goose fat, inspire instant adulation. ✉ *13 E. 12th St., between 5th Ave. and University Pl., Greenwich Village* ☎ *212/328–0000* ▭ *AE, DC, MC, V* ⊙ *No lunch weekends.*

Thai

¢–$$ ✕ **Little Basil.** This is a West Village favorite. The vibrant food—enlivened by chilies, opal basil, and kaffir lime—comes carefully composed in layer-cake form. Taste buds awaken to the spicy *som tum* (green papaya salad) and rich *tom kah gai* (chicken and coconut-milk soup), not to mention anything in *kaw praw* (a traditional curried preparation). A large and informative wine list is an added bonus. ✉ *39 Greenwich Ave., at Charles St., Greenwich Village* ☎ 212/645–8965 ▭ MC, V ⊙ *No lunch.*

East Village & Lower East Side

Once Manhattan's bohemian and immigrant enclave, the East Village has become another high-rent neighborhood. The influx of deeper pockets is changing the restaurant scene, too; amid the cheap Ukrainian diners, sushi houses, and tiny Thai restaurants is an army of mid-priced Italian spots and a handful of high-end reservations-only eateries.

American

$–$$$$ ✕ **Prune.** This adorable restaurant serves a quirky brand of eclectic American food that matches perfectly with the offbeat, homey decor. Roasted capon is served over garlicky toasted bread, homemade lamb sausages are grilled, and marrow bones are roasted and served with parsley salad. Sides cost extra. The home-style touches are evident in an appetizer of house-made bologna and a dessert of buttered bread with sugar. The Bloody Marys at weekend brunch are gaining a cult following. There's usually a wait, and the quarters are very cramped, so don't expect to linger at your table. ✉ *54 E. 1st St., between 1st and 2nd Aves., East Village* ☎ 212/677–6221 ✍ *Reservations essential* ▭ AE, MC, V ⊙ *No lunch.*

$–$$ ✕ **First.** Sam DeMarco was an East Village serious-food pioneer when he opened First in 1995. This quintessentially downtown restaurant—stylish waiters, loud music, and dark, horseshoe-shape banquettes—remains a primo option in the neighborhood. DeMarco oversees an open kitchen that makes everything from the bread to the mayonnaise. As at his other restaurants, Merge and District, you are sure to find seafood tacos, buffalo "lollipop" chicken wings, and some form of roasted pork. Several fine vintages from the carefully chosen wine list are available by the glass, but the "tiny 'tinis," dwarf martinis in luscious flavors, are the drink of choice at First, where late hours prevail. ✉ *87 1st Ave., between E. 5th and E. 6th Sts., East Village* ☎ 212/674–3823 ✍ *Reservations essential* ▭ AE, MC, V ⊙ *No lunch.*

American Casual

¢–$ ✕ **Radio Perfecto.** The music is loud, the wine comes in water glasses, and the owner really cares about his guests. Radio Perfecto is a part of the Avenue B restaurant revolution and it is a perfect neighborhood spot, lively but completely casual, with such decent, inexpensive food as hamburgers, pasta, french fries, and an exemplary roast chicken served with a choice of sauces each night. The waitstaff, all dressed according to the prevailing neighborhood aesthetic, are friendly and personable, if occasionally forgetful. ✉ *190 Ave. B, between E. 11th and E. 12th Sts., East Village* ☎ 212/477–3366 ▭ AE, DC, MC, V ⊙ *No lunch.*

Cafés

¢–$ ✕ **Le Gamin.** It's easy to confuse New York for Paris at this hip little haven, where the menu includes all the French café standards: croque monsieur, quiche Lorraine, salade niçoise, crepes (both sweet and savory), and big bowls of café au lait. Service can be desultory, but the upside is that you're free to lounge for hours. ✉ *536 E. 5th St., between Aves. A and B, East Village* ☎ 212/254–8409 ▭ AE, MC, V.

¢ ✕ **Goupil and DeCarlo.** The almond croissants at this small bakery-café rival any baked in France. There's a complete selection of French baked goods, sandwiches (the foot-long baguette stuffed with merguez and potato gratin is satisfying), and a special dish of the day (the likes of beef bourguignonne). ✉ *244 E. 13th St., between 2nd and 3rd Aves., East Village* ☎ *212/473–3320* ▭ *MC, V.*

¢ ✕ **Newsbar.** This ultracasual resting place has good coffee and tea, a generous selection of magazines, and CNN on the tube. ✉ *107 University Pl., between W. 10th and W. 11th Sts., East Village* ☎ *212/260–4192* ▭ *No credit cards.*

¢ ✕ **Saint's Alp Teahouse.** Join the hip Asian youth crowding the small tables at Saint's Alp Teahouse, part of a Hong Kong–based international chain. They're here for bubble tea—frothy, pastel-color, flavored black or green tea speckled with beads of tapioca or sago (they look like tadpoles). Passion-fruit green tea with chewy tapioca is refreshing. You can also order snacks such as spring rolls, dumplings, or sweets. ✉ *39 3rd Ave., between 9th and 10th Sts., East Village* ☎ *212/598–1890* ▭ *No credit cards.*

¢ ✕ **Veniero's Pasticceria.** More than a century old, this bustling bakery-café sells every kind of Italian *dolci* (sweet), from cherry-topped cookies to creamy cannoli. A new liquor license means you can top off an evening with a nightcap of Kahlua-spiked cappuccino or a dessert wine. ✉ *342 E. 11th St., near 1st Ave., East Village* ☎ *212/674–7264* ✍ *Reservations essential* ▭ *AE, DC, MC, V.*

Cajun/Creole

¢–$ ✕ **Great Jones Cafe.** When you pass through the bright orange door into this small, crowded Cajun joint you'll feel like you're in a honky-tonk. The daily changing menu, posted on the brightly colored walls, always features cornmeal-fried or blackened catfish, gumbo, jambalaya, popcorn shrimp, and rice. Brunch is also festive, and if the strong coffee isn't enough to wake you up, the spicy food definitely will be. ✉ *54 Great Jones St., between the Bowery and Lafayette St., East Village* ☎ *212/674–9304* ▭ *No credit cards.*

Contemporary

¢–$$$ ✕ **Tasting Room.** Ignoring any sense of proportion, this eight-table spot on East 1st Street's restaurant row fits more than 300 different bottles on its American-only wine list. There's an ever-changing list of about 10 wines by the glass, and the menu depends on the season. Owners Collin and Renée Alevras want you to have a full tasting experience, so the menu items such as roast suckling pig, oven-roasted quail with foie gras ravioli, or daikon radish and pomelo salad come in small ("tastes") and large ("shares") portions. Collin must be a magician: you won't believe his food was cooked on a four-burner stove in the basement. ✉ *72 E. 1st St., between 1st and 2nd Aves., East Village* ☎ *212/358–7831* ✍ *Reservations essential* ▭ *AE, DC, MC, V* ⊗ *Closed Sun.–Mon. No lunch.*

★ $$ ✕ **71 Clinton Fresh Food.** The name does little to indicate the sophisticated experience that awaits at this off-the-beaten-path fashionista favorite (Calvin Klein and Michael Kors are spotted here). Food really is the focus—Matt Reguin's short seasonal menu tempts with clean modern dishes with clever twists. Winter might bring pan-roasted monkfish with a cranberry bean *brandade,* or tender and rare rack of wild boar in a smoked mushroom consommé. The cramped dining room adds to the friendly, neighborhood charm of the place. Reservations can be hard to come by, so call in advance. ✉ *71 Clinton St., between Stanton and Rivington Sts., Lower East Side* ☎ *212/614–6960* ✍ *Reservations essential* ▭ *AE, MC, V* ⊗ *No lunch.*

$–$$ ✕ **industry (food).** Young chef Alex Freij, who has worked under Jean-Louis Palladin and Jean-Georges Vongerichten, opened this instant East Village hit. Intended as a hangout for restaurant folk, industry (food) lures hip people from all walks of life into its quasi–Val d'Isère chalet dining room, all woody and snug. Chef de cuisine Kenneth Tufo, a Veritas alum, fools around with food in a thoroughly fun and fabulous way. Rich pork confit, coated in cumin and coriander, on flageolets is his way of saying "pork and beans," and a lobster roll comes as sweet meat on toasted brioche. ✉ *509 E. 6th St., between Aves. A and B, East Village* ☎ *212/777–5920* ✍ *Reservations essential* ▭ *AE, D, DC, MC, V* ⏲ *No lunch Mon.–Sat.*

Delicatessens

$–$$ ✕ **Second Avenue Deli.** A face-lift may have removed the wrinkles of time, but the kosher food is as good as ever at this East Village landmark. The deli's bevy of Jewish classics includes chicken in the pot, matzo-ball soup, chopped liver, Romanian tenderloin, and *cholent* (a Sabbath dish of meat, beans, and grain). A better pastrami sandwich you can't find (don't ask for it lean). A welcome bowl of pickles, sour green tomatoes, and coleslaw satisfies from the start, but at the finish forego dessert—it's nondairy to comply with the rules of kashruth. ✉ *156 2nd Ave., at E. 10th St., East Village* ☎ *212/677–0606* ▭ *AE, DC, MC, V.*

¢–$ ✕ **Katz's Delicatessen.** Everything and nothing has changed at Katz's since it first opened in 1888, when the neighborhood was dominated by Jewish immigrants. The rows of Formica tables, the long self-service counter, and such signs as "send a salami to your boy in the army" are all completely authentic. What's different are the area's demographics, but the locals still flock here for succulent hand-carved corned beef and pastrami sandwiches, soul-warming soups, juicy hot dogs, crisp half-sour pickles, and a little old-school attitude thrown in for good measure. ✉ *205 E. Houston St., at Ludlow St., Lower East Side* ☎ *212/254–2246* ▭ *AE, MC, V.*

Italian

$$–$$$ ✕ **Il Buco.** The unabashed clutter of antique kitchen gadgets, vintage tableware, and old pine cabinets harkens back to Il Buco's past as an antiques store. The tables, some of which are communal, are each unique—the effect is a festive, almost romantic country-house atmosphere. A long menu of Mediterranean tapaslike appetizers lets you try many different dishes such as Angus carpaccio with Umbrian black truffles, and sweet red- and golden-beet raviolis balanced by goat cheese and house-cured pancetta. Chef Jeremy Griffiths uses meats and produce from local farms for the daily entrées such as slow-roasted suckling pig and house-made pastas. Book the inspirational wine cellar for dinner: there are more than 300 varieties down there, and it prompted Edgar Allen Poe to write *The Cask of Amontillado.* ✉ *47 Bond St., between the Bowery and Lafayette St., East Village* ☎ *212/533–1932* ▭ *AE* ⏲ *No lunch Sun.–Mon.*

¢–$$ ✕ **Il Bagatto.** You have to be a magician (*il bagatto* in Italian) to get a table before 11:30 PM at this hip, inexpensive restaurant, but as the reservationist says in her Italian-accented drawl "you go home, take a shower, relax, everyone else will be tired and drunk, you will come to dinner refreshed and happy." How true, and Il Bagatto is just the kind of restaurant where you want to arrive refreshed—so as to enjoy its electric ambience, rich Italian food (order the lasagna special), and fun, rustic decor. It's like being at a party, only the food is better. ✉ *192 E. 2nd St., between Aves. A and B, East Village* ☎ *212/228–0977* ✍ *Reservations essential* ▭ *No credit cards* ⏲ *Closed Mon. No lunch.*

¢–$ ✕ **Gnocco.** The East Village is packed with cheap-and-chic Italian joints. One that stands out when it comes to food is Gnocco. Owners Pierluigi Palazzo and Rossella Tedesco named the place after a regional specialty (they're from Emilia-Romagna)—deep-fried dough, sort of like wontons, served with salami and prosciutto. Head to the roomy rear canopied garden for savory salads, house-made pastas (tagliatelle with lamb ragù is a winner), and hearty entrées like sliced beef tenderloin on a bed of arugula (perfect for Atkins addicts). Homesick expats come here for a dose of comfort. ✉ *337 E. 10th St., between Aves. A and B, East Village* ☎ *212/677–1913* ▭ *No credit cards* ⊙ *No lunch weekdays.*

Japanese

$$ ✕ **Bond Street.** The minimalist setting of sheer curtains, sleek black tables, and taupe screens doesn't seem as chic as it once did, nor does the crowd. But that means you can fully concentrate on the cooking of Linda Rodriguez and creative sushi of Hiroshi Nakahara, neither of which have lost their luster. The kitchen does an admirable job with dishes such as lobster tempura with yuzu and tomato dressing, or rib-eye steak with caramelized shallot teriyaki. As for the sushi bar: you won't find a selection of 10 kinds of hamachi or four types of yellowtail in many other restaurant around town. ✉ *6 Bond St., between Broadway and Lafayette St., East Village* ☎ *212/777–2500* ✍ *Reservations essential* ▭ *AE, MC, V* ⊙ *No lunch.*

$$ **Jewel Bako.** In a minefield of cheap, often inferior, sushi houses gleams tiny Jewel Bako (the Japanese pronunciation of "jewel box"). This is indisputably the best sushi restaurant in the East Village, and seats are hard to come by. The futuristic bamboo tunnel of a dining room is gorgeous, but try to nab a place at the sushi bar and put yourself in the hands of Kazuo Yoshida (his *omakase* starts at $50). He will serve you only the best fish of the day, perhaps even denying you a request because he feels it's not up to par. And like all precious gems, this one will cost you. ✉ *239 E. 5th St., between 2nd and 3rd Aves., East Village* ☎ *212/979–1012* ✍ *Reservations essential* ▭ *AE, DC, MC, V* ⊙ *Closed Sun. No lunch.*

★ **¢–$$** ✕ **Takahachi.** Of the pack of inexpensive East Village Japanese restaurants, Takahachi is one of the best. You'll find well-done sushi standards that attract a loyal following including the occasional celebrity. The food is not exactly distinctive, but the freshness and the price make the restaurant stand out. ✉ *85 Ave. A, between E. 5th and E. 6th Sts., East Village* ☎ *212/505–6524* ✍ *Reservations not accepted* ▭ *AE, MC, V* ⊙ *No lunch.*

¢ ✕ **Otafuku.** A tiny hole-in-the-wall with barely any standing room, Otafuku brings Japanese street food to New York. There are only two things on the menu, *okonomiyaki* (an eggy vegetable pancake native to Hiroshima) and *takoyaki* (octopus balls). The pocketlike pancakes are stuffed with your choice of beef, shrimp, pork, or squid. The octopus balls are made in cast-iron molds. Both are topped with a swirl of mayo, special sauce, and a sprinkling of dried bonito (tuna) flakes. ✉ *236 E. 9th St., between 2nd and 3rd Sts., East Village* ☎ *212/353–8503* ▭ *No credit cards.*

¢ ✕ **Rai Rai Ken.** In the East Village's first true ramen (noodle) shop, sit at the counter overlooking the kitchen and order from the limited menu of appetizers (*gyoza*, or panfried Japanese dumplings) and ramen with miso broth or *shoyu* (soy sauce) broth. Choose from toppings like barbecued pork and snow peas, and some simple condiments (like seven-flavor pepper); that's all the kitchen offers and that's all any self-respecting Japanese diner would want. ✉ *214 E. 10th St., between 1st and 2nd Aves., East Village* ☎ *212/477–7030* ▭ *No credit cards.*

Korean

¢–$ ✕ **Dok Suni's.** If anyone in New York is responsible for making Korean food cool, it is the mother-daughter team behind this perennially popular (and hip) East Village restaurant and its Greenwich Village sister, Do Hwa. Jenny Kwak and her mother Myung Ja serve home cookin' in the form of *kalbi jim* (braised short ribs), bibimbop, and other favorites that may not be as pungent as they are in Little Korea, but are satisfying nevertheless. ✉ *119 1st Ave., between 7th St. and St. Marks Pl., East Village* ☎ *212/477–9506* ▭ *No credit cards* ⏲ *No lunch.*

Latin

¢–$ ✕ **Paladar.** Kitsch 'n' cool Paladar is a party cabana where the drinks are fruity and the pan-Latin dishes snappy updates of old favorites. Corn *arepas* come topped with artfully arranged chorizo and crème fraîche; a plantain "canoe" is split down the middle and stuffed with a bacalao mash. The bold flavors (and meek prices) are courtesy of chef-heartthrob Aaron Sanchez, the son of restaurateur Zarela Martinez. On weekends the place fills up, so be prepared to perch at the bar with a passion-fruit agua fresca or two. ✉ *161 Ludlow St., between Houston and Stanton Sts., Lower East Side* ☎ *212/473–3535* ▭ *No credit cards* ⏲ *No lunch.*

Mexican

$–$$ ✕ **La Palapa.** The menu at this regional Mexican restaurant is about as far from Tex-Mex as El Paso is from Oaxaca. Aztec-style pottery inset into the wall, embossed-tin mirrors, and a terra-cotta tiled floor provide a cozy setting in which to explore traditional ingredients like *epazote* (an herb), *guajillo* (a chili), and *chayote* (a crunchy vegetable). Revelatory sauces combine ingredients such as chilies, tamarind, and chocolate to create multidimensional flavor. Cod fillet with green pumpkin seed sauce and ancho chile barbecue lamb shank are among several dishes that will ruin you for other Mexican restaurants. ✉ *77 St. Marks Pl., between 1st and 2nd Aves., East Village* ☎ *212/777–2537* ✍ *Reservations essential* ▭ *AE, DC, MC, V.*

Middle Eastern

★ ¢–$ ✕ **Moustache.** The focal point here is the pita, steam-filled pillows of dough rolled before your eyes and baked in a searingly hot oven. They are the perfect vehicle for the tasty salads—lemony chickpea and spinach, and hearty lentil and bulghur among them. For entrées, try the leg of lamb or merguez sausage sandwiches or, if you are feeling particularly hungry, tackle the ouzi, a large phyllo package stuffed with chicken and fragrant rice. Although the service can be slow, it's always friendly. ✉ *265 E. 10th St., between Ave. A and 1st Ave., East Village* ☎ *212/228–2022* ✍ *Reservations not accepted* ▭ *No credit cards.*

Moroccan

$–$$ ✕ **Le Souk.** In a city of too many anemic couscous royales and tagines, Le Souk's dishes are packed with authentic Moroccan flavor. Besides those staples, you can order meze such as calves' liver and "cigars" (phyllo filled with chicken, beef, or vegetables), as well as grilled fish. Moroccan tile, camel-skin chairs, luminous lanterns, and a belly dancer enrich the experience. ✉ *47 Ave. B, between 3rd and 4th Sts., East Village* ☎ *212/777–5454* ▭ *AE, MC, V* ⏲ *No lunch.*

¢–$ ✕ **Mogador Cafe.** Whether it's for the Middle Eastern breakfast, espresso in the afternoon, or belly dancing on Wednesday night, East Villagers don't mind a wait at this neighborhood fixture. The menu occasionally strays beyond couscous and hummus with dishes such as butternut squash ravioli. ✉ *101 St. Marks Pl., between 1st Ave. and Ave. A, East Village* ☎ *212/677–2226* ✍ *Reservations not accepted* ▭ *AE, MC, V.*

Pizza

¢-$$ × **Serafina.** Mediterranean-hue friezes, an inviting upstairs terrace, and a steady stream of models and celebrities grace this very Italian café adorned with wine racks and paper wall sconces. Scene aside, the real draw here is some of Manhattan's most authentic Neopolitan pizza. Beyond the pies are antipasti, salads, pastas including a number of ravioli dishes, and second courses like veal scallopini. ✉ *393 Lafayette St., at E. 4th St., East Village* ☎ *212/995–9595* ▭ *AE, DC, MC, V.*

Scandinavian

¢-$ × **Good World Bar and Grill.** An old sign for the Good World Barber Shop, the original tenant, marks the storefront of this downtown hangout with a Swedish bent on the fringes of Chinatown. The groovy crowd of non-blonds smoking cigarettes in the shabby, bohemian space snacks on potato pancakes that are sweet and salty with lingonberries and bacon, Swedish meatballs, fish soup, and a tasting plate of herring. ✉ *3 Orchard St., at Division St., Lower East Side* ☎ *212/925–9975* ▭ *AE, D, DC, MC, V.*

Southwestern

$-$$ × **Miracle Grill.** In fair weather, your long wait for an outdoor table will be rewarded by a seat in a large and pretty garden. The margaritas are fabulous and the food reasonably priced and tasty—after all, this is where Bobby Flay got his start. Appetizers such as cornmeal-crusted catfish soft tacos are crowd pleasers. Entrée portions are huge, and vegetarians will appreciate the grilled or roasted vegetable dishes. ✉ *112 1st Ave., between E. 6th and E. 7th Sts., East Village* ☎ *212/254–2353* ✍ *Reservations not accepted* ▭ *AE, MC, V* ⊙ *No lunch weekdays.*

Thai

¢-$ × **Holy Basil.** It's not often you get to enjoy good Thai food within a clubby setting of dark-wood floors, brick-face walls, huge gilt-framed mirrors, and old-fashioned paintings. The vibrant food—enlivened by chilies, opal basil, and kaffir lime—comes carefully composed in layer-cake form. Taste buds awaken to the spicy som tum and rich tom kah gai, not to mention anything in kaw praw. A large and informative wine list is an added bonus. ✉ *149 2nd Ave., between E. 9th and E. 10th Sts., East Village* ☎ *212/460–5557* ▭ *AE, DC, MC, V* ⊙ *No lunch.*

Murray Hill, Flatiron District & Gramercy

Quiet, residential Murray Hill is home to some of the city's most charming boutique hotels, and notable restaurants are starting to appear. Lexington Avenue between 26th and 28th streets is known as Curry Hill for its wall-to-wall subcontinental restaurants and take-out joints. Little Korea is near Herald Square in the West 30s. South of Murray Hill, genteel Gramercy is dotted with fashionable eateries in the neighborhood's stately buildings, especially on lower Madison Avenue. Part of the Flatiron District, Park Avenue South and the streets leading off it may be the city's hottest restaurant district, packed with crowd pleasers like Dos Caminos and top-tier foodie havens such as Union Pacific.

American

$$$$ Fodor'sChoice ★ × **Gramercy Tavern.** Danny Meyer's ever-popular restaurant is near the top of most New Yorkers' "favorite restaurant" list. In front, the first-come, first-served tavern offers a light menu prepared in the wood-burning oven on view, plus a menu of small dishes and desserts between lunch and dinner service. The more formal dining room has a prix-fixe American table d'hôte menu carefully conceived by executive chef John Schaefer. For $65 (plus an occasional supplement), choose from seasonal dishes such as roasted cod in a sauce of cèpes or a trio of beef sirloin,

short ribs, and duck foie gras. Meyer's restaurants (which include Tabla and Union Square Cafe) are renowned for their knowledgable, accommodating service, and Gramercy Tavern sets the gold standard. ✉ 42 *E. 20th St., between Broadway and Park Ave. S, Flatiron District* ☎ *212/477–0777* ✍ *Reservations essential* ▭ *AE, DC, MC, V.*

$$–$$$$ **Fodor's Choice ★** ✕ **Craft.** Crafting your ideal meal here is like picking and choosing from a gourmand's well-stocked kitchen—one overseen by Tom Colicchio, who is also chef at Gramercy Tavern. The bounty of simple yet intriguing starters and sides on the menu makes it easy to forget there are main courses to pair them with as well. Seared scallops, braised veal, seasonal vegetables—just about everything is exceptionally prepared with little fuss. The serene dining room is an impressive modern American Arts and Crafts experiment, with dark wood, custom tables, a curved leather wall, and sculptural light arrangements of radiant bulbs. ✉ *43 E. 19th St., between Broadway and Park Ave. S, Flatiron District* ☎ *212/780–0880* ✍ *Reservations essential* ▭ *AE, D, DC, MC, V* ⊗ *No lunch weekends.*

$–$$$ ✕ **Union Square Cafe.** When he opened Union Square Cafe in 1985, Danny Meyer changed the American restaurant landscape. The combination of upscale food and unpretentious low-key service sparked a revolution. Today executive chef Michael Romano still draws devotees (reservations remain hard to get) with his crowd-pleasing menu. Mahogany moldings outline white walls hung with bright modern paintings; in addition to the three main dining areas, there's a long bar perfect for solo diners. The cuisine is American with a thick Italian accent: for example, the signature tuna burger with Asian slaw can land on the same table as homemade gnocchi. ✉ *21 E. 16th St., between 5th Ave. and Union Sq. W, Flatiron District* ☎ *212/243–4020* ✍ *Reservations essential* ▭ *AE, D, DC, MC, V* ⊗ *No lunch Sun.*

$$ ✕ **Kitchen 22.** Chef and budding restaurant mogul Charlie Palmer (Aureole, Métrazur) made an astute move when he shut down his restaurant Alva to open streamlined Kitchen 22. Where a single entrée once cost about $25, now you get a three-course prix-fixe for the same price. A young, professional crowd waits up to 45 minutes on weeknights (reservations aren't accepted) for the basic fare with nice flair. Choose from five starters and five entrées—say pepper-seared tuna followed by a chewy New York strip steak. Homey desserts like white-chocolate pudding sit in big bowls on a table, and your waiter will scoop up as many of them as you want. The '50s airport-lounge look of teal booths and white plastic chairs is so chic, you'll feel like you should be paying more for dinner. ✉ *36 E 22nd St., between Broadway and Park Ave. S, Flatiron District* ☎ *212/228–4399* ▭ *AE, DC, MC, V* ⊗ *Closed Sun. No lunch.*

American Casual

¢ ✕ **Eisenberg's Sandwich Shop.** Since the 1930s this narrow coffee shop with its timeworn counter and cramped tables has been providing the city with some of the best tuna, chicken, and egg-salad sandwiches. During the lunch rush, counter workers shout orders at one another down the line as they make sandwiches, ladle soups, and slice dill pickles. They still use the cryptic language of soda jerks and diner cooks, in which "whisky down" means rye toast and "Adam and Eve on a raft" means two eggs on toast. Considering the feeling of mayhem in the place, it's always a pleasant surprise when you actually get your sandwich, quickly and precisely as ordered. ✉ *174 5th Ave., between E. 22nd and E. 23rd Sts., Flatiron District* ☎ *212/675–5096* ▭ *AE* ⊗ *Closed Sun.*

Cafés

¢–$ ✕ **Le Pain Quotidien.** This international Belgian chain brings its homeland ingredients with it, treating New Yorkers to crusty breads and

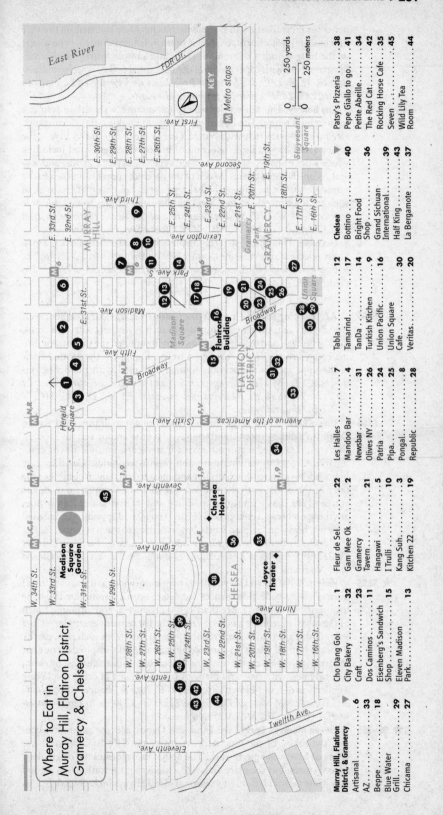

Where to Eat in Murray Hill, Flatiron District, Gramercy & Chelsea

Murray Hill, Flatiron District, & Gramercy ▼

Artisanal 6
AZ 33
Beppe 18
Blue Water Grill 29
Chicama 27
Cho Dang Gol 1
City Bakery 32
Craft 23
Dos Caminos 11
Eisenberg's Sandwich Shop 15
Eleven Madison Park 13
Fleur de Sel 22
Gam Mee Ok 2
Gramercy Tavern 21
Hangawi 5
I Trulli 10
Kang Suh 3
Kitchen 22 19
Les Halles 7
Mandoo Bar 4
Newsbar 31
Olives NY 26
Patria 24
Pipa 25
Pongal 8
Republic 28
Tabla 12
Tamarind 17
TanDa 14
Turkish Kitchen 9
Union Pacific 16
Union Square Cafe 30
Veritas 20

Chelsea ▼

Bottino 40
Bright Food Shop 36
Grand Sichuan International 39
Half King 43
La Bergamote 37
Patsy's Pizzeria 38
Pepe Giallo to go 41
Petite Abeille 34
The Red Cat 42
Rocking Horse Cafe . . . 35
Seven 45
Wild Lily Tea Room 44

delicious jams. Best of all is the Belgian chocolate sweetening the café mochas and hot chocolate. For a more substantial meal, take a seat at the long wooden communal table and sample hearty sandwiches like roast beef with caper mayonnaise or roasted turkey with herb dressing. ✉ *38 E. 19th St., between Broadway and Park Ave S., Flatiron District* ☎ *212/673–7900* ▭ *No credit cards.*

¢ ✕ **City Bakery.** This self-service bakery-restaurant has the urban aesthetic to match its name. The baked goods—giant cookies, flaky croissants, elegant tarts—are rich with butter. One of the major draws here is the pricey salad bar—a large selection of impeccably fresh food including whole sides of baked salmon, roasted vegetables, pasta salads, and several Asian-flavored dishes. Much of the produce comes from the nearby farmers' market. In winter, the bakery hosts a hot chocolate festival; in summer it's lemonade time. Weekend brunch includes some table-side service. ✉ *3 W. 18th St., between 5th and 6th Aves., Flatiron District* ☎ *212/366–1414* ▭ *AE, MC, V* ⊙ *Closed Sun. No dinner.*

¢ ✕ **Newsbar.** This ultracasual resting place has good coffee and tea, a generous selection of magazines, and CNN on the tube. ✉ *2 W. 19th St., between 5th and 6th Aves., Flatiron District* ☎ *212/255–3996* ▭ *No credit cards.*

Contemporary

$$$$ ✕ **AZ.** Star chef Patricia Yeo's Asian fusion food has garnered her raves. At AZ you can taste her signature dishes such as tempura soft-shell crabs, duck schnitzel, and tea-smoked chicken. In summer, the third-floor dining room's roof retracts for auto alfresco dining. On the ground floor is the appetizers-and-cocktails lounge crammed with postwork imbibers. ✉ *21 W. 17th St., between 5th and 6th Aves., Flatiron District* ☎ *212/691–8888* ✍ *Reservations essential* ▭ *AE, D, DC, MC, V* ⊙ *No lunch weekends.*

$$$$ Fodor's Choice ★ ✕ **Union Pacific.** In a neighborhood of serious restaurants, chef Rocco DiSpirito's dining room stands out as a favorite among serious foodies. Every meal is an education in exotic ingredients, unusual flavor combinations, elegant presentations, and precise technique. Consider raw bay scallops with fresh sea urchin and mustard oil, which combines the taste of the ocean with the temperature of a hot summer's day, or the entrée of sea bass with squash pudding and saffron sauce. Rarely does anything on his seasonal prix-fixe ($65) menus disappoint. An unusual wine list, heavy on German labels, has something to teach you, too. ✉ *111 E. 22nd St., between Broadway and Park Ave. S, Flatiron District* ☎ *212/995–8500* ✍ *Reservations essential* ▭ *AE, MC, V* ⊙ *Closed Sun. No lunch Sat.*

★ $$$$ ✕ **Veritas.** What do you do when you own more wine than you can drink? Veritas's wine-collecting owners decided to open a restaurant. The wine list originally boasted more than 1,300 producers, and although much of the initial inventory has been drunk, the list remains exemplary. Chef Scott Bryan's prix-fixe contemporary menu runs from such rich, earthy dishes as braised veal with parsnip puree to an Asian-inspired arctic char tartare with pickled cucumbers. The dining room is distinguished by clean, natural lines, with one wall made of Italian tile and another displaying a collection of hand-blown vases. ✉ *43 E. 20th St., between Broadway and Park Ave. S, Flatiron District* ☎ *212/353–3700* ✍ *Reservations essential* ▭ *AE, DC, MC, V* ⊙ *No lunch.*

★ $$–$$$ ✕ **Eleven Madison Park.** Like Tabla this Danny Meyer restaurant occupies the lobby of the landmark Metropolitan Life Building and has views of Madison Square Park. The design incorporates the original art deco fixtures, but the place feels like a modern train station—in a good way. Chef Kerry Heffernan's seasonal menu always includes a delicious braised beef dish (the short ribs are superb), plus skate, squab, lobster, and rarities, such as pig's feet, each prepared in his simple, elegant French manner. The bar is beautiful. ✉ *11 Madison Ave., at E. 24th St., Flatiron District* ☎ *212/889–0905* ✍ *Reservations essential* ▭ *AE, D, DC, MC, V* ⏲ *No lunch Sun.*

Eclectic

$$–$$$$ ✕ **Tabla.** In concert with restaurant guru Danny Meyer, chef Floyd Cardoz creates exciting cuisine based on the tastes and traditions of his native India, filtered through his formal European training. Indian ingredients, condiments, and garnishes, such as *kasundi* (tomato sauce), *rawa* (a blend of spices), and *kokum* (dried black plum) garnish familiar fish and meats like skate, lobster, oxtail, and chicken. Your server will explain unfamiliar terms in a friendly, unintimidating way. At the more casual Bread Bar downstairs, you can get in and out faster and for less money while watching fresh naan come out of the tandoor ovens. ✉ *11 Madison Ave., at E. 25th St., Flatiron District* ☎ *212/889–0667* ✍ *Reservations essential* ▭ *AE, D, DC, MC, V* ⏲ *No lunch weekends.*

French

$$$–$$$$ ✕ **Fleur de Sel.** Chef-owner Cyril Renaud, who's danced behind the stoves at such high falutin restaurants as La Caravelle and Bouley, has settled down in his own restaurant. The results of his personal endeavor, from the exceptional, precise cooking to the professional service, are nothing short of excellent. He's brought his watercolors (which adorn the walls and the menus), his thirst for creativity, and his beloved salt from Brittany, which gives the restaurant its name. The prix-fixe menu is limited but perfectly tuned to the season and the scale of the dining room. A lobster salad is dressed with tangy lemongrass vinaigrette; crisp *poussin* (baby chicken) is bathed in a rich foie gras sauce. The professionalism of the service is commendable. ✉ *5 E. 20th St., between 5th Ave. and Broadway, Flatiron District* ☎ *212/460–9100* ✍ *Reservations essential* ▭ *AE, MC, V.*

$–$$$$ ✕ **Artisanal.** This isn't so much a French brasserie as it is a shrine to cheese, the favorite food of chef-owner Terrence Brennan (Picholine) and master cheese man Max McCalman. You can spot it aging to perfection in the back corner of the dining room, in a temperature-controlled "cave." You can order it in myriad forms from the menu: fondu, gougères, onion soup, or just piece after piece from the ever-changing, 200-plus cheese list. The other contemporary brasserie fare—braised lamb shank, chicken under a brick—is disappointing in comparison. But that's not the reason you came—*c'est* cheese. ✉ *2 Park Ave., at E. 32nd St., Murray Hill* ☎ *212/725–8585* ▭ *AE, MC, V.*

¢–$$ ✕ **Les Halles.** Chef Anthony Bourdain has become famous not for his cooking, but for his best-selling books *Kitchen Confidential* and *A Cook's Tour* (the latter has spawned a Food Network show starring the reed-thin Bourdain). But his original restaurant remains strikingly unpretentious, like a French bistro–cum–butcher shop. Butcher paper on the tables, French posters, a tin ceiling, and a windowed kitchen contribute to the atmosphere. A good bet is the *côte de boeuf* with béarnaise sauce, a massive rib steak for two served on a wooden board. Other prime choices include crispy duck-leg confit and frisée salad, warm sausages with lentils, and heaping plates of garlicky cold cuts. ✉ *411 Park Ave. S, between E. 28th and E. 29th Sts., Murray Hill* ☎ *212/679–4111* ✍ *Reservations essential* ▭ *AE, DC, MC, V.*

Indian

$–$$$ ✕ **Tamarind.** Trading the usual brass, beads, and dark tones for a contemporary skylighted dining room awash in soothing neutral color, this modern Indian restaurant breaks from tradition. A multiregional menu contains some familiar dishes, such as tandoori chicken (prepared in a glass-encased display kitchen), while also offering fusion-inspired options like Cornish game hen with tamarind and garlic, and she-crab soup with saffron, ginger juice, and sweet spices. As a rule, the more intriguing a dish sounds (lotus seed dumplings, Goan shrimp, Hyderabad biryani), the better it is. Be sure to order a selection of breads (many versions of naan and roti are available) to sop up any excess sauce. A tiny teahouse next door serves as a casual café and take-out shop. ✉ *41–43 E. 22nd St., between Broadway and Park Ave. S, Flatiron District* ☎ *212/674–7400* ✍ *Reservations essential* ▭ *AE, DC, MC, V.*

¢–$ ✕ **Pongal.** One of the city's best Indian restaurants is also vegetarian-only and kosher. Its menu is a mix of southern Indian comfort foods (many that would be served at breakfast or on the streets of Bombay) and expertly prepared home-style dishes. Try the spicy, potato-filled samosas or chickpea-battered vegetable *pakoras* (unapologetically served with the traditional ketchup, in addition to tamarind and coconut dipping sauces). One of the restaurant's specialties is *dosas*—giant, wafer-thin, crisp crepes made from fermented grains such as lentil and rice and filled with spiced potatoes. For some home cooking, don't miss the *saag paneer* (fresh curd cheese with spinach) and *kala chana* (seasoned black chickpeas in a rich sauce). ✉ *110 Lexington Ave., between E. 27th and E. 28th Sts., Murray Hill* ☎ *212/696–9458* ▭ *D, DC, MC, V.*

Italian

$$–$$$ ✕ **I Trulli.** Rough-hewn gold walls, a fireplace, a garden for summer dining, and a whitewashed open grill with the traditional beehive shape of early Pugliese houses distinguish this Italian winner from its competitors. An out-of-the-ordinary glass of wine from a little-known producer and one of the enticing appetizers—shrimp bruschetta or grilled zucchini-stuffed squid—are a great way to start. Almost all the pasta is handmade by chef Mauro Mafrici and his staff, who also construct superior *secondi,* such as grilled lamb with fava bean puree. Entrées of game, meat, and fish are cooked in the wood-fired oven. Enoteca, a lovely casual wine bar next door, has a simple menu of exquisite food and an impressive selection of wines, available by the glass or in tasting flights. ✉ *122 E. 27th St., between Lexington Ave. and Park Ave. S, Murray Hill* ☎ *212/481–7372* ✍ *Reservations essential* ▭ *AE, DC, MC, V* ⏲ *Closed Sun. No lunch Sat.*

$–$$$ ✕ **Beppe.** There are a lot of restaurants claiming to be Tuscan in New York, but Cesare Casella's labor of love is one of the few who honestly wear the mantle. Born to a restaurant family outside Florence, Casella (formerly of Coco Pazzo) offers a large, playful menu of Tuscan specialties, such as farro soup, and clever concoctions, such as "Tuscan fried chicken" and "cowboy-style" spareribs. The seasonally changing home-made pastas may be the best part of the satisfying menu. The bright dining room simulates a cheery trattoria. ✉ *45 E. 22nd St., between Broadway and Park Ave. S, Flatiron District* ☎ *212/982–8422* ▭ *AE, MC, V* ⏲ *Closed Sun. No lunch Sat.*

Korean

¢–$$ ✕ **Cho Dang Gol.** A few blocks away from the main drag of Little Korea, this restaurant specializes in tofu (*doo-boo* in Korean). Myriad varieties of bean curd are made on the premises and then incorporated into a vast array of traditional Korean dishes of varying heat and spice. Anyone who thinks of tofu as a bland, jiggling substance should try *doo-boo* *dong-ka-rang-deng,* puffy rounds of tofu filled with shredded vegetables and beef, or *cho-dan-gol jung-sik,* a three-part dish of tofu dregs, pork stew, and rice. The only drawback is that the staff members, who are lovely and eager to please, don't speak enough English to be of much help. ✉ *55 W. 35th St., between 5th and 6th Aves., Murray Hill* ☎ *212/695–8222* ▭ *AE, DC, MC, V.*

¢–$$ ✕ **Gam Mee Ok.** The deconstructed industrial design, inexpensive menu, and late-night hours attract a young and stylish crowd to this restaurant in the heart of Little Korea. As soon as you sit down, an aloof waitress will approach your table and snip whole turnip and cabbage kimchi into bite-size pieces. Every item on the very limited menu has a photo to help you order. But all you need to remember are oxtail-and-bone-marrow soup—a subtle, satisfying milky-white bowl of soup with rice noodles and beef that you season at your table with Korean sea salt and chopped scallions—and mung bean pancakes, made fresh with scallions, and fried until crisp and chewy. ✉ *43 W. 32nd St., between 5th and 6th Aves., Murray Hill* ☎ *212/695–4113* ✍ *Reservations not accepted* ▭ *No credit cards.*

¢–$$ ✕ **Kang Suh.** "Seoul" food at its best is served at this lively, second-floor restaurant. Cook thin slices of ginger-marinated beef (*bul go gui*) or other meats over red-hot coals; top them with hot chilies, bean paste, and pickled cabbage; and wrap them all up with lettuce for a satisfying meal. Dinner starts with 10 or more delicious types of kimchi, spicy pickles, and other condiments that are almost a meal in themselves. A crisp oyster-and-scallion pancake, sautéed yam noodles, and other traditional dishes are all expertly prepared. The waitstaff speaks little English but the menu has lots of pictures, so you can just point and smile. ✉ *32 W. 32nd St., between 5th and 6th Aves., Murray Hill* ☎ *212/947–8482* ▭ *AE, MC, V.*

¢–$ ✕ **Mandoo Bar.** At this appealing little dumpling shop on Little Korea's main drag, you can watch the ladies making the little oval treats in the window on your way to one of the blond-wood cafeteria-like tables in the back. There are plenty of dumplings, or *mandoo,* to choose from, such as broiled shrimp and sea cucumber, Korean kimchi, beef, pork, or leek. Rounding out the menu are noodle and rice dishes and a couple of specialties like *tangsuyook*—fried pork with sweet-and-sour sauce. ✉ *2 W. 32nd St., between 5th Ave. and Broadway, Murray Hill* ☎ *212/279–3075* ▭ *AE, MC, V.*

Latin

$$–$$$ ✕ **Chicama.** Enter the castle of the king of Nuevo Latino cooking—chef Douglas Rodriguez. Located in the home-furnishings store ABC Carpet & Home (along with his Spanish tapas restaurant Pipa), Chicama is done up like a rustic hacienda—much of the wood-panel interior was imported from Brazil. There's a ceviche bar, from which a wide array of creative fish "cocktails" are served. The menu changes frequently, but if you can find roasted goat or suckling pig, order it. Same goes for stewed turkey, roasted meats with chimichurri sauce, or anything that includes coconut. Warm *churros* (doughnuts) are served with melted chocolate for dipping. ✉ *35 E. 18th St., between Broadway and Park Ave. S, Flatiron District* ☎ *212/505–2233* ✍ *Reservations essential* ▭ *AE, D, DC, MC, V.*

$$–$$$ ✕ **Patria.** Bright colors and festive mosaics are the right match for Andrew DiCataldo's electric cooking. His menu echoes not one, but all of Latin America's cuisines. Contemporary variations on traditional appetizers, such as black lobster empanadas, and an impressive array of ceviches provide an exciting start. Entrées build to a Guatamalan-style chicken, a Brazilian-style seafood stew, and tuna with a citrus mojo sauce.

The wine list focuses on Spain, Argentina, and California. Arrive early to enjoy one of the signature cocktails. ✉ *250 Park Ave. S, at E. 20th St., Flatiron District* ☎ *212/777–6211* *Reservations essential* ▭ *AE, D, MC, V* ⏲ *No lunch weekends.*

Mediterranean

$$–$$$ ✕ **Olives NY.** The New York branch of Boston-based Todd English's growing Olives empire resides in the lobby of the hopping W Hotel on Union Square. English's menu raises calorie counts to new levels, and you'll be glad about it. A mousse of chicken, foie gras, and truffles fills his chicken wing, which is then simmered in duck fat until crisp. The delicate, overstuffed pastas are made by hand, and most come dripping in butter. The hearty entrées all have a creative twist, such as the Dover sole that's served with foie gras sauce and chanterelles. Unfortunately, the design of the room is so drab it almost detracts from the food. But not quite. ✉ *201 Park Ave. S, at E. 17th St., Flatiron District* ☎ *212/353–8345* *Reservations essential* ▭ *AE, D, DC, MC, V.*

Mexican

$–$$ ✕ **Dos Caminos.** Stephen Hanson, the man behind Blue Water Grill, has created a fiesta of a restaurant that maintains the kind of sophistication New York professionals expect. The dramatic interior has the feel of a Mazatlan beach at sunset, and the 150 kinds of tequila will put you in the mood for anything executive chef Dudley Nieto, who hails from Puebla, sends your way. Food ranges from the prosaic (chicken enchiladas with rice and beans) to the eye-opening (pork slow-roasted in banana leaves until the meat is soft and moist as pudding). The noise level is comparable to the climax at a stag party. ✉ *373 Park Ave. S, between 26th and 27th Sts., Flatiron District* ☎ *212/294–1000* *Reservations essential.* ▭ *AE, DC, MC, V* ⏲ *No lunch.*

Pan-Asian

$$ ✕ **TanDa.** In this fever dream of an opium den dotted with pillow-covered banquettes in shades of orange and pink, Vietnamese, Thai, and Malaysian influences mix in boldly flavored dishes such as Balinese roasted duck—a Southeast Asian take on Peking duck. While the ground-floor dining room is tranquil enough for you to enjoy the food, flesh-baring partyers head upstairs to the jumping bar—the owners were behind the Moomba, the late hot spot that attracted the likes of Leonardo and Gisele. ✉ *331 Park Ave. S, between 24th and 25th Sts., Flatiron District* ☎ *212/253–8400* *Reservations essential.* ▭ *AE, D, MC, V* ⏲ *Closed Sun.*

¢ ✕ **Republic.** Epicureans on a budget flock to this Asian noodle emporium that looks like a cross between a downtown art gallery and a Japanese school cafeteria. The young waitstaff dressed in black T-shirts and jeans hold remote-control ordering devices to speed the already speedy service. Sit at the long, bluestone bar or at the picnic-style tables and order appetizers such as smoky grilled eggplant and spicy fried wantons. Entrées are based on noodles or rice. The spicy coconut chicken soup and the Vietnamese-style barbecued pork are particularly delicious. ✉ *37 Union Sq. W, between E. 16th and E. 17th Sts., Flatiron District* ☎ *212/627–7172* ▭ *AE, DC, MC, V.*

Pizza

¢–$ ✕ **Patsy's Pizzeria.** The original Patsy's opened back in 1933 in East Harlem, when the neighborhood was largely Italian. The pizzeria still serves some of the best slices in New York. The secret is in the thin, crisp, coal-oven-baked crust, topped with thick sauce and fresh toppings. ✉ *509 3rd Ave., between E. 34th and E. 35th Sts., Murray Hill* ☎ *212/689–7500* ▭ *No credit cards.*

Seafood

$–$$$$ ✕ **Blue Water Grill.** A copper-and-tile raw bar anchors one end of this warm, sweeping room of indigo, siena, and yellow. The original 1904 molded ceiling and marble everywhere recall the space's former life as a bank. Strong on fresh seafood served neat (chilled whole lobster, shrimp in the rough), the menu also has international flair—lobster fra diavolo, Maryland crab cakes, Chilean sea bass with ginger and soy—and simple preparations that issue forth from a wood-burning oven. For dessert, go for the brownie ice-cream sundae. A lounge and dining room in the basement vault has live jazz. ✉ *31 Union Sq. W, at E. 16th St., Flatiron District* ☎ *212/675–9500* *Reservations essential* *AE, DC, MC, V.*

Spanish

$–$$ ✕ **Pipa.** Douglas Rodriguez turns his attention to Spain at this festive tapas bar, located in ABC Carpet & Home, as is his pan-Latin Chicama. The menu has 50-plus items including *cocas,* flavorful pizzalike flat breads covered with savory toppings such as delicious garlicky clams, tender sautéed porcini mushrooms, and white beans and serrano ham. More traditional tapas such as garlic shrimp and grilled chorizo come in traditional clay dishes, and are perfect for nibbling with one of the many sherries on the wine list. ABC's design team did the decorating, and the result is that of a Victorian designer gone mad: chandeliers hang on top of one another, and one concrete wall is oozing with shells. The atmosphere, however, is calm. ✉ *38 E. 19th St., between Broadway and Park Ave. S, Flatiron District* ☎ *212/677–2233* *Reservations essential* *AE, MC, V.*

Turkish

$–$$ ✕ **Turkish Kitchen.** This striking multilevel room with lipstick-red walls, chairs with skirted slipcovers, and colorful kilims is Manhattan's busiest Turkish restaurant. The authentic recipes are served by a young staff dressed in long white chefs' aprons. For appetizers choose from such delectable offerings as velvety char-grilled eggplant or octopus salad, creamy hummus, or stewed beans. The stuffed cabbage, whole-roasted whitefish, and bulghur-wheat patties filled with ground lamb, pine nuts, and currants are highly recommended. ✉ *386 3rd Ave., between E. 27th and E. 28th Sts., Murray Hill* ☎ *212/679–1810* *AE, D, DC, MC, V* *No lunch weekends.*

Vegetarian

$–$$$ ✕ **Hangawi.** Hangawi, serving "vegetarian mountain Korean cooking," holds a special place in the city's small collection of vegetarian restaurants. For the full experience choose the "emperor's menu," a parade of more than 10 courses designed as a complete introduction to this unusual cuisine. Offerings include delicate soups, such as miso broth or pumpkin puree; stuffed tofu; marinated wild mountain herbs; and a main-course spread of more than 15 bowls of assorted kimchi—some taste like earth, some are brazenly spiced. Exotic teas, including one made from a puree of dates, or an unfiltered milky white Korean sake served from a wooden bowl are good accompaniments to the meal. ✉ *12 E. 32nd St., between 5th and Madison Aves., Murray Hill* ☎ *212/213–0077* *Reservations essential* *AE, DC, MC, V.*

Chelsea

Soon after the art galleries and gay men surged into the area, Chelsea underwent a residential building boom, bringing a new wave of luxury-condo dwellers to this relentlessly trendy neighborhood. But there has been no congruent influx of great restaurants. Chelsea may not be a white-hot dining destination like, say, its Flatiron neighbor to the east, but you can eat very well if you know where to go.

American

$$–$$$ ✕ **The Red Cat.** Chef-owner Jimmy Bradley oversees this comfortable neighborhood restaurant. Seasonal appetizers include sautéed zucchini with almonds and pecorino, clam and octopus stew, and a signature chicken-and-apple sausage served with braised cabbage. Satisfying entrées include sautéed skate with capers and brown butter, steak and golden potatoes with fennel and cabernet sauce, and whole trout in beurre blanc. Be sure to order a side of tempura green beans. The service is friendly and welcoming, and the wine list is reasonably priced. ✉ *227 10th Ave., between W. 23rd and W. 24th Sts., Chelsea* ☎ *212/242–1122* ▭ *AE, DC, MC, V* ⊗ *No lunch.*

$–$$ ✕ **Seven.** In the culinary wasteland around Macy's and Penn Station, there actually is a serious restaurant. The contemporary American menu runs the gamut from overstuffed sandwiches (at lunch), to seasonal soups, to homemade pastas, to creative entrées such as roasted cod with aioli-crushed potatoes in saffron broth. The decor, like the menu, plays it safe but sophisticated. In another neighborhood this restaurant might not warrant mention, but as an oasis in a desert of fast-food outlets and diners it deserves special mention. ✉ *350 7th Ave., between W. 29th and W. 30th Sts., Chelsea* ☎ *212/967–1919* ▭ *AE, MC, V.*

Belgian

$–$$ ✕ **Petite Abeille.** There are only a few tables in this small outpost of the expanding chain of Belgian bistros. The menu tempts with salads, frites, sandwiches, omelets, poached salmon, and other light fare. Two styles of waffles are always available: de Bruxelles (made fresh to order and topped with ice cream, whipped cream, and fresh fruit) and the true Belgian waffle, de Liège (imported from Belgium and reheated until the subtle caramelized sugar coating crunches and melts in your mouth). ✉ *107 W. 18th St., between 6th and 7th Aves., Chelsea* ☎ *212/604–9350* ⊗ *Closes at 7PM* ▭ *AE, MC, V.*

Cafés

¢ ✕ **Goupil and DeCarlo.** The almond croissants at this small bakery-café rival any baked in France. There's a complete selection of French baked goods, sandwiches (the foot-long baguette stuffed with merguez and potato gratin is satisfying), and a special dish of the day (the likes of beef bourguignonne). ✉ *Chelsea Market, 75 9th Ave., between 15th and 16th Sts., Chelsea* ☎ *212/807–1908* ▭ *MC, V.*

¢ ✕ **La Bergamote.** Exemplary French pastries are served in this simple café. Try the buttery pain au chocolat and chewy meringues with a steaming bowl of café au lait. ✉ *169 9th Ave., at W. 20th St., Chelsea* ☎ *212/627–9010* ▭ *No credit cards.*

¢ ✕ **Le Gamin.** It's easy to confuse New York for Paris at this hip little haven, where the menu includes all the French-café standards: croque monsieur, quiche Lorraine, salade niçoise, crepes (both sweet and savory), and big bowls of café au lait. Service can be desultory, but the upside is that you're free to lounge for hours. ✉ *183 9th Ave., at W. 21st St., Chelsea* ☎ *212/243–8864* ▭ *AE, MC, V.*

Chinese

¢–$ ✕ **Grand Sichuan International.** This regional Chinese restaurant serves a vast menu of specialties you won't find anywhere else. The emphasis is on fiery Sichuan (Szechuan) cooking, but Cantonese, Hunan, Shanghai, and even American Chinese food are represented (a handy treatise and guide on Chinese food comes with the menu). Spicy *dan dan* noodles, shredded potatoes in vinegar sauce, crab soup dumplings, minced pork with cellophane noodles or fermented green beans, and sautéed loofah are among the hauntingly delicious dishes. ✉ *229 9th Ave., at W. 24th St., Chelsea* ☎ *212/620–5200* ▭ *AE, MC, V.*

Eclectic

$ ✕ **Bright Food Shop.** Asia and the American Southwest converge at this former coffee shop. It may look like an early-20th-century lunch counter, but the food is from some futuristic place. Don't be scared by bizarre-sounding concoctions such as "salmon wonton tostadas" and "moo shu mex vegetable handrolls with chipotle peanut sauce"—somehow the kitchen pulls these mega-fusion recipes off with finesse. The flavors are bold and the portions are filling. An equally eclectic menu is available for breakfast, brunch, and lunch, and a simpler take-out menu is available next door at Kitchen Market. ✉ *216 8th Ave., between W. 21st and W. 22nd Sts., Chelsea* ☎ *212/243–4433* ▭ *No credit cards.*

¢–$ ✕ **Wild Lily Tea Room.** A true gem worthy of its setting among the Chelsea galleries, this tearoom provides endless serenity. Food is served on china lily pads, and the menu describes teas with such eloquence that it could be a book of poetry. Afternoon tea comes complete with dainty finger sandwiches, desserts, and delectable scones with jam and clotted cream, or choose from savory Asian treats, such as shu mai dumplings with shrimp, crab, or vegetables; spicy Thai sausage in puff pastry; or an ingenious ginger chicken "hamburger." ✉ *511A W. 22nd St., between 10th and 11th Aves., Chelsea* ☎ *212/691–2258* *Reservations essential* ▭ *AE, MC, V* *Closed Mon.*

Irish

¢–$ ✕ **Half King.** *Perfect Storm* author Sebastian Junger and his writer friends opened this low-key Irish pub so people could hang out, meet friends, drink pints, and eat hearty Irish food. Chelsea desperately needed such a down-to-earth place amidst the chic galleries and trendy bistros, and Half King succeeds in its mission. The pub has large booths, friendly service, plenty of beer on tap, and inexpensive dishes served in generous portions. As you'd expect, potatoes and cabbage are given a prominent role on the menu; there are also lamb, roast pork, steak, and fish-and-chips. ✉ *505 W. 23rd St., between 10th and 11th Aves., Chelsea* ☎ *212/462–4300* ▭ *AE, DC, MC, V.*

Italian

$–$$$ ✕ **Bottino.** Chelsea's chic art crowd seems to want good food, good prices, and a good atmosphere at their hangouts. They get it *alla italiana* at this smartly designed, inexpensive west Chelsea restaurant. The menu is straightforward—mixed fry of seafood and vegetables, arugula salad with fennel, halibut with olives, stewed rabbit. Service is slow but attractive and friendly. The take-out shop of the same name, next door, has a nice selection of Italian lunch items. ✉ *246 10th Ave., between W. 24th and W. 25th Sts., Chelsea* ☎ *212/206–6766* *Reservations essential* ▭ *AE, D, DC, MC, V* *No lunch Sun.–Mon.*

¢–$ ✕ **Pepe Giallo to Go.** The crown of a chain of four tiny Italian eateries, this Chelsea branch is the most spacious and charming of the lot. A long list of specials changes daily, but the menu always includes generously portioned pastas (prepared fresh in the open kitchen), antipasti, salads, entrées, and sandwiches. The gnocchi are as light as little clouds, the pesto sauce is fragrant with basil and garlic, and the veal is tender. Inexpensive wine is available in carafes or by the bottle. Considering dinner can cost less than $17, these restaurants may be the best Italian value in the city. ✉ *253 10th Ave., at W. 25th St., Chelsea* ☎ *212/242–6055* ▭ *AE, MC, V.*

Mexican

$–$$ ✕ **Rocking Horse Cafe.** The modern Mexican interior of this restaurant puts it a cut above the others on the 8th Avenue strip. Twenty-eight oblong white resin lamps draw attention to the bar, walls are done in blue mosaic tiles and gold leaf, and stone lines the floor. Riffs on nouveau Mexican cuisine include crispy calamari dressing, duck confit in blue corn–*epazote* (a wild Mexican herb) crepes, and seared salmon in a roasted tomatillo sauce. Take in the buff Chelsea crowd while enjoying a potent margarita and some homemade tortilla chips served in a metal bucket at the bar. ✉ *182 8th Ave., between W. 19th and W. 20th Sts., Chelsea* ☎ *212/463–9511* ▭ *AE, MC, V.*

Pizza

¢–$ ✕ **Patsy's Pizzeria.** The original Patsy's opened back in 1933 in East Harlem, when the neighborhood was largely Italian. The pizzeria still serves some of the best slices in New York. The secret is in the thin, crisp, coal-oven-baked crust, topped with thick sauce and fresh toppings. ✉ *318 W. 23rd St., between 8th and 9th Aves., Chelsea* ☎ *646/486–7400* ▭ *No credit cards.*

Thai

¢–$$ ✕ **The Basil.** It's not often you get to enjoy good Thai food in such a trendy setting. The vibrant food—enlivened by chilies, opal basil, and kaffir lime—comes carefully composed in layer-cake form. Taste buds awaken to the spicy som tum and rich tom kah gai, not to mention anything in kaw praw. A large and informative wine list is an added bonus. ✉ *206 W. 23rd St., between 7th and 8th Aves., Chelsea* ☎ *212/242–1014* ▭ *AE, MC, V* ⊙ *Closed Mon. No lunch.*

Midtown West

Big hotels, big businesses, and blockbuster Broadway shows dominate the western half of midtown, and that means there's a lot of people to feed. Capitalizing on that fact is an ever-burgeoning plethora of restaurants ranging from inexpensive ethnic eateries and theme restaurants to fine French dining rooms. Be sure to make an informed choice, or you could find yourself in a tourist trap. Now that Times Square and the theater district resemble theme parks and Hell's Kitchen has been gentrified (you'll hear it called Clinton or even Upper Chelsea), the seedy edge of the area is all but gone.

American

$$–$$$$ ✕ **District.** The plush design of this contemporary American restaurant in the Muse Hotel incorporates clever stage references meant to evoke the (theater) district for which it is named. Sam DeMarco, chef of the popular late-night haunt First, is following his muse while creating grown-up food with an irrepressible sense of humor. The menu has a section called the "luxury box," where foie gras is available in three sizes—Huey, Dewey, and Louis—and an entire truffle can be yours for the asking. There are several dishes for two, drawn truffle butter for your bread, and a get-in-and-out pre-theater prix fixe. ✉ *130 W. 46th St., between 5th and 6th Aves., Midtown West* ☎ *212/485–2999* ⚠ *Reservations essential* ▭ *AE, D, DC, MC, V.*

★ $$–$$$$ ✕ **JUdson Grill.** Owner Jerome Kretchmer conceived JUdson Grill on an even grander scale than his flagship Gotham Bar & Grill. The bi-level space has a freestanding bar that hosts a lively after-work crowd. The main dining room and balcony have red velour banquettes, soaring ceilings, and immense gold vases. In the open kitchen, chef Bill Telepan produces such sumptuous dishes as foie gras terrine with luscious Sauternes-onion marmalade, clever comfort food like baby pumpkin overflowing with supple gnocchi, inventive fish entrées, and perfectly executed seasonal preparations. Beth von Benz's wine list is beautifully organized, with many hard-to-find bottles. ✉ *152 W. 52nd St., between 6th and 7th Aves., Midtown West* ☎ *212/582–5252* *Reservations essential* *AE, D, DC, MC, V* *Closed Sun. No lunch Sat.*

$$–$$$$ ✕ **"21" Club.** It's undeniably exciting to hobnob with celebrities and tycoons at this four-story brownstone landmark, a former speakeasy that opened on December 31, 1929. The Grill Room features roomy banquettes and a ceiling hung with toys, while the new Upstairs at "21" is an intimate 32-seat restaurant with a luscious $85 four-course prix-fixe menu. Thus, chef Erik Blauberg can satisfy everyone, retaining signature dishes like the famous "21" burger" and other New American food downstairs, while offering more eclectic fare upstairs, like cinnamon lavender duck and pistachio mint poached turbot. Service is seamless throughout. ✉ *21 W. 52nd St., between 5th and 6th Aves., Midtown West* ☎ *212/582–7200* *Reservations essential* *Jacket and tie* *AE, D, DC, MC, V* *Closed Sun. No lunch Sat.*

$–$$$$ ✕ **Beacon.** Chef Waldy Malouf has established himself as a master of fire in this multilevel restaurant with an emphasis on wood-roasting. Meat, fish, and even vegetables are cooked to a succulent crisp-but-juicy in his wood-fired ovens, and just about everything on the seasonal menu sounds delectable. The crusty bread, baked on the premises, is notable, and the rich desserts by pastry chef Ebrahima Sisho are satisfying. Although the atmosphere is midtown business, the simple, almost rustic food pleases people from all walks of life. ✉ *25 W. 56th St., between 5th and 6th Aves., Midtown West* ☎ *212/332–0500* *AE, D, MC, V* *Closed Sun. No lunch Sat.*

American Casual

¢ ✕ **Island Burgers and Shakes.** Belly-busting burgers rule at this bright and cheery café with multicolored round tables and funky chairs. Every sandwich can be ordered with grilled chicken instead of the usual beef patty, but true believers stick to the real thing and choose from a wide variety of toppings. If you're in the mood for even more calories, the tempting selection of milk shakes is extremely difficult to resist. The only drawback is that there are no french fries—you'll have to settle for potato chips. ✉ *766 9th Ave., between W. 51st and W. 52nd Sts., Midtown West* ☎ *212/307–7934* *No credit cards.*

Barbecue

$–$$ ✕ **Virgil's Real BBQ.** Neon, wood, and Formica set the scene at this massive roadhouse in the theater district. Start with stuffed jalapeños or buttermilk onion rings with blue-cheese dip. Then go for the "pig out"—a rack of pork ribs, Texas hot links, pulled pork, rack of lamb, chicken, and more. If you prefer seafood, the New Orleans–style barbecued shrimp are giant and tasty. There are also five domestic microbrews on tap and a good list of top beers from around the world. ✉ *152 W. 44th St., between 6th Ave. and Broadway, Midtown West* ☎ *212/921–9494* *Reservations essential* *AE, MC, V.*

Brazilian

★ $$$$ ✕ **Churrascaria Plataforma.** This sprawling, boisterous shrine to meat, with its generous all-you-can-eat prix-fixe menu, is best experienced with a group of hungry friends. Order a full pitcher of *caipirinhas* (a cocktail of sugarcane liquor and lime), and head for the vast salad bar that beckons with vegetables (including fresh hearts of palm), meats, and cheeses, plus hot tureens of *fejoida* (the Brazilian national dish of beans, pork, greens, and manioc). But exercise restraint—the real show begins with the parade of lamb, beef, chicken, ham, sausage, and innards,

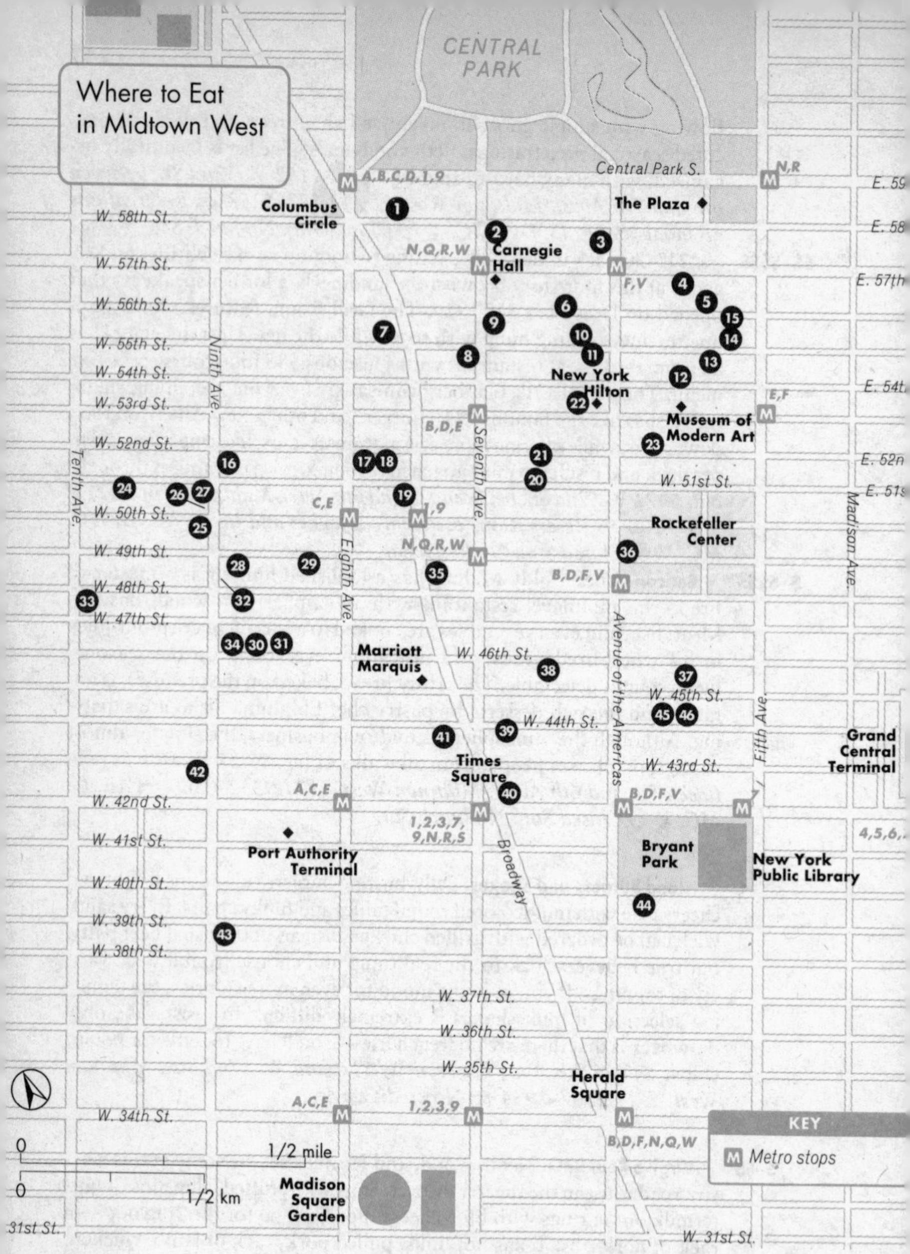

- Alain Ducasse New York 1
- Aquavit 12
- Barbetta 31
- Beacon 6
- Becco 30
- Carnegie Deli. 8
- Churrascaria Plataforma. 29
- Citarella. 36
- Coffee Pot 28
- Cupcake Café. 43
- db bistro moderne. 45
- District. 37
- Esca. 42
- ESPN Zone 40
- Estiatorio Milos 10
- Firebird 34
- Gallagher's Steak House 18
- Grand Sichuan 27
- Hallo Berlin. 24
- Ilo 44
- Island Burgers and Shakes. 16
- Jeckyll and Hyde 3
- Joe's Shanghai 15
- JUdson Grill. 21
- La Caravelle. 14
- La Côte Basque 13
- La Locanda Vini 25
- Le Bernardin 20
- Le Marais. 38
- Mangia-57th Street 4
- Mars 2112. 19
- Meskerem 33
- Molyvos. 9
- Noche 35
- Ollies. 41
- Osteria del Circo 11
- Petrossian 2
- Pigalle. 32
- Remi 22
- Sugiyama 7
- Town 5
- Triomphe. 46
- "21" Club. 23
- Uncle Nick's 26
- Victor's Café 52 17
- Virgil's Real BBQ. 39

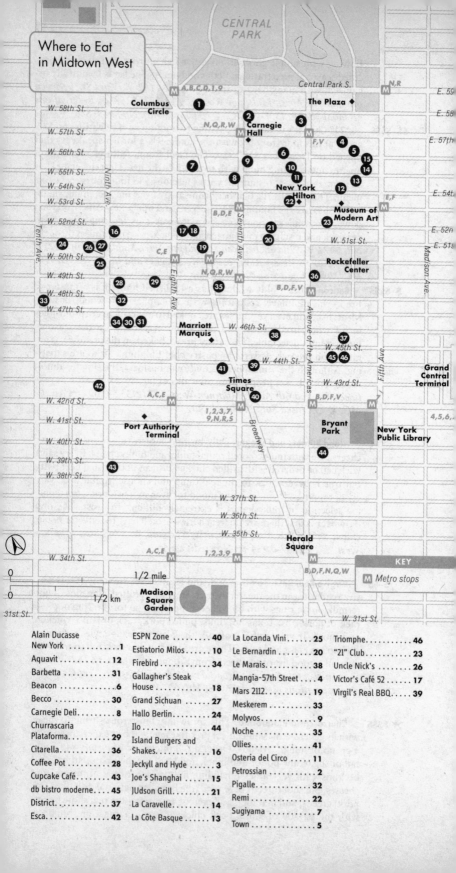

brought to the table on skewers. Simple sides and gooey desserts complete the authentic Brazilian experience. ✉ *316 W. 49th St., between 8th and 9th Aves., Midtown West* ☎ *212/245–0505* ✍ *Reservations essential* ▭ *AE, DC, MC, V.*

Cafés

¢ ✕ **Coffee Pot.** Overstuffed sofas and chairs, mirrors, brass chandeliers, good deals on the coffee of the day, and pleasant service make this one of the theater district's most pleasant options. ✉ *350 W. 49th St., at 9th Ave., Midtown West* ☎ *212/265–3566* ▭ *No credit cards.*

¢ ✕ **Cupcake Café.** Intensely buttery, magnificently decorated cakes and cupcakes, as well as doughnuts, pies, coffee cake, and hearty soup are worth the trek to this funky spot on the western flank of the Port Authority Bus Terminal (a somewhat sketchy area). ✉ *522 9th Ave., at W. 39th St., Midtown West* ☎ *212/465–1530* ▭ *No credit cards.*

Chinese

¢–$$ ✕ **Joe's Shanghai.** Joe opened his first Shanghai restaurant in Queens, but buoyed by the accolades accorded his steamed soup dumplings—magically filled with a rich, fragrant broth and a pork or pork-and-crabmeat mixture—he saw fit to open in Manhattan's Chinatown, and then here in midtown. Menu highlights include turnip shortcakes and dried bean curd salad to start, and succulent braised pork shoulder, ropey homemade Shanghai noodles, and traditional lion's head—rich pork meatballs braised in brown sauce—to follow. Other more familiar Chinese dishes are also excellent. ✉ *24 W. 56th St., between 5th and 6th Aves., Midtown West* ☎ *212/333–3868* ▭ *AE, DC, MC, V.*

¢–$ ✕ **Grand Sichuan International.** This regional Chinese restaurant serves a vast menu of specialties you won't find anywhere else. The emphasis is on fiery Sichuan (Szechuan) cooking, but Cantonese, Hunan, Shanghai, and even American Chinese food are represented (a handy treatise and guide on Chinese food comes with the menu). Spicy dan dan noodles, shredded potatoes in vinegar sauce, crab soup dumplings, minced pork with cellophane noodles or fermented green beans, and sautéed loofah are among the hauntingly delicious dishes. ✉ *745 9th Ave., between W. 50th and W. 51st Sts., Midtown West* ☎ *212/582–2288* ▭ *AE, MC, V.*

¢–$ ✕ **Ollie's.** This no-frills Chinese chain is a blessing for locals in search of a quick budget meal. The best dishes are the noodle soups (available with a number of ingredients including dumplings, vegetables, and meat) and the dim sum prepared by speedy chefs with nimble maneuverings that you can watch while you wait for a table. The many other standard dishes include shrimp with lobster sauce and sesame chicken. The portions are generous, but don't expect any culinary revelations. ✉ *200 W. 44th St., at Broadway, Midtown West* ☎ *212/921–5988* ✍ *Reservations not accepted* ▭ *AE, MC, V.*

Contemporary

$$$$ ✕ **Town.** It's difficult to say which is more chic in this bi-level restaurant: the design or the crowd. Ubiquitous architect David Rockwell has created a contemporary restaurant with an international feel, manipulating scale and using a variety of materials, like plastic and glass. Geoffrey Zakarian's cooking is every bit as sophisticated as the environment. The menu's descriptions are far simpler than the food that arrives. Quail with foie gras fritters, cod in porcini puree, and duck steak with buckwheat pilaf are intricate exercises in culinary craft. The "Balcony" lounge has a limited selection of light fare. ✉ *15 W. 56th St., between 5th and 6th Aves., Midtown West* ☎ *212/582–4445* ✍ *Reservations essential* ▭ *AE, D, DC, MC, V.*

$$–$$$$ ✕ **Ilo.** Rick Laakkonen's elegant cooking is almost lost in this oddly shaped, cramped dining room in the lobby of the Bryant Park Hotel. The signature appetizer is a "tidal pool" of oysters and sea urchin in a warm broth, and the stuffed duck neck is great. The menu changes seasonally, but stand-out dishes include rabbit with dandelion and sheep's milk ricotta cannelloni, and roasted lamb with curried couscous. ✉ *40 W. 40th St., between 5th and 6th Aves., Midtown West* ☎ *212/642–2255* ✍ *Reservations essential* ▭ *AE, DC, MC, V.*

Continental

$$–$$$ ✕ **Petrossian.** The only way to begin a meal at Petrossian is with caviar—beluga, osetra, or sevruga—presented in a Christofle server, or with a selection of smoked salmon, eel, and other delicacies. The rest of executive chef Michael Lipp's menu features a mélange of contemporary dishes, such as truffle-stuffed saddle of lamb, solidly prepared and satisfying. The dining room is enhanced by art deco accents, a granite bar, and *objets* by Erté and Lalique. The café next door sells fine pastries and a selection of creative treats—plus caviar, of course. ✉ *182 W. 58th St., at 7th Ave., Midtown West* ☎ *212/245–2214* ✍ *Reservations essential* ▭ *AE, DC, MC, V.*

Cuban

¢–$$$ ✕ **Victor's Café 52.** You can smell the authentic Cuban cooking as you enter this technicolor restaurant, a neighborhood fixture since 1963. The high-back booths, tile floor, rattan chairs, and skylight evoke golden-age movies set in Old Havana. Better than average, the food is a contemporary transcription of Cuban, Puerto Rican, and Latin dishes, such as hearty adobo, black bean soup, and fried plantains. The staff couldn't be friendlier. ✉ *236 W. 52nd St., between Broadway and 8th Ave., Midtown West* ☎ *212/586–7714* ▭ *AE, DC, MC, V.*

Delicatessens

$–$$ ✕ **Carnegie Deli.** Although not what it once was, this no-nonsense deli is still a favorite with out-of-towners. The portions are so huge you feel like a child in a surreal culinary fairy tale. Two giant matzo balls come in a bowl of soup, the knishes hang off the edge of the plates, and some combination sandwiches are so tall they have to be held together with bamboo skewers, not toothpicks. Don't miss the cheesecake, to our palates the best (and, of course, biggest) in the city. You pay for that excessive amount of food, but you can take home what you don't eat. ✉ *854 7th Ave., at W. 55th St., Midtown West* ☎ *212/757–2245* ▭ *No credit cards.*

Ethiopian

¢–$ ✕ **Meskerem.** Ethiopian art adorns the walls in this Hell's Kitchen storefront. The tasty delicacies include *kitfo* (spiced ground steak), which can be ordered raw, rare, or well-done, and *yebeg alecha,* tender pieces of lamb marinated in Ethiopian butter flavored with curry, rosemary, and an herb called *kosart,* and then sautéed with fresh ginger and a bit more curry. The vegetarian combination, an array of five vegetable and grain preparations served on injera (a yeasty flat bread used as a utensil to sop up the food) is a terrific deal. ✉ *468 W. 47th St., near 10th Ave., Midtown West* ☎ *212/664–0520* ▭ *AE, DC, MC, V.*

French

$$$$ ✕ **Alain Ducasse New York.** The only question New Yorkers ask about the restaurant created by France's most decorated chef is: "How many times can I afford to go?" This is by far New York's most expensive restaurant. But there's value behind that exorbitant price tag: you get an upholstered stool for your purse, an ever-changing menu of seasonal delights (including white truffles, black truffles, caviar), a superb wine list, and an array of petit fours to rival any Parisian bakery (you're even encouraged to take some home). These flourishes elevate Ducasse's deceptively simple riffs on classic French preparations—venison medallions Rossini, roasted sole—into an art form. ✉ *Essex House, 155 W. 58th St., between 6th and 7th Aves., Midtown West* ☎ *212/265–7300* ✍ *Reservations essential* 🧥 *Jacket and tie* 💳 *AE, D, DC, MC, V* ⏲ *Closed Sun. No lunch.*

$$$$ ✕ **La Caravelle.** When it opened in 1960, La Caravelle was one of New York's most opulent dining rooms. Since 1988, owners Rita and André Jammet have been celebrating the good life in the anachronistic dining room, Parisian style. (The bartender, Adelberto Alonso, has been there since 1960.) Although the decor may be worse for the wear, it is enlivened by Jean Pagé's murals, mirrors, flowers, and a star-studded clientele. Now under the direction of chef Troy Dupuy (formerly of Lespinasse), the prix-fixe menu features both classic (pike quenelles) and contemporary (baby lamb with buckwheat sprouts and curry) creations. ✉ *33 W. 55th St., between 5th and 6th Aves., Midtown West* ☎ *212/586–4252* ✍ *Reservations essential* 🧥 *Jacket required* 💳 *AE, DC, MC, V* ⏲ *Closed Sun. No lunch Sat.*

$$$$ ✕ **La Côte Basque.** Though not in its original location, Jean-Jacques Rachou's landmark French restaurant preserves many elements of its original design: dark wooden cross beams, murals by Bernard Lamotte, faux windows, and even the revolving door. The cuisine is classic French—begin with the trio of pâtés or one of the gossamer soufflés. The roast duckling with honey, Grand Marnier, and black-cherry sauce is prepared for two and carved table-side. A hearty cassoulet will leave you happily sated. The prix-fixe-only menu offers reasonable value given the quality of the food and the service. ✉ *60 W. 55th St., between 5th and 6th Aves., Midtown West* ☎ *212/688–6525* ✍ *Reservations essential* 🧥 *Jacket required* 💳 *AE, DC, MC, V* ⏲ *No lunch Sun.*

$$$$ ✕ **Le Bernardin.** Owner Maguy LeCoze presides over the power scene in the plush, teak-paneled dining room at this trend-setting French seafood restaurant. Chef-partner Eric Ripert works magic with anything that swims—preferring at times not to cook it at all. Deceptively simple dishes such as Spanish mackerel tartare with osetra caviar and steamed halibut on a pea puree are typical of his style. In Ripert's hands, a lowly croque monsieur becomes a four-star feast. There's no beating Le Bernardin for fine French cooking, seafood or otherwise, coupled with some of the finest desserts in town. ✉ *155 W. 51st St., between 6th and 7th Aves., Midtown West* ☎ *212/489–1515* ✍ *Reservations essential* 🧥 *Jacket required* 💳 *AE, DC, MC, V* ⏲ *Closed Sun. No lunch Sat.*

Fodor'sChoice ★

$$–$$$ ✕ **db bistro moderne.** Daniel Boulud's "casual bistro" (it's neither, really) consists of two elegantly appointed rooms, one in front where the tables are not clothed, and one in back where they are. The menu is organized by the French names of seasonal ingredients—lobster (*homard*), beet (*betterave*), beef (*boeuf*), and mushroom (*champignon*), *par exemple.* Within each category, appetizers and main courses are offered. Much has been made of the $28 hamburger. But considering it is superbly stuffed with braised short ribs, foie gras, and black truffles, it's almost a deal. ✉ *55 W. 44th St., between 5th and 6th Aves., Midtown West* ☎ *212/391–5353* ✍ *Reservations essential* 💳 *AE, MC, V* ⏲ *No lunch Sun.*

$$–$$$ ✕ **Triomphe.** You have to be mighty confident to name your restaurant Triomphe, and indeed the team behind this jewel box in the Iroquois Hotel has triumphed. The dining room is pleasing but unfussy, and chef Steve Zobel's wide-ranging menu is ambitious yet understated. Appetizers usually include chicken livers with sherry and onions, perfectly grilled quail, and seared scallops with a light licking of truffle oil. Zobel's rabbit coq au vin is a robust entrée, and crisp-tender arctic char flaunts its mustard crust. Desserts are simple but impeccable, especially the tarte Tatin, which is caramelized to a fare-thee-well. ✉ *49 W. 44th St., between 5th and 6th Aves., Midtown West* ☎ *212/453–4233* ✍ *Reservations essential* 💳 *AE, D, MC, V* ⊙ *Closed Sun. No lunch Sat.*

¢–$$ ✕ **Pigalle.** A good choice for a pre- or post-theater meal, this brasserie has removed any obstacle for those craving French food—rich duck foie gras is made in-house by the French chef, the prices are extremely reasonable, and the 24-hour kitchen turns out anything from steak au poivre to omelets. Sauces and vinaigrettes never overwhelm the main ingredients in dishes such as salmon tartare, duck confit, or salubrious steamed salmon tournedos. Some dishes can be ordered as half portions. The friendly waitstaff is knowledgeable about both the menu and wine selection. ✉ *790 8th Ave., at W. 48th St., Midtown West* ☎ *212/489–2233* 💳 *AE, MC, V.*

German

¢–$ ✕ **Hallo Berlin.** When nothing but bratwurst will do, head to this Hell's Kitchen café. In addition to "brat" there are more than 10 varieties of wurst, accompanied by traditional German side dishes such as sauerkraut, spaetzle, or addictive panfried potatoes. The atmosphere is low-budget Berlin beer garden, and the low, low prices match the lack of pretension. There are other authentic dishes on the menu, but none can compete with a sausage paired with a cold pint of German beer. ✉ *402 W. 51st St., between 9th and 10th Aves., Midtown West* ☎ *212/541–6248* 💳 *No credit cards* ⊙ *No lunch Sun.*

Greek

$$–$$$$ ✕ **Estiatorio Milos.** Like a stylized version of the Plaka in Athens, this dramatic restaurant comes dazzlingly alive with whitewashed walls, table umbrellas, iced displays of glimmering fresh fish, and beautiful European diners. Your meal begins with the snipping of fresh herbs into a bowl of olive oil. Classic salads—of lentil, chickpea, or smoked carp roe—and a signature pile of paper-thin fried vegetables make delicious appetizers. You can select a fish from the display of fresh Mediterranean seafood flown in everyday, and have it weighed (you pay by the pound) and grilled whole. You almost have to be a shipping tycoon to afford it all. ✉ *125 W. 55th St., between 6th and 7th Aves., Midtown West* ☎ *212/245–7400* ✍ *Reservations essential* 💳 *AE, D, MC, V.*

$$–$$$ ✕ **Molyvos.** Fresh ingredients, bold flavors, fine olive oil, and fragrant herbs emerge from Jim Botsacos's marvelous kitchen at this upscale taverna. Meals start with a selection of salads, or *meze*. They include gigantes beans stewed with tomatoes, *taramasalata* (a creamy spread made with smoked carp roe), garlicky *skordalia* (potato puree), *saganaki* (fried *kefalotiri* cheese), and a real Greek salad with vegetables, olives, and feta—but no lettuce. Seasonal entrées include traditional Greek dishes, such as supreme *pastitsio* (baked pasta casserole), moussaka, and whole grilled snapper. ✉ *871 7th Ave., between W. 55th and W. 56th Sts., Midtown West* ☎ *212/582–7500* ✍ *Reservations essential* 💳 *AE, D, DC, MC, V.*

¢–$$ ✕ **Uncle Nick's.** The long dining room of this inexpensive taverna has a navy blue pipe-lined tin ceiling, an exposed kitchen, and a wood floor. Appetizing displays of whole red snapper, porgy, and striped bass summon the spirit of restaurants throughout Greece. Uncle Nick's owners, Tony and Mike Vanatakis, prepare each fish selection with simplicity and care. A few excellent appetizers—crispy fried smelts, tender grilled baby octopus, marvelous sweetbreads, and giant lima beans with tomatoes and herbs—make a satisfying meal. In temperate weather there's outdoor dining in a quiet rear garden. ✉ *747 9th Ave., between W. 50th and W. 51st Sts., Midtown West* ☎ *212/245–7992* 💳 *MC, V.*

Italian

$–$$$$ ✕ **Carmine's.** Savvy New Yorkers line up early for the affordable family-style meals served at this large, busy eatery. The dining room has dark woodwork and old-fashioned black-and-white tiles. There are no reservations taken for parties of fewer than six people after 7 PM, but those who wait are rewarded with truly huge portions of such popular items as fried calamari, linguine with white clam sauce, chicken parmigiana, and lobster fra diavolo. You will inevitably order too much, but it all tastes just as satisfying the next day. ✉ *200 W. 44th St., between Broadway and 8th Ave., Midtown West* ☎ *212/221–3800* ▭ *AE, D, DC, MC, V.*

$$–$$$ ✕ **Osteria del Circo.** Opened by the sons of celebrity restaurateur Sirio Maccioni (Le Cirque 2000), this less formal place celebrates the Tuscan cooking of their mother Egi. The contemporary menu offers a wide selection and includes some traditional Tuscan specialties, such as Egi's ricotta-and-spinach-filled ravioli, tossed in butter and sage and gratinéed with imported Parmesan. The pizza *pazza* (crazy pizza) has a delicate layer of mascarpone cheese and tomato topped with thin slices of prosciutto di Parma. Don't miss the fanciful Circo desserts, especially the filled *bomboloncini* doughnuts. ✉ *120 W. 55th St., between 6th and 7th Aves., Midtown West* ☎ *212/265–3636* ⛵ *Reservations essential* ▭ *AE, DC, MC, V* ⏲ *No lunch Sun.*

$$–$$$ ✕ **Remi.** A Venetian sensibility pervades this stylish restaurant designed by Adam Tihany. A skylighted atrium, blue-and-white striped banquettes, Venetian glass chandeliers, and a soaring room-length mural of the city of canals make this the perfect spot for a power lunch or a meal before a night on the town. Chef Francesco Antonucci's contemporary Venetian cuisine is highly favored among Italians living in New York. Fresh sardines make a lovely beginning, with their contrasting sweet-and-sour onion garnish, and you can't go wrong with the sumptuous pastas, expertly prepared rack of lamb, or any of the wonderful desserts. ✉ *145 W. 53rd St., between 6th and 7th Aves., Midtown West* ☎ *212/581–4242* ⛵ *Reservations essential* ▭ *AE, DC, MC, V* ⏲ *No lunch weekends.*

$–$$$ ✕ **Barbetta.** Operated by the same family since it opened in 1906, Barbetta offers a uniquely authentic Piemontese experience in a throwback of a dining room that evokes the tired, old-world charm of Turin, once the seat of the Savoy kingdom. The vast menu highlights dishes from the restaurant's past, as well as traditional Piemontese cooking. Pasta, like the eggy tajarin, and risotto stand out. A beautiful garden affords a lovely summertime setting. ✉ *321 W. 46th St., between 8th and 9th Aves., Midtown West* ☎ *212/246–9171* ▭ *AE, D, DC, MC, V* ⏲ *Closed Sun.–Mon.*

$–$$$ ✕ **Becco.** An ingenious concept makes Becco a prime Restaurant Row choice for time-constrained theatergoers. There are two pricing scenarios: one includes an all-you-can-eat selection of antipasti and three pastas served hot out of pans that waiters circulate around the dining room; the other adds a generous entrée. Either way you'll be in and out quickly, and you won't leave hungry. The selection changes daily but often includes gnocchi, fresh ravioli, and something in a cream sauce. The entrées include braised lamb shank, veal, and various fish. Try to save room for bread pudding. ✉ *355 W. 46th St., between 8th and 9th Aves., Midtown West* ☎ *212/397–7597* ⛵ *Reservations essential* ▭ *AE, DC, MC, V.*

$–$$ ✕ **La Locandadei Vini.** On a strip of popular restaurants, this trattoria stands out for its authenticity and cozy charm. Tawny wood paneling is topped by a shelf of wine bottles that runs the length of the restaurant, and frosted glass fixtures create a soft glow. After nibbling the bread and olives, quiz your Italian waiter about the hearty pastas that go well beyond fettuccine and tagliatelle and include duck ragout and homemade sausage in the mix. The antipasti portions are generous, and there's a wide range of salads. Grilled meats and veal are also tempting. ✉ *737 9th Ave., at W. 50th St., Midtown West* ☎ *212/258–2900* ▭ *AE, MC, V.*

¢–$ ✕ **Mangia–57th Street.** Office workers looking for out-of-the-ordinary takeout come here for sandwiches and salads that include fresh mozzarella, prosciutto, focaccia, grilled eggplant, and sun-dried tomatoes. In the sit-down restaurant upstairs, small pizzas and pastas are a regular feature, and special dishes might include grilled swordfish with *puttanesca* sauce or rib-eye steak with porcini mushrooms. It's one of the most reasonably priced lunches in midtown. ✉ *50 W. 57th St., between 5th and 6th Aves., Midtown West* ☎ *212/582–5882* ▭ *AE, D, DC, MC, V* ⏲ *Closed weekends. No dinner.*

Japanese

$$$$ ✕ **Sugiyama.** Introduce yourself to the Japanese style of eating known as *kaiseki* (a meal of small tasting portions presented in a ritualized order) at this charming prix-fixe-only restaurant. First timers should order the *omikase,* or chef's tasting, to appreciate the true breadth of the genre. It may start with a wild mountain plum floating in a glassy cube of gelatin, and proceed to a gurgling pot of blowfish or to sweet lobster or delicate squid to be cooked on a hot stone. The experience is exhilarating. ✉ *251 W. 55th St., between Broadway and 8th Ave., Midtown West* ☎ *212/956–0670* ▭ *AE, D, MC, V* ⏲ *Closed Sun.–Mon. No lunch.*

Kosher

$$–$$$ ✕ **Le Marais.** The appetizing display of meats and terrines at the entrance, the bare wood floors, tables covered with butcher paper, the French wall posters, and maroon banquettes may remind you of a Parisian bistro. Yet the clientele (mostly male) is strictly kosher (as is the food), and they don't speak French. A cold *terrine de boeuf en gelée façon pot au feu* (marinated short ribs) starts the meal on the right note, and rib steak for two is cooked until it is tender and juicy. The accompanying fries are perfect. ✉ *150 W. 46th St., between 6th and 7th Aves., Midtown West* ☎ *212/869–0900* ▭ *AE, MC, V* ⏲ *Closed Sat. No dinner Fri.*

Latin

$$–$$$ ✕ **Noche.** Ignore the pedestrian bar at street level, and ride the glass elevator to Noche's soaring main dining room, where dazzling white leather banquettes line a vast, complex space that the ubiquitous Rockwell design group intended to resemble one of Rio's dance halls. One end of the vast space ends with a 180-degree revolving stage upon which, on certain nights, Latin American music is performed. Ramiro Jimenez's pan-Latin cuisine features big flavors and portions all around: spicy ceviches, succulent suckling pig, addictive *arepas* (freshly fried corn cakes), and luscious *churros*—Mexican crullers filled with bittersweet chocolate and sauced with dulce de leche. ✉ *1604 Broadway, between 48th and 49th Sts., Midtown West* ☎ *212/541–7070* ✍ *Reservations essential* ▭ *AE, D, MC, V* ⏲ *No dinner Sun.*

Pan-Asian

$–$$ ✕ **Ruby Foo's.** This is the midtown branch of the Upper West Side, Pan-Asian hot spot. The menu incorporates favorites from most Asian cuisines, including a pungent Thai hot-and-sour soup with shrimp and ginger wontons. There are also dim sum and a sushi menu available. If some of the food doesn't quite measure up to the grand setting, the place is so lively and amusing no one seems to mind a bit. ✉ *1626 Broadway, at W. 49th St., Midtown West* ☎ *212/489–5600* ✍ *Reservations essential* ▭ *AE, MC, V.*

Russian

$$$ × **Firebird.** Eight dining rooms full of objets d'art and period antiques lie within these two brownstones resembling a pre-Revolutionary St. Petersburg mansion. Staples of the regional cuisine range from caviar and *zakuska* (assorted Russian hors d'oeuvres) to tea with cherry preserves, and great desserts (an assortment of Russian cookies steals the show). Don't fail to sample the extraordinary vodka selection. And the elegant caviar presentation—steaming hot blini drenched in butter, slathered with sour cream, and filled with beluga, sevruga, or osetra by waiters in white gloves—is a giddy indulgence. ☒ *365 W. 46th St., between 8th and 9th Aves., Midtown West* ☎ *212/586–0244* ✍ *Reservations essential* ▭ *AE, DC, MC, V* ⊗ *Closed Mon. No lunch Sun.*

4

Scandinavian

★ $$–$$$$ × **Aquavit.** Cool as a dip in the Baltic Sea, this airy atrium that was once Nelson Rockefeller's town house is decorated with contemporary art and an inspiring waterfall. The nouveau Swedish fare of wunderkind chef Marcus Sammuelsson is dressed in chic contemporary garb. Forget herring, lingonberries, and pea soup (although they're better here than anywhere else): think molten foie gras ganache with truffle ice cream. Desserts are equally creative and scrumptious. An upstairs dining room is less formal and less expensive. New York's largest selection of aquavits (a strong Scandinavian liquor) partners the well-chosen wine list. Sunday brunch is literally a smorgasbord. ☒ *13 W. 54th St., between 5th and 6th Aves., Midtown West* ☎ *212/307–7311* ✍ *Reservations essential* ▭ *AE, DC, MC, V.*

Seafood

$$–$$$$ × **Citarella.** Citarella's enormously popular trio of stores in Manhattan demonstrates some of the best fish-market connections in town, so the emergence of a state-of-the-art seafood restaurant from the fold was inevitable. Cozily ensconced in a four-story, highly aquatic and luxurious space (yet another Rockwell Group design), the restaurant showcases chef Brian Bistrong's culinary wiles. You won't find fresher, tastier striped bass, a hunk of which is served with fava beans, morels, and a red wine reduction. Two tender sweet pink snapper filets arrive over a tangle of white and green asparagus. William Yosses's glorious desserts include warm vanilla cake with 12-bean vanilla ice cream and chocolate-cherry jubilee bonbon with caramelized pistachios. ☒ *1240 6th. Ave., at 49th St., Midtown West* ☎ *212/332–1515* ✍ *Reservations essential* ▭ *AE, D, DC, MC, V.*

$$–$$$ × **Esca.** Mario Batali's Esca, Italian for "bait," lures diners in with delectable raw preparations called *cruda*—scallops with tangerine oil or fluke with a douse of olive oil and sprinkle of crunchy sea salt—and hooks them with entrées like whole, salt-crusted *branzino* (sea bass), or *bucatini* pasta with crab or octopus. The dining room conjures images of sea and sand, though the high-powered media crowd could only exist in Manhattan. Batali's partner, Joe Bastianich, is in charge of the wine cellar, so expect an adventurous list of esoteric Italian bottles. ☒ *402 W. 43rd St., at 9th Ave., Midtown West* ☎ *212/564–7272* ✍ *Reservations essential* ▭ *AE, DC, MC, V* ⊗ *No lunch Sun.*

Steak

$$–$$$$ × **Gallagher's Steak House.** The most casual of the great New York steak houses, with red-and-white check tablecloths, photos of sports greats on the walls, and a large, friendly bar, Gallagher's has almost no pretensions and nothing to hide—through the street window you can even peer into the dry-aging room where slabs of meat ripen to perfection. You won't be disappointed with the famous aged sirloin steaks, over-

SPECIAL EXPERIENCES

CRAVING KOREAN AT 2 AM? *Want to catch some rays along with a dish of homemade pasta? New York City can fulfill your every dining desire, whether for a really good brunch or a side of celebrities. All of these special spots are reviewed in this chapter.*

ALFRESCO: *Although New York is an asphalt jungle, there are still a few restaurants where you can dine in the open air—and not just on the sidewalk. Old-world charm flows from the fountain in the middle of* **Barbetta***'s handsome garden on Restaurant Row in the theater district. For a romantic dinner over a dish of handmade Pugliese pasta try the garden at* **I Trulli** *in Murray Hill. If margarita-induced mayhem is more your East Village speed, the lovely backyard of* **Miracle Grill** *beckons.*

BRUNCH: *Brunch with a few friends and the Sunday paper is a weekly tradition. Upper West Side institutions such as* **Barney Greengrass** *and* **Sarabeth's** *offer good food at good prices (and often a good long wait for a table), while* **Avenue** *serves French pastries along with fine brunch fare. On the Upper East Side,* **Le Pain Quotidien** *serves up Belgian treats. In TriBeCa,* **Bubby's** *always has a line on weekend mornings, but these days the overflow is handled by* **Kitchenette.** *Long before the Meatpacking District became trendy,* **Florent** *had a loyal brunch following amongst night crawlers.* **Home** *in Greenwich Village and the various outposts of* **Petite Abeille** *offer cozy environments and good food. In the Flatiron District,* **City Bakery** *has a brunch that allows you to pick from the salad bar and order some delicious table-service entrées, as well. For nontraditional brunch fare, try the Spanish tapas at* **Pipa,** *also in the Flatiron District. For a big appetite, try the Swedish smorgasbord at* **Aquavit** *in Midtown West.*

CELEBRITY SPOTTING: *True New Yorkers will never admit to choosing a dining destination based on the chance of seeing a celebrity, but if star-studded glam is the evening's aim, some excellent restaurants usually come through. Everyone from Jerry Seinfeld to Martha Stewart has been caught with a hand in the bread basket at SoHo's* **Balthazar.** *Giorgio Armani, Sandra Bernhard, and Isaac Mizrahi have been seen getting take-out food from* **Second Avenue Deli** *in the East Village. For the billionaire celebrity set, like Ron Perlman, Donald Trump, and Larry Tish, nothing but midtown's* **Le Cirque 2000** *will do, but for media moguls, such as Edgar Bronfman and Barbara Walters, the Grill Room at* **Four Seasons** *is the place to lunch. (These days you may see everyone "slumming it" at Daniel Boulud's* **db bistro moderne,** *also in midtown.) There's bound to be someone famous at* **Jean-Georges, Daniel,** *or* **Nobu** *any night of the week.*

LATE-NIGHT: *If you'd rather eat at 3 AM than wake up early to stand on line for Sunday brunch, there are a wealth of late-night dining options to choose from. In TriBeCa you can wind down to the wee hours at* **Grace.** *In SoHo,* **Balthazar** *seats until 1:30 AM, and you can eat your way around the world at* **Blue Ribbon** *until 4 AM. In the Meatpacking District* **Pastis** *serves French bistro fare almost as late, and* **Florent** *is open 24 hours from Thursday through Sunday, and until 5 AM the rest of the week. The French brasserie* **Pigalle** *on 8th Avenue in midtown is open 24 hours and has a changing shift of menus. If wine's your thing, head to the East Village's* **Tasting Room** *(open until 2 AM) for an excellent selection of American labels and contemporary cooking, but if it's martinis and creative American fare you desire, your first priority should be* **First** *(until 3 AM). If you want a more ethnic experience, try the 24-hour* **Kang Suh** *Korean barbecue place in Murray Hill, or Chinese noodles at* **Great New York Noodletown,** *where you can get mei fun until 4 AM.*

size lobsters, or any of the fabulous potato dishes (try the potatoes O'Brien, with sweet pepper and onion). Don't miss the creamy rice pudding. ✉ *228 W. 52nd St., between Broadway and 8th Ave., Midtown West* ☎ *212/245–5336* *Reservations essential* *AE, DC, MC, V.*

$$–$$$$ ✕ **Palm West.** They may have added tablecloths, but it would take more than that to hide the brusque, no-nonsense nature of this West Side branch of the legendary steak house. The steak is always impeccable, and the lobsters are so big there may not be room at the table for such classic side dishes as rich creamed spinach. The "half and half" side combination of cottage-fried potatoes and fried onions is addictive. ✉ *250 W. 50th St., between Broadway and 8th Ave., Midtown West* ☎ *212/333–7256* *Reservations essential* *AE, DC, MC, V* *Closed Sun. No lunch Sat.*

Midtown East

Power brokers like to seal their deals over lunch on the East Side, so that means lots of suits and ties at the restaurants during the day. At night the streets are deserted, but the restaurants are filled with people celebrating success over some of the finest, most expensive, and most formal food in town.

American

$$$$ ✕ **Four Seasons.** The landmark Seagram Building houses one of America's most famous restaurants, designed by architect Philip Johnson in a timeless moderne style. The stark Grill Room, birthplace of the power lunch, has inviting leather banquettes, a floating sculpture, and one of the best bars in New York. Illuminated trees and a gurgling Carrara marble pool distinguish the more romantic Pool Room. The eclectic menu changes seasonally; the pre-theater prix-fixe dinner is relatively inexpensive. Otherwise, the menu is among the priciest in town. You can't go wrong with Dover sole, steak tartare, truffled bison, or crispy duck. ✉ *99 E. 52nd St., between Park and Lexington Aves., Midtown East* ☎ *212/754–9494* *Reservations essential* *Jacket required* *AE, DC, MC, V* *Closed Sun. No lunch Sat.*

American-Casual

¢–$ ✕ **Comfort Diner.** Looking for a quick, casual, and satisfying meal? Comfort Diner is glad to oblige, with a menu of typical American fare like buffalo wings, Caesar salad, grilled chicken club sandwich, macaroni and cheese, meat loaf, and burgers. The pies and cakes are baked fresh daily. The chrome and teratza may look a bit faded, but at least the price is right. Prepare to wait on line for the popular weekend brunch. ✉ *214 E. 45th St., between 2nd and 3rd Aves., Midtown East* ☎ *212/867–4555* *Reservations not accepted* *D, DC, MC, V.*

Chinese

$–$$ ✕ **Shun Lee Palace.** If you want inexpensive Cantonese food without pretensions, head to Chinatown; but if you prefer to be pampered and don't mind spending a lot of money, this is the place. The cuisine is classic Chinese. Giant prawns with black bean sauce make a good starter, and rack of lamb Szechuan style is a popular entrée. ✉ *155 E. 55th St., between Lexington and 3rd Aves., Midtown East* ☎ *212/371–8844* *Reservations essential* *AE, DC, MC, V.*

Contemporary

$$$$ ✕ **March.** With its travertine floor and working fireplace, this romantic, understated restaurant is tucked into a small town house. Co-owner Joseph Scalice supervises the polished service and the expert wine list that complement the cuisine of partner-chef Wayne Nish, master of

Brasserie 11
Docks Oyster Bar 21
Felidia 1
Fifty-Seven Fifty-Seven 6
Four Seasons .12
Guastavino's ...4
Heartbeat 17
Kuruma Zushi .18
La Grenouille .13
Le Cirque 2000 14
Lespinasse 8
L'Impero 26
Lutèce 16
Maloney & Porcelli 15
March 3
Marichu 23
Oyster Bar ...19
The Palm 24
Pazo 9
Rosa Mexicano 2
Shallots NY 7
Sparks Steak House 22
Sushi Yasuda 25
Tao Asian Bistro 5
Tuscan Steak 20
Vong 10

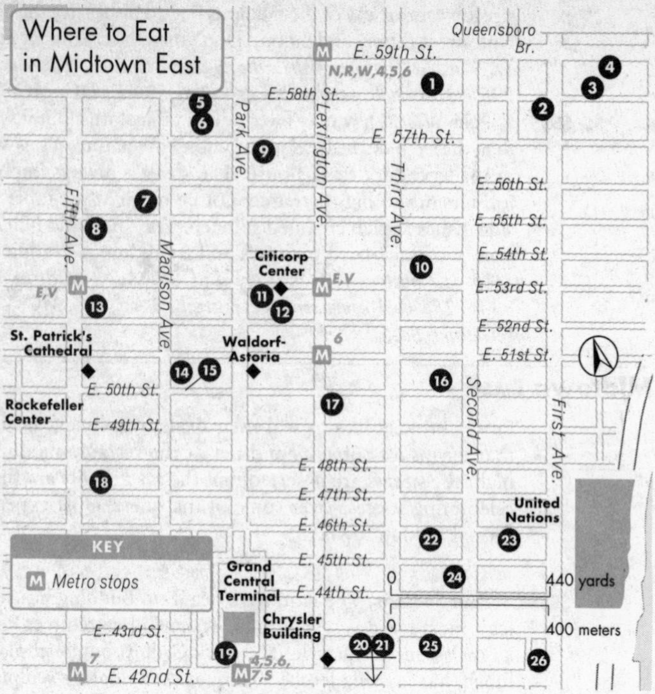

classical French technique with a strong Asian influence. The table d'hôte prix-fixe menu is organized into tasting categories. Select any number of courses, then choose from a long list of seasonal dishes, such as salmon with leeks in miso rice vinegar, and luxury offerings, like the "Beggar's Purses," filled with caviar and crème fraîche. ✉ *405 E. 58th St., between 1st Ave. and Sutton Pl., Midtown East* ☎ *212/754–6272* ✍ *Reservations essential* ▭ *AE, DC, MC, V* ⏲ *No lunch.*

$$–$$$ ✕ **Fifty Seven Fifty Seven.** I. M. Pei's strikingly sleek Four Seasons Hotel houses this restaurant and a sophisticated adjacent bar. Even locals come in to be wowed by the 22-ft coffered ceilings, inlaid maple floors, onyx-studded bronze chandeliers, and the contemporary American menu. Creative interpretations of familiar dishes such as lobster Caesar salad are very well prepared, and it's hard to choose between the pepper-crusted tuna niçoise or the perfectly cooked herb-roasted veal chop with artichokes and oven-roasted tomatoes. For breakfast, don't miss the lemon ricotta pancakes. ✉ *57 E. 57th St., between Madison and Park Aves., Midtown East* ☎ *212/758–5757* ✍ *Reservations essential* ▭ *AE, DC, MC, V.*

$$–$$$ ✕ **Heartbeat.** The omnipresent Drew Nieporent opened this unfortunately named restaurant in the W New York hotel. The colorful, geometric design by David Rockwell makes you think you're sitting in a Mondrian painting. Chef Michel Nischan has devised a menu of modern-day spa food, which emphasizes healthful preparations full of flavor, not fat. The focus is on seafood and lean meats, and bean or squash purees add richness. Highlights include sautéed trout with lump crab cake and succotash and a spiced seared venison chop. Don't worry, desserts are full of fat. Finish with a selection from the impressive tea menu. ✉ *149 E. 49th St., at Lexington Ave., Midtown East* ☎ *212/407–2900* ▭ *AE, DC, MC, V* ⏲ *No lunch weekends.*

$$–$$$ ✕ **Maloney & Porcelli.** Known for generous portions of whimsical American food, this friendly, comfortable restaurant (named for the owner's lawyers) is ideal when you're dining with a hungry crowd of people (especially men) who can't agree on a restaurant. The definitive dish is a huge, juicy crackling pork shank served on a bed of poppy-seed sauerkraut with a Mason jar of tangy, homemade "Firecracker" jalapeño-spiced apple sauce. The drunken doughnuts, served warm with three small pots of liqueur-flavored jam, are one of the fun desserts. The inventive wine list includes 40 wines priced under $40. A large, square bar centers the bi-level space. ✉ *37 E. 50th St., between Madison and Park Aves., Midtown East* ☎ *212/750–2233* *Reservations essential* *AE, DC, MC, V.*

$$–$$$ ✕ **Pazo.** Fresh from the triumphant Asian fusion cuisine at her flagship Chelsea restaurant, AZ, chef Patricia Yeo is here reinterpreting Mediterranean cuisine, and she and her coexecutive chef Pino Maffeo are no less successful. Pazo's perfectly lighted space has Spanish and Moroccan touches in the decor, reflecting influences prevalent in the kitchen. Yeo's *pissaladière* (onion-Parmesan tart) is draped with milk-soaked sardines. Maple-crusted quail rests on a bed of raisin and Gorgonzola-studded risotto. Roasted dourade is plated on a bed of spaghetti squash strands, with rock shrimp hush puppies alongside. Don't miss Nicole Plue's sumptuous desserts, like cinnamon-dusted beignets with Catalan cream. ✉ *106 E. 57th St., between Lexington and Park Aves., Midtown East* ☎ *212/752–7470* *Reservations essential* *AE, D, DC, MC, V* *Closed Sun. No lunch Sat.*

Eclectic

$–$$ ✕ **Guastavino's.** Under the 59th Street Bridge lies this incredible space that shows the pristine tile work of Raphael Guastavino. It is something of a marvel to New Yorkers, who remember when this was nothing but a deserted tunnel. It took Terence Conran, a Brit with a penchant for soaring, out-of-the-way spaces in his native London, to envision this site as a restaurant. Two dining rooms showcase chef Daniel Orr's eclectic cuisine. The downstairs menu offers fish-and-chips, matzo-ball soup, and just about everything else. The more refined upstairs prix-fixe menu leans toward French cuisine (pheasant with whiskey sauce, fish ragout). ✉ *409 E. 59th St., between 1st Ave. and Sutton Pl., Midtown East* ☎ *212/980–2455* *AE, DC, MC, V.*

French

$$$$ ✕ **La Grenouille.** This is such a quintessential Manhattan French restaurant that it almost feels like a retro theme restaurant. The menu, written only in French, presents a $90 prix fixe of three courses (with several tempting supplements that fatten your bill). Possible choices include salmon tartare with caviar vinaigrette, or frogs' legs and escargot to start, followed by duck breast with chestnuts, or a flambé of kidneys with mustard sauce. Expect to add anywhere from $3.50 to $85 for lobster, sole, foie gras, steak, or beluga. This isn't just about having memorable food—it's about having a wonderful experience. ✉ *3 E. 52nd St., between 5th and Madison Aves., Midtown East* ☎ *212/752–1495* *Reservations essential* *AE, DC, MC, V* *Closed Sun.*

$$$$ ✕ **Lutèce.** A renovation and the young French chef David Féau have breathed robust life back into this tired restaurant, which was once an international sensation. Féau's enticing creations, such as black and white scallops, which arrive on pools of squid ink and cream sauces that look like an abstract painting, and yellowfin tuna mille-feuille, a stack of glistening raw tuna slices, are as beautiful as they are delicious. State-of-the-art roast farm-raised chicken (for two) comes dribbled with black truffle jus. Toothsome sautéed veal chop is partnered by a Swiss chard

gratin with Parmesan and rhubarb jelly. ✉ *249 E. 50th St., between 2nd and 3rd Aves., Midtown East* ☎ *212/752–2225* ✍ *Reservations essential* ▭ *AE, DC, MC, V* ⊙ *Closed Sun.*

$$$–$$$$ ✕ **Le Cirque 2000.** Owner Sirio Maccioni has fed the world's elite for more than 25 years. His restaurant's current incarnation in the landmark Villard House at the New York Palace Hotel continues the tradition. But the celebrities and moguls are now surrounded by Adam Tihany's controversial, futuristic, circus-chic interior. French native Pierre Schaedlin has injected contemporary overtones into the classic French menu (roasted red snapper with anchovy cream, for example) and has included a few homages to Sirio's Italian roots. Over-the-top desserts come in Venetian-glass goblets and sugar domes. The wine list spans the spectrum of the world's varietals. ✉ *455 Madison Ave., between E. 50th and E. 51st Sts., Midtown East* ☎ *212/303–7788* ✍ *Reservations essential* *Jacket and tie* ▭ *AE, DC, MC, V* ⊙ *No lunch Sun.*

$–$$$ ✕ **Brasserie.** This midtown ultramodern brasserie has an unmistakable downtown vibe. The design by architects Diller & Scofidio uses molded pear wood, lime-green resin, pastry-bag sculptures, and digital flat-screen technology to create an otherworldly eating environment. As an added bonus, the contemporary brasserie fare—served from morning to late night—is excellent. The baguettes are superb and the daily specials speak French without an accent. Don't leave without sampling dessert or taking a trip to the cool bathroom. ✉ *100 E. 53rd St., between Lexington and Park Aves., Midtown East* ☎ *212/751–4840* ✍ *Reservations essential* ▭ *AE, D, DC, MC, V.*

Italian

$–$$$ ✕ **Felidia.** Manhattanites frequent this *ristorante* as much for the winning enthusiasm of owner/cookbook author/Public Television chef Lidia Bastianich as for the food. The menu emphasizes authentic regional Italian cuisines, with a bow to dishes from Bastianich's homeland, Istria, on the Adriatic. Sit in an attractive front room with a wooden bar, a rustic room beyond, or in the elegant second-floor dining room. Seasonal dishes feature white truffles and exceptional game preparations (in autumn). Order risotto, fresh homemade pasta, or roasted whole fish, and choose from a wine list representing Italy's finest vineyards. ✉ *243 E. 58th St., between 2nd and 3rd Aves., Midtown East* ☎ *212/758–1479* ✍ *Reservations essential* *Jacket and tie* ▭ *AE, DC, MC, V* ⊙ *Closed Sun. No lunch Sat.*

$–$$$ ✕ **L'Impero.** Rather than flaunt its proximity to the United Nations by offering a view, L'Impero instead offers a most comfortable escape. Scott Conant's Italian cooking is highly respectful of the cuisine's fine traditions. Pastas are superb, especially a braised rabbit ravioli with roasted parsnips, tomato, and mint. Spaghetti with tomato and basil sounds too simple, but every aspect of the dish is absolutely perfect, especially those magically sweet tomatoes. Don't miss *capretto*—baby goat that is slow-roasted beyond tenderness, and served with flash-sautéed artichoke. Finish with sesame cannoli or supple quince crostata. ✉ *45 Tudor City Pl., between W. 42nd and W. 43rd Sts., Midtown East* ☎ *212/599–5045* ▭ *AE, DC, MC, V* ⊙ *Closed Sun. No lunch Sat.*

Japanese

★ $–$$$$ ✕ **Kuruma Zushi.** Only a small sign in Japanese indicates the location of this extraordinary restaurant that serves only sushi and sashimi. Bypass the tables, sit at the sushi bar, and put yourself in the hands of Toshihiro Uezu, the owner and chef. Uezu imports hard-to-find fish from Japan, and on a typical night he will offer several different types of tuna, the prices of which vary according to the degree of fattiness and the size of the fish from which they are cut. The most quietly attentive service staff in the city completes the wildly expensive experience, and makes it worth every penny. ✉ *7 E. 47th St., 2nd floor, between 5th and Madison Aves., Midtown East* ☎ *212/317–2802* ✍ *Reservations essential* ▭ *AE, MC, V* ⊙ *Closed Sun.*

$–$$$ ✕ **Sushi Yasuda.** The chic bamboo-lined space in which chef Maomichi Yasuda works his aquatic sorcery is as clean and elegant as his food. It couldn't be more out of place, surrounded by car-rental companies on a nondescript block near Grand Central Station. But whether he's using fish flown in daily from Japan or the creamiest sea urchin, Yasuda makes sushi so fresh and delicate it melts in your mouth. A number of special appetizers change daily (crispy fried eel backbone is a surprising treat), and a fine selection of sake and beer complements the food. ✉ *204 E. 43rd St., between 2nd and 3rd Aves., Midtown East* ☎ *212/972–1001* ▭ *AE, D, MC, V* ⊙ *Closed Sun. No lunch Sat.*

Kosher

$$–$$$$ ✕ **Shallots NY.** The owners and chef of this ambitious kosher restaurant want to be taken seriously by diners, whether they are observant or not. The decor is tasteful and romantic with colored glass panels, low lighting, and impressive floral arrangements. The food comes on oversized, colored, frosted-glass plates, and tends to be porcini-dusted sweetbreads and parsnip and garlic soup, rather than knishes and corned beef sandwiches. Everything is attractively presented and priced for the big leagues. The only time you'll realize you're not in a secular restaurant is when you first look at the wine list, which is—you guessed it—all kosher. ✉ *The Sony Atrium, 550 Madison Ave., between E. 55th and E. 56th Sts., Midtown East* ☎ *212/833–7800* ✍ *Reservations essential* ▭ *AE, D, MC, V* ⊙ *Closed Sun. No lunch Sat. No dinner Fri.*

Mexican

★ $–$$$ ✕ **Rosa Mexicano.** When a waiter slips open a parchment package containing a lamb shank braised in a three-chili sauce, the dining room fills with the fragrance of Oaxaca. Duck enchiladas and chicken steamed in beer stand out among the interesting regional dishes. A better guacamole, prepared table-side and served with warm corn tortillas, cannot be found—not even in Mexico. The assortment of chilled seafood served as an appetizer is terrific, and the chocolate-chili mousse cake has real kick. The jam-packed bar room in the front makes you feel as though you've happened upon a Mexican fiesta (or a frat party). ✉ *1063 1st Ave., at E. 58th St., Midtown East* ☎ *212/753–7407* ✍ *Reservations essential* ▭ *AE, DC, MC, V* ⊙ *No lunch.*

Pan-Asian

$$–$$$$ ✕ **Tao Asian Bistro.** The scene here offers none of the serenity suggested by the restaurant's name. Housed in a vast former movie theater, this is a see-and-be-seen eatery with every guest "hip-checking" the next. With its soaring brick walls, the place seems to go on forever in every direction, not unlike the menu, which explores all Asian cuisines with serious creative license. Sushi-style appetizers will satisfy nonpurists, and dishes such as dragon tail spareribs in sweet-and-sour sauce, and Chilean sea bass in soy will delight those with more purist leanings. Naturally dominating the dining room is a 40-ft gilt Buddha. He seems thoroughly amused by the spectacle. ✉ *42 E. 58th St., between Park and Madison Aves., Midtown East* ☎ *212/888–2288* ✍ *Reservations essential* ▭ *AE, D, MC, V.*

$–$$$$ ✕ **Vong.** A tour of duty at Bangkok's Oriental Hotel inspired Jean-Georges Vongerichten to create this radiant restaurant of potted palms and gold-leaf ceilings. Presentation is vital here: the food is showcased on dazzling dishes of varying sizes, colors, and shapes. The menu changes seasonally, but reliable standbys include quail rubbed with Thai spices and grilled beef and noodles in a ginger broth. As is often the case these days, appetizers are better than entrées. Order two or three and you'll be very happy. Desserts are also terrific. It's not authentic Thai—more like French-Thai fusion—but the food is intensely delicious. ✉ *200 E. 54th St., at 3rd Ave., Midtown East* ☎ *212/486–9592* *Reservations essential* *AE, DC, MC, V* ⊙ *No lunch weekends.*

Seafood

¢–$$$ ✕ **Oyster Bar.** Deep in the belly of Grand Central Station, the Oyster Bar has been a worthy seafood destination for nine decades. The cavernous tile space combines the camp of a 1970s airport-style lounge, the noir style of a serpentine lunch counter, and the appealing tackiness of a smoke-filled commuter tavern. Sit at the counter and slurp an assortment of bracingly fresh oysters, or a steaming bowl of clam chowder, and wash it down with an ice-cold brew. Or experience the forgotten pleasure of fresh, unadorned seafood such as lobster with drawn butter or matjes herring in season. Avoid anything that sounds newfangled. ✉ *Grand Central Station, dining concourse, 42nd St. and Vanderbilt Ave., Midtown East* ☎ *212/490–6650* *Reservations essential* *AE, D, MC, V* ⊙ *Closed Sun.*

¢–$$ ✕ **Docks Oyster Bar.** As the name implies, this casual spot serves oysters galore (both raw and fried) as well as raw clams, shrimp cocktail, steamed lobster, and all the other nautical goodies you would expect from a New York seafood restaurant. There's also a large selection of grilled fish including red snapper, swordfish, and tuna. Desserts are worth saving room for, including a pleasantly tart key lime pie. ✉ *633 3rd Ave., at E. 40th St., Midtown East* ☎ *212/986–8080* *AE, D, DC, MC, V.*

Spanish

$$–$$$ ✕ **Marichu.** Natural brick, old beams, and a lovely garden grace this Basque restaurant, an overlooked find just steps from the United Nations. A fascinating list of Spanish wines nicely complements the refined cuisine, which is particularly strong on seafood. There's no better way to start than with Rioja peppers stuffed with a puree of salt cod. Other preparations, such as Florida snapper in garlic vinaigrette and baby squid in black ink sauce, are fresh and boldly seasoned. The small, bright dining room with white walls and wooden tables doesn't feel like Manhattan. ✉ *342 E. 46th St., between 1st and 2nd Aves., Midtown East* ☎ *212/370–1866* *Reservations essential* *AE, DC, MC, V* ⊙ *No lunch weekends.*

Steak

$$–$$$$ ✕ **Sparks Steak House.** Magnums of wines that cost more than most people earn in a week festoon the large dining rooms of this classic New York steak house. Black-tie waiters at the door seem so sincerely pleased to see you it's startling to realize there are about 600 other people inside. Although seafood is given fair play on the menu, Sparks is about dry-aged steak. The lamb chops and veal chops are also noteworthy. Classic sides of hash browns, spinach (not creamed!), mushrooms, onions, and broccoli are all you need to complete the experience. ✉ *210 E. 46th St., between 2nd and 3rd Aves., Midtown East* ☎ *212/687–4855* *Reservations essential* *AE, D, DC, MC, V* ⊙ *Closed Sun. No lunch Sat.*

$–$$$$ ✕ **The Palm.** They may have added tablecloths, but it would take more than that to hide the brusque, no-nonsense nature of this legendary steak house. The steak is always impeccable, and lobsters are so big there may not be room at the table for such classic side dishes as rich creamed spinach. The "half and half" side combination of cottage-fried potatoes and fried onions is addictive. Overflow from the restaurant caused the owners to open Palm Too, a slightly less raffish version of the original, across the street. ✉ *837 2nd Ave., between E. 44th and E. 45th Sts., Midtown East* ☎ *212/687–2953* ✉ *Palm Too, 840 2nd Ave., between E. 44th and E. 45th Sts., Midtown East* ☎ *212/697–5198* *Reservations essential* *AE, DC, MC, V* ⏲ *Closed Sun. No lunch Sat.*

$$–$$$$ ✕ **Tuscan Steak.** "Tuscan Steak" is somewhat misleading. It's not Tuscan, but at the entryway is a 30-ft backlit photo of a stone wall in Tuscany. It's not really a steak house, either, but they do serve better-than-average meat prepared Florentine style. This is a huge, glitzy American restaurant, with oversized black booths and a rocking downstairs lounge, which serves family-style Italian food. You can eat well if you order correctly. The steak is a sure bet, as are the huge Caesar salad, addictive garlic bread with truffle oil, lemony pasta topped with chicken piccata, and fragrant mushroom risotto. ✉ *622 3rd Ave., at E. 40th St., Midtown East* ☎ *212/404–1700* *Reservations essential* *AE, D, MC, V* ⏲ *No lunch weekends.*

Upper East Side

Long viewed as an enclave of the privileged, the Upper East Side has plenty of elegant restaurants to serve ladies who lunch and bankers who look forward to a late-night meal and single malt at the end of the day. However, the eastern and northern reaches of the area have some quite affordable spots, too. Whether you want to celebrate a special occasion or have simply worked up an appetite after a long museum visit, you're sure to find something appropriate for almost any budget.

American

$$–$$$ ✕ **The Dining Room.** As the simple name suggests, Mark Spangenthal's neighborhood restaurant has no other motive than to satisfy people's hunger, and food takes center stage. (The setting is plush just to help local Upper East Siders feel at home.) The zingy panfried artichokes are a favorite, along with a copious raw bar with several types of oysters and ceviche. Seasonal entrées include roasted halibut with Swiss chard, fava beans, bacon, and fingerling potatoes. ✉ *154 E. 79th St., at Lexington Ave., Upper East Side* ☎ *212/327–2500* *AE, D, MC, V* ⏲ *No lunch Sat.*

$–$$$ ✕ **Butterfield 81.** This contemporary American restaurant is a popular retreat for the young professionals living in the area. The intimate dining room has the feel of a French bistro, with brown leather banquettes, mirrored walls, white tablecloths, and a pressed-tin ceiling. The menu includes such choices as tuna tartare with avocado salad and cedar-planked salmon. ✉ *170 E. 81st St., between Lexington and 3rd Aves., Upper East Side* ☎ *212/288–2700* *AE, D, DC, MC, V* ⏲ *No lunch.*

$–$$ ✕ **Lenox.** Formerly called the Lenox Room, this small neighborhood restaurant keeps a low profile; nevertheless, insiders know it's a serious place to dine. The menu changes seasonally, but there are normally such items as shrimp cocktail, oysters, and organic pan-roasted chicken with spinach and mushrooms. Thanks to congenial and charming host Tony Fortuna, the red-color dining room is always comfortable. The lounge is often crowded with well-heeled locals. ✉ *1278 3rd Ave., between E. 73rd and E. 74th Sts., Upper East Side* ☎ *212/772–0404* *AE, D, MC, V.*

American Casual

$–$$ ✕ **Sarabeth's.** Filled with bric-a-brac and imbued with a homespun charm, Sarabeth's is loved by locals for its eclectic menu featuring such dishes as hazelnut-crusted sea bass and butternut squash risotto with duck con-

Atlantic Grill . . 13
Aureole 28
Butterfield 81 . . 7
Café Boulud . . 15
Caffe Bianco . . 12
Comfort Diner . . 2
Daniel 22
The Dining Room 10
Etats-Unis. 8
Jo Jo 24
Le Pain Quotidien . 1,19,25
Lenox 18
Luca 5
Manhattan Grille 26
Maya 23
Nicole's 30
Orsay 16
Park Avenue Cafe 27
Patsy's Pizzeria . . . 4, 21
Payard Pâtisserie & Bistro 17
rm 29
Saigon Grill . . . 3
Serafina Fabulous Pizza 9
Serendipity 3 . 31
Sushi of Gari . 11
Taperia Madrid 14
Toraya 20
Zócalo 6

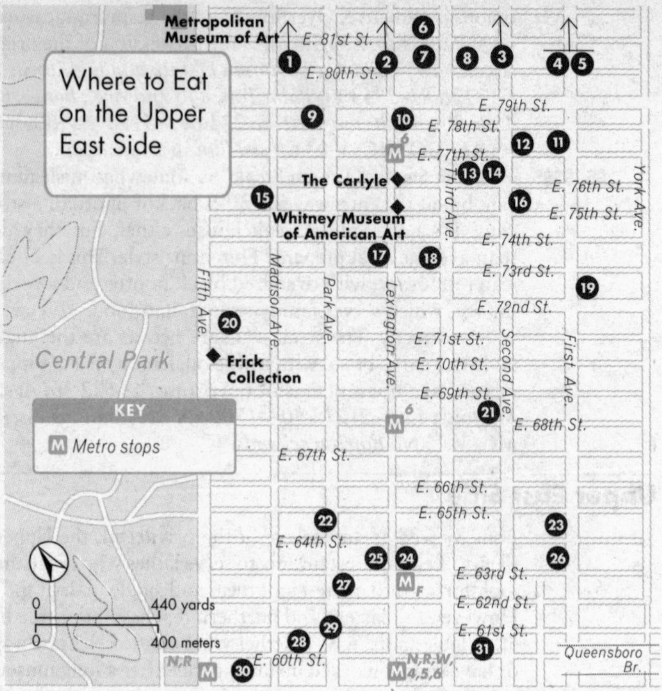

fit. The baked goods like muffins, scones, and a cranberry-pear bread pudding are outstanding. The affordable wine list includes some unexpected bottles from small producers. ✉ *1295 Madison Ave., between E. 92nd and E. 93rd Sts., Upper East Side* ☎ *212/410–7335* ✉ *945 Madison Ave., at E. 75th St. (in Whitney Museum of Art), Upper East Side* ☎ *212/570–3670* ✍ *Reservations not accepted* ▭ *AE, DC, MC, V.*

¢–$$ ✕ **Serendipity 3.** A neighborhood favorite since 1954, this fun ice-cream parlor bedecked with stained-glass lamps also dishes out excellent burgers, foot-long hot dogs, French toast, omelets, salads, and special sandwiches. However, most people come for the huge, naughty, and decadent sundaes, as well as Serendipity's most famous dessert—frozen hot chocolate (now available in a mix you can prepare at home). As demonstrated by John Cusack and Kate Beckinsale in the movie *Serendipity,* this is the perfect spot for a break after a sweep through nearby Bloomingdales. ✉ *225 E. 60th St., between 2nd and 3rd Aves., Upper East Side* ☎ *212/838–3531* ▭ *AE, DC, MC, V.*

¢–$ ✕ **Comfort Diner.** Looking for a quick, casual, and satisfying meal? Comfort Diner is glad to oblige, with a menu of typical American fare like buffalo wings, Caesar salad, grilled chicken club sandwiches, macaroni and cheese, meat loaf, and burgers. The pies and cakes are baked fresh daily. The chrome and teratza may look a bit faded, but at least the price is right. Prepare to wait on line for the popular weekend brunch. ✉ *142 E. 86th St., at Lexington Ave., Upper East Side* ☎ *212/426–8600* ✍ *Reservations not accepted* ▭ *D, DC, MC, V.*

Cafés

¢–$ ✕ **Caffé Bianco.** Settle in for excellent coffee, espresso, cappuccino, and sinful desserts like dark chocolate torte and intoxicating tiramisu. Light meals of salads, sandwiches, and pasta are also available, and in warm weather you can relax in the back garden with its pint-size pond. The waitstaff is very accommodating and prices are reasonable, making this a choice spot. ✉ *1486 2nd Ave., between E. 77th and E. 78th Sts., Upper East Side* ☎ *212/988–2655* ▭ *AE, MC, V.*

¢–$ ✕ **Le Pain Quotidien.** This international Belgian chain brings its homeland ingredients with it, treating New Yorkers to crusty breads and delicious jams. Best of all is the Belgian chocolate sweetening the café mochas and hot chocolate. For a more substantial meal, take a seat at the long wooden communal table and sample hearty sandwiches like roast beef with caper mayonnaise or roasted turkey with herb dressing. ✉ *1131 Madison Ave., between E. 84th and E. 85th Sts., Upper East Side* ☎ *212/327–4900* ✉ *833 Lexington Ave., between E. 63rd and E. 64th Sts., Upper East Side* ☎ *212/755–5810* ▭ *No credit cards.*

¢–$ ✕ **Toraya.** A traditional and serene Japanese tearoom, Toraya is tucked into a row of town houses off 5th Avenue. Along with green tea, you can try some of the seasonal *wagashi,* a sweet treat that's often shaped like flowers or leaves. A lunch menu includes such creative items as a salad of shiitake mushrooms, bacon, and *mochi* (lightly fried rice cakes), and a smoked turkey sandwich with miso and wasabi mayonnaise. Takeout is also available. ✉ *17 E. 71st St., between 5th and Madison Aves., Upper East Side* ☎ *212/861–1700* ▭ *AE, DC, MC, V* ⏲ *Closed Sun. No dinner.*

Contemporary

$$$$ ✕ **Aureole.** Celebrity chef Charlie Palmer's protégé Dante Boccuzzi has taken over the kitchen at Palmer's top-rated restaurant. The food is presented as striking architectural constructions, but taste remains paramount. Several distinct flavors work their way into single dishes such as seared foie gras with Comice pears, mâche salad, and pomegranate vinaigrette, or shallot-basted salmon with toasted chestnuts, kabocha squash, and chanterelles. Desserts, too, are breathtaking. The town-house setting on two floors has striking floral displays, and a small, pristine garden is open in season. For a romantic evening, reserve a table on the ground floor. ✉ *34 E. 61st St., between Madison and Park Aves., Upper East Side* ☎ *212/319–1660* ✍ *Reservations essential* ▭ *AE, DC, MC, V* ⏲ *Closed Sun. No lunch Sat.*

$$–$$$$ ✕ **Park Avenue Cafe.** Folk art, antique toys, and sheaves of dried wheat decorate this inviting New American restaurant. Chef David Burke's presentations are imaginative and often whimsical—salmon is cured like pastrami and arrives on a marble slab with warm corn blini, and "Duck, Duck, Duck!" includes a duck breast, duck meat loaf, and a foie gras corn cake. The bread basket and desserts are visual masterpieces presented with equal flair by the exuberant waitstaff. Some critics complain that the food isn't as good as it used to be, but a reservation can still be hard to come by. ✉ *100 E. 63rd St., between Park and Lexington Aves., Upper East Side* ☎ *212/644–1900* ✍ *Reservations essential* ▭ *AE, DC, MC, V* ⏲ *No lunch Sat.*

$$–$$$ ✕ **Etats-Unis.** The food is the main focus at this small restaurant, as evidenced by the open kitchen and shelves filled with cookbooks. Dishes lean toward the traditional, with some modern combinations to liven things up. Good examples are the crispy boneless chicken with seedless red grapes and saffron Italian couscous, and the charcoal-grilled swordfish with lemon mashed potatoes and compote of tomatoes, onions, and peppers. The same dinner menu served at Etats-Unis is also available across the street at The Bar@Etats-Unis. ✉ *242 E. 81st St., between 2nd and 3rd Aves., Upper East Side* ☎ *212/517–8826* ▭ *AE, DC, MC, V* ✉ *Bar@Etats-Unis, 247 E. 81st St., Upper East Side* ☎ *212/396–9928* ▭ *AE, DC, MC, V.*

$$–$$$ ✕ **Nicole's.** After a morning of shopping for the casually elegant designs of London hot fashion talent Nicole Farhi, why not take the elevator to the lower level for lunch in the equally stylish restaurant? The dining room includes a view of the kitchen through a glass window, as well as a glimpse of the street above. The food is simple, including crisp salads and light desserts, as well as entrées like grilled halibut with wild rice and roasted beets. At lunch the crowd is a mix of fashionistas, publishing-world players, and ladies who lunch. At dinner, it's hardly a crowd at all. ✉ *Nicole Farhi, 10 E. 60th St., between 5th and Madison Aves., Upper East Side* ☎ *212/223–2288* ▭ *AE, D, MC, V.*

French

$$$$ ✕ **Daniel.** In this grand space inside the historic Mayfair Hotel, celebrity chef Daniel Boulud has created one of the most memorable dining experiences available in Manhattan today. The lengthy prix-fixe-only menu is predominantly French, with such modern classics as chestnut-crusted venison with braised red cabbage and sweet potato puree. Equally impressive is the professional service and primarily French wine list. Don't forget the decadent desserts and overflowing cheese trolley. For a more casual evening, you can reserve a table in the lounge area. ✉ *60 E. 65th St., between Madison and Park Aves., Upper East Side* ☎ *212/288–0033* ✍ *Reservations essential* 👔 *Jacket required* ▭ *AE, DC, MC, V* ⊙ *Closed Sun. No lunch.*

Fodor'sChoice ★

★ **$$–$$$$** ✕ **Café Boulud.** Both the food and service are top-notch at Daniel Boulud's conservative (but not overly stuffy) bistro in the Surrey Hotel. The kitchen is run by chef Andrew Carmellini, who has teamed up with Boulud to create a four-part menu. Under *La Tradition* you'll find such classic French dishes as baked fresh pork belly with lentils; *Le Potager* has tempting vegetarian dishes like oven-roasted vegetable casserole; *La Saison* reflects the bounty of the market with white truffles, fresh fava beans, and other delicacies; and *Le Voyage* is where the kitchen reinterprets the myriad cuisines of the world. ✉ *20 E. 76th St., between 5th and Madison Aves., Upper East Side* ☎ *212/772–2600* ✍ *Reservations essential* ▭ *AE, DC, MC, V* ⊙ *No lunch Sun.–Mon.*

$$–$$$$ ✕ **Orsay.** It's hard to believe that this elegant, sedate brasserie was once the socialite hangout Mortimers—gone are the party favors, the mini-hamburgers, and the staff's snooty attitude. Instead, you will discover a serious French restaurant featuring a menu that includes a long list of tartares and an array of house-smoked items. Both the traditional brasserie fare such as steak frites and more creative options like Thai bouillabaisse with ginger and lemongrass are skillfully executed. A reasonably priced wine list and professional service complete the dining experience. ✉ *1057 Lexington Ave., at E. 75th St., Upper East Side* ☎ *212/517–6400* ✍ *Reservations essential* ▭ *AE, D, MC, V.*

$$–$$$ ✕ **Payard Pâtisserie & Bistro.** Pastry chef François Payard is the force behind this combination bistro and pastry shop. The room looks thoroughly traditional, until you notice such details as the croissant motifs in the mosaic tile floor. Appetizers on the bistro menu include an adventurous salad of crispy pig's feet, haricots verts, and frisée, and the entrée list has such interesting combinations as roasted squab with cipollini onions, black trumpet mushrooms, and bok choy. Payard's tarts, soufflés, and other French pastries are truly memorable. ✉ *1032 Lexington Ave., between E. 73rd and E. 74th Sts., Upper East Side* ☎ *212/717–5252* ✍ *Reservations essential* ▭ *AE, MC, V* ⊙ *Closed Sun.*

$–$$$ ✕ **Jo Jo.** Following a million-dollar face-lift, this gorgeous town-house restaurant is once again serving refined French cuisine to crowds of appreciative New Yorkers. It was the first restaurant in the now vast empire of chef Jean-Georges Vongerichten (Jean-Georges, Vong, The

Mercer Kitchen), and the food reflects his method of combining classic cooking techniques with infused oils, juices, and reductions in place of heavy sauces. The goat cheese and potato terrine is typical of Vongerichten's culinary style, as is the simple chicken roasted with ginger, green olives, and coriander. ✉ *160 E. 64th St., between Lexington and 3rd Aves., Upper East Side* ☎ *212/223–5656* ✍ *Reservations essential* ▭ *AE, MC, V.*

Italian

$$ ✕ **Luca.** This casual spot happens to serve some of the best Italian food on the Upper East Side, including fresh pastas like pappardelle with duck ragù and ravioli filled with spinach and ricotta. Main courses—including lamb shank braised with red wine and served with polenta—leave regulars satisfied. The clean, sparse restaurant has bright yellow walls and a small bar in front. ✉ *1712 1st Ave., between E. 88th and E. 89th Sts., Upper East Side* ☎ *212/987–9260* ▭ *MC, V* ⊙ *No lunch.*

Japanese

$–$$$$ ✕ **Sushi of Gari.** Options at this popular sushi restaurant range from the ordinary (Alaska maki, California roll) to exotic, with items such as tuna sushi with a creamy tofu sauce, or salmon sushi with tomato and onion on rice. Japanese noodles (udon or soba) and meat dishes such as teriyaki are all well prepared. Reservations are strongly recommended. ✉ *402 E. 78th St., at 1st Ave., Upper East Side* ☎ *212/517–5340* ▭ *AE, D, MC, V* ⊙ *Closed Mon. No lunch.*

Mexican

★ $$ ✕ **Maya.** The upscale hacienda look of this popular restaurant is an appropriate setting for some of the best Mexican food in the city. Begin with a delicious mango margarita, then order such flavorful dishes as *mole poblano*—a grilled chicken breast covered with mole sauce and accompanied by cilantro rice and plantains, or lobster and shrimp marinated in adobo seasoning and paired with roasted corn puree and watercress salad. Service can be a little rushed at times, especially on a busy weekend night. ✉ *1191 1st Ave., between E. 64th and E. 65th Sts., Upper East Side* ☎ *212/585–1818* ✍ *Reservations essential* ▭ *AE, DC, MC, V* ⊙ *No lunch.*

$–$$ ✕ **Zócalo.** Explore the unusual menu while enjoying a first-class margarita and chunky guacamole served in a traditional *molcajete* (lava rock mortar). Among the inventive entrées are grilled tuna rubbed with red chili, and marinated grilled hanger steak. There are also such classics as quesadillas and enchiladas. Burnt-orange and blue walls add zest to the attractive main dining room, although it can get a bit crowded. ✉ *174 E. 82nd St., between Lexington and 3rd Aves., Upper East Side* ☎ *212/717–7772* ✍ *Reservations essential* ▭ *AE, DC, MC, V* ⊙ *No lunch.*

Pizza

¢–$$ ✕ **Serafina Fabulous Pizza.** Mediterranean-hue friezes, an inviting upstairs terrace, and a steady stream of models and celebrities grace this very Italian café adorned with wine racks and paper wall sconces. Scene aside, the real draw here is some of Manhattan's most authentic Neopolitan pizza. Beyond the pies are antipasti, salads, pastas including a number of ravioli dishes, and second courses like veal scallopini. ✉ *1022 Madison Ave., at E. 79th St., Upper East Side* ☎ *212/734–2676* ✉ *29 E. 61st St., between Madison and Park Aves., Upper East Side* ☎ *212/702–9898* ▭ *AE, DC, MC, V.*

¢–$ ✕ **Patsy's Pizzeria.** Opened back in 1933 when East Harlem was largely Italian, Patsy's is one of the few survivors of that era in the now highly mixed neighborhood. The pizzeria still serves some of the best slices in New York, and while there are a number of other Patsy's throughout

Manhattan, most believe the original location is still the best. The secret is in the thin, crisp, coal-oven-baked crust, topped with thick sauce and fresh toppings. A newly built dining room with a congenial bar has minimal atmosphere. ✉ *2287-91 1st Ave., between E. 117th and E. 118th Sts., Upper East Side* ☎ *212/534–9783* ✉ *1312 2nd Ave., at E. 69th St., Upper East Side* ☎ *212/639–1000* ▭ *No credit cards.*

Seafood

★ **$$$$** ✕ **rm.** For eight magical years, Rick Moonen regularly demonstrated that he understood more about seafood than most chefs will ever know. Now ensconced in a beautiful new restaurant he co-owns, his seafood mastery really sings. Blue Island oysters are paired with cucumber sorbet and paddlefish caviar. Seared coriander-crusted yellowtail is soothed with tangerine, avocado, and cinnamon oil. Pancetta-wrapped striped bass is dribbled with littleneck clam vinaigrette. Pastry chef Pichet Ong knows precisely how to follow such virtuosity: with delicious whimsy. Try his banana-rice crispy "pillbox" with chocolate caramel Bavarian and bourbon pecans. ✉ *33 E. 60th St., between Madison and Park Aves., Upper East Side* ☎ *212/319–3800* ✍ *Reservations essential* ▭ *AE, D, MC, V* ⊙ *Closed Sun. No lunch Sat.*

$–$$ ✕ **Atlantic Grill.** It may be one of Manhattan's most popular dining rooms, but few people outside of New York have heard of this seafood restaurant. The combination of friendly service, fair prices, and reliably fresh fish means the large dining room is often filled to capacity. Traditional appetizers are joined by sushi and sashimi starters. Grilled items like Atlantic salmon and wild striped bass are a better choice than fancier concoctions such as barbecue-glazed mahimahi. ✉ *1341 3rd Ave., between E. 76th and E. 77th Sts., Upper East Side* ☎ *212/988–9200* ✍ *Reservations essential* ▭ *AE, MC, V.*

Spanish

$–$$ ✕ **Taperia Madrid.** A ceramic-tile facade and communal tables set the stage for a well-conceived culinary journey to Spain. The deliciously fruity red sangria is perfect for washing down plates of tapas, including such standard items as tangy chorizo, perfectly grilled squid, and shrimp in garlic sauce. Entrées include paella Valenciana with seafood, chorizo, and chicken. Throw in the weekday happy hour and occasional flamenco dancing, and you have all the ingredients for a delightful and festive evening. ✉ *1471 2nd Ave., between E. 76th and E. 77th Sts., Upper East Side* ☎ *212/794–2923* ▭ *No credit cards* ⊙ *No lunch.*

Steak

$$–$$$$ ✕ **Manhattan Grille.** Cut flowers, Victorian chandeliers, Persian carpets, mahogany moldings, and a warm greeting past the bronze doorway make for a sophisticated alternative to the typical burly New York beef parlor. The huge dry-aged double sirloin or porterhouse steaks can rival practically any in town. Seafood items include grilled swordfish, halibut, salmon, and tuna. The wine list is easy to negotiate and has several good choices under $30. ✉ *1161 1st Ave., between E. 63rd and E. 64th Sts., Upper East Side* ☎ *212/888–6556* ▭ *AE, DC, MC, V.*

Vietnamese

¢–$ ✕ **Saigon Grill.** A prime example of excellent and affordable dining on the Upper East Side is Saigon Grill, which serves some of the best Vietnamese food in New York. The appetizers are so delicious you might never make it to the entrées—standout starters include the shrimp summer roll, chicken satay, and barbecued spareribs with plum sauce. Main courses like basil shrimp and grilled marinated pork chops are also worth a try. The sparse dining room is nothing special to look at, but the waiters are both speedy and polite. ✉ *1700 2nd Ave., at E. 88th St., Upper*

East Side ☎ *212/996–4600* ✍ *Reservations not accepted* ▭ *AE, D, DC, MC, V.*

Upper West Side & Harlem

Considering the fact that Lincoln Center's theaters can seat more than 18,000 audience members at one time, you would certainly expect the Upper West Side to be jammed with competitive, wonderful restaurants catering to all tastes and budgets. While the area has made some impressive gustatory progress in the last few years, the overall pickings remain a bit slim for Lincoln Center denizens in a hurry. The main avenues are indeed lined with restaurants, but many of them are mediocre; they survive by catering to a local population that has neither the time nor the inclination to cook at home. Still, there are strong signs of continuing improvement.

American Casual

$–$$ ✕ **Sarabeth's.** Lining up for brunch here is as much an Upper West Side tradition as taking a sunny Sunday afternoon stroll in nearby Riverside Park. Filled with bric-a-brac and imbued with a homespun charm, Sarabeth's is loved by locals for its eclectic menu featuring such dishes as hazelnut-crusted sea bass and butternut squash risotto with duck confit. The baked goods like muffins, scones, and a cranberry-pear bread pudding are outstanding. The affordable wine list includes some unexpected bottles from small producers. ✉ *423 Amsterdam Ave., between W. 80th and W. 81st Sts., Upper West Side* ☎ *212/496–6280* ✍ *Reservations not accepted* ▭ *AE, DC, MC, V.*

¢–$ ✕ **Barney Greengrass.** The self-proclaimed "Sturgeon King," this Jewish deli dates back to 1908 and offers the basic formula of high-quality food, abrupt service, Formica tables, wooden chairs, and plenty of salt. Order a platter with smoked salmon, sturgeon, or whitefish and you'll get a bagel, cream cheese, tomato, and onion on the side. Omelets are also available, with such scrumptious fillings as salami and caramelized onions. Beware: the wait for a table can last an hour or more during weekend brunch time. ✉ *541 Amsterdam Ave., between W. 86th and W. 87th Sts., Upper West Side* ☎ *212/724–4707* ✍ *Reservations not accepted* ▭ *No credit cards* ⊙ *Closed Mon.*

¢–$ ✕ **Kitchenette.** This small, comfy restaurant lives up to its name with tables so close together you're likely to make new friends. There are no frills, just good, solid cooking, friendly service, and a long line at peak times. For brunch don't miss the pancakes, cranberry-cinnamon swirl French toast, and thick-cut bacon. If you come for a dinner of turkey meat loaf or chicken potpie, do like the Columbia University profs and students and BYOB. ✉ *1272 Amsterdam Ave., between 122nd and 123rd Sts., Morningside Heights* ☎ *212/531–7600* ▭ *AE, DC, MC, V.*

Cafés

¢–$$ ✕ **Cafe Mozart.** Images of Mozart cover the walls at this festive spot near Lincoln Center. Patrons stop in after a night at the opera or ballet to sample the specialties—luscious desserts including linzer torte and banana mousse cake. Cappuccino, espresso, and hot chocolate are also available, as well as a variety of soups, salads, and sandwiches. Playing up the café's musical theme, classical and jazz pianists perform regularly. On Friday and Saturday nights it's open until 3 AM, and on other nights until 1 AM. ✉ *154 W. 70th St., between Broadway and Columbus Ave., Upper West Side* ☎ *212/595–9797* ▭ *AE, DC, MC, V.*

¢–$ ✕ **Cafe Lalo.** The plentiful offerings at this café attract enough people to make seating at the small tables a squeeze, but the plate-glass windows, vintage posters, classical music, and an enormous selection of pies,

Arties's Delicatessen . 15
Avenue 12
Barney Greengrass . . 11
Bayou 4
Cafe Con Leche 5, 20
Café des Artistes 30
Café Lalo 16
Café Luxembourg . 28
Cafe Mozart 29
Calle Ocho . . 22
Carmine's 8
Compass 27
Docks Oyster Bar 10
Drip 17
Gabriela's 6, 26
Gennaro 7
Jean-Georges 35
La Grolla 21
Miss Maude's Spoonbread Too 3
Ocean Grill . . 23
Ollie's 1, 13, 32
Ouest 14
Picholine . . . 34
Rain 18
Ruby Foo's . . 24
Saigon Grill . . 9
Sarabeth's . . 19
Shark Bar . . . 25
Shun Lee West 33
Tavern on the Green 31
Turkuaz 2

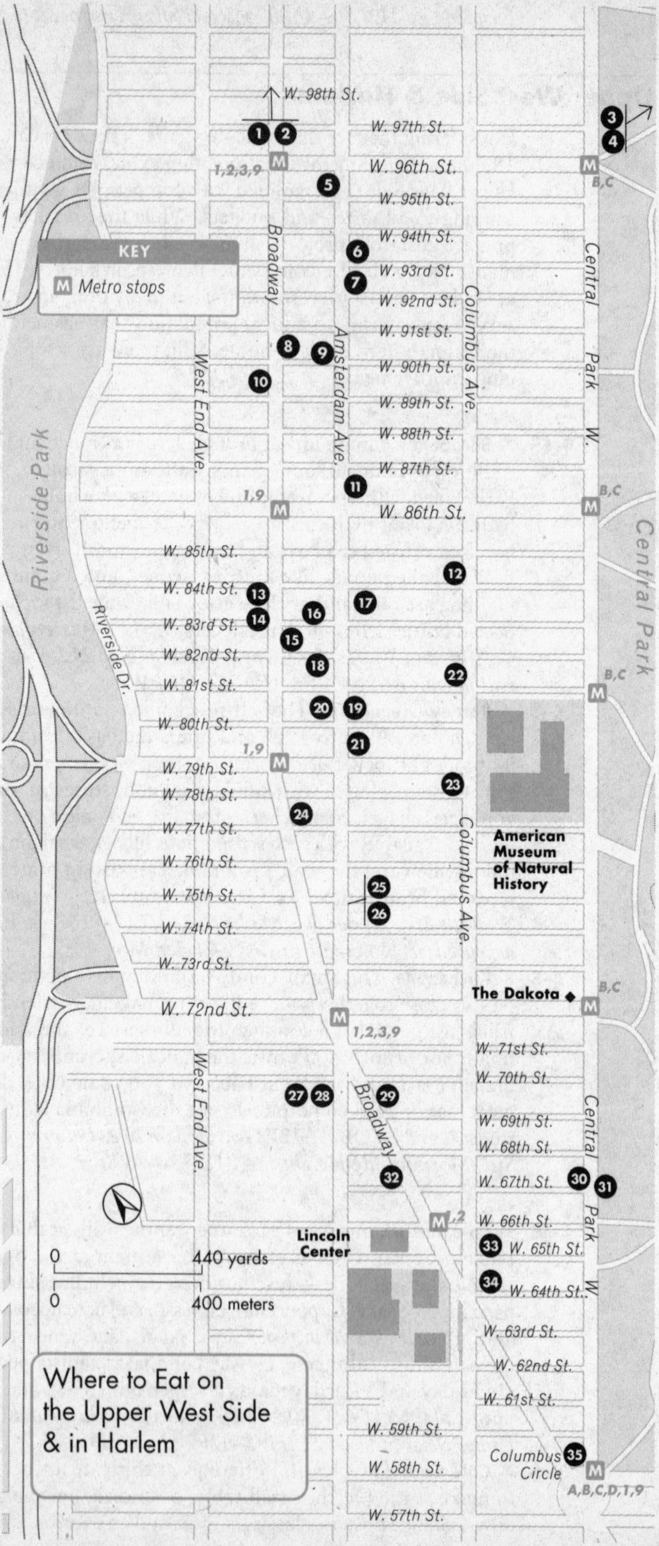

cakes, tarts, and cheesecakes are worth it. Somehow a camera crew fit in here to film Tom Hanks and Meg Ryan parleying in *You've Got Mail.* Anything from sardines to sandwiches and brunch items are served daily. ✉ *201 W. 83rd St., between Broadway and Amsterdam Ave., Upper West Side* ☎ *212/496–6031* ✍ *Reservations essential* ▭ *No credit cards.*

¢ ✕ **Drip.** A café, bar, and dating service all in one, Drip is definitely not your ordinary neighborhood hangout. Blind-date notebooks contain the personal ads of other patrons, and the vintage 1970s couches are perfect for lounging on while you sip drinks and check out the list of potential dates. Snacks available include sandwiches, soups, and desserts like chocolate mud cake and cheesecake. ✉ *489 Amsterdam Ave., between W. 83rd and W. 84th Sts., Upper West Side* ☎ *212/875–1032* ▭ *MC, V.*

Chinese

$–$$ ✕ **Shun Lee West.** If you want inexpensive Cantonese food without pretensions, head to Chinatown; but if you prefer to be pampered and don't mind spending a lot of money, this is the place. The dramatically lighted dining room is accented by images of white dragons and monkeys. The cuisine is classic Chinese. Giant prawns with black bean sauce make a good starter, and rack of lamb Szechuan style is a popular entrée. The adjacent Shun Lee Cafe is less expensive and serves some of the best dim sum around. ✉ *43 W. 65th St., between Columbus Ave. and Central Park W, Upper West Side* ☎ *212/595–8895* ✍ *Reservations essential* ▭ *AE, DC, MC, V.*

¢–$ ✕ **Ollie's.** This no-frills Chinese chain is a blessing for locals and Lincoln Center patrons in search of a quick budget meal. The best dishes are the noodle soups (available with a number of ingredients including dumplings, vegetables, and meat) and the dim sum prepared by speedy chefs with nimble maneuverings that you can watch while you wait for a table. The many other standard dishes include shrimp with lobster sauce and sesame chicken. The portions are generous, but don't expect any culinary revelations. ✉ *1991 Broadway, at W. 67th St., Upper West Side* ☎ *212/595–8181* ✉ *2315 Broadway, at W. 84th St., Upper West Side* ☎ *212/362–3111* ✉ *2957 Broadway, at W. 116th St., Morningside Heights* ☎ *212/932–3300* ✍ *Reservations not accepted* ▭ *AE, MC, V.*

Contemporary

$$–$$$$ ✕ **Tavern on the Green.** A meal here is not about the erratic food or service: it's about eating in Central Park with out-of-towners. This visual fantasy is a maze of dining rooms, each with a different theme: the Chestnut Room, the Crystal Room, and the garden area, which is under a beautiful canopy of lighted trees. The simplest dishes on the menu are normally the best bet, including wonderful prime rib and linguine with seafood. Desserts such as the decadent ice-cream sundae are also well worth ordering. ✉ *In Central Park at W. 67th St., Upper West Side* ☎ *212/873–3200* ✍ *Reservations essential* ▭ *AE, DC, MC, V.*

$$–$$$ ✕ **Compass.** With an up-to-the-minute decor, a quicksilver staff, and Neil Annis, one of the best chefs on the West Side, Compass will guide you in the right gustatory direction. Start with citrus-cured salmon with the most succulent fried oysters in town. Wild striped bass arrives in a mussel-bound bouillabaisse with Jerusalem artichokes. Bulbous, juicy guinea hen is perfectly roasted and plated with sautéed chanterelle mushrooms. Marc Aumont's fanciful desserts are all about textures and contrasts. Passion Napoleon interlopes crepes and fried discs of tuile with fresh fruit, sour cream sorbet, kiwi sauce, and passion-fruit curd. ✉ *208 W. 70th St., between Amsterdam and West End Aves., Upper West Side* ☎ *212/875–8600* ▭ *AE, MC, V.*

$–$$ ✕ **Ouest.** Finally, the Upper West Side has an upscale contemporary American restaurant to call its own. Ouest's menu is the brainchild of well-known chef Tom Valenti, who rewards his loyal patrons with such signature dishes as braised short ribs with soft polenta. There are also simple grilled meats, and lighter but equally satisfying dishes like oyster pan roast with potatoes and mushrooms. Request one of the circular red-leather booths near the open kitchen to see Valenti and his crew at work. ✉ *2315 Broadway, between W. 83rd and W. 84th Sts., Upper West Side* ☎ *212/580–8700* ✍ *Reservations essential* ▭ *AE, D, MC, V* ⊙ *No lunch.*

Continental

$$$ ✕ **Café des Artistes.** Howard Chandler Christy's murals of naked nymphs at play grace the walls of this thoroughly romantic restaurant, which first opened in 1917. Although the haute French food may no longer be among the best in New York, a meal here should still leave you thoroughly satisfied. The salmon entrée is available either sautéed or smoked, and roasted duckling comes with fresh fruit compote. Desserts like chocolate mousse and almond tart are classic and appealing. The prix-fixe dinner is $39 (no substitutions allowed). ✉ *1 W. 67th St., at Central Park W, Upper West Side* ☎ *212/877–3500* ✍ *Reservations essential* 🧥 *Jacket required* ▭ *AE, DC, MC, V.*

Creole

$–$$ ✕ **Bayou.** Harlem is still known for its casual soul-food spots, but trendy restaurants like Bayou are beginning to move into the area. The modern Creole menu includes such classics as shrimp rémoulade and crawfish étouffée, as well as more inventive fare like a grilled pork loin chop with green peppercorn demi-glace. Also unusual for the neighborhood is Bayou's upscale dining room complete with a pressed-tin ceiling and brass lamps, as well as its accommodating waitstaff. There's even a small wine list. ✉ *308 Lenox Ave., between W. 125th and W. 126th Sts., Harlem* ☎ *212/426–3800* ▭ *AE, D, MC, V* ⊙ *No dinner Sun. No lunch Sat.*

Delicatessen

¢–$ ✕ **Artie's Delicatessen.** The dining room at Artie's may have the look of an old-timer, but this popular Jewish deli has only been open a few years. The pastrami is served hot, moist, and appropriately fatty. In fact, pretty much everything else on the menu—from the coleslaw and pickles to the homemade hot dogs and fresh roasted turkey—is worth traveling out of your way to enjoy. ✉ *2290 Broadway, between W. 82nd and W. 83rd Sts., Upper West Side* ☎ *212/579–5959* ✍ *Reservations not accepted* ▭ *AE, D, MC, V.*

French

$$$$ FodorsChoice ★ ✕ **Jean-Georges.** Celebrity chef Jean-Georges Vongerichten's prix-fixe restaurant near Central Park is a true culinary destination. The main dining room is dressed in neutral colors, with beige banquettes and minimal decoration. Vongerichten's cooking shows a like-minded restraint, with some unusual combinations: sea scallops in caper-raisin emulsion with caramelized cauliflower is an outstanding example. Elegant desserts, exceedingly personalized service, and a well-selected wine list contribute to the overall experience. The **Nougatine** serves a more moderate à la carte menu in the front area, with a view of the open kitchen. ✉ *1 Central Park W, at W. 59th St., Upper West Side* ☎ *212/299–3900* ✍ *Reservations essential* 🧥 *Jacket required* ▭ *AE, DC, MC, V* ⊙ *Closed Sun.*

★ $$$–$$$$ ✕ **Picholine.** The elegant dining room in this mellow restaurant features soft colors, wood floors, and gorgeous dried flowers. Chef Terrance Brennan's French food with Mediterranean accents is considered by many to be among the very best in Manhattan. Top dishes include the wild mushroom and duck risotto, roasted loin of lamb, and tournedos of salmon with horseradish crust, cucumbers, and salmon caviar. The wine list is extensive, including a good selection of wine by the glass. The celebrated cheese course is also outstanding. ✉ *35 W. 64th St., between Broadway and Central Park W, Upper West Side* ☎ *212/724–8585* ✍ *Reservations essential* ▭ *AE, DC, MC, V* ⊙ *No lunch Sun.–Mon.*

$–$$ ✕ **Avenue.** This French-American family-friendly bistro remains a beacon of hope for this stretch of Columbus Avenue, which has long faced a shortage of good restaurants. During the day diners can select lighter fare including eggs, pancakes, sandwiches, and salads. The seasonal menu at night is more ambitious, with such items as warm wild mushroom and black truffle tart, and grilled leg of lamb with garlic potato puree. Show up early for the enormously popular weekend brunch. ✉ *520 Columbus Ave., at W. 85th St., Upper West Side* ☎ *212/579–3194* ▭ *AE, MC, V.*

$–$$ ✕ **Café Luxembourg.** Lively and sophisticated Café Luxembourg has a definite downtown vibe, rare among the restaurants in this low-key neighborhood. It's a terrific spot for a meal after visiting nearby Lincoln Center, and as a result the dining room is often crowded. The menu includes classic bistro dishes such as cassoulet, steak frites, and Long Island duck with roasted parsnips and endive. There's also a decent selection of wines. ✉ *200 W. 70th St., between Amsterdam and West End Aves., Upper West Side* ☎ *212/873–7411* ✍ *Reservations essential* ▭ *AE, DC, MC, V.*

Italian

$–$$$$ ✕ **Carmine's.** Savvy New Yorkers line up early for the affordable family-style meals served at this large, busy eatery. The dining room has dark woodwork and old-fashioned black-and-white tiles, and outdoor seating is available in the front. There are no reservations taken for parties of fewer than six people after 7 PM, but those who wait are rewarded with truly huge portions of such popular items as fried calamari, linguine with white clam sauce, chicken parmigiana, and lobster fra diavolo. You will inevitably order too much, but it all tastes just as satisfying the next day. ✉ *2450 Broadway, between W. 90th and W. 91st Sts., Upper West Side* ☎ *212/362–2200* ▭ *AE, D, DC, MC, V.*

$–$$ ✕ **La Grolla.** In an area bursting at the seams with mediocre Italian restaurants, this refined trattoria is a welcome alternative. The cuisine of the Val d'Aosta, a tiny region in the North of Italy, is the focal point of the menu. Try their tantalizing take on veal *Milanese,* served with arugula, tomato, and mozzarella. Pastas include linguine with cockles, zucchini, and parsley. Next door to La Grolla is their sister café, a more casual and less expensive option. ✉ *413 Amsterdam Ave., between 79th and 80th Sts., Upper West Side* ☎ *212/496–0890* ✉ *Café La Grolla, 411A Amsterdam Ave., between W. 79th and W. 80th Sts., Upper West Side* ☎ *212/579–9200* ▭ *AE, DC, MC, V.*

¢–$ ✕ **Gennaro.** A small dining room and excellent food make for long waits at this neighborhood restaurant, but an expansion has helped ease the crush. The pleasant dining room has brick walls and tables covered with white tablecloths. Start with the huge antipasto platter filled with hot and cold vegetables, prosciutto, fresh mozzarella, and shrimp, and then move on to the pastas or entrées like roasted Cornish hen or braised lamb shank. ✉ *665 Amsterdam Ave., between W. 92nd and W. 93rd Sts., Upper West Side* ☎ *212/665–5348* ✍ *Reservations not accepted* ▭ *No credit cards.*

Latin

$–$$$ ✕ **Calle Ocho.** Named for the main drag of Miami's Little Havana district, Calle Ocho cultivates a festive vibe with bright colors, murals, and a terra-cotta fireplace. Chef Jorge Adriazola serves a pan-Latin menu that incorporates dishes from various countries. You can dine on Cuban-style steak frites with yucca fries, or try the roasted chicken with *mole verde* (green sauce) and spring vegetables. All of the dishes are best when washed down with one of the restaurant's snappy specialty drinks, such as a refreshing *mojito* (rum with soda, mint, and sugar syrup). ✉ *446 Columbus Ave., between W. 81st and W. 82nd Sts., Upper West Side* ☎ *212/873–5025* ▭ *AE, DC, MC, V* ⊙ *No lunch.*

¢–$ ✕ **Café con Leche.** The Cuban and Dominican food here is both inexpensive and satisfying, and the brightly lighted space makes an effort at decor with soothing pastel-color walls covered with brightly colored masks. The counter area in front is perfect for enjoying one of the filling pressed sandwiches and a café con leche. The menu also has numerous rice dishes and hefty entrées like *cerdo guisado* (pork stew). It gets crowded during the popular weekend brunch. ✉ *424 Amsterdam Ave., between W. 80th and W. 81st Sts., Upper West Side* ☎ *212/595–0936* ✉ *726 Amsterdam Ave., between W. 95th and W. 96th Sts., Upper West Side* ☎ *212/678–7000* ▭ *AE, MC, V.*

Mexican

$–$$$ ✕ **Rosa Mexicano.** When a waiter slips open a parchment package containing a lamb shank braised in a three-chili sauce, the dining room fills with the fragrance of Oaxaca. Duck enchiladas and chicken steamed in beer stand out among the interesting regional dishes. A better guacamole, prepared table-side and served with warm corn tortillas, cannot be found. The assortment of chilled seafood served as an appetizer is terrific, and the chocolate-chili mousse cake has real kick. ✉ *51 Columbus Ave., at W. 62nd St., Upper West Side* ☎ *212/977–7700* ✍ *Reservations essential* ▭ *AE, DC, MC, V* ⊙ *No lunch.*

¢–$ ✕ **Gabriela's.** For authentic Mexican cuisine at rock-bottom prices, these modest cantinas are the way to go. The menu is filled with such interesting choices as tacos with marinated roast pork, and tamales stuffed with mushrooms and other vegetables. The house specialty is a whole rotisserie chicken, served moist and spicy with rice, beans, and plantains. Ceramic parrots hang from the ceiling in the noisy and festive dining room. Parents with small children particularly appreciate Gabriela's for its welcoming attitude. ✉ *311 Amsterdam Ave., at W. 75th St., Upper West Side* ☎ *212/875–8532* ✉ *685 Amsterdam Ave., at W. 93rd St., Upper West Side* ☎ *212/961–0574* ▭ *AE, DC, MC, V.*

Pan-Asian

$–$$ ✕ **Rain.** Healthful Thai- and Vietnamese-inspired food is the focus here, at prices reasonable enough to attract a fairly young crowd. The menu has a number of Southeast Asian favorites, including steamed striped bass with lemongrass, ginger, and a fresh lime broth, and Thai-style duck fajitas with Asian vegetables. The spices and flavorings are toned down, but the food still manages to satisfy most diners' cravings. The spacious restaurant is adorned with modern Asian touches, including a pretty bar area with rattan furniture. ✉ *100 W. 82nd St., between Amsterdam and Columbus Aves., Upper West Side* ☎ *212/501–0776* ✍ *Reservations essential* ▭ *AE, DC, MC, V.*

$–$$ ✕ **Ruby Foo's.** In a vast departure from the normally staid restaurants in the area, Ruby Foo's has a spacious dining room filled with oversize Chinese pottery and sculpture, and a dramatic staircase ascending from its center. The menu incorporates favorites from most Asian cuisines, including a pungent Thai hot-and-sour soup with shrimp and ginger wontons. There are also dim sum and a sushi menu available. If some of the food doesn't quite measure up to the grand setting, the place is so lively and amusing no one seems to mind a bit. ✉ *2182 Broadway, at W. 77th*

St., Upper West Side ☎ *212/724–6700* ✍ *Reservations essential* ▭ *AE, MC, V.*

Pizza

¢–$ ✕ **Patsy's Pizzeria.** The original Patsy's opened back in 1933 in East Harlem, when the neighborhood was largely Italian. The pizzeria still serves some of the best slices in New York. The secret is in the thin, crisp, coal-oven-baked crust, topped with thick sauce and fresh toppings. ✉ *61 W. 74th St., between Columbus Ave. and Central Park W, Upper West Side* ☎ *212/579–3000* ▭ *No credit cards.*

Seafood

¢–$$ ✕ **Docks Oyster Bar.** As the name implies, this casual spot serves oysters galore (both raw and fried) as well as raw clams, shrimp cocktail, steamed lobster, and all the other nautical goodies you would expect from a New York seafood restaurant. There's also a large selection of grilled fish including red snapper, swordfish, and tuna. Desserts are worth saving room for, including a pleasantly tart key lime pie. Overall the waiters are not particularly friendly, but most are fairly efficient. ✉ *2427 Broadway, between W. 89th and W. 90th Sts., Upper West Side* ☎ *212/724–5588* ▭ *AE, D, DC, MC, V.*

$–$$ ✕ **Ocean Grill.** Known for its expansive raw bar filled with copious amounts of oysters, clams, and other seafood delights, this popular spot is also a good choice for those seeking satisfyingly fresh and well-prepared fish dishes. Simply grilled entrées including tuna, salmon, and swordfish are usually the best bet, although there are also more elaborate selections like pan-seared halibut with leeks and artichoke ravioli. The lengthy wine list includes many good choices under $40. Ocean Grill has one of the largest and most attractive dining rooms in the area, as well as competent service and reasonable prices. ✉ *384 Columbus Ave., between W. 78th and W. 79th Sts., Upper West Side* ☎ *212/579–2300* ▭ *AE, D, DC, MC, V.*

Southern

$–$$ ✕ **Shark Bar.** With its contemporary take on Southern cooking, this popular restaurant has plenty to keep you interested. Check out the "soul roll," a playful variation on an egg roll made with chicken, collard greens, and black-eyed peas. Tasty chicken wings come two ways: Harlem style (floured and deep fried) or barbecued. There are three separate dining areas plus a bar in front, all decorated with African and American paintings. ✉ *307 Amsterdam Ave., between W. 74th and W. 75th Sts., Upper West Side* ☎ *212/874–8500* ▭ *AE, D, DC, MC, V* ⏲ *No lunch Mon.–Tues.*

¢–$ ✕ **Miss Mamie's/Miss Maude's Spoonbread Too.** There are more soul-food restaurants in Harlem than anywhere else in New York City, and two of the newest and best are Miss Mamie's/Miss Maude's. They're the brainchild of cookbook-author Norma Jean Darden. Her renditions of Southern favorites like fried chicken and barbecue ribs come with a choice of sides, including collard greens and candied yams. The dining rooms are pleasantly decorated. ✉ *Miss Mamie's Spoonbread Too, 366 W. 110th St., between Columbus and Manhattan Aves., Upper West Side* ☎ *212/865–6744* ✉ *Miss Maude's Spoonbread Too, 547 Lenox Ave., between W. 137th and W. 138th Sts., Harlem* ☎ *212/690–3100* ✍ *Reservations not accepted* ▭ *AE, MC, V.*

Turkish

¢–$$ ✕ **Turkuaz.** As the northernmost reaches of the Upper West Side become increasingly gentrified, the local dining scene is slowly evolving. Enter Turkuaz, a surreal Turkish restaurant with flavorful and authentic food, fabric-draped ceilings, and waiters in traditional costume. The salads will look familiar to anyone who enjoys Middle Eastern food, but entrées such as *balik kebabi* (salmon wrapped in vine leaves) are more unconventional. Yogurt and lamb also factor heavily. Service is sporadic but personable, which is more than you can expect from most restaurants in the area. ✉ *2637 Broadway, at W. 100th St., Upper West Side* ☎ *212/665–9541* ✍ *Reservations essential* ▭ *AE, D, MC, V.*

Vietnamese

¢–$ ✕ **Saigon Grill.** A prime example of excellent and affordable dining on the Upper West Side is Saigon Grill, which serves some of the best Vietnamese food in New York. The appetizers are so delicious you might never make it to the entrées—standout starters include the shrimp summer roll, chicken satay, and barbecued spareribs with plum sauce. Main courses like basil shrimp and grilled marinated pork chops are also worth a try. ✉ *620 Amsterdam, at W. 90th St., Upper West Side* ☎ *212/875–9072* ✍ *Reservations not accepted* ▭ *AE, D, DC, MC, V.*

OUTER-BOROUGH RESTAURANTS

Manhattan is where most of New York City's dining excitement occurs, but you can find plenty of great food in the city's other four boroughs. Brooklyn in particular has a plethora of great neighborhood restaurants, and Queens has some of the best ethnic food in the country—and the price is usually right.

The Bronx

When it comes to food, one of the few areas of the Bronx worth exploring is Arthur Avenue, a strip of Italian bakeries, food stores, and butcher shops located near Fordham University.

American

$–$$ ✕ **Jimmy's Bronx Cafe.** A huge complex featuring a sports bar, nightclub, restaurant, and outdoor patio, Jimmy's is one of the few destinations in the Bronx able to attract New Yorkers from the other boroughs (nearby Yankee Stadium is another). There's a regular lineup of Latino performers, as well as special events. The kitchen serves a selection of American, Spanish, and Caribbean food, and every dish comes with a choice of sides like rice and beans or plantains. ✉ *281 W. Fordham Rd., between Cedar Ave. and Major Deegan Expressway, University Heights* ☎ *718/329–2000* ✍ *Reservations essential* ▭ *AE, DC, MC, V.*

Italian

¢–$$$ ✕ **Dominick's.** Dominick's is one of the best and most popular Italian restaurants on Arthur Avenue. No-nonsense waiters preside over communal tables in the sparsely decorated dining room, where huge portions of garlic-laden food vie for attention. There are no printed menus, but typical Southern Italian items like veal parmigiana, spaghetti with meat sauce, and shrimp scampi are normally available. If you aren't sure what to order, just ask your waiter. ✉ *2335 Arthur Ave., at E. 187th St., Belmont* ☎ *718/733–2807* ✍ *Reservations not accepted* ▭ *No credit cards* ⊗ *Closed Tues.*

¢ ✕ **Press Café.** Catercorner to Gate 6 of Yankee Stadium is this diminutive restaurant serving delicious salads and pressed Italian-style sandwiches—all for $8 or less. Ingredients like fennel sausage, prosciutto, and mascarpone cheese come from the Italian Arthur Avenue Retail Market. Just look for the striped awning and take a seat at one of the seven bar stools or six tables. Stella Artois and wheat beer are on tap. ✉ *114 E. 157th St., between River and Gerard Aves., Highbridge* ☎ *718/401–0545* ▭ *AE, MC, V* ⊗ *Closed Sun. except on game days.*

Brooklyn

New York's most populous borough inspires fierce loyalty in the hearts of its residents; many maintain that everything in Brooklyn—including the restaurant scene—is equal to what you can find in Manhattan. Although this may be a bit of an exaggeration, there is certainly plenty to be excited about. In particular, Smith Street in Carroll Gardens and the Park Slope and Williamsburg neighborhoods have some hot kitchens.

American

$$ ✕ **The Grocery.** After elbowing its way onto the crowded Smith Street restaurant scene, this American bistro quickly became known as one of the top restaurants in the borough. The Grocery is a class act, with attentive service and a calm backyard patio. Carroll Garden residents turn out for flavorful dishes such as roasted beets with homemade goat cheese ravioli, and pan-roasted monkfish with bacon, manila clams, and an herb broth. ✉ *288 Smith St., between Sackett and Union Sts., Carroll Gardens* ☎ *718/596–3335* ▭ *MC, V* ⏲ *Closed Sun. No lunch.*

¢–$ ✕ **Diner.** It may be located in an old diner car at a windblown crossroads, but this trendy hangout's menu features such fancy fare as mussels, mesclun salad, and hanger steak, in addition to great burgers and fries. Bottles of alcohol, not cream puff pies, are displayed behind the marble countertop. Service is friendly, and the price is right for the resident bohemians. ✉ *85 Broadway, at Berry St., Williamsburg* ☎ *718/486–3077* ✍ *Reservations not accepted* ▭ *AE, D, MC, V.*

American Casual

¢–$$$ ✕ **Junior's.** While it may be a relic of the 1950s, Junior's remains a popular destination for locals. The huge menu still has the Jewish specialties that made the restaurant famous, including corned beef, pastrami, chopped liver, and other sandwiches served on freshly baked rye bread. Complete dinners of roast chicken, ribs, meat loaf, and the like come with a wide choice of sides. The sinfully rich cheesecake is famous worldwide, and deservedly so. There's takeout for those with late-night cravings. ✉ *386 Flatbush Ave. Ext., at DeKalb Ave., Downtown Brooklyn* ☎ *718/852–5257* ✍ *Reservations essential* ▭ *AE, DC, MC, V.*

Contemporary

$$$$ ✕ **River Café.** When this gorgeous prix-fixe-only restaurant opened in 1977, no one imagined that such top New York chefs as Charlie Palmer of Aureole would get their start here; however, owner Buzzy O'Keefe has always been able to attract new talent (and customers) by promoting the concept of seasonal-based American cuisine. Chef Brad Steelman's menu remains true to this philosophy, with such tantalizing dishes as Maine lobster poached with artichokes and basil. The flower-filled main dining room has an amazing view of the Brooklyn Bridge and lower Manhattan. ✉ *1 Water St., at Old Fulton St., Brooklyn Heights* ☎ *718/522–5200* ✍ *Reservations essential* 👔 *Jacket required* ▭ *AE, DC, MC, V.*

$$ ✕ **Saul.** This creative American restaurant run by Saul Bolton is one of the main reasons why Manhattanites venture to Smith Street for dinner. The dining room is small but uncluttered, with brick walls and a pleasant bar area. Everything on the seasonal menu is well prepared, from such simple dishes as a grilled hanger steak to more involved items like crispy duck confit with poached pear, Gorgonzola, and walnuts. ✉ *140 Smith St., between Dean and Bergen Sts., Cobble Hill* ☎ *718/935–9844* ▭ *MC, V.*

Eclectic

★ $–$$$ ✕ **Blue Ribbon Brooklyn.** This is the Brooklyn branch of the SoHo original. The menu *appears* standard but it's not. Instead of the usual fried calamari, exceptionally tender squid is lightly sautéed in olive oil and garlic and served like a savory pudding in a Japanese rice bowl. Sweetbreads cleverly mix with shiitakes. As Eric and Bruce Bromberg's empire slowly grows, so does its quality. ✉ *280 5th Ave., between Garfield and 1st Sts., Park Slope* ☎ *718/840–0404* ✍ *Reservations not accepted* ▭ *AE, MC, V* ⊙ *No lunch Tues.–Fri.*

¢–$ ✕ **Rice.** Choose from an array of rice varieties, such as basmati, brown, Thai black, or Bhutanese red, and create a meal by adding a savory topping such as Jamaican jerk chicken wings, warm lentil stew, or Indian chicken curry. The fresh, well-seasoned, budget-price menu affords a satisfying mix of multicultural cuisine and comfort food. Ask to sit in the plant-filled outdoor patio, or try the downstairs lounge if you're interested in live performances. ✉ *81 Washington St., between Front and York Sts., DUMBO* ☎ *718/222–9880* ✍ *Reservations not accepted* ▭ *No credit cards.*

French

$–$$ ✕ **La Bouillabaisse.** This French bistro with a friendly staff serves simple but delicious food to a mostly local clientele. The menu is presented on a blackboard brought to your table; it always includes their signature fish soup, a huge portion of seafood bathed in a rich, aromatic fish broth. Other French favorites like mussels and sweetbreads also transcend the ordinary. ✉ *145 Atlantic Ave., between Clinton and Henry Sts., Brooklyn Heights* ☎ *718/522–8275* ▭ *No credit cards* ⊙ *No lunch weekends.*

$ ✕ **Banania Cafe.** By offering quality French fare at welcoming prices, this bistro has managed to stand out from the pack of ensuing arrivals that now line Smith Street. However, the small dining room can mean long waits for a table. Popular dishes include sautéed foie gras with quince puree, cornmeal-crusted Blue Point oysters, and braised lamb shank with rosemary sauce. ✉ *241 Smith St., at Douglass St., Carroll Gardens* ☎ *718/237–9100* ✍ *Reservations not accepted* ▭ *No credit cards* ⊙ *No lunch Mon.–Thurs.*

Italian

$$ ✕ **Cucina.** Long before Park Slope became a serious dining destination, Cucina was known for serving some of the best Italian food in New York. New chef Mark Strausman, of Campagna in Manhattan, has brought in several signature dishes, but there's still a wide selection of antipasti and appetizers to choose from, for $8–$10 per person. Try luscious pasta creations as spinach and ricotta ravioli with pesto tomato cream sauce. Entrées include grilled Florentine steak for two, "Day Boat" cod *pepperonata*, and half chicken *al diavolo.* ✉ *256 5th Ave., between Carroll St. and Garfield Pl., Park Slope* ☎ *718/230–0711* ✍ *Reservations essential* ▭ *AE, DC, MC, V* ⊙ *Closed Mon. No lunch.*

$–$$ ✕ **al di la.** You'll know you're nearing al di la when you see groups of people waiting outside for a table. The dining room is comfortably rustic, with a pressed-tin ceiling and communal tables. Generous amounts of browned butter and oils, and plenty of care go into the authentic Italian dishes. The *primi* portions are on the small side, so be sure to treat yourself to one of the tempting appetizers. Homemade pastas are rich in flavor, particularly the *malfatti*—a vegetable dumpling with ricotta and Parmesan. Entrées such as charred hanger steak *tagliata* with arugula truly hit the spot. ✉ *248 5th Ave., at Carroll St., Park Slope* ☎ *718/783–4565* ✍ *Reservations not accepted* ▭ *MC, V* ⊙ *Closed Tues. No lunch.*

¢–$ × **Miss Williamsburg Diner.** The name and look of this neighborhood spot say diner, but in reality this is a well-regarded Italian restaurant with a loud, hospitable vibe and a large outdoor garden. Chef Massimiliano Bartoli offers a small menu of simple salads, creative pastas and lasagnas, plus such entrées as sautéed monkfish with braised endives. And there isn't a burger in sight. ✉ *206 Kent Ave., between Metropolitan Ave. and N. 3rd St., Williamsburg* ☎ *718/963–0802* ✍ *Reservations essential* ▭ *No credit cards* ⊙ *Closed Mon. No lunch.*

¢–$ × **Pepe Viola to Go.** A long list of specials changes daily here, but the menu always includes generously portioned pastas (prepared fresh in the open kitchen), antipasti, salads, entrées, and sandwiches. The gnocchi are as light as little clouds, the pesto sauce is fragrant with basil and garlic, and the veal is tender. Inexpensive wine is available in carafes or by the bottle. ✉ *200 Smith St., at Baltic St., Carroll Gardens* ☎ *718/222–8279* ▭ *AE, MC, V.*

Pizza

$–$$$$ × **Grimaldi's.** When you think of a classic New York–style pizza parlor, this one near the Brooklyn Bridge is exactly what comes to mind. The tables are covered in red-and-white checkered cloths, the walls are filled with autographed photos, and Frank Sinatra croons from the jukebox. Everyone is happy with the luscious pies that emerge from the coal-fired oven. Toppings are $2 each, and include such items as Italian sausage and roasted red peppers. ✉ *19 Old Fulton St., between Front and Water Sts., DUMBO* ☎ *718/858–4300* ▭ *No credit cards.*

Seafood

$–$$ × **Gage & Tollner.** A true Brooklyn institution, this classic old-world dining room with arched mirrors, red velvet fabric, and brass gas-lamp chandeliers has been at the same downtown location since 1879. The menu includes such longtime standards as fried oysters, crab cakes, New York sirloin steak, and lobster Newburg, as well as Southern dishes like shrimp Creole. ✉ *372 Fulton St., between Jay and Smith Sts., Downtown Brooklyn* ☎ *718/875–5181* ▭ *AE, D, DC, MC, V* ⊙ *Closed Sun. No lunch Sat.*

Steak

$$$$ Fodor'sChoice ★ × **Peter Luger Steak House.** Sure, steak houses in Manhattan have better lighting, more elegant dining, bigger wine lists, and comfortable chairs instead of wooden benches, but if you're after the best porterhouse steak in New York, then Peter Luger's is well worth the trip to Brooklyn. Serving the same highest quality beef since 1873, it originally opened as a German beer hall. You probably won't see a menu, but here's all you need to know: shrimp cocktail, beefsteak tomato and onion salad, home fries, creamed spinach, pecan pie, and of course steak—ordered according to how many are in your party. Free parking is available. ✉ *178 Broadway, at Driggs Ave., Williamsburg* ☎ *718/387–7400* ✍ *Reservations essential* ▭ *No credit cards.*

Thai

¢–$$ × **Planet Thailand.** Some of the best Thai cuisine in New York is available at this trendy spot, along with respectable Japanese and Korean fare. The artists and musicians who live in the area also appreciate the restaurant's cheap prices, with most entrées costing less than $10. The large, funky space is always crowded at night, but the bar area in front is a good place to wait for a table. Thai dishes include such staples as pad thai and chicken curry. ✉ *133 North 7th St., between Bedford Ave. and Berry St., Williamsburg* ☎ *718/599–5758* ✍ *Reservations not accepted* ▭ *No credit cards.*

Queens

The most ethnically diverse borough in New York City has a wide range of restaurants where immigrant owners, chefs, and patrons ensure authenticity. Lower Manhattan may contain Chinatown, but the Flushing section of Queens is home to some of the city's top Asian restaurants. There are Greek tavernas in Astoria, Indian cuisine in Jackson Heights, and additional ethnic pockets scattered throughout the huge borough.

American

$$$$ ✕ **Water's Edge.** This formal riverside restaurant provides its own free shuttle service from Manhattan. The breathtaking view of midtown alone is worth the trip, but the international wine list and upscale prix-fixe-only menu are sublime. You can start off with a nice selection of East and West Coast oysters, or opt for angel hair pasta with manila clams and broccoli rabe. Entrées include butter-roasted halibut with sautéed porcini mushrooms and artichoke hearts, and roasted suckling pig with sweet and sour glazed apples. This is literally a transporting experience. ✉ *44th Dr., at Vernon Blvd. (East River), Long Island City* ☎ *718/482–0033* ✍ *Reservations essential* 👔 *Jacket required* ▭ *AE, D, DC, MC, V* ⊙ *Closed Sun. No lunch Mon.*

Barbecue

¢–$ ✕ **Pearson's Texas Barbecue.** When you say barbecue, Southerners think of meltingly tender meat that has been slowly cooked in an outdoor pit. In New York City, food prepared in this style is understandably hard to find, but Pearson's (located in the back of Legends Sports Bar) is the real deal. In addition to Texas-style beef brisket, there are chicken, pork shoulder, beef ribs, and other barbecued items, all at reasonable prices. Reservations are taken for parties of six or more. ✉ *71-04 35th Ave., at 71st St., Jackson Heights* ☎ *718/779–7715* ▭ *No credit cards* ⊙ *Closed Mon.–Tues. No lunch Wed.*

Brazilian

$$ ✕ **Green Field Churrascaria.** The sprawling dining room in this all-you-can-eat, prix-fixe Brazilian restaurant includes a copious salad bar, as well as a *rodizio* (a Brazilian version of all-you-can-eat) with huge amounts of grilled meats. Waiters arrive at your table in a seemingly endless parade, carrying skewers of flank steak, chicken, duck, sausage, roast pork, and more, which they slice directly onto your plate. Let them know when to stop by using the chip on your table (green means continue, red means stop). ✉ *108-01 Northern Blvd., at 108th St., Corona* ☎ *718/672–5202* ✍ *Reservations essential* ▭ *AE.*

Chinese

¢–$$ ✕ **Joe's Shanghai.** This is the original location of the popular dumpling house, best known for its steamed soup dumplings filled with pork, crabmeat, and broth. Menu highlights include turnip shortcakes and dried bean curd salad to start, and succulent braised pork shoulder, ropey homemade Shanghai noodles, and traditional lion's head—rich pork meatballs braised in brown sauce—to follow. Other more familiar Chinese dishes are also excellent. ✉ *136-21 37th Ave., between Main and Union Sts., Astoria* ☎ *718/539–3838* ✉ *82-74 Broadway, between 45th and Whitney Aves., Elmhurst* ☎ *718/639–6888* ▭ *No credit cards.*

¢–$$ ✕ **Ping's Seafood.** This is the original location of this popular restaurant, and it still has the most elaborate menu with the most extensive selection of live seafood. Helpful menus have pictures of most of the specialties. Among them are Dungeness crab in black bean sauce, crisp fried tofu, silken braised *e-fu* noodles, and Peking duck. ✉ *83-02 Queens Blvd.,* *at Goldsmith St., Elmhurst* ☎ *718/396–1238* ✍ *Reservations essential* ▭ *MC, V.*

¢–$ ✕ **Shanghai Tang.** The Shanghai cuisine here is a standout among the many Chinese restaurants in Flushing. The menu includes such specialties as soup dumplings, pork shoulder with Chinese vegetables, and simply prepared fresh fish. Live fish and other marine life inhabit the tanks within the bright and spacious dining room. ✉ *135-20 40th Rd., at Main St., Flushing* ☎ *718/661–4234* ▭ *MC, V.*

Greek

$–$$ ✕ **Karyatis.** The best Greek restaurants in New York are in Queens, and the multilevel Karyatis is among the oldest and most elegant of these neighborhood spots. The traditional appetizers, grilled octopus, lamb, and grilled fish entrées are all menu highlights, served by friendly and professional waiters. End the meal with a glass of anise-flavored ouzo, followed by gooey baklava and a cup of thick Greek coffee. With live music at night you can make a festive evening of it. ✉ *35-03 Broadway, between 35th and 36th Sts., Astoria* ☎ *718/204–0666* ▭ *AE, DC, MC, V.*

¢–$$ ✕ **Elias Corner.** There's always a line and never a menu in this casual Greek fish restaurant. Start with the crisp fried smelts or the tender grilled octopus. Then choose whatever seafood is fresh from the market that morning, including such items as whole red snapper, swordfish, St. Peter's fish, and grilled shrimp. The traditional Greek appetizers are also good, particularly a garlicky *tsatsiki* (homemade yogurt dip). Wines are limited to Greek selections, and beer is available. Weather permitting, head for the charming garden. ✉ *24-02 31st St., at 24th Ave., Astoria* ☎ *718/932–1510* ✍ *Reservations not accepted* ▭ *No credit cards* ⏲ *No lunch.*

¢–$$ ✕ **Stamatis.** Both these inexpensive, family-run Greek restaurants serve a home-style menu of favorites like hearty moussaka and grilled fish and lamb. The standard salads and dips are solidly prepared, including *taramasalata* (fish roe dip), *skordalia* (potato and garlic), and hummus. Grilled octopus is flavorful and tender, and the grilled pork souvlaki will satisfy most any appetite. ✉ *29-12 23rd Ave., between 29th and 30th Sts., Astoria* ☎ *718/932–8596* ✉ *31-14 Broadway, between 31st and 32nd Sts., Astoria* ☎ *718/204–8964* ▭ *AE, MC, V.*

Indian

¢–$$ ✕ **Jackson Diner.** Enjoy the Indian cuisine in this modern dining room filled with spice-color accents. Everyone from neighborhood folk to Manhattanites flock here for cheap, spicy, and authentic fare served in generous portions. Popular choices include chicken tandoori and any of the curry dishes, as well as the many vegetarian specialties. ✉ *37-47 74th St., between Roosevelt and 37th Aves., Jackson Heights* ☎ *718/672–1232* ▭ *No credit cards.*

Italian

$–$$ ✕ **Manducatis.** This classic Southern Italian restaurant, on a deserted street in Long Island City, serves up hearty dishes that put it a cut above its family-style counterparts. On weekends the large bar area and three main dining rooms jump with a loyal clientele, who are warmly greeted by the friendly owners and accommodating waitresses. Homemade pastas and basic entrées like veal marsala are good choices, and the menu is complemented by a large, well-chosen wine list with reasonable prices. ✉ *13-27 Jackson Ave., at 47th Ave., Long Island City* ☎ *718/729–4602* ✍ *Reservations essential* ▭ *AE, MC, V* ⏲ *Closed Sun. July–Aug. and last 2 weeks in Aug. No lunch Sat.*

Malaysian

¢–$ × **Penang.** There are branches of this inexpensive Malaysian restaurant scattered throughout Manhattan, but this original location in Queens is the only one that still serves superb, authentic Malaysian food. Start with an order of the freshly made *roti canai* (an Asian pancake served with curried chicken dipping sauce), and you'll likely want another by the time you choose an entrée. The coconut-fried shrimp is also a standout dish. If you can't figure out what else to order from the vast menu, the considerate staff will be happy to help out. ✉ *38-04 Prince St., at Main St.,* ☎ *718/321–2078* ▭ *AE, MC, V.*

Middle Eastern

$–$$ × **Mombar.** While Mombar is a bit of a walk from the nearest subway station (G, R at Steinway Street), it's certainly worth the trip if you're interested in Egyptian cooking. Artist Moustafa El Sayed designed the mosaic-filled dining room. He also runs the kitchen, and his signature *mombar* (a lamb sausage) is both light and delicious. Familiar Middle Eastern spreads and salads such as hummus and baba ghanouj make great starters. Entrées include braised rabbit, lamb, and a vegetarian special that changes daily. ✉ *25-22 Steinway St., at 25th Ave., Astoria* ☎ *718/726–2356* ▭ *No credit cards.*

Steak

$$$$ × **Uncle Jack's Steakhouse.** As lived-in and comfortable as any steak house in the five boroughs, Uncle Jack's features 28-day-dry-aged porterhouse steaks—22.5 ounce per person—that will leave you panting. But don't miss the seafood platter *or* the perfect crab cakes, bound by just a few Japanese bread crumbs and served on warm shrimp sauce. The restaurant regularly receives Australian lobster tails that are so large they're actually served carved. The wine list is very good, service is focused and friendly, and the splendid cheesecake will round out you and your meal. ✉ *39-40 Bell Blvd., at 40th Ave., Bayside* ☎ *718/229–1100* ☞ *BYOB.*

Staten Island

The least urban of New York's five boroughs, Staten Island is a residential area where most diners prefer quantity without surprises.

Contemporary

$–$$ × **Aesop's Tables.** Though Manhattan dwellers rarely venture to Staten Island, this charming little restaurant is worth a visit. Near the ferry terminal, it's easy to get to by public transportation (S51 bus to Highland Avenue). There's a pretty garden, and the contemporary American food is reasonably priced and well prepared. The menu changes daily, but look for dishes like bacon-wrapped monkfish medallions and pan-seared duck breast with winter squash and pancetta risotto. ✉ *1233 Bay St., at Maryland Ave., Rosebank* ☎ *718/720–2005* ✍ *Reservations essential* ▭ *AE, MC, V* ⏲ *Closed Mon. No lunch.*

WHERE TO STAY

5

FODOR'S CHOICE

The Carlyle, *Upper East Side*
Four Seasons, *Midtown East*
The Gershwin, *Murray Hill*
Howard Johnson's Express Inn, *Lower East Side*
The Inn at Irving Place, *Gramercy*
Larchmont Hotel, *Greenwich Village*
The Lowell, *Upper East Side*
Mercer Hotel, *SoHo*
The Paramount, *Midtown West*
Roger Williams Hotel, *Murray Hill*
W Times Square, *Midtown West*

HIGHLY RECOMMENDED

Broadway Inn, *Midtown West*
Empire Hotel, *Upper West Side*
Holiday Inn Wall Street, *Lower Manhattan*
Hotel Beacon, *Upper West Side*
Library Hotel, *Midtown East*
The Mark, *Upper East Side*
The Michelangelo, *Midtown West*
Regent Wall Street, *Lower Manhattan*
The Ritz-Carlton New York, *Battery Park*
The Ritz-Carlton New York, Central Park South, *Midtown West*
Roger Smith, *Midtown East*
The Royalton, *Midtown West*
The Shoreham, *Midtown West*
The St. Regis, *Midtown East*
60 Thompson, *SoHo*
Warwick, *Midtown West*

Updated by Elise Harris

PERHAPS NOT SINCE THE JAZZ AGE DAYS of the Waldorf-Astoria and The Plaza have New York hotels been so intertwined in city life. Whether a New Yorker is invited to a wedding, a premiere, or dinner, there's a fair chance it will take place in one of the luxurious old standbys of yesteryear or in one of the chic newcomers. When Miramax unspools a new film for the viewing pleasure of local VIPs, the basement screening room in the Bryant Park will likely play host. When epicures gather for adventurous gastronomic delight, odds are it will be in one of the umpteen hotel hot spots such as Thom in the stylish 60 Thompson Street. For world-class cuisine and power dining, the elite gather at such upscale boîtes as Alain Ducasse in the Essex House, Town in Chambers, and Jean-Georges at Trump International Hotel and Towers—to name but a few. And when a publicist needs an intimate space in which to launch a new product or showcase a celebrity, the firelight penthouse suites at Hotel Giraffe spring to mind.

It's always amusing to observe New York hotel trends, which will filter down not only to second-tier hostelries, but also to residences far and wide. One ubiquitous visual element is the bed crowned with an oversize, high-style headboard that manages to condense a hotel's style into a few square feet of metaphor. Did we mention mosaics, the glitzier the better? And bathrooms limned with every kind of marble? With the city at the center of the art world, it's no wonder that at several newer hotels, every room and hallway is an informal gallery, from the Chambers' display of emerging international artists to the vintage cityscape photos at the Park South Hotel. Increasingly, you'll find high-tech accessories like plasma TVs, wireless laptops, and DVD vending machines. Wherever you stay, one design standard is universal: you'll be pampered with 400-plus thread counts, goose-down duvets, satin coverlets, and gratis terry-cloth slippers in abundance.

For those who seek the most exciting lodging experience, nearly every upscale New York hotel has an extravagant penthouse or suite. Even if you are accustomed to staying in a standard room at a five-star hotel, for a similar price you might consider staying in one of these spectacular spaces at a less credentialed hotel. The Alchemist Suite in the Dylan, an otherwise unremarkable hotel, is a Gothic wonder with soaring ceilings, and the penthouse duplex at the Mansfield is slightly down at heel, but grand.

Lower Manhattan

★ $$$$ **Regent Wall Street.** The centerpiece of this palatial Financial District gem, originally a U.S. Custom House where novelist Herman Melville toiled, is a 12,000-square-ft grand ballroom with a unique Wedgwood dome. Rooms may start at $495, but the price approaches justification when the little things add up—elevators of exceptional speed, sumptuous Bulgari toiletries, personalized service. The accommodations are both stately and luxurious, and the immense, marble-clad bathrooms have what seem like the deepest tubs in town. Courtyard rooms are most impressive, with plenty of light and an elongated design that makes standard rooms feel like suites. ✉ *55 Wall St., at William St., Lower Manhattan 10005* ☎ *212/845–8600 or 800/545–4000* 📠 *212/845–8601* 🌐 *www.regenthotels.com* *97 rooms, 47 suites* *Restaurant, room service, in-room data ports, in-room fax, in-room safes, minibars, cable TV with movies, in-room DVD players, in-room VCRs, gym, bar, dry cleaning, laundry service, concierge, business services, meeting rooms, parking (fee), some pets allowed, no-smoking floors* 💳 *AE, D, DC, MC, V.*

Watever your preference, hotels are the dreamscapes of New York. The room where you sleep may be a highlight of your stay. The lodgings we list are the cream of the crop in each price category. Properties are assigned price categories based on the range from their least expensive standard double room at high season (excluding holidays) to the most expensive. We always list the facilities that are available—but we don't specify whether they cost extra: when pricing accommodations, always ask what's included and what costs extra.

Services

Unless otherwise noted in the individual descriptions, all the hotels listed have private baths, central heating, air-conditioning, and private phones. Almost all hotels have data ports and phones with voice mail, as well as valet service. Most large hotels have video or high-speed checkout capability, and many can arrange baby-sitting.

Pools are a rarity, but most properties have gyms or health clubs, and sometimes full-scale spas; hotels without facilities usually have arrangements for guests at nearby gyms, sometimes for a fee. Among those hotels with pools (all listed in this chapter) are Le Parker Meridien, The Peninsula, the Millennium Hilton, the Millennium Hotel New York UN Plaza, Trump International Hotel and Towers, and the New York Marriott Brooklyn; on the other end of the price spectrum is the Vanderbilt YMCA.

Bringing a car to Manhattan can be the source of any number of headaches and can significantly add to your lodging expenses. Many properties in all price ranges do have parking facilities, but they are often at independent garages that charge as much as $20 or more per day, and valet parking can cost up to $40 a day. The city's exorbitant 18¾% parking tax makes leaving your lemon out of the Big Apple a smart idea.

New York has gone to great lengths to attract family vacationers, and hotels have followed the family-friendly trend. One result is that properties that once drew mostly business travelers are finding themselves suddenly full of families—and are scrambling to add child-friendly amenities. Some properties provide such diversions as Web TV and in-room video games; others have suites with kitchenettes and fold-out sofa beds. Most full-service Manhattan hotels provide roll-away beds, baby-sitting, and stroller rental, but be sure to make arrangements when booking the room, not when you arrive. Ask the reservations agent specific questions, since the list of services and amenities is constantly expanding.

Reservations

Hotel reservations are an absolute necessity when planning your trip to New York—hotels fill up quickly, so book your room as far in advance as possible. Fierce competition means properties undergo frequent improvements, so when booking inquire about any ongoing renovations lest you get a room within earshot of noisy construction. In this ever-changing city, travelers can find themselves temporarily, and most inconveniently, without commonplace amenities such as room service or spa access if their hotel is upgrading.

Once you decide on a hotel, use a major credit card to guarantee the reservation—another essential in a market where "lost" reservations are not unheard of. When signing in, take a pleasant but firm attitude; if there's a mix-up, chances are the outcome will be an upgrade or a free night.

What It Costs

With square footage coming at a hefty premium in this town, some accommodations provide more space for more money, while others can only entreat you with more amenities. The style-conscious set seduced by Ian Schrager's Paramount and Hudson hotels pay for cell-size rooms in exchange for the exciting public spaces, while spacious rooms at hotels like the Inn at Irving Place and the Kitano attract those who hanker for privacy. It's up to you to choose your priority: do you yearn for Bulgari toiletries, a four-star restaurant in the building, spectacular views, or room to maneuver? If it's a bargain you long for, that's one amenity few New York hotels provide. But don't be put off by printed rates—the priciest hotels often have deals that cut room rates nearly in half.

The lodgings we list are the cream of the crop in each price category. Properties are assigned price categories based on the range from their least expensive standard double room at high season (excluding holidays) to the most expensive. We always list the facilities that are available—but we don't specify whether they cost extra: when pricing accommodations, always ask what's included and what costs extra.

WHAT IT COSTS

	$$$$	$$$	$$	$	¢
DOUBLE ROOMS	over $475	$350–$475	$225–$350	$110–$225	under $110

The lodgings we list are the top selections of their type in each price category. Price categories are assigned based on the range between their least and most expensive standard double room in non-holiday high season, based on the European Plan (with no meals) unless otherwise noted. City and state taxes (13.625%) are extra. In listings, we always name the facilities that are available, but we don't specify whether they cost extra. When pricing accommodations, always ask what's included and what entails an additional charge.

★ $$$–$$$$ **The Ritz-Carlton New York, Battery Park.** A stone's throw from the financial district, this hotel has stunning views of the city's waterfront. The rooms are minimalist and monochromatic, with down pillows, feather beds, duvets wrapped in Frette linens, and luxurious marble baths. A fleet of service providers includes water sommelier, bath and technology butlers, and on-call aestheticians and masseurs. Come evening, locals flock to the Rise bar to drink martinis while admiring New York Harbor and the Statue of Liberty at sunset. ✉ *2 West St., at Battery Pl., Battery Park 10004* ☎ *212/344–0800 or 800/241–3333* 📠 *212/344–3801* 🌐 *www.ritzcarlton.com* *254 rooms, 44 suites* *Restaurant, in-room data ports, minibars, cable TV with video games, in-room DVD players, 2 bars, laundry service, Internet, meeting rooms, parking (fee), no-smoking rooms* 💳 *AE, D, DC, MC, V.*

★ $–$$ **Holiday Inn Wall Street.** You know the future has arrived when a Holiday Inn provides T-1 Internet access in every room, express check-in lobby computers that dispense key cards, and both Web TV and Nintendo on

27-inch televisions. Half the rooms have desktop PCs, and on the "smart floor" wireless laptops and printers are at the ready. The comfortable rooms are surprisingly spacious—many have 14-ft ceilings. Thoughtful touches include ergonomically designed work spaces with L-shape desks, full-length mirrors that open to reveal ironing boards, and oversize showerheads that simulate falling rain. ✉ *15 Gold St., at Platt St., Lower Manhattan 10038* ☎ *212/232–7700 or 800/465–4329* 🖷 *212/425–0330* 🌐 *www.holidayinnwsd.com* *136 rooms, 1 suite* *Restaurant, room service, in-room data ports, in-room safes, minibars, cable TV with movies and video games, gym, bar, dry cleaning, laundry service, Internet, business services, meeting rooms, parking (fee), some pets allowed (fee), no-smoking floors* *AE, D, DC, MC, V.*

$ **Best Western Seaport Inn.** This thoroughly pleasant, restored 19th-century building is one block from the waterfront, close to South Street Seaport. Its cozy, library-like lobby has the feel of a Colonial sea captain's house, though the reasonably priced rooms are clearly those of a chain hotel. For $25–$35 extra, you can have a room with a whirlpool tub and/or an outdoor terrace with a view of the Brooklyn Bridge. ✉ *33 Peck Slip, between Front and Water Sts., Lower Manhattan 10038* ☎ *212/766–6600 or 800/468–3569* 🖷 *212/766–6615* 🌐 *www.bestwestern.com* *72 rooms* *In-room data ports, in-room safes, refrigerators, cable TV with video games, in-room VCRs, gym, dry cleaning, laundry service, parking (fee), no-smoking floors* *AE, D, DC, MC, V.*

Chinatown, SoHo & TriBeCa

$$$–$$$$ Fodor's Choice ★ **Mercer Hotel.** Owner Andre Balazs, known for his Château Marmont in Hollywood, has a knack for channeling a neighborhood sensibility. Here, it's SoHo loft all the way. In the hushed lobby, the reception desk is unmarked. Guest rooms are generously sized with long entryways, high ceilings, and walk-in closets. Dark African woods and custom-designed furniture upholstered in muted solids lend serenity. The bathrooms steal the show with their decadent two-person marble tubs—some surrounded by mirrors—but beware: not all rooms come with a tub. Downstairs is the happening Mercer Kitchen, where the cool still congregate. ✉ *147 Mercer St., at Prince St., SoHo 10012* ☎ *212/966–6060 or 888/918–6060* 🖷 *212/965–3838* 🌐 *www.mercerhotel.com* *67 rooms, 8 suites* *Restaurant, room service, in-room data ports, in-room safes, minibars, cable TV with movies and video games, in-room VCRs, 2 bars, concierge, business services, some pets allowed, no-smoking rooms* *AE, D, DC, MC, V.*

$$$–$$$$ **SoHo Grand.** This hardy pioneer of SoHo's hotel boom still holds its own against the newer arrivals. Guest rooms have custom-designed furnishings, including drafting table–style desks, nightstands that mimic sculptors' stands, and minibars made of old chests. All rooms have stereos with CD players, and suites come equipped with Web TV. The lounge is outfitted in pony hair and mohair, with antique fixtures and a flirtation-stimulating "tête-à-tête" sofa. ✉ *310 West Broadway, at Grand St., SoHo 10013* ☎ *212/965–3000 or 800/965–3000* 🖷 *212/965–3244* 🌐 *www.sohogrand.com* *365 rooms, 4 suites* *Restaurant, room service, in-room data ports, in-room safes, minibars, cable TV with movies, in-room VCRs, exercise equipment, gym, hair salon, massage, 2 bars, baby-sitting, dry cleaning, laundry service, concierge, Internet, business services, meeting rooms, parking (fee), some pets allowed, no-smoking rooms, no-smoking floor* *AE, D, DC, MC, V.*

$$–$$$$ **Tribeca Grand.** Enter this industrial-looking giant via a curving, 30-ft cleft-stone ramp and you'll find yourself looking up into an eight-story

LODGING ALTERNATIVES

Apartment Rentals

If you want a money-saving home base that's roomy enough for a family and comes with cooking facilities, consider a furnished rental. Home-exchange directories sometimes list rentals as well as exchanges. International agents include:

Hideaways International *(✉ 767 Islington St., Portsmouth, NH 03802 ☎ 603/430–4433 or 800/843–4433 📠 603/430–4444 🌐 www.hideaways.com), membership $129.*
Hometours International *(✉ 1108 Scottie La., Knoxville, TN 37919 ☎ 865/690–8484 or 866/367–4668 🌐 http://thor.he.net/~hometour/).*

Local agents include: ***Gamut Realty Group, Inc.*** *(✉ 301 E. 78th St., ground floor, between 2nd and 1st., Upper East Side, New York, NY 10021 ☎ 800/437–8353 or 212/879–4229 📠 212/517–5356 🌐 www.gamutnyc.com), which arranges rentals of furnished apartments that are not someone's private home.*

Bed-and-Breakfasts

Most bed-and-breakfasts in New York City are residential apartments. B&Bs booked through a service may be either hosted (you're the guest in someone's quarters) or unhosted (you have full use of someone's vacated apartment, including kitchen privileges). Reservation services include:

A Hospitality Company *(✉ 247 W. 35th St., between 7th and 8th Aves., Midtown West, New York, NY 10001 ☎ 800/987–1235 or 212/965–1102 📠 212/965–1149 🌐 www.hospitalitycompany.com).*
Abode Bed and Breakfasts Ltd. *(📭 Box 20022, New York, NY 10021 ☎ 212/472–2000 or 800/835–8880 🌐 www.abodenyc.com).*
All Around the Town *(✉ 150 5th Ave., Suite 711, between 19th and 20th Sts., Gramercy, New York, NY 10011 ☎ 212/675–5600 or 800/443–3800 📠 212/675–6366).*
Bed-and-Breakfast (and Books) *(✉ 35 W. 92nd St., Apt. 2C, between Central Park W and Columbus Ave., Upper West Side, New York, NY 10025 ☎📠 212/865–8740 [please call only weekdays 10 AM–5 PM]).*
Bed-and-Breakfast in Manhattan *(📭 Box 533, New York, NY 10150 ☎ 212/472–2528 📠 212/988–9818).*
Bed-and-Breakfast Network of New York *(✉ 134 W. 32nd St., Suite 602, between 6th and 7th Aves., Midtown West, New York, NY 10001 ☎ 212/645–8134 or 800/900–8134).*
City Lights Bed-and-Breakfast *(📭 Box 20355, Cherokee Station, New York, NY 10021 ☎ 212/737–7049 📠 212/535–2755).*
Manhattan Home Stays *(📭 Box 20684, Cherokee Station, New York, NY 10021 ☎ 212/737–3868 📠 212/265–3561 🌐 www.manhattanstays.com).*
New World Bed and Breakfast *(✉ 150 5th Ave., Suite 711, between 19th and 20th Sts., Gramercy, New York, NY 10011 ☎ 212/675–5600; 800/443–3800 in the U.S. 📠 212/675–6366).*
New York Habitat *(✉ 307 7th Ave., Suite 306, between 27th and 28th Sts., Chelsea, New York, NY 10001 ☎ 212/647–9365 📠 212/627–1416 🌐 www.nyhabitat.com).*
Urban Ventures *(✉ 38 W. 32nd St., Suite 1412, between 5th and 6th Aves., Midtown West, New York, NY 10001 ☎ 212/594–5650 📠 212/947–9320).*
West Village Reservations *(📭 Village Station, Box 347, New York, NY 10014-0347 ☎ 212/614–3034 📠 425/920–2384).*

Home Exchanges

If you would like to exchange your home for someone else's, join a home-exchange organization, which will send you its updated listings of available exchanges for a year and will include your own listing in at least one of them. It's up to you to make specific arrangements. Exchange clubs include:

HomeLink International *(📭 Box 47747, Tampa, FL 33647 ☎ 813/975–9825 or 800/638–3841 📠 813/910–8144* *www.homelink.org); $110 yearly for a listing, on-line access, and catalog; $40 without catalog.*

Intervac U.S. *(✉ 30 Corte San Fernando, Tiburon, CA 94920 ☎ 800/756–4663 📠 415/435–7440 www.intervacus.com); $105 yearly for a listing, on-line access, and a catalog; $50 without catalog.*

Hostels

No matter what your age, you can save on lodging costs by staying at hostels. In some 4,500 locations in more than 70 countries around the world, Hostelling International (HI), the umbrella group for a number of national youth-hostel associations, offers single-sex, dorm-style beds and, at many hostels, rooms for couples and family accommodations. Membership in any HI national hostel association, open to travelers of all ages, allows you to stay in HI-affiliated hostels at member rates; one-year membership is about $28 for adults (C$35 for a two-year minimum membership in Canada, £13.50 in the U.K., A$52 in Australia, and NZ$40 in New Zealand); hostels charge about $10–$30 per night. Members have priority if the hostel is full; they're also eligible for discounts around the world, even on rail and bus travel in some countries.

In New York, hostels are often full of international travelers.

To contact the organizations: ***Hostelling International—USA*** *(✉ 8401 Colesville Rd., Suite 600, Silver Spring, MD 20910 ☎ 301/495–1240 📠 301/495–6697 www.hiayh.org).*

Hostelling International—Canada *(✉ 400–205 Catherine St., Ottawa, Ontario K2P 1C3 ☎ 613/237–7884 or 800/663–5777 📠 613/237–7868 www.hihostels.ca).*

YHA England and Wales *(✉ Trevelyan House, Dimple Rd., Matlock, Derbyshire DE4 3YH, U.K. ☎ 0870/870–8808 📠 0870/770–6127 www.yha.org.uk).*

YHA Australia *(✉ 422 Kent St., Sydney, NSW 2001 ☎ 02/9261–1111 📠 02/9261–1969 www.yha.com.au).*

YHA New Zealand *(✉ Level 3, 193 Cashel St., Box 436, Christchurch ☎ 03/379–9970 or 0800/278–299 📠 03/365–4476 www.yha.org.nz).*

atrium. The popular Church Lounge serves as bar, café, and dining room well into the night—sometimes to the dismay of quiet-minded guests. Twin glass elevators housed in a steel cage whisk you to hallways overlooking the atrium. The well-appointed, average-size rooms have a subdued color scheme of blue and cream. Like its sister, the SoHo Grand, the Tribeca Grand welcomes pets. ✉ *2 Ave. of the Americas, between Walker and White Sts., TriBeCa 10013* ☎ *212/519–6600 or 800/965–3000* 📠 *212/519–6700* 🌐 *www.tribecagrand.com* *196 rooms, 8 suites* *Restaurant, café, room service, in-room data ports, in-room fax, in-room safes, minibars, cable TV with movies and video games, in-room VCRs, gym, bar, dry cleaning, laundry service, concierge, Internet, business services, meeting rooms, parking (fee), some pets allowed, no-smoking rooms, no-smoking floors* 💳 *AE, D, DC, MC, V.*

★ $$$ **60 Thompson.** A superb and original design by Thomas O'Brien, along with a popular lounge and restaurant, instantly anchored this stunning hotel into the downtown scene. The generous use of dark woods and full-wall leather headboards give the retro-classic rooms a welcoming warmth. The high-backed Thompson Chair has become a signature style statement. Amenities such as CD stereos and linens by Frette cater thoroughly to the demands of the enlightened guest. Marble-swathed bathrooms are positively hedonistic. The Eurasian restaurant Thom is popular among young Wall Streeters and media and fashion types. ✉ *60 Thompson St., between Broome and Spring Sts., SoHo 10012* ☎ *212/431–0400* 📠 *212/431–0200* 🌐 *www.60thompson.com* *90 rooms, 11 suites* *Restaurant, in-room data ports, minibars, cable TV with movies, in-room DVD players, 2 bars, Internet, meeting rooms, parking (fee), no-smoking rooms* 💳 *AE, D, DC, MC, V.*

$–$$ **Holiday Inn Downtown.** Historical features such as oversize arched windows, high ceilings, and a classic exterior remain in this former factory building, but the lobby is a cross-cultural affair mixing marble and Asian accents. Excellent dim sum at Pacifica Restaurant attracts plenty of Asian business travelers. Many Europeans and young budget travelers are also drawn by the reasonable rates and proximity to Little Italy, TriBeCa, and SoHo. The rooms are standard issue, but are clean and well maintained. The staff is well trained and works hard to please. Nearby bustling Canal Street is full of shops selling discounted (contraband?) perfumes, handbags, and watches. ✉ *138 Lafayette St., near Canal St., Chinatown 10013* ☎ *212/966–8898 or 800/465–4329* 📠 *212/966–3933* 🌐 *www.holidayinn-nyc.com* *215 rooms, 12 suites* *Restaurant, room service, in-room data ports, refrigerators, cable TV with movies, bar, dry cleaning, laundry service, concierge, parking (fee), no-smoking floors* 💳 *AE, D, DC, MC, V.*

Greenwich Village

$ **Washington Square Hotel.** This low-key hotel with a Continental feel is catercorner to Washington Square Park's magnificent arch. Most striking is its ornate wrought iron and gleaming brass gate in the small lobby. Rooms are small and well maintained. It's convenient to New York University, but alas, service is less than desirable. Complimentary Continental breakfast is served. ✉ *103 Waverly Pl., at MacDougal St., Greenwich Village 10011* ☎ *212/777–9515 or 800/222–0418* 📠 *212/979–8373* 🌐 *www.washingtonsquarehotel.com* *170 rooms* *Restaurant, in-room data ports, cable TV, gym, bar* 💳 *AE, MC, V.*

¢–$ Fodor's Choice ★ **Larchmont Hotel.** You might miss the entrance to this beaux arts town house, whose geranium boxes and lanterns blend right in with the old New York feel of West 11th Street. If you don't mind shared bathrooms and no room service, the residential-style accommodations are all any-

- Best Western Seaport Inn 17
- Carlton Arms.......... 3
- Chelsea Inn.......... 5
- Chelsea Savoy Hotel 2
- Gramercy Park Hotel.... 4
- Holiday Inn Downtown. 14
- Holiday Inn Wall Street. 16
- Howard Johnson...... 10
- The Inn at Irving Place .. 7
- Inn on 23rd.......... 1
- Larchmont Hotel....... 8
- Mercer Hotel......... 11
- New York Marriott Brooklyn............ 20
- The Regent Wall Street. 18
- Ritz-Carlton Battery Park 19
- 60 Thompson 12
- SoHo Grand 13
- Tribeca Grand......... 15
- W New York Union Square 6
- Washington Square Hotel.......... 9

one could ask for, for the price. The small rooms have a tasteful safari theme; your own private sink and stocked bookshelf will make you feel right at home. Guests have use of a communal kitchen. ✉ *27 W. 11th St., between 5th and 6th Aves., Greenwich Village 10011* ☎ *212/989–9333* 📠 *212/989–9496* 🌐 *www.larchmonthotel.com* *60 rooms, none with bath* *Café, fans, business services, no-smoking rooms* 💳 *AE, D, DC, MC, V.*

The East Village & the Lower East Side

$ Fodor's Choice ★ **Howard Johnson's Express Inn.** This hotel at the nexus of East Village and Lower East Side nightlife is perfect if you want to check out the downtown scene. A corner location increases your chances of having a view when you eventually rise to meet the day, and next door is a century-old knish bakery. The tastefully done rooms each have enough space for a desk; a few have hot tubs or microwaves and mini-refrigerators. With amenities such as in-room hair dryers, irons, coffeemakers, and voice mail, plus free local calls, you're getting more than your money's worth in New York's hotel market. ✉ *135 E. Houston St., at Forsyth St., Lower East Side 10002* ☎ *212/358–8844 or 800/446–4656* 📠 *212/473–3500* 🌐 *www.hojo.com* *46 rooms* *In-room data ports, microwaves in some rooms, cable TV, laundry service, no-smoking floors* 💳 *AE, D, DC, MC, V.*

Flatiron District & Gramercy

$$–$$$$ Fodor's Choice ★ **The Inn at Irving Place.** The city's most charming small inn occupies two grand 1830s town houses just steps from Gramercy Park. Its cozy tea salon (complete with a working fireplace), antiques-filled living room, and original curving banister evoke a more genteel era. Rooms have ornamental fireplaces, four-poster beds with embroidered linens, wood shutters, and glossy cherrywood floors. The room named after Madame Olenska (the lovelorn Edith Wharton character) has a bay window with sitting nook. In the morning, steaming pots of tea and coffee are served in the tea salon, along with a free Continental breakfast including homemade pastries and breads. ✉ *56 Irving Pl., between E. 17th and E. 18th Sts., Gramercy 10003* ☎ *212/533–4600 or 800/685–1447* 📠 *212/533–4611* 🌐 *www.innatirving.com* *5 rooms, 6 suites* *Restaurant, room service, in-room data ports, minibars, refrigerators, cable TV with movies, in-room VCRs, massage, bar, dry cleaning, laundry service, business services, parking (fee); no kids under 8* 💳 *AE, D, DC, MC, V.*

$$$ **W New York Union Square.** Starwood's W Hotel brand has owned Union Square since it bought the landmark Guardian Life building at the park's northeast corner. Both the interior and exterior of the 1911 beaux arts–style building retain many original granite and limestone details. Modernism permeates each room, from shiny sharkskin bed coverings to overstuffed velvet armchairs. Generally, the service staff look as though they just stepped out of a photo shoot, and at times it feels like that's where they'd rather be. Celebrity chef Todd English's first New York restaurant, Olives NY, and the comfortable lobby bar draw huge crowds. ✉ *201 Park Ave. S, at E. 17th St., Flatiron District 10003* ☎ *212/253–9119 or 877/946–8357* 📠 *212/779–0148* 🌐 *www.whotels.com* *270 rooms, 16 suites* *Restaurant, room service, in-room data ports, in-room fax, in-room safes, minibars, cable TV with movies, in-room VCRs, gym, health club, 2 bars, dry cleaning, laundry service, concierge, Internet, business services, meeting rooms, parking (fee), some pets allowed, no-smoking rooms, no-smoking floors* 💳 *AE, D, DC, MC, V.*

$–$$ **Gramercy Park Hotel.** Long past its prime as a rock star hideaway, this 1920s curio has the air of a proud retiree living on a fixed income. From the lobby's mishmash attempts at grandeur—chandeliers, tufted Naugahyde arm chairs, knotty pine paneling—to the depressing rooms with their floral coverlets and haphazard furniture selection, it's a time capsule of a better-forgotten era. The classic bar, replete with dark woods and red hurricane candles, is B-movie noir and attracts a loyal clientele. Guests earn a key to the coveted private Gramercy Park. This hotel manages to soothe those who feel safest when time stands still. ✉ *2 Lexington Ave., at Gramercy Park, Gramercy 10010* ☎ *212/475–4320 or 800/221–4083* 🖷 *212/505–0535* 🌐 *www.gramercyparkhotel.com* *360 rooms, 149 suites* *Restaurant, room service, kitchenettes, refrigerators, cable TV, hair salon, bar, dry cleaning, laundry service, Internet, parking (fee), some pets allowed, no-smoking floors* 💳 *AE, D, DC, MC, V.*

Murray Hill

$$$$ **The Kitano.** A large Botero bronze of a stylized dog presides over the chic mahogany and marble lobby of this luxe hotel with an austere grandeur. Handsome cherry and mahogany furnishings, Japanese tea makers, and watercolor still lifes impart an air of serenity to the rooms; soundproof windows make them among Manhattan's quietest. The Nadaman restaurant is known for high-priced but authentic Japanese cuisine; the second-floor lounge hosts a jazz band on Friday nights. For business meetings, two of the top-floor banquet rooms have floor-to-ceiling glass doors leading to expansive balconies with dazzling city views. ✉ *66 Park Ave., at E. 38th St., Murray Hill 10016* ☎ *212/885–7000 or 800/548–2666* 🖷 *212/885–7100* 🌐 *www.kitano.com* *141 rooms, 8 suites* *2 restaurants, room service, in-room data ports, in-room fax, in-room safes, in-room hot tubs, minibars, cable TV with movies, bar, baby-sitting, dry cleaning, laundry facilities, laundry service, concierge, business services, meeting rooms, parking (fee), no-smoking floors* 💳 *AE, D, DC, MC, V.*

$$–$$$$ **W New York–The Court and W New York–The Tuscany.** Big black "W"s transform guest-room headboards into billboards at these self-consciously stylish sister properties. The design-for-design's-sake lobbies might strike some as cold, but an exceedingly attentive staff goes a long way toward warming things up. Spacious rooms have vaguely Oriental black-and-blond wood furnishings and ottomans with chenille throws (which can be purchased through the in-room W catalog). Both uphold the W chain's hip nightlife standards with Tuscany's Cherry, a rock-and-roll vision in red; the Court's popular Wet Bar; and the starkly elegant, steamship-deco Icon restaurant. ✉ *Court: 130 E. 39th St., between Lexington and Park Aves., Murray Hill 10016* ☎ *212/685–1100 or 877/946–8357* 🖷 *212/889–0287* ✉ *Tuscany: 120 E. 39th St., near Lexington Ave., Murray Hill 10016* ☎ *212/779–7822; 800/223–6725 for reservations* 🖷 *212/696–2095* 🌐 *www.whotels.com* *Court: 150 rooms, 48 suites; Tuscany: 110 rooms, 12 suites* *Restaurant, café, room service, in-room data ports, in-room safes, minibars, cable TV with movies, in-room VCRs, exercise equipment, gym, 2 bars, baby-sitting, dry cleaning, laundry service, concierge, business services, meeting rooms, parking (fee), no-smoking rooms, no-smoking floors* 💳 *AE, D, DC, MC, V.*

$$–$$$ **Hotel Giraffe.** Inspired by the colors and sleek lines of European Moderne, this retro-glam property aspires to the sophisticated and indulgent comfort of the 1920s and 1930s. Guest rooms with 10-ft ceilings are adorned with antique-rose velveteen armchairs, larger-than-life headboards, sorbet-color sheer curtains, diamond-quilted satin bedcovers, and pearlized platinum wall covers. Deluxe rooms have French doors opening onto private balconies from which you can survey Park

CloseUp

KID-FRIENDLY HOTELS

*TOTS AND TEENS IN TOW? Here's where to rest easy with your family. The **Iroquois** has family-size suites, in-room Nintendo, afternoon board games in the parlor, and child-size bathrobes at no extra charge. With basketball and racquetball courts and a rooftop pool with a lifeguard, **Le Parker Meridien** is loads of fun. The underage set indulges in the NYPD Special (Krispy Kreme donuts stuffed with raspberry and chocolate whipped cream) at Norma's restaurant. And kids can bring their pets.*

*At the midtown **Library Hotel,** kids receive a Harry Potter, Madeline, or Winnie-the-Pooh kit, which includes theme sheets and pillows. The group of properties operated by **Manhattan East Suite Hotels** (☎ 212/465–3690 🌐 www.mesuite.com), including the Benjamin, Plaza Fifty, and the Beekman Tower, tends to have fully equipped suites at very reasonable rates. The rooms and suites at **Trump International Hotel and Towers** resemble mini-apartments: all have fully equipped kitchens, entertainment centers, and mini-telescopes overlooking Central Park. There's also an indoor pool.*

*Upon check-in at the **Omni Berkshire Place,** kids under 11 get a goodie bag and a backpack loaner. Both contain toys galore from cards and puzzles to coloring books and bedtime reading. On the room's Web TV, kids can log on to www.omnikidsrule.com to participate in polls and contests.*

Avenue. For the ultimate in entertaining (or an exorbitant romantic getaway), reserve the spectacular penthouse suite with baby grand piano and rooftop garden. ✉ *365 Park Ave. S, at E. 26th St., Murray Hill 10016* ☎ *212/685–7700 or 877/296–0009* 📠 *212/685–7771* 🌐 *www.hotelgiraffe.com* *73 rooms, 21 suites* *Restaurant, room service, in-room data ports, in-room safes, minibars, cable TV, in-room VCRs, 2 bars, dry cleaning, laundry service, concierge, business services, parking (fee), no-smoking rooms, no-smoking floors* 💳 *AE, DC, MC, V.*

$$ **Jolly Hotel Madison Towers.** The Italian Jolly Hotels chain brings a European air to this friendly hotel on a residential Murray Hill corner. Operators answering phones in Italian provide atmosphere. The tasteful and traditional rooms have dark-wood furnishings. Deluxe rooms on top floors have views of the Empire State Building, minimalist walnut furniture, beds with Frette linens and duvets, and marble bathrooms. Suites are downright luxurious, with huge bathrooms. Cinque Terre serves Northern Italian cuisine, and the cozy Whaler Bar has a fireplace and a wood-beam ceiling. A separate concession on the premises offers shiatsu massage and a Japanese sauna. ✉ *22 E. 38th St., between Madison and Park Aves., Murray Hill 10016* ☎ *212/802–0600 or 800/225–4340* 📠 *212/447–0747* 🌐 *www.jollymadison.com* *243 rooms, 6 suites* *Restaurant, in-room data ports, in-room safes, minibars, cable TV with movies and video games, massage, sauna, steam room, bar, dry cleaning, laundry service, concierge, Internet, business services, meeting rooms, parking (fee), some pets allowed, no-smoking floors* 💳 *AE, DC, MC, V.*

$$ **Morgans.** Überhotelier Ian Schrager launched New York's boutique hotel craze way back in 1984 when he opened this hipster, but Morgans is still up-to-the-minute. Your first clue is the studied lack of a sign outside. Inside, the stunning rooms have a minimalist, high-tech look, with low-lying, futonlike beds and 27-inch TVs on wheels; the tiny bathrooms have crystal shower doors, steel surgical sinks, and poured-granite floors. The chic Asia de Cuba restaurant has long, communal tables and delectable nibbles. The cavelike, candlelit Morgans Bar downstairs also lives up to all its hype. ✉ *237 Madison Ave., between E. 37th and E. 38th Sts., Murray Hill 10016* ☎ *212/686–0300 or 800/334–3408* 📠 *212/779–8352* 🌐 *www.ianschragerhotels.com* *87 rooms, 26 suites* *Room service, in-room data ports, in-room safes, minibars, refrigerators, cable TV with movies, in-room VCRs, 2 bars, baby-sitting, dry cleaning, laundry service, concierge, Internet, business services, meeting rooms, parking (fee), some pets allowed, no-smoking rooms, no-smoking floors* 💳 *AE, D, DC, MC, V.*

$–$$ **Doral Park Avenue.** The lobby rotunda of this stately Park Avenue hotel is neoclassical with a twist: a giant painting of an ancient Roman city is offset by palm trees and art deco details. Styled headboards and throw pillows in muted colors grace the warm, inviting guest rooms. The swanky lounge off the lobby has big windows facing Park Avenue, and the restaurant, 70 Park Bar and Grill, is your classic bistro serving American dishes. ✉ *70 Park Ave., at E. 38th St., Murray Hill 10016* ☎ *212/687–7050* 📠 *212/973–2497 or 212/808–9029* 🌐 *www.doralparkavenue.com* *184 rooms, 4 suites* *Restaurant, room service, in-room data ports, in-room safes, minibars, cable TV with movies, bar, baby-sitting, dry cleaning, laundry service, concierge, Internet, business services, meeting rooms, parking (fee), some pets allowed, no-smoking rooms* 💳 *AE, D, DC, MC, V.*

$–$$ **Park South Hotel.** In this beautifully transformed 1906 office building, rooms are smartly contemporary and even a bit regal, given the majestic, oversize wooden headboards. Some have views of the Chrysler Building. The New York flavor permeates from a mezzanine library focusing on local history to the ubiquitous black-and-white photos of city scenes from the 1880s through 1950s. The Black Duck bar and restaurant warms patrons with its wood-burning fireplace. Unlike at other boutique hotels where locals have made the lounges their watering holes, you won't have to contend with crowds here. ✉ *122 E. 28th St., between Lexington and Park Aves., Murray Hill 10016* ☎ *212/448–0888 or 800/315–4642* 📠 *212/448–0811* 🌐 *www.parksouthhotel.com* *143 rooms* *Restaurant, room service, in-room data ports, in-room fax, minibars, cable TV, in-room DVD players, gym, bar, dry cleaning, laundry service, concierge, business services* 💳 *AE, D, DC, MC, V.*

$–$$ Fodor's Choice ★ **Roger Williams Hotel.** A masterpiece of industrial chic, the cavernous Rafael Viñoly–designed lobby—clad with sleek maple walls accented with fluted zinc pillars—was dubbed "a shrine to modernism" by *New York* magazine. What rooms lack in space, they make up for in high-style, custom-made blond-birch furnishings—including sliding shoji screens behind the beds—and dramatic downlighting. Some baths have a cedar-wood-floor shower stall. There's complimentary fresh fruit in the evenings, as well as 24-hour cappuccino. ✉ *131 Madison Ave., at E. 31st St., Murray Hill 10016* ☎ *212/448–7000 or 877/847–4444* 📠 *212/448–7007* 🌐 *www.rogerwilliamshotel.com* *187 rooms, 2 suites* *In-room data ports, cable TV, in-room VCRs, exercise equipment, gym, piano, concierge, Internet, business services, parking (fee), some free parking, no-smoking rooms, no-smoking floors* 💳 *AE, D, MC, V.*

$–$$ **Red Roof Inn.** Two blocks from the Empire State Building, Penn Station, Madison Square Garden, and Macy's, this chain hotel has pleasant rooms and a mezzanine bar overlooking the smart lobby. Weekday newspapers are free, as is the Continental breakfast. ✉ *6 W. 32nd St., between 5th Ave. and Broadway, Murray Hill 10001* ☎ *212/643–7100* *or 800/567–7720 212/643–7101 www.applecorehotels.com 171 rooms In-room data ports, microwaves, refrigerators, cable TV with movies and video games, health club, bar, dry cleaning, laundry service, concierge, Internet, business services, meeting rooms, parking (fee), no-smoking rooms AE, D, DC, MC, V.*

¢–$$ Fodor'sChoice ★ **The Gershwin.** Young, foreign travelers flock to this budget hotel–cum–hostel, housed in a converted 13-story Greek revival building adjacent to the Museum of Sex. A giant Plexiglas and metal sculpture of glowing pods by Stefan Lindfors creeps down the facade and winds its way into the lobby. With Andy Warhol as muse, there's pop art on every floor. Rooms are painted in bright colors. Dormitories have 2 to 10 beds and a remarkable $29.99 to $59.99 rate. On any given night there's something going on—film series, stand-up comedy, performance art—at this slightly cheesy center for avant-garde activities. *7 E. 27th St., between 5th and Madison Aves., Murray Hill 10016 212/545–8000 212/684–5546 www.gershwinhotel.com 120 rooms, 64 beds in dorm rooms, 12 suites Café, cable TV, Internet, no-smoking floors; no TV in some rooms AE, MC, V.*

$ **Ramada Inn.** The least antiseptic of Manhattan's three Apple Core hotels, this East-sider on a pleasant residential block has sunny, simple rooms done in primary colors. A small gym and a tiny business center with a credit card–operated fax, photocopier, and computer are in the basement. *161 Lexington Ave., at E. 30th St., Murray Hill 10016 212/545–1800 or 800/567–7720 212/481–7270 www.applecorehotels.com 95 rooms Café, in-room data ports, in-room safes, cable TV with movies and video games, exercise equipment, gym, business services, airport shuttle, parking (fee), no-smoking floors AE, D, DC, MC, V.*

¢–$ **Herald Square Hotel.** Sculpted cherubs on the facade and vintage magazine covers adorning the common areas hint at this building's previous incarnation as *Life* magazine's 1886 headquarters. Rooms are basic and clean; all have TVs and phones with voice mail. There's no concierge and no room service, but nearby restaurants will deliver. A no-frills option, to be sure, but where else in the city can you find a clean, single room for the downright suburban sum of $60 (doubles start at $99). *19 W. 31st St., between 5th Ave. and Broadway, Murray Hill 10001 212/279–4017 or 800/727–1888 212/643–9208 www.heraldsquarehotel.com 120 rooms Room service, in-room safes, cable TV, Internet, airport shuttle, some pets allowed AE, D, MC, V.*

¢ **Carlton Arms.** So creepy, it's cool—every wall and ceiling in this bohemian dive is covered with a mural. Each room has a theme. The Versailles Room is an outré symphony of trompe l'oeil trellises and classical urns, while the "child's dream" room has a puzzle-covered floor and a bed the shape of a car with monsters underneath. But these are tame compared to the room devoted to sadomasochism. Children are allowed, but you may consider leaving them with relatives. All rooms have double-glazed windows but none have TVs. Many are almost free of furniture, and some of baths. *160 E. 25th St., at 3rd Ave., Murray Hill 10010 212/684–8337; 212/679–0680 for reservations www.carltonarms.com 54 rooms, 20 with bath Some pets allowed; no a/c, no room phones, no room TVs MC, V.*

Chelsea

$–$$ **Inn on 23rd.** Innkeepers Annette and Barry Fisherman were inspired to restore this 19th-century commercial building in the heart of Chelsea, making each of the 14 guest rooms spacious and unique. One exotic and elegant room is outfitted in bamboo, another in the art moderne style of the 1940s. There's also a suite with an incomparable view of the quintessential New York landmark, the Empire State Building. Although it's small and homey, the inn provides private baths and satellite TV in all rooms, an elevator, and, of course, breakfast. ✉ *131 W. 23rd St., between 6th and 7th Aves., Chelsea 10011* ☎ *212/463–0330* 🖷 *212/463–0302* *14 rooms, 1 suite* *In-room data ports, Internet; no smoking* *AE, MC, V.*

$ **Chelsea Inn.** The eclectic, country ambience here is a refreshing change from the characterless hotels that dominate this price category. Housed in an old brownstone, it's a favorite of young budget travelers, who don't mind not having an elevator and appreciate the funky style and in-room cooking facilities. (Most rooms have kitchenettes; others have a refrigerator and sink.) Rooms, with shared or private bath, are a hodgepodge of country quilts and thrift-shop antiques. A few in back overlook a little courtyard with an ivy-draped fence, and quiet prevails even though next door sits one of the largest gay bars in town. ✉ *46 W. 17th St., between 5th and 6th Aves., Chelsea 10011* ☎ *212/645–8989 or 800/640–6469* 🖷 *212/645–1903* 🌐 *www.chelseainn.com* *26 rooms, 4 with bath* *In-room safes, some kitchenettes, some microwaves, refrigerators, cable TV* *AE, D, MC, V.*

¢–$ **Chelsea Savoy Hotel.** Affordable rates and a friendly though often harried young staff make this a sensible choice. Jade-green carpets, butterscotch wood furniture, and perhaps a framed van Gogh print enliven the small, basic rooms. The Bull Run Grill is next to the bland lobby. ✉ *204 W. 23rd St., at 7th Ave., Chelsea 10011* ☎ *212/929–9353 or 866/929–9353* 🖷 *212/741–6309* 🌐 *www.chelseasavoy.qpg.com* *90 rooms* *Restaurant, café, room service, in-room data ports, in-room safes, refrigerators, cable TV, bar, no-smoking rooms* *AE, MC, V.*

Midtown West

★ $$$$ **Ritz-Carlton New York, Central Park South.** Formerly the St. Moritz, this glamour palace sits on a strategic spot with some of the best views in the city. Its renovation yielded larger but fewer rooms, and the 1930s facade was kept intact. Adding to the value are technology butlers, butlers who draw your bath, on-call personal trainers, complimentary Bentley limousine service within midtown, and a La Prairie salon. Rooms and suites are furnished in shades of celadon, taupe, and pale rose, with plush upholsteries, brocade drapes, and richly patterned carpets. Innovative French cuisine is served at Atelier. ✉ *50 Central Park S, at 6th Ave., Midtown West 10019* ☎ *212/308–9100 or 800/241–3333* 🖷 *212/207–8831* 🌐 *www.ritzcarlton.com* *237 rooms, 40 suites* *Restaurant, in-room data ports, minibars, cable TV, in-room DVD players, bar, Internet, meeting rooms* *AE, D, DC, MC, V.*

$$$–$$$$ **Chambers.** Midtown is the new downtown in David Rockwell's gorgeous showcase, where more than 500 works of art hang and each guestroom floor has a mural installation. Loftlike rooms with hand-troweled cement walls are decorated warmly, and the bathroom floors of poured concrete shimmer with glass mosaic tiles. After entering through the magnificent carved teak doors and passing through the intimate yet grand lobby with soaring ceilings, double-sided fireplace, and Hugo Boss–uniformed staff, head downstairs to the restaurant Town for one of the most sublime culinary experiences around. ✉ *15 W. 56th St., off 5th Ave., Midtown West 10019* ☎ *212/974–5656 or 866/204–5656* 🖷 *212/974–5657* 🌐 *www.chambershotel.com* *72 rooms, 5 suites* *Restaurant, in-room data ports, in-room safes, minibars, cable TV with movies, in-room DVD players, bar, lounge, dry cleaning, laundry service, con-*

Where to Stay in Murray Hill, Midtown & Uptown
W. 86th St.
Metropolitan Museum of Art
Riverside Park
Riverside Dr.
1,9
W.79th St.
Museum of Natural History
B,C
West End Ave.
Amsterdam Ave.
1,2,3,9
W. 72nd St.
Columbus Ave.
Broadway
Central Park W.
Central Park
Fifth Ave.
Madison Ave.
Lincoln Center
Hudson River
Columbus Circle
A,B,C,D,1,9
Central Park S.
N,Q,R,W
F
N,R,W
W. 57th St.
Seventh Ave.
Eighth Ave.
Avenue of the Americas (Sixth Ave.)
B,D,E
E,V
W. 52nd St.
Rockefeller Center
C,E
B,D,F,V
Twelfth Ave.
Eleventh Ave.
Tenth Ave.
Ninth Ave.
W. 46th St.
Times Square
West Side Highway
Port Authority Bus Terminal
W. 42nd St.
A,C,E
1,2,3,7,9, N,Q,R,S,W
7
Public Library
W. 38th St.
Javits Convention Center
B,D,F,N, Q,R,V,W
Empire State Building
W. 34th St.
Penn Station
Herald Square
E. 32nd St.
Madison Square Garden
1 2 4 5 6 7 8 9 14 15 16 17 18 19 21 22 23 24 26 29 30 31 32 33 34 35 36 37 38 40 41 50 51 52 53 54 55 56 57 58 59 60 61 62 63 64 65 66 67 68 69 70 77 82 83

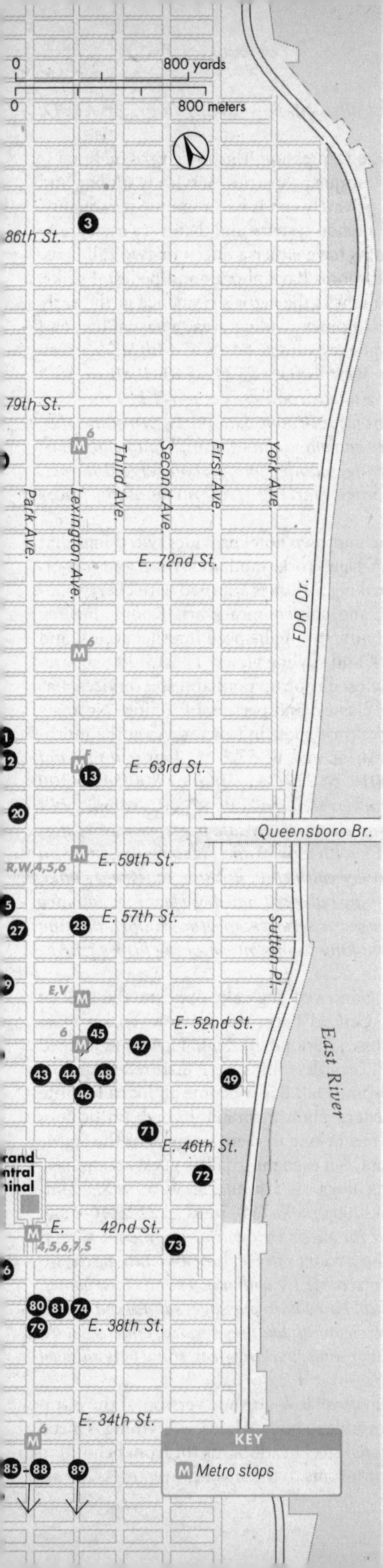

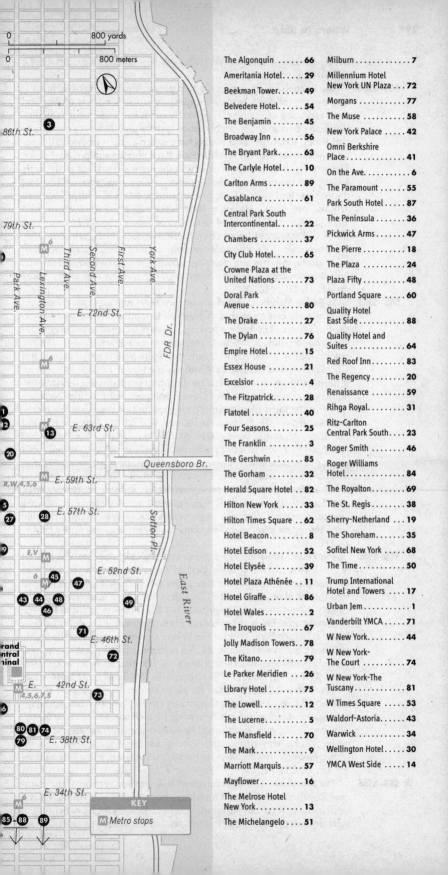

The Algonquin 66
Ameritania Hotel. 29
Beekman Tower. 49
Belvedere Hotel. 54
The Benjamin 45
Broadway Inn 56
The Bryant Park. 63
The Carlyle Hotel. 10
Carlton Arms 89
Casablanca 61
Central Park South Intercontinental. 22
Chambers 37
City Club Hotel. 65
Crowne Plaza at the United Nations 73
Doral Park Avenue 80
The Drake 27
The Dylan 76
Empire Hotel 15
Essex House 21
Excelsior 4
The Fitzpatrick. 28
Flatotel 40
Four Seasons. 25
The Franklin 3
The Gershwin 85
The Gorham 32
Herald Square Hotel . . 82
Hilton New York 33
Hilton Times Square . . 62
Hotel Beacon. 8
Hotel Edison 52
Hotel Elysée 39
Hotel Plaza Athénée . . 11
Hotel Giraffe 86
Hotel Wales 2
The Iroquois 67
Jolly Madison Towers. . 78
The Kitano. 79
Le Parker Meridien . . . 26
Library Hotel 75
The Lowell. 12
The Lucerne. 5
The Mansfield 70
The Mark. 9
Marriott Marquis 57
Mayflower 16
The Melrose Hotel New York. 13
The Michelangelo 51
Milburn 7
Millennium Hotel New York UN Plaza . . . 72
Morgans 77
The Muse 58
New York Palace 42
Omni Berkshire Place 41
On the Ave. 6
The Paramount 55
Park South Hotel 87
The Peninsula 36
Pickwick Arms 47
The Pierre 18
The Plaza 24
Plaza Fifty 48
Portland Square 60
Quality Hotel East Side 88
Quality Hotel and Suites 64
Red Roof Inn. 83
The Regency 20
Renaissance 59
Rihga Royal. 31
Ritz-Carlton Central Park South. . . . 23
Roger Smith 46
Roger Williams Hotel. 84
The Royalton. 69
The St. Regis 38
Sherry-Netherland 19
The Shoreham. 35
Sofitel New York 68
The Time 50
Trump International Hotel and Towers 17
Urban Jem 1
Vanderbilt YMCA 71
W New York. 44
W New York-The Court 74
W New York-The Tuscany 81
W Times Square 53
Waldorf-Astoria. 43
Warwick 34
Wellington Hotel. 30
YMCA West Side 14

cierge, parking (fee), some pets allowed, no-smoking floors ▭ *AE, D, DC, MC, V.*

$$$–$$$$ **The Iroquois.** Built during the Depression, this once prosaic hotel is now among the city's better boutique properties. Service is smiling and top-notch, and as the hotel is privately run it has a unique personality. Children can enjoy in-room Nintendo systems and their very own Frette bathrobes. Cozy standard rooms have either a queen or two full beds, and the marble-and-brass bathrooms have phones and pedestal sinks. The street-side James Dean suite was the actor's residence in the early 1950s. Off the tiny lobby are a homey reading area, a casual bar, and the intimate and refined Triomphe restaurant. ✉ *49 W. 44th St., between 5th and 6th Aves., Midtown West 10036* ☎ *212/840–3080 or 800/332–7220* 🖷 *212/398–1754* 🌐 *www.iroquoisny.com* *114 rooms, 9 suites* *Restaurant, room service, in-room data ports, in-room safes, minibars, cable TV with movies and video games, gym, health club, massage, sauna, spa, bar, dry cleaning, laundry service, concierge, Internet, business services, meeting rooms, parking (fee), no-smoking floors* ▭ *AE, D, DC, MC, V.*

$$$–$$$$ **Le Parker Meridien.** This chic midtown hotel provides two things that don't always come together in New York: modern styling and top-of-the-line service. The lobby's striking atrium is adorned with cherry paneling, hand-painted columns, and contemporary art. Rooms include ergonomically sound Aeron chairs, free high-speed Internet access, and CD players—and Central Park and skyline views. The 15,000-square-ft health club, with a glass-enclosed rooftop pool and spa services, has numerous machines, aerobics classes, and personal training. Norma's is one of the most popular breakfast spots in town, serving the morning meal from 6:30 AM to 3 PM. ✉ *118 W. 57th St., between 6th and 7th Aves., Midtown West 10019* ☎ *212/245–5000 or 800/543–4300* 🖷 *212/307–1776* 🌐 *www.parkermeridien.com* *701 rooms, 249 suites* *2 restaurants, room service, in-room data ports, in-room safes, minibars, microwaves, cable TV with movies and video games, in-room DVD/VCR players, indoor pool, health club, hot tub, massage, sauna, spa, basketball, racquetball, bar, baby-sitting, dry cleaning, laundry service, concierge, Internet, business services, meeting rooms, parking (fee), some pets allowed, no-smoking rooms, no-smoking floors* ▭ *AE, D, DC, MC, V.*

$$$–$$$$ **The Plaza.** Towering like a giant wedding cake opposite the fleet of horse-drawn carriages lining Central Park, this is New York's most beloved hotel. The fictional Eloise ran riot in it, Zelda Fitzgerald jumped into the fountain outside of it, countless films have featured it, and its comely Palm Court and handsome Oak Bar welcome all like a favorite aunt and uncle. The management carefully maintains its high-traffic public areas, which New Yorkers feel belong to them as much as the Statue of Liberty. Suites are magnificent, but even the smallest guest rooms have crystal chandeliers and 14-ft ceilings. ✉ *5th Ave. at W. 59th St., Midtown West 10019* ☎ *212/759–3000 or 800/759–3000* 🖷 *212/546–5324 for reservations; 212/759–3167 for guests* 🌐 *www.fairmont.com* *805 rooms, 60 suites* *4 restaurants, room service, in-room data ports, in-room safes, minibars, refrigerators, cable TV with movies and video games, in-room VCRs, gym, health club, hair salon, massage, sauna, spa, steam room, 2 bars, baby-sitting, dry cleaning, laundry service, concierge, Internet, business services, meeting rooms, parking (fee), some pets allowed* ▭ *AE, D, DC, MC, V.*

★ **$$$–$$$$** **The Shoreham.** This is a miniature, low-attitude version of the ultra-cool Royalton—and it's comfortable to boot. Almost everything is metal or of metal color, from perforated steel headboards (lit from behind) to steel sinks in the shiny, tiny bathrooms to the silver-gray carpets. Pleasant touches include CD players and cedar-lined closets. Guests can enjoy a complimentary Continental breakfast, and the Shoreham Bar and Grille serves an eclectic, light menu of sandwiches and salads. The legendary French restaurant La Caravelle is downstairs. ✉ *33 W. 55th St., between 5th and 6th Aves., Midtown West 10019* ☎ *212/247–6700 or 877/847–4444* 📠 *212/765–9741* 🌐 *www.shorehamhotel.com* *174 rooms, 37 suites* *2 restaurants, room service, in-room data ports, in-room safes, minibars, refrigerators, cable TV, in-room VCRs, massage, bar, baby-sitting, dry cleaning, laundry service, concierge, Internet, business services, parking (fee), some pets allowed, no-smoking floors* 💳 *AE, DC, MC, V.*

$$–$$$$ **The Bryant Park.** Carved out of the bones of the former American Radiator Building that towers over the New York Public Library and Bryant Park, this brilliant blend of '20s Gothic revival exterior and sleekly modern rooms delivers the pizzazz worthy of the city's moniker, Gotham. Though the stark red lobby disappoints, rooms are furnished at the apex of minimalist chic with sumptuous travertine bathrooms, hardwood floors, killer views, and wireless laptops that connect to the Internet via large TV monitors. Ilo, a rave-garnering restaurant, rises a few steps from the lobby bar popular with the after-work crowd. ✉ *40 W. 40th St., between 5th and 6th Aves., Midtown West 10018* ☎ *212/869–0100 or 877/640–9300* 📠 *212/869–4446* 🌐 *www.bryantparkhotel.com* *107 rooms, 22 suites* *Restaurant, room service, in-room data ports, in-room safes, minibars, cable TV with movies, gym, massage, spa, steam room, 2 bars, dry cleaning, laundry service, concierge, Internet, business services, meeting rooms, some pets allowed (fee), no-smoking floors* 💳 *AE, DC, MC, V.*

$$–$$$$ **City Club Hotel.** Like Cary Grant's ocean-liner suites, City Club rooms are brisk, bright, and masculine, with Jonathan Adler ceramics, baseball photos from the '50s, Hermes bathroom products, and "City Club" banner wool blankets. The bathroom marble is chocolate color, and the wallpaper flecked with mica. Privacy, not publicity, is the emphasis at this luxe property owned by young man-about-town Jeff Klein and designed by celebrity decorator Jeffrey Bilhuber. The lobby is tiny, and guests who wish to drink are sent across the street to the Royalton. Top chef Daniel Boulud opened his db Bistro Moderne downstairs. ✉ *55 W. 44th St., between 5th and 6th Aves., Midtown West 10036* ☎ *212/921–5500* 📠 *212/944–5544* 🌐 *www.cityclubhotel.com* *62 rooms, 3 suites* *Restaurant, minibars, cable TV with movies, in-room DVD players, Internet, parking (fee), no-smoking rooms* 💳 *AE, D, DC, MC, V.*

$$–$$$$ **The Muse.** In the heart of the theater district, the Muse has a display of artwork that includes photos of such "muses" as Katharine Hepburn and Nureyev. The rooms are oversize and crammed with state-of-the-art amenities such as multiline cordless phones and high-speed Internet access. The beds are dressed in fine linens with feather duvets, and some rooms have a DVD player, wide-screen TV, exercise equipment, and desktop computer. In the hotel's happening, stagelike restaurant, District, chef Sam DeMarco prepares outstanding, globally influenced American cuisine. There's also a "midnight pantry," where you can enjoy a complimentary post-theater buffet. ✉ *130 W. 46th St., between 6th and 7th Aves., Midtown West 10036* ☎ *212/485–2400 or 877/692–6873* 📠 *212/485–2900* 🌐 *www.themusehotel.com* *200 rooms, 19 suites* *Restaurant, room service, in-room data ports, in-room safes, minibars, cable TV with movies, gym, massage, bar, dry cleaning, laundry service, concierge, business services, meeting rooms, parking (fee), some pets allowed, no-smoking floors* 💳 *AE, D, DC, MC, V.*

$$–$$$$ **W Times Square.** Times Square finally goes hip on a grand scale with
Fodor'sChoice ★ the opening of this super-sleek 57-floor monolith, the flagship of the white-hot W line. After passing through an entrance of cascading, glass-enclosed water, you alight to the seventh-floor lobby where Kenneth Cole–clad "welcome ambassadors" await. The Jetsons experience continues in the space-age, white-on-white lobby and the futuristic rooms with their glowing resin boxes and multiple shades of gray. The bi-level Blue Fin restaurant with its sushi bar and floor-to-ceiling windows caps the architectural wonderment. ✉ *1567 Broadway, at W. 47th St., Midtown West 10036* ☎ *212/930–7400 or 877/946–8357* 🖷 *212/930–7500* 🌐 *www.whotels.com* *466 rooms, 43 suites* *Restaurant, café, room service, in-room data ports, in-room safes, minibars, cable TV with movies, in-room DVD players, exercise equipment, gym, massage, 4 bars, shop, dry cleaning, laundry service, concierge, Internet, business services, parking (fee), some pets allowed (fee), no-smoking rooms, no-smoking floors* 💳 *AE, D, DC, MC, V.*

★ $$–$$$$ **Warwick.** Astonishingly, this palatial hotel was built by William Randolph Hearst in 1927 as a private hotel for his friends and family. The midtown favorite is well placed for the Theater District. The elegant, marble-floor lobby buzzes with activity; the Randolph restaurant is on one side, and Ciao Europa, an Italian restaurant, is on the other. Handsome, Regency-style rooms have soft pastel color schemes, mahogany armoires, and marble bathrooms, and some have fax machines. The Cary Grant suite was the actor's New York residence. ✉ *65 W. 54th St., at 6th Ave., Midtown West 10019* ☎ *212/247–2700 or 800/223–4099* 🖷 *212/713–1751* 🌐 *www.warwickhotels.com* *358 rooms, 68 suites* *2 restaurants, room service, in-room data ports, in-room safes, minibars, cable TV with movies and video games, exercise equipment, gym, bar, dry cleaning, laundry service, concierge, Internet, business services, meeting rooms, parking (fee), no-smoking rooms* 💳 *AE, DC, MC, V.*

$–$$$$ **Central Park South InterContinental.** This 1929 property has not only a swank address near Carnegie Hall and 5th Avenue shopping, but also very polished service and fine art on virtually every wall. Everything about the hotel is first-class. Guest rooms are graced with rich brocades, polished woods, and marble bathrooms; some have breathtaking Central Park views. By joining the "Six Continents Club" ($135 for the first year), you earn a free upgrade, a daily in-room fruit basket, the *New York Times* delivery, a free movie, 4 PM checkout, and a certificate for a weekend night stay at any Inter-Continental Hotel. ✉ *112 Central Park S, between 6th and 7th Aves., Midtown West 10019* ☎ *212/757–1900 or 800/327–0200* 🖷 *212/757–9620* 🌐 *new-york-central.intercontinental.com* *200 rooms, 16 suites* *Restaurant, room service, in-room data ports, in-room safes, minibars, cable TV with movies and video games, exercise equipment, health club, sauna, steam room, bar, babysitting, dry cleaning, laundry service, concierge, business services, meeting rooms, parking (fee), some pets allowed, no-smoking rooms, no-smoking floors* 💳 *AE, D, DC, MC, V.*

$–$$$$ **The Paramount.** The Paramount caters to a somewhat bohemian,
Fodor'sChoice ★ fashionable, yet cost-conscious clientele. The tiny rooms have white furnishings and walls, gilt-framed headboards, and conical steel bathroom sinks. In the lobby, a sheer platinum wall and a glamorous sweep of staircase lead to the Mezzanine Restaurant, where you can enjoy cocktails or dinner while gazing down on the action below. The bar, once fiercely trendy, draws a somewhat diluted crowd now that other Whiskey Bars have opened in many of the W Hotels around town. Hotel drawbacks include limited room amenities and a sometimes harried staff. ✉ *235 W. 46th St., between Broadway and 8th Aves., Midtown West 10036* ☎ *212/764–5500 or 800/225–7474* 🖷 *212/354–5237* *590 rooms,*

10 suites ♨ *2 restaurants, café, room service, in-room data ports, in-room safes, minibars, cable TV, in-room VCRs, gym, 2 bars, dry cleaning, laundry service, concierge, Internet, business services, meeting rooms, no-smoking floors* ▭ *AE, D, DC, MC, V.*

$–$$$$ **The Time Hotel.** This spot half a block from the din of Times Square tempers trendiness with a touch of humor. A ridiculously futuristic glass elevator—eggshells line the bottom of the shaft—transports guests to the second-floor lobby. In the adjoining bar, nature videos lighten up the low-flung, serious gray-scale furnishings. The smallish guest rooms, each themed on one of the primary colors, have mood lighting and even specific aromas that create a unique, if contrived, hotel experience. Pino Luongo operates the popular Coco Pazzo Teatro restaurant on the first floor. ✉ *224 W. 49th St., between Broadway and 8th Ave., Midtown West 10019* ☎ *212/320–2900 or 877/846–3692* 📠 *212/245–2305* 🌐 *www.thetimeny.com* 🛏 *164 rooms, 30 suites* ♨ *Restaurant, room service, in-room data ports, in-room fax, in-room safes, minibars, refrigerators, cable TV with movies, gym, bar, dry cleaning, laundry service, concierge, business services, parking (fee), no-smoking floors* ▭ *AE, D, DC, MC, V.*

$$$ **Marriott Marquis.** This brash behemoth in the heart of the theater district is a place New Yorkers love to hate. With its own little city of restaurants, a sushi bar, shops, meeting rooms, and ballrooms—there's even a Broadway theater—it virtually defines "over-the-top." As at other Marriotts, all of the nearly 2,000 rooms here look alike and are pleasant and functional. Some have more dramatic urban views than others. The View, the revolving restaurant and bar on the 49th floor, provides one of the most spectacular panoramas in New York, but make a reservation to get in. ✉ *1535 Broadway, at W. 45th St., Midtown West 10036* ☎ *212/398–1900 or 800/843–4898* 📠 *212/704–8930 or 212/704–8931* 🌐 *www.marriott.com* 🛏 *1,889 rooms, 58 suites* ♨ *3 restaurants, café, coffee shop, room service, in-room data ports, in-room safes, minibars, cable TV with movies, exercise equipment, health club, hair salon, hot tub, massage, 3 bars, theater, baby-sitting, dry cleaning, laundry service, concierge, Internet, business services, meeting rooms, parking (fee), some pets allowed, no-smoking rooms* ▭ *AE, D, DC, MC, V.*

$$–$$$ **The Algonquin.** Even Matilda the resident cat, who holds court in the parlorlike lobby, seems to know that the draw here is the ghost of its literary past. The signed works of former Round Table raconteurs can be checked out of the library, while their witticisms grace guest room doors. Small and boxy, the rooms have a less than cheerful feel, but the hotel has recently been upgraded to meet a higher technological standard. The renowned Oak Room is one of the city's premier cabaret performance venues, and the publike Blue Bar makes visitors from around the world feel at home. ✉ *59 W. 44th St., between 5th and 6th Aves., Midtown West 10036* ☎ *212/840–6800 or 800/555–8000* 📠 *212/944–1419* 🌐 *www.algonquinhotel.com* 🛏 *150 rooms, 24 suites* ♨ *2 restaurants, room service, in-room data ports, in-room safes, cable TV with movies, gym, bar, cabaret, library, piano, dry cleaning, laundry service, concierge, Internet, business services, meeting rooms, parking (fee), no-smoking floors* ▭ *AE, D, DC, MC, V.*

$$–$$$ **Ameritania Hotel.** Guests at this busy crash pad just off Broadway are divided pretty evenly: half come for business, half for pleasure. Dimly lit hallways create a feeling of perpetual nighttime—an impression that lingers in the bedrooms, where black metal furniture dominates. The hotel's Bar 54 plays Top-40 music until 2 AM. Rates may drop by as much as $100 a night off-season, depending on occupancy. ✉ *230 W. 54th St., at Broadway, Midtown West 10019* ☎ *212/247–5000 or 888/664–6835* 📠 *212/247–3316* 🌐 *www.nychotels.com/ameritania.html*

195 rooms, 12 suites Restaurant, room service, in-room data ports, in-room safes, cable TV with movies, gym, bar, dry cleaning, laundry service, concierge, business services, parking (fee), no-smoking rooms AE, D, DC, MC, V.

$$–$$$ **The Gorham.** An inviting lobby with maple-panel walls, marble floors, Persian rugs, and potted plants sets the cosmopolitan mood for this midtown gem, which prides itself on its cozy breakfast room and sunny, immaculate gym. Fully equipped kitchenettes and work desks make the spacious rooms a bargain, whether or not you like the Euro-modern red-lacquer furniture and marbleized countertops. Bathrooms have their own phones and nifty digital water-temperature settings. The quietest rooms are in the front of the hotel, on West 55th Street. *136 W. 55th St., between 6th and 7th Aves., Midtown West 10019 212/245–1800 or 800/735–0710 212/582–8332 www.gorhamhotel.com 70 rooms, 45 suites Restaurant, room service, in-room data ports, in-room safes, kitchenettes, microwaves, cable TV with movies and video games, exercise equipment, gym, dry cleaning, laundry service, concierge, Internet, business services, meeting rooms, parking (fee), no-smoking rooms, no-smoking floors AE, DC, MC, V.*

$$–$$$ **Hilton New York.** New York City's largest hotel and the epicenter of the city's hotel-based conventions, the Hilton has a Vegas-size range of business facilities, eating establishments, and shops, all designed for convenience. Considering the size of this property, guest rooms are well maintained, and all have coffeemakers, hair dryers, and ironing boards. A variety of local ethnic cuisines is available at the New York Marketplace, a mall-style food court in the hotel lobby. *1335 6th Ave., between W. 53rd and W. 54th Sts., Midtown West 10019 212/586–7000 or 800/445–8667 212/315–1374 www.newyorktowers.hilton.com 2,079 rooms, 2 penthouses, 5 suites 2 restaurants, café, room service, in-room data ports, in-room safes, minibars, cable TV, gym, health club, hair salon, hot tub, massage, sauna, 2 bars, sports bar, shops, baby-sitting, dry cleaning, laundry service, concierge, concierge floors, business services, parking (fee) AE, D, DC, MC, V.*

★ $$–$$$ **The Michelangelo.** Italophiles will feel that they've been transported to the boot at this deluxe hotel, whose long, wide lobby lounge is clad with multihue marble and Veronese-style oil paintings. Upstairs, the decor of the relatively spacious rooms (averaging 475 square ft) varies. You can choose contemporary, neoclassic, art deco, or French country—but all have marble foyers and marble bathrooms equipped with bidets and oversize 55-gallon tubs. The larger rooms have sitting areas and king beds. Complimentary cappuccino, pastries, and other Italian treats are served each morning in the baroque lobby lounge. *152 W. 51st St., at 7th Ave., Midtown West 10019 212/765–1900 or 800/237–0990 212/581–7618 www.michelangelohotel.com 123 rooms, 55 suites Restaurant, room service, in-room data ports, in-room fax, in-room safes, minibars, cable TV with movies, in-room DVD players, exercise equipment, gym, bar, baby-sitting, dry cleaning, laundry service, concierge, business services, meeting rooms, parking (fee), no-smoking floors AE, D, DC, MC, V.*

$–$$$ **Sofitel New York.** The European hotel group's property is a dramatic, contemporary 30-story curved tower overlooking 5th Avenue. The place feels professional, with a spacious, quiet lobby, an elegant French brasserie (Gaby, named for a Parisian model who made a name for herself in the Big Apple in the 1920s), and courteous staff who are always on hand. Upstairs, the rooms are what you expect to find in a big corporate hotel—lots of earth tones and mahogany—but what they lack in aesthetics they more than make up for in amenities such as high-speed Internet access and plush bedding. *45 W. 44th St., between 5th and*

6th Aves., Midtown West 10036 ☎ *212/354–8844* 🖷 *212/782–3002* 🌐 *www.sofitel.com* *398 rooms, 52 suites* *Restaurant, room service, in-room data ports, minibars, cable TV with movies, gym, massage, piano bar, dry cleaning, laundry service, concierge, Internet, business services, meeting rooms, parking (fee), some pets allowed, no-smoking floors* 💳 *AE, D, DC, MC, V.*

$$ **Casablanca.** This Morocco comes by way of Disney: mosaic tiles, framed Berber scarves and rugs, and a mural of a North African city. Rattan furniture, ceiling fans, and Moroccan-style wood shutters dress up the smallish and mysteriously tatty rooms, which have elaborately tiled bathrooms. In the spacious lounge with a fireplace, a piano, a 41-inch movie screen, and bookshelves stocked with Bogart-abilia, join guests for the popular nightly wine and cheese fest and free Continental breakfast in the morning. The rooftop garden bar with views of the lights fantastic is one of the best outdoor spots in town. ✉ *147 W. 43rd St., between 6th Ave. and Broadway, Midtown West 10036* ☎ *212/869–1212 or 888/922–7225* 🖷 *212/391–7585* 🌐 *www.casablancahotel.com* *48 rooms, 5 suites* *Restaurant, room service, in-room data ports, in-room safes, minibars, refrigerators, cable TV, in-room VCRs, lounge, piano, baby-sitting, dry cleaning, laundry service, Internet, business services, meeting rooms, parking (fee), no-smoking floors* 💳 *AE, DC, MC, V.*

$$ **Essex House, a Westin Hotel.** The lobby of this stately Central Park South property is an art deco masterpiece, with inlaid marble floors and bas-relief elevator doors. Reproductions of Chippendale or Louis XIV antiques decorate guest rooms, all of which have marble baths—some with walk-in showers. Many rooms have breathtaking views of the park, and in-room extras include ironing facilities and personal fax-copier-printers. Michelin-starred chef Alain Ducasse opened his first Stateside restaurant here; the *New York Times* saw fit to bestow its rare four-star accolade. ✉ *160 Central Park S, between 6th and 7th Aves., Midtown West 10019* ☎ *212/247–0300 or 800/937–8461* 🖷 *212/315–1839* 🌐 *www.starwood.com* *516 rooms, 81 suites* *2 restaurants, room service, in-room data ports, in-room fax, in-room safes, minibars, cable TV with movies and video games, in-room VCRs, exercise equipment, gym, health club, spa, bar, baby-sitting, dry cleaning, laundry service, concierge, Internet, business services, meeting rooms, parking (fee), no-smoking rooms* 💳 *AE, D, DC, MC, V.*

$$ **Flatotel.** Its name gives it away. This 46-story tower started life as British-built condominium apartments (flats), but has been transformed into a hotel full of spacious, minimalist rooms. Quite recently, public spaces were glammed up as well. At cocktail time, the lobby lounge is a hub of genteel carousing; later, diners sup at the Milan-style Moda. The beds are custom-designed with attached night-lights and anchored at their feet by built-in drawers, and fitted with goose-down duvets and luxe linens. Bathrooms have oversize marble Jacuzzi tubs. ✉ *135 W. 52nd St., between 6th and 7th Aves., Midtown West 10019* ☎ *212/887–9400 or 800/352–8683* 🖷 *212/887–9442 for reservations; 212/887–9795 for guests* 🌐 *www.flatotel.com* *210 rooms, 70 suites* *Restaurant, room service, in-room data ports, in-room safes, kitchenettes, minibars, microwaves, refrigerators, cable TV, exercise equipment, gym, bar, concierge, Internet* 💳 *AE, DC, MC, V.*

$$ **Hilton Times Square.** The Hilton Times Square sits atop a 335,000-square-ft retail and entertainment complex that includes a 25-theater movie megaplex and Madame Tussaud's Wax Museum. The building has a handsome Mondrian-inspired facade, but room decor is chain-hotel bland. Nonetheless, the rooms are comfortable, with amenities from in-room coffeemakers to bathrobes. The hotel is efficiently run and the staff is pleasant. Because all guest rooms are above the 21st floor, many afford excellent views of Times Square and midtown. Chef Larry Forgione's Restaurant Above is off the "sky lobby" on the 21st floor. ✉ *234 W. 42nd St., between 7th and 8th Aves., Midtown West 10036* ☎ *212/642–2500 or 800/445–8667* 🖷 *212/840–5516* 🌐 *www.hilton.com* *444 rooms, 15 suites* *Restaurant, room service, in-room data ports, in-room safes, minibars, cable TV, gym, bar, laundry service, concierge, business services, meeting rooms, parking (fee)* ▭ *AE, D, DC, MC, V.*

$$ The Mansfield. Built in 1904 as lodging for distinguished bachelors, this small, clubby hotel has an Edwardian sensibility from the working fireplace in the lounge to the lobby's coffered ceiling and marble and cast-iron staircase. Rooms, with their black-marble bathrooms, dark-wood venetian blinds, and sleigh beds, never disappoint. And suites are especially grand. A machine dispenses complimentary cappuccino from 7 to 11 AM, and the hotel's swank M Bar serves cocktails, caviar, and desserts until 2 AM. For a romantic, if refined, getaway, ensconce yourself in the duplex penthouse suite. ✉ *12 W. 44th St., between 5th and 6th Aves., Midtown West 10036* ☎ *212/944–6050 or 800/255–5167* 🖷 *212/764–4477* 🌐 *www.mansfieldhotel.com* *124 rooms, 25 suites* *Room service, in-room data ports, in-room safes, cable TV, in-room VCRs, bar, library, dry cleaning, laundry service, concierge, Internet, business services, meeting rooms, parking (fee), some free parking, pets allowed, no-smoking rooms, no-smoking floors.* ▭ *AE, D, DC, MC, V.*

$$ Renaissance. This link in the chain is a business hotel, but vacationers often take advantage of its low promotional rates and its location at the head of Times Square. For the businessperson, each spacious and plush room comes with a work desk, a duo of two-line speakerphones, call waiting, a fax, and a voice-mail system. For the diva, the marble bathrooms have deep soaking tubs and a princess phone. Elevators lead from street level to the third-floor art deco–style reception area. On the second floor are two bars and Foley's Restaurant & Bar, a restaurant with up-close views of Times Square. ✉ *714 7th Ave., between W. 47th and W. 48th Sts., Midtown West 10036* ☎ *212/765–7676 or 800/628–5222* 🖷 *212/765–1962* 🌐 *www.renaissancehotels.com* *300 rooms, 5 suites* *Restaurant, room service, in-room data ports, in-room safes, minibars, cable TV with movies, in-room VCRs, exercise equipment, gym, massage, 2 bars, baby-sitting, dry cleaning, laundry service, concierge, Internet, business services, meeting rooms, parking (fee), some pets allowed (fee), no-smoking floors* ▭ *AE, D, DC, MC, V.*

$$ Rihga Royal. This discreet establishment—the only luxury all-suites hotel in Manhattan—has a loyal following among celebrities and business travelers. Each of its contemporary-style suites—many of them quite spacious—has a living room, bedroom, and large marble bath with glass-enclosed shower and separate tub. Some suites have French doors and bay windows, and the pricier Pinnacle Suites include CD players, cellular phones, printer-copiers, and even complimentary town-car service from and to airports. The hotel's spectacular Sunday brunch, served in the top-floor banquet rooms, has become a local favorite. ✉ *151 W. 54th St., between 6th and 7th Aves., Midtown West 10019* ☎ *212/307–5000 or 800/937–5454* 🖷 *212/765–6530* 🌐 *www.rihgaroyalny.com* *500 suites* *Restaurant, room service, in-room data ports, in-room fax, in-room safes, in-room hot tubs, kitchenettes, minibars, refrigerators, cable TV with movies and video games, in-room VCRs, gym, health club, massage, bar, baby-sitting, dry cleaning, laundry service, concierge, Internet, business services, meeting rooms, parking (fee), no-smoking floors* ▭ *AE, D, DC, MC, V.*

★ $$ **The Royalton.** During the '90s, the lobby craze of local media, music, and fashion fol boîtes. While many of the movers and sh imalist Philippe Starck space with its su ous Vodka Bar still gives off a cool vibe. custom-made bed, tasteful lighting, anc have working fireplaces, and all have stainless-steel and glass fixtures may also fea tubs. ✉ *44 W. 44th St., between 5th and 6th Aves., 10036* ☎ *212/869–4400 or 800/635–9013* 📠 *212/575–0012 ianschragerhotels.com* ⟹ *145 rooms, 23 suites* ⚐ *Restaurant, room service, in-room data ports, in-room safes, minibars, cable TV with movies, in-room VCRs, gym, massage, 2 bars, baby-sitting, dry cleaning, laundry service, concierge, business services, meeting rooms, parking (fee), some pets allowed, no-smoking rooms* ▭ *AE, D, DC, MC, V.*

$–$$ **Belvedere Hotel.** This affordable hotel has some fun with its art deco café and playful floor patterning, but the rooms are surprisingly conservative, with patterned bedspreads and curtains and traditional wooden headboards (an odd juxtaposition to the modern art prints on the walls). Still, the rooms are newly renovated and large enough for kitchenettes and two full beds if you need them (you can also request a queen- or king-size bed). Plenty of theaters and restaurants are nearby. ✉ *319 W. 48th St., between 8th and 9th Aves., Midtown West 10036* ☎ *212/245–7000 or 888/468–3558* 📠 *212/245–4455* 🌐 *www.newyorkhotel.com* ⟹ *398 rooms, 2 suites* ⚐ *Restaurant, café, in-room data ports, in-room safes, kitchenettes, microwaves, refrigerators, cable TV with movies and video games, shop, dry cleaning, laundry facilities, laundry service, concierge, Internet, business services, parking (fee)* ▭ *AE, D, MC, V.*

★ $–$$ **Broadway Inn.** In the heart of the theater district, this Midwestern-friendly B&B welcomes with a charmingly comfy brick-walled reception room with hump-backed sofa, bentwood chairs, fresh flowers, and stocked book shelves that encourage lingering. Impeccably clean neo-deco–style rooms with black-lacquer beds are basic, but cheerful. An extra $70 or $80 gets you a suite with an additional fold-out sofa bed, and a kitchenette hidden by closet doors. Single travelers can get their own room for as little as $89, which very well might be one of the best deals in town. ✉ *264 W. 46th St., between Broadway and 8th Ave., Midtown West 10036* ☎ *212/997–9200 or 800/826–6300* 📠 *212/768–2807* 🌐 *www.broadwayinn.com* ⟹ *28 rooms, 13 suites* ⚐ *Restaurant, some in-room data ports, some kitchenettes, some microwaves, refrigerators, cable TV, concierge, parking (fee), no-smoking rooms* ▭ *AE, D, DC, MC, V.*

$–$$ **Wellington Hotel.** This large, old-fashioned property's main advantages are reasonable prices and its proximity to Central Park and Carnegie Hall. The lobby has an aura of faded glamor, from the lighted-up red awning outside to the chandeliers and ornate artwork inside. The hotel appeals to families, groups, and those traveling on a budget. Rooms are small but clean, baths are serviceable, and the staff is helpful. ✉ *871 7th Ave., at W. 55th St., Midtown West 10019* ☎ *212/247–3900 or 800/652–1212* 📠 *212/581–1719* 🌐 *www.wellingtonhotel.com* ⟹ *500 rooms, 100 suites* ⚐ *Restaurant, coffee shop, in-room data ports, microwaves, cable TV with movies, hair salon, bar, laundry facilities, laundry service, parking (fee), no-smoking floors* ▭ *AE, D, DC, MC, V.*

¢–$$ **Quality Hotel and Suites.** This small prewar hotel shares its block with a plethora of Brazilian restaurants and is near many theaters and Rockefeller Center. The peculiar lobby has a narrow corridor that snakes off around a corner and is decorated with some rather handsome art deco Bakelite lamps. The rooms are very plain, but most are well maintained and clean. This block is one of midtown's most deserted at night, so travelers should be alert. ⊠ *59 W. 46th St., between 5th and 6th Aves., Midtown West 10036* ☎ *212/790–2710 or 800/567–7720* 🖷 *212/290–2760* 🌐 *www.applecorehotels.com* ⇨ *209 rooms* ☞ *Cafeteria, in-room data ports, in-room safes, cable TV with movies and video games, hair salon, bar, business services, meeting rooms, parking (fee), no-smoking rooms* ▭ *AE, D, DC, MC, V.*

$ **Hotel Edison.** This offbeat old hotel is a popular budget stop for tour groups from both the United States and abroad. The simple, serviceable guest rooms are clean and fresh, but the bathrooms tend to show their age. The loan-shark murder scene in *The Godfather* was shot in what is now Sophia's restaurant, and the pink-and-blue plaster Edison Café, known half jokingly as the Polish Tea Room, is a theater-crowd landmark consistently recognized as New York City's best coffee shop. ⊠ *228 W. 47th St., between Broadway and 8th Ave., Midtown West 10036* ☎ *212/840–5000 or 800/637–7070* 🖷 *212/596–6850* 🌐 *www.edisonhotelnyc.com* ⇨ *770 rooms, 30 suites* ☞ *Restaurant, coffee shop, cable TV, gym, 2 bars, dry cleaning, Internet, business services, meeting rooms, airport shuttle, parking (fee), no-smoking floors* ▭ *AE, D, DC, MC, V.*

¢–$ **Portland Square Hotel.** You can't beat this theater district old-timer for value, given its clean, simple rooms that invite with flower-print bedspreads and curtains. James Cagney once lived in the building, and—as the story goes—a few of his Radio City Rockette acquaintances lived upstairs. *Life* magazine used to have its offices here, and everything from the gilt-edged entryway to the original detailing evokes old New York. There are no no-smoking rooms, but if you check into one with a smoky scent, they'll move you to another. Rooms on the east wing have oversize bathrooms. ⊠ *132 W. 47th St., between 6th and 7th Aves., Midtown West 10036* ☎ *212/382–0600 or 800/388–8988* 🖷 *212/382–0684* 🌐 *www.portlandsquarehotel.com* ⇨ *142 rooms, 112 with bath* ☞ *In-room safes, cable TV, gym, laundry facilities, Internet, business services* ▭ *AE, MC, V.*

Midtown East

$$$$ **The Drake.** Off Park Avenue in the center of corporate Manhattan, this Swissôtel property caters to business travelers with modern, comfortable rooms that are a cut above the average corporate variety. The deco-style accommodations are a welcome alternative to the traditional look of many hotels in this price category. The Q-56 restaurant is sleek and contemporary, and a branch of Fauchon—the first time this luxury food emporium has ventured beyond Paris—has a shop and a lovely tearoom off the lobby. ⊠ *440 Park Ave., at E. 56th St., Midtown East 10022* ☎ *212/421–0900 or 800/372–5369* 🖷 *212/371–4190* 🌐 *www.swissotel.com* ⇨ *387 rooms, 109 suites* ☞ *Restaurant, tea shop, room service, in-room data ports, in-room fax, in-room safes, minibars, some refrigerators, cable TV with movies, gym, health club, massage, sauna, spa, steam room, bar, baby-sitting, dry cleaning, laundry service, concierge, Internet, business services, meeting rooms, parking (fee), some pets allowed* ▭ *AE, D, DC, MC, V.*

$$$$ Fodor's Choice ★ **Four Seasons.** Architect I. M. Pei designed this limestone-clad stepped spire amid the prime shops of 57th Street. Everything here comes in epic proportions—from the rooms averaging 600 square ft (and *starting* at $595) to the sky-high Grand Foyer, with French limestone pillars, marble, onyx, and acre upon acre of blond wood. The soundproof guest rooms have 10-ft-high ceilings, enormous English sycamore walk-in clos-

KEEP AN EYE ON

THE LAST DECADE may go down in architectural history as a period when New York hotel construction reached a pitch rivaling the Gilded and Jazz Ages' love for grand public spaces. But as room rates are slashed in a slow economy, developers are losing interest, and the boom has finally begun to bust. While 2002 saw 14 new hotels, in 2003 there were only about four.

*Pickings for 2004 look slim indeed. In late 2003, the trendy Meatpacking District will receive its first hotel, the **Hotel Gansevoort.** But several projects that had design-savvy New Yorkers very excited, including a new Andre Balas hotel on Grand Street, have been called off. Ian Schrager's Rem Koolhaas–designed stainless-steel edifice on Astor Place, which had been heralded with messianic fervor, now seems less likely to happen. There will be one last hurrah, however: the 250-room **Mandarin Oriental Hotel.** This luxe hotel will occupy the north tower of the gargantuan AOL/Time Warner building at Columbus Circle, one of the largest, most obsessively watched construction projects New York has seen in decades. The Mandarin Oriental will have a 6,000-square-ft ballroom overlooking Central Park and a Jean-Georges Vongerichten steak house. The complex will also host Jazz at Lincoln Center and a movie multiplex.*

ets, and blond-marble bathrooms with tubs that fill in 60 seconds. If you really want epic, a night in the new duplex presidential suite may run to $20,000. ✉ *57 E. 57th St., between Park and Madison Aves., Midtown East 10022* ☎ *212/758–5700 or 800/487–3769* 🖷 *212/758–5711* 🌐 *www.fourseasons.com* *310 rooms, 62 suites* *Restaurant, room service, in-room data ports, in-room fax, in-room safes, minibars, some microwaves, cable TV with movies and video games, in-room VCRs, gym, health club, massage, sauna, spa, steam room, bar, lobby lounge, piano, baby-sitting, dry cleaning, laundry service, concierge, business services, meeting rooms, car rental, parking (fee), some pets allowed, no-smoking floors* 💳 *AE, D, DC, MC, V.*

$$$$ **The Peninsula.** Step past the beaux arts facade of this 1905 gem and into the luxurious lobby with original art nouveau accents. Guest rooms, many with sweeping views down 5th Avenue, have a modern sensibility. King-size beds have formal covers that are ingeniously tucked away in built-in drawers. The high-tech amenities are excellent, from a bedside console that controls the lighting, sound, and thermostat for the room to a TV mounted over the tub for bath-time viewing (in all but standard rooms). The rooftop health club, indoor pool, and seasonal open-air bar—which is something of a local hot spot—all have dazzling views of midtown. ✉ *700 5th Ave., at E. 55th St., Midtown East 10019* ☎ *212/247–2200 or 800/262–9467* 🖷 *212/903–3943* 🌐 *www.peninsula.com* *185 rooms, 54 suites* *2 restaurants, room service, in-room data ports, in-room fax, in-room safes, minibars, cable TV with movies, indoor pool, gym, health club, hot tub, massage, sauna, spa, steam room, 2 bars, lobby lounge, dry cleaning, laundry service, concierge, business services, meeting rooms, parking (fee), some pets allowed, no-smoking floors* 💳 *AE, D, DC, MC, V.*

$$$–$$$$ **Omni Berkshire Place.** Omni Berkshire's East Coast flagship hotel brings sophistication to the Omni name. Although the reception area is less than inviting, a dramatic, two-story atrium lounge with a fireplace, an elaborately stained dark-wood floor, and a piano more than compensates. The spacious guest rooms (all of them 375 square ft) have a contemporary, Asian-influenced simplicity as well as plush bedding, tasteful furnishings, spacious bathrooms, and Web TV. Kids receive their own welcome bag of treats. *21 E. 52nd St., between 5th and Madison Aves., Midtown East 10022 212/753–5800 or 800/843–6664 212/754–5020 www.omnihotels.com 396 rooms, 47 suites Restaurant, room service, in-room data ports, in-room fax, in-room safes, minibars, cable TV with movies and video games, exercise equipment, health club, massage, bar, baby-sitting, dry cleaning, laundry facilities, laundry service, concierge, Internet, business services, meeting rooms, parking (fee), some pets allowed (fee), no-smoking floors AE, D, DC, MC, V.*

★ $$$–$$$$ **The St. Regis.** A one-of-a-kind New York classic, this 5th Avenue beaux arts landmark is a hive of activity in its unparalleled public spaces. The King Cole Bar is an institution in itself with its famous Maxfield Parrish mural. Even the elevators have crystal chandeliers. Guest rooms, all serviced by accommodating butlers, are straight out of the American Movie Channel, with high ceilings, crystal chandeliers, silk wall coverings, Louis XV antiques, and world-class amenities such as Tiffany silver services. Marble bathrooms, with tubs, stall showers, and double sinks, are outstanding. *2 E. 55th St., at 5th Ave., Midtown East 10022 212/753–4500 or 800/325–3589 212/787–3447 www.stregis.com 222 rooms, 92 suites 2 restaurants, room service, in-room data ports, in-room fax, in-room safes, minibars, cable TV, in-room VCRs, gym, health club, hair salon, massage, bar, shops, baby-sitting, dry cleaning, laundry service, concierge, business services, meeting rooms, parking (fee), no-smoking rooms, no-smoking floors AE, D, DC, MC, V.*

$$–$$$$ **The Dylan.** This 1903 beaux arts–style building with ornate plasterwork on its facade and a stunning marble staircase spiraling up its three floors once housed the Chemists Club. The 11-ft ceilings give the modern guest rooms a touch of grandeur, and the Carrara cut-marble bathrooms show the hotel's opulent intentions. Soaring columns and vaulted ceilings make the splendid Alchemy Suite—built in the 1930s to replicate a medieval laboratory—a Gothic confection. *52 E. 41st St., between Park and Madison Aves., Midtown East 10017 212/338–0500 212/338–0569 www.dylanhotel.com 107 rooms, 2 suites Restaurant, in-room data ports, in-room safes, minibars, health club, bar, concierge, business services, meeting rooms AE, D, DC, MC, V.*

$$–$$$$ **New York Palace.** Connected mansions built in the 1880s by railroad baron Henry Villard make up this palatial hotel. Entering through a gated courtyard, guests can dine at perhaps the city's most famous restaurant, the five-star Le Cirque 2000. The lobby, with its sweeping staircases and arched colonnades fit for royalty, is host to the stunning New American restaurant Istana. The tower provides a choice of glamorous deco-style guest rooms or traditional Empire-style rooms. For terrific views of St. Patrick's Cathedral head to the 7,000-square-ft health club, where TVs with videos and headphones await at every treadmill. *455 Madison Ave., at E. 50th St., Midtown East 10022 212/888–7000 or 800/697–2522 212/303–6000 www.newyorkpalace.com 797 rooms, 100 suites 2 restaurants, room service, in-room data ports, in-room fax, in-room safes, minibars, some refrigerators, cable TV with movies, health club, massage, spa, 2 bars, baby-sitting, dry cleaning, laundry service, concierge, concierge floors, business services, meeting rooms, park-*

ing (fee), some pets allowed, no-smoking rooms, no-smoking floors ▭ *AE, D, DC, MC, V.*

$$–$$$$ **Sherry-Netherland.** The marble-lined lobby of this grande dame wows with fine, hand-loomed carpets, crystal chandeliers, and wall friezes from the Vanderbilt mansion. The enormous, utterly luxurious suites—some with unsurpassed midtown views—have separate living and dining areas, serving pantries, decorative fireplaces, antiques, and glorious marble baths. All rooms are individually decorated. The cramped and stupendously expensive Harry Cipriani's provides room service (a liter of water costs about $20). Continental breakfast is complimentary for guests, and at lunch it's the best people-watching in town. ✉ *781 5th Ave., at E. 59th St., Midtown East 10022* ☎ *212/355–2800 or 800/247–4377* 🖷 *212/319–4306* 🌐 *www.sherrynetherland.com* *40 rooms, 35 suites* *Restaurant, room service, in-room safes, refrigerators, cable TV, in-room VCRs, gym, hair salon, massage, bar, dry cleaning, laundry service, concierge, Internet, business services, meeting rooms, parking (fee)* ▭ *AE, D, DC, MC, V.*

$$–$$$$ **W New York.** This W brought nature to midtown with calming earth tones and flowing curtains meant to conjure up the wind. Vast floor-to-ceiling windows pour sunlight into the airy lobby, where a fireplace and bar flank a sunken sitting area. Although tiny, the rooms display custom craftsmanship in natural materials, and soothe with feather beds and CD players. In the slate-floor baths, not a sliver of the all-too-familiar polished marble is to be found. Downstairs, Heartbeat Restaurant serves heart-healthy foods; a mezzanine dining area makes breakfast a quick buffet affair. In the attached Whiskey Blue you'll find a young, hip, and moneyed crowd. ✉ *541 Lexington Ave., between E. 49th and E. 50th Sts., Midtown East 10022* ☎ *212/755–1200 or 877/946–8357* 🖷 *212/319–8344* 🌐 *www.whotels.com* *551 rooms, 62 suites* *Restaurant, snack bar, room service, in-room data ports, in-room fax, in-room safes, minibars, cable TV with movies, health club, massage, spa, steam room, bar, lobby lounge, dry cleaning, laundry facilities, laundry service, concierge, business services, meeting rooms, no-smoking floors* ▭ *AE, D, DC, MC, V.*

$–$$$$ **Waldorf-Astoria.** The lobby of this landmark 1931 art deco masterpiece, full of murals, mosaics, and elaborate plaster ornamentation, features a grand piano once owned by Cole Porter and still played daily. Astoria-level rooms have the added advantages of great views, fax machines, and access to the Astoria lounge, where a lovely, free afternoon tea is served. The Bull and Bear Bar is a 1940s throwback complete with cigar smoke, miniature soda bottles, and no-nonsense barkeeps. Well known to U.S. presidents and other international luminaries, the ultra-exclusive Waldorf Towers (the 28th floor and above) has a separate entrance and management. ✉ *301 Park Ave., between E. 49th and E. 50th Sts., Midtown East 10022* ☎ *212/355–3000 or 800/925–3673* 🖷 *212/872–7272* 🌐 *www.waldorfastoria.com* *1,176 rooms, 276 suites* *4 restaurants, room service, in-room data ports, in-room fax, some in-room safes, minibars, refrigerators, cable TV with movies, gym, health club, hair salon, massage, sauna, steam room, 3 bars, shops, babysitting, dry cleaning, laundry service, concierge, concierge floors, business services, meeting rooms, parking (fee), some pets allowed, no-smoking floors* ▭ *AE, D, DC, MC, V.*

$$$ **Crowne Plaza at the United Nations.** This 20-story building built in 1931 is in historic Tudor City, a stone's throw from the United Nations and Grand Central Terminal. Interior spaces are classic and unassuming, with marble floors, handmade carpets, and hardwood reproduction furniture upholstered in brocades and velvets. The traditional, well-kept rooms all come with irons, ironing boards, and coffeemakers. With a guest coupon, you can get a free drink at the bar. ✉ *304 E. 42nd St., between 1st and 2nd Aves., Midtown East 10017* ☎ *212/986–8800 or 800/879–8836* 🖷 *212/297–3440* 🌐 *www.united-nations.crowneplaza.com* *300 rooms, 12 suites* *Restaurant, room service, in-room data ports, in-room safes, minibars, cable TV, exercise equipment, gym, massage, sauna, spa, bar, lounge, baby-sitting, dry cleaning, laundry service, concierge, Internet, business services, meeting rooms, parking (fee), some pets allowed (fee), no-smoking rooms* 💳 *AE, D, DC, MC, V.*

$$$ **The Regency.** Rough-hewn travertine punctuated by Regency-style furnishings, potted palms, and burnished gold sconces lines an understated lobby—the better to cloak heads of state and other VIP guests in modesty. Guest rooms have taupe-color silk wallpaper, velvet throw pillows, and polished Honduran mahogany, but the smallish bathrooms with their marble countertops are unspectacular. Goose-down duvets and ergonomic leather desk chairs reinforce the pleasingly modern feel. Feinstein's at the Regency hosts some of the hottest (and priciest) cabaret acts in town, and 540 Park has become a destination in its own right among restaurant-savvy locals. ✉ *540 Park Ave., at E. 61st St., Midtown East 10021* ☎ *212/759–4100 or 800/235–6397* 🖷 *212/826–5674* 🌐 *www.loewshotels.com* *266 rooms, 86 suites* *Restaurant, room service, in-room data ports, in-room fax, in-room safes, some kitchenettes, minibars, refrigerators, cable TV with movies, in-room VCRs, gym, hair salon, massage, sauna, bar, lobby lounge, cabaret, baby-sitting, dry cleaning, laundry service, concierge, business services, meeting rooms, parking (fee), some pets allowed, no-smoking floors* 💳 *AE, D, DC, MC, V.*

$$–$$$ **Beekman Tower.** Three blocks north of the United Nations, this jazzy hotel is an art deco architectural landmark. Its swanky Top of the Towers lounge, a rooftop bar with live piano, is a superb place to take in the view of the East River and beyond; downstairs, the Zephyr Grill looks out on 1st Avenue. Suites, which range from studios to one-bedrooms, are all very spacious, and all have kitchens. Rooms are attractively decorated with chintz and dark-wood furniture, and all have separate sitting areas. The one-bedroom suites have dining tables as well. ✉ *3 Mitchell Pl., at 1st Ave. and E. 49th St., Midtown East 10017* ☎ *212/320–8018 or 800/637–8483* 🖷 *212/465–3697* 🌐 *www.mesuite.com* *174 suites* *2 restaurants, room service, in-room data ports, in-room fax, in-room safes, kitchenettes, minibars, microwaves, cable TV, exercise equipment, gym, sauna, 2 bars, lounge, piano bar, dry cleaning, laundry facilities, laundry service, concierge, Internet, business services, meeting rooms, parking (fee), no-smoking floors* 💳 *AE, D, DC, MC, V.*

$$–$$$ **The Benjamin.** From the elegant marble-and-silver lobby with 30-ft ceilings and a sweeping staircase to the high-tech argon gas–filled windows that reduce street noises to near whispers, this place pleases in ways seen and unseen. Rooms are done in warm beiges and golds, custom mattresses and Frette linens make up the beds, and extensive in-room offices come with personalized business cards. Bathrooms are disappointingly small, but you might be too busy eating at Larry Forgione's An American Place, choosing from the "pillow menu," or being pampered at the on-site Woodstock Spa to notice. ✉ *125 E. 50th St., at Lexington Ave., Midtown East 10022* ☎ *212/715–2500 or 888/423–6526* 🖷 *212/715–2525* 🌐 *www.thebenjamin.com* *109 rooms, 100 suites* *Restaurants, room service, in-room data ports, in-room safes, minibars, cable TV, gym, health club, massage, spa, bar, baby-sitting, dry cleaning, laundry service, concierge, concierge floors, business services, meeting rooms, parking (fee)* 💳 *AE, D, DC, MC, V.*

★ **$$–$$$** **Library Hotel.** This handsome landmark building (1900) gets its intellectual inspiration from the nearby New York Public Library. Each of its 10 floors is dedicated to one of the 10 categories of the Dewey

Decimal System (such as technology or literature) with modern rooms stocked with art and books relevant to a subtopic (such as medicine or poetry). Neil Armstrong's preference is the astronomy room; a green thumb might choose Room 500.004, the botany room. The property delivers tremendous comfort, and you can unwind in front of the fire in the library or relax in the roof garden. Continental breakfast is complimentary. ✉ *299 Madison Ave., at E. 41st St., Midtown East 10017* ☎ *212/983–4500 or 877/793–7323* 🖷 *212/499–9099* 🌐 *www.libraryhotel.com* *60 rooms* *Restaurant, room service, in-room data ports, in-room safes, minibars, cable TV with movies, in-room VCRs, massage, bar, 3 lounges, baby-sitting, dry cleaning, laundry service, concierge, Internet, business services, meeting rooms, parking (fee), no-smoking floors* 💳 *AE, DC, MC, V.*

$$–$$$ **Millennium Hotel New York UN Plaza.** A name change and major renovation have modernized this sky-high tower near the United Nations. Rooms, which begin on the 28th floor, command breathtaking views, make generous use of warm woods and neutral tones, and have an array of up-to-the-minute telecommunications gadgets. The multilingual staff caters to a discerning clientele that includes heads of state. The views also dazzle from the elegant 27th-floor pool and health club, and the rooftop tennis court attracts name players. Service throughout the hotel is first-rate, and the business center is open until 11 PM. ✉ *1 United Nations Plaza, at E. 44th St. and 1st Ave., Midtown East 10017* ☎ *212/758–1234 or 800/222–8888* 🖷 *212/702–5051* 🌐 *www.millenniumhotels.com* *387 rooms, 40 suites* *Restaurant, room service, in-room data ports, in-room fax, in-room safes, some kitchens, minibars, cable TV with movies, tennis court, indoor pool, health club, massage, sauna, bar, shop, baby-sitting, dry cleaning, laundry service, concierge, business services, meeting rooms, parking (fee), no-smoking floors* 💳 *AE, D, DC, MC, V.*

$$–$$$ **Plaza Fifty.** This hotel has a distinctly businesslike mood—witness the granite-wall lobby outfitted with mirrors, stainless steel, and leather furniture—but it's also supremely comfortable. The spacious rooms and suites have a clean, modern design with abstract art and oversize chairs and couches. There's no restaurant in the hotel, but a restaurant next door provides room service 5 PM–10:30 PM. ✉ *155 E. 50th St., at 3rd Ave., Midtown East 10022* ☎ *212/751–5710 or 800/637–8483* 🖷 *212/753–1468* 🌐 *www.mesuite.com* *74 rooms, 138 suites* *Room service, in-room data ports, in-room fax, in-room safes, kitchens, microwaves, refrigerators, cable TV, exercise equipment, gym, hair salon, dry cleaning, laundry facilities, laundry service, concierge, Internet, business services, meeting rooms, parking (fee), no-smoking floors* 💳 *AE, D, DC, MC, V.*

$$ **Hotel Elysée.** Best known as the site of the Monkey Bar, a legendary watering hole, this intimate, Euro-style hotel has relatively affordable rates, given its location. All guests have access to the comfortable Club Room, where complimentary coffee, tea, and snacks are available all day. You can grab a breakfast pastry there in the morning and free wine and hors d'oeuvres on weeknights—a blessing, since room service is limited and there are no minibars in the guest rooms. Many of the old-world guest rooms have terraces; request one far in advance. ✉ *60 E. 54th St., between Madison and Park Aves., Midtown East 10022* ☎ *212/753–1066 or 800/535–9733* 🖷 *212/980–9278* 🌐 *www.elyseehotel.com* *89 rooms, 12 suites* *Restaurant, room service, in-room data ports, in-room safes, some kitchenettes, microwaves, refrigerators, cable TV, in-room VCRs, massage, bar, piano, baby-sitting, dry cleaning, laundry service, concierge, Internet, business services, meeting rooms, parking (fee), no-smoking floors* 💳 *AE, DC, MC, V.*

$–$$ **The Fitzpatrick Manhattan Hotel.** This cozy hotel south of Bloomingdale's brings Irish charm to the New York hotel scene, which might explain why Gregory Peck, Liam Neeson, various Kennedys, Sinead O'Connor, and the Chieftains have all been guests. More than half of the units are suites, and all have emerald carpets and traditional darkwood furniture. Guests have free access to the Excelsior Athletic Club next door. Fitzer's, the publike bar at the heart of the hotel, is as welcoming as any in Dublin. ✉ *687 Lexington Ave., at E. 57th St., Midtown East 10022* ☎ *212/355–0100 or 800/367–7701* 🖷 *212/355–1371* 🌐 *www.fitzpatrickhotels.com* *42 rooms, 50 suites* *Restaurant, room service, in-room data ports, some in-room safes, some kitchenettes, minibars, some refrigerators, cable TV, health club, massage, bar, pub, baby-sitting, dry cleaning, laundry service, concierge, business services, meeting rooms, airport shuttle, parking (fee), no-smoking rooms* 💳 *AE, D, DC, MC, V.*

$–$$ **The Melrose Hotel New York.** A women's residence club from 1927 to 1981, the Melrose, formerly the Barbizon, was home at various times to Grace Kelly, Joan Crawford, and Liza Minelli. The lobby has a beautiful marble-and-limestone floor and gilt chairs with mohair upholstery. Guest rooms, decorated in shades of shell-pink or celadon, are modest but pleasant. The on-site health club has a lap pool. Since most rooms are minuscule, ask for one of the few larger ones when booking; some tower suites have balconies. If you want space at any cost, ask for the penthouse suite, which has a lovely view of Central Park. ✉ *140 E. 63rd St., at Lexington Ave., Midtown East 10021* ☎ *212/838–5700 or 800/635–7673* 🖷 *212/888–4271* 🌐 *www.melrosehotel.com* *274 rooms, 32 suites* *Café, room service, in-room data ports, in-room safes, some in-room hot tubs, minibars, cable TV, some in-room VCRs, indoor pool, health club, hair salon, massage, spa, bar, baby-sitting, dry cleaning, laundry service, concierge, business services, parking (fee), no-smoking rooms* 💳 *AE, D, DC, MC, V.*

★ $–$$ **Roger Smith.** The elusive Roger Smith (see if *you* can find out who he is) lends his name to this colorful boutique hotel and adjacent gallery. Riotous murals cover the walls in Lily's, the café. The art-filled rooms are homey and comfortable, and some have stocked bookshelves and fireplaces. An eclectic mix of room service is provided by five local restaurants. Guests have access to the nearby New York Sports Club ($10 fee). Rates can drop by as much as $75 per night in winter and summer, so ask when booking. A complimentary Continental breakfast is included. ✉ *501 Lexington Ave., between E. 47th and E. 48th Sts., Midtown East 10017* ☎ *212/755–1400 or 800/445–0277* 🖷 *212/758–4061* 🌐 *www.rogersmith.com* *102 rooms, 28 suites* *Restaurant, room service, in-room data ports, some kitchenettes, refrigerators, cable TV with movies and video games, massage, bar, baby-sitting, dry cleaning, laundry service, Internet, meeting rooms, parking (fee), some pets allowed, no-smoking floors* 💳 *AE, D, DC, MC, V.*

$ **Pickwick Arms Hotel.** This no-frills but convenient East Side establishment is regularly booked solid by bargain hunters. Privations you endure to save a buck start and end with the lilliputian size of some rooms, all of which have cheap-looking furnishings. However, some rooms look over the Manhattan skyline, and all are renovated on a regular basis. There's also a rooftop garden. ✉ *230 E. 51st St., between 2nd and 3rd Aves., Midtown East 10022* ☎ *212/355–0300 or 800/742–5945* 🖷 *212/755–5029* 🌐 *www.pickwickarms.com* *360 rooms, 175 with bath* *Café, in-room data ports, some refrigerators, cable TV, bar, airport shuttle, parking (fee)* 💳 *AE, DC, MC, V.*

¢–$ **Vanderbilt YMCA.** Of the various Manhattan Ys that provide overnight accommodations, this one has the best facilities, including a full-scale fitness center. Rooms are little more than dormitory-style a bed (bunks in doubles), dresser drawer, and TV; singl Only six rooms have phones and private baths (these cos communal showers and toilets are clean. The Turtle Bay neig is safe and convenient; Grand Central Terminal and the United are both a few blocks away. ✉ *224 E. 47th St., between 2nd a Aves., Midtown East 10017* ☎ *212/756–9600* 🖷 *212/752–0210* 🌐 *ymcanyc.org* 🛏 *375 rooms, 6 with bath* ♨ *Restaurant, refrigera 2 indoor pools, fitness classes, gym, health club, hot tub, massag sauna, steam room, basketball, volleyball, laundry facilities, meeting rooms, airport shuttle; no phones in some rooms* 💳 *AE, D, MC, V.*

Upper East Side

$$$$ **The Carlyle.** European tradition and Manhattan swank come together at New York's most lovable grand hotel. Everything about this Madison Avenue landmark suggests refinement, from the Mark Hampton–designed rooms, with their fine antique furniture and artfully framed Audubons and botanicals, to the first-rate service. Cabaret luminaries Barbara Cook and Bobby Short take turns holding court at the clubby Café Carlyle, but the canny Peter Mintun steals the show at Bemelmans Bar, named after the illustrator responsible for the bar's wall murals and the beloved children's book character, Madeline. ✉ *35 E. 76th St., between Madison and Park Aves., Upper East Side 10021* 🖷 *212/717–5737* 🌐 *www.thecarlyle.com* 🛏 *145 rooms, 45 suites* ♨ *Restaurant, café, room service, in-room data ports, in-room safes, some in-room hot tubs, kitchenettes, minibars, microwaves, cable TV, in-room VCRs, gym, health club, massage, spa, bar, dry cleaning, laundry service, concierge, business services, meeting room, parking (fee), some pets allowed, no-smoking floors* 💳 *AE, DC, MC, V.*

Fodor'sChoice ★

$$$$ **The Lowell.** This old-money refuge was built as an upscale apartment hotel in the 1920s and still delivers genteel sophistication. Guest rooms, most of which are suites, have all the civilized comforts of home, including stocked bookshelves and even umbrellas. Thirty-three of the suites have working fireplaces, and 10 have private terraces, the better for spying on posh neighboring abodes. A gym suite has its own fitness center, and a garden suite has two beautifully planted terraces. The Pembroke Room serves a fine afternoon tea, and the Post House serves some of the best steaks in town. ✉ *28 E. 63rd St., between Madison and Park Aves., Upper East Side 10021* ☎ *212/838–1400 or 800/221–4444* 🖷 *212/319–4230* 🌐 *www.lhw.com* 🛏 *21 rooms, 47 suites* ♨ *2 restaurants, room service, in-room data ports, in-room fax, in-room safes, kitchenettes, minibars, refrigerators, cable TV, in-room VCRs, exercise equipment, health club, massage, bar, baby-sitting, dry cleaning, laundry service, concierge, Internet, business services, parking (fee), some pets allowed* 💳 *AE, D, DC, MC, V.*

Fodor'sChoice ★

$$$$ **Hotel Plaza Athénée.** At this elegant French property in a building of a certain age, no two rooms share the same floor plan and all have ample space. Even the most modest rooms have sitting areas with inviting sofas, and generous closet space. Handsomely furnished suites come with dining tables or dining rooms, and 12 suites have balconies. Rooms above the 12th floor have over-the-rooftops views. The revamped cocktail lounge is a romantic Moroccan fantasy, and the restaurant Arabelle serves world-class food. Ask about weekend packages, which can be much less expensive than the standard rates. ✉ *37 E. 64th St., at Madison Ave., Upper East Side 10021* ☎ *212/734–9100 or 800/447–8800* 🖷 *212/772–0958* 🌐 *www.plaza-athenee.com* 🛏 *117 rooms, 35 suites* ♨ *Restaurant, room service, in-room data ports, some in-room faxes, in-room* *itchenettes, minibars, refrigerators, cable TV, exercise ..., massage, bar, lounge, baby-sitting, dry cleaning, laun... ...erge, Internet, business services, meeting rooms, park... ... allowed, no-smoking floors* ▭ *AE, D, DC, MC, V.* ...mber of the Mandarin Oriental hotel group, the ...is "No jacket, no tie, no attitude," is refreshingly ...onsidering its luxurious atmosphere. An art deco mar... ...eads into a clubby bar where even lone women travelers feel ...ortable, and to the Mark's restaurant, where afternoon tea is served. Elegant bedrooms have English and Italian furnishings and prints, Frette linens, and deep soaking tubs in the sleek marble bathrooms. Special touches here include hidden pantries with small kitchenettes in many of the rooms, a free shuttle to Wall Street, and free cell phones. ✉ *25 E. 77th St., at Madison Ave., Upper East Side 10021* ☎ *212/744–4300 or 800/843–6275* 📠 *212/472–5714* 🌐 *www.mandarinoriental.com* ☞ *123 rooms, 54 suites* ♖ *Restaurant, room service, in-room data ports, in-room fax, in-room safes, some kitchenettes, minibars, cable TV, in-room VCRs, exercise equipment, health club, massage, sauna, steam room, bar, baby-sitting, dry cleaning, laundry service, concierge, Internet, business services, meeting rooms, parking (fee), some free parking, some pets allowed, no-smoking floors* ▭ *AE, D, DC, MC, V.*

$$–$$$$ **The Pierre.** The Pierre remains a grand presence among the Four Seasons hotel group's properties, all of which are known for their exceptional service (the staff will scan an image for a business presentation or hand wash your delicates). As ornate as the Four Seasons hotel on 57th Street is minimalist, the Pierre's landmark building owes a lot to the Palace of Versailles, with chandeliers, murals depicting putti, and Corinthian columns in the Rotunda lounge. Chintz and dark wood adorn the grand and traditional guest rooms, whose gleaming black-and-white art deco bathrooms are spacious for New York. ✉ *2 E. 61st St., between 5th and Madison Aves., Upper East Side 10021* ☎ *212/838–8000 or 800/332–3442* 📠 *212/758–1615* 🌐 *www.fshr.com* ☞ *149 rooms, 52 suites* ♖ *2 restaurants, room service, in-room data ports, in-room safes, minibars, cable TV, exercise equipment, health club, hair salon, massage, bar, baby-sitting, dry cleaning, laundry service, concierge, Internet, business services, meeting rooms, travel services, parking (fee), some pets allowed, no-smoking floors* ▭ *AE, D, DC, MC, V.*

$$–$$$ **Hotel Wales.** Every effort has been made to retain the turn-of-the-20th-century mood of this 1901 Carnegie Hill landmark—from the cavernous lobby to the Pied Piper parlor, where vintage children's illustrations cover the walls. A $10 European-style breakfast is served in the parlor, along with free coffee and cappuccino. Guest rooms are small and show signs of wear and tear, but they do have fine oak woodwork, and all are equipped with CD players. Most of the suites face Madison Avenue. ✉ *1295 Madison Ave., between E. 92nd and E. 93rd Sts., Upper East Side 10128* ☎ *212/876–6000 or 877/847–4444* 📠 *212/860–7000* 🌐 *www.waleshotel.com* ☞ *46 rooms, 41 suites* ♖ *2 restaurants, room service, in-room safes, some kitchenettes, minibars, cable TV with video games, in-room VCRs, exercise equipment, bar, baby-sitting, dry cleaning, laundry service, Internet, business services, parking (fee), some pets allowed, no-smoking floors* ▭ *AE, D, DC, MC, V.*

$ **The Franklin.** The Upper East Side's hippest, funkiest hotel has a pint-size lobby decorated with black granite, brushed steel, and cherrywood. Most rooms are also tiny (some measure 100 square ft), but what they lack in size they make up for in style: all have custom-built steel furniture, gauzy white canopies over the beds, cedar closets, and CD players. Added bonuses are the generous complimentary breakfast (with homemade granola), fresh fruit in the evenings, and 24-hour cappuc-

cino. ✉ *164 E. 87th St., between Lexington and*
Side 10128 ☎ *212/369–1000 or 877/847–4444*
🌐 *www.franklinhotel.com* ⇆ *48 rooms* ♁ *In-room*
room safes, cable TV, in-room VCRs, lounge, library,
laundry service, parking (fee), some free parking, no-smoking f
DC, MC, V.

Upper West Side

$$$$ **Trump International Hotel and Towers.** Rooms and suites in this expensive, showy hotel resemble mini-apartments: all have fully equipped kitchens with black-granite countertops, entertainment centers with stereos and CD players, and mini-telescopes, which you can use to gaze through the floor-to-ceiling windows. Creamy-beige marble bathrooms are equipped with Jacuzzis and Frette bathrobes, and slippers hang in the closets. Complimentary cellular phones and personalized stationery and business cards are also offered. The restaurant, Jean-Georges, is one of the city's finest, and for a price a Jean-Georges sous-chef will prepare a meal in your kitchenette. ✉ *1 Central Park W, between W. 59th and W. 60th Sts., Upper West Side 10023* ☎ *212/299–1000 or 888/448–7867* 📠 *212/299–1023* 🌐 *www.trumpintl.com* ⇆ *37 rooms, 130 suites* ♁ *Restaurant, café, room service, in-room data ports, in-room fax, in-room safes, in-room hot tubs, kitchenettes, minibars, microwaves, refrigerators, cable TV with movies and video games, in-room DVD/VCR players, indoor pool, gym, health club, massage, sauna, spa, steam room, bar, baby-sitting, dry cleaning, laundry service, concierge, Internet, business services, meeting rooms, parking (fee), no-smoking rooms* ▭ *AE, D, DC, MC, V.*

★ $$–$$$$ **Hotel Beacon.** The Upper West Side's best budget buy is three blocks from Central Park and Lincoln Center, and footsteps from Zabar's gourmet bazaar. All of the generously sized rooms and suites include marble bathrooms, kitchenettes with coffeemakers, pots and pans, stoves, and ironing facilities. Closets are huge, and some of the bathrooms have Hollywood dressing room–style mirrors. High floors have views of Central Park, the Hudson River, or the midtown skyline. ✉ *2130 Broadway, at W. 75th St., Upper West Side 10023* ☎ *212/787–1100 or 800/572–4969* 📠 *212/787–8119* 🌐 *www.beaconhotel.com* ⇆ *129 rooms, 110 suites* ♁ *Café, in-room safes, kitchens, kitchenettes, microwaves, refrigerators, cable TV, baby-sitting, laundry facilities, business services, meeting rooms, parking (fee), no-smoking rooms* ▭ *AE, D, DC, MC, V.*

$–$$$$ **Mayflower.** This spot across the street from Central Park has a long, low, wood-paneled lobby, with gilt-framed oils of tall ships. Although a bit dowdy, the rooms are large and comfortable (spend the extra few bucks for a park view). All have dark-wood colonial-style furniture and walk-in closets; most also have walk-in pantries with a refrigerator and sink. Service has been shaky at times, but most of the staff are friendly and helpful, and complimentary coffee and cookies are served in the evenings. ✉ *15 Central Park W, between W. 61st and W. 62nd Sts., Upper West Side 10023* ☎ *212/265–0060 or 800/223–4164* 📠 *212/265–0227* 🌐 *www.mayflowerhotel.com* ⇆ *169 rooms, 196 suites* ♁ *Restaurant, room service, some in-room data ports, refrigerators, cable TV, exercise equipment, gym, bar, baby-sitting, dry cleaning, laundry service, meeting rooms, parking (fee), some pets allowed, no-smoking floors* ▭ *AE, D, DC, MC, V.*

$$–$$$ **On the Ave.** A slice of sophistication and service on the Upper West Side, this reasonably priced boutique hotel appeals to those who will do anything to avoid midtown. There's no restaurant or room service, but the amenities in the basic rooms, like hair dryers and terry robes,

…uate, and penthouse floors afford views of Central …dson River. On the Ave. combines modern style—… other moderately priced Upper West Side hotels—…es guests a little taste of what it's like to live in New …adway, at W. 77th St., Upper West Side 10024 … 800/509–7598 ☏ 212/787–9521 🌐 www.ontheave-… …ms, 24 suites ♁ Room service, in-room data ports, …sitting, dry cleaning, laundry service, concierge, In-…ices, parking (fee), some pets allowed, no-smoking …C, MC, V.

…y across the street from the American Museum of Natural History, this well-kept spot rubs shoulders with fine prewar doorman apartment buildings (make sure to spring for a room with museum views). Fine traditional rooms come with amenities such as Web TV, Q-Tips, cotton balls, a pants press, and an iron and ironing board. The second-floor breakfast room serves a good, if slightly pricey for the neighborhood, breakfast. The library lounge, with leather sofas, a cozy fireplace, and tables with built-in game boards, is an unexpected plus. ✉ *45 W. 81st St., between Central Park W and Columbus Ave., Upper West Side 10024* ☎ *212/362–9200 or 800/368–4575* ☏ *212/721–2994* 🌐 *www.excelsiorhotelny.com* *118 rooms, 80 suites* ♁ *Restaurant, dining room, in-room data ports, in-room fax, in-room safes, gym, library, dry cleaning, laundry service, concierge, Internet, meeting rooms, some pets allowed, no-smoking floors* ▭ *AE, D, DC, MC, V.*

★ $ **Empire Hotel.** One of the city's better buys, this property has an unbeatable location across from Lincoln Center. The 1929 building, with its warm, inviting medieval-style lobby, was bought by boutique hotel maverick Ian Schrager. Rooms and suites—with their great views of Broadway or an inner courtyard—are small but appealing; all have textured teal carpets, dark-wood furnishings, and entertainment centers with CD players. A nearby New York Sports Club is accessible for a small fee, and a well-stocked lending library provides videos and CDs for a fee. ✉ *44 W. 63rd St., between Broadway and Columbus Ave., Upper West Side 10023* ☎ *212/265–7400 or 888/822–3555* ☏ *212/245–3382* 🌐 *www.empirehotel.com* *382 rooms, 40 suites* ♁ *Restaurant, dining room, room service, in-room data ports, cable TV, in-room VCRs, bar, dry cleaning, laundry service, parking (fee), no-smoking floors* ▭ *AE, D, DC, MC, V.*

$ **The Lucerne.** The opulent and spacious multihue marble lobby of this exquisite landmark building has more pizzazz than the predictable guest rooms, with their requisite dark-wood reproduction furniture and chintz bedspreads. Health-conscious adults might like the gym on the top floor, with its city views, and children may be glued to the in-room Nintendo games. The affluent residential neighborhood is filled with an impressive array of boutiques and gourmet food shops, and the American Museum of Natural History is a short walk away. A complimentary Continental breakfast is served. ✉ *201 W. 79th St., at Amsterdam Ave., Upper West Side 10024* ☎ *212/875–1000 or 800/492–8122* ☏ *212/721–1179* 🌐 *www.newyorkhotel.com* *209 rooms, 41 suites* ♁ *Restaurant, room service, in-room data ports, some kitchenettes, some microwaves, some refrigerators, cable TV, gym, bar, lobby lounge, baby-sitting, dry cleaning, laundry service, concierge, Internet, business services, meeting rooms, parking (fee), no-smoking floors* ▭ *AE, D, DC, MC, V.*

$ **Milburn.** In a converted prewar apartment building on a quiet, residential side street, the spacious rooms are homey and a notch classier than your usual value-conscious hostelry. All have kitchenettes equipped with a microwave and coffeemaker (Zabar's is blocks away), and toiletries from Caswell & Massey. Convenient to Lincoln Center, Central

Park, and a host of wonderful shops and dining est… bohemian hotel has a lobby that resembles a Bavar… ing tapestry, black-and-white marble floors, an… *W. 76th St., between Broadway and West En… 10023 ☎ 212/362–1006 or 800/833–9622 📠 21… milburnhotel.com ⇨ 50 rooms, 50 suites ♁ In-room safes, … microwaves, laundry facilities ▭ AE, DC, MC, V.*

¢–$ **YMCA West Side.** Although the fitness center here is not quite as polished as the one at the Vanderbilt YMCA in Midtown East, you can't beat this Y for value, location, and atmosphere. Two blocks from Lincoln Center and a short jaunt from Central Park, it's housed in a building that looks like a Spanish cloister, with gargoyles adorning its arched neo-Byzantine entrance. Rooms are as tiny as jail cells, but red carpeting and spreads make them a little more cheerful. Those with private bath cost extra. ✉ *5 W. 63rd St., at Central Park W, Upper West Side 10023 ☎ 212/875–4100 or 800/348–9622 📠 212/875–1334 ⇨ 500 rooms, 33 with bath ♁ Cafeteria, cable TV, 2 indoor pools, health club, massage, sauna, steam room, paddle tennis, racquetball, laundry facilities, Internet, meeting rooms, airport shuttle; no room phones, no smoking ▭ AE, MC, V.*

Harlem

$ **Urban Jem.** Innkeeper Jane Mendelson restored this 1878 brownstone (across the street from President Clinton's office) to its former grandeur. The parlor has gleaming woodwork and 12-ft ceilings, and the rooms exude an old-world charm with their marble fireplaces. Choose from a pair of spacious studio apartments replete with private kitchens and baths or two rooms with semiprivate kitchen and bath that can be converted into a one-bedroom suite. The Studio Museum of Harlem, Apollo Theater, and soul-food mecca Sylvia's are all within three blocks. A complimentary Continental breakfast is served in the parlor. ✉ *2005 5th Ave., between W. 124th and W. 125th Sts., Harlem 10035 ☎ 212/831–6029 📠 212/831–6940 🌐 www.urbanjem.com ⇨ 4 rooms ♁ In-room data ports, kitchens, microwaves, in-room VCRs, baby-sitting, laundry facilities, laundry service, Internet, business services, meeting room, no-smoking rooms ▭ AE, D, MC, V.*

Brooklyn

$$ **New York Marriott Brooklyn.** Don't discount staying in Brooklyn. What Manhattan hotel has room for an Olympic-length lap pool, a 1,100-car valet parking garage, and even a dedicated Kosher kitchen? Large (if plain) guest rooms are enhanced by niceties such as 11-ft ceilings, massaging showerheads, and rolling desks. Beautiful trompe l'oeil ceilings transform the multilevel foyer into a virtual open-air atrium. Major subway lines only a block away make for a mere 10-minute commute into Manhattan. Five-minute walks bring you to the Brooklyn Bridge's pedestrian path and the charming neighborhood of Brooklyn Heights. ✉ *333 Adams St., between Johnson and Willoughby Sts., Downtown Brooklyn 11201 ☎ 718/246–7000 or 800/843–4898 📠 718/246–0563 🌐 www.marriott.com/nycbk ⇨ 355 rooms, 21 suites ♁ Restaurant, room service, in-room data ports, in-room fax, in-room safes, minibars, cable TV, indoor pool, health club, hot tub, massage, sauna, bar, baby-sitting, dry cleaning, laundry service, concierge, Internet, business services, meeting rooms, airport shuttle, parking (fee), no-smoking floors ▭ AE, D, DC, MC, V.*

NIGHTLIFE

6

FODOR'S CHOICE

Bowery Ballroom, *Lower East Side*
Campbell Apartment, *Midtown East*
The Carlyle, *Upper East Side*
Club Shelter, *Midtown West*
Royalton, *Midtown West*
Village Vanguard, *Greenwich Village*

HIGHLY RECOMMENDED

Algonquin Hotel Lounge, *Midtown West*
Blue Note, *Greenwich Village*
Bottom Line, *Greenwich Village*
Chicago City Limits, *Upper East Side*
Chumley's, *Greenwich Village*
Cornelia Street Café, *Greenwich Village*
Exit, *Midtown West*
Fez, *East Village*
Irving Plaza, *Gramercy*
Joe's Pub, *East Village*
Ludlow Bar, *Lower East Side*
MercBar, *SoHo*
Telephone Bar, *East Village*

Updated by John J. Donohue

WHATEVER THE STATE OF THE ECONOMY or the hour they have to and shine the next morning, New Yorkers like going out, and that's ev night of the week. Having a drink or a turn on a dance floor with frien is as much about checking out what's new in town as it is about socializing Downtown, talented bands play back-to-back in 45-minute sets, while uptown, a cabaret singer holds her audience in rapt attention for an entire evening. Most bars don't have a so-called cabaret license (without which dancing is not allowed—you can sing all you want), although some lounges employ DJs who tempt patrons with insistent grooves anyway.

The nightlife scene is still largely downtown—in drab-by-day East Village dives, classic jazz joints in the West Village, and TriBeCa see-and-be-seen boîtes—but the idea of downtown now includes Brooklyn: Manhattan's neighbor is now the place for rock and roll, with new clubs in Williamsburg and Park Slope. Preppy hangouts are also still alive and well on the Upper East and Upper West sides. And all over town you can find lounges. You'll know you're in one if you see lots of crushed velvet and a zinc-top bar.

There are enough committed club crawlers in Manhattan to support venues for almost every idiosyncratic taste. But keep in mind that *when* you go is just as important as *where* you go. These days, night prowlers are more loyal to floating parties, DJs, even party promoters, than they are to addresses. A spot is only hot when it's hopping, and you may find the same party or bar that raged last night completely empty tonight. The other thing to remember is to dress properly, something that is easily accomplished by wearing black and leaving your sneakers at home.

For the totally hip, ***Paper*** magazine's "P.M. 'Til Dawn" and bar sections have as good a listing as exists of the roving parties and the best of the fashionable crowd's hangouts. ***Time Out New York*** provides a comprehensive weekly listing of amusements by category. The more-staid Friday ***New York Times*** "Weekend/Movies and Performing Arts" section runs "Pop and Jazz" and "Cabaret" columns that can clue you in to what's in the air, as can the ***Village Voice,*** a free weekly newspaper that probably has more club ads than any other rag in the world. Look also for that weekly's competitor, the ***New York Press,*** which has pages and pages of nightlife listings. Flyers about and passes to coming events are stacked in the entry at **Tower Records** (✉ 692 Broadway, at 4th St., East Village ☎ 212/505–1500 ✉ 1961 Broadway, at W. 66th St., Upper West Side ☎ 212/799–2500). You may also get good tips from a suitably au courant hotel concierge. Keep in mind that events change almost weekly, and venues have the life span of a tsetse fly, so phone ahead to make sure your target hasn't closed or turned into a polka hall. Most charge a cover, which can range from $5 to $25 or more, depending on the club and the night. And take cash, because many places don't accept plastic.

As of March 30, 2003, smoking is prohibited in all enclosed public places in New York City, *including restaurants and bars*. Some bars have installed fully-enclosed smoking rooms for those who wish to light up, but in most places you will have to step outside if you wish to smoke.

CLUBS & ENTERTAINMENT

Quintessential New York

These are the crème de la crème of New York's nightlife venues—distinguished by locale, age (you'd think even the newest of these has been there for years), style (elegance prevails), or a peerless combination of the three. Reservations are essential.

Fodor's Choice ★ **The Carlyle.** Bobby Short plays the hotel's discreetly sophisticated Café Carlyle when he's in town, and Barbara Cook and Eartha Kitt also often purr by the piano. Stop by on a Monday night and take in Woody Allen, who swings on the clarinet with his New Orleans Jazz Band. Bemelmans Bar, with murals by the author of the Madeline books, regularly stars pianist-singers Loston Harris and Peter Mintun. ✉ *35 E. 76th St., between Madison and Park Aves., Upper East Side* ☎ *212/744–1600.*

Four Seasons. Miró tapestries in the lobby greet you as you enter this power bar in the Grill Room. New York City (and American) history is made here. Watch for politicos and media moguls. ✉ *99 E. 52nd St., between Park and Lexington Aves., Midtown East* ☎ *212/754–9494.*

Oak Room. One of the great classic cabarets, the Oak Room is formal (jacket and tie for men) and offers pre-theater dining; diners get better tables. You might find the hopelessly romantic singer Andrea Marcovicci, among other top-notch performers, crooning here. ✉ *Algonquin Hotel, 59 W. 44th St., near 6th Ave., Midtown West* ☎ *212/840–6800.*

Rainbow Room. Heavenly views top the bill of fare at this romantic, 65th-floor institution, where the revolving dance floor and 12-piece orchestra ensure high spirits, even on a cloudy night. ✉ *30 Rockefeller Plaza, between 5th and 6th Aves., Midtown West* ☎ *212/632–5000.*

River Café. If you're looking for an eminently romantic locale, head out to this restaurant hidden at the foot of the Brooklyn Bridge. The bar has smashing views of the downtown Manhattan skyline across the East River, and after cocktails you can enjoy a splendid meal. ✉ *1 Water St., near Old Fulton St., DUMBO, Brooklyn* ☎ *718/522–5200.*

"21" Club. Famous for its clubby atmosphere even before it became a setting in *All About Eve,* this New York classic still has a conservative air that evokes a sense of connections, power, and prestige. ✉ *21 W. 52nd St., between 5th and 6th Aves., Midtown West* ☎ *212/582–7200.*

Dance Clubs

The city's busiest clubs are as much places to shake your booty as to strut your style and admire that of others. Revelers come to socialize, to find romance, to show off their glad rags, or to be photographed rubbing shoulders with stars. Some clubs are cavernous spaces filled with throbbing music and a churning sea of bodies. Others are like parties thrown by a mutual friend for people who don't know one another; comers are drawn by a common interest, a likeness of spirit, which can be created almost any place. Parties—dance and otherwise—with DJs, salsa bands, and themes ranging from '60s bossa-nova nights to soul-and-drag galas have been known to crop up at such places as Irving Plaza and Opaline. So read some rags of the paper variety and make some calls. Be aware that weeknight parties don't make allowances for early-morning risers: the crowd doesn't arrive or warm up until after midnight.

Arc. Video installations and a mammoth DJ booth that runs the width of the room enhance the vibe at this gallery-like TriBeCa space, which once housed the legendary dance hall Vinyl. Perhaps the no-alcohol policy here draws a more determined gang, but whatever the reason, the crowd is friendly, the vibe is good, and the dancing is among the city's hottest. Expect house music and a great time. ✉ *6 Hubert St., at Hudson St., TriBeCa* ☎ *212/226–9212.*

Bang the Party. A diverse crowd with energy to burn revels to house beats at this $5 Friday-night party. ✉ *667 Bar Gallery Lounge, 667 Fulton St., between Ashland and Rockwell Sts., Fort Greene, Brooklyn* ☎ *212/726–1322.*

Centro-Fly. This eye-popping lounge and dance hall is a geometric wonderland—black and white circles and other geometric patterns cover its

DANCE WITH ME!

BALLROOM: *In summer there's dancing under the stars at the popular* **Midsummer Night Swing** *(☎ 212/875–5766) at Lincoln Center's Fountain Plaza. The legendary* **Roseland Ballroom** *(✉ 239 W. 52nd St., between Broadway and 8th Ave., Midtown West ☎ 212/247–0200) is Manhattan's most spacious place to waltz, fox-trot, and rumba with a crowd that remembers when. A popular option for serious hoofers is the dance socials held at ballroom studios, such as* **Dance New York** *(✉ 237 W. 54th St., between 7th and 8th Aves., Midtown West ☎ 212/246–5797). What they lack in atmosphere (canned music, folding chairs, no booze), studios such as* **DanceSport** *(✉ 1845 Broadway, between W. 60th and W. 61st Sts., Upper West Side ☎ 212/307–1111) make up for by providing an enthusiastic, learning-oriented environment. The skill level is mixed but generally high at more-established schools, such as* **Dance Manhattan** *(✉ 39 W. 19th St., between 5th and 6th Aves., Chelsea ☎ 212/807–0802). You can trip the light fantastic at* **Pierre Dulaine Dance Club** *(✉ 25 W. 31st St., between 5th and 6th Aves., Midtown West ☎ 212/244–8400).*

SALSA/MAMBO/MERENGUE: *"On 2" salseros shouldn't ignore* **Bistro Latino** *(✉ 1711 Broadway, between W. 54th and W. 55th Sts., Upper West Side ☎ 212/956–1000). The later the better at the swank* **Copacabana** *(✉ 560 W. 34th St., between 10th and 11th Aves., Midtown West ☎ 212/239–2672). For pop-salsa music and a younger crowd, try* **Babalu** *(✉ 327 W. 44th St., between 8th and 9th Aves., Midtown West ☎ 212/262–1111). Latin bands rule at* **SOB's** *(✉ 204 Varick St., at W. Houston St., SoHo ☎ 212/243–4940).*

SWING: *The subterranean space of* **Cache** *(✉ 221 W 46 St., between Broadway and 8th Ave., Midtown West ☎ 212/391–6881) has all the charm of a down-at-the-heels Las Vegas lounge, but the top-notch bands and dedicated dancers don't mind. Tasty food and a sizable dance floor are seductive at the* **Cotton Club** *(✉ 656 W. 125th St., between Broadway and Riverside Dr., Upper West Side ☎ 212/663–7980). The Roy Gerson Orchestra fills the dance floor on Savoy Sundays, organized by the* New York Swing Dance Society *(☎ 212/696–9737), at* **Irving Plaza** *(✉ 17 Irving Pl., at E. 15th St., Gramercy ☎ 212/777–6800). Hop, swing, and jump to bands nightly at* **Swing 46** *(✉ 349 W. 46th St., between 8th and 9th Aves., Midtown West ☎ 212/262–9554).*

TANGO: *Tango between courses on Tuesday at* **Il Campanello** *(✉ 136 W. 31st St., between 6th and 7th Aves., Midtown West ☎ 212/695–6111). A balcony view of the pros who dance at romantic* **La Belle Epoque** *(✉ 827 Broadway, between E. 12th and E. 13th Sts., Greenwich Village ☎ 212/254–6436) most Fridays could make you swoon. Practice your ochos at the comfortable* **Lafayette Grill** *(✉ 54 Franklin St., between Broadway and Lafayette St., TriBeCa ☎ 212/732–5600) on Saturday. At laid-back* **La Nacional** *(✉ 239 W. 14th St., between 7th and 8th Aves., Greenwich Village ☎ 212/243–9308) the* milonga *fires up late on Thursday.*

KNOW BEFORE YOU GO: *Expect a cover charge ($5–$25) and, at some places, a drink minimum. Latin clubs usually have less expensive cover charges for women and are more expensive after 10 PM. Heels and skirts for women and suits for men are required at upscale and Latin places. Swing parties attract couples in retro costume; ballroom dancing is done in everything from gowns to jeans. Going solo is common; both men and women can expect to find willing partners in most clubs and studios. Many clubs offer lessons for a small additional fee. Schedules change often, so call to confirm or check the listings in* Time Out *or the* New York Press, *or hit 🌐 www.nycdc.com*

— Karen Deavers

interior. You'll find world-famous DJs, house music on the weekends, and an enthusiastic mainstream crowd. ✉ *51 W. 21st St., between 5th and 6th Aves., Flatiron District* ☎ *212/627–7770.*

Cheetah. No longer one of the hot spots, Cheetah still draws a solid crowd that loves to pay homage to the '70s by disco dancing in a faux-leopard setting. ✉ *12 W. 21st St., between 5th and 6th Aves., Flatiron District* ☎ *212/206–7770.*

China Club. This symbol of high-living excess has relocated from its original Upper West Side location to an 8,000-square-ft bilevel space in Hell's Kitchen. The exclusionary velvet ropes are again in place, but there's also a mass-market gift shop. ✉ *268 W. 47th St., between Broadway and 8th Ave., Midtown West* ☎ *212/398–3800.*

Fodor'sChoice ★ **Club Shelter.** This warehouse-like space is the home to some of the best dancing in the city, which is no surprise, as it takes its name and its low-key attitude from a long-running after-hours party that was once found at the old TriBeCa club Vinyl. ✉ *20 W. 39th St., between 5th and 6th Aves., Midtown West* ☎ *212/719–4479.*

Cream. Five rooms, two dance floors, and wildly eclectic decor (everything from Persian rugs to fake snow) induce a crowd of young professionals to cut the rug. In this neighborhood Cream can't be beat for dancing. ✉ *246 Columbus Ave., between W. 71st and W. 72nd Sts., Upper West Side* ☎ *212/633–9800.*

Culture Club. From the Pacman illustration on the outside awning to the interior murals of Adam Ant and the cast from *The Breakfast Club,* if you're desperately seeking a dose of '80s nostalgia, this is your place. ✉ *179 Varick St., between Charlton and King Sts., SoHo* ☎ *212/243–1999.*

Discotheque. The name may say '70s, but the excessiveness of the decor here speaks of the '80. There is no shortage of glitzy effects and Grecian artifacts, or for that matter, twentysomething professionals from the Upper East Side. They gather to dance to house music and to ogle the male strippers, who do their thing from 8 until 10 PM. ✉ *17 W. 19th St., between 5th and 6th Aves., Chelsea* ☎ *212/352–9999.*

Estate. At the end of 2002 the up-and-coming local promoter John Blair reopened this notorious haunt once known as the Limelight, housed in a former church. The interior is completely new—think modern and mirrored rather than Gothic and foreboding—but you still never know what amusement you might find in the dark corners of the labyrinthine space. ✉ *47 W. 20th St., at 6th Ave., Chelsea* ☎ *212/807–7780.*

★ **Exit.** This extravagant multilevel club has everything from a massive dance floor to an outdoor patio. You'll find A-list DJs spinning for an enthusiastic crowd that can often include a hip-hop star or two. ✉ *610 W. 56th St., between 11th and 12th Aves., Midtown West* ☎ *212/582–8282.*

Filter 14. In the former space of the famed Mother bar, Filter 14 has a refreshingly unpolished feel thanks to a tenant-landlord dispute that brought a halt to renovations. The crowd during the week is young and passionate about the famously obscure electronica DJs who work here. On Friday and Saturday nights a slightly older crowd dominates the dance floor. ✉ *432 W. 14th St., between 9th and 10th Aves., Greenwich Village* ☎ *212/366–5680.*

Float. Skinny trust-fund girls and the bankers who chase them crowd into this three-level dance hall that feels like a fun house. A maze of VIP rooms and small lounges leads off the main dance floor. On Sunday nights Float often hosts top-notch Spanish rock bands. ✉ *240 W. 52nd St., between Broadway and 8th Ave., Midtown West* ☎ *212/581–0055.*

Le Bar Bat. This bamboo-encrusted, multitier monster fits right in with the touristy Hard Rock Cafe–type places on 57th Street's theme-restaurant row, but you can have a flashy good time here among the Euro and prepster poseurs. ✉ *311 W. 57th St., between 8th and 9th Aves., Midtown West* ☎ *212/307–7228.*

Nell's. Nell Campbell (of *Rocky Horror* fame) opened this sophisticated club back in the '80s, and it's still going strong. The tone in the upstairs live-music jazz salon is Victorian; downstairs the DJ spins everything from R&B to reggae. ✉ *246 W. 14th St., near 8th Ave., Greenwich Village* ☎ *212/675–1567.*

Roxy. Most nights this huge hall is a standard bridge-and-tunnel magnet, mostly attracting those who live in other New York boroughs and in New Jersey and occasionally drawing a mixed rave crowd. Wednesday is roller-disco night. Call ahead for special events. ✉ *515 W. 18th St., between 10th and 11th Aves., Chelsea* ☎ *212/645–5156.*

Saci. Don't let the midtown address fool you. This airy dance hall draws an ultra-fashion-conscious crowd. They appreciate the minimalistic elevated bars and pulsing walls of light, which look just as good as the patrons. ✉ *135 W. 41st St., between 6th Ave. and Broadway, Midtown West* ☎ *212/278–0988.*

Sapphire. A veteran of the Lower East Side scene, tiny Sapphire is still going strong. The party gets started late, but the DJ keeps the lively, diverse crowd going with every kind of music from ska to disco. Ultra-friendly patrons might drag you onto the floor to strut your stuff. Drinks are half price before 10 PM. ✉ *249 Eldridge St., between E. Houston and Stanton Sts., Lower East Side* ☎ *212/777–5153.*

Shine. The specialty of this intimate club seems to be variety—everyone from rocker Sheryl Crow to rapper Jay Z has appeared here. On nights when bands aren't rocking the folks on the dance floor, DJs keep the crowds moving. ✉ *285 West Broadway, at Canal St., TriBeCa* ☎ *212/941–0900.*

Sound Factory. A cavernous, super-high-energy dance mecca, this club is only open on Friday and Saturday nights, though the action continues through noon on Sunday. ✉ *618 W. 46th St., between 11th and 12th Aves., Midtown West* ☎ *212/489–0001.*

Spa. Before working out to the R&B and hip-hop beats on the dance floor, massage your psyche by the bar, which is backed by cascading water. The super fit and attractive set can be found in the exclusive alabaster banquettes of the White Room. The sound system is remarkably poor, given the $20-to-$25 cover. ✉ *76 E. 13th St., between Broadway and 4th Ave., East Village* ☎ *212/388–1060.*

Webster Hall. Five kinds of music are played on the four floors of this fave among New York University students and out-of-towners looking for the most bang for their buck. The barely clad go-go dancers certainly do work hard for the crowd. ✉ *125 E. 11th St., between 3rd and 4th Aves., East Village* ☎ *212/353–1600.*

Jazz Clubs

Greenwich Village is still New York's jazz mecca, with more than a dozen jazz nightclubs, although many others are strewn around town. Jazz at Lincoln Center moves in fall 2004 to a new 100,000-square-ft complex on Columbus Circle at West 59th Street. The facility will house AOL Time Warner's new headquarters, which will include two auditoriums, a jazz café, rehearsal studios, classrooms, and a Jazz Hall of Fame.

Arthur's Tavern. Unless there's a festival in town, you won't find any big names jamming here. But you will find live jazz nightly, without a cover charge, amid the dark-wood ambience of the Greenwich Village of old. ✉ *57 Grove St., between 7th Ave. S and Bleecker St., Greenwich Village* ☎ *212/675–6879.*

Birdland. At the place that gets its name from saxophone great Charlie Parker, you'll find serious, up-and-coming groups. The dining room serves moderately priced Southern cuisine. If you sit at the bar your $20 cover charge includes a drink. ✉ *315 W. 44th St., between 8th and 9th Aves., Midtown West* ☎ *212/581–3080.*

★ **Blue Note.** Considered by many to be the jazz capital of the world, the Blue Note could see on an average month Spyro Gyra, Ron Carter, and Jon Hendricks. Expect a steep music charge except on Monday, when record labels promote their artists' new releases for an average ticket price of less than $20. ✉ *131 W. 3rd St., near 6th Ave., Greenwich Village* ☎ *212/475–8592.*

Cajun. You'll think you've ended up in New Orleans when you settle into this charming old restaurant. Mardi Gras masks and beads line the walls, and there's music nine times a week (that's nightly plus a champagne jazz brunch on Sunday and a lunchtime combo on Wednesday). If you long for the sounds of the '20s and '30s, don't miss Vince Giordano and his 12-piece Nighthawks orchestra on Monday and Thursday. ✉ *129 8th Ave., at 16th St., Chelsea* ☎ *212/691–6174.*

Garage Restaurant and Cafe. There's no cover at this bilevel Village hot spot, where you can hear live jazz seven nights a week; a fireplace sets the mood upstairs. ✉ *98 7th Ave. S, near Grove St., Greenwich Village* ☎ *212/645–0600.*

Iridium. This cozy club is a sure bet for big-name talent. It has good sight lines, and the sound system was designed with the help of Les Paul, the inventor of the solid-body electric guitar, who takes the stage on Monday night. ✉ *1650 Broadway, at W. 51st St., Midtown West* ☎ *212/582–2121.*

Jazz Standard. This sizable underground room is a reliable spot to hear the top names in the business. As a part of Danny Meyer's Southern-food restaurant Blue Smoke, it's one of the few spots where you can get dry-rubbed ribs to go with your bebop. ✉ *116 E. 27th St., between Park and Lexington Aves., Murray Hill* ☎ *212/576–2232.*

Knickerbocker. Piano-and-bass duets are the fare at this reliable steak house with an old New York feel. Think red meat and good jazz. ✉ *33 University Pl., at E. 9th St., Greenwich Village* ☎ *212/228–8490.*

Knitting Factory. This laid-back, three-level space in TriBeCa stages avant-garde jazz in a variety of settings, from a small homey, room to a black-box theater. ✉ *74 Leonard St., between Broadway and Church St., TriBeCa* ☎ *212/219–3055.*

Lenox Lounge. This art deco lounge opened in the 1930s and currently hosts jazz ensembles, blues acts, and jam sessions in its Zebra Room. ✉ *288 Malcolm X Blvd., between W. 124th and W. 125th Sts., Harlem* ☎ *212/427–0253.*

Smoke. This small, sleek lounge near Columbia University draws some of the top names in the business, including turban-wearing organist Dr. Lonnie Smith and the drummer Jimmy Cobb (who laid down the beat on Miles Davis's seminal album *Kind of Blue*). ✉ *2751 Broadway, between W. 105th and W. 106th Sts., Upper West Side* ☎ *212/864–6662.*

Fodor's Choice ★ **Village Vanguard.** This former Thelonious Monk haunt and prototypical old-world jazz club lives on in a cellar, where you might hear jams from the likes of Wynton Marsalis and James Carter, among others. ✉ *178 7th Ave. S, between W. 11th and Perry Sts., Greenwich Village* ☎ *212/255–4037.*

Zinc Bar. This tiny underground spot features Brazilian jazz on weekends. During the week the live music ranges from straight-ahead guitar work to Cuban tunes. ✉ *90 W. Houston St., between Thompson St. and LaGuardia Pl., Greenwich Village* ☎ *212/477–8337.*

Rock Clubs

Arlene Grocery. This rock club on the Lower East Side is known for recruiting new bands with promising futures. Low cover charges (usually only on weekends), a welcoming atmosphere, and punk-rock/heavy-metal karaoke sessions on Monday night set it apart. ✉ *95 Stanton St., between Ludlow and Orchard Sts., Lower East Side* ☎ *212/358–1633.*

Bitter End. This old Village standby has served up its share of talent; Billy Joel, David Crosby, and Dr. John are among the stars who have played here. These days you're more likely to find unknown but talented musicians on their way up. Patrons, mostly seated in front of the stage, rotate with the bands billed each night—blues, country, rock, and jazz all make an appearance here. ✉ *147 Bleecker St., between Thompson St. and LaGuardia Pl., Greenwich Village* ☎ *212/673–7030.*

Fodor'sChoice ★ **Bowery Ballroom.** This tastefully clean, balconied space is the city's premier midsize concert venue. You can sit at one of the few tables upstairs or stand and dance on the main floor. P. J. Harvey, Shelby Lynne, and Superchunk are the caliber of musicians who perform here. There's a comfortable bar in the basement. ✉ *6 Delancey St., near the Bowery, Lower East Side* ☎ *212/533–2111.*

CBGB & OMFUG. American punk rock and New Wave (the Ramones, Blondie, the Talking Heads) were born in this long, black tunnel of a club. Today expect Shirley Temple of Doom, Xanax 25, and other inventively named performers. **CB's 313 Gallery,** next door at 313 Bowery, attracts a quieter (and older) crowd with mostly acoustic music. ✉ *315 Bowery, at Bleecker St., East Village* ☎ *212/982–4052.*

Continental. A favorite haunt of NYU students, this dive is loud, cheap, and lots of fun, in a delightfully sophomoric way. Local up-and-coming rock bands keep the place lively. ✉ *25 3rd Ave., at St. Marks Pl., East Village* ☎ *212/529–6924.*

Don Hill's. At this downtown favorite, you'll find a mixed crowd of gays and straight folk who gather for hot dancing and cool rock and roll from bands both popular and not yet signed. ✉ *511 Greenwich St., at Spring St., SoHo* ☎ *212/334–1390.*

★ **Irving Plaza.** Looking for Joan Osborne, Weezer, or Wilco? You'll find them in this perfect-size place for general-admission live music. There's a small balcony with a bar and a tiny lounge area. ✉ *17 Irving Pl., at E. 15th St., Gramercy* ☎ *212/777–6800.*

Luna Lounge. Downtown hipsters pack the back room of this Ludlow Street staple to catch two to four local rock acts a night except on Monday, when stand-up comedy is on the bill. ✉ *171 Ludlow St., between E. Houston and Stanton Sts., Lower East Side* ☎ *212/260–2323.*

Luxx. If the words indie, postpunk, or electroclash mean anything to you, this is your place. If they sound like gibberish, but you're still curious about the city's newest music, you'll find it in this candy-striped club where young creative types down cheap drinks while shaking their hips and checking each other out. ✉ *256 Grand St., between Driggs Ave. and Roebling St., Williamsburg, Brooklyn* ☎ *718/599–1000.*

Maxwells. It's actually in New Jersey, but if you're looking for a small room to see some big names in indie rock, it's well worth the short PATH train ride. ✉ *1039 Washington St., at 11th St., Hoboken, NJ* ☎ *201/798–0406.*

Mercury Lounge. With one of the best sound systems in the city, this small club holds a quiet cachet with bands and industry insiders. One small problem: there's no coat check, and it can get hot in there. ✉ *217 E. Houston St., between Ludlow and Essex Sts., Lower East Side* ☎ *212/260–4700.*

Northsix. Housed in an old factory, this spacious indie-rock club has cheap beer, low cover charges, and a set of bleachers straight out of a high school gym. Expect to find up-and-coming national acts and some of the best local bands you've never heard of. ✉ *66 N. 6th St., between Wythe and Kent Aves., Williamsburg, Brooklyn* ☎ *718/599–5103.*

Southpaw. Like its upscale Brooklyn neighborhood, this Park Slope club is polished and plush. You can catch the latest rock act in comfort, thanks to an elevated area of sleek tables and cushioned benches. A wooden floor in front of the stage enables you to press yourself against more rabid fans, if that's what rock and roll means to you. ✉ *125 5th Ave., between St. Johns Pl. and Sterling Pl., Park Slope, Brooklyn* ☎ *718/230–0236.*

TriBeCa. This downtown rock club was once known for its blues acts. Now it books the music's distant descendants—contemporary jam bands that in previous days would have been found at the defunct club Wetlands or, to go back a bit further, San Francisco's Haight-Ashbury neighborhood. ✉ *16 Warren St., between Broadway and Church St., TriBeCa* ☎ *212/766–1070.*

Warsaw. The sparkling and sizable ballroom of the Polish National Home in Brooklyn often features independent rock and old soul bands booked by legendary impresario Steve Weitzman (who also lines up the acts for the Village Underground). Next door there's a beer hall and restaurant with Polish treats and a pool table. ✉ *261 Driggs Ave., between Eckford and Leonard Sts., Greenpoint, Brooklyn* ☎ *718/387–0505.*

World Music Venues

A former mayor once called New York a "gorgeous mosaic" for the rich ethnic mix of its inhabitants, and the music in some of its clubs reflects that. Brazilian, Celtic, and of course Latin—salsa, samba, merengue—integrate with the ever-present energy of the streets.

Connolly's. This trilevel Irish pub with a *Cheers*-like atmosphere plays host to the Irish rock-and-roots hybrid Black 47 (named for the year of the Great Famine) on Saturday night. ✉ *121 W. 45th St., between Broadway and 6th Ave., Midtown West* ☎ *212/597–5126.*

Copacabana. The granddaddy of Manhattan dance clubs (it has been open almost continuously since 1940) moved into a massive new space in fall 2002. In typical Copa fashion, little restraint was shown, and the club now hosts music and dancing on three levels. From the disco on the lower level to the main ballroom where the top names in salsa and merengue perform, few other clubs can compare. ✉ *560 W. 34th St., between 10th and 11th Aves., Midtown West* ☎ *212/239–2672.*

Knitting Factory. This cross-genre venue regularly hosts performers from far and wide. The intimate Old Office space is a great place to catch a Cuban guitarist or an African folk singer. ✉ *74 Leonard St., between Broadway and Church St., TriBeCa* ☎ *212/219–3055.*

SOB's. The initials stand for Sounds of Brazil at *the* place for reggae, Trinidadian carnival, zydeco, African, and especially Latin tunes and salsa rhythms. The decor is à la Tropicana; the favored drink, a *caipirinha*, a mixture of Brazilian sugarcane liquor and lime. Dinner is served as well. ✉ *204 Varick St., at W. Houston St., SoHo* ☎ *212/243–4940.*

Blues, Acoustic & R&B Venues

B. B. King Blues Club & Grill. It ain't no Mississippi juke joint. This lavish Times Square club is vast and shiny and host to a range of musicians from Bo Diddley to Peter Frampton. Every so often the relentlessly touring owner stops by as well. ✉ *237 W. 42nd St., between 7th and 8th Aves., Midtown West* ☎ *212/997–4144.*

★ **Bottom Line.** Clubs come and go, but this one prevails. Its reputation is for showcasing talents on their way up, as it did for Stevie Wonder and Bruce Springsteen. Recent visitors include Buster Poindexter, Jane Siberry, and Loudon Wainwright III. When a name pulls in a crowd, patrons are packed like sardines at mostly long, thin tables. ✉ *15 W. 4th St., at Mercer St., Greenwich Village* ☎ *212/228–6300.*

Hogs & Heifers Uptown. The sibling of the downtown bar of the same name draws a slightly preppier but equally inebriated crowd. During the week, the country, blues, and rockabilly music is free; on Friday and Saturday there's a cover charge. ✉ *1843 1st Ave., between E. 95th and E. 96th Sts., Upper East Side* ☎ *212/722–8635.*

Rodeo Bar. There's never a cover at this Texas-style roadhouse, complete with barn-wood siding, a barbecue and Tex-Mex menu, and music with American roots—country, rock, rockabilly, swing, bluegrass, and blues. ✉ *375 3rd Ave., at 27th St., Murray Hill* ☎ *212/683–6500.*

Terra Blues. A second-story haven for blues lovers, this cozy Village club is surprisingly short on NYU students and rowdy folk. It must be the candlelit tables. Great national and local acts grace the stage. ✉ *149 Bleecker St., between Thompson and LaGuardia Sts., Greenwich Village* ☎ *212/777–7776.*

Village Underground. It may be a tiny subterranean space but is has a huge booking agent: Steve Weitzman, who draws the same type of top-notch blues, rock, country, and soul acts that he presented at the now-defunct Tramps for 10 years. ✉ *130 W. 3rd St., near 6th Ave., Greenwich Village* ☎ *212/777–7745.*

Comedy Clubs

Neurotic New York comedy is known the world over, and a few minutes watching these Woody Allen types might just make your own problems seem laughable. Expect to pay about $15 per person on a weekend, sometimes topped off by a drink minimum, and reservations are usually necessary. Only those skilled in the art of repartee should sit in the front. The rest are advised to hide in a corner or risk being relentlessly heckled.

Caroline's on Broadway. This high-gloss club presents established names as well as comedians on the edge of stardom. Janeane Garofalo, Bill Bellamy, Colin Quinn, and Gilbert Gottfried have appeared. ✉ *1626 Broadway, between W. 49th and W. 50th Sts., Midtown West* ☎ *212/757–4100.*

★ **Chicago City Limits.** This troupe's been doing improvisational comedy for a long time, and it seldom fails to whip its audiences into a laughing frenzy. Chicago City Limits performs in a renovated movie theater and is very strong on audience participation. ✉ *1105 1st Ave., at E. 61st St., Upper East Side* ☎ *212/888–5233.*

Comedy Cellar. Laughter fills this space beneath the Olive Tree Café. The bill is a good barometer of who's hot. ✉ *117 MacDougal St., between W. 3rd and Bleecker Sts., Greenwich Village* ☎ *212/254–3480.*

Comic Strip Live. The atmosphere here is strictly corner bar ("More comfortable than a nice pair of corduroys," says the daytime manager). The stage is brilliantly lighted but minuscule; the bill is unpredictable but worth checking out. ✉ *1568 2nd Ave., between 81st and 82nd Sts., Upper East Side* ☎ *212/861–9386.*

Dangerfield's. Since 1969 this has been an important showcase for prime comic talent. Prices are reasonable ($12.50 during the week and $15–$20 on the weekends, with no drink minimum). It's owned by comedian Rodney Dangerfield. ✉ *1118 1st Ave., between E. 61st and E. 62nd Sts., Upper East Side* ☎ *212/593–1650.*

Freestyle Repertory Theater. These roving improv comedians specialize in "theater sport" matches in which teams compete head-to-head for laughs. ☎ *212/642–8202 for locations.*

Gotham Comedy Club. Housed in a landmark building, this club—complete with a turn-of-the-20th-century chandelier and copper bars—showcases popular headliners such as Chris Rock and David Brenner. Once a month there's a Latino comedy show. ✉ *34 W. 22nd St., between 5th and 6th Aves., Flatiron District* ☎ *212/367–9000.*

Luna Lounge. On Monday night the back room at this watering hole hosts no-name stand-ups as well as big-name stars such as Janeane Garofalo. ✉ *171 Ludlow St., between E. Houston and Stanton Sts., Lower East Side* ☎ *212/260–2323.*

Surf Reality. At this downtown loft space, a showcase for alternative comedy, you won't find anyone telling jokes on a stage backed by an exposed brick wall. Instead, expect oddball skits. ✉ *172 Allen St., between Stanton and Rivington Sts., Lower East Side* ☎ *212/673–4182.*

Upright Citizens Brigade Theatre. Sketch comedy, audience-initiated improv, and even classes are available at this venue. ✉ *161 W. 22nd St., between 6th and 7th Aves., Chelsea* ☎ *212/366–9176.*

Cabaret & Performance Spaces

Cabaret takes many forms in New York, from a lone crooner at the piano to a full-fledged song-and-dance revue. Some nightspots have stages; almost all have a cover and a minimum food and/or drink charge. In addition to the Carlyle and the Oak Room (⇨ Quintessential New York, *above*), here are some of the best venues.

Danny's Skylight Room. Housed in Danny's Grand Sea Palace, this fixture on Restaurant Row presents a little bit of everything: jazz performers, crooners, and ivory ticklers. ✉ *346 W. 46th St., between 8th and 9th Aves., Midtown West* ☎ *212/265–8133.*

Don't Tell Mama. Composer-lyricist hopefuls and established talents show their stuff until 4 AM at this convivial theater-district cabaret. Extroverts will be tempted by the piano bar's open-mike policy. In the club's two rooms you might find singers, comedians, or female impersonators. ✉ *343 W. 46th St., between 8th and 9th Aves., Midtown West* ☎ *212/757–0788.*

The Duplex. Since 1951 this music-scene veteran on busy Sheridan Square has hosted young singers on the rise, drop-ins fresh from Broadway at the open mike, and comediennes polishing their acts. Joan Rivers got her start here and came back for an encore in 2001. No matter who's performing, the largely gay audience hoots and hollers in support. Plays and rock bands round out the entertainment. ✉ *61 Christopher St., at 7th Ave. S, Greenwich Village* ☎ *212/255–5438.*

Feinstein's at the Regency. That the world-touring Michael Feinstein performs here only a few times a year and still gets a room named after him speaks volumes about the charismatic cabaret star. When he's not in town, Feinstein's presents some of the top names in the business. ✉ *540 Park Ave., at E. 61st St., Upper East Side* ☎ *212/339–4095.*

Firebird Cafe. On Restaurant Row beside the Russian restaurant of the same name, this swank spot with red walls and a mosaic of Gustave Klimt's *Kiss* is the place to hear leading crooners. Choose from the vast selection of rare vodkas. ✉ *363 W. 46th St., between 9th and 10th Aves., Midtown West* ☎ *212/586–0244.*

★ **Joe's Pub.** Wood paneling, red-velvet walls, and comfy sofas make a lush setting for top-notch performers and the A-list celebrities who come to see them. There's not a bad seat in the house, but if you want to sit, arrive a half hour early and enjoy the finger foods. ✉ *425 Lafayette St., between E. 4th St. and Astor Pl., East Village* ☎ *212/539–8770.*

Judy's Restaurant and Cabaret. Both cabaret and piano bar, Judy's is known for singing pianists with a flair for drama in the Michael Feinstein mold. ✉ *169 8th Ave., between 18th and 19th Sts., Chelsea* ☎ *212/929–5410.*

Laurie Beechman Theater. This polished theater below the attractive West Bank Café is often home to moonlighting musical-comedy triple threats (actor-singer-dancers). ✉ *407 W. 42nd St., between 8th and 9th Aves., Midtown West* ☎ *212/695–6909.*

Rose's Turn. This unpretentious, unpolished landmark cabaret draws a lively, friendly crowd that enjoys singers, sketch-comedy groups, and various other performers. Downstairs at the piano bar you can join the singing bartenders: they don't mind duets, or choruses for that matter. ✉ *55 Grove St., near Bleecker St. and 7th Ave. S, Greenwich Village* ☎ *212/366–5438.*

BARS

No matter if they're working 70 hours a week, are unemployed, or obsessed with keeping fit, New Yorkers will never cease supporting bars and drinking establishments, which continue to thrive and multiply. You'll find a glut of mahogany-encrusted historic taverns in Greenwich Village; chichi lounges in SoHo and TriBeCa; yuppie and collegiate minifrats on the Upper West and Upper East sides; and hipster bars all over downtown, especially in the East Village's Alphabet City and on the Lower East Side. Most pubs and taverns have a wide draught selection, and bars and lounges often have a special drink menu of concoctions no one would ever think up on their own. A single martini of the increasingly creative variety can send your tab into double digits. If velvet ropes or shoulder-to-shoulder crowds ever rub you the wrong way, feel free to move on and find a more comfortable spot, because there's always another one nearby. The city's liquor law allows bars to stay open until 4 AM.

Lower Manhattan, SoHo & TriBeCa

Bar 89. This bilevel lounge has the most entertaining bathrooms in town; the high-tech doors of unoccupied stalls are transparent, and (ideally) turn opaque as you lock the door. Like the neighborhood, the crowd at the perennially popular spot is hip and monied, but the help manages to be remarkably friendly. ✉ *89 Mercer St., between Spring and Broome Sts., SoHo* ☎ *212/274–0989.*

Bridge Café. Just a hop away from South Street Seaport, this busy little restaurant flanking the Brooklyn Bridge is a world apart from that touristy district. The bar is one of the oldest in Manhattan, and though it's small, its inventory is huge: you can choose from a list of 80 domestic wines and about 50 single-malt scotches. ✉ *279 Water St., at Dover St., Lower Manhattan* ☎ *212/227–3344.*

Broome Street Bar. A hangout that's been in business since 1972, back when the neighborhood was known as the cast-iron district, this SoHo standard has a fine selection of draught beers, simple wooden chairs and tables, and a hardwood floor. Artsy types like the mellow vibe. ✉ *363 West Broadway, at Broome St., SoHo* ☎ *212/925–2086.*

Double Happiness. On a block where the boundary between Little Italy and Chinatown blurs, a stairwell descends into a dark former speakeasy where friends converse in nooks beneath a low ceiling. Drinks are as diverse as a green-tea martini and tap beer. The music is often trip-hop and loungy. ✉ *174 Mott St., between Broome and Grand Sts., Chinatown* ☎ *212/941–1282.*

El Teddy's. You can't miss the gigantic Lady Liberty crown out front, and the Judy-Jetson-goes-to-art-camp decor at this enduring TriBeCa bar. The margaritas (straight up, *por favor*) are phenomenal. ✉ *219 West Broadway, between White and Franklin Sts., TriBeCa* ☎ *212/941–7070.*

Fanelli. On Sunday many carry the fat *New York Times* under their arms when they come to this casual SoHo neighborhood bar and restaurant. ✉ *94 Prince St., at Mercer St., SoHo* ☎ *212/226–9412.*

Lucky Strike. Now that the supermodels party elsewhere, this ultracool SoHo bistro is more quiet. Young Euro types pose at the cozy back tables. DJs play funky tunes at crowded weekend parties. ✉ *59 Grand St., between Broadway and Wooster St., SoHo* ☎ *212/941–0479.*

Lush. One of TriBeCa's hottest lounges, this modern-looking space has a cool banquette running the length of its loftlike room, as well as a couple of round chambers where celebrities retire. ✉ *110 Duane St., between Church St. and Broadway, TriBeCa* ☎ *212/766–1295.*

★ **MercBar.** A chic European crowd and New Yorkers in the know come to this dark, nondescript bar for the wonderful martinis. Its street number is barely visible—look for the French doors, which stay open in summer. ✉ *151 Mercer St., between Prince and W. Houston Sts., SoHo* ☎ *212/966–2727.*

Naked Lunch. Dazzlingly popular, this William Burroughs–inspired, earth-tone SoHo haunt is frequented by celebrities and other beautiful people. On weekends the crowd dances late into the night. ✉ *17 Thompson St., at Grand St., SoHo* ☎ *212/343–0828.*

Pravda. Martinis are the rule at this stylish Russian-theme bar and lounge, which is warm with color but cellarlike with a vaulted ceiling and columns. Choose from more than 70 brands of vodka and nearly as many types of martinis. Appetizers and entrées are also available, and you can call to reserve a table. ✉ *281 Lafayette St., between Prince and E. Houston Sts., SoHo* ☎ *212/226–4944.*

Raoul's. One of the first trendy spots in SoHo, this French restaurant has yet to lose its touch. Expect a chic bar scene filled with model-pretty men and women. ✉ *180 Prince St., between Sullivan and Thompson Sts., SoHo* ☎ *212/966–3518.*

Red Bench. This small, dark lounge, which was reportedly once a mob hangout, is popular with attractive locals who want a break from the usual SoHo scene. This place is far from trendy, which, oddly enough, accounts for its cachet. ✉ *107 Sullivan St., between Prince and Spring Sts., SoHo* ☎ *212/274–9120.*

The Room. It can get rather cozy in this minimalist but comfortable spot where the great selection of wine and beer draws a friendly international crowd. ✉ *144 Sullivan St., between W. Houston and Prince Sts., SoHo* ☎ *212/477–2102.*

Screening Room. Have dinner, drinks, and a night out at the movies, all in the same place. Although the movie theater here is small, it has comfy couches and serves good food, making it a favorite with the TriBeCa crowd and couples on dates. Above the candelit bar area is a mezzanine lounge with velvety chairs and ottomans where you can sip your cocktail under the gaze of indie-film stars, or at least of their photographs. ✉ *54 Varick St., at Canal St., TriBeCa* ☎ *212/334–2100.*

Sweet and Vicious. The crowd at this bar is friendly and 25 to 45 years old. Dim lighting and loud music can make eye contact and conversation a challenge. The back garden is more quiet. Feel free to order in a pie from the nearby pizzerias. ✉ *5 Spring St., between Bowery and Elizabeth St., NoLita* ☎ *212/334–7915.*

Veruka. Getting past the velvet rope at this ultrahot lounge is as difficult as driving a ground ball past New York Yankee shortstop Derek Jeter, who frequents this spot, along with other celebrities such as Serena

Altschul. ✉ *525 Broome St., between Thompson and Sullivan Sts., SoHo* ☎ *212/625–1717.*

Walker's. First-precinct N.Y.P.D. detectives, TriBeCa artists, Wall Street suits, and the odd celeb kick back at this cozy restaurant-bar. ✉ *16 N. Moore St., at Varick St., TriBeCa* ☎ *212/941–0142.*

Chelsea & Greenwich Village

Automatic Slim's. A cramped, sweaty, eternally popular joint where the patrons often end up dancing on the bar to loud music, Slim's also has amazingly good food. ✉ *733 Washington St., at Bank St., Greenwich Village* ☎ *212/645–8660.*

Bar Six. This elegant bar and restaurant with French doors opening onto the street is an idyllic stop on a soft summer night. ✉ *502 6th Ave., between W. 12th and W. 13th Sts., Greenwich Village* ☎ *212/691–1363.*

Café Loup. This French restaurant is something of a neighborhood institution, and its cozy bar serves some of the best margaritas in the city—only fresh fruit juices are used. ✉ *105 W. 13th St., between 5th and 6th Aves., Greenwich Village* ☎ *212/255–4746.*

Cedar Tavern. This old-fashioned tavern is one block from the site of the original, which was a haunt of abstract expressionists during the 1950s. College students and blue-collar workers enjoy the tap beer and dark-wood, old-world ambience. The spacious upstairs room has a skylight and plants. There are frequent poetry readings. ✉ *82 University Pl., at W. 12th St., Greenwich Village* ☎ *212/741–9754.*

Chelsea Commons. Construction workers mingle with Chelsea dandies at this longtime neighborhood fave. It's got a welcoming fireplace and a lamplighted brick courtyard straight out of olde London. ✉ *242 10th Ave., at W. 24th St., Chelsea* ☎ *212/929–9424.*

★ **Chumley's.** There's no sign to help you find this place—they took it down during Chumley's speakeasy days—but when you reach the corner of Bedford and Barrow streets, you're very close (just head a little north on Barrow, and use the doorway on the east side of the street). A fireplace warms the relaxed dining room, where the burgers are hearty and the clientele collegiate. ✉ *86 Bedford St., at Barrow St., Greenwich Village* ☎ *212/675–4449.*

Ciel Rouge. Sip titillating cocktails such as Lady Love Fizz and Bitches Brew in a wicked all-red room straight out of the Left Bank. During warmer months the leafy garden in back is open. Don't miss cool happenings like live jazz and piano music on Tuesday nights. ✉ *176 7th Ave., between 20th and 21st Sts., Chelsea* ☎ *212/929–5542.*

★ **Cornelia Street Café.** Share a bottle of merlot at a street-side table on a quaint West Village lane. Downstairs you can groove to live jazz from Wednesday through Saturday. ✉ *29 Cornelia St., between W. 4th and Bleecker Sts., Greenwich Village* ☎ *212/989–9319.*

Corner Bistro. Founded in 1966, this pub-and-grub-style bar serves the best hamburgers in town. The cozy place is so inviting and the young, professional crowd so friendly, you might think you're in a small town. ✉ *331 W. 4th St., at 8th Ave., Greenwich Village* ☎ *212/242–9502.*

Grange Hall. Decorated in art deco style with W.P.A.-ish murals, this restaurant is an American classic, just like its all-domestic wine list. ✉ *50 Commerce St., at Barrow St., Greenwich Village* ☎ *212/924–5246.*

Half King. Adventure-writer Sebastian Junger (*The Perfect Storm*) is one of the owners of this mellow pub, which draws a friendly crowd of media types and stragglers from nearby Chelsea galleries. ✉ *505 W. 23rd St., between 10th and 11th Aves., Chelsea* ☎ *212/462–4300.*

Hogs & Heifers. This raucous place is all about the saucy barkeeps berating men over their megaphones and baiting women to get up on the bar and dance (and add their bras to the collection on the wall). Celebrities drop in to get their names in the gossip columns. ✉ *859 Washington St., at W. 13th St., Greenwich Village* ☎ *212/929–0655.*

Lot 61. This cavernous restaurant with sliding doors, rubber sofas, and contemporary art is as good-looking, and coolly distant, as its model and movie-star patrons. ✉ *550 W. 21st St., between 10th and 11th Aves., Chelsea* ☎ *212/243–6555.*

Lotus. Use your nose to help find this unmarked West Side hot spot: incense burns in the entry to its blond-wood-paneled quarters, where unexpectedly mature patrons try not to get caught admiring the celebrities (Denis Leary, Mick Jagger) in their midst. ✉ *409 W. 14th St., between 9th and 10th Aves., Greenwich Village* ☎ *212/243–4420.*

Madame X. The bordello atmosphere here is enhanced by blood-red walls and a sexy crowd. Madame X is across West Houston Street from SoHo, which means it's got an attractive clientele, but less attitude. From Sunday through Wednesday there's live jazz. The garden is a pleasure in warm months. ✉ *94 W. Houston St., between LaGuardia Pl. and Thompson St., Greenwich Village* ☎ *212/539–0808.*

The Park. This multistory, former taxi garage is like an imaginary mansion: you can wander from the patio to the various rooms and feel like a bicoastal millionaire. Check out the 30-ft yucca palm tree in the dining room. Be warned: the doorman may very well tell you a "reservation" is needed to enter on the weekends, after 8 PM. ✉ *118 10th Ave., at W. 17th St., Chelsea* ☎ *212/352–3313.*

Peculier Pub. Nearly 500 beers, representing 43 countries, including Peru, Vietnam, and Zimbabwe, are the draw at this heart-of-the-Village pub, where you can get some grub, too. ✉ *145 Bleecker St., at LaGuardia Pl., Greenwich Village* ☎ *212/353–1327.*

Rio-Mar. This run-down throwback to Spain serves tapas until about 1 AM. With an adjoining dining room and great sangria, Rio-Mar is a friendly respite from the surrounding trendy Meatpacking District. ✉ *7 9th Ave., at Little W. 12th St., Greenwich Village* ☎ *212/243–9015.*

Serena. This remarkably stylish subterranean lounge with fresh pink paint is the creation of top New York City caterer Serena Bass. Her chic friends are its most reliable patrons. ✉ *Chelsea Hotel, 222 W. 23rd St., between 7th and 8th Aves., Chelsea* ☎ *212/255–4646.*

Tortilla Flats. The back room here is a tribute to the stars of Vegas, from Lewis and Martin to Siegfried and Roy, but the real action is in the rambunctious crowd that packs the tight quarters for drinking games (Bingo on Monday and Tuesday, hula-hooping on Wednesday), tequila, margaritas, and Mexican food. The Flats is a prime bachelorette-party destination. ✉ *767 Washington St., at 12th St., Greenwich Village* ☎ *212/243–1053.*

Village Idiot. George Thorogood plays on the jukebox, the drinks are nearly as cheap as a subway ride, and the crowd of young college students just loves it. ✉ *355 W. 14th St., at 9th Ave., Greenwich Village* ☎ *212/989–7334.*

White Horse Tavern. According to (dubious) New York legend, Dylan Thomas drank himself to death in 1953 at this historic tavern founded in 1889. From April through October there's sidewalk seating. ✉ *567 Hudson St., at W. 11th St., Greenwich Village* ☎ *212/989–3956.*

Lower East Side & East Village Through East 20s

B Bar. Long lines peer through venetian blinds at the fabulous crowd within this trendy bar-restaurant formerly known as the Bowery Bar. If the bouncer says there's a private party going on, more likely than not it's his way of turning you away nicely. ✉ *358 Bowery, at E. 4th St., East Village* ☎ *212/475–2220.*

Beauty Bar. Grab a seat in a barber chair or under a hair dryer at this former parlor. During happy hour, if the manicurist is around, you can get your nails done. There's no room to dance, but a DJ spins funky tunes on weekends. ✉ *231 E. 14th St., between 2nd and 3rd Aves., East Village* ☎ *212/539–1389.*

Cloister Café. With one of Manhattan's largest and leafiest outdoor gardens, the Cloister is a perfect perch for lingering and elbow-bending. Be warned though: the frozen margaritas are not very good. ✉ *238 E. 9th St., between 2nd and 3rd Aves., East Village* ☎ *212/777–9128.*

Coyote Ugly. At this grimy dive the raucous patrons can be heard across the 'hood singing along with the Skynyrd wailing from the jukebox. The attractive female bartenders are an ironic twist on the bar's name. ✉ *153 1st Ave., between E. 9th and E. 10th Sts., East Village* ☎ *212/477–4431.*

★ **Fez.** Tucked away in the popular Time Café, this Moroccan-theme Casbah hosts nightly events, including drag and comedy shows, readings, and jazz and pop music (make reservations in advance for big-name bands). ✉ *380 Lafayette St., between E. 4th and Great Jones Sts., East Village* ☎ *212/533–2680.*

Idlewild. Just outside the border of the East Village, this kitschy bar pays homage to jet travel—it takes its name from the airstrip that became John F. Kennedy International Airport and succeeds as a cool drinking destination. The booths were created from coach seats, the modular bathrooms remain intact, and waitresses are decked out in stewardess uniforms. ✉ *145 E. Houston St., between Forsyth and Eldridge Sts., Lower East Side* ☎ *212/477–5005.*

Jules. This *très français, très romantique* bistro with wine bar is fronted by a perfect people-watching patio. ✉ *65 St. Marks Pl., between 1st and 2nd Aves., East Village* ☎ *212/477–5560.*

Lansky Lounge and Grill. A former speakeasy and haunt of gangster Myer Lansky, this spot was such a hit when it opened a few years back that it has since expanded to take over the bulk of what was once Ratner's Deli, upstairs. Girls in high heels and guys hoping to meet them love traipsing down an alley to swill steeply priced cocktails. Food is also served. ✉ *104 Norfolk St., between Delancey and Rivington Sts., Lower East Side* ☎ *212/677–9489.*

Local 138. If you're looking for a neighborly spot to catch the Yankees, Knicks, or the World Cup, head to this cozy, low-lighted outpost run by Irish lads who love football, er, soccer. The friendly bartenders and relaxed customers are a nice change of pace from the typical Ludlow Street scene. ✉ *138 Ludlow St., between Stanton and Rivington Sts., Lower East Side* ☎ *212/477–0280.*

Lucky Cheng's. Cheng's is known for its mediocre Asian fare and for drag queens of all colors. They can often be found cavorting with Jersey brides-to-be and tourists from the Heartland in front of the cellar's goldfish pond. ✉ *24 1st Ave., between E. 1st and E. 2nd Sts., East Village* ☎ *212/473–0516.*

★ **Ludlow Bar.** This bar is one of the main draws on the main drag of the Lower East Side. The nearly subterranean space (you descend four steps at the entrance) has a pool table and a tiny dance floor. The DJs spin everything from house music to R&B to Brazilian soul. ✉ *165 Ludlow St., between E. Houston and Stanton Sts., Lower East Side* ☎ *212/353–0536.*

Luna Park. This open-air café near the green-market stalls at the northern end of Union Square is open only in summer. To get a seat, arrive before the nine-to-five crowd. It's a great place for a romantic date, too. ✉ *Union Sq. between Broadway and Park Ave. S, Flatiron District* ☎ *212/475–8464.*

Max Fish. This crowded, kitschy palace on a gentrified Lower East Side strip has one of the most eclectic jukeboxes in town, a pool table in back, and a young crowd. It's a good bet for the last drink of the evening. ✉ *178 Ludlow St., between E. Houston and Stanton Sts., Lower East Side* ☎ *212/529–3959.*

McSorley's Old Ale House. One of New York's oldest saloons (they claim to have opened in 1854) and immortalized by *New Yorker* writer Joseph Mitchell, this is a must-see for beer-loving first-timers to Gotham, even if only two kinds of brew are served: McSorley's light and McSorley's dark. Go on a weekday or go early. The line on Friday and Saturday often stretches down the block. ✉ *15 E. 7th St., between 2nd and 3rd Aves., East Village* ☎ *212/473–9148.*

Old Town Bar and Restaurant. This proudly unpretentious watering hole is heavy on the mahogany and redolent of old New York—it's been around since 1892. ✉ *45 E. 18th St., between Broadway and Park Ave. S, Flatiron District* ☎ *212/529–6732.*

Otto's Shrunken Head. A bamboo bar and fish lamps floating overhead help set the South Seas mood at this East Village bar. You'll also find a Playboy pinball machine and a DJ with a taste for punk. Call ahead to see when the charming Hawaiian-swing band called the Moonlighters is playing. ✉ *538 E. 14th St., between Aves. A and B, East Village* ☎ *212/228–2240.*

Pete's Tavern. This saloon is famous as the place where O. Henry is alleged to have written *The Gift of the Magi* (at the second booth to the right as you come in). These days it's crowded with noisy, friendly souls. ✉ *129 E. 18th St., at Irving Pl., Gramercy* ☎ *212/473–7676.*

Remote. The tables here have science-fiction-movie video consoles on them, and you control the cameras that scan the room. For a technology that's designed to work over long distances, the effect, strangely enough, is to bring people closer together. Perhaps there are just more show-offs in New York City than elsewhere. It might be just a novelty, but it's a fun one. ✉ *327 Bowery, at 2nd St., East Village* ☎ *212/228–0228.*

★ **Telephone Bar.** Imported English telephone booths and a polite, handsome crowd mark this pub, which has great tap brews and killer mashed potatoes. ✉ *149 2nd Ave., between E. 9th and E. 10th Sts., East Village* ☎ *212/529–5000.*

Temple Bar. Romantic and upscale, this unmarked haunt is famous for its martinis and is a treat at any price. Look for the painted iguana skeleton on the facade, and walk past the slim bar to the back, where, in near-total darkness, you can lounge on a plush banquette surrounded by velvet drapes. ✉ *332 Lafayette St., between Bleecker and E. Houston Sts., East Village* ☎ *212/925–4242.*

219 Flamingo. Kidney-shape sofas, style-mad patrons, and moody lighting make this bar a cool good time. The boîte is host to a variety of parties each week; call ahead for details. In warm months the balcony overlooking 2nd Avenue is a treat. ✉ *219 2nd Ave., between E. 13th and E. 14th Sts., East Village* ☎ *212/533–2860.*

Midtown & the Theater District

★ **Algonquin Hotel Lounge.** This venerable hotel bar plays up its heritage as the site of the fabled literary Algonquin Roundtable. The clubby, oak-paneled lobby and overstuffed easy chairs encourage lolling over cocktails and conversation. ✉ *59 W. 44th St., between 5th and 6th Aves., Midtown West* ☎ *212/840–6800.*

Barrymore's. The requisite show posters hang on the wall at this pleasantly downscale theater-district bar. ✉ *267 W. 45th St., between Broadway and 8th Ave., Midtown West* ☎ *212/391–8400.*

Café Un Deux Trois. In a charming converted hotel lobby, this small bar is fashionably peopled; it hops before and after the theater. ✉ *123 W.*

44th St., between Broadway and 6th Ave., Midtown West ☎ *212/354–4148.*

Fodor's Choice ★ **Campbell Apartment.** One of Manhattan's more beautiful rooms, this restored space inside Grand Central Terminal dates to the 1930s, when it was the private office of an executive named John W. Campbell. He knew how to live, and you can enjoy his good taste from an overstuffed chair. ✉ *15 Vanderbilt Ave., at E. 41st St., Midtown East* ☎ *212/953–0409.*

Divine Bar. Zebra-stripe bar chairs downstairs and cozy velvet couches upstairs make this bar unusually chic for midtown. There's a selection of tapas, wines, and beers, but no hard liquor is served. Wine samplers, known as flights, are organized by country and varietal. The wine list is updated each quarter and includes such hard-to-come-by bottles as those produced by Robert Mondavi's Opus One label. ✉ *244 E. 51st St., between 2nd and 3rd Aves., Midtown East* ☎ *212/319–9463.*

ESPN Zone. When there's a play-off game and a New York team is involved, expect a line at the door of this block-long, multi-story sports bar. With two 16-ft video screens and scores of other TVs, there isn't a bad seat in the house. Try the sports-theme video game lounge on the top floor, or dig into the kitchen's full menu. ✉ *1472 Broadway, at 42nd St., Midtown West* ☎ *212/921–3776.*

Fantino. In the Central Park InterContinental, this restaurant-bar is dressy and traditional—a very double-martini place. ✉ *112 Central Park S, between 6th and 7th Aves., Midtown West* ☎ *212/757–1900.*

Joe Allen. At this old reliable on Restaurant Row, celebrated in the musical version of *All About Eve,* everybody's en route to or from a show. The posters that adorn the "flop wall" are from Broadway musicals that bombed. ✉ *326 W. 46th St., between 8th and 9th Aves., Midtown West* ☎ *212/581–6464.*

Keens Steakhouse. Just around the corner from Madison Square Garden, this restaurant dates to 1885 and is stocked with more than 140 single-malt scotches. Take a look at the ceilings, which are lined with clay pipes that once belonged to patrons. ✉ *72 W. 36th St., between 5th and 6th Aves., Midtown West* ☎ *212/947–3636.*

King Cole Bar. A famed Maxfield Parrish mural is a welcome sight at this classic, gorgeous midtown meeting place, which happens to be the birthplace of the Bloody Mary. ✉ *St. Regis Hotel, 2 E. 55th St., near 5th Ave., Midtown East* ☎ *212/753–4500.*

Landmark Tavern. This aged redbrick pub (it opened in 1868) is warmed by the glow of potbellied stoves on each of its three floors. The original mahogany bar and hand-pressed tin ceilings and walls give the tavern a 19th-century feel. The waiters insist it's haunted. ✉ *626 11th Ave., at W. 46th St., Midtown West* ☎ *212/757–8595.*

Monkey Bar. Once a fabled spot where the likes Tennessee Williams and hard-living actress Tallulah Bankhead gathered, this lounge was restored in the '90s. Despite the monkey decor (simian light fixtures, rugs, murals, and drink specials), there's very little barbarism in the mannered banker types who shoot back scotch here. ✉ *60 E. 54th St., between Park and Madison Aves., Midtown East* ☎ *212/838–2600.*

Morgans Bar. This dark, barless lounge (the drinks are prepared in back, out of your sight) in the basement of Ian Schrager's namesake boutique hotel draws supermodels and their kin. Note that there's no sign at the street entrance. ✉ *Morgans, 237 Madison Ave., between E. 37th and E. 38th Sts., Midtown East* ☎ *212/726–7600.*

Morrell Wine Bar and Café. Run by the wine purveyors of the same name (their store is next door), this cozy bar has one of the city's best selections of wine by the glass. In summer you can sip your Viognier at outdoor tables in the heart of Rockefeller Center. ✉ *1 Rockefeller Center, W. 49th St. between 5th and 6th Aves., Midtown West* ☎ *212/262–7700.*

Oak Bar. Bedecked with plush leather chairs and oak walls, this old favorite continues to age well. The three Everett Shinn murals of early 20th-century city life were restored in 2001. Its great location draws sophisticates, shoppers, businesspeople, tourists in the know, and stars. ✉ *Plaza Hotel, 768 5th Ave., at W. 59th St., Midtown West* ☎ *212/759–3000.*

Pen Top Bar and Lounge. Take a break from 5th Avenue shopping at this glass-lined penthouse bar on the 22nd floor. Drinks are pricey, but the views are impressive, and it's well worth a visit during hot months for its open-air, rooftop seating area. ✉ *Peninsula Hotel, 700 5th Ave., at W. 55th St., Midtown West* ☎ *212/247–2200.*

P. J. Clarke's. Mirrors and polished wood adorn New York's most famous Irish bar, where scenes from the 1954 movie *Lost Weekend* were shot. An after-work crowd unwinds here. ✉ *915 3rd Ave., at E. 55th St., Midtown East* ☎ *212/759–1650.*

Fodor'sChoice ★ **Royalton.** Philippe Starck's modernistic hotel has two places to drink—the large lobby bar furnished with armchairs and chaise longues and, specifically for vodka and champagne, the banquette-lined Round Bar in a separate, circular room to your right as you enter. The entrance to the hotel is hidden (look for the curved silver railings). ✉ *44 W. 44th St., between 5th and 6th Aves., Midtown West* ☎ *212/869–4400.*

Sardi's. "The theater is certainly not what it was," crooned a cat in the long-running *Cats,* the same could be said for this Broadway institution. Still, if you care for the theater, make time for a drink in one of the red-leather booths, which are surrounded by caricatures of stars past and present. ✉ *234 W. 44th St., between Broadway and 8th Ave., Midtown West* ☎ *212/221–8440.*

Top of the Tower. There are higher hotel-top lounges, but this one on the 26th floor still feels halfway to heaven. The atmosphere is elegant and subdued. There's piano music every night save Monday. ✉ *Beekman Tower, 3 Mitchell Pl., near 1st Ave. at E. 49th St., Midtown East* ☎ *212/355–7300.*

Water Club. Right on the East River, with a pleasing outside deck (you're not on a boat, but you'll somehow feel you are), this is a special-occasion place—especially for those who've already been to all the special landlocked watering holes in town. ✉ *500 E. 30th St., at F.D.R. Dr., Midtown East* ☎ *212/683–3333.*

Whiskey Park. At the noted nightlife impresario Rande Gerber's sleek, dark-wood lounge, buxom waitresses attend to visiting businessmen and wayward Wallstreeters. The candlelit outpost is across the street from Central Park. ✉ *100 Central Park S, at 6th Ave., Midtown West* ☎ *212/307–9222.*

Upper East Side

American Trash. The name refers to the decor, not necessarily to the clientele. Old pipes, bike wheels, and golf clubs line the walls and ceilings. ✉ *1471 1st Ave., between E. 76th and E. 77th Sts., Upper East Side* ☎ *212/988–9008.*

Auction House. There's a modest, loosely enforced dress code (no baseball hats, no sneakers) at this lounge with high ceilings and candlelight, so the neighborhood crowd is a little better in appearance, and behavior, than at many other bars. ✉ *300 E. 89th St., between 1st and 2nd Aves., Upper East Side* ☎ *212/427–4458.*

Big Easy. This sprawling watering hole is decorated with Mardi Gras masks, and the happy hour lasts until 10 PM. With eight TVs, a pool table, and darts, there's no shortage of ways to while the evening away. A DJ gets the patrons dancing on weekends. ✉ *1768 2nd Ave., at E. 92nd St., Upper East Side* ☎ *212/348–0879.*

Elaine's. The food's nothing special, and you will be relegated to an inferior table, but go to gawk; try going late at night, when the stars rise in Elaine's firmament. Woody Allen's favorite table is by the cappuccino machine. ✉ *1703 2nd Ave., at E. 88th St., Upper East Side* ☎ *212/534–8103.*

Metropolitan Museum of Art. On Friday and Saturday evenings, until 9, unwind to the sounds of a string quartet at the Great Hall Balcony Bar. In summer, be sure to visit the bar on the Iris and B. Gerald Cantor Roof Garden for a view of Central Park and the skyline that's as stunning as anything in the museum's vast collections. ✉ *1000 5th Ave., at E. 82nd St., Upper East Side* ☎ *212/879–5500.*

Session 73. Live music sets this sizable bar and restaurant above other bars in the neighborhood. Young locals crowd the pale wood-trimmed interior for jazz and blues nightly. If the songs don't set your heart racing, there's always the generous assortment of tequila and tap beer. ✉ *1359 1st Ave., at E. 73rd St., Upper East Side* ☎ *212/517–4445.*

Taperia Madrid. Pitchers of tart and tasty sangria flow easily at this local piece of Spain where bullfighting posters line the walls. Flamenco dancers liven up the scene on Thursday night. ✉ *1471 2nd Ave., between E. 76th and E. 77th Sts., Upper East Side* ☎ *212/794–2923.*

Upper West Side

Café des Artistes. George Lang's restaurant, as well known for its glorious art-nouveau murals as for its food, has a small, warm bar where interesting strangers tell their life stories and the house drink is pear champagne. It's one of the city's special hideaways. ✉ *1 W. 67th St., near Central Park W, Upper West Side* ☎ *212/877–3500.*

Gabriel's. This highly regarded Northern Italian restaurant has a cool, modern interior, a 35-ft curved mahogany bar, and a stupendous selection of grappas. ✉ *11 W. 60th St., between Broadway and Columbus Ave., Upper West Side* ☎ *212/956–4600.*

Hi-Life. Dark-wood fixtures, padded black walls, large round mirrors, and a curved wooden bar give this spot the look of a 1940s cocktail lounge. Settle into a banquette and watch the neighborhood bons vivants in action. ✉ *477 Amsterdam Ave., at W. 83rd St., Upper West Side* ☎ *212/787–7199.*

Peter's. A staple of the Upper West Side singles scene since the early 1980s, this vast, noisy bar and restaurant, adorned with copies of the wall paintings at Pompeii, hosts an ambitious crowd in its late 20s and early 30s. ✉ *182 Columbus Ave., between W. 68th and W. 69th Sts., Upper West Side* ☎ *212/877–4747.*

Potion Lounge. More of a downtown spot than you'd expect in this neighborhood, this attractive lounge serves eye-catching, multicolor drinks, or "potions," to a slightly more mature crowd. On weekends a DJ gets the everybody dancing. ✉ *370 Columbus Ave., between W. 77th and W. 78th Sts., Upper West Side* ☎ *212/721–4386.*

Shark Bar. A classy, loungy kind of place, this bar fills with eye candy every night. Rapper LL Kool J has been known to stop by, and it's very popular among young black professionals. ✉ *307 Amsterdam Ave., between W. 75th and W. 76th Sts., Upper West Side* ☎ *212/874–8500.*

Soha. The name is short for South of Harlem, but the SoHo allusion is right on target. There's a funky, friendly, art-house vibe, and in between games of pool you can stretch out on one of the many couches. ✉ *988 Amsterdam Ave., between W. 108th and W. 109th Sts., Upper West Side* ☎ *212/678–0098.*

Brooklyn

Galapagos. Neighborhood hipsters and visiting Europeans file past the dark reflecting pool before bellying up to the long tables at this former mayonnaise factory. A small stage holds DJs and bands, and on Monday night there's an old-fashioned burlesque show. Ocularis hosts its popular Sunday-night independent-film series here. Take the L train to Bedford Avenue. ✉ *70 N. 6th St., between Wythe and Kent Aves., Williamsburg* ☎ *718/782–5188.*

Gay & Lesbian Bars

Any night of the week gay men and lesbians can find plentiful entertainment of every description in New York City. The thriving community enjoys gay-specific theater, concerts, comedy, readings, dining, parties, dance clubs, and bars. For listings of gay events and places, check out ***Homo Xtra (HX), Next, New York Blade, Time Out New York, MetroSource,*** the ***Village Voice,*** and ***Paper.***

Dance Clubs & Parties

Big Apple Ranch. You won't find house or disco beats at this mixed Saturday night party. Instead you'll get country-western music and two-stepping lessons (at 8 PM). ✉ *Dance Manhattan, 39 W. 19th St., between 5th and 6th Aves., Chelsea* ☎ *212/358–5752.*

1984. On Friday energetic guys hit the boxy dance floor at this East Village institution and relive the '80s in all their new-wave, syntho-trash glory. Theme nights have honored Madonna and the TV show *Dallas.* Downstairs there's a lounge where you can catch your breath. ✉ *Pyramid, 101 Ave. A, between 6th and 7th Sts., East Village* ☎ *212/462–9077.*

Trannie Chaser. Three times a week, from Thursday to Saturday, Glorya Wholesome plays hostess for her transvestite girlfriends. ✉ *Nowbar, 22 7th Ave. S, at Leroy St., Greenwich Village* ☎ *212/802–9502.*

Men's Bars

Barracuda. The comfy couches in back are the big draw at this hangout, where the pool table draws a crowd. ✉ *275 W. 22nd St., between 7th and 8th Aves., Chelsea* ☎ *212/645–8613.*

Boiler Room. A neighborhood gathering spot with a pool table, a jukebox, and cheap drinks, this bar gets packed with twenty- and thirtysomething locals late weeknights and on weekends. ✉ *86 E. 4th St., between 1st and 2nd Aves., East Village* ☎ *212/254–7536.*

Cleo's 9th Avenue Saloon. Near the theater district, this small, narrow neighborhood bar draws a convivial, laid-back older group. ✉ *656 9th Ave., at W. 46th St., Midtown West* ☎ *212/307–1503.*

g. A huge circular bar and two airy, relaxed rooms lined with leather settees bring an upscale, mostly male crowd to this Chelsea favorite. ✉ *223 W. 19th St., between 7th and 8th Aves., Chelsea* ☎ *212/929–1085.*

The Lure. Here, at the ultimate parade of black leather, chains, and Levi's, the bark is always bigger than the bite. ✉ *409 W. 13th St., between 9th Ave. and Washington St., Greenwich Village* ☎ *212/741–3919.*

SBNY. At the large, perennially crowded Chelsea dance club formerly known as Splash, go-go dancers writhe in translucent shower cubicles, and the bartenders are clad only in their briefs. ✉ *50 W. 17th St., between 5th and 6th Aves., Chelsea* ☎ *212/691–0073.*

Stonewall. With its odd assortment of down-to-earth locals and tourists chasing gay history (though the famed riots actually started at the original Stonewall, which used to be next door), the scene here is definitely democratic. ✉ *53 Christopher St., near 7th Ave. S, Greenwich Village* ☎ *212/463–0950.*

The Townhouse. On some nights it's like stepping into a Brooks Brothers catalog—cashmere sweaters, Rolex watches, distinguished gentlemen—and it's surprisingly festive. ✉ *236 E. 58th St., between 2nd and 3rd Aves., Midtown East* ☎ *212/754–4649.*

Ty's. Although its clientele is close-knit and fiercely loyal, this small, jeans-and-flannel neighborhood saloon never turns away friendly strangers. ✉ *114 Christopher St., near Bleecker St., Greenwich Village* ☎ *212/741–9641.*

The Works. The crowd is usually J. Crew–style or disco-hangover at this Upper West Side institution. ✉ *428 Columbus Ave., between W. 80th and W. 81st Sts., Upper West Side* ☎ *212/799–7365.*

XL. Promoter John Blair and his partners poured a reported $2.5 million into this super-stylish lounge, but all eyes are on the friendly, bare-chested bartenders. Watch out for the fish tanks in the bathroom. ✉ *375 W. 16th St., between 8th and 9th Aves., Chelsea* ☎ *212/995–1400.*

Mixed Bars

Hanna's Lava Lounge. Christmas lights and wood paneling give this friendly hangout the look and feel of a well-worn basement. There are tarot card readings on most nights. ✉ *923 8th Ave., between W. 54th and W. 55th Sts., Midtown West* ☎ *212/974–9087.*

hell. This groovy Meatpacking District lounge with crystal chandeliers and red drapes attracts a hip, mixed crowd of Chelsea-ites and downtowners. ✉ *59 Gansevoort St., between Washington and Greenwich Sts., Greenwich Village* ☎ *212/727–1666.*

The Monster. A long-standing Village contender, the Monster has a piano bar upstairs and a pitch-black disco downstairs that continue to draw a busy blend of ages, races, and genders. ✉ *80 Grove St., between W. 4th St. and 7th Ave. S, Greenwich Village* ☎ *212/924–3558.*

Wonder Bar. A youngish crowd fills this friendly, popular lounge that has low sofas, and a DJ spinning hypnotic music on the speakers. ✉ *505 E. 6th St., between Aves. A and B, East Village* ☎ *212/777–9105.*

Women's Bars

Crazy Nanny's. The hairstyles here range from mullet to shaved head, and you'll find more of a racial mix than at most of Manhattan's lesbian bars. Different nights of the week have different themes and events. ✉ *21 7th Ave. S, between Leroy and Carmine Sts., Greenwich Village* ☎ *212/366–6312.*

Cubby Hole. Early on the crowd is mixed at this small institution with colorful plastic fish floating overhead. Later on the men move on and the room belongs to the women. ✉ *281 W. 12th St., at W. 4th St., Greenwich Village* ☎ *212/243–9041.*

Henrietta Hudson. Two rooms, a pool table, and party nights attract young professionals, out-of-towners, and longtime regulars to this laid-back bar. ✉ *438 Hudson St., at Morton St., Greenwich Village* ☎ *212/924–3347.*

Meow Mix. The East Village's only lesbian bar hosts live music, literary readings, cheap drinks, and the cutest girls in town. The young, sometimes outrageous, crowd pushes the fashion envelope way out there. ✉ *269 E. Houston St., at Suffolk St., East Village* ☎ *212/254–0688.*

SPORTS & THE OUTDOORS

7

FODOR'S CHOICE

Ice-skating, Rockefeller Center, *Midtown West*

Rent a Rowboat, Loeb Boathouse, *Central Park*

HIGHLY RECOMMENDED

Driving Range, Golf Club at Chelsea Piers, *Chelsea*

Rock Climbing, Extra Vertical Climbing Center, *Upper West Side*

Running, New York City Marathon, *New York City*

Tennis, U.S. Open Tennis Championships, *Queens*

Yoga, Jivamukti Yoga Center, *East Village*

Updated by Evelyn Kanter

LOOK AT ANY SUBWAY RIDER with a newspaper, and chances are they're perusing not the front page, but the sports section. New Yorkers are diehard sports fans, supporting their home teams whether it's the Yankees on top of their game or the Knicks struggling to make the play-offs. But this isn't just a city of watchers, it's a city of doers. From rock climbing to billiards, no matter what the sport or activity, there's a place to pursue it. You'll find oases of greenery all over New York—14% of the city, or approximately 28,500 acres, is parkland. Head to Central Park and join cyclists zooming by on thousand-dollar bikes, blissed-out runners circling the Reservoir, bird-watchers spying the latest avian arrivals, in-line skaters literally dancing in the streets, and even cross-country skiers when there's a bounty of winter snow. If you strike up a conversation while waiting to rent a bike, stretching before a jog, or before sliding your kayak into the Hudson River, you'll discover a friendly, relaxed side of the city. Just one word before you set out: weekends are very busy. If you need to rent equipment or secure space—a bicycle or a tennis court, for instance—go very early or very late, or be prepared to wait.

BEACHES

Good weather brings sun-worshiping New Yorkers out in force. Early in the season, Central Park's Sheep Meadow or even a "tar beach" rooftop is just fine for catching rays, but later on everyone heads for the beach in the city or on Long Island.

City Beaches

Brooklyn's **Brighton Beach,** in a largely Russian community sometimes called "Odessa by the Sea," is reached easily via the Q train. Be sure to stock up on homemade pierogies and other munchables en route to the boardwalk. The tame waves of adjacent **Coney Island** (☎ 718/946–1350) are the closest many New Yorkers get to the surf all year. Across the street from the last Brooklyn stop on the F, N, W, and Q lines, the beach here has a boardwalk and the famous amusement-park skyline of the Cyclone and the Wonderwheel as its backdrop. It's busy every day in summer. To see surfers riding the waves in wet suits, venture out on the A train to the beaches in the **Rockaways** (☎ 718/318–4000) section of Queens—at 9th Street, 23rd Street, or between 80th and 118th streets. The least crowded beaches are north of the last subway stop at 116th Street.

Long Island

The Long Island Railroad (LIRR ☎ 718/217–5477 🌐 www.mta.nyc.ny.us) provides easy access to all Long Island beaches. New Yorkers' favorite strand may be **Jones Beach** (☎ 516/785–1600), one of the world's great man-made beaches, built in the late 1920s under the reign of former parks commissioner Robert Moses. The train station nearest to Jones Beach is Freeport, where you can catch a shuttle to the water. The LIRR will take you directly to suburban **Long Beach,** where the beach and boardwalk are only a five-minute walk from the station. Stores and eateries line the main street, but there are no concessions along the boardwalk. On the west end of Fire Island, a narrow barrier island that runs along the southern coast of Long Island, there's a good beach at **Robert Moses State Park** (☎ 631/669–0449), also reachable via the LIRR and a bus.

PARKS & PLAYGROUNDS

Few New Yorkers have either a yard or a car, so the parks are necessary and much-appreciated getaways. In neighborhoods like the East Village, some residents even grow their vegetables in the small plots of community gardens. The most renowned park of all is, of course, **Central Park,** which beyond its verdant beauty serves the city as a gym, entertainment venue, and meeting point. Strictly for the kids are the 21 playgrounds full of slides, bridges, bars, swings, towers, and tunnels; they're carpeted with sand or soft rubber matting and are often cooled in summer by sprinklers or fountains. Good playgrounds can be found along 5th Avenue at 67th Street near the zoo, at 71st and 77th streets, at 85th Street near the Metropolitan Museum, and at 96th Street. Along Central Park West, the best playgrounds are at 68th, 82nd, 85th, 93rd, and 96th streets. The **Hecksher Playground,** at West 62nd Street, is the park's largest. Central Park's comprehensive Web site, www.centralpark.org, includes several virtual tours, including a "Kid's Day Out Tour."

The **Asser Levy Playground** (✉ E. 23rd St., 1 block from East River, Gramercy ☎ 212/447–2020) is the first in Manhattan to cater fully to children with disabilities, with giant, multicolor mazelike structures; helter-skelter slides with wheelchair stations; and textured pavement for children who are blind. An activity center and a playground near Vesey Street keep the kids giggling at **Battery Park City Parks** (✉ River Terr., between Chambers and Vesey Sts., Lower Manhattan ☎ 212/267–9700 🌐 www.bpcparks.org). Hundreds of free activities and events are scheduled here between May and October. **Hudson River Park's** Pier 25 at North Moore Street provides all sorts of free activities. Kids may try their hand at fishing in summer, as well as enjoy Ping-Pong, miniature golf, and other fun stuff. In **Riverside Park** (✉ W. 72nd through W. 158th Sts., west of Riverside Dr., Upper West Side), the best playgrounds are at 77th and 91st streets; the one at 77th Street has a circle of spouting elephant fountains. The amphitheater-shape hill behind the park at 91st Street is one of the best sledding hills in the city after a snowfall. **Washington Square Park** (✉ south end of 5th Ave. between Waverly Pl. and W. 4th St., Greenwich Village) has a shady playground, as well as jugglers, magicians, and musicians in summertime. *New York* magazine, sold at most newsstands, lists performances and activities for kids, or check listings at www.newyorkmetro.com.

SPORTS & FITNESS

For information about athletic facilities in Manhattan as well as a calendar of sporting events, pick up a copy of *MetroSports* at sporting-goods stores or health clubs. The magazine also has a good Web site, 🌐 www.metrosportsny.com. The sports section of *Time Out New York,* sold at most newsstands, lists upcoming events, times, dates, and ticket information. The City of New York's Parks & Recreation Web site, 🌐 www.nyc.gov/parks, lists all of the recreational facilities and activities available through New York's Parks Department.

Arenas

Many events—ranging from boxing to figure skating—take place at **Madison Square Garden** (✉ 7th Ave., between W. 31st and W. 33rd Sts., Midtown West 🌐 www.thegarden.com); tickets can be purchased in person at the box office (☎ 212/465–6741) or by phone through Ticketmaster (☎ 212/307–7171 🌐 www.ticketmaster.com). Check out the Garden's Web site for game and event schedules, plus a comprehensive overview of all the teams that call this gigantic structure home. Several pro teams, including New York's two football teams and New Jersey's basketball and hockey teams, play across the Hudson River at the **Meadowlands Sports Complex** (✉ Rte. 3 and New Jersey Tpke. Exit 16W,

East Rutherford, NJ ☎ 201/935–3900 for box office and information; 201/507–8900 for tickets 🌐 www.meadowlands.com), which includes the **Continental Airlines Arena** and **Giants Stadium.** Whenever there's a game, buses run directly from the Port Authority Bus Terminal in Manhattan. On the day of a sold-out game you can sometimes pick up a ticket outside the particular venue from a fellow sports fan. Ticket agencies, listed in the Manhattan Yellow Pages and the sports pages of the *Daily News*, can be helpful—for a price.

Baseball

New York baseball fans still reminisce about the Subway Series of 2000, when their two champions slugged it out in the World Series. The subway will get you directly to the stadiums, but the *Yankee Clipper* and *Mets Express* ferries (New York Waterways) also cruise from Manhattan's east side to the respective stadiums on game nights. For departure information call 800/533–3779. The regular baseball season runs from April through September.

The **New York Mets** play at **Shea Stadium** (✉ Roosevelt Ave. off Grand Central Pkwy., Flushing ☎ 718/507–8499), at the penultimate stop on the No. 7 train, in Queens. The **New York Yankees** reigned supreme in the 1996, 1998, 1999, and 2000 World Series, rallied a beleaguered city's spirits with their second-place finish in October 2001, and disappointed the city with a nonfinish in 2002. See them play at **Yankee Stadium** (✉ 161st St. and River Ave., Highbridge ☎ 718/293–6000), accessible by the No. 4 train to 161st Street or the B or D to 167th Street in the Bronx.

Founded in 2001, the minor league **Brooklyn Cyclones** (✉ 1904 Surf Ave., at 19th St., Coney Island ☎ 718/449–8497 🌐 www.brooklyncyclones.com) feeds into the New York Mets. The Cyclones won the New York–Penn League championship their very first year and were sold out at every home game. The season's 38 home games take place at KeySpan Park, on the Boardwalk with views of the Atlantic over the right-field wall and views of historic Astroland over the left-field wall. Most people make a day of it, with time at the beach and amusement rides before an evening game. Take the F, N, W, and Q subway lines to the end stop, and walk one block to the right of the original Nathan's Famous Hotdog Stand.

For a fun, family-oriented experience, check out the **Staten Island Yankees** (✉ Richmond County Bank Ballpark at St. George, Staten Island ☎ 718/720–9265), one of New York's minor league teams, which warms up many future New York Yankees players. The stadium, a five-minute walk from the Staten Island Ferry terminal, has magnificent panoramic views of Lower Manhattan and the Statue of Liberty.

Basketball

Watching pro basketball at Madison Square Garden is a legendary experience—if you can get a ticket. If the professional games are sold out, try to attend a college game where New York stalwarts Fordham, Hofstra, and St. John's compete against national top 25 teams during invitational tournaments. Log on to the Garden Web site, 🌐 www.thegarden.com, for game schedules. The Web site also provides listings of special basketball events, such as the Harlem Globetrotters.

The **New York Knicks** arouse intense hometown passions, which means tickets for home games at Madison Square Garden are still hard to come by, despite several losing seasons. For up-to-date game roundups, phone the **New York Knicks Fan Line** (☎ 212/465–5867) or log on to www.nyknicks.com for the latest scoop on the team. The **New Jersey Nets** play at the Meadowlands in the Continental Airlines Arena. For tickets—which are remarkably easy to obtain—call the **Meadowlands box office** (☎ 201/935–3900) or **Ticketmaster** (☎ 201/507–8900). The men's basketball season goes from late October through April.

The **Liberty** (☎ 877/962–2849 for tickets; 212/564–9622 fan hot line), New York's Women's NBA team, captured the 1999 and 2000 Eastern Conference Championships. Some of the team's more high-profile players are already legendary. In the stands you'll see many more women and girls than usually attend pro sports games, and there are followers who believe the women play a more skilled game than the guys. The season runs from Memorial Day weekend through August, with home games played at Madison Square Garden.

Bicycling

Even in tiny apartments, many locals keep a bicycle for transportation—the intrepid ones swear it's the best (and fastest) way to get around—and for rides on glorious days. A sleek pack of dedicated racers zooms around Central Park at dawn and at dusk daily, and on weekends the parks swarm with recreational cyclists. **Central Park** has a 6-mi circular drive with a couple of decent climbs. It's closed to automobile traffic from 10 AM to 3 PM (except the southeast portion between 6th Avenue and East 72nd Street) and 7 PM to 10 PM on weekdays, and from 7 PM Friday to 6 AM Monday. On holidays it's closed to automobile traffic from 7 PM the night before until 6 AM the day after. The bike lane along the **Hudson River Park's** esplanade parallels the waterfront from West 59th Street south to the esplanade of Battery Park City. The lane also heads north, connecting with the bike path in **Riverside Park,** the promenade between West 72nd and West 110th streets, and continuing all the way to the George Washington Bridge. From Battery Park it's a quick ride to the Wall Street area, which is deserted on weekends, and over to South Street and a bike lane along the East River. The 3⅓-mi circular drive in Brooklyn's **Prospect Park** is closed to cars weekends year-round and from 9 AM to 5 PM and 7 PM to 10 PM weekdays from April to November. It has a long, gradual uphill that tops off near the Grand Army Plaza entrance.

Bike Rentals

Expect to leave a deposit or a credit card and a photo ID when renting a bike. **Bicycle Rentals at Loeb Boathouse** (✉ Midpark near E. 74th St., Central Park ☎ 212/517–2233) provides sturdy cycles for the whole family at $6 to $20 per hour. **Hub Station** (✉ 517 Broome St., at Thompson St., SoHo ☎ 212/965–9334) rents electric bikes, tandems, recumbents, manual scooters, and old-fashioned two-wheelers at some of the lowest rates in the city. **Larry's & Jeff's Bicycles Plus** (✉ 1690 2nd Ave., at E. 87th St., Upper East Side ☎ 212/722–2201) rents mountain bikes and hybrids. **Pedal Pusher** (✉ 1306 2nd Ave., between E. 68th and E. 69th Sts., Upper East Side ☎ 212/288–5592) has everything from three-speeds to racing bikes to hybrids in its rental fleet. Also available are audio guides that describe the sights along a specified loop through Central Park—a great way to learn the history behind some of the park's many statues and areas of interest. **Toga Bike Shop** (✉ 110 West End Ave., at W. 64th St., Upper West Side ☎ 212/799–9625) rents all kinds of bikes.

Group Trips

For organized rides with other cyclists, call or write before you come to New York. **Bike New York** (✉ 891 Amsterdam Ave., at W. 103rd St.,

Upper West Side ☎ 212/932–2300 Ext. 111 🌐 www.bikenewyork.org) runs the five-borough bike ride in May and Sept. The **Five Borough Bicycle Club** (✉ 891 Amsterdam Ave., at W. 103rd St., Upper West Side ☎ 212/932–2300 Ext. 115 🌐 www.5bbc.org) organizes day and weekend rides. The **New York Cycle Club** (📭 Box 20541, Columbus Circle Station, 10023 ☎ 212/828–5711 🌐 www.nycc.org) sponsors weekend rides for every level of ability. **Time's Up!** (☎ 212/802–8222 🌐 www.times-up.org), a nonprofit environmental group, leads free recreational rides at least twice a month for cyclists as well as skaters; the Central Park Moonlight Ride, departing from Columbus Circle at 10 PM the first Friday of every month, is a favorite. **Transportation Alternatives** (✉ 115 W. 30th St., between 6th and 7th Aves., Suite 1207, Midtown West 10001 ☎ 212/629–8080 🌐 www.transalt.org) lists group rides throughout the metropolitan area in its bimonthly newsletter, which is distributed in many local bike stores.

Billiards

Pool halls used to be dusty, grimy, sticky places—and there are still a few of those around. But in New York they're outnumbered by a group of spots with deluxe decor, gourmet food, high prices, and even classical music or jazz in the background. Most halls are open late weekdays, even later on weekends.

Amsterdam Billiard Club (✉ 344 Amsterdam Ave., between W. 76th and W. 77th Sts., Upper West Side ☎ 212/496–8180) can satisfy your hustling desires until 3 AM weekdays and 4 AM weekends—365 days a year. A side benefit are the stargazing opportunities, as the club counts Jerry Seinfeld, Bruce Willis, Paul Sorvino, and Eric Clapton among its "regulars." The club has 31 pool tables and a full bar. **Amsterdam Billiard Club East** (✉ 210 E. 86th St., between 2nd and 3rd Aves., Upper East Side ☎ 212/570–4545) has 30 pool tables, three professional Ping-Pong tables, a café, and a full bar. You might spot a celebrity here, too. **Billiard Club** (✉ 220 W. 19th St., between 7th and 8th Aves., Chelsea ☎ 212/206–7665) has 16 tables and a classy look and plays loud rock music. **Corner Billiards** (✉ 85 4th Ave., at E. 11th St., East Village ☎ 212/995–1314) draws a college crowd to its 28 tables on weekends and is busy with league play during the week. **East Side Amusements** (✉ 163 E. 86th St., between 3rd and Lexington Aves., Upper East Side ☎ 212/831–7665) has 11 tables, plus a video game arcade. **SoHo Billiards** (✉ 56 E. Houston St., between Mott and Mulberry Sts., SoHo ☎ 212/925–3753) has a great location to attract weary bar hoppers. On the two floors of **Slate Restaurant Bar & Billiard** (✉ 54 W. 21st St., between 5th and 6th Aves., Flatiron District ☎ 212/989–0096) you'll find 30 pool tables and three for snooker downstairs.

Bird-Watching

New York's green parks and woodlands provide habitats for thousands of birds, everything from fork-tailed flycatchers to common nighthawks. Because the city is on the Atlantic flyway, a major migratory route, you can see birds that nest as far north as the high Arctic. April and May are the best months. The songbirds are in their freshest colors then, and so many sing at once that you can hardly distinguish their songs. Fall is also an excellent season for birding in New York. To find out what's been seen where and when, call in to hear the thorough recording of the **Rare Bird Alert** (☎ 212/979–3070). For information on the best bird-watching spots in city parks, contact the **Urban Park Rangers** (☎ 866/692–4295 🌐 www.nyc.gov/parks), a uniformed division of the Parks

Department. In addition to birding information, the Urban Park Rangers provide numerous educational programs focusing on conservation, nature exploration, history, and more.

The Ramble in Manhattan's **Central Park** is full of warblers in springtime and may attract as many birders as it does birds. In Brooklyn, **Green-wood Cemetery** (✉ 5th Ave. and 25th St., Sunset Park ☎ 718/768–7300 for permission to enter grounds) features Victorian-era headstones, as well as a woodland that attracts hawks and songbirds. Walks often take place in **Prospect Park.** In Queens try **Jamaica Bay Wildlife Refuge,** where birds are drawn to the 9,155 acres of salt marshes, fresh and brackish ponds, open water, and upland fields and woods. Stop first at the **visitor center** (✉ Crossbay Blvd., Broad Channel ☎ 718/318–4340) to get a free permit, which lists the rules for this National Park Service site. The Bronx's 1,146-acre **Van Cortlandt Park** (✉ Riverdale ☎ 718/430–1890) is reachable via the No. 1 or 9 subway to West 242nd Street and has varied habitats, including freshwater marshes and upland woods. In Staten Island, head for the mostly undeveloped 312-acre **Wolfe's Pond Park** (✉ Cornelia Ave. and Hylan Blvd., Huguenot ☎ 718/984–8266), where the pond and the nearby shore can be dense with geese and ducks during migrations. From the Staten Island Ferry station, transfer to the Staten Island Rapid Transit, getting off at the Huguenot Avenue station. It's a short walk from there.

Guided Walks

The **New York City Audubon Society** (✉ 71 W. 23rd St., between 5th and 6th Aves., Flatiron District ☎ 212/691–7483 🌐 www.nycas.org) conducts frequent bird-watching outings; call weekdays 10–4 for information. Also check with the Urban Park Rangers at the number listed above.

Boating & Kayaking

Fodor'sChoice ★

Central Park has rowboats (plus one Venetian gondola for glides in the moonlight) on the 18-acre Central Park Lake. Rent your boat at **Loeb** Boathouse (☎ 212/517–2233), near East 74th Street, from spring through fall. **Floating the Apple** (✉ W. 44th St. and the Hudson River, Midtown West ☎ 212/564–5412) has free rows and sails in community group–made boats from Pier 84 at West 43rd Street; Pier 40 at West Houston Street; Erie Basin in Red Hook, Brooklyn; and from the ferry stop in Weehauken, New Jersey.

At the **Downtown Boathouse** (✉ Pier 26, N. Moore St. and the Hudson River, TriBeCa ☎ 212/385–2790 🌐 www.downtownboathouse.org) you can take a sturdy kayak out for a paddle for free on summer weekends and weekday evenings. Beginners learn to paddle in the calmer embayment area closest to shore until they feel ready to venture farther out onto open water. More experienced kayakers can partake in the three-hour trips offered every weekend and on holiday mornings. Sign-ups for these extremely popular tours end at 8 AM. Due to high demand, names are entered into a lottery to see who gets to go out each morning. No reservations are taken in advance. **Manhattan Kayak Company** (✉ Chelsea Piers, Pier 60, W. 23rd St. and the Hudson River, Chelsea ☎ 212/924–1788 🌐 www.manhattankayak.com) runs trips (these are not free) and gives lessons for all levels.

Bowling

Bowling may not be the first thing that comes to mind when you think of New York City, but local bowling alleys are perfect for group outings, especially when the weather is terribly cold, or unbearably hot. **AMF**

Chelsea Piers Bowling Center (✉ between Piers 59 and 60, W. 18th St. and the Hudson River, Chelsea ☎ 212/835–2695) has 40 lanes and all the latest bowling trends—glow-in-the-dark and "extreme" bowling on Thursday, Friday, and Saturday nights after 8 PM—and fine finger foods. Bowl to dance tunes at the funky **Bowlmor Lanes** (✉ 110 University Pl., between E. 12th and E. 13th Sts., Greenwich Village ☎ 212/255–8188), a 42-lane bi-level operation that can have a two-hour wait for a lane on weekend nights. If you're lucky, you can stay inside with a beeper so you can eat, drink at the bar, or wander upstairs to the pool tables while you wait. After 6 PM it's strictly 21-and-over. **Leisure Time Bowling & Recreation Center** (✉ Port Authority Bus Terminal, south bldg., 2nd level, W. 42nd St. and 8th Ave., Midtown West ☎ 212/268–6909) offers 30 lanes and New York's most traditional bowling alley atmosphere. It's more affordable than Manhattan's other lanes, which brings out families on weekends.

Boxing

Major and minor boxing bouts are staged in Madison Square Garden throughout the year. Log on to www.thegarden.com for match listings. **Church Street Boxing Gym** (✉ 25 Park Pl., between Church St. and Broadway, Lower Manhattan ☎ 212/571–1333) has amateur boxing and kickboxing fights on some Friday nights; call for the schedule. Several of the trainers here are Golden Gloves champions.

If you're interested in getting in the ring yourself, **Chelsea Piers Sports Center** (✉ W. 23rd St. and the Hudson River, Chelsea ☎ 212/336–6000) has a boxing ring and equipment circuit. **Crunch Fitness** (✉ 404 Lafayette St., at E. 4th St., East Village ☎ 212/614–0120) gives classes in its boxing ring. Brooklyn's venerable **Gleason's** (✉ 83 Front St., between Washington and Main Sts., DUMBO ☎ 718/797–2872), home of more than 100 world champs, including Muhammad Ali, instructs visitors and allows spectators for a small fee. Don't miss the monthly White Collar Fight Night; it's exactly what it sounds like.

Chess & Checkers

In **Central Park,** the Chess & Checkers House (✉ Midpark at 64th St., Central Park) perches atop a massive stone outcrop. Twenty-four outdoor tables are available during daylight hours. Bring your own or pick up playing pieces at The Dairy (✉ Midpark at 64th St., Central Park ☎ 212/794–6564) Tuesday–Sunday 11–5; there's no charge, but a photo ID is required. Downtown, the **Village Chess Shop** (✉ 230 Thompson St., between Bleecker and W. 3rd Sts., Greenwich Village ☎ 212/475–9580) has 30 boards that it rents by the hour for play in the store, along with timers for speed chess. Outdoor players congregate at the tables in the southwest corner of **Washington Square Park** (✉ W. 4th and MacDougal Sts., Greenwich Village), where, for a small donation to the regulars, you can borrow pieces and a timer. You can even play against the people in charge—good luck trying to win.

Classes & Cardio

Chelsea Piers Sports Center (✉ W. 23rd St. and the Hudson River, Chelsea ☎ 212/336–6000) sells a day pass for $50 that includes access to all the impressive facilities and classes this sports behemoth has to offer. **Crunch Fitness** (✉ 404 Lafayette St., at E. 4th St., East Village ☎ 212/614–0120 ✉ 54 E. 13th St., between Broadway and University Pl., Greenwich Village ☎ 212/475–2018 ✉ 162 W. 83rd St., between Columbus and Amsterdam Aves., Upper West Side ☎ 212/875–1902 ✉ 1109 2nd Ave., at E. 59th St., Midtown East ☎ 212/758–3434 🌐 www.crunch.com) offers everything from straight-up cardio to kickboxing, yoga, pilates, and body sculpting. Day passes are $24. **New York Sports Clubs** (✉ 30 Wall St., between Nassau and William Sts., Lower Manhattan ☎ 212/482–4800 ✉ 1601 Broadway, at W. 49th St., Midtown West ☎ 212/977–8880 ✉ 200 Madison Ave., at E. 36th St., Murray Hill ☎ 212/686–1144 ✉ 125 7th Ave. S, at W. 10th St., Greenwich Village ☎ 212/206–1500 🌐 www.nysc.com) are well equipped and have conditioning and strength-training classes at times and locations likely to suit any schedule. A day pass is $25. The **Vanderbilt YMCA** (✉ 224 E. 47th St., between 2nd and 3rd Aves., Midtown East ☎ 212/756–9600) schedules nearly 200 drop-in exercise classes every week. Day passes are $25, and include the swimming pool.

Football

The football season runs from September through December. The enormously popular **New York Giants** (☎ 201/935–8111 for tickets) play at Giants Stadium in the Meadowlands Sports Complex. Most seats for Giants games are sold on a season-ticket basis—and there's a very long waiting list for those. However, single tickets are occasionally available at the stadium box office. The **New York Jets** (☎ 516/560–8200 for tickets; 516/560–8288 for fan club) also play at Giants Stadium. Although they're not as scarce as Giants tickets, most Jets tickets are snapped up by fans before the season opener.

Golf

Queens has a 6,053-yard, par-70 course at **Forest Park** (✉ 101 Forest Park Dr., Woodhaven ☎ 718/296–0999). The greens fee runs $21–$24; a cart costs $27. Staten Island has the 6,138-yard, par-69 **Silver Lake Golf Course** (✉ 915 Victory Blvd., 1 block south of Forest Ave., Silver Lake Park ☎ 718/447–5686). The greens fee ranges from $21 to $30; a two-person cart costs $27. Of the 14 city courses, the 6,281-yard, par-71 **Split Rock** (✉ 870 Shore Rd., Pelham Bay Park ☎ 718/885–1258) in the Bronx is the most challenging. Slightly easier is its sister course, the 6,307-yard, par-71 Pelham Bay, which has fewer trees. Both courses cost $21–$27 plus $27 for a cart. Van Cortlandt Park, in the Bronx, has the nation's first public golf course, established in 1895: the hilly 6,102-yard, par-70 **Van Cortlandt** (✉ Bailey Ave., Van Cortlandt Park ☎ 718/543–4595). The greens fee runs $21–$30, and a cart costs $27.

The 18-hole miniature golf course at **Pier 25** (✉ Hudson River at Reade St., TriBeCa ☎ 212/766–1104), open seasonally, has a great riverside location and fabulous fresh lemonade.

Driving Ranges

★ Jutting out into the Hudson, the **Golf Club at Chelsea Piers** (✉ Pier 59, W. 23rd St. and the Hudson River, Chelsea ☎ 212/336–6400) has a 200-yard artificial-turf fairway, a computerized tee-up system, and 52 heated hitting stalls ($15 for a bucket of balls). In the middle of the East River, the **Randall's Island Golf Center** (✉ Randall's Island ☎ 212/427–5689) has a 300-yard driving range with 80 heated stalls ($6 for a bucket of balls) and lessons. There are also batting cages and two 18-hole miniature golf courses. A shuttle bus departs from 3rd Avenue between East 86th and 87th streets every hour on the hour weekdays 3–8 and weekends 10–5. The round-trip cost is $10.

Hockey

The hockey season runs from October through April. Tickets for the Islanders and Devils are usually available at game time; Rangers tickets are more difficult to find. The **New Jersey Devils** (☎ 201/935–6050) fight for the puck at the Continental Airlines Arena at the Meadowlands. The **New York Islanders** (✉ Nassau Veterans Memorial Coliseum, Uniondale ☎ 631/888–9000 for tickets) skate in Long Island. Take the LIRR to Westbury station, from which it's a 10-minute cab ride to the Coliseum. The Stanley Cup Champion **New York Rangers** (☎ 212/465–6741 for ticket office) play at Madison Square Garden.

Horse Racing & Horseback Riding

Modern **Aqueduct Racetrack** (✉ 110th St. and Rockaway Blvd., Ozone Park, Queens ☎ 718/641–4700), with its abundant lawns and gardens, holds Thoroughbred races late October–early May, Wednesday–Sunday. In May the action moves to **Belmont Park** (✉ Hempstead Tpke., Elmont, Long Island ☎ 718/641–4700), home of the third jewel in horse racing's triple crown, the Belmont Stakes. The horses run here May–June and early September–October, Wednesday–Sunday. The **Meadowlands** (☎ 201/935–8500 for race information) has Thoroughbred racing September–mid-December and harness racing the rest of the year (late December–mid-August). **Yonkers Raceway** (✉ Yonkers and Central Aves., Yonkers ☎ 718/562–9500) features harness racing every evening except Wednesday and Sunday year-round.

If you'd rather ride than watch, there are two riding academies in the city. The **Claremont Riding Academy** (✉ 175 W. 89th St., between Columbus and Amsterdam Aves., Upper West Side ☎ 212/724–5100) is the city's oldest riding academy (established in 1892). Experienced English riders can rent horses for an unescorted walk, trot, or canter on nearby Central Park's bridle path; escorted rides are also available by special arrangement for experienced riders. Call ahead to reserve, preferably a week in advance. **New York City Riding Academy** (✉ Randall's Island ☎ 212/860–2986) rents to the general public (English and Western saddles available) for rides on outdoor rings; trail rides may also be available provided you pass a riding test. Take the No. 4, 5, or 6 subway to East 125th Street, and then transfer to the M35 bus.

Ice-Skating

The city's outdoor rinks are open from mid-October through mid-April, depending on the weather, and each has its own character. Central Park's **Lasker Rink** (✉ Midpark near E. 106th St., Central Park ☎ 212/534–7639), at the north end of the park, is smaller and usually less crowded than Wollman Memorial Rink. The outdoor rink in **Rockefeller Center** (✉ 50th St. at 5th Ave., lower plaza, Midtown West ☎ 212/332–7654) is fairly small (and very busy, so be prepared to wait—there are no advance ticket sales) yet utterly romantic, especially when the enormous Christmas tree towers above it. If you're a self-conscious skater, note that there are usually huge crowds watching. Chelsea Piers' **Sky Rink** (✉ Pier 61, W. 23rd St. and the Hudson River, Chelsea ☎ 212/336–6100) has two year-round indoor rinks overlooking the Hudson; one is almost always open for general skating, and the other hosts leagues, lessons, and special events. The beautifully situated **Wollman Memorial Rink** (✉ 6th Ave. at 59th St., north of park entrance, Central Park ☎ 212/439–6900) offers skating until 11 PM beneath the lights of the city. Be prepared for daytime crowds on weekends. Prospect Park's **Kate Woll-**

Fodor'sChoice ★

man Memorial Rink (✉ Ocean Ave. and Parkside Ave., Prospect Park, Brooklyn ☎ 718/287–6431) borders the lake, and has a picture-postcard setting. Rentals are available at all locations.

In-Line Skating

In-line skating remains a popular form of both recreation and transportation for many New Yorkers. **Central Park** is headquarters for city skaters. Most seem to prefer circling the park, though not everyone is strong enough to make it up the hill at the park's northwest corner; to skip it, take the cutoff near 103rd Street. On weekends, between the Mall and Bethesda Fountain, dancing skaters whirl and twirl to disco music emanating from the huge speakers they set up. On weekends from April through October the **Central Park Skate Patrol** (☎ 212/439–1234) holds $20 clinics for skaters of all levels. Call for times and registration information. The **Hudson River Park Esplanade,** from West 59th Street down to Battery Park, is a scenic, flat skate on a marked lane (there are separate marked lanes for joggers and strollers).

The outdoor roller rink at **Chelsea Piers** (✉ Pier 62, W. 23rd St. and the Hudson River, Chelsea ☎ 212/336–6200) is open from April through October and rents in-line skates and provides classes, Rollaerobics, and hip-hop dance parties by special arrangement. There's also a skate park, with ramps, half-pipes, rails, and other in-line challenges; it's open to skateboarders as well. The **Roxy** (✉ 515 W. 18th St., between 10th and 11th Aves., Chelsea ☎ 212/645–5156), a downtown dance club, goes roller-disco on Wednesday nights. You must be 21 or older to enter.

Blades (✉ 160 E. 86th St., between 3rd and Lexington Aves., Upper East Side ☎ 212/996–1644 ✉ 120 W. 72nd St., between Broadway and Columbus Ave., Upper West Side ☎ 212/787–3911 ✉ 659 Broadway, between Bleecker and Bond Sts., Greenwich Village ☎ 212/477–7350) has several Manhattan stores selling and renting skates along with all the protective gear. **Empire Skate Club** (☎ 212/774–1774) runs skate trips for members and fields skating questions. **Peck & Goodie** (✉ 917 8th Ave., at W. 54th St., Midtown West ☎ 212/246–6123) sells and rents skates. Skaters are welcome on all **Time's Up!** (☎ 212/802–8222) bike rides.

Rock Climbing

For rock jocks and beginners alike, New York's indoor climbing walls provide hand-cramping challenges of the vertical sort. Lessons and equipment rentals (harness and climbing shoes) are available at the walls listed below, and experienced climbers should expect to take a belay test before they're free to belay their partners. You can usually find a partner if you're solo. **Chelsea Piers** (✉ W. 23rd St. and the Hudson River, Chelsea ☎ 212/336–6000) has two climbing areas: a 10-ft wall in the field house designed for children (but adults are welcome, too), and a 46-ft-high, 10,000-square-ft climbing wall plus separate bouldering wall in the Sports Center. Both allow nonmembers, though the day rate ★ is higher in the Sports Center. The **Extra Vertical Climbing Center** (✉ 61 W. 62 St., at Broadway, Upper West Side ☎ 212/586–5718) has an indoor-outdoor (covered) wall ranging from 30 to 50 ft high. Taking a climb above gawking pedestrians is an only-in-NYC experience. It's a great place to watch, and there's a $10 "challenge" package for beginners that includes instruction, equipment, and two climbs. The **Manhattan Plaza Health Club Climbing Wall** (✉ 482 W. 43rd St., between 9th and 10th Aves., Midtown West ☎ 212/563–7001) has an indoor 5,000-square-ft wall with overhangs, geometric forms, a 40-ft lead climbing roof, and a bouldering cave. Experienced climbers can drop in for $15 a day; beginners should call in advance for a $40 orientation lesson.

Squirrel Island Expeditions (☎ 203/966–2569 🌐 www.squirrelislandexpeditions.com) offers day and weekend climbing and kayaking instruction trips out of New York City, including round-trip transportation from Manhattan.

Soccer

Since 1996 the tri-state area has had a national major-league soccer team, the **MetroStars** (☎ 201/583–7000). Games take place at Giants Stadium from April to September. Tickets are easy to get. **The New York Power** (✉ Mitchel Athletic Complex, Uniondale, Long Island ☎ 866/769–7849 🌐 www.nypower.com), New York's first professional women's soccer team, began play in April 2001. You can catch a glimpse of some of the world's finest female soccer players from April to August. Take the Long Island Railroad to the Mineola Station and transfer to the stadium via shuttle bus.

Swimming

Asphalt Green (✉ 1750 York Ave., between E. 90th and E. 92nd Sts., Upper East Side ☎ 212/369–8890) has a breathtaking 50-m pool (known as AquaCenter), which is usually sectioned off into 25-yard and 20-yard lap areas, and a full fitness center; the daily drop-in fee is $20 for either the pool or the fitness center. Nonmembers are not allowed in the pool between 3 PM and 8 PM. The **Carmine Recreation Center** (✉ 7th Ave. S and Clarkson St., Greenwich Village ☎ 212/242–5228) has a 23-yard indoor pool and a 105-yard outdoor pool (only one is open at a time). The $25 annual membership fee allows access to the pool, fitness facilities, and classes. Bring your own padlock, towel, and shower shoes; it's a no-frills kind of place. **Chelsea Piers Sports Center** (✉ Pier 60, W. 23rd St. and the Hudson River, Chelsea ☎ 212/336–6000) has a six-lane, 25-yard lap pool surrounded by windows overlooking the Hudson, with an adjacent whirlpool and sundeck. Day passes for the exercise club, including the pool, are $50. **Lasker Pool** (✉ Central Park between E. 106th and E. 107th Sts. ☎ 212/534–7639) offers free swimming in its outdoor pool from July 4th weekend through Labor Day weekend—if you can brave the crowds. The **Vanderbilt YMCA** (✉ 224 E. 47th St., between 2nd and 3rd Aves., Midtown East ☎ 212/756–9600) has two clean, brightly lighted lap pools open to nonmembers for a $25 day fee. The sparkling 25-yard lap pool at the **YWCA** (✉ 610 Lexington Ave., at E. 53rd St., Midtown East ☎ 212/755–4500) is available for $25.

Tennis

The New York City Parks Department maintains scores of tennis courts. Scenic—and economical—are the 26 clay courts and four hard courts in **Central Park** (✉ Midpark near 96th St., Central Park ☎ 212/280–0206), set in a thicket of trees with the skyline beyond. **Riverside Park** (☎ 212/496–2006) has 10 clay courts at 96th Street and 10 hard courts at 119th Street, with the bonus of being cooled by Hudson River breezes. Admission to all of these courts is available without reservations or seasonal permits, for $5 per hour, from April through November. These courts can be extremely busy so be prepared to wait several hours.

Several local clubs will book courts to nonmembers: **Crosstown Tennis** (✉ 14 W. 31st St., between 5th Ave. and Broadway, Murray Hill ☎ 212/

947–5780) has four indoor hard courts; fees range from $45 to $95 hourly. The five hard-surface courts at **Manhattan Plaza Racquet Club** (✉ 450 W. 43rd St., between 9th and 10th Aves., Midtown West ☎ 212/594–0554) see the soles of some famous regulars. The hourly fee for same-day reservations is $70 to $90, but the hours nonmembers can play are limited. At **Midtown Tennis Club** (✉ 341 8th Ave., between W. 26th and W. 27th Sts., Chelsea ☎ 212/989–8572 🌐 www.midtowntennis.com) it's best to make reservations for one of the eight courts (some outdoor in summer, bubbled in winter) a couple of days in advance. Hourly rates are $50–$75. **Sutton East Tennis Club** (✉ York Ave. at 60th St., Upper East Side ☎ 212/751–3452) charges hourly rates ranging from $46 to $125 for its eight indoor clay courts.

The **USTA National Tennis Center** (✉ Flushing Meadows–Corona Park, Queens ☎ 718/760–6200), site of the U.S. Open Tennis Championships, has 42 courts (33 outdoor and 9 indoor, all Deco Turf II) open to the public all year except August and September. Reservations are accepted up to two days in advance, and prices are $15–$44 hourly.

ON THE SIDELINES ★ If you want to see the pros battle it out on the courts, don't miss the annual **U.S. Open Tennis Championships,** held from late August through early September at the **USTA National Tennis Center.** This is one of the high points of the tennis buff's year, and tickets to watch the late rounds are some of the hottest in town. Early round matches are entertaining, too, and with a stadium-court ticket you can also view matches in outlying courts. The championships are played at the 23,000-seat Arthur Ashe Stadium. Tickets go on sale in May through the **USTA box office** (☎ 718/760–6200 🌐 www.usta.com).

Volleyball

Both beach and lawn courts await those looking for a good volley. **Central Park** (✉ Midpark at 66th St. and 86th St.) has two areas for pick-up game play: a sand court east of Sheep Meadow, midpark at 66th Street, and three lawn courts near the Great Lawn, midpark at 86th Street. Pick-up games are on a first-come, first-served basis, and you need to bring your own volleyball. You must also bring your own net if playing on the Sheep Meadow court. **Chelsea Piers Sports Center** (✉ Pier 60, W. 23rd St. and the Hudson River, Chelsea ☎ 212/336–6000) has Manhattan's only indoor sand volleyball court. Day passes for the entire complex are $50. On Monday nights a volleyball fundamental class is offered at 8 PM. Hudson River Park's **Pier 25** (✉ N. Moore St. and the Hudson River, TriBeCa ☎ 212/766–1104) has three sand courts available for groups, but you should call ahead to reserve one. On weekends, courts are $10 per hour; on weeknights the fee jumps to $30 per hour. The **New York Urban Professionals Volleyball League** (✉ 200 W. 72nd St., Suite 68, Upper West Side ☎ 212/877–3614) offers open-play volleyball most Friday nights 7–10:30 for $10 per person at Brandeis High School on West 84th Street between Amsterdam and Columbus avenues, and at LaGuardia High School at West 65th Street and Amsterdam Avenue. Call to find out which location has a game at your skill level. There are also games on Sunday afternoons at Brandeis for $12.

Walking, Jogging & Running

Walking

Touring the streets of New York will keep you on your feet from morning until night, but if you're interested in joining locals on a walking work-out, try one of these walking clubs. **Take a Walk, New York!** (☎ 212/379–8339 🌐 www.WalkNY.org) draws scores of locals with its free three-hour walks that cover 4 to 6 mi. The city's Department of Health and the Neighborhood Open Space Coalition are cosponsors of the weekend walks that often take place along parklands in the outer boroughs and over city bridges. A fact sheet and commentary on local history and environmental issues are part of the exercise.

Racewalkers can move as fast as some joggers, the great difference being that their heels are planted firmly with every stride. Competitive racewalking events are held regularly by the **Park Race Walkers' Club** (✉ 320 E. 83rd St., 10028 ☎ 212/628–1317).

Jogging

All kinds of New Yorkers jog, some with dogs or babies in tow, so you'll always have company on the regular jogging routes. What's not recommended is to set out on a lonely park path at dusk. Jog when and where everybody else does. On Manhattan streets, figure 20 north–south blocks per mile.

In Manhattan, **Central Park** is the busiest spot, specifically along the 1⅗-mi path circling the **Jacqueline Kennedy Onassis Reservoir.** A runners' lane has been designated along the park roads. A good 1¾-mi route starts at Tavern on the Green along the West Drive, heads south around the bottom of the park to the East Drive, and circles back west on the 72nd Street park road to your starting point; the entire loop road is a hilly 6 mi. **Riverside Park,** along the Hudson River bank in Manhattan, is glorious at sunset. You can cover 4½ mi by running from West 72nd to 116th Street and back, and the **Greenbelt** trail extends 4 more miles north to the George Washington Bridge at 181st Street.

Other favorite Manhattan circuits are the **Battery Park City** esplanade (about 2 mi), which connects to the longer **Hudson River Park** (about 1½ mi), and the **East River Esplanade** (just over 3 mi from East 59th to East 125th streets). Tiny, but pleasant loops are around **Gramercy Park** (⅕ mi) and **Washington Square Park** (½ mi). In Brooklyn try the **Brooklyn Heights Promenade** (⅓ mi), which faces the Manhattan skyline, or the loop in **Prospect Park** (3⅓ mi).

Running

The **Achilles Track Club** (☎ 212/354–0300 🌐 www.achillestrackclub.org), for runners with disabilities, has free two-hour guided workouts on Tuesday and Saturday at 10 AM leaving from the New York Roadrunners Club. The **Hash House Harriers** organize runs with a purpose: they always end up at a bar. There's usually more than one run in New York City each week. Call 212/427–4692 for times, fees, and locations.

The **New York Road Runners Club** (✉ 9 E. 89th St., between Madison and 5th Aves., Upper East Side ☎ 212/860–4455) organizes a year-round schedule of races and group runs. The latter begin at 6:30 AM and 6:30 PM on weekdays and at 10 AM on weekends. Runners meet at the club kiosk along the bridal path near the Central Park entrance at East 90th Street and 5th Avenue. The runs are open to runners—members or not—of all levels. At the 4-mi Midnight Run, held on New Year's Eve in Central Park, runners show up wearing costumes, and the night culminates with fireworks.

ON THE SIDELINES ★ If you prefer to watch other people run, the **New York City Marathon** has rocked the city on the first Sunday in November every year since 1970. Millions of spectators cheer on the pack of more than 30,000 international participants (some 98% of whom finish). World-class marathoners, racewalkers, senior citizens, competitors with disabilities, runners in costume, and thousands of volunteers help to make this an incredibly spirited event. New Yorkers line rooftops and sidewalks, promenades, and terraces along the route, which covers ground in all five boroughs. Don't go near the finish line in Central Park around 2 PM unless you relish mob scenes. Contact the **New York Road Runners Club** (✉ 9 E. 89th St., between Madison and 5th Aves., Upper East Side ☎ 212/860–4455).

Yoga

Has the pace of New York City gotten you wound up? Are you yearning to both stretch your limbs and center yourself? Yoga studios across the city offer classes with reasonable drop-in rates. Hatha yoga classes take place every day of the week at all levels at the **Integral Yoga Institute** (✉ 227 W. 13th St., between 7th and 8th Aves., Greenwich Village ☎ 212/929–0586 ✉ 200 W. 72nd St., between Broadway and West End Ave., Upper West Side ☎ 212/721–4000). Chanting and meditation is ★ part of the vigorous practice at **Jivamukti Yoga Center** (✉ 404 Lafayette St., between Astor Pl. and E. 4th St., East Village ☎ 212/353–0214 ✉ 853 Lexington Ave., between E. 64th and E. 65th Sts., Upper East Side ☎ 212/396–4200). Classes last 1 hour and 35 minutes and are accompanied by taped music. Evening sessions fill up fast; arrive early or call ahead to secure your $17 spot. Mat rental is $2. Don't be surprised to see celebrities here. The soothingly decorated **SoHo Sanctuary** (✉ 119 Mercer St., between Prince and Spring Sts., SoHo ☎ 212/334–5550) is for women only. Hatha, Iyengar, and Vinyasa are among the classes that take place every day but Monday. The one-class rate of $25 includes use of a yoga mat, showers, locker, and steam bath. "Ishta," or the integrated traditions of Hatha, Tantra, and Ayurveda yoga, is practiced at **Yoga Zone** (✉ 160 E. 56th St., between Lexington and 3rd Aves., Midtown East ☎ 212/935–9642 ✉ 138 5th Ave., between E. 18th and E. 19th Sts., Flatiron District ☎ 212/647–9642), which has a full schedule of classes at both locations. A single class costs $20.

SHOPPING

8

FODOR'S CHOICE

ABC Carpet & Home, *Flatiron District*
B & H Photo Video and Pro Audio, *Midtown West*
Barneys New York, *Upper East Side*
Century 21, *Lower Manhattan*
Enchanted Forest, *SoHo*
Madison Avenue and 57th Street
Kate's Paperie, *SoHo*
Kiehl's Since 1851, *East Village*
NoLita's pint-sized boutiques
Tiffany & Co, *Midtown East*

HIGHLY RECOMMENDED

Crawford Doyle Booksellers, *Upper East Side*
F.A.O. Schwarz, *Midtown East*
Kirna Zabête, *SoHo*
La Maison du Chocolat, *Upper East Side*
Louis Vuitton, *Midtown East*
Moss, *SoHo*
Other Music, *East Village*
Richart Design et Chocolat, *Midtown East*
St. Mark's Bookshop, *East Village*

By Jennifer Paull

TRUE TO ITS NATURE, New York shops on a grand scale at the world's finest department stores, glossy couture houses along Madison Avenue, fashionable boutiques downtown, and renowned antiques dealers all over the city. NoLita practically steams with chic, its streets full of upstart clothing lines and exotic home-design stores, and hip retailers continue to waft into Chelsea. No matter which threshold you cross, shopping in New York is an event.The city whets acquisitive appetites with widely varied shopping experiences. For every bursting department store, there's an echoing, minimalist boutique; for every nationally familiar brand, there's a local favorite. The foremost American and international designers stake their flagship stores here; meanwhile, small neighborhood shops guarantee a reservoir of both the down-to-earth and the unexpected. National chains often make their New York stores something special, with unique sales environments and merchandise.

One of Manhattan's biggest shopping lures is the bargain—a temptation fueled by Loehmann's, H&M, and other discount divas. Hawkers of not-so-real Rolex watches and Kate Spade bags are stationed at street corners, even on Madison Avenue, and Canal Street is lined with counterfeit Gucci logos and Burberry plaid. There are uptown thrift shops where socialites send their castoffs, and downtown spots where the fashion crowd turns in last week's supertrendy must-haves. And of course, thousands of eyes train on the cycles of sales.

SALES

If a seasonal sale makes New Yorkers' eyes gleam, a sample sale throws the city's shoppers into a frenzy. With so many designer flagships and corporate headquarters in town, merchandise fallout periodically leads to tremendous deals. Sample sales typically comprise leftover, already discounted stock, sample designs, and show models. Location adds a bit of an illicit thrill to the event—sales are held in hotels, warehouses, or loft space. Clothes incredible and unfortunate jam a motley assortment of racks, tables, and bins. Generally, there is a makeshift communal dressing room, and mirrors are scarce. Veteran sample-sale shoppers come prepared for wriggling in the aisles; some wear skirts, tights, and tank tops for modest quick-changes. Two rules of thumb: grab first and inspect later, and call in advance to find out what methods of payment are accepted.

The level of publicity and regularity of sales vary. Be sure to check out *New York* magazine's "Sales and Bargains" column, which often lists sales in manufacturers' showrooms that are not otherwise promoted publicly, and *Time Out New York*'s "Shoptalk" page, which includes sales. The *Village Voice* is also a good source for tip-off ads. High season for sales is August–September and February–March, but these days an offloading of goods can happen year-round. One of the ultimate experiences is the Barneys Warehouse Sale, held in February and August in the über-stylish department store's Chelsea location. Other luscious sales range from the Vera Wang bridal-gown sale (early winter) and TSE cashmere (spring and late fall) to the downtown chic of Katayone Adeli (late summer). If you're interested in specific designers, call their shops and inquire—you may get lucky. If it's not a sale period, you can always get a bargain fix at **Woodbury Commons** (☎ 845/928–4000), a giant outlet village in Central Valley, New York, where businesses such as Brooks Brothers, DKNY, and Williams-Sonoma offer deep discounts. **Shortline Coach USA** (☎ 800/631–8405) buses shuttle from New York City to the outlet several times a day.

Get your MetroCard ready and save enough cash for cab fare to lug all your packages home from these shopping itineraries. They're arranged by special interest; exact addresses can be found in the store listings below.

Antiques Spend two hours at the **Manhattan Art & Antiques Center,** on 2nd Avenue at East 55th Street; then swing over to East 57th Street for an even posher array of European, American, and Asian treasures. Stroll westward across East 57th Street, stopping at **Israel Sack Inc.,** nearby on 5th Avenue, for its superb American antique furniture. Then head up Madison Avenue to **Didier Aaron, Barry Friedman Ltd.,** and **Leigh Keno** in the East 60s, and **DeLorenzo, Leo Kaplan,** and **Florian Papp** in the East 70s.

Bargains Begin by checking for any sample sales—you're bound to find some—and hit them first. Then head down to the lower tip of Manhattan to discount emporium **Century 21.** Take a cab to Hester and Orchard streets and shop north along Orchard Street to East Houston Street; be sure to stop in at **Klein's of Monticello.** By mid-afternoon take a cab to Chelsea; check out **Find Outlet** for boutique fashions, then tackle **Loehmann's** for a range of men's and women's clothing, from inexpensive basics to designer items. A reminder: many Lower East Side shops are closed Saturday.

Home Furnishings Start with a bang at **ABC Carpet & Home** on Broadway; this phenomenal emporium could eat up hours on end, so keep an eye on the time and move on to Greenwich Village to **William–Wayne & Co.** for elegant decorative items (or try to stop by the uptown branches, which are larger). If your bags aren't too heavy yet, head down to SoHo, making sure not to miss **Moss,** then walk east and poke around the pocket-size boutiques on Elizabeth Street between East Houston and Spring streets. Get back into a big frame of mind at the new **Crate & Barrel** at the corner of Houston and Broadway, then cab it back uptown to the **Terence Conran Shop** for something modish. Finally, if you're looking for basics, head over to **Bloomingdale's,** open late on Thursday, or to **Macy's,** open late Monday, Thursday, and Friday.

SHOPPING NEIGHBORHOODS

New York City does not have a mall culture. The closest thing you'll find are the stores in Grand Central Terminal, in the South Street Seaport, and in the underground promenades below Rockefeller Center; the Manhattan Mall has a big neon light display and not much else. However, many New Yorkers complain that some chain-store-packed neighborhoods are beginning to resemble malls, without the food courts or free parking. So save the chain stores for home, and seek out the shops that are unique to New York, or at least unique to the world's shopping capitals. Stores tend to cluster in a few main neighborhoods, which makes shopping a good way to get to know the area. If you head off in search of an outlying store, you may end up discovering something else—new boutiques are constantly springing up, even on previously deserted streets. Below are the shopping highlights in each neighborhood. Addresses for shops can be found in the store listings later in the chapter.

SoHo

Once an abandoned warehouse district, then lined with artists' studios and galleries, the cobbled streets of SoHo are now packed with high-rent boutiques and national chains. Big fashion guns such as **Louis Vuitton, Chanel, Burberry,** and **Prada** have established themselves, raising local retail a notch above the secondary-line designer outposts, such as **D&G, DKNY,** and **Miu Miu.** Adornment advances further in a flock of makeup stores, including **Shu Uemura, Nars,** and French import **Sephora.** Much to the distress of longtime residents, the mall element (Victoria's Secret, **Old Navy, J. Crew,** French Connection, and many more) has a firm foothold; however, there are still many unique shops, especially for housewares and clothing. Some well-known stops include **Dean & DeLuca,** a gourmet food emporium; **Moss,** full of well-designed home furnishings and gifts; and the **Enchanted Forest** toy store. There are the two Kates as well: **Kate's Paperie,** for stationery and other paper products, and **Kate Spade,** for handbags and accessories. On Lafayette Street below East Houston Street, a fashionable strip includes shops outside the mainstream, dealing in urban streetwear and vintage 20th-century furniture. Many SoHo stores are open seven days a week.

NoLita

Fodor's Choice ★ This Nabokovian nickname, shorthand for "*No*rth of *Li*ttle *Ita*ly," describes a neighborhood that has taken the commercial baton from SoHo and run with it. Like SoHo, NoLita has gone from a locals-only area with businesses thin on the ground to a crowded weekend shopping destination, though its stores remain mostly one-of-a-kind. NoLita's parallel north–south spines are Elizabeth, Mott, and Mulberry streets, between East Houston and Kenmare streets. Tiny boutiques continue to sprout like mushrooms after rain. A cache of stylish shops—such as **Mayle, Tracy Feith, Seize sur Vingt,** and the various **Calypso**s—will start your sartorial engines running. Accessories are hardly neglected; **Blue Bag** provides swish purses, while spots like Coclico, Geraldine, and Hollywould play to women's shoe cravings. **Sigerson Morrison** covers both bases with smart shoes and handbags. Meanwhile, **Me + Ro** and **Femmegems** beckon with jewelry.

Lower East Side & the East Village

Once home to millions of Jewish immigrants from Russia and Eastern Europe, the Lower East Side has traditionally been New Yorkers' bargain beat. The center of it all is Orchard Street. The spirit of "Have I got a bargain for you!" still fills the narrow street crammed with tiny, no-nonsense clothing and lingerie stores and open stalls. A lot of the merchandise here is of dubious quality, but there are some finds to be made. Increasingly, these scrappy vendors are giving way to edgy boutiques, particularly in the first block south of East Houston Street, where places like **DDC Lab** and **Seven New York** show newly hatched clothing concepts. Among the Orchard Street veterans, essential stops include **Fine & Klein** for handbags, **Forman's** for women's clothing, and **Klein's of Monticello** for deals on dressy clothes. Many shops on or near Orchard Street sell candy, nuts, dried fruit, and Israeli sweets. Note that many Orchard Street stores are closed Saturday in observance of the Jewish Sabbath. Ludlow Street, one block east of Orchard, is buzzing with little storefronts selling hipster gear such as electric guitars, vintage '60s and '70s furniture, and clothing and accessories from local designers. To the north, the East Village offers diverse, offbeat specialty stops, plenty of collectible kitsch, and some great vintage-clothing boutiques, especially along East 7th and East 9th streets. East 9th Street between Second Avenue and Avenue A merits a ramble for its variety: an herbalist, a couple of gown boutiques, a few music specialists, and casual new threads at spots like Meg and A. Cheng. There's even an "interactive design" place, In the Pink, where you can whip up your own creations.

Chelsea, the Flatiron District & the Meatpacking District

Fodor's Choice ★ Fifth Avenue south of 23rd Street, along with the streets fanning east and west, nurses a lively downtown shopping scene. In stores here, you'll find a mix of the hip, such as **Emporio Armani, Intermix,** and **Paul Smith,** and the hard-core, such as the mega-discounter **Loehmann's** on 7th Avenue. Broadway has a smattering of stores dear to New Yorkers' hearts, including the richly overstuffed **ABC Carpet & Home** and the comprehensive **Paragon Sporting Goods.** In the teens on 6th Avenue is a cluster of superstores, including the colossal **Bed, Bath & Beyond.** Several blocks west, between 10th and 11th avenues, a few intrepid retailers, such as the cutting-edge **Comme des Garçons** and the first U.S. **Balenciaga,** took root amid the flourishing art galleries in what was until recently the desolate fringe of Chelsea. Farther south, the Meatpacking District—an area that until the late 1990s was home primarily to biker bars, after-hours clubs, and suppliers to the city's steak houses—has become chic, thanks to high-fashion temple **Jeffrey;** the two mega-Mcs, **Stella McCartney** and **Alexander McQueen**; a few fresh galleries; and a slew of restaurants-of-the-moment.

5th Avenue

Fifth Avenue from Rockefeller Center to Central Park South still wavers between the money-is-no-object crowd and an influx of more accessible stores. The flag-bedecked **Saks Fifth Avenue** faces **Rockefeller Center,** which harbors branches of Banana Republic and **J. Crew** as well as smaller specialty shops, both along the outdoor promenade and in the underground marketplace. The perennial favorites will eat up a lot of shoe leather: **Cartier** jewelers and **Salvatore Ferragamo,** at 52nd Street; **Takashimaya,** at 54th Street; **Henri Bendel,** at 56th Street; **Tiffany** and **Bulgari** jewelers, at 57th Street; and **F.A.O. Schwarz** and **Bergdorf Goodman,** at 58th Street. Exclusive design houses such as **Versace, Prada,** and **Gucci** are a stone's throw from the über-chain Gap and a souped-up branch of good old **Brooks Brothers.** Swedish retailer **H&M** adds affordable designer knockoffs to the mix.

57th Street

Fodor's Choice ★ Despite the tougher economic climate, luxury houses have reclaimed more 57th Street frontage. **Louis Vuitton** now wraps the northeast corner of 5th Avenue, and **Yves Saint Laurent** became its neighbor in summer 2003. The angular, white-glass Louis Vuitton Moët Hennesy headquarters, on the north side of East 57th Street between 5th and Madison avenues, houses **Christian Dior** and **Bliss,** the SoHo-born superspa. These glamazons are surrounded by big-name art galleries and other swank flagships such as **Burberry** and **Chanel.** The block isn't limited to top-echelon shopping, however; a **NikeTown** sits cheek by jowl with the couture houses. To the west of 5th Avenue are less monolithic shops, such as **Smythson of Bond Street** and the oak-paneled **Rizzoli** bookstore.

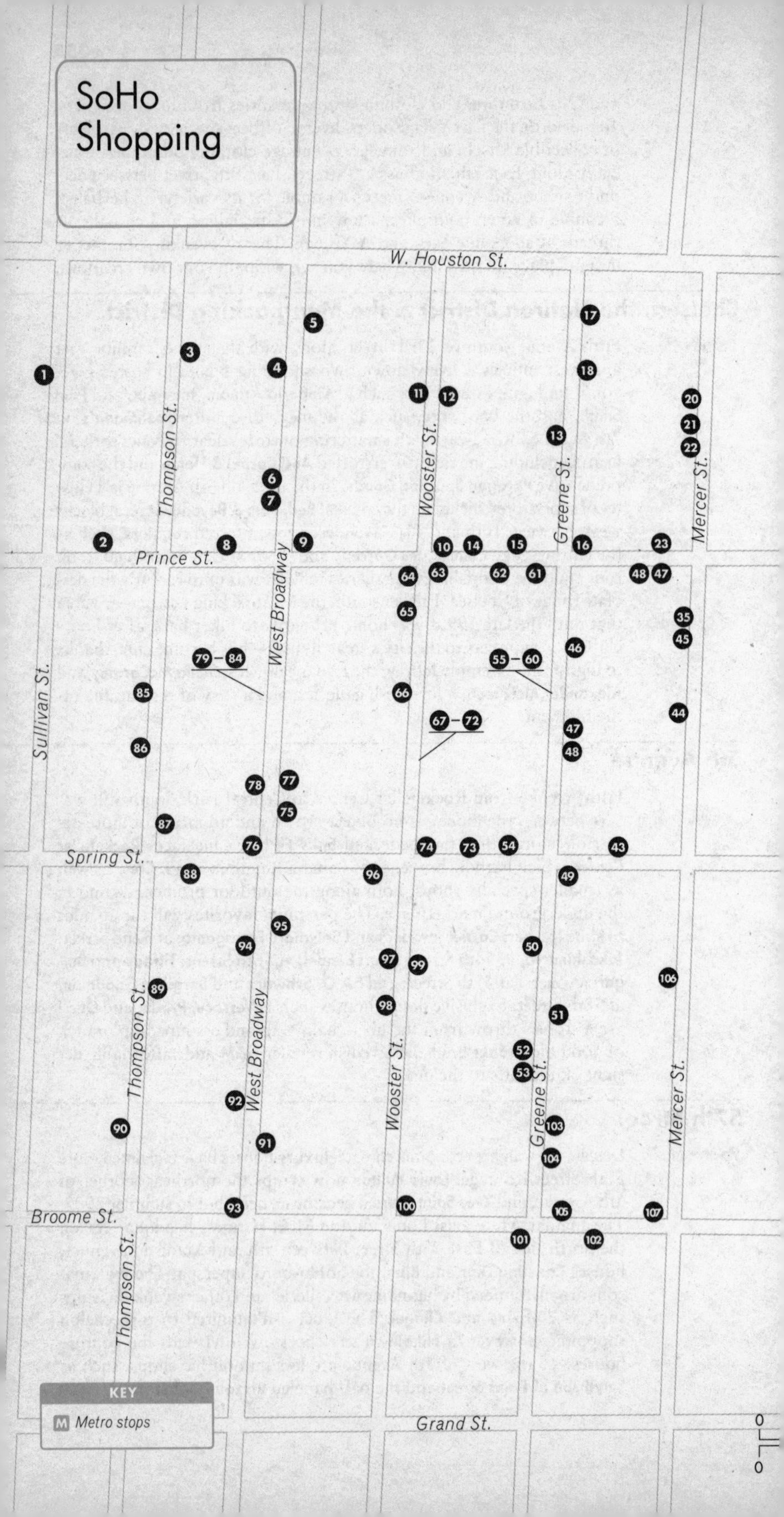
SoHo
Shopping
W. Houston St.
Prince St.
Spring St.
Broome St.
Grand St.
Sullivan St.
Thompson St.
West Broadway
Wooster St.
Greene St.
Mercer St.
KEY
Metro stops

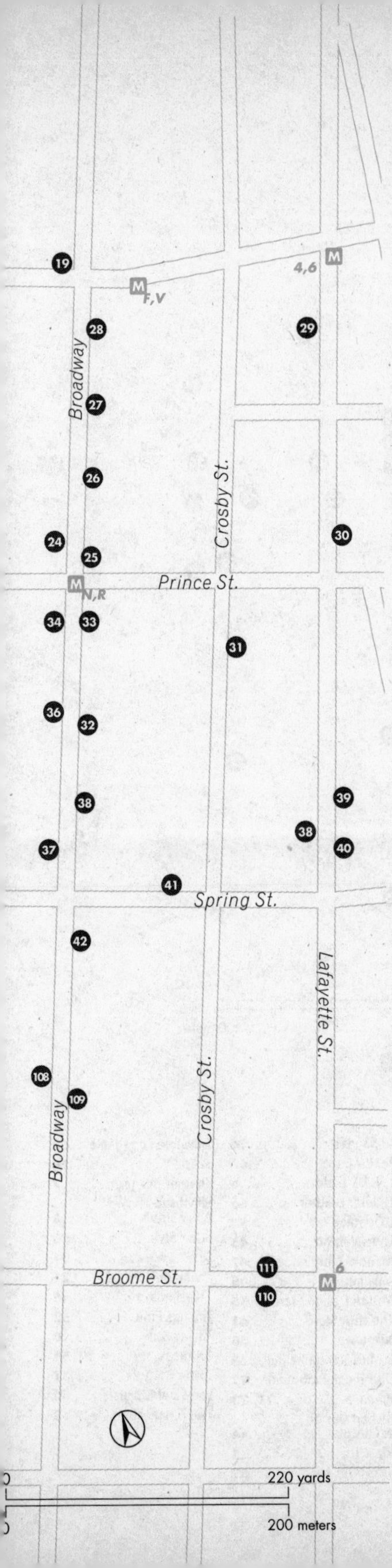
Broadway
Crosby St.
Prince St.
Spring St.
Lafayette St.
Broome St.
4,6
F,V
N,R
6
M
19
28
29
27
26
30
24
25
34
33
31
36
32
38
39
37
40
41
42
108
109
111
110
220 yards
200 meters

57th Street/5th Avenue Shopping

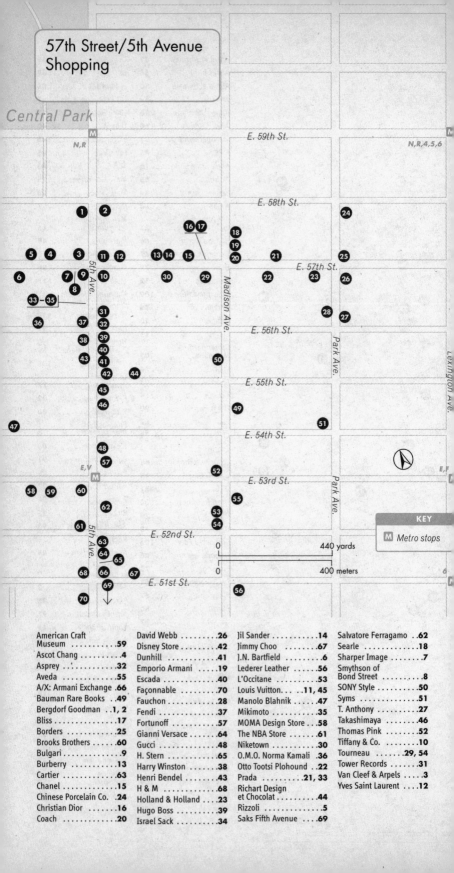

- American Craft Museum 59
- Ascot Chang 4
- Asprey 32
- Aveda 55
- A/X: Armani Exchange .66
- Bauman Rare Books . .49
- Bergdorf Goodman . .1, 2
- Bliss 17
- Borders 25
- Brooks Brothers 60
- Bulgari 9
- Burberry 13
- Cartier 63
- Chanel 15
- Chinese Porcelain Co. .24
- Christian Dior 16
- Coach 20
- David Webb 26
- Disney Store 42
- Dunhill 41
- Emporio Armani 19
- Escada 40
- Façonnable 70
- Fauchon 28
- Fendi 37
- Fortunoff 57
- Gianni Versace 64
- Gucci 48
- H. Stern 65
- Harry Winston 38
- Henri Bendel 43
- H & M 68
- Holland & Holland 23
- Hugo Boss 39
- Israel Sack 34
- Jil Sander 14
- Jimmy Choo 67
- J.N. Bartfield 6
- Lederer Leather 56
- L'Occitane 53
- Louis Vuitton. 11, 45
- Manolo Blahnik 47
- Mikimoto 35
- MOMA Design Store . . .58
- The NBA Store 61
- Niketown 30
- O.M.O. Norma Kamali .36
- Otto Tootsi Plohound . .22
- Prada 21, 33
- Richart Design et Chocolat 44
- Rizzoli 5
- Saks Fifth Avenue 69
- Salvatore Ferragamo . .62
- Searle 18
- Sharper Image 7
- Smythson of Bond Street 8
- SONY Style 50
- Syms 51
- T. Anthony 27
- Takashimaya 46
- Thomas Pink 52
- Tiffany & Co. 10
- Tourneau 29, 54
- Tower Records 31
- Van Cleef & Arpels 3
- Yves Saint Laurent 12

Madison Avenue

Fodor's Choice ★ Madison Avenue from East 57th to about East 79th streets can satisfy almost any couture craving. **Cerruti, Giorgio Armani, Dolce & Gabbana, Valentino, Gianni Versace,** and **Prada** are among the avenue's Italian compatriots, while French houses assert themselves with **Yves Saint Laurent Rive Gauche, Hermès, Jean Paul Gaultier, Givenchy,** and a pair of **Chanel** specialty boutiques. New York's hometown designer Donna Karan posts both **DKNY** and **Donna Karan** collections. Many of these stores occupy much larger spaces than traditional, one-level Madison boutiques; still, some smaller shops, such as perfumer **Creed,** are able to squeeze in. The full-fledged department store **Barneys** fits right in with its recherché roll call. Madison Avenue isn't just a fashion funnel, however; there are a couple of marvelous bookstores, several outstanding antiques dealers, and numerous art galleries here as well.

DEPARTMENT STORES

Most of these stores keep regular hours on weekdays and are open late (until 8 or 9) at least one night a week. Many have personal shoppers who can walk you through the store at no charge, as well as concierges who will answer all manner of questions. Some have restaurants or cafés that offer decent meals and pick-me-up snacks.

Fodor's Choice ★ **Barneys New York.** Barneys continues to provide fashionistas with irresistible objects of desire at its uptown flagship store. The extensive menswear selection has introduced a handful of edgier designers, though made-to-measure is always available. The women's department showcases cachet designers of all stripes, from the subdued lines of Armani and Jil Sander to the irrepressible Alaïa and Gaultier. The shoe selection trots out Prada boots and strappy Blahniks; the makeup department will keep you in Kiehl's. Expanded versions of the less expensive Co-op department occupy the old Barneys' warehouse space on West 18th Street and a niche on Wooster Street. ✉ *660 Madison Ave., between E. 60th and E. 61st Sts., Upper East Side* ☎ *212/826–8900* ✉ *Barneys Co-op, 236 W. 18th St., between 7th and 8th Aves., Chelsea* ☎ *212/716–8817* ✉ *116 Wooster St., between Prince and Spring Sts., SoHo* ☎ *212/965–9964.*

Bergdorf Goodman. Good taste reigns in an elegant and understated setting, but remember that elegant doesn't necessarily mean sedate. Bergdorf's carries some brilliant lines, such as John Galliano's sensational couture and Philip Treacy's dramatic hats. In the basement Level of Beauty, find a seat at the manicure bar (no appointments) for a bit of impromptu pampering. The home department has rooms full of wonderful linens, tableware, and gifts. Across the street is another entire store devoted to menswear: made-to-measure shirts, custom suits, designer lines by the likes of Ralph Lauren and Gucci, and scads of accessories, from hip flasks to silk scarves. ✉ *754 5th Ave., between W. 57th and W. 58th Sts., Midtown West* ✉ *men's store, 745 5th Ave., at 58th St., Midtown East* ☎ *212/753–7300.*

Bloomingdale's. Only a handful of department stores occupy an entire city block; Macy's is one, and this New York institution is another. The main floor is a stupefying maze of cosmetic counters, mirrors, and black walls. Get past this, and you'll find some good buys on dependable designers, bedding, and housewares. Don't mind the harried salespeople or none-too-subtle promotions—chalk it up to the Bloomie's experience. At this writing, Bloomingdale's was at work on a Soho branch, at 504 Broadway between Spring and Broome streets. ✉ *1000 3rd Ave., main*

THE FOOD-LOVERS' MANHATTAN BLITZ TOUR

ATTENTION FOODIES! *Loosen your belts, as Manhattan has more destinations for food lovers than ever before. Start early to cover downtown by lunchtime. Begin in Chinatown, at* **Kam-Man** *(✉ 200 Canal St., at Mott St., Chinatown ☎ 212/571–0330), packed with dried squid, steamed bread, edible birds' nests, and dried shark fins. Next stop:* **Mott Street** *(below Grand Street), where markets and stalls sell ginger root, vegetables, meat, and live fish. Take another dip into the briny deep with a taste of herring or salmon at* **Russ & Daughters** *(✉ 179 E. Houston St., between Allan and Orchard Sts. Lower East Side ☎ 212/475–4880). Then zip over to Broadway where the brilliantly white* **Dean & DeLuca** *(✉ 560 Broadway, at Prince St., SoHo ☎ 212/226–6800) artfully displays intriguing produce and prepared food such as horned melons and stuffed quail; gleaming racks of cookware are in back. For more affordable kitchen gear, try* **Broadway Panhandler** *(✉ 477 Broome St., between Greene and Wooster Sts., SoHo ☎ 212/966–3434), where Calphalon, Le Creuset, and other professional-level makers are priced lower than retail.*

Monday, Wednesday, Friday, and Saturday, farmers and other food producers arrive at dawn at the **Union Square Greenmarket** *bearing organic produce, flowers, homemade bread, preserves, fish, and seasonal fare. A square block of foodie heaven,* **Chelsea Market** *(✉ 75 9th Ave., between W. 15th and W. 16th Sts., Chelsea ☎ 212/243–6005) is home to butchers, bakers, and a dozen other specialty food purveyors.*

The next three destinations require a subway or taxi ride. **Macy's Cellar** *(✉ 151 W. 34th St., between 6th and 7th Aves., Midtown West ☎ 212/695–4400) is a great place to rummage through kitchen gadgets. Head uptown to* **Citarella** *(✉ 2135 Broadway, at W. 75th St., Upper West Side ☎ 212/874–0383) for a gander at their seafood department and heady treats like white truffles or foie gras. A few blocks north at* **Zabar's** *(✉ 2245 Broadway, at W. 81st St., Upper West Side ☎ 212/787–2000), grab a loaf of the fabled bread, examine the smoked fish and cheeses, and climb upstairs to the well-priced kitchenware section.*

The East Side has plenty of stores to focus on. If you're passing through Grand Central Terminal, stop by **Oliviers & Co.** *(✉ Grand Central Terminal, Midtown East ☎ 212/973–1472) for superb olive oil from all around the Mediterranean, then duck into the* **Grand Central Market** *area to check out the vendors of spices, cheese (from the Village's Murray's Cheese Shop), pasta, and other specialties. At* **Bridge Kitchenware** *(✉ 214 E. 52nd St., between 2nd and 3rd Aves., Midtown East ☎ 212/688–4220), a dusty, unpretentious hideaway, you can scoop up tiny ramekins and countless doodads. Farther uptown, the* **Vinegar Factory** *(✉ 431 E. 91st St., between York and 1st Aves., Upper East Side ☎ 212/987–0885) carries bread from the other Zabar brother, Eli, who sells a great selection of vinegar and oils, plus fresh produce and cheese, and has a loft space for weekend brunch. If you don't want to go quite so far east, hit* **Eli's Manhattan** *(✉ 1411 3rd Ave., between E. 80th and E. 81st Sts., Upper East Side ☎ 212/717–8100), a second, equally well-stocked branch. Nearby,* **Kitchen Arts & Letters** *(✉ 1435 Lexington Ave., between E. 93rd and E. 94th Sts., Upper East Side ☎ 212/876–5550) has thousands of cookbooks and other titles on food and wine. For a fitting conclusion, head back down to* **Payard Pâtisserie & Bistro** *(✉ 1032 Lexington Ave., between E. 73rd and E. 74th Sts., Upper East Side ☎ 212/717–5252), a glossy, Parisian-perfect patisserie where you can sample impeccable pastries and pick up elegant chocolates or succulent pâtes de fruits (fruit jellies).*

entrance at E. 59th St. and Lexington Ave., Midtown East ☎ *212/355–5900.*

Fodor's Choice ★ **Century 21.** For many New Yorkers, this is the mother lode of discount shopping. Four large floors are crammed with everything from J. P. Tod's driving moccasins to Ralph Lauren bedding—on a good day it may seem to lack nothing but a private dressing room. The rows of half-price ties, designer briefs, and shoes are most appealing in the men's merchandise. Scouring the full floor of women's designer clothing can turn up such deals as a Dolce & Gabbana suit for about $370 or Vera Wang silk tops for less than $150. Don't pass up lingerie, where you can find La Perla lace. The basement linens department has choice buys on pure cotton sheets and wool blankets, but watch for IRREGULAR stickers. There's also a collection of name-brand luggage, from gym bags to rolling suitcases. Cosmetics are the only goods not directly discounted, but a purchase elicits coupons good for deductions on other store merchandise. ✉ *22 Cortlandt St., between Broadway and Church St., Lower Manhattan* ☎ *212/227–9092.*

Henri Bendel. Behind the graceful Lalique windows you'll discover more than the usual fashion suspects. Bendel's dedication to the unusual begins on the ground-floor cosmetic area, filled with lines like Vincent Longo, and percolates through the floors of women's clothing and accessories. Designers such as Yeohlee, Bernhard Willhelm, Trina Turk, and Diane von Furstenberg have room to breathe; also look into Bendel's own line of sophisticated sweaters. Brave the Lair by Tiffany Dubin for retro-kitsch housewares. Shoe lovers should be forewarned that there is no true footwear department, just as there is no lingerie department. ✉ *712 5th Ave., between W. 55th and W. 56th Sts., Midtown West* ☎ *212/247–1100.*

Lord & Taylor. Refined, comfortably conservative, and never overwhelming, Lord & Taylor is a stronghold of classic American designer clothes. Instead of unpronounceable labels, you'll find Dana Buchman, Jones New York, and a lot of casual wear. It also has a large selection of reasonably priced full-length gowns. ✉ *424 5th Ave., between W. 38th and W. 39th Sts., Midtown West* ☎ *212/391–3344.*

Macy's. Macy's headquarters store claims to be the largest retail store in America; expect to lose your bearings at least once. Fashion-wise, there's a concentration on the mainstream rather than the luxe. For cooking gear and housewares, the Cellar nearly outdoes Zabar's. ✉ *Herald Sq., 151 W. 34th St., between 6th and 7th Aves., Midtown West* ☎ *212/695–4400.*

Pearl River Mart. Now ensconced on Broadway, Pearl River Mart has a less adventurous, jam-packed feel than it did in its previous digs. The ground floor devotes plenty of space to clothing (embroidered jackets, rayon brocade dresses) and some housewares. Wooden birdcages dangle from the ceiling, dragon heads grin over a counter, and there's a special tea counter. A waterfall guides you downstairs for a motley assortment of slippers, paper lanterns, Buddha figures, and more furnishings. ✉ *477 Broadway, between Broome and Grand Sts., SoHo* ☎ *212/431–4770.*

Saks Fifth Avenue. A fashion-only department store, Saks sells an astonishing array of apparel. The choice of American and European designers is impressive without being esoteric—the women's selection includes Gucci and Marc Jacobs, plus devastating ball gowns galore. The footwear collections are gratifyingly broad, from Ferragamo to Nine West. In the men's department, conservative stars like Oxxford Clothes and Alan Flusser counterbalance current trends. ✉ *611 5th Ave., between E. 49th and E. 50th Sts., Midtown East* ☎ *212/753–4000.*

Takashimaya New York. This pristine branch of Japan's largest department store carries stylish accessories, beauty products, and fine household items, all of which reflect a combination of Eastern and Western designs. In the Tea Box downstairs, you can have a *bento* box lunch in the serene, softly lighted tearoom or stock up on green tea. The florist-cum-front-window-display provides a refreshing mini botanical garden. ✉ *693 5th Ave., between E. 54th and E. 55th Sts., Midtown East* ☎ *212/350–0100.*

SPECIALTY SHOPS

Many specialty stores have several branches in the city; in these cases, we have listed the locations in the busier shopping neighborhoods.

Antiques

Antiquing is a fine art in Manhattan. Goods include everything from rarefied museum-quality to wacky and affordable. Premier shopping areas are on Madison Avenue north of 57th Street, and East 60th Street between 2nd and 3rd avenues, where more than 20 shops, dealing in everything from 18th-century French furniture to art deco lighting fixtures, cluster on one block. Around West 11th and 12th streets between University Place and Broadway, a tantalizing array of settees, bedsteads, and rocking chairs can be seen in the windows of about two dozen dealers, many of whom have TO THE TRADE signs on their doors; a card from your architect or decorator, however, may get you inside. Finally, for 20th-century furniture and fixtures, head south of Houston Street, especially along Lafayette Street. Most dealers are closed Sunday.

Many small dealers cluster in a few antiques "malls."

Chelsea Antiques Building. With a full 12 floors of antiques and collectibles here, the options run the gamut from antique books to vintage Georg Jensen silver to lunch boxes. ✉ *108–110 W. 25th St., between 6th and 7th Aves., Chelsea* ☎ *212/929–0909.*

Manhattan Art & Antiques Center. Art-nouveau perfume bottles and samovars, samurai swords, pewter pitchers, and much more fill 100-plus galleries. The level of quality is not, as a rule, up to that of Madison Avenue, but then neither are the prices. ✉ *1050 2nd Ave., between E. 55th and E. 56th Sts., Midtown East* ☎ *212/355–4400.*

American & English

Florian Papp. The shine of gilt—on ormolu clocks, chaise longues, and marble-top tables—lures casual customers in, but this store has an unassailed reputation among knowledgeable collectors. ✉ *962 Madison Ave., between E. 75th and E. 76th Sts., Upper East Side* ☎ *212/288–6770.*

Hyde Park Antiques. For 18th- and 19th-century English furniture, such as Georgian mahogany chests and Regency rosewood bookcases, visit this spacious showroom. ✉ *836 Broadway, between E. 12th and E. 13th Sts., East Village* ☎ *212/477–0033.*

Israel Sack Inc. This is widely considered one of the best places in the country for 17th-, 18th-, and early-19th-century American furniture. Although the store is reputed to be very expensive, there's actually plenty of furniture for less than $25,000. ✉ *730 5th Ave., between W. 56th and W. 57th Sts., Midtown West* ☎ *212/399–6562.*

Kentshire Galleries. Elegant furniture is displayed in room settings on eight floors, with an emphasis on formal English pieces from the 18th and 19th centuries, particularly the Georgian and Regency periods. Period and estate jewelry spans more decades, with Victorian brooches and deco diamond bracelets. ✉ *37 E. 12th St., between University Pl. and Broadway, Greenwich Village* ☎ *212/673–6644.*

Leigh Keno American Antiques. Twins Leigh and Leslie Keno set an auction record in the American antiques field by paying $2.75 million for a hairy paw–foot Philadelphia wing chair. They have a good eye and an interesting inventory; gaze up at a tall case clock or down at the delicate legs of a tea table. It's best to make an appointment. ✉ *127 E. 69th St., between Park and Lexington Aves., Upper East Side* ☎ *212/734–2381.*

Newel Art Galleries. Near the East Side's interior-design district, this huge collection roams from the Renaissance to the 20th century. The nonfurniture finds, from figureheads to bell jars, make for prime conversation pieces. ✉ *425 E. 53rd St., between 1st Ave. and Sutton Pl., Midtown East* ☎ *212/758–1970.*

Steve Miller American Folk Art. This gallery is run by one of the country's premier folk-art dealers, the author of *The Art of the Weathervane.* ✉ *17 E. 96th St., between Madison and 5th Aves., Upper East Side* ☎ *212/348–5219.*

Woodard & Greenstein. Americana, antique quilts and rugs, and 19th-century country furniture are among the specialties of this prestigious dealer. ✉ *506 E. 74th St., between York Ave. and FDR Dr., Upper East Side* ☎ *212/794–9404.*

Asian

Chinese Porcelain Company. Though the name of this prestigious shop indicates one of its specialties, its stock covers more ground, ranging from lacquerware to Khmer sculpture to 18th-century French furniture. ✉ *475 Park Ave., at E. 58th St., Midtown East* ☎ *212/838–7744.*

Flying Cranes Antiques. Here you'll find a well-regarded collection of rare, museum-quality pieces from the Meiji period, the time known as Japan's Golden Age. Items include ceramics, cloisonné, metalwork, carvings, ikebana baskets, and Samurai swords and fittings. ✉ *Manhattan Art and Antiques Center, 1050 2nd Ave., between E. 55th and E. 56th Sts., Midtown East* ☎ *212/223–4600.*

Jacques Carcangues, Inc. Carrying goods from Japan to India, this SoHo gallery offers an eclectic array of objects, from pillboxes to 18th-century Burmese Buddhas. ✉ *106 Spring St., at Mercer St., SoHo* ☎ *212/925–8110.*

Old Japan. This little Village shop specializes in antique textiles and kimonos. You'll also find furniture, such as chests and low tables, plus small items such as 100-year-old sake bottles, bamboo baskets, and sewing boxes (which can double as jewelry boxes). Contemporary gift items are also available. ✉ *382 Bleecker St., between Perry and Charles Sts., Greenwich Village* ☎ *212/633–0922.*

European

Newel Art Galleries and Florian Papp, covered under American and English antiques, and the Chinese Porcelain Company, listed under Asian antiques, also carry European pieces.

Barry Friedman Ltd. Having championed 20th-century art for decades, Barry Friedman now turns to contemporary decorative objects, such as art glass by Dale Chihuly. Vintage and contemporary photographs are also available. ✉ *32 E. 67th St., between Park and Madison Aves., Upper East Side* ☎ *212/794–8950.*

DeLorenzo. Come here for the sinuous curves and highly polished surfaces of French art deco furniture and accessories. ✉ *956 Madison Ave., between E. 75th and E. 76th Sts., Upper East Side* ☎ *212/249–7575.*

Didier Aaron. This esteemed gallery specializes in superb 18th- and 19th-century French decorative arts and paintings. ✉ *32 E. 67th St., between Park and Madison Aves., Upper East Side* ☎ *212/988–5248.*

L'Antiquaire & The Connoisseur, Inc. Proprietor Helen Fioratti has written a guide to French antiques, but she is equally knowledgeable about her Italian and Spanish furniture and decorative objects from the 15th through the 18th centuries, as well as the medieval arts. ✉ *36 E. 73rd St., between Madison and Park Aves., Upper East Side* ☎ *212/517–9176.*

Leo Kaplan Ltd. The impeccable items here include art nouveau glass and pottery, porcelain from 18th-century England, antique and modern paperweights, and Russian artwork. ✉ *114 E. 57th St., between Park and Lexington Aves., Upper East Side* ☎ *212/249–6766.*

Les Pierre Antiques. Pierre Deux popularized French Provincial through reproductions; come here for a strong selection of the real thing. ✉ *369 Bleecker St., at Charles St., Greenwich Village* ☎ *212/243–7740.*

20th-Century Furniture & Memorabilia

City Barn Antiques. Come for your fill of the blond-wood Heywood-Wakefield originals (many refinished) and streamlined pieces mostly from the '50s. ✉ *269 Lafayette St., at Prince St., SoHo* ☎ *212/941–5757.*

Darrow's Fun Antiques. A leader among the city's nostalgia shops, the store is full of whimsy: antique toys, animation art, and other collectibles. ✉ *1101 1st Ave., between E. 60th and E. 61st Sts., Upper East Side* ☎ *212/838–0730.*

Las Venus. Step into this kitsch palace and you'll feel as though a time machine has zapped you back to the groovy '70s. Look for bubble lamps, lots of brocade, and Knoll knockoffs. ✉ *163 Ludlow St., between E. Houston and Stanton Sts., Lower East Side* ☎ *212/982–0608.*

Lost City Arts. In addition to mod furniture, like pod and Eames chairs, and industrial memorabilia, such as neon gas-station clocks, Lost City can help you relive the Machine Age with an in-house, retro-modern line of furniture. ✉ *18 Cooper Sq., at E. 5th St., East Village* ☎ *212/375–0500.*

Beauty

Aveda. Natural ingredients and plant extracts are the basis of Aveda's shampoos and hair treatments. You can concoct your own perfumes from the impressive selection of essential oils. The Spring Street and West Broadway locations also have hair-salon services. ✉ *509 Madison Ave., at E. 53rd St., Midtown East* ☎ *212/832–2416* ✉ *140 5th Ave., at W. 19th St., Flatiron District* ☎ *212/645–4797* ✉ *233 Spring St., at 6th Ave., SoHo* ☎ *212/807–1492* ✉ *456 West Broadway, between Prince and W. Houston Sts., SoHo* ☎ *212/473–0280.*

Creed. Choose from an array of existing fragrances—many of which were named and created for royalty such as Princess Diana and Grace Kelly—or have one custom-made for you. ✉ *9 Bond St., between Lafayette St. and Broadway, East Village* ☎ *212/228–1940* ✉ *897 Madison Ave., between E. 72nd and E. 73rd Sts., Upper East Side* ☎ *212/794–4480* ✉ *680 Madison Ave., between E. 61st and E. 62nd Sts., Upper East Side* ☎ *212/838–2780.*

FACE Stockholm. Besides the pretty pastels and neutrals, FACE carries some brazenly colored nail polish (emerald green, sky blue), juicy red glosses, and little pots of jewel-tone glitter. Swabs and tissues at hand make a quick do-it-yourself tryout refreshingly easy. ✉ *110 Prince St., at Greene St., SoHo* ☎ *212/966–9110* ✉ *226 Columbus Ave., between W. 70th and W. 71st Sts., Upper West Side* ☎ *212/769–1420.*

Floris of London. Floral English toiletries beloved of the British royals fill this re-creation of the cozy London original. If you love lathering, look for the wooden bowls of shaving or bath soap. ✉ *703 Madison Ave., between E. 62nd and E. 63rd Sts., Upper East Side* ☎ *212/935–9100.*

Fresh. Many of these products sound (and smell) good enough to eat: a brown-sugar skin-care line, apple-cranberry body wash, pear-cassis cologne. The beautifully wrapped soaps make first-rate instant gifts. ☒ *1061 Madison Ave., between E. 80th and E. 81st Sts., Upper East Side* ☎ *212/396–0344* ☒ *57 Spring St., between Lafayette and Mulberry Sts., SoHo* ☎ *212/925–0099* ☒ *388 Bleecker St., between Perry and W. 11th Sts., Greenwich Village* ☎ *917/408–1850.*

Helena Rubenstein. This is not your mother's Helena Rubenstein. Ladylike peaches and beiges in the makeup lines have been joined by bold citrine, blue, and glitter. Skin-care products line the walls; there are also several skin tests (oil, UV damage). ☒ *135 Spring St., between Greene and Wooster Sts., SoHo* ☎ *212/343–9966.*

Jo Malone. Consider this extra incentive to visit the landmark Flatiron Building. Unisex scents like lime blossom and vetiver can be worn alone or, in the Malone style, layered. (Since Malone uses colognes, not perfumes, it's not overpowering.) ☒ *949 Broadway, at 5th Ave., Flatiron District* ☎ *212/673–2220.*

Fodor's Choice ★ **Kiehl's Since 1851.** At this favored haunt of top models and stylists, white-smocked assistants can advise you on the relative merits of the incredibly effective and somewhat expensive skin lotions and hair potions, all packaged in disarmingly simple bottles. The employees dole out generous take-home samples. ☒ *109 3rd Ave., between E. 13th and E. 14th Sts., East Village* ☎ *212/677–3171.*

L'Occitane. Extra-mild soaps, shampoos, and creams here pack an olfactory punch with Provençal scents (think almond, rosemary, and the ever-present lavender). ☒ *1046 Madison Ave., at E. 80th St., Upper East Side* ☎ *212/639–9185* ☒ *510 Madison Ave., between E. 52nd and E. 53rd Sts., Midtown East* ☎ *212/826–5020* ☒ *146 Spring St., at Wooster St., SoHo* ☎ *212/343–0109* ☒ *198 Columbus Ave., at W. 69th St., Upper West Side* ☎ *212/362–5146* ☒ *412 Lexington Ave., at E. 43rd St., Midtown East* ☎ *212/557–6754* ☒ *247 Bleecker St., at Leroy St., Greenwich Village* ☎ *212/367–8428.*

M.A.C. Fashion hounds and stylists pile into these boutiques for the basics (foundation and concealer for a huge range of skin tones) and the far-out.Salespeople can offer expert advice—many of them also work as professional makeup artists. ☒ *113 Spring St., between Mercer and Greene Sts., SoHo* ☎ *212/334–4641* ☒ *14 Christopher St., between 6th and 7th Aves., Greenwich Village* ☎ *212/243–4150* ☒ *1 E. 22nd St., between 5th Ave. and Broadway, Flatiron District* ☎ *212/677–6611.*

Make Up For Ever. The makeup from this Paris-based boutique does not hew to the natural look. The products are pigment-rich and boldly colored; liquid eyeliner could be bright green as well as dark brown, mascara pearly white as well as black. The staff applications help nonprofessionals navigate the spectrum for everyday wear. ☒ *409 West Broadway, between Prince and Spring Sts., SoHo* ☎ *212/941–9337.*

Ricky's. Shopping at any one of these wacky stores is a uniquely New York experience. The loud and fun drugstores attract an eclectic, mostly young crowd who come just as often for the crazy-color wigs or fishnet stockings as they do for the body glitter and Neutrogena soap. Every fall the stores turn into Halloween central. ☒ *590 Broadway, at Prince St., SoHo* ☎ *212/226–5552* ☒ *718 Broadway, at Astor Pl., East Village* ☎ *212/979–5232* ☒ *466 6th Ave., at W. 12th St., Greenwich Village* ☎ *212/924–3401* ☒ *44 E. 8th St., between Broadway and University Pl., Greenwich Village* ☎ *212/254–5247* ☒ *988 8th Ave., at W. 59th St., Midtown West* ☎ *212/586–0114.*

Sephora. This black-and-crimson chain has already conquered France, and is now saturating major U.S. cities. A huge roster of perfumes is arranged alphabetically down the walls, and the comprehensive makeup selection ranges from Urban Decay to Stila to Sephora's own brand. Skin-care lines include hard-to-find names such as Peter Thomas Roth. Most important, try-on stations, complete with tissues, cotton pads, makeup remover, and disinfectant, make trying on the goods a low-commitment proposition. ✉ *555 Broadway, between Prince and Spring Sts., SoHo* ☎ *212/625–1309* ✉ *119 5th Ave., at E. 19th St., Flatiron District* ☎ *212/674–3570* ✉ *1500 Broadway, at W. 44th St., Midtown West* ☎ *212/944–8168.*

Shu Uemura. One of downtown's many beauty spots, this is a good place to scoop up top-of-the-line Japanese skin-care products, makeup, and tools such as dozens of brushes and an excellent eyelash curler. One clever touch: there are four light simulators, which allow you to test makeup colors under officelike and simulated outdoor lighting. ✉ *121 Greene St., between Prince and W. Houston Sts., SoHo* ☎ *212/979–5500.*

Books

Manhattan supports dozens of bookstores, small and large, chain and independent. A few of the city's landmark independent stores have been in flux. At this writing, for instance, Gotham Book Mart was still on the lookout for a new space, while Coliseum Books had settled on a new location at 11 West 42nd Street.

The biggest bookstore presence in the city is **Barnes & Noble** (✉ 396 6th Ave., at W. 8th St., Greenwich Village ☎ 212/674–8780 ✉ 33 E. 17th St., at Union Sq., Flatiron District ☎ 212/253–0810 ✉ 4 Astor Pl., at Lafayette St., East Village ☎ 212/420–1322 ✉ 600 5th Ave., at W. 48th St., Midtown West ☎ 212/765–0592 ✉ 1972 Broadway, at W. 66th St., Upper West Side ☎ 212/595–6859 ✉ 2289 Broadway, at W. 82nd St., Upper West Side ☎ 212/362–8835 ✉ 240 E. 86th St., between 2nd and 3rd Aves., Upper East Side ☎ 212/794–1962). **Borders** (✉ 461 Park Ave., at E. 57th St., Midtown East ☎ 212/980–6785 ✉ 550 2nd Ave., at E. 32nd St., Murray Hill ☎ 212/685–3938) is another chain in the city.

Children's Books

Books of Wonder. A friendly staff can help select gifts for all reading levels from the extensive stock of children's books here; Oziana is a specialty. ✉ *16 W. 18th St., between 5th and 6th Aves., Chelsea* ☎ *212/989–3270.*

Foreign Language

Librairie de France/Libraria Hispanica. This store offers one of the country's largest selections of foreign-language books, videos, and periodicals, mostly in French and Spanish. You'll also find dozens of dictionaries, phrase books, and other learning materials. ✉ *610 5th Ave., Rockefeller Center Promenade, Midtown West* ☎ *212/581–8810.*

Gay & Lesbian

Oscar Wilde Bookshop. Opened in 1967, this was the first gay and lesbian bookstore in the city and is now the oldest existing one in the country, having weathered a close brush with closure in 2003. It's just steps from the site of the Stonewall riots. The shelves hold everything from cultural studies and biographies to fiction and first editions by the likes of Djuna Barnes and Paul Monette. ✉ *15 Christopher St., between 6th and 7th Aves., Greenwich Village* ☎ *212/255–8097.*

General Interest

Archivia Books. In this second-floor store, you can pore over a tome on Japanese gardens or the catalog of a landmark modernism exhibition.

The new, used, and out-of-print books cover all sorts of design and decorative arts, particularly architecture, gardening, and interior design. ✉ *1063 Madison Ave., between E. 80th and E. 81st Sts., 2nd floor, Upper East Side* ☎ *212/439–9194.*

Biography Bookshop. Published diaries, letters, biographies, and autobiographies fill this neighborly store; there's also a careful selection of general nonfiction, fiction, guidebooks, and children's books. ✉ *400 Bleecker St., at W. 11th St., Greenwich Village* ☎ *212/807–8655.*

★ **Crawford Doyle Booksellers.** You're as likely to see a volume of poetry or an old edition of Wodehouse as a best-seller in the window of this shop. There's a thoughtful selection of fiction, nonfiction, biographies, etc., plus some rare books on the tight-fit balcony. Salespeople offer their opinions *and* ask for yours. ✉ *1082 Madison Ave., between E. 81st and E. 82nd Sts., Upper East Side* ☎ *212/288–6300.*

Gotham Book Mart. The late Frances Steloff opened this store in 1920 with just $200 in her pocket, half of it on loan. But she helped launch James Joyce's *Ulysses,* D. H. Lawrence, and Henry Miller and is now legendary among bibliophiles—as is her bookstore. There's a wealth of signed editions of deliciously macabre Edward Gorey books. ✉ *41 W. 47th St., between 5th and 6th Aves., Midtown West* ☎ *212/719–4448.*

Lenox Hill Bookstore. Narrow in shape but not in spirit, this shop carries many copies of books signed by their authors and often hosts readings. ✉ *1018 Lexington Ave., between E. 72nd and E. 73rd Sts., Upper East Side* ☎ *212/472–7170.*

Posman Books. Good to know of if you're about to embark on a long train ride out of Grand Central, the last remaining Posman store in the city carries mostly best-sellers and new releases, often at a discount. ✉ *9 Grand Central Terminal, at Vanderbilt Ave. and E. 42nd St., Midtown East* ☎ *212/983–1111.*

Rizzoli. A marble entrance and oak paneling create a refined setting for books and magazines on art, architecture, dance, design, photography, and travel. ✉ *31 W. 57th St., between 5th and 6th Aves., Midtown West* ☎ *212/759–2424.*

★ **St. Mark's Bookshop.** Extending far beyond the *New York Times* best-seller list, this store's New Titles section might have a study of postmodernism next to the latest Nick Hornby. Cultural and critical theory books are right up front; it also has a rich store of literature, literary journals, and even a rack of self-published booklets. ✉ *31 3rd Ave., at 9th St., East Village* ☎ *212/260–7853.*

Shakespeare & Co. Booksellers. The stock here represents what's happening in just about every field of publishing today: students can grab a last-minute Gertrude Stein for their literature class, then rifle through the homages to cult pop-culture figures. Late hours at the downtown location ('til midnight on Friday and Saturday, 11 PM the rest of the week) are a plus. ✉ *939 Lexington Ave., between E. 68th and E. 69th Sts., Upper East Side* ☎ *212/570–0201* ✉ *137 E. 23rd St., at Lexington Ave., Gramercy* ☎ *212/505–2021* ✉ *716 Broadway, at Washington Pl., Greenwich Village* ☎ *212/529–1330* ✉ *1 Whitehall St., at Beaver St., Lower Manhattan* ☎ *212/742–7025.*

The Strand. The Broadway branch proudly claims to have "8 miles of books"; craning your neck among the tall-as-trees stacks will likely net you something from the mix of new and old. Rare books are next door, at 826 Broadway, on the third floor. The Fulton Street branch is near South Street Seaport; it's decidedly less overwhelming. ✉ *828 Broadway, at E. 12th St., East Village* ☎ *212/473–1452* ✉ *95 Fulton St., between Gold and William Sts., Lower Manhattan* ☎ *212/732–6070.*

Three Lives & Co. On a picture-perfect corner, Three Lives has one of the city's most impeccable selections of books. The display tables and counters highlight the latest literary fiction and serious nonfiction, classics, quirky gift books, and gorgeously illustrated tomes. ✉ *154 W. 10th St., at Waverly Pl., Greenwich Village* ☎ *212/741–2069.*

Music

Joseph Patelson Music House. A huge collection of scores has long made this the heart of the music-lover's New York; fittingly, it's right by Carnegie Hall. ✉ *160 W. 56th St., between 6th and 7th Aves., Midtown West* ☎ *212/582–5840.*

Mystery & Suspense

Murder Ink. Mystery lovers have relied on this institution for years; ask the knowledgeable staff for recommendations. ✉ *2486 Broadway, between W. 92nd and W. 93rd Sts., Upper West Side* ☎ *212/362–8905.*

The Mysterious Bookshop. Come to this atmospheric shop to uncover one of the largest selections of mystery, suspense, and detective fiction in the city—new, used, and out-of-print volumes, as well as first editions. ✉ *129 W. 56th St., between 6th and 7th Aves., Midtown West* ☎ *212/765–0900.*

Partners & Crime. Imported British paperbacks, helpful staff, a rental library, and whodunits galore—new, out-of-print, and first editions—make this a must-browse for fans. Revered mystery writers give readings here. Check out the "radio mystery hour" on the first Saturday of every month. ✉ *44 Greenwich Ave., between 6th and 7th Aves., Greenwich Village* ☎ *212/243–0440.*

Rare & Used Books

Archivia, Crawford Doyle Booksellers, and the Strand, covered under General Interest, also carry rare and used titles.

Argosy Bookstore. This sedate landmark, established in 1921, keeps a scholarly stock of books and autographs. It's also a great place to look for low-price maps and prints. ✉ *116 E. 59th St., between Park and Lexington Aves., Midtown East* ☎ *212/753–4455.*

Bauman Rare Books. This successful Philadelphia firm now offers New Yorkers the most impossible-to-get titles, first editions, and fine leather sets. The Madison Avenue store has become their flagship store, eight times the size of their boutique in the Waldorf-Astoria. ✉ *535 Madison Ave., between E. 54th and E. 55th Sts., Midtown East* ☎ *212/751–0011* ✉ *Waldorf-Astoria, lobby level, 301 Park Ave., at E. 50th St., Midtown East* ☎ *212/759–8300.*

J. N. Bartfield. A legend in the field offers old and antiquarian books distinguished by binding, author, edition, or content. ✉ *30 W. 57th St., between 5th and 6th Aves., 3rd floor, Midtown West* ☎ *212/245–8890.*

Skyline Books and Records, Inc. Come here for out-of-print and unusual books in all fields. The store handles literary first editions, as well as a small handful of jazz records. ✉ *13 W. 18th St., between 5th and 6th Aves., Chelsea* ☎ *212/675–4773.*

Westrider Rare & Used Books. This wonderfully crammed space is a bibliophile's lifesaver in the otherwise sparse Upper West Side. Squeeze in among the stacks of art books and fiction; clamber up the steep stairway and you'll find all sorts of rare books. ✉ *2246 Broadway, between W. 80th and W. 81st Sts., Upper West Side* ☎ *212/362–0706.*

Theater

Drama Book Shop. If you're looking for a script, be it a lesser-known Russian translation or a Broadway hit, chances are you'll find it here. The range of books spans film, music, dance, TV, and biographies. ✉ *250 W. 40th St., between 7th and 8th Aves., Midtown West* ☎ *212/944–0595.*

Cameras & Electronics

Apple Store SoHo. A former post office now displays the darlings of the e-mail set. Find some elbow room and try out the latest in PowerBooks, iMacs, digital moviemaking, and more. Head up the glass staircase for software, a demo area, and a troubleshooting desk. ✉ *103 Prince St., at Greene St., SoHo* ☎ *212/226–3126.*

Fodor's Choice ★ **B & H Photo Video and Pro Audio.** As baskets of purchases trundle along on tracks overhead, you can plunge into the excellent selection of imaging, audio, video, and lighting equipment. The staff willingly give advice and compare merchandise. Low prices, good customer service, and a liberal returns policy make this a favorite with pros and amateurs alike. Be sure to leave a few extra minutes for the checkout procedure; also, keep in mind that the store is closed Saturday. ✉ *420 9th Ave., between W. 33rd and W. 34th Sts., Midtown West* ☎ *212/444–5000.*

Bang & Olufsen. Bang & Olufsen stereos are unmistakable—slim, flat cases, with transparent doors that open when you reach toward them, revealing the whirling CDs inside. In the back of the store is a mock living room, where you can test the impressive surround-sound. ✉ *952 Madison Ave., at E. 75th St., Upper East Side* ☎ *212/879–6161.*

Harvey Electronics. A well-informed staff offers top-of-the-line audio-visual equipment. ✉ *2 W. 45th St., between 5th and 6th Aves., Midtown West* ☎ *212/575–5000* ✉ *888 Broadway, at E. 19th St., in ABC Carpet & Home, Flatiron District* ☎ *212/228–5354.*

J&R Music and Computer World. Just south of City Hall, J&R has emerged as the city's most competitively priced one-stop electronics outlet, with video equipment, computers, stereos, and cameras. Home-office supplies are at No. 17, computers at No. 15, small appliances at No. 27. ✉ *23 Park Row, between Beekman and Ann Sts., Lower Manhattan* ☎ *212/238–9000.*

SONY Style. This equipment and music store comes in a glossy package, with imaginative window displays and a posh downstairs demonstration area for the integrated systems. The latest stereo and entertainment systems, video cameras, and portable CD and mp3 players preen on the shelves. ✉ *550 Madison Ave., at E. 55th St., Midtown East* ☎ *212/833–8800.*

Willoughby's. Having started more than 100 years ago as a camera store, Willoughby's now includes DVD players, scanners, and other electronics alongside digital cameras, manual models, and point-and-shoots. ✉ *136 W. 32nd St., between 6th and 7th Aves., Midtown West* ☎ *212/564–1600.*

CDs, Tapes & Records

The city's best record stores provide browsers with a window to New York's groovier subcultures. The East Village is especially good for dance tracks and used music.

Academy Records & CDs. You can walk into Academy with just $15 and walk out happy. The new and used CDs, DVDs, and records are well organized, low-priced, and in good condition; sometimes they've never even been opened. ✉ *12 W. 18th St., between 5th and 6th Aves., Chelsea* ☎ *212/242–3000.*

Bleecker Bob's Golden Oldies Record Shop. The staff sells punk, new wave, and reggae, plus good old rock on vinyl until the wee hours. ✉ *118 W. 3rd St., at MacDougal St., Greenwich Village* ☎ *212/475–9677.*

Footlight Records. Stop here to browse through New York's largest selection of old and new musicals and movie sound tracks (hello Judy Garland!), as well as a good choice of jazz and American popular standards.

It's closed Monday. ✉ *113 E. 12th St., between 3rd and 4th Aves., East Village* ☎ *212/533–1572.*

Gryphon Record Shop. One of the city's best rare-record stores, it stocks some 90,000 out-of-print and rare LPs. ✉ *233 W. 72nd St., between Broadway and West End Ave., Upper West Side* ☎ *212/874–1588.*

HMV. These record superstores stock hundreds of thousands of discs, tapes, and videos, and provide lots of listening stations to check out what's new. ✉ *565 5th Ave., at E. 46th St., Midtown East* ☎ *212/681–6700* ✉ *234 W. 42nd St., between 7th and 8th Aves., Midtown West* ☎ *212/302–1451* ✉ *308 W. 125th St., between St. Nicholas and 8th Aves., Harlem* ☎ *212/932–9619.*

House of Oldies. The specialty here is records made between 1950 and the late 1980s—45s and 78s, as well as LPs; there are more than a million titles. ✉ *35 Carmine St., between Bleecker St. and 6th Ave., Greenwich Village* ☎ *212/243–0500.*

Jazz Record Center. The city's well-known jazz-record specialist also stocks collectibles. ✉ *236 W. 26th St., between 7th and 8th Aves., 8th floor, Chelsea* ☎ *212/675–4480.*

J&R Music World. This store has a huge selection of pop music and videos, as well as Latin, jazz, and classical, with good prices on major releases. You can even buy music by telephone. ✉ *23 Park Row, between Beekman and Ann Sts., Lower Manhattan* ☎ *212/238–9000.*

Kim's Video & Music. Scruffy and eclectic, Kim's crystallizes the downtown music scene. Its top-20 list is a long, long way from the Top 40; instead, there's a mix of electronica, jazz, lounge, and experimental. ✉ *6 St. Marks Pl., between 2nd and 3rd Aves., East Village* ☎ *212/598–9985* ✉ *144 Bleecker St., between Thompson St. and La Guardia Pl., Greenwich Village* ☎ *212/387–8250* ✉ *2906 Broadway, between W. 113th and W. 114th Sts., Morningside Heights* ☎ *212/864–5321.*

★ **Other Music.** Across the way from Tower Records, both spatially and spiritually, this spot carries hard-to-find albums on CD and vinyl, from Japanese remixes to French free jazz to American roots music. ✉ *15 E. 4th St., between Lafayette St. and Broadway, East Village* ☎ *212/477–8150.*

Tower Records. The scene in each branch is pure New York: at the Village location, many customers are multipierced and rainbow-haired, while at the Lincoln Center branch, patrons discuss jazz in the store café. The East 4th Street branch features discount selections. ✉ *692 Broadway, at E. 4th St., East Village* ☎ *212/505–1500* ✉ *1961 Broadway, at W. 66th St., Upper West Side* ☎ *212/799–2500* ✉ *725 5th Ave., basement level of Trump Tower, between E. 56th and E. 57th Sts., Midtown East* ☎ *212/838–8110* ✉ *20 E. 4th St., at Lafayette St., East Village* ☎ *212/228–7317.*

Virgin Megastore. There's a polished Megastore planted in each major square: Times and Union. Despite the rows upon rows of CDs, videos, books, and DVDs, there's plenty of room for live band appearances—and if you're weak in the knees afterward, you can drop into a chair at the in-store café. ✉ *1540 Broadway, between W. 45th and W. 46th Sts., Midtown West* ☎ *212/921–1020* ✉ *52 E. 14th St., at Broadway, East Village* ☎ *212/598–4666.*

Chocolate

Elk Candy Co. This slice of old Yorkville carries European treats such as Mozartkugeln along with specialty chocolates and wonderful marzipan. Bahlsen spice cookies and chocolate advent calendars arrive for the holidays. ✉ *1628 2nd Ave., between E. 84th and E. 85th Sts., Upper East Side* ☎ *212/650–1177.*

Fauchon. Stroll into the U.S. branches of the Parisian fine-food purveyor to pick up house blends of tea and coffee and some luscious jams for a future *petit déjeuner*, then study the chocolate counter's bonbons. ✉ *442 Park Ave., at E. 56th St., Midtown East* ☎ *212/308–5919* ✉ *1000 Madison Ave., between E. 77th and E. 78th Sts., Upper East Side* ☎ *212/570–2211* ✉ *1383 3rd Ave., Upper East Side* ☎ *No phone at press time.*

★ **La Maison du Chocolat.** Stop in at this chocolatier's small tea salon to dive into a cup of thick, heavenly hot chocolate. The Paris-based outfit sells handmade truffles, chocolates, and pastries that could lull you into a chocolate stupor. ✉ *1018 Madison Ave., between E. 78th and 79th Sts., Upper East Side* ☎ *212/744–7117* ✉ *30 Rockefeller Center, between 5th and 6th Aves., Midtown West* ☎ *212/265–9404.*

Li-Lac Chocolates. This charming nook has been feeding the Village's sweet tooth with traditional homemade American treats, such as turtles, bark, and butter crunch, since 1923. You can also snatch a hand-dipped treat at their stand in the Grand Central Market at Grand Central Terminal. ✉ *120 Christopher St., between Bleecker and Hudson Sts., Greenwich Village* ☎ *212/242–7374.*

Lunettes et Chocolat. Eyeglasses and candy? The better to see your chocolate with, my dear. Gaze at the rows of dashing frames by New Yorker favorite Selima and various designer shades for as long as you can withstand the beckoning smell of cocoa. Then melt for the chocolates, with their delectable ganache, praline, and cream-based fillings. ✉ *25 Prince St., between Elizabeth and Mott Sts., NoLita* ☎ *212/925–8800.*

Neuchatel Chocolates. Neuchatel's velvety chocolates, which come in five dozen varieties, are all made in New York to approximate the Swiss chocolates. ✉ *Plaza Hotel, 2 W. 59th St., between 5th and 6th Aves., Midtown West* ☎ *212/751–7742* ✉ *60 Wall St., between William and Pearl Sts., Lower Manhattan* ☎ *212/480–3766.*

Neuhaus. When they say "Belgian chocolates" they mean it—the treats are flown in from Brussels. Try the pralines or the flavored crème fraîche–filled chocolates. ✉ *922 Madison Ave., between E. 73rd and E. 74th Sts., Upper East Side* ☎ *212/861–2800* ✉ *Grand Central Terminal, at Vanderbilt Pl. and E. 42nd St., Midtown East* ☎ *212/972–3740.*

★ **Richart Design et Chocolat.** This French shop is worth its weight in cacao beans. Many of the sophisticated chocolates use high percentages of cacao, the ganaches and fillings are intense, and many are imprinted with impossibly intricate and colorful patterns. ✉ *7 E. 55th St., between 5th and Madison Aves., Midtown East* ☎ *212/371–9369.*

Teuscher Chocolates of Switzerland. Fabulous chocolates (try the champagne truffles) made in Switzerland are flown in weekly for sale in these jewel-box shops, newly decorated each season. ✉ *620 5th Ave., in Rockefeller Center, Midtown West* ☎ *212/246–4416* ✉ *25 E. 61st St., between 5th and Madison Aves., Upper East Side* ☎ *212/751–8482.*

Clothing

Children's Clothing

Au Chat Botté. Besides little-princess party dresses, this store has delicate, snowy layettes. ✉ *1192 Madison Ave., at E. 87th St., Upper East Side* ☎ *212/722–6474.*

Bonpoint. The sophistication here lies in the beautiful designs and impeccable workmanship—velvet-tipped coats with matching caps and hand-embroidered jumpers and blouses. ✉ *1269 Madison Ave., at E. 91st St., Upper East Side* ☎ *212/722–7720* ✉ *811 Madison Ave., at E. 68th St., Upper East Side* ☎ *212/879–0900.*

Bu and the Duck. Clothes for the young in an old setting sets this infant and children's clothing shop apart from the rest. Owner Susan Lane designs the shop's complete line of clothing and accessories. Everything else in the store is vintage furniture, which is also for sale. ✉ *106 Franklin St., at Church St., TriBeCa* ☎ *212/431–9226.*

Calypso Enfant et Bébé. Sailor-stripe tops, polka-dot PJs, lovely party dresses . . . you may find yourself dressing vicariously through your children. ✉ *426 Broome St., between Lafayette and Crosby Sts., NoLita* ☎ *212/966–3234.*

Infinity. Mothers gossip near the dressing rooms as their daughters try on slinky Les Tout Petits dresses and cheeky Juicy tees. The aggressively trendy and the rather sweet meet in a welter of preteen accessories. ✉ *1116 Madison Ave., at E. 83rd St., Upper East Side* ☎ *212/517–4232.*

Jacadi. The classic clothes here, such as toggle coats and appliquéd sweaters, evoke Madeline's "two straight lines." ✉ *787 Madison Ave., at E. 67th St., Upper East Side* ☎ *212/535–3200* ✉ *1296 Madison Ave., at E. 92nd St., Upper East Side* ☎ *212/369–1616.*

La Petite Etoile. These *petit* European imports might cost as much as lunch at one of the neighboring French bistros, but they are unique; keep an eye out for Floriane jumpers or shirts decorated with Babar. ✉ *746 Madison Ave., between E. 64th and E. 65th Sts., Upper East Side* ☎ *212/744–0975.*

Les Petits Chapelais. Scarves with built-in pockets and cotton play aprons show that comfort and usefulness are high priorities here—but the clothes are also adorable. ✉ *142 Sullivan St., between Prince and W. Houston Sts., SoHo* ☎ *212/505–1927.*

Lilliput. At both locations, which are across the street from each other, kids can up their coolness quotient with cashmere onesies, taxicab-yellow raincoats, or sequinned party dresses. The difference is that the shop at No. 265 carries it all up to size 12, whereas the original shop stops at size 8. ✉ *240 Lafayette St., between Prince and Spring Sts., SoHo* ☎ *212/965–9201* ✉ *265 Lafayette St., between Prince and Spring Sts., SoHo* ☎ *212/965–9567.*

Little Eric. Hip adult styles—Camper knockoffs, brogues—play footsie alongside the familiar loafers and mary janes. ✉ *1331 3rd Ave., at E. 76th St., Upper East Side* ☎ *212/288–8987* ✉ *1118 Madison Ave., at E. 83rd St., Upper East Side* ☎ *212/717–1513.*

Morris Bros. This gold mine of boys' and girls' active wear carries Bear down jackets, mesh shorts, Quiksilver swim trunks, and stacks of Levi's. ✉ *2322 Broadway, at W. 84th St., Upper West Side* ☎ *212/724–9000.*

Oilily. Stylized flowers, stripes, and animal shapes splash across these brightly colored play and school clothes. ✉ *870 Madison Ave., between E. 70th and E. 71st Sts., Upper East Side* ☎ *212/628–0100.*

Petit Bateau. Fine cotton is spun into comfortable underwear, play clothes, and pajamas; T-shirts come in dozens of colors and to every specification, with V-necks, round necks, snap-fronts, and more. ✉ *1094 Madison Ave., at E. 82nd St., Upper East Side* ☎ *212/988–8884.*

Shoofly. Children's shoes and accessories range from Mary Janes, moc crocs, and wing tips to hats, socks, tights, and jewelry. ✉ *465 Amsterdam Ave., between W. 82nd and W. 83rd Sts., Upper West Side* ☎ *212/580–4390* ✉ *42 Hudson St., between Thomas and Duane Sts., TriBeCa* ☎ *212/406–3270.*

Space Kiddets. The funky (Elvis-print rompers) mixes with the tried-and-true (fringed cowboy/cowgirl outfits) at this casual, trendsetting store. ✉ *46 E. 21st St., between Broadway and Park Ave., Flatiron District* ☎ *212/420–9878.*

Z'Baby Company. Outfit the eight-and-unders for dress-up or play with overalls, tulle-skirted party dresses, even motorcycle jackets. An offshoot, Z'Girl, continues the look for girls 10 and up. ✉ *100 W. 72nd St., at Columbus Ave., Upper West Side* ☎ *212/579–2229* ✉ *996 Lexington*

Ave., at E. 72nd St., Upper East Side ☎ *212/472–2229* ✉ *Z'Girl, 976 Lexington Ave., between E. 70 and E. 71st Sts., Upper East Side* ☎ *212/879–4990.*

Discount Clothing

Eisenberg and Eisenberg. Bargain hunters have relied on this store for well-priced men's suits for decades. ✉ *16 W. 17th St., between 5th and 6th Aves., Flatiron District* ☎ *212/627–1290.*

Find Outlet. These outlets are like year-round sample sales. Both locations stock up-and-coming and established designer merchandise for 50%–80% off the original price. It's easy to make finds on a regular basis, as the stock is replenished daily. For a wider selection visit the Chelsea shop; it's open only Thursday through Sunday, however. ✉ *229 Mott St., between Prince and Spring Sts., NoLita* ☎ *212/226–5167* ✉ *361 W. 17th St., between 8th and 9th Aves., Chelsea* ☎ *212/243–3177.*

Forman's. The selection of discounted designer sportswear is particularly good at the Orchard Street store—plenty of conservative clothes by Ralph Lauren, Jones New York, and Liz Claiborne, and lots of options for petite and plus sizes. ✉ *82 Orchard St., between Broome and Grand Sts., Lower East Side* ☎ *212/228–2500* ✉ *145 E. 42nd St., between Lexington and 3rd Aves., Midtown East* ☎ *212/681–9800* ✉ *560 5th Ave., at W. 46th St., Midtown West* ☎ *212/719–1000* ✉ *59 John St., at William St., Lower Manhattan* ☎ *212/791–4100.*

Klein's of Monticello. One of the most genteel stores in the Lower East Side (no fluorescent lighting!), Klein's has authentic labels—Malo cashmere sweaters, Les Copains separates—normally for 20%–30% off. ✉ *105 Orchard St., at Delancey St., Lower East Side* ☎ *212/966–1453.*

Loehmann's. Label searchers can turn up $40 Polo/Ralph Lauren chinos and Donna Karan and Dolce & Gabbana suits in the men's department here on a regular basis. The women's designer section also carries American and European labels, though you may need to make a repeat visit or two before emerging victorious. ✉ *101 7th Ave., at W. 16th St., Chelsea* ☎ *212/352–0856.*

Moe Ginsburg. In this calm store, you can browse through Joseph Abboud suits, Boss tuxedos, and Kenneth Cole or Rockport shoes without getting frazzled. ✉ *162 5th Ave., at W. 21st St., Flatiron District* ☎ *212/242–3482.*

Syms. There are some excellent buys to be had for designer suits and separates. Men can flip through racks of Bill Blass and Cerruti, while women can uncover Calvin Klein and Versus Versace without even trying. Nondesigner racks can be uninspiring. ✉ *400 Park Ave., at E. 54th St., Midtown East* ☎ *212/317–8200* ✉ *42 Trinity Pl., at Rector St., Lower Manhattan* ☎ *212/797–1199.*

Men's & Women's Clothing

Abercrombie & Fitch. Ostensibly wholesome, Abercrombie clothes legions of college kids in jeans, branded tees, and plaid shirts. ✉ *199 Water St., South Street Seaport, Lower Manhattan* ☎ *212/809–9000.*

A.P.C. This hip French boutique proves to be deceptively simple. Watch your step on the uneven wooden floorboards while choosing perfectly cut narrow gabardine and corduroy suits, plus dark denim jeans and jackets. The back room holds such odds and ends as a careful selection of CDs and bottles of olive oil, plus sale items. ✉ *131 Mercer St., between Prince and Spring Sts., SoHo* ☎ *212/966–9685.*

A/X: Armani Exchange. A/X's affordable basics make it possible for most people to own an Armani . . . something. T-shirts and dark-washed jeans abound, but there are also sharp zip-front jackets, pea coats, and stretchy knits. ✉ *568 Broadway, at Prince St., SoHo* ☎ *212/431–6000* ✉ *645 5th Ave., at E. 51st St., Midtown East* ☎ *212/980–3037.*

Brooks Brothers. The clothes at this classic American haberdasher are, as ever, traditional, comfortable, and fairly priced. A modernizing trend has resulted not only in slightly modified styles, but also in a foray into digital tailoring. At the Madison Avenue store, you can step into a computer scanner to get precisely measured for a custom shirt or suit. Summer seersucker, navy blue blazers, and the peerless oxford shirts have been staples for generations. The women's selection has variations thereof. ✉ *666 5th Ave., at W. 53rd St., Midtown West* ☎ *212/261–9440* ✉ *346 Madison Ave., at E. 44th St., Midtown East* ☎ *212/682–8800.*

Burberry. The signature plaid is hardly square these days, as bikinis, leather pants, and messenger-style bags join the traditional gabardine trench coats. The flagship store on East 57th Street is the mother lode; the SoHo branch has an abbreviated assortment. ✉ *9 E. 57th St., between 5th and Madison Aves., Midtown West* ☎ *212/407–7100* ✉ *131 Spring St., between Greene and Wooster Sts., SoHo* ☎ *212/925–9300.*

Calvin Klein. The stark flagship store emphasizes the luxe end of the designer's clothing line. Men's suits tend to be soft around the edges; women's evening gowns are often a fluid pouring of silk. There are also shoes, accessories, housewares, makeup, and, yes, underwear. ✉ *654 Madison Ave., at E. 60th St., Upper East Side* ☎ *212/292–9000.*

Cerruti. Having earned a sterling reputation for men's suits, Cerruti opened its first American boutique here. Move beyond the tailoring to slink into buttery leather, substantial knits, and even specially designed Manolo Blahnik shoes. ✉ *789 Madison Ave., at E. 67th St., Upper East Side* ☎ *212/327–2222.*

Club Monaco. This chain strikes the balance among manageable prices, neutral palettes, and mild designer knockoffs. You won't do too much damage if you cave in to distressed leather or tuxedo pants. ✉ *121 Prince St., between Wooster and Greene Sts., SoHo* ☎ *212/533–8930* ✉ *2376 Broadway, at W. 87th St., Upper West Side* ☎ *212/579–2587* ✉ *160 5th Ave., at W. 21st St., Flatiron District* ☎ *212/352–0936* ✉ *8 W. 57th St., between 5th and 6th Aves., Midtown West* ☎ *212/459–9863* ✉ *1111 3rd Ave., at E. 65th St., Upper East Side* ☎ *212/355–2949* ✉ *520 Broadway, between Broome and Spring Sts., SoHo* ☎ *212/941–1511.*

Comme des Garçons. The designs in this stark, white, swoopy space consistently push the fashion envelope. ✉ *520 W. 22nd St., between 10th and 11th Aves., Chelsea* ☎ *212/604–9200.*

Costume National. Dipping into this murky space brings to light sexy, slim-cut styles for both genders, like leather overcoats or black leather-and-lace shirts. ✉ *108 Wooster St., between Prince and Spring Sts., SoHo* ☎ *212/431–1530.*

DDC Lab. One of the first contemporary boutiques to strike into Orchard Street, DDC continues to equip downtowners with denim and accessories like stingray leather card cases. ✉ *180 Orchard St., at E. Houston St., Lower East Side* ☎ *212/375–1647.*

D&G. This was the first U.S. store for the secondary Dolce & Gabbana line, which aims for younger customers addicted to the over-the-top Sicilian-influenced designs. Look for striped sweaters and skinny pants for men, crocheted dresses and embroidered fabrics for women, and flamboyant accessories all around. ✉ *434 West Broadway, between Prince and Spring Sts., SoHo* ☎ *212/965–8000.*

Diesel. The display windows styled like washing machines at the Lexington Avenue superstore will tip you off to Diesel's industrial edge. They give their mainstay, denim, various finishes, from a dusty-looking indigo to superfaded. **Diesel Style Lab** carries a secondary line with futuristic leanings in graphic prints and souped-up fabrics. The **Diesel Denim Gallery** will even launder your purchase for you. ✉ *770 Lexington Ave.,* *at E. 60th St., Upper East Side* ☎ *212/308–0055* ✉ *1 Union Sq. W, at 14th St.* ☎ *646/336–8552* ✉ *Diesel Style Lab, 416 West Broadway, between Prince and Spring Sts., SoHo* ☎ *212/343–3863* ✉ *Diesel Denim Gallery, 68 Greene St., between Spring and Broome Sts., SoHo,* ☎ *212/966–5593.*

DKNY. Not only does DKNY embrace the lifestyle store concept, but it's a lifestyle with a relatively short attention span. New merchandise arrives frequently, so there's always something new to wish for. Cocktail-party ensembles, chunky-knit sweaters, and knockaround denim vie for attention; the "pure" line is reserved for all-natural fibers. A scattering of vintage pieces, such as leather bomber jackets or 1930s jet jewelry, ensures that you can have something no one else has. Scout out the non-wearables too; the candles, toiletries, and home accessories are unfailingly cool. Then you can belly up to the juice bar, log on to an in-store iMac, or listen to a featured CD. ✉ *655 Madison Ave., at E. 60th St., Upper East Side* ☎ *212/223–3569* ✉ *420 West Broadway, between Prince and Spring Sts., SoHo* ☎ *646/613–1100.*

Dolce & Gabbana. It's easy to feel like an Italian movie star amid these extravagant (in every sense) clothes. Pinstripes are a favorite; for women, they could be paired with something sheer, furred, or leopard-print, while for men they elongate the sharp suits. ✉ *825 Madison Ave., between E. 68th and E. 69th Sts., Upper East Side* ☎ *212/249–4100.*

Donna Karan. Luxurious materials meet "ravaged" design in Karan's first collection store. Devoré velvet, cashmere flannel, and deerskin are drawn into carefully un-precious pieces. A Zen garden lets you relieve sticker shock. ✉ *819 Madison Ave., between E. 68th and E. 69th Sts., Upper East Side* ☎ *212/861–1001.*

Emporio Armani. At this "middle child" of the Armani trio, the clothes are dressy without quite being formal, often in cream, muted blues, and the ever-cool shades of soot. ✉ *601 Madison Ave., between E. 57th and E. 58th Sts., Midtown East* ☎ *212/317–0800* ✉ *110 5th Ave., at W. 16th St., Flatiron District* ☎ *212/727–3240* ✉ *410 West Broadway, at Spring St., SoHo* ☎ *646/613–8099.*

Etro. There are echoes of 19th-century luxury in Etro's clothing, along with a strong whiff of the exotic and a dash of levity. Trademark paisleys sprawl over richly covered suits, dresses, and lustrous pillows. ✉ *720 Madison Ave., between E. 63rd and E. 64th Sts., Upper East Side* ☎ *212/317–9096.*

Gianni Versace. The five-story flagship store, in a restored turn-of-the-20th-century landmark building on 5th Avenue, hums with colored neon lights. Although the sometimes outrageous designs and colors of Versace clothes might not be to everyone's taste (or budget), they're never boring. A second five-story store has a steely, modern take; it focuses on higher-end clothes and accessories. ✉ *647 5th Ave., near E. 51st St., Midtown East* ☎ *212/317–0224* ✉ *815 Madison Ave., between E. 68th and E. 69th Sts., Upper East Side* ☎ *212/744–6868.*

Giorgio Armani. Armani managed to beat out Calvin Klein on the exterior-minimalism front; inside, the space has a museumlike quality, reinforced by the refined clothes. Suits for men and women have a telltale perfect drape, and women's might be accessorized with a broad, striking, beaded necklace. ✉ *760 Madison Ave., between E. 65th and E. 66th Sts., Upper East Side* ☎ *212/988–9191.*

Gucci. The white-hot label shows no signs of cooling off—even the traditional red-and-green ribbon is chic again. The most touted designs are often overtly sexy, but there's also subtler attire. The home and lifestyle accessories can go over the top, as is the case with the multihundred-dollar yoga mat. ✉ *685 5th Ave., between 54th and 55th Sts., Midtown*

East ☎ *212/826–2600* ✉ *840 Madison Ave., between E. 69th and E. 70th Sts., Upper East Side* ☎ *212/717–2619.*

Guess? The denim here seizes on all kinds of trends at once: wide legs and tight low-riders, shredded waistbands, lace-up flys, studs, streaks, and whatever else takes teenagers' fancy. ✉ *537 Broadway, between Prince and Spring Sts., SoHo* ☎ *212/226–9545.*

Helmut Lang. Lang's men's and women's clothes and accessories—mostly in black, white, and gray—are tough distillations of his skinny-pants aesthetic. Black, mirror-ended walls slice up the space, which is punctuated by the digital ticker tape designed by artist Jenny Holzer. Cross the street to sniff a unisex scent at Lang's even more spare perfume boutique. ✉ *80 Greene St., between Spring and Broome Sts., SoHo* ☎ *212/334–3921* ✉ *80 Greene St., between Spring and Broome Sts., SoHo* ☎ *212/925–7214.*

Hermès. Sweep up and down the curving stairway in this contemporary flagship while on the prowl for the classic, distinctively patterned silk scarves and neckties, the coveted Kelly and Birkin handbags, or the beautifully simple separates. True to its equestrian roots, Hermès still stocks saddles and dressage items. ✉ *691 Madison Ave., at E. 62nd St., Upper East Side* ☎ *212/751–3181.*

H&M. Crowds of locals and tourists swarm over the racks in search of up-to-the-minute trends at unbelievably low prices. While you can get the latest in flared jeans or glittery tees, it's not all for teenyboppers; turtleneck sweaters, shifts, and button-downs have their place, too. Fitting-room lines are frustratingly long, the pop music overhead relentless, and the clothing rather cheaply made, but the investment fits the quality. ✉ *1328 Broadway, at W. 34st St., Midtown West* ☎ *646/473–1165* ✉ *558 Broadway, between Prince and Spring Sts., SoHo* ☎ *212/343–2722* ✉ *125 W. 125 St., between Lenox Ave. and Adam Clayton Powell Jr. Blvd., Harlem* ☎ *212/665–8300.*

Hugo Boss. While Hugo Boss is known for its menswear, women will have no trouble occupying themselves. Choose a business-meeting wool suit, then cut a dash with something leather or a wild striped shirt. ✉ *717 5th Ave., at E. 56th St., Midtown East* ☎ *212/485–1800.*

Issey Miyake. Pleats of a Fortuny-like tightness are the Miyake signature—but instead of Fortuny's silks, these clothes are in polyester or ultra-high-tech textiles, often forming sculptural shapes. **Pleats Please** carries a line with simpler silhouettes, from tunics to long dresses. ✉ *992 Madison Ave., between E. 76th and E. 77th Sts., Upper East Side* ☎ *212/439–7822* ✉ *119 Hudson St., at N. Moore St., TriBeCa* ☎ *212/226–0100* ✉ *Pleats Please, 128 Wooster St., at Prince St., SoHo* ☎ *212/226–3600.*

J. Crew. At these hubs of apple-cheeked East Coast style, you can get turned out for a job interview or a week in the Adirondacks. Wool crepe suits, roll-neck sweaters, chinos, and mix-and-match bikini swimwear are among the regulars in the basic-but-not-boring line. Remember, there's not a complete overlap between the store and catalog merchandise. ✉ *99 Prince St., between Mercer and Greene Sts., SoHo* ☎ *212/966–2739* ✉ *203 Front St., at Fulton St., Lower Manhattan* ☎ *212/385–3500* ✉ *91 5th Ave., between E. 16th and E. 17th Sts., Flatiron District* ☎ *212/255–4848* ✉ *30 Rockefeller Plaza, W. 51st St. between 5th and 6th Aves., Midtown West* ☎ *212/765–4227* ✉ *347 Madison Ave., at E. 45th St., Midtown East* ☎ *212/949–0570.*

Jean Paul Gaultier. The powder-pink padded walls give the impression of a style sanctum—but the calm certainly doesn't extend to the clothes. Look for nomad-inspired layers, deconstructed pinstripe suits, and sexy takes on the striped sailor shirt for both sexes. ✉ *759 Madison Ave., between E. 66th and E. 65th Sts., Upper East Side* ☎ *212/249–0235.*

Jeffrey. The Meatpacking District really arrived when this Atlanta-based mini-Barneys opened its doors. You'll find an incredible array of shoes, both in terms of design and size, plus the ultimate in labels like Marc Jacobs, Gucci, and Collette Dinnigan. ✉ *449 W. 14th St., between 9th and 10th Aves., Chelsea* ☎ *212/206–1272.*

Jil Sander. A herringbone coat or a bit of neon trim is about as unruly as this label gets. The designs are unflappable, whether for shirtdresses or boxy jackets, and the colors urban. ✉ *11 E. 57th St., between 5th and Madison Aves., Midtown East* ☎ *212/838–6100.*

Keiko New York. End bathing-suit trauma once and for all by getting your swimsuit customized here—or pick out one of the ready-made, brightly colored numbers. ✉ *62 Greene St., between Spring and Broome Sts., SoHo* ☎ *212/226–6051.*

Kenzo. Lavish layers of color and texture distinguish these designs; you can count on florals, be it a dress sprayed with embroidered buds or a men's shirt printed with blossoms. ✉ *80 Wooster St., between Spring and Broome Sts., SoHo* ☎ *212/966–4142.*

Marc Jacobs. Next door to a SoHo garage lies Jacobs's sleek boutique displaying piles of perfect (and pricey) cashmere, silk, and wool. But the luscious fabrics aren't always treated with complete gravitas: details like oversize buttons or circular patch pockets add a sartorial wink. The Bleecker Street spaces carry relatively casual clothes with a stronger sense of humor, such as stripes in sherbet colors. Pop into the accessories boutique next door for toothsome handbags and shoes. ✉ *163 Mercer St., between W. Houston and Prince Sts., SoHo* ☎ *212/343–1490* ✉ *accessories boutique, 385 Bleecker St., at Perry St., Greenwich Village* ☎ *212/924–6126* ✉ *403-405 Bleecker St., at W. 11th St., Greenwich Village* ☎ *212/924–0026.*

Nicole Farhi. The designer's New York store represents the convergence of her many design talents and endeavors—men's and women's apparel, home furnishings, and restaurants. On entering the store, you can look from the walkway to the inviting tables below. The clothing can be engrossing, especially the knits. The housewares, also downstairs, mix modern and vintage. ✉ *10 E. 60th St., between 5th and Madison Aves., Upper East Side* ☎ *212/223–8811.*

Old Navy. The Gap's kissing cousin has quickly garnered legions of fans with its kick-around clothes at low prices. While sportswear's the general rule, there are some funkier, club-oriented styles called One Below (think Diesel on a budget) available at the Herald Square branch. ✉ *610 6th Ave., at W. 18th St., Chelsea* ☎ *212/645–0663* ✉ *503 Broadway, between Broome and Spring Sts., SoHo* ☎ *212/226–0838* ✉ *150 W. 34th St., at Broadway, Midtown West* ☎ *212/594–0049.*

Patricia Field. After many years in two locations, Field's off-kilter style and outlandish taste are now all under one roof. This is *the* resource for club gear. Think of Carrie Bradshaw's wilder outfits on *Sex and the City*—Field is the costume designer for the show. Fetishes are good-humoredly indulged, with teeny kilts, mesh tops, lamé, marabou, and vinyl thrown into the mix. ✉ *382 West Broadway, between Spring and Broome Sts., SoHo* ☎ *212/966–4066.*

Paul Frank. The flat visage of Julius the monkey, the original Paul Frank character, plasters vinyl wallets, flannel PJs, skateboards, and, of course, T-shirts. Also look for tees evoking such formative elements of '80s youth as corn dogs and break dancing. ✉ *195 Mulberry St., at Kenmare St., NoLita* ☎ *212/965–5079.*

Paul Stuart Inc. The fabric selection is interesting, the tailoring superb, and the look traditional but not stodgy. ✉ *Madison Ave., at E. 45th St., Midtown East* ☎ *212/682–0320.*

Polo/Ralph Lauren. One of New York's most distinctive shopping experiences, Lauren's flagship store is in the turn-of-the-20th-century Rhinelander mansion. Clothes range from summer-in-the-Hamptons madras to exquisite silk gowns and Purple Label men's suits. **Polo Sport** (✉ 888 Madison Ave., at 72nd St., Upper East Side ☎ 212/434–8000 ✉ 381 West Broadway, between Spring and Broome Sts., SoHo ☎ 212/625–1660) carries casual clothes and sports gear, from puffy anoraks to wick-away tanks. At **Double RL** (✉ 271 Mulberry St., between Prince and E. Houston Sts., NoLita ☎ 212/343–0841) vintage flannel shirts, denim, motorcycle leathers, and accessories provide the models for new jeans, barn jackets, and the like. An outpost for children opened on Madison at East 70th Street in spring 2003. ✉ *867 Madison Ave., at E. 72nd St., Upper East Side* ☎ *212/606–2100.*

Prada. Prada's gossamer silks, slick black techno-fabric suits, and luxe shoes and leather goods are among the last great Italian fashion coups of the last millennium. The uptown stores pulse with pale "verdolino" green walls (remember this if you start questioning your skin tone). The 57th Street branch carries just the shoes, bags, and other accessories. The SoHo location, an ultramodern space designed by Rem Koolhaas, incorporates so many technological innovations that it was written up in *Popular Science*. The dressing-room gadgets alone include liquid crystal displays, changeable lighting, and scanners that link you to the store's database. ✉ *724 5th Ave., between W. 56th and W. 57th Sts., Midtown West* ☎ *212/664–0010* ✉ *45 E. 57th St., between Madison and Park Aves., Midtown East* ☎ *212/308–2332* ✉ *841 Madison Ave., at E. 70th St., Upper East Side* ☎ *212/327–4200* ✉ *575 Broadway, at Prince St., SoHo* ☎ *212/334–8888.*

Roberto Cavalli. Rock-star style (at rock-star prices) delivers denim decked with fur, feathers, prints, even shredded silk overlays. ✉ *711 Madison Ave., at E. 63rd St., Upper East Side* ☎ *212/755–7722.*

Seize sur Vingt. In bringing a contemporary sensibility to custom tailoring, this store realized an ideal fusion. Brighten a men's wool suit or cotton moleskin flat-front pants with a checked or striped shirt; all can be made to order. Women are also the beneficiaries of their crisp button-downs and single-pleat trousers. ✉ *243 Elizabeth St., between Prince and Houston Sts., NoLita* ☎ *212/343–0476.*

Seven New York. For Björk-worthy levels of experimental clothing, investigate the efforts of designers like As Four, Imitation of Christ, and Sophia Kokosalaki. ✉ *180 Orchard St., between E. Houston and Stanton Sts., Lower East Side* ☎ *646/654–0156.*

Shanghai Tang. Slide into a loose crepe de chine or velvet Tang jacket, silk pajamas, or a form-fitting cheongsam dress; these modern adaptations of Chinese styles come in soft colors or eye-popping lime and fuschia. ✉ *714 Madison Ave., between E. 63rd and E. 64th Sts., Upper East Side* ☎ *212/888–0111.*

Thomas Pink. London's Jermyn Street shirtmaker hopped the pond with its traditional, impeccably tailored shirts in several styles; besides the British-favored spread collars and French cuffs, there are button-down collars and buttoned cuffs. Silk ties, cuff links, and two lines of women's shirts round out the selection at both locations. ✉ *520 Madison Ave., at E. 53rd St., Midtown East* ☎ *212/838–1928* ✉ *1155 6th Ave., at E. 44th St., Midtown East* ☎ *212/840–9663.*

Tommy Hilfiger. Patriotic red, white, and blue dominates these casual clothes. If jeans, bandanna-print shirts, and other standards don't do it for you, search out the vintage choices, such as sports jerseys or denim jackets. ✉ *372 West Broadway, at Broome St., SoHo* ☎ *917/237–0774.*

Trash and Vaudeville. Punk out in skintight pants, spiderwebby dresses, and other night-crawler garb. ✉ *4 St. Marks Pl., between 2nd and 3rd Aves., East Village* ☎ *212/982–3590.*

TSE. The soft delicacy of the cashmere here doesn't stop at the fabric; TSE's designs are hopelessly refined. ✉ *827 Madison Ave., at E. 69th St., Upper East Side* ☎ *212/472–7790.*

Urban Outfitters. This national hipster chain has been making trends affordable for the student masses for years. The clothes can be cheaply made and the home furnishings may not last a lifetime, but fashions change as often as semesters anyway. ✉ *162 2nd Ave., between E. 10th and E. 11th Sts., East Village* ☎ *212/375–1277* ✉ *374 6th Ave., at Waverly Pl., Greenwich Village* ☎ *212/677–9350* ✉ *582 6th Ave., at W. 14th St., Greenwich Village* ☎ *646/638–1646* ✉ *628 Broadway, between Bleecker and E. Houston Sts., East Village* ☎ *212/475–0009* ✉ *2081 Broadway, at W. 72nd St., Upper West Side* ☎ *212/579–3912.*

Valentino. The mix here is at once audacious and beautifully cut; the fur or feather trimmings, low necklines, and opulent fabrics are about as close as you can get to celluloid glamour. ✉ *747 Madison Ave., at E. 65th St., Upper East Side* ☎ *212/772–6969.*

Yohji Yamamoto. Although almost entirely in black and white, these clothes aren't as severe as they seem. Jackets could gesture toward track suits, or a wool coat could have sleeves of neoprene. ✉ *103 Grand St., at Mercer St., SoHo* ☎ *212/966–9066.*

Yves Saint Laurent Rive Gauche. The sharp-edged store on Madison became the template for all YSL boutiques. Tom Ford's designs for women have been using ruchings, lacings, fringe, and braided leather to moody, rich effect. Hedi Slimane's suits—meant for men but sometimes pilfered by women—follow boyishly slender, narrow lines. A second location opened on East 57th Street in summer 2003. ✉ *855 Madison Ave., between E. 70th and E. 71st Sts., Upper East Side* ☎ *212/988–3821.*

Zara. The tags covered with prices in international currencies all boil down to one thing: inexpensive clothes and accessories for the office or a night out. ✉ *750 Lexington Ave., between E. 59th and E. 60th Sts., Midtown East* ☎ *212/754–1120* ✉ *101 5th Ave., between E. 17th and E. 18th Sts., Flatiron District* ☎ *212/741–0555* ✉ *580 Broadway, between Prince and E. Houston Sts., SoHo* ☎ *212/343–1725.*

Men's Clothing

Agnès b. Homme. This French designer's love for the movies makes it easy to come out looking a little Godard around the edges. Turtleneck sweaters, lean black suits, and black leather porkpie hats demand the sangfroid of Belmondo. ✉ *79 Greene St., between Broome and Spring Sts., SoHo* ☎ *212/431–4339.*

Ascot Chang. Perfect tailoring is a given here, from the worsted-wool suits to the ready-made shirts, but the custom-made shirts are truly outstanding. (There's a four-shirt minimum for the first order.) ✉ *7 W. 57th St., between 5th and 6th Aves., Midtown West* ☎ *212/759–3333.*

Dunhill. Corporate brass come here for finely tailored clothing, both ready-made and custom-ordered, and smoking accessories; the walk-in humidor upstairs stores top-quality tobacco and cigars. ✉ *711 5th Ave., between E. 56th and E. 55th Sts., Midtown East* ☎ *212/753–9292.*

Façonnable. This French company has a lock on the Euro-conservative look. Their sport coats (about $800) and Italian-made suits may be expensive, but the tailoring and canvas fronting will make them withstand years of dry cleaning. ✉ *5th Ave., at W. 51st St., Midtown West* ☎ *No phone at press time.*

Holland & Holland. This is no Ralph-Lauren-does-country-squire; Holland & Holland provides the Prince of Wales (and wealthy colonials) with country clothing and accessories such as leather falcon hoods. There's a special safari tailoring section and a gun room on the fifth floor. ✉ *50 E. 57th St., between Madison and Park Aves., Midtown East* ☎ *212/752–7755.*

J. Press. Oxford-cloth shirts, natural-shoulder suits, madras-patch Bermuda shorts, and amusing club ties will help you join the old boy network—or just look the part. ✉ *7 E. 44th St., between 5th and Madison Aves., Midtown East* ☎ *212/687–7642.*

John Varvatos. After years with Calvin Klein and Ralph Lauren, Varvatos set off on his own and quickly started racking up design awards. A degree of ease marks his soft-shoulder suits, long overcoats, tweedy trousers, and denim. ✉ *149 Mercer St., between W. Houston and Prince Sts., SoHo* ☎ *212/965–0700.*

Nautica. As the name implies, there are seafaring influences at work, manifesting themselves in water-resistant jackets and thick-knit sweaters, often in deep blue or stripes. Dress shirts and suits with a bit of stretch apply for when you're not on deck. ✉ *50 Rockefeller Center, between 5th and 6th Aves., Midtown West* ☎ *212/664–9594.*

Paul Smith. Dark mahogany Victorian cases complement the foppish British styles they hold. Embroidered vests, brightly colored socks and shirts, and quirky cuff links and other accessories leaven the classic, dark, double-back-vent suits. ✉ *108 5th Ave., at E. 16th St., Flatiron District* ☎ *212/627–9770.*

Sean. A welcome antidote to the omnipresent minimalist boxes, these snug shops carry low-key, well-priced, and comfortable apparel from France—wool and cotton painter's coats, very-narrow-wale corduroy pants, and a respectable collection of suits and dress shirts. ✉ *132 Thompson St., between W. Houston and Prince Sts., SoHo* ☎ *212/598–5980* ✉ *224 Columbus Ave., between W. 70th and W. 71st Sts., Upper West Side* ☎ *212/769–1489.*

Vilebrequin. Allow St-Tropez to influence your swimsuit; these striped, floral, and solid-color French-made trunks come in sunny hues. Waterproof pocket inserts keep your essentials safe from beachcombers. Many styles come in boys' sizes, too. ✉ *1070 Madison Ave., at E. 81st St., Upper East Side* ☎ *212/650–0353* ✉ *436 West Broadway, between Prince and Spring Sts., SoHo* ☎ *212/431–0673.*

Vintage & Consignment Clothing

Alice Underground. Alice may not be subterranean, but it has what almost all vintage-clothing stores lack—elbow room. Some finds are hardly vintage, but staples include cashmere sweaters and beaded shells for under $100, track pants, tuxes, and Hawaiian shirts. ✉ *481 Broadway, between Broome and Grand Sts., SoHo* ☎ *212/431–9067.*

Allan & Suzi. The proprietors, whom you'll no doubt find sitting behind the counter, are the godfather and -mother of fashion collecting. Their wacky shop preserves 1980s shoulder pads and 1940s gowns for posterity (or sale). ✉ *416 Amsterdam Ave., between W. 79th and W. 80th Sts., Upper West Side* ☎ *212/724–7445.*

Cheap Jack's. Three floors are jammed with almost everything you could wish for: track suits, bomber jackets, early 1980s madras shirts, old prom dresses, and fur-trimmed wool ladies' suits with the eau-de-mothball stamp of authenticity. Often, though, Jack's is not so cheap. ✉ *841 Broadway, between E. 13th and E. 14th Sts., Greenwich Village* ☎ *212/995–0403.*

INA. Although you may spot something vintage, like a 1960s Yves Saint Laurent velvet bolero, most clothing at these small boutiques harks back only a few seasons, and in some cases, it's never been worn. The Mott Street location racks up menswear; the other three stores carry women's resale. ✉ *101 Thompson St., between Prince and Spring Sts., SoHo*

☎ *212/941–4757* ✉ *21 Prince St., between Elizabeth and Mott Sts., NoLita* ☎ *212/334–9048* ✉ *262 Mott St., between Prince and E. Houston Sts., NoLita* ☎ *212/334–2210* ✉ *208 E. 73rd St., between 2nd and 3rd Aves., Upper East Side* ☎ *212/249–0014.*

Resurrection. With original Courrèges, Puccis, and foxy boots, this store is a retro-chic gold mine. It's also responsible for the vintage selection at Henri Bendel's uptown. ✉ *217 Mott St., between Prince and Spring Sts., NoLita* ☎ *212/625–1376.*

Screaming Mimi's. Vintage 1960s and 1970s clothes and retro-wear include everything from lingerie to soccer shirts to prom dresses. ✉ *382 Lafayette St., between 4th and Great Jones Sts., East Village* ☎ *212/677–6464.*

What Comes Around Goes Around. Thanks to the staff's sharp eyes, the denim and leather racks here are reliably choice. The tidy selection also provides hip-again items like rabbit-fur jackets and decorative belt buckles. ✉ *351 West Broadway, between Grand and Broome Sts., SoHo* ☎ *212/343–9303.*

Women's Clothing

Agnès b. With this quintessentially French line you can look like a Parisienne schoolgirl—in snap-front tops, slender pants, sweet floral prints—or like her chic *maman* in tailored dark suits and leather jackets. ✉ *79 Greene St., between Prince and Spring Sts., SoHo* ☎ *212/925–4649* ✉ *13 E. 16th St., between 5th Ave. and Union Sq. W, Flatiron District* ☎ *212/741–2585* ✉ *1063 Madison Ave., between E. 80th and E. 81st Sts., Upper East Side* ☎ *212/570–9333.*

Alexander McQueen. No matter how flouncy McQueen's ensembles become, they retain idiosyncratic, unsettling elements. Copper rings might pierce and pucker a shirt; a narrow wool skirt could have rows of suture-like stitches. Leather, meanwhile, could be used for harnesslike straps or be perforated like lace. ✉ *417 W. 14th St., between 9th and 10th Aves., Meatpacking District* ☎ *212/645–1797.*

Alicia Mugetti. Silks and velvets are layered, softly shaped, and sometimes hand-painted. ✉ *999 Madison Ave., between E. 77th and E. 78th Sts., Upper East Side* ☎ *212/794–6186.*

Anna Sui. The violet-and-black salon, hung with Beardsley prints and neon alterna-rock posters, is the perfect setting for Sui's bohemian, flapper- and rocker-influenced designs. ✉ *113 Greene St., between Prince and Spring Sts., SoHo* ☎ *212/941–8406.*

Anne Fontaine. The white blouses here might make you swear off plain oxford shirts forever. Rows of snowy blouses, most in cotton poplin or organdy, are jazzed up with lacings, embroidery, or billowing sleeves. Other styles, like a tuxedo-bib front, are executed in black. ✉ *93 Greene St., between Prince and Spring Sts., SoHo* ☎ *212/343–3154* ✉ *791 Madison Ave., at E. 67th St., Upper East Side* ☎ *212/639–9651.*

Balenciaga. Nicolas Ghesquière, a recent *amour fou* in the fashion world, took a page from the neighboring galleries for the first. U.S. store. The lighting and background sounds shift subtly as you make discoveries: a sueded silk lining or a pair of pumps in a grotto. ✉ *54 W. 22nd St., between 10th and 11th Aves., Chelsea* ☎ *212/206–0872.*

Barbara Bui. Leave it to the French to successfully mix feminine details (jackets with a thin edging of leather or mink) with a cold, industrial edge (shirts from the secondary line come encased in vacuum-sealed plastic pouches). ✉ *115-117 Wooster St., between Prince and Spring Sts., SoHo* ☎ *212/625–1938.*

BCBG. If flirtation's your sport, you'll find your sportswear here among the fluttering skirts, beaded camisoles, and leather pants. ✉ *120 Wooster*

St., between Prince and Spring Sts., SoHo ☎ 212/625–2723 ✉ 770 Madison Ave., at E. 66th St., Upper East Side ☎ 212/717–4225.

Betsey Johnson. The SoHo store departs from the traditional (if such a word can be applied) hot pink interior; instead its walls are sunny yellow with painted roses, and there's a bordello-red lounge area in back. Besides the quirkily printed dresses, available in all stores, there's a slinky upscale line. This is not the place for natural fibers—it's ruled by rayon, stretch, and the occasional faux fur. ✉ *138 Wooster St., between Prince and W. Houston Sts., SoHo ☎ 212/995–5048 ✉ 251 E. 60th St., between 2nd and 3rd Aves., Upper East Side ☎ 212/319–7699 ✉ 248 Columbus Ave., between W. 71st and W. 72nd Sts., Upper West Side ☎ 212/362–3364 ✉ 1060 Madison Ave., between E. 80th and E. 81st Sts., Upper East Side ☎ 212/734–1257.*

Bond 07. The clothing by edgy designers certainly piques interest, but the accessories here are the standouts: Selima two-tone glasses, inventive handbags, hats, gloves, perhaps even ruffled parasols. ✉ *7 Bond St., between Lafayette St. and Broadway, East Village ☎ 212/677–8487.*

Calypso. Spring for something with a tropical vibe, like a sweeping, ruffled skirt in guava-color silk, an embroidered kurta-style top, or a fringed shawl. The jewelry offshoot at 252 Mott Street can doll you up in equally colorful semiprecious stones or shells. Search out something for your *homme* at the men's branch. ✉ *424 Broome St., at Crosby St., SoHo ☎ 212/274–0449 ✉ 280 Mott St., between E. Houston and Prince Sts., NoLita ☎ 212/965–0990 ✉ 935 Madison Ave., at E. 74th St., Upper East Side ☎ 212/535–4100 ✉ Bijoux, 252 Mott St., between Prince and E. Houston Sts., NoLita ☎ 212/334–9730 ✉ Calypso Homme, 405 Broome St., between Lafayette and Centre Sts., NoLita ☎ 212/343–0450.*

Carolina Herrera. This couture deserves a truly outstanding occasion; the beading and sequinning work are stunning. Expect anything from demure, shimmering bands of decoration to a knockout zebra-ish pattern. ✉ *954 Madison Ave., at E. 75th St., Upper East Side ☎ 212/249–6552.*

Catherine Malandrino. More monochromatic than in years past—with cream and black nudging out the lavender and red—these designs still get worked over with shirring, ruching, appliquéing, and crochet. ✉ *468 Broome St., at Greene St., SoHo ☎ 212/925–6765.*

Chanel. The midtown flagship has often been compared to a Chanel suit—slim, elegant, and timeless. Inside wait the famed suits themselves, along with other pillars of Chanel style: chic little black dresses and evening gowns, chain-handled bags, and yards of pearls. Frédéric Fekkai's five-story, Provence-saturated salon perches upstairs. Downtown's branch concentrates on more contemporary forays, including ski gear, while Madison's boutique is dedicated to shoes, handbags, and other accessories. ✉ *139 Spring St., at Wooster St., SoHo ☎ 212/334–0055 ✉ 15 E. 57th St., between 5th and Madison Aves., Midtown East ☎ 212/355–5050 ✉ 737 Madison Ave., at E. 64th St., Upper East Side ☎ 212/535–5505.*

Chloé. Phoebe Philo stepped up to the plate as house designer after Stella McCartney's departure; her saucy trousers and puffed-sleeve blouses may induce you to roll out some Philo dough. ✉ *850 Madison Ave., at E. 70th St., Upper East Side ☎ 212/717–8220.*

Christian Dior. The New York outpost of one of France's most venerable fashion houses makes its home in the dazzlingly modern LVMH tower. The designs bring elements of everything from raceways to skate punks to haute couture. If you're not in the market for an investment gown, peruse the glam accessories, like the latest stirrup bag. The Dior jewelry boutique glitters just next door. ✉ *21 E. 57th St., at Madison Ave., Midtown East ☎ 212/931–2950 ✉ jewelry boutique, 21 E. 57th St., Midtown East ☎ 212/207–8448.*

Christopher Totman. Relish the handmade Peruvian alpaca knits, from the sweaters studded with semiprecious stones to the crochet hats. Whatever the season, the colors are bright. ✉ *262 Mott St., between E. Houston and Prince Sts., NoLita* ☎ *212/925–7495.*

Diane von Furstenberg. Mirrored disks spread like confetti across the ceiling here. Flit through the perennial wrap dresses or tops with a deep-V neckline, some with ruffles along the edge to accentuate the plunge. ✉ *389 W. 12th St., between Washington and West Sts., West Village* ☎ *646/486–4800.*

Emanuel Ungaro. The vibrant shocking pink of the stairway will keep you alert as you browse through swell ladies-who-lunch daytime suits and grande dame, sometimes bead-encrusted, evening wear. ✉ *792 Madison Ave., at E. 67th St., Upper East Side* ☎ *212/249–4090.*

Escada. Not for the color-shy, Escada cruises on with royal purple or crimson suits, white resort knits, and a helping of gold lamé. ✉ *715 5th Ave., between E. 55th and E. 56th Sts., Midtown East* ☎ *212/755–2201.*

Givenchy. After years under British enfant terrible Alexander McQueen, Givenchy throttles back with designer Julien Macdonald's less aggressive styles, which include full skirts and diaphanous fabrics. ✉ *710 Madison Ave., at E. 63rd St., Upper East Side* ☎ *212/688–4338.*

Intermix. The trend-conscious will find one-stop shopping for upscale items from designers such as Katayone Adeli, Catherine Malandrino, and Marc Jacobs, plus a just-enough layout of shoes and accessories. ✉ *125 5th Ave., between E. 19th and E. 20th Sts., Flatiron District* ☎ *212/533–9720* ✉ *210 Columbus Ave., between W. 69th and W. 70th Sts., Upper West Side* ☎ *212/769–9116* ✉ *1003 Madison Ave., between E. 77th and E. 78th Sts., Upper East Side* ☎ *212/249–7858.*

Katayone Adeli. While Adeli pants show up in several city boutiques, here you can see the full collection of subtly sexy basics, with pieces exclusive to the store. Consider pairing the trousers or jeans (on the small side) with a filmy silk and lace blouse. ✉ *35 Bond St., between Lafayette and the Bowery, East Village* ☎ *212/260–3500.*

★ **Kirna Zabête.** A heavy-hitting lineup of cachet designers—Balenciaga, Cacharel, Clements Ribiero—is managed with an exceptionally cheerful flair. Step downstairs for Burberry dog coats, e.vil tees to announce your true colors ("Little Miss Drama"), and even giant gum balls. ✉ *96 Greene St., between Spring and Prince Sts., SoHo* ☎ *212/941–9656.*

Language. The first of the "lifestyle" fashion boutiques, Language supplements its noteworthy racks (Chloé, Lucien Pellat-Finet cashmere sweaters, its own chic knits) with Taschen art books and cult editions of *Visionaire.* ✉ *238 Mulberry St., between Prince and Spring Sts., NoLita* ☎ *212/431–5566.*

Laura Ashley. Laura Ashley's last Manhattan holdout still purveys the hyperfloral look, although some flower prints are nearly abstract and there are simple linen sundresses. ✉ *398 Columbus Ave., at W. 79th St., Upper West Side* ☎ *212/496–5110.*

Liz Lange Maternity. By using lots of stretch fabrics, even stretch leather, this designer can conjure up maternity versions of the latest trends. ✉ *958 Madison Ave., between E. 75th and E. 76th Sts., Upper East Side* ☎ *212/879–2191.*

Marina Rinaldi. These plus-size tailored suits, cocktail dresses, and sweeping coats know just how to flatter. ✉ *800 Madison Ave., between E. 67th and E. 68th Sts., Upper East Side* ☎ *212/734–4333.*

Max Mara. Think subtle colors and enticing fabrics—straight skirts in cashmere or heathered wool, tuxedo-style evening jackets, and several choices of wool and cashmere camel overcoats. ✉ *813 Madison Ave., at E. 68th St., Upper East Side* ☎ *212/879–6100* ✉ *450 West Broadway, between Prince and Spring Sts., SoHo* ☎ *212/674–1817.*

Mayle. This little shotgun boutique basks in the ineffable vapor of cool. Designer Jane Mayle, who is often found lounging in the store, designs close-fitting knit tops, ultrasuede bags, and retro-style dresses, which are displayed alongside vintage items she culls from flea markets around the world. Word has it she is the hottest young designer around. ✉ *252 Elizabeth St., between E. Houston and Prince Sts., NoLita* ☎ *212/625–0406.*

Michael Kors. In his deft reworkings of American classics, Kors gives sportswear the luxury treatment, as with car coats using cashmere or fur. The approach continues in the secondary line at **Kors** (✉ 159 Mercer St., between Prince and W. Houston Sts., SoHo ☎ 212/966–5880), where wrap skirts could appear in silk twill or jeans in silver leather. ✉ *974 Madison Ave., at E. 76th St., Upper East Side* ☎ *212/452–4685.*

Miu Miu. Prada front woman Miuccia Prada established a secondary line (bearing her childhood nickname, Miu Miu) to showcase her more experimental ideas. Look for Prada-esque styles in more daring colors and fabrics, such as jersey culottes or bright yellow patent leather boots. ✉ *100 Prince St., between Mercer and Greene Sts., SoHo* ☎ *212/334–5156* ✉ *831 Madison Ave., at E. 69th St., Upper East Side* ☎ *212/249–9660.*

Morgane Le Fay. The clothes here borrow from centuries past (billowing silk, high waists); you almost have to be tall and willowy, or French, to carry it off. ✉ *746 Madison Ave., between E. 64th and E. 65th Sts., Upper East Side* ☎ *212/879–9700* ✉ *67 Wooster St., between Broome and Spring Sts., SoHo* ☎ *212/219–7672.*

Moschino. IT'S BETTER TO DRESS AS YOU WISH THAN AS YOU SHOULD! proclaims one of the walls of the multistory Moschino flagship. People with a penchant for comedic couture won't have any trouble finding their wardrobe soul mate in this whirligig store. ✉ *803 Madison Ave., between E. 67th and E. 68th Sts., Upper East Side* ☎ *212/639–9600.*

Nanette Lepore. The insouciant looks here put retro references—pompom trim, yoked tops, floral, tapestry, and paisley prints—to good use. ✉ *423 Broome St., between Lafayette and Crosby Sts., NoLita* ☎ *212/219–8265.*

O.M.O. Norma Kamali. Dim corners and dislocated stairs characterize this bunkerlike store—an odd setting for evening gowns, long tunics, resort-ready bathing suits, and a little gathering of vintage Kamali. ✉ *11 W. 56th St., between 5th and 6th Aves., Midtown West* ☎ *212/957–9797.*

Philosophy di Alberta Ferretti. The designer's eye for delicate detailing is evident in the seaming and sprinklings of beads across gauzy fabrics or soft knits. ✉ *452 West Broadway, between W. Houston and Prince Sts., SoHo* ☎ *212/460–5500.*

Searle. Strung along the East Side, these stores have a devoted following for their coats: pea coats, long wool coats, shearlings, leather, or even llama hair. There are plenty of other designer things to layer, too, from cowl-neck sweaters to fitted tees. ✉ *1051 3rd Ave., at E. 62nd St., Upper East Side* ☎ *212/838–5990* ✉ *609 Madison Ave., at E. 58th St., Midtown East* ☎ *212/753–9021* ✉ *805 Madison Ave., between E. 67th and E. 68th Sts., Upper East Side* ☎ *212/628–6665* ✉ *1296 3rd Ave., between E. 74th and E. 75th Sts., Upper East Side* ☎ *212/717–5200* ✉ *1035 Madison Ave., at E. 79th St., Upper East Side* ☎ *212/717–4022* ✉ *1124 Madison Ave., at E. 84th St., Upper East Side* ☎ *212/988–7318.*

Sonia Rykiel. Paris's "queen of knitwear" sets off strong colors such as fuchsia or orange with, *naturellement,* black. ✉ *849 Madison Ave., between E. 70th and E. 71st Sts., Upper East Side* ☎ *212/396–3060.*

Stella McCartney. A devout vegetarian setting up shop in the Meatpacking District may seem odd, but it's further proof that chic trumps many other considerations. You could put together an outfit of head-to-toe satin or chiffon, but it's more in keeping to mix it with shredded denim. As leather is verboten, shoes and accessories come in satin, canvas, and synthetics. ✉ *429 W. 14th St., at Washington St., Meatpacking District* ☎ *212/255–1556.*

Tracy Feith. Mr. Feith makes the most of feminine curves with vibrant dresses and separates. Necklines on tees scoop wide and low, skirts flirt with flounces and yokes, and the sexy printed silk dresses are light as a feather. Peer into the cases for a bauble or two. ✉ *209 Mulberry St., between Spring and Kenmare Sts., NoLita* ☎ *212/334–3097.*

Ventilo. Eastern elements, such as paisley patterns and sari-like strong pinks and golds, enliven Occident-ready tweeds and mohair. ✉ *69 Greene St., between Spring and Broome Sts., SoHo* ☎ *212/625–3660* ✉ *810 Madison Ave., between E. 67th St. and E. 68th Sts., Upper East Side* ☎ *212/535–9362.*

Vera Wang. The made-to-order bridal and evening wear glows with satin, beading, and embroidery. Periodic pret-a-porter sales offer the dresses for a (relative) song. ✉ *991 Madison Ave., at E. 77th St., Upper East Side* ☎ *212/628–3400.*

Vivienne Tam. Tam is known for her playful, "China chic" take on familiar Asian images: embroidered flowers and Chinese dragons spill down soft net dresses, and Mao's image gazes impassively from PVC jackets or throw pillows. ✉ *99 Greene St., between Prince and Spring Sts., SoHo* ☎ *212/966–2398.*

Vivienne Westwood. Up front, the grande dame of British fashion offers rocker clothes from her Anglomania line; move toward the back for the dandyish fabrics and tongue-in-cheek touches (oversize buttons, elaborate necklines) of the couture line. ✉ *71 Greene St., between Spring and Broome Sts., SoHo* ☎ *212/334–5200.*

Crystal

Baccarat. "Life is worth Baccarat," say the ads—in other words, the quality of crystal shown here is priceless. ✉ *625 Madison Ave., at E. 59th St., Midtown East* ☎ *212/826–4100.*

Galleri Orrefors Kosta Boda. Stop here for striking Swedish crystal, including work from the imaginative and often brightly colored Kosta Boda line. ✉ *685 Madison Ave., between E. 61st and E. 62nd Sts., Upper East Side* ☎ *212/752–1095.*

Steuben. The bowls and vases make for knockout table centerpieces, but if all this shopping gives you sweaty palms, wrap your fingers around a miniature sculpted-animal hand cooler, then head downstairs to view one of the rotating glass exhibitions. ✉ *667 Madison Ave., between E. 60th and E. 61st Sts., Upper East Side* ☎ *212/752–1441.*

Gadgets

Hammacher Schlemmer. The store that gave America its first pop-up toaster still ferrets out the outrageous, the unusual, and the best of home electronics. ✉ *147 E. 57th St., between 3rd and Lexington Aves., Midtown East* ☎ *212/421–9000.*

Sharper Image. The assortment of things to make the good life even better includes massage chairs, ionic air purifiers, and whatsits such as miniature replicas of classic cars. ✉ *Pier 17, South Street Seaport, Lower Manhattan* ☎ *212/693–0477* ✉ *98 Greene St., between Prince and Spring Sts., SoHo* ☎ *917/237–0221* ✉ *4 W. 57th St., at 5th Ave., Midtown West* ☎ *212/265–2550* ✉ *900 Madison Ave., at E. 72nd St., Upper East Side* ☎ *212/794–4974.*

Home Furnishings

Fodor's Choice ★ **ABC Carpet & Home.** ABC seems to cover most of the furnishings alphabet; over several floors it encompasses everything from rustic furniture to 19th-century repros, refinished Chinese chests and Vitra chairs, not to mention that loose category "country French." The ground floor teems with a treasure-attic's worth of accessories. ✉ *888 Broadway, at E. 19th St., Flatiron District* ☎ *212/473–3000.*

Aero. On street level, accessories such as ebonized wood trays and opalescent glass pieces do the talking. Upstairs, you can parley with quietly luxurious furniture. ✉ *132 Spring St., between Greene and Wooster Sts., SoHo* ☎ *212/966–1500.*

The Apartment. In this apartment moonlighting as a store—or is it the other way around?—you can stroll the multilevels, admire the artwork and cool decor, and flip through a book. Anything you see can be yours. ✉ *101 Crosby St., between Prince and Spring Sts., SoHo* ☎ *212/219–3661.*

Armani Casa. In keeping with the Armani aesthetic, the clean lines and subdued color schemes (cream, black, a crimson accent here and there) bring attention to detail and texture. Among the understated furnishings and tableware, the gleam of gold-flecked glass or the striations of carved mango-wood accessories stand out. ✉ *97 Greene St., between Prince and Spring Sts., SoHo* ☎ *212/334–1271.*

Avventura. Glory in Italian design in all its streamlined beauty here. Tabletop items and mouth-blown glass accessories are all stunning. ✉ *463 Amsterdam Ave., at W. 82nd St., Upper West Side* ☎ *212/769–2510.*

Bed, Bath & Beyond. These megastores stock some 80,000 different household items, from bedding to kitchenware, at reasonable prices. Weekends are mob scenes, but the Upper East Side branch is often the quieter of the two. ✉ *620 6th Ave., between W. 18th and W. 19th Sts., Chelsea* ☎ *212/255–3550* ✉ *410 E. 61st St., between 1st and York Aves., Upper East Side* ☎ *646/215–4702.*

c.i.t.e. Housewares in this showroom wander from industrial (Pyrex containers) to amusing (bulbous fiberglass chairs) to kid-friendly (chairs that double as toy storage). ✉ *100 Wooster St., between Prince and Spring Sts., SoHo* ☎ *212/431–7272.*

Clio. Take a shortcut to find the accessories you've seen in the shelter mags. This boutique sets its table with delicate Czech glass vases, bone china with raised dots, and colorful handblown glass bottles. ✉ *92 Thompson St., between Prince and Spring Sts., SoHo* ☎ *212/966–8991.*

Crate & Barrel. Each of these bright stores carries a terrific selection of household items for every imaginable room. The careful coordination table- and kitchenwares on the ground floor may sway you into buying any number of doodads. Upstairs, couples wander among sets of easy-to-please furniture, consulting each other on leather club chairs and coffee tables. ✉ *650 Madison Ave., at E. 59th St., Upper East Side* ☎ *212/308–0011* ✉ *611 Broadway, at Houston St., SoHo* ☎ *212/308–0011.*

Fishs Eddy. The dishes, china, and glassware for resale here come from all walks of crockery life—corporate dining rooms, failed restaurants, etc. New wares often look retro, such as a service with a ticker-tape border, and there are lots of oddball pieces such as finger bowls. ✉ *2176 Broadway, at W. 77th St., Upper West Side* ☎ *212/873–8819* ✉ *889 Broadway, at E. 19th St., Flatiron District* ☎ *212/420–9020.*

Hable Construction. Vivid colors, graphic shapes (stripes, dots, leaves), and a soft nap give these wool felt and cotton-linen pillows all-around warmth. Appliqued felt stockings are hung up for the holidays. ✉ *230 Elizabeth St., between Prince and Houston Sts., NoLita* ☎ *212/343–8555.*

Jonathan Adler. The blunt graphics (stripes, crosses, circles) that emblazon the handmade pottery (ranging from a tiny $30 vase to a chunky $400 lamp), hand-loomed wool pillow covers, throws, and even ponchos are Adler's trademark. If the store is out of stock, place a special order at no extra cost. ✉ *465 Broome St., at Greene St., SoHo* ☎ *212/941–8950.*

Let There Be Neon. Browse among the terrific collection of new and antique neon signs, clocks, and tabletop accessories. ✉ *38 White St., between Broadway and Church St., Lower Manhattan* ☎ *212/226–4883.*

Ligne Roset. These showcases of modern French furniture, filled with pieces such as beech nesting tables topped with ribbed aluminum and armchairs curvy or boxy, also include uncommon vases, decorative bowls, and other accessories. ✉ *250 Park Ave., between E. 19th and E. 20th Sts., Gramercy* ☎ *212/375–1036* ✉ *155 Wooster St., between W. Houston and Prince Sts., SoHo* ☎ *212/253–5629* ✉ *1090 3rd Ave., at E. 64th St., Upper East Side* ☎ *212/794–2903.*

Maurice Villency. The company may be venerable, but the furniture is strictly modern. The lines cut sharp corners for a boxy sofa and curve for a chaise or ottoman, but they're always uncluttered. This flagship introduces home accessories, too, including kimonos and vases. ✉ *200 E. 57th St., at 3rd Ave., Upper East Side* ☎ *212/725–4840.*

Miya Shoji Interiors. This shop offers a superb selection of neatly crafted Japanese folding screens, plus *tonsu* chests and tatami platforms. ✉ *109 W. 17th St., between 6th and 7th Aves., Chelsea* ☎ *212/243–6774.*

Mood Indigo. For a retro rush, drift through Stork Club paraphernalia, Bakelite bangles, novelty salt-and-pepper sets, martini shakers, and Fiestaware. ✉ *181 Prince St., between Sullivan and Thompson Sts., SoHo* ☎ *212/254–1176.*

★ **Moss.** International designers, many of them Italian or Scandinavian, put a fantastic spin on even the most utilitarian objects, which are carefully brought together by Murray Moss at his store–cum–design museum. The latest innovations from Droog Design or Philippe Starck are interspersed with Nymphenburg porcelain and evergreen designs from the early 20th century. ✉ *146 Greene St., between W. Houston and Prince Sts., SoHo* ☎ *212/226–2190.*

Mxyplyzyk. Hard to pronounce (*mixyplitsick*) and hard to resist, this is a trove of impulse buys—creative riffs on household standbys such as soap dispensers (here a stylized bird) and night-lights (magic lanterns). ✉ *125 Greenwich Ave., at W. 13th St., Greenwich Village* ☎ *212/989–4300.*

Pottery Barn. With its all-occasion glassware, artsy knickknacks, and relatively grounded prices, Pottery Barn has become one of the most visible American purveyors of contemporary interior design. ✉ *600 Broadway, at E. Houston St., SoHo* ☎ *212/219–2420* ✉ *1965 Broadway, at W. 67th St., Upper West Side* ☎ *212/579–8477.*

Restoration Hardware. There's a touch of retro goodness in the wares here, such as bathroom and cabinet fixtures, tools, a smattering of furniture and lamps, and cleaning supplies, plus little buy-mes like bar towels and bookends. ✉ *935 Broadway, at E. 22nd St., Flatiron District* ☎ *212/260–9479.*

Room. New Yorkers have welcomed the first freestanding store from the Australian home-product line of the same name. The assortment is random but complete—everything from doormats to bicycles to vases. ✉ *182 Duane St., between Hudson and Greenwich Sts., TriBeCa* ☎ *212/226–1045.*

Scully & Scully. Leather footstools in animal shapes and small pieces of reproduction antique furniture exemplify this store's high-WASP style. ✉ *504 Park Ave., between E. 59th and E. 60th Sts., Upper East Side* ☎ *212/755–2590.*

Shabby Chic. An invitation to lengthy lounging, these slipcovered sofas, love seats, armchairs, and pillows are often, as they say, "squadgy." Fabrics run to the floral and faded. ✉ *83 Wooster St., between Spring and Broome Sts., SoHo* ☎ *212/274–9842.*

Terence Conran Shop. The British style monger has made a victorious return to New York City. The small glass pavilion beneath the 59th Street Bridge caps a vast underground showroom of kitchen and garden implements, fabrics, furniture, and glassware. ✉ *407 E. 59th St., at 1st Ave., Midtown East* ☎ *212/755–9079.*

Totem. Combining a shop and design house, Totem treats you to avant-garde items that range from the inexpensive (neon-tone plastic dish racks) to the luxurious (glossy red folding screens), not to mention some of the friendliest salespeople in the city. ✉ *71 Franklin St., between Broadway and Church St., TriBeCa* ☎ *212/925–5506* ✉ *83 Grand St., between Wooster and Greene Sts., SoHo* ☎ *212/219–2446.*

Troy. In this spare space, the clean lines of Lucite, leather, cedar, and resin furniture and home accessories may well wreak havoc with your credit card. In addition to the seriously sleek furnishings, you'll find limited-edition playthings—puzzles, toys, and board games. ✉ *138 Greene St., between Prince and W. Houston Sts., SoHo* ☎ *212/941–4777.*

Waterworks. While bathroom fittings may not be on the top of your trip's shopping list, Waterworks is more than a faucet shop. Be tempted by European toiletries, densely plush cotton towels, or tissue holders, soap dishes, and other accessories in mother-of-pearl, resin, pewter, and mercury glass. ✉ *225 E. 57th St., between 2nd and 3rd Aves., Midtown East* ☎ *212/371–9266* ✉ *469 Broome St., at Greene St., SoHo* ☎ *212/966–0605.*

William-Wayne & Co. Silver julep cups, Viennese playing cards, butler's trays: these whimsical decorative items are hard to resist. A low-key monkey theme puts smiling simians on dishes, candleholders, wall sconces, and tea towels. ✉ *40 University Pl., at E. 9th St., Greenwich Village* ☎ *212/533–4711* ✉ *846 Lexington Ave., at E. 64th St., Upper East Side* ☎ *212/737–8934* ✉ *850 Lexington Ave., at E. 64th St., Upper East Side* ☎ *212/288–9243.*

Jewelry, Watches & Silver

Most of the world's premier jewelers have retail outlets in New York, and the nation's wholesale diamond center is on West 47th Street between 5th and 6th avenues. At this writing, Boucheron was under construction, gearing to join its bijoux brethren on Fifth Avenue near 55th Street.

A La Vieille Russie. Stop here to behold bibelots by Fabergé and others, enameled or encrusted with jewels. ✉ *781 5th Ave., at E. 59th St., Midtown East* ☎ *212/752–1727.*

Asprey. Having split from Garrard, Asprey is spreading its net to cater to all kinds of luxury tastes, from leather goods to rare books to its famed jewelry. The house now has its own eponymous diamond cut, with A-shape facets. The store plans to expand in 2003. ✉ *725 5th Ave., at E. 56th St., Midtown East* ☎ *212/688–1811.*

Beads of Paradise. Enjoy a rich selection of African trade-bead necklaces, earrings, and rare artifacts. You can also create your own designs. ✉ *16 E. 17th St., between 5th Ave. and Broadway, Flatiron District* ☎ *212/620–0642.*

Bulgari. This Italian company is certainly not shy about its name, which encircles gems, watch faces, even lighters. There are beautiful, weighty rings, pieces mixing gold with stainless steel or porcelain, as well as the lighter Lucea line. ✉ *730 5th Ave., at W. 57th St., Midtown West*

☎ 212/315–9000 ✉ 783 Madison Ave., between E. 66th and E. 67th Sts., Upper East Side ☎ 212/717–2300.

Cartier. The 5th Avenue mansion location was obtained by Pierre Cartier by trading two strands of perfectly matched natural pearls to Mrs. Morton Plant. The jewelry is still incredibly persuasive, from established favorites like the interlocking rings and the riveting Love bracelet to the more recent, streamlined designs. ✉ *653 5th Ave., at E. 52nd St., Midtown East* ☎ *212/753–0111* ✉ *828 Madison Ave., at E. 69th St., Upper East Side* ☎ *212/472–6400.*

Chanel Fine Jewelry. Besides the showstopper pieces based on Chanel's own jewels, there are stars and comets sparkling with diamonds and gold worked into a quilted design. ✉ *733 Madison Ave., at E. 64th St., Upper East Side* ☎ *212/535–5828.*

David Webb. The gem-studded pieces sold here are often enameled and in animal forms. Styles and prices have a tendency to go over the top. ✉ *445 Park Ave., at E. 57th St., Midtown East* ☎ *212/421–3030.*

David Yurman. The signature motifs here—cables, quatrefoil shapes—add up to a classic, go-anywhere look, while the use of semiprecious stones keeps prices within reason. ✉ *729 Madison Ave., at E. 64th St., Upper East Side* ☎ *212/752–4255.*

Dinosaur Designs. Translucent and colorful, this antipodean work uses an untraditional medium: resin. Some look like semiprecious stone, such as onyx or jade; the rest delve into stronger colors like aqua or crimson. Cruise the stacks of chunky bangles and cuffs or rows of rings; prices start under $50. There's some striking tableware, too. ✉ *250 Mott St., between Prince and Spring Sts., NoLita* ☎ *212/680–3523.*

Femmegems. Finicky tastes can be as choosy as they like here. On one side dangle necklaces and bracelets designed by the staff, on the other hang strands of stones ready for customization. Pick out the beads you like (mostly semiprecious like quartz, carnelian, and jade), fish out a porcelain or carved-stone pendant, and have the perfect bauble assembled in short order. ✉ *280 Mulberry St., between Prince and Houston Sts., NoLita,* ☎ *212/625–1611.*

Fortunoff. Good prices on jewelry, flatware, and hollowware draw crowds to this large, multilevel store. ✉ *681 5th Ave., between E. 53rd and E. 54th Sts., Midtown East* ☎ *212/758–6660.*

Fragments. This SoHo spot glitters with pieces by nimble new jewelry designers, whose work is splashed across the pages of glossy fashion magazines. ✉ *116 Prince St., between Greene and Wooster Sts., SoHo* ☎ *212/334–9588.*

H. Stern. Sleek designs pose in an equally modern 5th Avenue setting; smooth cabochon-cut stones, most from South America, glow in pale wooden display cases. The designers make notable use of semiprecious stones such as citrine, tourmaline, and topaz. ✉ *645 5th Ave., between E. 51st and E. 52nd Sts., Midtown East* ☎ *212/688–0300* ✉ *301 Park Ave., between E. 49th and E. 50th Sts., in Waldorf-Astoria, Midtown East* ☎ *212/753–5595.*

Harry Winston. Oversize stones of impeccable quality sparkle in Harry Winston's inner sanctum—no wonder the jeweler was immortalized in the song "Diamonds Are a Girl's Best Friend." ✉ *718 5th Ave., at W. 56th St., Midtown West* ☎ *212/245–2000.*

James Robinson. This family-owned business sells handmade flatware, antique silver, fine estate jewelry, and 18th- and 19th-century china (mostly in sets, rather than individual pieces). ✉ *480 Park Ave., at E. 58th St., Midtown East* ☎ *212/752–6166.*

Jean's Silversmiths. Where to find a replacement for the butter knife that's missing from your great-aunt's set? Try this dusty, crowded shop. ✉ *16 W. 45th St., between 5th and 6th Aves., Midtown West* ☎ *212/575–0723.*

Me + Ro. Eastern styling has gained these designers a cult following. The Indian-inspired, hand-finished gold bangles and earrings covered with tiny dangling rubies or sapphires may look bohemian, but the prices target the well-to-do. ✉ *239 Elizabeth St., between Prince and E. Houston Sts., NoLita* ☎ *917/237–9215.*

Mikimoto. The Japanese originator of the cultured pearl, Mikimoto presents a glowing display of perfectly formed, high-luster pearls. Besides the creamy strands from their own pearl farms, there are dazzlingly colored South Sea pearls and some freshwater varieties. ✉ *730 5th Ave., between W. 56th and W. 57th Sts., Midtown West* ☎ *212/664–1800.*

Robert Lee Morris. Gold and silver take on simple, fluid shapes here, as waving cuff bracelets or dimpled disk earrings. Some pieces incorporate semiprecious stones like turquoise or citrine. ✉ *400 West Broadway, between Broome and Spring Sts., SoHo* ☎ *212/431–9405.*

Stuart Moore. Many designs here are minimalist or understated, but stunning: the twinkle of a small diamond offset by gold or brushed platinum. Pieces tend to be modest in scale. ✉ *128 Prince St., at Wooster St., SoHo* ☎ *212/941–1023.*

Fodor'sChoice ★ **Tiffany & Co.** The display windows can be elegant, funny, or just plain breathtaking. Alongside the $80,000 platinum-and-diamond bracelets, a lot here is affordable on a whim—and everything comes wrapped in that unmistakable Tiffany blue. ✉ *727 5th Ave., at E. 57th St., Midtown East* ☎ *212/755–8000.*

Tourneau. Each of these stores stocks a wide range of watches, but the three-level 57th Street TimeMachine, a high-tech merchandising extravaganza, steals the scene. A museum downstairs has timepiece exhibits, both temporary and permanent. The shops carry more than 70 brands, from status symbols such as Patek Philippe, Cartier, and Rolex, to more casual styles by Swatch, Seiko, and Swiss Army. ✉ *500 Madison Ave., between E. 52nd and E. 53rd Sts., Midtown East* ☎ *212/758–6098* ✉ *12 E. 57th St., between 5th and Madison Aves., Midtown East* ☎ *212/758–7300* ✉ *200 W. 34th St., at 7th Ave., Midtown West* ☎ *212/563–6880.*

Van Cleef & Arpels. The jewelry here (lots of classically set diamonds) is sheer perfection. ✉ *744 5th Ave., at W. 57th St., Midtown West* ☎ *212/644–9500.*

Linens

Madison Avenue has an inviting handful of high-end linen shops; move downtown for less expensive—and less conventional—lines. Grand Street on the Lower East Side has a spate of dry-goods merchants.

D. Porthault. Porthault's showcase beds are virtual cocoons of pale, crisp linens and pillows. It's no wonder the money-is-no-object crowd covets these sheets. ✉ *18 E. 69th St., between 5th and Madison Aves., Upper East Side* ☎ *212/688–1660.*

Frette. Thread counts rise well above 250 here; there are also ultrafine table linens, alpaca throws, and such. Loungewear lurks in back, including extremely decadent mink-lined mules. ✉ *799 Madison Ave., between E. 67th and E. 68th Sts., Upper East Side* ☎ *212/988–5221.*

Pratesi. To complement its pristine bedding, Pratesi has layettes, fragrances, and home gift lines, including damask table linens so fine they could almost stand in for the bedding. ✉ *829 Madison Ave., at E. 69th St., Upper East Side* ☎ *212/288–2315.*

Lingerie

Agent Provocateur. The bustiest mannequins in Manhattan vamp in the front window of this British underpinnings phenom. Showpieces include boned corsets, lace sets with contrast-color trim, and bottoms tied with satin ribbons. ✉ *133 Mercer St., between Prince and Spring Sts., SoHo* ☎ *212/965–0229.*

Eres. The sheer net underthings, from demi-cups to garters, prove that simple can be effective. Eres also turns out a line of refined bathing suits. ✉ *621 Madison Ave., between E. 58th and E. 59th Sts., Midtown East* ☎ *212/223–3550* ✉ *98 Wooster St., between Prince and Spring Sts., SoHo* ☎ *212/431–7300.*

Joovay. This tiny store has tempting underwear from floor to ceiling: bras by Rigby & Peller, La Mystère, and Sybaris, plus chemises and bathrobes. ✉ *436 West Broadway, between Prince and Spring Sts., SoHo* ☎ *212/431–6386.*

La Perla. From the Leavers lace, soutache, and embroidery to unadorned tulle, these underthings are so perfect they've inspired a trilogy of books. Look for the sets of sheer underwear embroidered with the days of the week in Italian—a grown-up alternative to Bloomie's classic bloomers. ✉ *777 Madison Ave., between E. 66th and E. 67th Sts., Upper East Side* ☎ *212/570–0050* ✉ *93 Greene St., between Prince and Spring Sts., SoHo* ☎ *212/219–0999.*

La Petite Coquette. Among the signed photos on the walls is one of ultimate authority—from Frederique, longtime Victoria's Secret model. The store's own line of silk slips, camisoles, and other underpinnings comes in a rainbow of colors, and as befits the name, they have special petite cuts. ✉ *51 University Pl., between E. 9th and E. 10th Sts., Greenwich Village* ☎ *212/473–2478.*

Le Corset. This lovely boutique naturally stocks its namesake, plus lacy underwear, nightgowns, and even powder-pink vintage girdles. ✉ *80 Thompson St., between Spring and Broome Sts., SoHo* ☎ *212/334–4936.*

Mixona. The minx-at-heart will have a field day among lace-encrusted Aubade, the gauzy bras of Capuchine Puerari and Passion Bait, and color-blocked silk nightgowns by Viamode. There's also a small selection of nightwear that will keep you warm in the winter. ✉ *262 Mott St., between Prince and E. Houston Sts., NoLita* ☎ *646/613–0100.*

Luggage, Leather Goods & Handbags

Altman Luggage. Great bargains (a Samsonite Pullman for a little more than $100) are the thing at this discount store, which also stocks tough Timberland and Jansport backpacks. ✉ *135 Orchard St., between Delancey and Rivington Sts., Lower East Side* ☎ *212/254–7275.*

Anya Hindmarch. While some of these divine British handbags in calf, satin, or velvet are ready for a very proper occasion, others cut loose with funny silk-screened photos or sequinned designs of candy or painkillers. ✉ *29 E. 60th St., between Madison and Park Aves., Upper East Side* ☎ *212/750–3974* ✉ *115 Greene St., between Prince and Spring Sts., SoHo* ☎ *212/343–8147.*

Blue Bag. The purses, satchels, and overnight bags here fill the bill by being diverse, novel, and not crushingly expensive. ✉ *266 Elizabeth St., between E. Houston and Prince Sts., NoLita* ☎ *212/966–8566.*

Bottega Veneta. The signature crosshatch weave graces leather handbags, slouchy satchels, and shoes; the especially satisfying brown shades extend from fawn to deep chocolate. ✉ *635 Madison Ave., between E. 59th and E. 60th Sts., Upper East Side* ☎ *212/371–5511.*

Coach. Coach's classic glove-tanned leather goes into handbags, briefcases, wallets, shoes, and dozens of other accessories. The identifying touches, like the turn lock, appear on fresher styles, such as mules and messenger bags, as well as the trusty older designs. ✉ *2321 Broadway, at W. 84th St., Upper West Side* ☎ *212/799–1624* ✉ *595 Madison Ave., at E. 57th St., Midtown East* ☎ *212/754–0041* ✉ *620 5th Ave., at Rockefeller Center, Midtown West* ☎ *212/245–4148* ✉ *342 Madison Ave., at E. 44th St., Midtown East* ☎ *212/599–4777* ✉ *193 Front St., at Fulton St., Lower Manhattan* ☎ *212/425–4350* ✉ *143 Prince St., at West Broadway, SoHo* ☎ *212/473–6925* ✉ *35 E. 85th St., at Madison Ave., Upper East Side* ☎ *212/879–9391.*

Crouch & Fitzgerald. Since 1839 this store has offered an unimpeachable selection of hard- and soft-sided luggage, as well as a huge number of attaché cases. ✉ *400 Madison Ave., at E. 48th St., Midtown East* ☎ *212/755–5888.*

Fendi. Come here for the most expensive baguettes and croissants in town—but not if you're looking for baked goods. Fendi's popular styles are named for the French breads they resemble. Each one is beaded, embroidered, and fantastically embellished, resulting in prices that skyrocket over $1,000. Fancy leathers, furs, and other accessories are available, too. ✉ *720 5th Ave., at W. 56th St., Midtown West* ☎ *212/767–0100.*

Fine & Klein. Among the Orchard Street veterans, this is a reliable stop for handbags. Some purses bear a marked resemblance to those of well-known designers. ✉ *119 Orchard St., between Rivington and Delancey Sts., Lower East Side* ☎ *212/674–6720.*

Flight 001. This is one-stop shopping for the contemporary sojourner. Travel in style and comfort with any of the luggage pieces, foldable maps, eye masks, and pampering kits. ✉ *96 Greenwich Ave., between W. 12th and Jane Sts., Greenwich Village* ☎ *212/691–1001.*

Furla. Shoulder bags, oblong clutches, and roomy totes are fashioned from calfskin either smooth, slightly textured, or imprinted with a reptilian pattern. ✉ *430 West Broadway, between Prince and Spring Sts., SoHo* ☎ *212/343–0048* ✉ *727 Madison Ave., between E. 63rd and E. 64th Sts., Upper East Side* ☎ *212/755–8986.*

Hiponica. Some of these breezy, colorful handbags come trimmed with grosgrain ribbon or with a coin-purse-like snapping closure. Others open like mini garment bags to disclose a wealth of inner pockets. ✉ *238 Mott St., between Prince and Spring Sts., NoLita* ☎ *212/966–4388.*

Kate Spade. These eminently desirable (and oft-copied) handbags come in various fabrics, from velvet to tweed, as well as inviting leathers. Partner up with matching mules, agendas, or a plush scarf. Around the corner at **Jack Spade** (✉ 56 Greene St., between Broome and Spring Sts., SoHo ☎ 212/625–1820), Kate's husband peddles his own line of bags, dopp kits, and other men's accessories in a nostalgic setting. The original storefront on Thompson Street now carries travel accessories. ✉ *454 Broome St., between Mercer and Greene Sts., SoHo* ☎ *212/274–1991* ✉ *59 Thompson St., between Spring and Broome Sts., SoHo* ☎ *212/965–8654.*

Lederer Leather Goods. The excellent selection here includes exotic skins such as ostrich, alligator, and lizard. ✉ *457 Madison Ave., at E. 51st St., Midtown East* ☎ *212/355–5515.*

LeSportsac. The ripstop parachute nylon's still in place, but nowadays the solid-color bags share space with gussied-up versions in plaid, floral, or leopard prints. In addition to the purses and totes, there are custom travel bags that won't break the bank. ✉ *176 Spring St., at West Broadway, SoHo* ☎ *212/625–2626* ✉ *1065 Madison Ave., between E. 80th and E. 81st Sts., Upper East Side* ☎ *212/988–6200.*

Longchamp. Its nylon bags have become an Upper East Side staple and can be spotted everywhere in the Hamptons. The store carries the entire line of classy luggage, wallets, and organizers in a rainbow of colors. ✉ *713 Madison Ave., between E. 63rd and E. 64th Sts., Upper East Side* ☎ *212/223–1500.*

★ **Louis Vuitton.** Vuitton's famous monogrammed pieces range from coin purses to extravagant steamer trunks. Joining the initials are the Damier check pattern and colorful striated leathers, not to mention devastatingly chic clothes and shoes designed by Marc Jacobs. A massive flagship is under construction at 5th Avenue and 5th Street, due to open in fall 2003. ✉ *703 5th Ave., between 54th and 55th Sts., Midtown East* ☎ *212/758–8877* ✉ *116 Greene St., between Prince and Spring Sts., SoHo* ☎ *212/274–9090.*

Lulu Guinness. Carrying off whimsical and retro touches with panache, from floral trim to poodle appliqués, these purses easily coax a smile. ✉ *394 Bleecker St., between W. 11th and Perry Sts., Greenwich Village* ☎ *212/367–2120.*

Manhattan Portage. You know you want one, so visit the source of the messenger-bag fad. Although they're a-dime-a-dozen around these parts, they cost real money—$20–$100—and will impress the folks back home. ✉ *333 E. 9th St., between 1st and 2nd Aves., East Village* ☎ *212/995–5490.*

Rugby North America. This Canadian-based store specializes in calfskin postman's bags, accessories, and unfussy men's and women's jackets and pants, often with a slightly crinkled finish. ✉ *115 Mercer St., between Prince and Spring Sts., SoHo* ☎ *212/431–3069.*

Sigerson Morrison. Poised to seduce your shoulder as well as your feet, Sigerson Morrison devises bags in calfskin, pigskin, suede, and the occasional fabric, often equipped with zippered exterior pockets for cell phones and other things you need close at hand. ✉ *242 Mott St., between Prince and E. Houston Sts., NoLita* ☎ *212/941–5404.*

T. Anthony. The trademark coated-canvas luggage with leather trim can be classic (black or beige) or eye-catching (red or purply blue). Those who like to carry it all with them can outfit themselves with hatboxes and shirt cases, plus totes, trunks, and hard- and soft-sided suitcases. ✉ *445 Park Ave., at E. 56th St., Midtown East* ☎ *212/750–9797.*

Tardini. For decades this Italian accessories maker has been making handbags from exotic materials such as alligator, lizard, and snakeskin. They've added an equally luxurious line of men's and women's footwear to complement the bags. ✉ *142 Wooster St., between W. Houston and Prince Sts., SoHo* ☎ *212/253–7692.*

Museum Stores

American Craft Museum. The tie-ins to ongoing exhibits can yield beautiful handmade glassware, unusual jewelry, or enticing textiles. ✉ *40 W. 53rd St., between 5th and 6th Aves., Midtown West* ☎ *212/956–3535.*

Metropolitan Museum of Art Shop. Of the three locations, the store in the museum has a phenomenal book selection, as well as posters, art videos, and computer programs. Reproductions of jewelry, statuettes, and other *objets* fill the gleaming cases in every branch. ✉ *5th Ave. at E. 82nd St., Upper East Side* ☎ *212/879–5500* ✉ *113 Prince St., between Greene and Wooster Sts., SoHo* ☎ *212/614–3000* ✉ *15 W. 49th St., between 5th and 6th Aves., Rockefeller Center, Midtown West* ☎ *212/332–1360.*

Museum of Modern Art Design Store. Although the museum's collection will be in Queens until late 2004 or early 2005, all of its shops will remain at their current locations. The Design Store is a hoard of good, eye-catching design: Frank Lloyd Wright furniture reproductions, vases designed by Alvar Aalto, and lots of clever trinkets. The **bookstore** (✉ 11 W. 53rd Sts., between 5th and 6th Aves., Midtown West ☎ 212/708–9700) adjacent to the museum has posters (from Mondrian to van Gogh's *Starry Night*) and a wide-ranging selection of books. The downtown branch combines most of the virtues of the two, although its book selection is smaller. ✉ *44 W. 53rd St., between 5th and 6th Aves., Midtown West* ☎ *212/767–1050* ✉ *81 Spring St., between Broadway and Crosby St., SoHo* ☎ *646/613–1367.*

Museum of the City of New York. Satisfy your curiosity about New York City's past, present, or future with this terrific selection of books, cards, toys, and photography posters. If you've something classic in mind, look for the Tin Pan Alley tunes and stickball sets. ✉ *1220 5th Ave., at E. 103rd St., Upper East Side* ☎ *212/534–1672.*

Paper, Greeting Cards & Stationery

Dempsey & Carroll. Supplying New York's high society for a century, this firm is always correct but seldom straitlaced. ✉ *110 E. 57th St., between Park and Lexington Aves., Midtown East* ☎ *212/486–7526* ✉ *19 E. 80th St., at Madison Ave., Upper East Side* ☎ *212/249–8411.*

Fodor's Choice ★ **Kate's Paperie.** Heaven for avid correspondents and gift-givers, Kate's rustles with fabulous wrapping papers, ribbons, blank books, writing implements of all kinds, and more. At this writing, a new branch on West 57th Street was due to open in summer 2003. ✉ *561 Broadway, between Prince and Spring Sts., SoHo* ☎ *212/941–9816* ✉ *8 W. 13th St., between 5th and 6th Aves., Greenwich Village* ☎ *212/633–0570* ✉ *1282 3rd Ave., between E. 73rd and E. 74th Sts., Upper East Side* ☎ *212/396–3670.*

Papivore. Yield to the array of fetching colors, either of the Marie Papier notebooks and albums or of the cotton-based stationary paper sold in sets or individually. ✉ *233 Elizabeth St., between Prince and Spring Sts., NoLita* ☎ *212/334–4330.*

Smythson of Bond Street. Keep notes on your purchases, deepest thoughts, or conquests in softbound leather notebooks with appropriate gilded titles like "Little Black Book" or "Snogs." They also carry blue blood–worthy stationery, diaries, and leather travel accessories. ✉ *4 W. 57th St., between 5th and 6th Aves., Midtown West* ☎ *212/265–4573.*

Untitled. One wall groans with art books, the other flutters with all kinds of greeting cards. There's also a long row of motley postcards alphabetized by topic, such as Degas pastels and fruit-crate labels. ✉ *159 Prince St., between Thompson St. and West Broadway, SoHo* ☎ *212/982–2088.*

Performing Arts Memorabilia

Drama Book Shop. The comprehensive stock here includes scripts, scores, and librettos. ✉ *250 W. 40th St., between 7th and 8th Aves., Midtown West* ☎ *212/944–0595.*

Motion Picture Arts Gallery. Vintage posters enchant collectors here. ✉ *133 E. 58th St., between Park and Lexington Aves., 10th floor, Upper East Side* ☎ *212/223–1009.*

Movie Star News. One look at the walls here and it's hard to doubt their claim that they have the world's largest variety of movie photos and posters. All around are signed pictures of stars such as Billy Crystal, Lauren Bacall, Anjelica Houston, and even Elvira, TV's Mistress of the Dark. Posters in the outer garage area run $10–$25. ✉ *134 W. 18th St., between 6th and 7th Aves., Chelsea* ☎ *212/620–8160.*

One Shubert Alley. Souvenir posters, tees, and other marketing knick-knacks memorializing past and present Broadway hits reign at this theater district shop. ✉ *311 W. 43rd St., at 8th Ave., Midtown West* ☎ *212/944–4133.*

Richard Stoddard Performing Arts Books. This veteran dealer, who offers out-of-print books, also has the largest stock of old Broadway *Playbills* in the world. It's closed Wednesday and Sunday. ✉ *41 Union Sq. W, Room 937, at W. 17th St., Flatiron District* ☎ *212/645–9576.*

Triton Gallery. Theatrical posters large and small can be found here for hits and flops. ✉ *323 W. 45th St., between 8th and 9th Aves., Midtown West* ☎ *212/765–2472.*

8

Shoes

For dressy, expensive footwear, Madison Avenue is always a good bet, but West 8th Street between 5th and 6th avenues is what most New Yorkers mean when they refer to Shoe Street; it's crammed with small shoe-storefronts that hawk funky styles, from steel-toe boots to outrageous platforms.

Men's & Women's Shoes

Arche. These molded natural latex soles make pounding the pavement decidedly less painful, and besides the usual brown and black, the soft leather or nubuck uppers come in colors like burgundy or forest green. ✉ *995 Madison Ave., at E. 77th St., Upper East Side* ☎ *212/439–0700* ✉ *123 Wooster St., between Prince and Spring Sts., SoHo* ☎ *646/613–8700.*

Bally. A few curveballs, like olive green or slate blue wing tips, liven up the mostly conservative selection. Carry-ons and clothing, such as deerskin or lamb jackets, join the shoe leather. ✉ *628 Madison Ave., at E. 59th St., Midtown East* ☎ *212/751–9082.*

Camper. Having established itself as the Euro-fave walking shoe, Camper hied itself to Manhattan; luckily, the nubby rubber soles work well on SoHo's rougher cobblestones. Whether you choose a slide-on or laced-to-the-toe style, all have comfortably round toes and a springy feel. ✉ *125 Prince St., at Wooster St., SoHo* ☎ *212/358–1841.*

Cole-Haan. With endless variations on the basic elements of its woven, moccasin, and loafer styles in brown and black, Cole-Haan provides reliably up-to-date styles for a conservative crowd. ✉ *620 5th Ave., at Rockefeller Center, Midtown West* ☎ *212/765–9747* ✉ *667 Madison Ave., at E. 61st St., Upper East Side* ☎ *212/421–8440.*

J. M. Weston. Specially treated calfskin for the soles and carefully hand-crafted construction have made these a French favorite; they could also double the price of your outfit. High heels, a more recent addition to the selection, started gradually with stacked-heel pumps. ✉ *812 Madison Ave., at E. 68th St., Upper East Side* ☎ *212/535–2100.*

Jimmy Choo. Pointy toes, low vamps, narrow heels, delicate sling backs—these British-made shoes are undeniably hot to trot, and sometimes more comfortable than they look. Although the men's selection is limited (and more sedate), the choices are subtly snazzy. ✉ *645 5th Ave., at E. 51st St., Midtown East* ☎ *212/593–0800.*

John Fluevog Shoes. The inventor of the Angelic sole (protects against water, acid . . . " and Satan"), Fluevog designs chunky, funky shoes and boots. ✉ *250 Mulberry St., at Prince St., NoLita* ☎ *212/431–4484.*

Otto Tootsi Plohound. Downtown New Yorkers swear by this large selection of supercool shoes. Many, including the store's own line, are Italian-made, and styles jump from vampy pumps to men's wing tips to Prada Sport boots. ✉ *413 West Broadway, between Prince and Spring Sts., SoHo* ☎ *212/925–8931* ✉ *273 Lafayette St., between Prince and E. Houston Sts., East Village* ☎ *212/431–7299* ✉ *137 5th Ave., between*

E. 20th and 21st Sts., Flatiron District ☎ *212/460–8650* ✉ *38 E. 57th St., between Park and Madison Aves., Midtown East* ☎ *212/231–3199.*

Rockport. After a day of pounding the sidewalk, a stop here may be just what you need. The comfort-first shoes run from athletic to dressy. ✉ *160 Columbus Ave., between W. 67th and W. 68th Sts., Upper West Side* ☎ *212/579–1301* ✉ *465 West Broadway, between W. Houston and Prince Sts., SoHo* ☎ *212/529–0209.*

Salvatore Ferragamo. Elegance typifies these designs, from black-tie patent to weekender ankle boots. The company reworks some of their women's styles from previous decades, like the girlish Audrey (as in Hepburn) flat, available in the original black or seasonal takes like bone or leopard. In midtown the lines get separate boutiques for men's and women's. A new flagship, expanding the 5th Avenue location, opened in spring 2003. ✉ *124 Spring St., at Greene St., SoHo* ☎ *212/226–4330* ✉ *661 5th Ave., between E. 52nd and E. 53rd Sts., Midtown East* ☎ *212/759–3822.*

Stuart Weitzman. The broad range of styles, from wing tips to strappy sandals, is enhanced by an even wider range of sizes and widths. ✉ *625 Madison Ave., between E. 58th and E. 59th Sts., Midtown East* ☎ *212/750–2555.*

Men's Shoes

Billy Martin's. Quality hand-tooled and custom-made boots for the Urban Cowboy are carried here. To complete the look, you'll also find everything from suede shirts to turquoise-and-silver belts. ✉ *220 E. 60th St., between 2nd and 3rd Aves., Upper East Side* ☎ *212/861–3100.*

John Lobb. These British shoes often use waxed leather, the better to contend with London levels of damp. Ankle boots with padded collars or zips join the traditional oxfords and derbys; some shoes have elegantly tapered toes. ✉ *680 Madison Ave., between E. 62nd and E. 61st Sts., Upper East Side* ☎ *212/888–9797.*

Santoni. Those who equate Italian with slightly flashy haven't seen these discreet, meticulously finished, handmade shoes. ✉ *864 Madison Ave., between E. 70th and E. 71st Sts., Upper East Side* ☎ *212/794–3820.*

Women's Shoes

Christian Louboutin. Bright-red soles are the signature of Louboutin's delicately sexy couture slippers and stilettos. Look for brocade, mink trim, and tassels. ✉ *941 Madison Ave., between E. 74th and E. 75th Sts., Upper East Side* ☎ *212/396–1884.*

Chuckies. The name may be aw-shucks, but the shoes certainly aren't. Pumps by Dolce & Gabbana, ankle-straps by Richard Tyler, and Jimmy Choo sky-high heels are joined by Chuckies' own cool, slightly lower-priced line. ✉ *1073 3rd Ave., between E. 63rd and E. 64th Sts., Upper East Side* ☎ *212/593–9898* ✉ *399 West Broadway, between Spring and Broome Sts., SoHo* ☎ *212/343–1717.*

Edmundo Castillo. There's a limited opportunity for window-shopping here, as only one design at a time gets the front-window spotlight. Inside you'll find rows of pointy toes, even on the flats, plus details like asymmetrical vamps or bow-tied straps. ✉ *219 Mott St., between Prince and Spring Sts., NoLita* ☎ *212/431–5320.*

Manolo Blahnik. These are, notoriously, some of the most expensive shoes money can buy. They're also devastatingly sexy, with pointed toes, low-cut vamps, and spindly heels. Mercifully, the summer stock includes plenty of flat (but still exquisite) sandals. Pray for a sale. ✉ *31 W. 54th St., between 5th and 6th Aves., Midtown West* ☎ *212/582–3007.*

Michel Perry. The intense pink interior cheers you along into teeteringly high strappy sling backs, lace-up sandals, and ankle boots. ✉ *320 Park Ave., at E. 51st St., Midtown East* ☎ *212/688–4968.*

Peter Fox. Combining old-fashioned lines, such as Louis heels, and such modern touches as thin platforms, these shoes defy categorization. There's also an extensive bridal section. ✉ *105 Thompson St., between Prince and Spring Sts., SoHo* ☎ *212/431–7426.*

Robert Clergerie. High-priced and highly polished, these shoes are not without their sense of fun. Pick up a pump and you may find an oval or triangular heel. ✉ *681 Madison Ave., between E. 61st and E. 62nd Sts., Upper East Side* ☎ *212/207–8600.*

8

Sergio Rossi. Here you can test-drive a pair of stilettos on plush carpet; the slender heels and sharp toes make for come-hither feet. Some styles get the full black-tie treatment with velvet, satin, or beading. Prices start around $300 and rapidly climb upward. ✉ *772 Madison Ave., at E. 66th St., Upper East Side* ☎ *212/327–4288.*

Sigerson Morrison. The details—just-right T-straps, small buckles, interesting two-tones—make these shoes irresistible. Prices hover around $300. ✉ *28 Prince St., between Mott and Elizabeth Sts., NoLita* ☎ *212/219–3893.*

Tod's. Diego Della Valle's coveted driving moccasins, casual loafers, and boots in colorful leather, suede, and ponyskin are right at home on Madison Avenue. ✉ *650 Madison Ave., near E. 60th St., Upper East Side* ☎ *212/644–5945.*

Unisa. Try on a gentle riff on a current trend, from satin slides to driving mocs; most pairs are under $100, sometimes well under. ✉ *701 Madison Ave., between E. 62nd and E. 63rd Sts., Upper East Side* ☎ *212/753–7474.*

Souvenirs of New York City

Major tourist attractions keep their gift shops well stocked, and dozens of souvenir shops dot the Times Square area. If you're looking for grungier souvenirs of downtown (T-shirts with salty messages, tattoos), troll St. Marks Place between 2nd and 3rd avenues in the East Village.

City Store. Discover all kinds of books and pamphlets that explain New York City's government and its various departments (building, sanitation, etc.), as well as pocket maps, Big Apple lapel pins, even official taxi medallions. It's closed weekends. ✉ *1 Centre St., at Chambers St., Lower Manhattan* ☎ *212/669–8246.*

New York City Transit Museum Gift Shop. In the symbolic heart of NYC's transit system, all the store's merchandise is somehow linked to the MTA, from "straphanger" ties to skateboards decorated with subway-line logos. A branch at the Transit Museum in Brooklyn Heights opened in the spring of 2003. ✉ *Grand Central Terminal, at Vanderbilt Pl. and E. 42nd St., Midtown East* ☎ *212/878–0106.*

New York Firefighter's Friend. NYFD logo sweats and tees join firefighter-theme toys and books, plus a few vintage items. The shop, though not officially affiliated with the fire department, donates a portion of its proceeds to widows' and children's funds for firefighters lost in the World Trade Center attacks. ✉ *263 Lafayette St., between Prince and Spring Sts., SoHo* ☎ *212/226–3142.*

The Pop Shop. Images from the late Keith Haring's unmistakable pop art cover a wealth of paraphernalia, from backpacks and umbrellas to key chains. ✉ *292 Lafayette St., between Houston and Prince Sts., SoHo* ☎ *212/219–2784.*

Spas

Avon Spa and Salon. Pay a call to the beauty giant's spa in Trump Tower; it offers the usual services, but is best known for its world-famous eyebrow guru Eliza Ptrescu. She heads her own division, **Eliza's Eyes,** staffed with several aestheticians. She's booked six months in advance and charges $100 for a first-time pluck, so plan ahead and save your pennies. ✉ *725 5th Ave., between E. 56th and E. 57th Sts., Midtown East* ☎ *212/755–2866.*

Away Spa. This Asian-influenced oasis provides a full menu of New Age delights. Go for a stone massage, or choose something more traditional like a full-body mud mask. ✉ *W Hotel, 541 Lexington Ave., near E. 49th St., Midtown East* ☎ *212/407–2970.*

Bliss Spa. Between its cheerful catalogs and its sought-after spa services, Bliss has sewn up a devoted customer base. Nibble on a brownie while awaiting your oxygen facial, detoxifying herbal hot wrap, or jet-lag-busting massage. ✉ *568 Broadway, at Prince St., 2nd floor, SoHo* ☎ *212/219–8970* ✉ *Bliss57, 19 E. 57th St., between 5th and Madison Aves., 3rd floor, Midtown East* ☎ *212/219–8970.*

Erbe. A little haven just off SoHo's beaten path, this is a good spot for waxing and facials. Breathe in the herbal scents of the house line of Italian-made lotions. ✉ *196 Prince St., between Sullivan and MacDougal Sts., SoHo* ☎ *212/966–1445.*

The Greenhouse Day Spa. The clean and serene space has a full range of spa and dermatological sessions, including Ayurvedic treatments. Concierge services are available; there's also a café and a shop filled with hard-to-find cosmetics and pampering brands. ✉ *127 E. 57th St., between Lexington and Park Aves., Midtown East* ☎ *212/644–4449.*

La Prairie The Art of Beauty. Hit the Ritz for a caviar facial or a treatment geared for sensitive skin. You can choose your own accompanying music, so you won't have to put up with the usual New Age stuff. ✉ *The Ritz-Carlton, 50 Central Park S, between 5th and 6th Aves., Midtown West* ☎ *212/521–6135.*

Oasis Day Spa. Head to either location for a very thorough massage; if your days are packed, you'll appreciate their late hours (until 10 on weekdays, 9 on weekends). The Park Avenue branch offers a larger selection of beauty services. ✉ *108 E. 16th St., between Union Sq. E and Irving Pl., Gramercy* ☎ *212/254–7722* ✉ *1 Park Ave., between E. 32nd and E. 33rd Sts., Murray Hill,* ☎ *212/254–7722.*

Paul Labreque Salon. Located inside the Reebok Sports Club near Lincoln Center, this luxurious salon is known for its top-notch facialist and fantastic and inventive massages, like the deep-stretching Thai massage. ✉ *160 Columbus Ave., at W. 67th St., Upper West Side* ☎ *212/595–0099.*

Rescue. The success of the manicure spot spawned a pair of "beauty lounges;" in all three, small treatment rooms invite gossip over a paraffin treatment. The Gansevoort branch has manicures and pedicures with La Mer products in its arsenal. ✉ *Rescue Nail Spa, 21 Cleveland Pl., between Spring and Kenmare Sts., Lower East Side* ☎ *212/431–3805* ✉ *Rescue Beauty Lounge, 8 Centre Market Pl., between Broome and Grand Sts., SoHo* ☎ *212/431–0449* ✉ *34 Gansevoort St., between Hudson and Greenwich Sts., 2nd floor, Meatpacking District* ☎ *212/206–6409.*

SoHo Sanctuary. It's women-only at this spa that somehow makes you feel like you're in Berkeley, California. Housed in a loft, it offers aromatherapy facials, massages, and a eucalyptus steam bath. There's a full yoga schedule. ✉ *119 Mercer St., between Prince and Spring Sts., SoHo* ☎ *212/334–5550.*

Sporting Goods

The NBA Store. Push through the bronze-armed door to hit the rows of pro basketball–theme merchandise. The ground floor has stacks of "lifestyle" items; wind down the ramp to score team jerseys, tear-away pants, and even baby clothes. Players grin in the digital-photo station, but they also make live appearances on the store's half-court. ✉ *666 5th Ave., at W. 52nd St., Midtown West* ☎ *212/515–6221.*

NikeTown. A fusion of fashion and sports arena, Nike's "motivational retail environment" is its largest sports-gear emporium. Inspirational quotes in the floor, computer-driven foot sizers, and a heart-pumping movie shown on an enormous screen in the entry atrium make it hard to leave without something in the latest wick-away fabric or footwear design. ✉ *6 E. 57th St., between 5th and Madison Aves., Midtown East* ☎ *212/891–6453.*

Paragon Sporting Goods. Tennis rackets, snowshoes, kayaks, swim goggles, hockey sticks, croquet mallets: Paragon stocks virtually everything any athlete needs, no matter what the sport. It keeps up with the trends (heart-rate monitors) and doesn't neglect the old-fashioned (Woolrich shirts). ✉ *867 Broadway, at E. 18th St., Flatiron District* ☎ *212/255–8036.*

Toys & Games

Most of these stores are geared to children, but a few shops that cater to grown-up toy-lovers are mixed in. During February's Toy Week, when out-of-town buyers come to place orders for the next Christmas season, the windows of the Toy Center at 23rd Street and 5th Avenue display the latest thing.

Big City Kite Co. Sport kites, traction kites, and single-line kites are the specialty here. The salespeople can talk winglets and wind windows or suggest a kite that can withstand crashing. ✉ *1210 Lexington Ave., at E. 82nd St., Upper East Side* ☎ *212/472–2623.*

Classic Toys. Collectors and children scrutinize the rows of miniature soldiers, toy cars, and other figures. It's a prime source for toy soldiers from Britain's Ltd., the United Kingdom's top manufacturer. ✉ *218 Sullivan St., between Bleecker and W. 3rd Sts., Greenwich Village* ☎ *212/674–4434.*

Compleat Strategist. This store puts on a great spread—from board games and classic soldier sets to fantasy games. ✉ *11 E. 33rd St., between 5th and Madison Aves., Murray Hill* ☎ *212/685–3880.*

Dinosaur Hill. These toys leave the run-of-the-mill far behind, with mini bongo drums, craft kits, and a throng of marionettes and hand puppets, from mermaids to farmers to demons. ✉ *306 E. 9th St., between 2nd and 1st Aves., East Village* ☎ *212/473–5850.*

Disney Store. All branches carry merchandise relating to Disney films and characters—pajamas, toys, figurines, you name it. The 5th Avenue store has the largest collection of Disney animation art in the country. ✉ *711 5th Ave., between E. 55th and E. 56th Sts., Midtown East* ☎ *212/702–0702* ✉ *218 W. 42nd St., at 7th Ave., Midtown West* ☎ *212/302–0595* ✉ *147 Columbus Ave., at W. 66th St., Upper West Side* ☎ *212/362–2386.*

Fodor's Choice ★ **Enchanted Forest.** Stuffed animals peer out from almost every corner of this fantastic shop. It's packed with all manner of curiosity-provoking gadgets; instead of video games, you'll find things like pinhole-camera kits, puppets, and vintage tin toys. ✉ *85 Mercer St., between Spring and Broome Sts., SoHo* ☎ *212/925–6677.*

★ **F.A.O. Schwarz.** Beyond the large mechanical clock at this wonderland are two floors of stuffed animals, dolls (including an inordinate number of Barbies), things with which to build, computer games, and much, much, much more. ✉ *767 5th Ave., at E. 58th St., Midtown East* ☎ *212/644–9400.*

Game Show. From Scrabble and Magic 8 Balls to backgammon and mah-jongg, this game- and puzzle-lover's paradise carries everything to challenge your IQ and tickle your funny bone. Intricate jigsaw puzzles are a specialty. ✉ *474 6th Ave., between 11th and 12th Sts, Greenwich Village* ☎ *212/633–6328* ✉ *1240 Lexington Ave., between E. 83rd and E. 84th Sts., Upper East Side* ☎ *212/472–8011.*

Geppetto's Toy Box. Many toys here are handmade. They carry everything from extravagant costumed dolls to tried-and-true rubber duckies. ✉ *10 Christopher St., at Greenwich Ave., Greenwich Village* ☎ *212/620–7511.*

Kidding Around. This unpretentious shop emphasizes old-fashioned wooden toys, fun gadgets, craft and science kits, and a small selection of infant clothes. ✉ *60 W. 15th St., between 5th and 6th Aves., Flatiron District* ☎ *212/645–6337.*

Tannen Magic Co. This magicians' supply house stocks sword chests, dove-a-matics, magic wands, and crystal balls, not to mention the all-important top hats with rabbits. ✉ *24 W. 25th St., between Broadway and 6th Ave., Chelsea* ☎ *212/929–4500.*

Toys R' Us. The Times Square branch of this megastore is so big that a three-story Ferris wheel revolves inside. With all the movie tie-in merchandise, video games, old favorites like pogo sticks, stuffed animals, and what seems to be the entire Mattel oeuvre, these stores have a lock on sheer volume. ✉ *1514 Broadway, at W. 44th St., Midtown West* ☎ *800/869–7787* ✉ *2432 Union Sq. E, at E. 15th St., Gramercy* ☎ *212/674–8697.*

West Side Kids. Legos and rubber animal figures share shelf space with arts-and-crafts sets. ✉ *498 Amsterdam Ave., at W. 84th St., Upper West Side* ☎ *212/496–7282.*

Wine

Acker Merrall & Condit. Known for its selection of red burgundies, this store has knowledgeable, helpful personnel. ✉ *160 W. 72nd St., between Amsterdam and Columbus Aves., Upper West Side* ☎ *212/787–1700.*

Astor Wines & Spirits. Plain and fluorescent-lighted it may be, but this is a key spot for everything from well-priced champagne to Poire William to Riesling. ✉ *12 Astor Pl., at Lafayette St., East Village* ☎ *212/674–7500.*

Best Cellars. In a novel move, the stock here is organized by the wine's characteristics (sweet, fruity) rather than region—and not only that, the prices are amazingly low, running between $8.50 and $14 a bottle. ✉ *1291 Lexington Ave., between E. 86th and E. 87th Sts., Upper East Side* ☎ *212/426–4200.*

Garnet Wines & Liquors. Its fine selection includes champagne at prices that one wine writer called "almost charitable." ✉ *929 Lexington Ave., between E. 68th and E. 69th Sts., Upper East Side* ☎ *212/772–3211.*

Morrell & Company. Peter Morrell is a well-regarded and very colorful figure in the wine business; his store reflects his expertise. Next door is his café, where dozens of fine wines are available by the glass. ✉ *1 Rockefeller Plaza, at W. 49th St., Midtown West* ☎ *212/688–9370.*

Sherry-Lehmann. This New York institution is an excellent place to go for good advice and to browse through sales on intriguing vintages. ✉ *679 Madison Ave., between E. 61st and E. 62nd Sts., Upper East Side* ☎ *212/838–7500.*

Union Square Wine & Spirits. The store stocks a great selection and has a regular schedule of wine seminars and special tasting events. ✉ *33*

Union Sq. W, at W. 16th St, Flatiron District ☎ *212/675–8100.*

Vintage New York. The vintages here, from cabernet sauvignon all the way to gewürztraminer, hail exclusively from New York State. Try your top choices at the tasting bar in the back; every wine sold is available by the glass. The business is open seven days a week. ✉ *482 Broome St., at Wooster St., SoHo* ☎ *212/226–9463* ✉ *2492 Broadway, between W. 92nd and W. 93rd Sts., Upper West Side* ☎ *212/721–9999.*

AUCTIONS & FLEA MARKETS

Auctions

New York is one of the world's major auctioning centers, where royal accoutrements, ancient art, and pop-culture memorabilia all have their moment on the block. Look for announcements in the *New York Times,* or in the weekly magazines *Time Out New York* and *New York.* If you plan to raise a paddle, be sure to attend the sale preview and review the catalog for price estimates.

Major Houses

Christie's. With more than 200 years of formidable history behind it, British born-and-bred Christie's has presided over the high-profile auctions of the late Princess Diana's gowns and the phenomenal Ganz Collection of 20th-century art. Special departments are devoted to such non-fine-art valuables as wine, cars, and cameras. ✉ *20 Rockefeller Plaza, at W. 49th St. between 5th and 6th Aves., Midtown West* ☎ *212/636–2000.*

Sotheby's. Established in London more than 250 years ago, Sotheby's is now American-run. It has sold off the effects of the Duke and Duchess of Windsor, paintings from the Whitney family (one of America's best private art collections), and "Sue," the largest and most complete *Tyrannosaurus rex* skeleton ever unearthed. Collectibles such as wine, vintage cars, animation art, and fashion have their own departments; there's even an Internet auction division. Their **Arcade,** at the same address, handles more affordable selections. ✉ *1334 York Ave., at E. 72nd St., Upper East Side* ☎ *212/606–7000.*

Smaller Houses

Guernsey's. This is a great source for modern memorabilia and collections; one auction put up hundreds of items that belonged to J.F.K. ✉ *108 E. 73rd St., between Park and Lexington Aves., Upper East Side* ☎ *212/794–2280.*

Phillips, de Pury & Luxembourg. The auctions here often have a modern bent; the house focuses on modern and contemporary painting, photography, and 20th-century design. ✉ *3 W. 57th St., between 5th and 6th Aves., Midtown West* ☎ *212/940–1200.*

Swann Galleries. Swann specializes in works on paper—letters, photographs, antiquarian books, and the like. ✉ *104 E. 25th St., between Park and Lexington Aves., 6th floor, Murray Hill* ☎ *212/254–4710.*

Tepper Galleries. General estate collections are sold here every other Saturday, with previews given the Friday before. ✉ *110 E. 25th St., between Park and Lexington Aves., Murray Hill* ☎ *212/677–5300.*

Flea Markets

The season runs from March or April through November or December at most of these markets in school playgrounds and parking lots. Certain markets charge a small admission fee.

Annex Antiques Fair and Flea Market. It can be more miss than hit, but it's open weekends year-round. ✉ *6th Ave. at W. 26th St., Chelsea* ☎ *212/243–5343.*

Chelsea Antiques Building. Looking for World War II photographs? Russian samovars? Out-of-print Austrian poetry books? This 12-story building is filled with specialized dealers, though prices can be steep. The best bargaining happens on weekends. ✉ *108–110 W. 25th St., between 6th and 7th Aves., Chelsea* ☎ *212/929–0909.*

The Garage Antique Shop. This indoor market in a 23,000-square-ft, two-story former parking garage is open weekends year-round. ✉ *112 W. 25th St., between 6th and 7th Aves., Chelsea* ☎ *212/647–0707.*

Green Flea. Green Flea runs the P.S.183 market on Saturday, and the I. S. 44 market on Sunday. ✉ *I.S. 44 Market: Columbus Ave. at W. 77th St., Upper West Side* ✉ *P.S. 183 Market: W. 84th St. between Columbus and Amsterdam Aves., Upper West Side* ☎ *212/721–0900 evening.*